RISE UP SINGING

THE GROUP SINGING SONGBOOK

Conceived, developed & edited by:

Peter Blood
& Annie Patterson

Illustrated by:

Kore Loy McWhirter

Introduction by:

Pete Seeger

Managing Editor: **Mark D. Moss**

Art Director: **Annie Patterson**

Editorial Assistance: **Pete Seeger**, **Judy Bell**, **Kate Kerman**

Chord System & Arrangements: **Peter Blood**

For the Revised Edition:

Editorial Supervisor: **Scott Atkinson**

Art Director: **Ed Courrier**

Musical Transcription of Rounds: **Grey Larsen**

A Sing Out! Publication – Bethlehem, Pennsylvania

ACKNOWLEDGEMENTS

This book took fifteen years to bring to birth. (Talk about a long labor!) *Many* people contributed to the project over the years – only a handful of whom can be mentioned here. We want to thank the Farm and Wilderness campers who first helped develop the idea of organizing a lyric book like this one – Peter's folks (Bob and Margaret Blood) who lent us generous "seed money" at early stages of the project – our long-suffering team of editorial assistants (Kate, Ada, and Ed Kerman, Deborah Halpern, Sally Yates, and Beth Bussiere-Nichols) who struggled to organize a mountain of lyrics, song sources and copyright data into useable form – our typists (Doris Patterson, Dorothy Patterson Lin and Varya Piper) who waded through hand-scrawled lyrics and complex formatting guidelines – all those (especially Johanna Halbeisen of New Song Library, Peggy Seeger, and Judy Bell) who helped us follow the trail of hard-to-find authors on both sides of the Atlantic – and all you who sang with us over the years, in helping us to choose which songs belonged in this book.

We are overwhelmed by the generosity of many artists, performers, folklorists, librarians, radio announcers, agents and copyright managers who lent their support and advice to this project. Over two hundred artists and publishers donated the use of their lyrics in this collection. Pete Seeger and Harold Leventhal played a decisive role in helping us obtain song permissions. Thank you all!

We want to give special thanks to Sing Out!'s wonderful Executive Director and magazine editor, Mark Moss, for endless months of typesetting and wrestling with us to a host of wise decisions about the book. Your work typified how a folk music organization like Sing Out! can (and did) help two of its members bring their dream into reality.

We just don't know how to thank all of you (family, friends, Friends, and neighbors – especially you, Nate, and you, Beth) who helped us keep at least a little perspective when we were totally overwhelmed by the magnitude of the job. We faced three great losses in the midst of the "final push to the printer" for the original 1988 edition – Peter's father Bob, our three-month old fetus (whom we named Little Heartfeather), and Peter's great aunt Mary Ashby Cheek – all of whom passed into a new place within the space of three days. With prayers and support and God's "Amazing Grace" we somehow kept going.

Finally: there's no doubt in our mind that we could not have finished the book without the strength and commitment of Kore Loy McWhirter, who left home for two months to do most of the layout for the book when Annie became ill and illustrated it so lovingly and lavishly. If you wish to make use of Loy's tremendous artistic talents on other projects, you can contact her at: 1115 Patton Thicket Rd., Burnsville NC 28714.

Addendum for the 2004 Edition: We'd like to also acknowledge two people whose contributions made the original editions of the book very special: Sam Hinton who contributed calligraphy for every song title in the book (now replaced by computer typesetting), and Meghan Merker, whose hand drawn music originally graced the "Rounds" and "Sacred Rounds" chapters for previous editions. Thanks to you both!

Peter Blood & Annie Patterson
Glen Mills, Pennsylvania
July 1988 & August 2004

Library of Congress Cataloguing in Publication Data

Rise Up Singing / edited by Peter Blood and Annie Patterson; introduction by Pete Seeger; illustrated by Kore Loy McWhirter with additional illustrations by Annie Patterson – Bethlehem, PA: Sing Out Corp., © 1988, 1992 & 2004.

ix, 279p.: ill.; 25 cm.

Song lyrics w/ guitar chord symbols, but without the tunes (except rounds). Acknowledgements dated July 1989. Includes six indices.

1. Songbooks, English-United States. I. Blood, Peter II. Patterson, Annie III. Title.

M1977.C5R56 1992 782.42'026'8-dc20 89-117888

ISBN 1-8813221-2-2 spiral-bound
ISBN 1-8813221-3-0 paperback
ISBN 1-8813221-4-9 large print leader's edition

Orders and inquiries should be directed to the publisher:
Sing Out!, PO Box 5460, Bethlehem PA 18015-0460. Ph: 610-865-5366. Web: <www.singout.org>.

INTRODUCTION

Once upon a time, wasn't singing a part of everyday life? As much as talking, physical exercise, and religion. Our distant ancestors, wherever they were in this world, sang while pounding grain, paddling canoes or walking long journeys. Nowadays we tend to put all these things in boxes.

Can we begin to make our lives once more "all of a piece?"

Finding the right songs and singing them over and over is a way to start. With friends you can learn harmony, rhythm, answer-back. Learning songs from different traditions and languages is possible, if we take the time to learn them well. We're building a world where everyone shares and no one is ostracized.

Don't say, "I can't sing." Take this book next time you ride in a car with friends. Locate some songs you'd like to hear next time you're at a party or a picnic. You'd be surprised how much better a song sounds when several voices join in together. Then, when you get a core of good singers and harmonizers, with maybe an instrument to help, you'll be the leaven in the loaf of bread. You'll get the rest of the dough bubbling, and the larger crowd will surprise themselves by how well they sing.

If a song seems too complicated, skip it. Come back later. When a song seems inappropriate to you, note that in the margin. No one would want to sing all the songs in this book. I don't. Change a word. Add a verse. This is known as "the folk process." Add pages, add illustrations. Glue a new cloth cover on top when the old cover is worn. Make it your own book.

You'll find some songs are best for certain places and certain times. Driving a car. Washing dishes. Or at a meeting, or at work, or at a demonstration. And when strangers meet and find they like the same song, then there is one more connection made for the future world network. And when eventually we have a world of peace and justice, the songs and those who sing them will be some of the millions of reasons why. Is such a world an impossibility? The alternative is no world at all.

Granted: no word means the same thing to everybody. Nor does any word mean the same thing at different times. But exploring how things change and how we differ is part of the fun. Getting that world of peace and justice will involve millions of smiles as we recognize and treasure our diversity, our different paths, our different values. And when one person taps out a beat while another leads into the melody, or when three people discover a harmony they never knew existed, or a crowd joins in on a chorus as though to raise the ceiling a few feet higher, then they also know: there's hope for the world.

A singing movement is a winning movement. We're putting a world together before it blows itself apart. Over the years you'll find the magic made by the right song at the right place at the right time.

Musicians can teach the politicians: it's fun to swap the lead. Musicians can teach the planners – economists, engineers, lawyers: *plan for improvisation.*

Our greatest songs are yet unsung. Maybe some of the users of this book will put them together.

Rise up singing.

Pete Seeger
Beacon, N.Y.

HOW TO USE THIS BOOK

How the Book Is Organized

Even though the book contains 1200 songs, you can flip to a particular song in seconds, as quickly as you can look up a word in a dictionary. How? Songs are grouped in chapter categories by subject matter. These chapters are arranged in alphabetical order (running from AMERICA through WORK). The songs within a given chapter are also arranged alphabetically by title.

As a result, if you remember or guess what category-chapter a given song is in, you don't have to use the index to find where the song is. Flip first to the chapter using the chapter headings at the upper corner of the page. Then locate the song title alphabetically within the chapter.

The key to finding songs this way is having a clear picture of what each chapter actually contains in terms of subject matter. Two good ways to familiarize yourself with this are to read the descriptions beside each chapter listing in the TABLE OF CONTENTS on the inside front cover, and to read through the SUBJECT INDEX on p. 267. There are also brief explanatory notes at the beginning of many chapters. Your guesses will get better as you use the book over time.

If you haven't any idea what chapter a given song is in, look the song up in the TITLES INDEX. Chapters are listed after each song in the TITLES INDEX to help you remember in the future which chapter the song is in.

• **Alternative Titles:** If you know a song by a different name than the title used in this book, you can find alternative titles and first lines of songs listed in the TITLES INDEX. First lines are in *italics*, alternate titles are regular type, titles used in the book are **bolded**. The arrow (→) in these listings refers you to the title we've used for the song. For example, some people know the song "Study War No More" as "Down by the Riverside." This alternative title is listed in the TITLES INDEX as:

Down by the Riverside → **Study War No More** ... PEACE ... 163

• **Finding Songs You Know:** Don't be overwhelmed by the number of songs you don't know in the book. There are 1200 songs altogether. Even if you know only one song in ten, that means the book contains over a hundred songs you know!

The ARTISTS INDEX on p.262 is a good way to find songs you know – check out performers/groups you are familiar with. Also, go to chapters likely to contain the kinds of songs you know best (like GOLDEN OLDIES, if you know a lot of old popular songs, or BALLADS & OLD SONGS, if you're familiar with traditional songs from the British Isles).

• **Finding Songs on a Specific Subject:** Teachers, songleaders, workshop leaders and others frequently need to find songs on a given topic for a special class, event, etc. This book has many ways of helping you do this. First, of course, turn to the chapter closest to the subject matter in question. At the end of each chapter there is a cross-listing of songs related to the subject of that chapter located elsewhere in the book. The CULTURES INDEX, HOLIDAYS INDEX, and SUBJECTS INDEX can also help.

The Format of Songs

• **Boldface:** Choruses appear in boldface. Lines or words that get repeated in later verses also appear in boldface. Songs that are mostly boldface are called "zipper songs." Only one or two words (underlined and in regular type) are changed ("zipped in") in each successive verse (eg. the first 3 verses of "If I Had a Hammer," p.215).

When a line or verse ends the same way in many verses, it will often be abbreviated with an ellipse ("...") in subsequent verses. After several verses, this repeated part may not be indicated at all ("This Land Is Your Land" on p.5). If some of the verses break this pattern, this is indicated on those verses (v. 4 & 5 of the same song).

• **Repeated Lines and Phrases:** If a single line of the song – or a phrase within a line – is to be repeated, this is indicated by "**(2x)**" or "**(3x)**". If, on the other hand, several lines are to be repeated together, it is indicated with the instruction "**(repeat)**" ("Were You There"; "Swing Low, Sweet Chariot" on p.212).

• **Lyrics in Italics:** Where someone other than the original author of a song has written new verses, these appear in italics ("Both Sides Now," p.27; "Green Rollin' Hills," p.145). Sometimes alternative words or phrases are indicated within a verse – usually as ways to avoid male labels for God or for people in general. These alternative ways to sing one or more bits of a song are indicated in italics and brackets ("Dear Lord and Father," p.41).

• **Beat Marks:** On songs with tricky rhythms we have at times underlined the syllables where main beats fall. These also show the places where the chords are to be played ("I Never Will Marry," "I Shall Be Released" on p.101-2).

We've tried as much as possible to group words so that each line has the same number of beats to the music. This may look a little funny now and then grammatically, but it helps fit the chords to the words and should also help you remember how the tune goes at times. For more on figuring out where beats fall, see the explanation of the chord notation system below.

• **Non-English Songs:** Singable translations get listed as regular verses to the song ("Mi Y'malel," "Mo'oz Tzur," p.45). Unsingable translations are given with copyright credits and sources in the notes following a song ("Guantanamera," p.24). On songs in Spanish, a slurred line between two words indicates that two vowels get blended together into one note of the music (Spanish verses of "Solidarity Forever," p.218).

Different people choose to sing songs in different ways. We have generally omitted instructions such as where to insert choruses or whether to repeat the first verse at the end of a song, on the assumption that you can decide for yourself what approach works best.

Learning Our Chord System

This songbook uses a unique system to indicate how chords fit with the music called "Chord Lines." They can be used with guitar, piano, organ, or any other instrument which plays chords. The system may seem tricky at first, but a lot of people find it works really well once they get the hang of it.

• **Chord Groups:** Each grouping of chords (separated by slashes "**/**") corresponds to one line of the lyrics. Thus, all the chords before the first slash go with the first line of the lyrics just above. The chords between the first and second slash correspond to the second line of the lyrics, etc. Notice that there are always the same number of chord groups as there are lines in the verse or chorus directly above.

• **Beats Per Chord:** In some songs each chord will stand for only one beat or strum of the guitar. But in most other songs each chord will correspond to two or more beats to the music. If songs are marked as being "in 3/4" then each chord represents 3, or in some cases 6, beats. If it is not marked as "in 3/4," then each chord represents 2, 4 or 8 beats. You will have to figure out by the flow of a given song how many beats one chord symbol represents in that particular song.

One way to figure this out is to add up the number of beats in the first line of the song. Then divide by the number of chords in the first chord group. (In "The Man on the Flying Trapeze," p.80, there are 12 beats in the first line of the song. There are two chords in the first chord group. This means that the chords in this song count for six beats each.) Once you have figured out how many beats each chord stands for in a given song, this will *always* stay the same throughout that song.

• **Repeated Chords:** A hyphen following a chord means to repeat the previous chord again. An empty space between two slashes means to repeat the previous chord group again. The chord line for "The Itsy Bitsy Spider" (p.172) is:

D - A D / / / /

The representation D - A D is shorthand for D D A D. Each chord equals two beats in this song, so this line is actually played DD DD AA DD. And since the next three chord groupings are "empty," it means that the 2nd, 3rd and 4th lines of this song are played exactly like the first line. The chords listed in the book fall on the main beats of each line. Here's how the chords actually fit: (the dashes indicate strums or beats where there is no chord change)

D - D - A - D -
The itsy bitsy spi-der climbed up the water spout

D - D - A - D -
Down came the rain and washed the spider out

• **Squeezed Chords:** When two chords are squeezed close together, each chord only gets half as many beats as regular chords in the same song. In other words, you change the chords twice as fast when two chords are squeezed together.

The chord line for "I've Been Working on the Railroad" (p.172) appears in the book as follows:

D - G D / - - E A / - D G F♯ / G D DA D

All the chords in this song correspond to 4 beats of the music except for the 2 squeezed chords in the last chord group, which get 2 beats each (ie. half of 4 beats). Here is where the chords get played with the words:

D - - - D - - - G - - - D - - -
I've been working on the rail-road, all the live-long day

D - - - D - - - E - - - A - - -
I've been working on the rail-road, just to pass the time a-way

A - - - D - - - G - - - F♯ - - -
Can't you hear the whistle blow-ing, rise up so early in the morn

G - - - D - - - D - A - D - - -
Can't you hear the captain shou-ting: "Di- nah blow your horn!"

• **Pickup Beats:** In the above examples, the main beats fall at the beginning of each line of the lyrics. This is often not the case, however. This is because chord groups throughout the book are written out with the first chord falling on a main downbeat of the music (corresponding with the beginning of a "measure" when you see the music written out.) Lines of lyrics, on the other hand, sometimes begin with several "pickup notes" that come just *before* the main downbeat where the chord group begins. In "When the Saints Go Marching In" (p.213) the first three words of the first verse are examples of "pickup notes." These are notes which come before the first main beat in a line of music. This verse appears in the book like this:

O when the Saints go marching in **(2x)**
O Lord I want to be in that number
When the Saints go marching in
D - / - A7 / D G / DA D

The first D in the chord line falls on the word "Saints." Each chord in this song gets 4 beats, except for the squeezed chords in the last line, which only get 2 beats each. The music below shows where the chords fit with the melody. Slashes indicate the end of a chord group. Notice how you begin singing 2-3 notes before you finish strumming each chord group in this song.

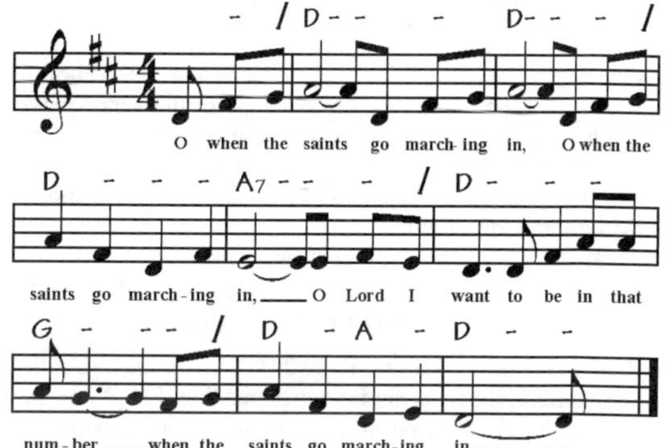

"This Land Is Your Land" (p.5) is another example of pickup beats. Each chord in this song gets 2 beats so the first line of the song is played GGGG DDDD. The first 3 words, however, are pickup beats, so you actually begin playing G on the word "your" and D on the word "my." On the second line of the music, don't start playing the chord "A" until you get to the syllable "for-" in the middle of "California."

• **Songs in Waltz Time:** Each chord in "Tell Me Why" (p.128) counts for 3 beats. The chords to the first two lines fit like this:

G - - G - - C - - G - -
Tell me why the stars do shine?

G - - G - - A - - D - -
Tell me why the i - vy twine?

Each regular chord in "The Holly and the Ivy" (p.11) also counts for 3 beats. The squeezed chords get one beat each, one-third as much as the regular chords. "The" is a pickup note.

The holly & the ivy when they are both full grown
Of all the trees that are in the wood, the holly bears the crown
DDG D DDG A / D GDD DDA D

Squeezed chords don't have to come in three's, however, for a song to be in 3/4 time. In the song "Goodnight Irene" (p.132), for example, each regular chord counts for 6 beats. In this case the squeezed chords E & E7 get 3 beats each, one-half as many as regular chords get in this song.

Are you still with us? If you understand the basic idea this far, you may now pass "Go" and collect $200! (What follows are the "fine points.")

• **Lines of Different Length:** We've generally tried to write out chord groups (and the lines of lyrics to which they correspond) so that they include the same number of beats throughout a given song. In some songs, however, (like "I Want a Girl Just Like the Girl," p.79), some chord groups have fewer chords than others. In this song regular chords count for 4 beats and squeezed chords get 2 beats each. This means that the first, second, and last lines are 8 beats long, while the 3rd & 4th lines are only 4 beats long.

• **Verse and Chorus:** If no chords are given after the chorus, it means that the chords are the same as for the verse above ("Loch Lomond," p.153). The same is true when the chorus comes first and there are no chords shown for the first verse ("This Land," p.5). Unless otherwise noted, assume the chords stay the same for all of the verses.

If the chords to the verse and chorus are given on the same chord line, a double slash "//" indicates where the chorus begins ("Angel Band," p.92).

• **Repeated Chord Groups, Part 2:** / **1st** / means to use the same chords as the first chord group of that line. / **1st 2** / means to repeat the chords used in the first and second groups. (In "Shine On Harvest Moon," p.81, use the same chords for the 3rd line of the chorus as you did on the first line. In "Everything Possible" on p.239, the 7th & 8th lines of the chorus are played the same as the 1st & 2nd lines of the chorus. In "Free At Last" on p.209, the 3rd & 4th lines of the verse are played the same as the 3rd & 4th lines (i.e. the repeated portion) of the chorus.

The "same as above" symbol / " / means to use the same chords as the corresponding chord group in the line of chords above. (In "Tenting Tonight," p.5, the 7th & 8th chord groups – that is the 3rd & 4th lines of the chorus–have the same chords as the 3rd & 4th lines of the verse.)

The "repeat sign" (:||) at the end of the chord line in "This Land Is Your Land" (p. 5) means that the third line is played the same as the first line and the fourth the same as the second. (In "Little Brown Jug," p.88, the two chord groups shown get repeated 4 times – twice through for the verse and two more times for the chorus.)

Finally, where a line of lyrics gets repeated, as indicated by "**(2x)**" at the end of that line, there will be two corresponding chord groups for this repeated line (When the Saints, p.213). If, on the other hand, **(2x)** or **(3x)** follows a word or phrase within a line of lyrics, then only one chord group is given for that line ("Goodnight Irene," p.132).

• **Keys:** **(In G)** indicates the key a song is in when this isn't obvious ("If Ever I Would Leave You," p.125). **(capo up)** indicates we have chosen an easy-to-play key which may be a bit low for many voices. If this is true for you, transpose the song to a higher key or capo up the song a few frets on the guitar.

• **Bass Runs:** Small letters appearing in parenthesis after a chord indicate bass notes to be played with the chord indicated. Thus in the song "Mandolin Man" (p.25), G(D,E,F#,E) is actually played as G(bass D) G(bass E) G(bass F#) G(bass E). This could have also been written as G G6 Gmaj7 G6.

A downward arrow after a chord indicates a descending bass run. Thus in "Mr. Bojangles" (also on p.25) C ↓ could have been written as C(C,B,A,G) using the notation described in the previous paragraph. In this song each chord gets 3 beats. You play C at the beginning of the song 4 times with 4 bass notes running down from C down to G and then switch to F. Here is how the chords fit:

```
C(C)    -  - C(B)    -  -   C(A)      -- C(G) - -
I knew a man Bo-jangles & he'd dance for you
F - -  F   - - G - - G - -
   In worn-out shoes
```

If all this has left you more puzzled than ever (or even if it hasn't!), you may want to consider acquiring a set of the Teaching CDs which accompany this book (see p.281) and try playing along with some of the songs while you are looking at the chord lines in the book.

Learning the Songs You Don't Know

We are often asked why this book includes no music (except for the two chapters of rounds). The answer lies in the basic purpose of the book. We wanted to create a large and diverse collection of songs that was compact and inexpensive enough that groups like camps, schools, and churches could actually acquire a quantity of these books for group singing. (See the inside back cover for information on bulk discounts available from the publisher.) These 1,200 songs would have required a huge and enormously costly book if music was included. We wanted a book with enough songs that groups could continue teaching each other new songs out of it year after year.

The second reason was copyrights. It is incredibly difficult and costly to obtain permission to reprint composed songs, even with the lyrics alone. We would have been unable to obtain permission to include many of the songs in this book if we had included music.

We recognize, however, many readers' keen frustration in not knowing the tunes to many of these songs. We hope you can look on this as a long-term journey of song learning through a wide variety of channels!

The best way to learn songs is directly from other people. If you get together and sing regularly with others, you will find that you know as a group many more songs than any one of you knows. Teaching each other songs is fun – that's what this book is basically for.

There are hundreds of places around North America where people gather regularly for "song circles." Many of these use this songbook. One way to connect with people in your area interested in this kind of singing is to become a member of Sing Out! (see the pullout card that comes with this book).

For those of us who learn by ear, we have produced a CD series with the tunes to all 1,200 songs in the songbook. Each CD has the tunes to all the songs in one or two chapters of *Rise Up Singing* in the same order as they appear in the book. Each song is presented in a simple vocal and guitar arrangement using the same chords as are used in the book. You'll find a small code after each song that tells you where you can find the song on the teaching CDs. For example, the A22 below "Tenting Tonight" on p.5 means that you can find the melody to this song on track 22 of Teaching Disc A. (This CD includes all the songs in the America and Golden Oldies chapters. For more information on these Teaching Discs see p.281.)

If the song on the teaching disk is not in the key shown in the book or as announced before the song on CD, a notation is made indicating how many frets you will have to capo up your guitar to play along with the CD for this track. For example, "Walk In Jerusalem" on p.212 is written out with chords in the key of C in this edition of the book, but the song is recorded in D on the teaching disk. The instruction **(TD ↑ 2)** means that you can play along with the teaching disk by putting your capo on the 2nd fret of your guitar.

Many of the songs in this book are written by contemporary singer-songwriters. A wealth of folk coffeehouses, festivals, folk music societies, and music networks have blossomed in recent years. These provide many rich opportunities to hear the songwriters performing their songs themselves. Each issue of *Sing Out!* magazine has information on these and other ways you can hear performers like these. As a Sing Out! member you can get assistance in contacting individual songwriters for booking information, recordings, etc.

• **Source Listings under Songs:** Songbook and recording titles are listed in regular ("roman") type within the italic resource listings at the bottom of each song. You can tell the print resources from the recordings by noting that songs are listed as ***in*** books or magazines, while they are listed as being ***on*** recordings. (Please also note that by buying the recordings or print music listed in this book you can not only learn some great songs but will be helping to support our music culture ... and you'll be enjoying some terrific music to boot!)

Hundreds of the songs in this book have appeared in *Sing Out! Magazine* – often their first time in print. "In *SO!* 31:3" means the song appeared in *Sing Out!* magazine, v.31#3. Many back issues of *Sing Out!* are still available. (Of particular interest is *Sing Out!* v.44#4, a special 50th anniversary issue containing 45 of the best-loved songs throughout *Sing Out!*'s history and this book.)

Beginning in 1959, *Sing Out!* began issuing Reprints volumes containing 50-60 songs which had been previously printed in the magazine. All twelve volumes of this series have been reissued by Sing Out Publications in larger-format collected editions of six volumes each. Thus, if a song is listed as "In *Reprints #4*" you can find the song in *Collected Reprints from Sing Out! Vols. 1-6*.

We are glad to receive corrections or comments on chords, lyrics or sources (and anything else!) in this book. Please forward these to the editors c/o Sing Out!, PO Box 5460, Bethlehem PA 18015-0460; <rus@singout.org>.

• **Music Publishers:** You can often obtain sources to tunes from music publishers: the sheet music for a specific song, collections of songs by one artist, or large "fakebooks" containing many songs administered by a given publisher. Here are some of the major publishers who generously agreed to let us use their songs in this collection. Smaller publishers which these companies administer are also listed. Please note: You need to contact these publishers directly (*not* Sing Out!) if you want to reprint any of the these publishers' songs found in this book.

Cherry Lane Music Co., PO Box 430, Port Chester NY 10573 (John Denver, Tom Paxton)

Columbia Pictures Publications, PO Box 4340, Miami FL 33014 – Famous, Irving, Leo Feist, Jobete (Motown), Peer-Southern (Donovan), Robbins, SBK, United Artists

Fall River Music, 250 W. 57th St, NY, NY 10107 – Appleseed, Sanga, Stormking (Seeger)

Hal Leonard Publishing, PO Box 13819, Milwaukee WI 53213 – April-Blackwood (Beatles, James Taylor), Chappell (many Broadway), Hudson Bay, MCA

Music Sales, 225 Park Ave S, NY, NY 10003 – Oak, G. Schirmer, Paul Simon, Bernstein

The Richmond Organization (TRO), 11 W. 19th, NY, NY 10011 – Ludlow (Guthrie, Lomax), Folkways (Weavers), Melody Trails (Seeger)

Warner-Chappell Music – Colgems-EMI (Carole King), Almo-Irving, Pepamar (Peter, Paul & Mary), Siquomb (Joni Mitchell). For licencing: 9000 Sunset Blvd, Los Angeles, CA 90069. For sheet music & songbooks: Warner Bros. Publications, 265 Secaucus Rd, Secaucus NJ 07094 or Jensen Publications, PO Box 248, New Berlin WI 53151.

Abbreviations Used in This Book:

abt = about
alb = album
Am = America, American
Anniv = anniversary
App = Appalachian
bal(s) = ballad(s)
B = book
Br = British
© = copyright
Celeb = Celebration
Conc = Concert
Cong = Congress
Ency = Encyclopedia
Eng = English
ESF = *Everybody Says Freedom*
FF = Flying Fish Records
FM = folk music
FS = folk song(s)
FW (FA, FG) = Folkways
Fam = Family
Fest = Festival
fr = from
FakeB = Fakebook
Fav = Favorite
FiresB = Fireside Book
Gold = Golden
Gr = Great, Greatest
GW = Gentle Wind tapes
H = Hits
in = in a songbook or musical
lulls = lullabies
M = Music
mtn = mountain
N = North
Nost = Nostalgic, Nostalgia
on = on a recording
orig = original(ly)
Pop = Popular
pub = public
pt = part
rec = recording
Reprints = *Reprints from SO!*
RUS = *Rise Up Singing*
RR = railroad
S = song(s)
SB = songbook
SFest = *Songfest*
SFF = *Sing For Freedom*
SO! = *Sing Out! Magazine*
So = southern
TD = teaching disc for RUS
Trav = Travelin'
Treas = Treasury
v = verse
V = Volume
Vang = Vanguard Records
w/ = with
WAS = World Around Songs
WB = Warner Bros.
WHATFG = Where Have All the Flowers Gone
yr = year
↑ = capo up

Three or four letter abbreviations in all caps refer to chapters of this book. *(FUN = FUNNY SONGS, BALS = BALLADS & OLD SONGS, etc.)*

Some Final Words (Finally!)

We created this book because we love to sing in groups. People have been sustained and uplifted for centuries by shared song – in their work, their play, their worship and their struggles for dignity.

This earth needs hopeful and refreshed people commited to its rebirth as a garden for all of God's creatures. We hope this book will play a small role in that process of transformation and renewal.

One of these mornings, you're gonna rise up singin'
*Then you'll spread your wings & you'll take to the sky**

Peter Blood & Annie Patterson
Cheyney, Pennsylvania
August 2004

** From the song "Summertime" by Dubose Heyward & George Gershwin.*

This songbook is dedicated to Nate, Ian, Bébé, Little Heartfeather ... and the song of the child within us all.

AMERICA

This chapter is about history, culture & experience in the USA. We've adopted the common usage of "America" for this even though we recognize this is inaccurate & unfair to people north & south of the border, who are every bit as much "Americans" as we are: as such we apologize. For help locating songs in this book on the rest of the Americas, see the end of this chapter.

America (Simon)

"Let us be lovers, we'll marry our fortunes together
I've got some real estate here in my bag"
So we bought a pack of cigarettes & Mrs. Wagner's pies
And walked off to look for America

C↓ - - F - - - /C↓ Am - - - /Em - A - (2x)/D C G C↓ Am -

"Kathy" I said as we boarded a Greyhound in Pittsburgh
"Michigan seems like a dream to me now
It took me four days to hitchhike from Saginaw
I've come to look for America"

/ " / " /G - - - /D G D Cmaj7 - C -

(interlude)
Laughing on the bus, playing games with the faces
She said the man in the gabardine suit was a spy
I said "Be careful, his bow tie is really a camera"

B♭ - - - C - - - / /F - - - C - - - (Fmaj7 - - -)

"Toss me a cigarette, I think there's one in my raincoat"
"We smoked the last one an hour ago"
So I looked at the scenery, she read her magazine
And the moon rose over an open field

Kathy I'm lost, I said, tho' I knew she was sleeping
I'm empty & aching & I don't know why
Counting the cars on the New Jersey Turnpike
They've all come to look for America

— **Paul Simon**

 — On his Live Rhymin' & Bookends. ©A02

America (West Side Story)

I like to be in America, OK by me in America
Everything free in America, for a small fee in America
I like the city of San Juan – I know a boat you can get on
Hundreds of flowers in full bloom – hundreds of people in each room

A D A E / C G F A // A - - Bm / D - Bm E

Automobile in America, chromium steel in America
Wire spoke wheel in America, very big deal in America
I'll drive a Buick through San Juan – if there's a road you can drive on
I'll give my cousins a free ride – how you fit all of them inside?

Immigrant goes to America, many helloes in America
Nobody knows in America, Puerto Rico's in America
When I will go back to San Juan – when you will shut up and get gone?
I'll give them new washing machine – what have they got there to keep clean?

I like the shores of America, comfort is yours in America
Knobs on the doors in America, wall to wall floors in America
I'll bring a TV to San Juan – if there's a current to turn on
Everyone there will give big cheer – everyone there will have moved here!

— **w: Stephen Sondheim** — **m: Leonard Bernstein**

 — From their musical West Side Story. ©A03

America the Beautiful

O beautiful for spacious skies for amber waves of grain
For purple mountain majesties above the fruited plain
America! America! God shed his *[all]* grace on thee
And crown thy good with brotherhood* from sea to shining sea
**[With brotherhood & sisterhood]*

G D - GD / G D A D / G D - G / C G CD G

O beautiful for pilgrim feet whose stern impassioned stress
A thoroughfare for freedom beat across the wilderness
America! America! God mend thine ev'ry flaw
Confirm thy soul in self control, thy liberty in law

O beautiful for heroes proved in liberating strife
Who more than self their country loved & mercy more than life
America! America! may God thy gold refine
Til all success be nobleness & ev'ry gain divine

O beautiful for patriot dream that sees beyond the years
Thine alabaster cities gleam undimmed by human tears
America! America! God shed his grace on thee
And crown thy good with brotherhood from ...

O beautiful for working folk who forged the wealth we see
In farm & mill, in home & school unsung in history
America! America! may race nor sex nor creed
No more divide, but side by side, all rise united, freed!

— **w: Katharine Lee Bates (last v. Pamela Haines)**
— **m: Samuel A. Ward**

 — On Leo Kottke Dream & All That Stuff, *Mormon Tab. Choir's* God Bless Amer. & *Limelighters'* Alive V2. *In* FS Ency V2, Treasury of FS, Sing to Children, Friends Hymnal, Gr Legal Fake B. ©A04

Battle of New Orleans

In 18 & 14 we took a little trip
Along with Col. Jackson down the mighty Mississip'
We took a little bacon & we took a little beans
And we met the bloody British near the town of New Orleans

G - C - / D - G - :||

We fired our guns & the British kept a-comin'
There wasn't nigh as many as they was a while ago
We fired once more & they commenced a-runnin'
On down the Mississippi to the Gulf of Mexico

G - - - / - - GD G :||

Well I see'd Marse Jackson a-walkin' down the street
And a-talkin' to a pirate by the name of Jean Lafitte
He gave Jean a drink that he'd brung from Tennessee
And the pirate said he'd help us drive the British in the sea
Well the French told Andrew "You had better run
Cuz Packenham's a-comin' with a bullet in his gun"
Old Hickory said he didn't give a damn
He's gonna whip the britches off of Col. Packenham"

We looked down the river & we seed the British come
There must have been a hundred of 'em beatin' on the drum
They stepped so high & they made their bugles ring
While we stood beside our cotton bales & didn't say a thing
Old Hick'ry said we'd take 'em by surprise
If we didn't fire a musket till we looked 'em in the eyes
We held our fire til we seed their faces well
Then we opened up our squirrel guns & really gave 'em hell

Interlude: (chords as in chorus)
Well they ran thru the briars & they ran thru the brambles
And they ran thru the bushes where a rabbit couldn't go
They ran so fast that the hounds couldn't catch 'em
On down the Mississippi to the Gulf of Mexico

They lost their pants & their pretty shiny coats
And their tails were all a-showin' like a bunch of billy goats
They ran down the river til their tongues were hangin' out
And they said they got a lickin' which there wasn't any doubt
Well we went back to town in our dirty ragged pants
And we danced all night with them pretty girls from France
We couldn't understand 'em but they had the sweetest charms
And we understood 'em better when we got 'em in our arms

Well the guide who brung the British from the sea
Came a-limpin' into camp just as sick as he could be
He said the dyin' words of Col. Packenham
Was "You'd better quit your foolin' with your cousin Uncle Sam"
Well we'll march back home but we'll never be content
Until we make Old Hickory the People's President
And every time we think about the bacon & the beans
We'll think about the fun we had way down in New Orleans

— w: Jimmy Driftwood — m: trad. ("8th of January")

© 1957, 1959 Warden Music Co. Inc. Used by permission. — On his Best of *(Monument SLP18043) & in* SO! *9:1, 44:4 &* Reprints *#3,* S of Independence, 1001 Jumbo S. OA05

Be Prepared

Be prepared! that's the Boy Scouts' marching song
Be prepared! as thru life you march along
Be prepared to hold your liquor pretty well
Don't write naughty words on walls if you can't spell

C - - - / G - - - / C E A - / D - G -

Be prepared! to hide that pack of cigarettes
Don't make book if you cannot cover bets
Keep those reefers hidden where you're sure that they will not be found
And be careful not to smoke them when the scoutmaster's around
For he only will insist that they be shared, be prepared!

/ " / " /C C7 F - /D - G - /C F D G C -

Be prepared! that's the Boy Scouts' solemn creed
Be prepared! & be clean in word & deed
Don't solicit for your sister, that's not nice
Unless you get a good percentage of her price

Be prepared! & be careful not to do
Your good deeds when there's no one watching you
If you're looking for adventure of a new & different kind
And you come across a Girl Scout who is similarly inclined
Don't be nervous, don't be flustered, don't be scared, be prepared!

— Tom Lehrer

© 1953 Tom Lehrer. Copyright renewed. Used by permission. On his Songs by *& in his* Too Many Songs by. OA06

Camptown Races

O the Camptown ladies sing this song, dooda dooda
The Camptown race track's five miles long, oh dooda day
Goin' to run all night, goin' to run all day
I bet my money on a bob-tailed nag, somebody bet on the bay

C - G - / C - G C // C - F C / - - G C

I went down South with my hat caved in, dooda dooda
I come back North with a pocket full of tin, oh dooda day

— Stephen Foster

On Pete Seeger Am Fav Bal V3 *& in* FS EncyV2, FiresB of FS, Read Em & Weep, Treas of Steph. Foster. OA07

Geronimo's Cadillac

They put Geronimo in jail down south
Where he couldn't look a gift horse in the mouth
Sergeant, Sergeant, don't you feel
There's something wrong with your automobile?
Governor, Governor, now ain't it strange
They didn't have no cars on the Indian range
Warden, Warden, listen to me:
Be brave & set Geronimo free

D A G D / G - D - :|| **(repeat 4x)**

Whoa, boys, take me back
I wanna ride in Geronimo's Cadillac (repeat 2x)

Warden, Warden, don't you know
That Indians have got no place to go?
Took Old Geronimo by storm
Ripped off the feathers from his uniform
Jesus tells me, I believe it's true
The red man has a place in the sunset too
Took all their land & they won't give it back
Sent Geronimo a Cadillac

— Charles Quarto & Michael M. Murphey

© Mystery Music Inc. Used by permission. — Orig rec by Michael Murphey. On Mary McCaslin & Jim Ringer Bramble & the Rose *& Bill Miller* Reservation Road. OA08

Little Boxes

Little boxes on the hillside, little boxes made of ticky tacky
Little boxes **(3x)** all the same
There's a green one & a pink one & a blue one & a yellow one
And they're all made out of ticky tacky & they all look just the same

A - D A / A E A E / A - D A / - E - A

And the people in the houses all go to the university
Where they all get put in boxes & they come out just the same
And there's doctors & lawyers & business executives **And...**

And they all play on the golf course & drink their martinis dry
And they all have pretty children & the children go to school
And the children go to summer camp & then to the university
Where they are put in boxes & they come out all the same

And the boys go into business & marry & raise a family
In boxes made of ticky tacky & they all look just the same
There's a green one & a pink one & a blue one & a yellow one
And they're all ...

— Malvina Reynolds

© 1962 by Schroder Music Co. (ASCAP) Berkeley, CA 94704. Used by permission. — On her Malvina *(CFS 2007),* Ear to the Ground *(CD on FW) & in her* SB *& her* Little Boxes. *French trans by Kate & Anna McGarrigle on* If I Had a S (S of Pete Seeger V2). *Also in* SO! *13:4,* S that Changed the World & A Time for Singing. *On Pete Seeger* World of & Gr H. OA09

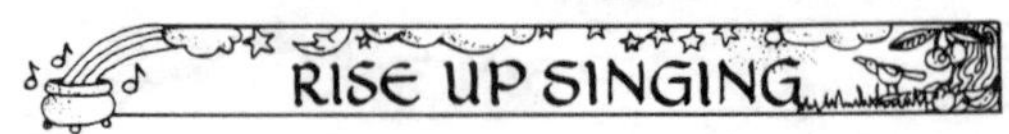

Mercedes-Benz

O Lord, won't you buy me a Mercedes-Benz?
My friends all have Porsches I must make amends
Worked hard all my lifetime, no help from my friends
O Lord ... **(repeat 1st line of each verse)**

D - G D / D - - A / D - - G / D - A D

O Lord won't you buy me a color TV?
Dialing for dollars is trying to find me
I'll wait for delivery each day until 3 / O Lord ...

O Lord won't you buy me a night on the town?
I'm countin' on you, Lord, please don't let me down
Prove that you love me & buy the next round ...

— Janis Joplin & Michael McClure

My Land Is a Good Land

My land is a good land, the grass is made of rainbow blades
Its fields & its rivers are blessed by God
It's a good land so they say **(2x)**

(in C) F G C Am **(2x)** / F G C Am / / F G C -

My land is a rich land, its hills & valleys are bound
Its highways go off to many good places
Where many good people are found **(2x)**

My land is a sweet land, it's a sweet land so I've heard
Its song is made up of many folks' hands
And the throat of a hummingbird **(2x)**

My land is a free land, it's a free land so I'm told
Freedom is a thing that money can't buy
If it's worth even more than gold **(2x)**

My land is my homeland, my homeland so strong & true
It starts where the sun is growing each morn
And ends where the skies are blue **(2x)**

— Eric Andersen

The Night They Drove Old Dixie Down

Virgil Caine is my name & I served on the Danville train
Til Stonewall's calvary came & tore up the tracks again
In the winter of '65 we were hungry, just barely alive
By May the 10th Richmond had fell, it was a night I remember o so well **(capo up)**

Am C F Dm / / Am F C F / Am F C - D D7

The night they drove old Dixie down & all the bells were ringing
The night ... & all the people were singing, they said Na nana ...

C F C F / / C Am D F C -

Back with my wife in Tennessee when one day she said to me
"Virgil, quick come see, there goes Robert E. Lee"
Now I don't mind choppin' wood & I don't care if the money's no good
Ya take what ya need & leave the rest but they should never have taken the very best

Like my father before me I will work the land
Like my brother above me who took a rebel stand
He was just 18, proud & brave, but a Yankee laid him in his grave
I swear by the mud below my feet, you can't raise a Caine back up when he's in defeat

— J. Robbie Robertson

Now That the Buffalo's Gone

Can you remember the times
That you have held your head high
And told all your friends of your Indian blood
Proud good lady & proud good man
Your great-great-grandfather from Indian blood sprang
And you feel in your heart for these ones

(in 3/4 in A) A E / G C#m / D A / E A / D A / E B7 E

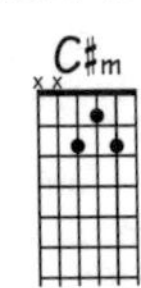

O it's written in books & in song
That we've been mistreated & wronged
Well over & over I hear the same words
From you, good lady, from you, good man
Well listen to me if you care where we stand
And you feel in your heart for these ones

Now when a war between nations is lost
The loser we know pays the cost
But even when Germany felt your hand
Consider, good lady, consider, good man
You left them their pride & you left them their land
And what have you done for these ones?

Has a change come about Uncle Sam
Or are you still taking our land?
A treaty forever George Washington signed
He did, dear lady, he did, dear man
And the treaty's being broken by Kinzua Dam
And what will you do for these ones?

O it's all in the past you can say
But it's still going on here today
The Government now wants the Iroquois land
That of the Seneca & the Cheyenne
It's here & it's now you must help us, dear man
Now that the Buffalo's gone

— Buffy Sainte-Marie

The Power and the Glory

C'mon & take a walk with me thru this green & growin' land
Walk thru the meadows & the mountains & the sand
Walk thru the valleys & the rivers & the plains
Walk thru the sun & walk thru the rain

C - / - G / - - / F G

Here's a land full of power & glory
Beauty that words cannot recall
O her power shall rest on the strength of her freedom
Her glory shall rest on us all

Am G / / C Em / F G **(last chorus: repeat** "on us all" C -)

From Colorado, Kansas & the Carolinas too
Virginia & Alaska, from the old to the new
Texas & Ohio & the California shore
Tell me who could ask for more?

Yet she's only as rich as the poorest of the poor
Only as free as a padlocked prison door
Only as strong as our love for this land
Only as tall as we stand

— Phil Ochs

 — On his All The News That's Fit To Sing *&* Chords of Fame *& Pete Seeger* God Bless the Grass. OA14

Putting On the Style

Young man in a carriage, driving like he's mad
With a pair of horses he borrowed from his dad
He cracks his whip so lively just to see his lady smile
But she knows he's only **putting on the style**

D - - A / - - - D :||

Putting on the agony, putting on the style
That's what all the young folks are doing all the while
And as I look around me, I'm very apt to smile
To see so many people putting on the style

Sweet 16 goes to church just to see the boys
Laughs & screams & giggles at every little noise
She turns this way a little then turns that way awhile
But everybody knows she's only **putting ...**

Young man in a restaurant smokes a dirty pipe
Looking like a pumpkin that's only halfway ripe
Smokin', drinkin', chewin', & thinkin' all the while
That there is nothing equal to ...

Young man just from college makes a big display
With a great big jawbreak which he can hardly say
It can't be found in Webster's & won't be for a while
But everybody knows he's only ...

Preacher in the pulpit shouting with all his might
Glory Hallelujah puts the people in a fright
You might think that Satan's coming up & down the aisle
But it's only the preacher ...

Movie star in Hollywood by the swimming pool
Never gets her feet wet, that lady ain't no fool
Sittin in a bathin suit, dark glasses & a smile
She don't know that we know she's putting ...

See the young executive in his charcoal gray
Talking with some union men who've come to have their say
Sitting at his office desk & wearing a toothpaste smile
But that's just the executive ...

Congressman from Washington, looking mighty slick
Wants to get elected & go back there right quick
Beats his breast & hollers & waves the flag awhile
But we know he's only ...

— new words & arr. by Norman Cazden (last 2 v. Jerry Walters)

 – The 1880's, when this song was 1st sung, was an era of tight corsets for the ladies & the phrase was current: "Let's take the agony out of putting on the style" — Pete Seeger. In SO! 5:1 *&* Reprints #1, FS EncyV1, Abecedary of FS, Am Fav Bal. *On Pete Seeger* Sampler. *Parodies in* SO! 8:2 *&* 9:4. OA15

Something to Sing About

From the eastern to western sea, pathway to liberty
Something to sing about, this land of ours
From Canada's northern glow, southward to Mexico
Something ...

A - D - / A - Bm E / A - D - / A - E A

Here's a land always young with a ballad that's still unsung
Small country farms to the great city towers
From the Great Lakes to Rio Grande, one great & friendly land
Something to sing about, this land of ours

E - A - / - E B7 E / " / " /

From Concord to Lexington, where free men fought & won ...
Midway, The Alamo, San Juan Hill, Anzio ...

From the Pilgrims who dared the waves, rather than live as slaves
To the thousands who come today, traveling freedom's way

Here's a haven to all who seek freedom to think & speak
Here's a land that has reached the heights, pow'rd by a Bill of Rights

— Oscar Brand

 — On his Amer Dreamer. OA16

Spoon River

All of the riverboat gamblers are losing their shirts
All of the brave Union soldier boys sleep in the dirt
But you know & I know there never was reason to hurt
When all of our lives were entwined to begin with here in Spoon River

(in 3/4) C Em F G (2x) / / C - C7 - F - Fm - / 1st

All of the calico dresses, the gingham & lace
Are up in the attic with grandfather's derringer case
There are words whispered down in the parlor, a shadowy face
The morning is heavy with one more beginning **here ...**

Come to the dance, Mary Perkins, I like you right well
The Union's preserved, if you listen you hear all the bells
There must be a heaven, God knows that I've seen mostly hell
My rig is outside, come & ride thru the morning here ...

— Michael Peter Smith

 — On Michael Smith *&* Claudia Schmidt. OA17

Stewball

There's a big race **(uh-huh)**, down in Dallas **(uh-huh)**
Don't you wish you **(...)** were there? **(...)**
You would bet your ( ) bottom dollar ( )
On that iron ( ) grey mare ( )
Bet on Stewball & you might win, win, win
Bet on Stewball & you might win! (repeat refrain)

C - / G C :||: F C / G C :||

Way out in / California / when old Stewball / was born
All the jockeys / in the nation / said he blew there / in a storm

Now the value / of his harness / has never / been told
His saddle / pure silver / & his bridle / solid gold

Old Stewball / was a racehorse / Old Molly / was too
Old Molly / she stumbled / Old Stewball / he flew

— trad. (US)

A skewbald horse is one that is brown & white. Based on a race which occured in Ireland in 1873. On Hot Mudd Family Meat & Potatoes, *M Cooney* Pure Unsweetened *& in* FS EncyV1 *& Lomax* Am Bal & FS *(1934). (A different version of this song is in* SO! 11:3 *&* Reprints #6 *& on Pete Seeger* Sings Leadbelly *– still another version is on* Peter Paul & Mary.*)* OA18

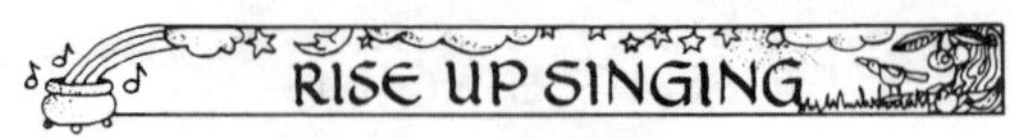

TV Song

TV, TV, gonna watch out so you won't get me!
Boob Tube, you lose, I'll turn you off any time I choose!

(in A) D A E - / Dm A E EA

I ain't gonna let you waste my time * (* = echo)
Tell me lies, & mess my mind *
I ain't gonna lay on the floor all day *
Lettin' my bones & brain decay! *

E - - - / A - - - / B7 - - - / E - - -

I ain't gonna eat all the junk you sell * (etc.)
I'll eat an apple, & I'll stay well
I think I'll go & have some fun
Ride my bike out in the sun

Same old stories, same cartoons
Chasin', punchin', killin' too
And tho' I love you, Kermit Frog
I'm off to catch some polliwogs

TV life ain't life at all
Life don't plug into the wall
C'mon everybody, get off your duff
Enough TV's enough's enough!

— **Carol Johnson**

© 1981 Carol Johnson. Noeldner Music (BMI), PO Box 6351, Grand Rapids MI 49506. All rights reserved. Used by permission. On her Might As Well Make It Love. ©A19

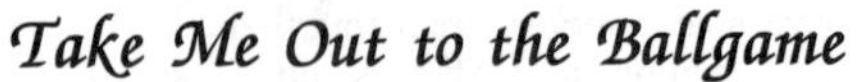

Take Me Out to the Ballgame

Take me out to the ballgame, take me out to the crowd
Buy me some popcorn & Cracker Jack, I don't care if we never get back
So it's root, root, root for the home team, if they don't win it's a shame
For it's 1, 2, 3 strikes you're out at the old ball game!

C G C G / A7 Dm D7 G / C G C A7 / F FC FG C

— **w: Jack Norworth m: Albert von Tilzer**

On Raffi One Light, One Sun *& in* M at the Turn of the Century *(Am Herit).* ©A20

Tennessee Stud

Along about 18 & 25
I left Tennessee very much alive
I never would have got thru the Arkansas mud
If I hadn't been a-ridin' on the Tennessee stud
I had some trouble with my sweetheart's pa
One of her brothers was a bad outlaw
I sent her a letter by my Uncle Fud
And I rode away on the Tennessee stud

D - - - / C - - - - - / D - - - / - - C D - - - :||

The Tennessee stud was long & lean
The color of the sun & his eyes were green
He had the nerve & he had the blood
And there never was a hoss like the Tennessee stud

D - C D/G - B♭ A - - - / " / " /

We drifted on down into no-man's land
We crossed the river called the Rio Grande
I raced my hoss with the Spaniards bold
Til I got me a skin full of silver & gold
Me & a gambler, we couldn't agree
We got in a fight over Tennessee
We jerked our guns, he fell with a thud
And I got away on the Tennessee stud

Well, I got as lonesome as a man can be
Dreamin' of my girl in Tennessee
The Tennessee stud's green eyes turned blue
Cuz he was a dreamin of a sweetheart too
We loped right on across Arkansas
I whipped her brother & I whipped her pa
I found that girl with the golden hair
And she was ridin' on a Tennessee mare

Stirrup to stirrup & side by side
We crossed the mountains & the valleys wide
We came to Big Muddy & we forded the flood
On the Tennessee mare & the Tennessee stud
Pretty little baby on the cabin floor
Little hoss colt playin' round the door
I love the girl with golden hair
And the Tennessee stud loves the Tennessee mare

— **Jimmy Driftwood**

© 1958 Warden Music Co. Inc. Used by permission. — On his Best of, *Jack Elliott* Country Style, *Doc Watson* Southbound *(Vanguard) &* & the Boys. *In* SO! *19:5 &* Reprints *#12.* ©A21

Tenting Tonight

We're tenting tonight on the old campground
Give us a song to cheer
Our weary hearts, a song of home
And friends we love so dear

E - AE / EB7 E / - AE / B7 E

Many are the hearts that are weary tonight
Wishing for the war to cease
Many are the hearts that are looking for the right
To see the dawn of peace
Tenting tonight (2x) tenting on the old campground

E A / E B7 / E AE / B7 E / E A B7 E

We've been tenting tonight on the old campground
Thinking of days gone by
Of the loved ones at home that gave us the hand
And the tear that says goodbye

We are tired of war on the old campground
Many are dead & gone
Of the brave & true who've left their homes
Others been wounded long

We've been fighting today on the old campground
Many are lying near
Some are dead & some are dying
Many are in tears

— **Walter Kittredge**

Fr the U.S. Civil War. (In the 19th c. a "campground" was not for vacationers, but a site for periodic religious gatherings for singing & preaching.) In SO! *3:5,* FS EncyV2, S that Changed the World, Treas of Am S, 120 Am S, Lift Every Voice*(SO!),* Best Loved S of the Am People, FiresB of Am S. ©A22

This Land Is Your Land

This land is your land, this land is my land
From California to the New York Island
From the redwood forest to the Gulf Stream waters
This land was made for you & me

(in D) G - D - / A - D - :||

As I was walking that ribbon of highway
I saw above me that endless skyway
I saw below me that golden valley
This land was made for you & me

I've roamed & rambled & I followed my footsteps
To the sparkling sands of her diamond deserts
And all around me, a voice was sounding: / **This land ...**

When the sun came shining & I was strolling
And the wheat fields waving & the dust clouds rolling
As the fog was lifting, a voice was chanting / This ...

As I went walking, I saw a sign there
On the sign it said "No Trespassing"
But on the other side it didn't say nothing
That side was made for you & me!

In the squares of the city, in the shadow of a steeple
By the relief office, I seen my people
As they stood there hungry I stood there asking
Is this land made for you & me?

Nobody living can ever stop me
As I go walking that freedom highway
Nobody living can make me turn back / This ...

(Canadian chorus) *This land is your land ...*
From Bonavista to Vancouver Island
From the Arctic Circle to the Great Lake Waters / This ...

— Woody Guthrie

 — In his SB *& on his* Hard Travelin, Gr S & 1940-46. *Also on* A Vision Shared / A Tribute to Woody Guthrie & Lead Belly, *Pete Seeger* I Can See a New Day, World of & Sings Woody Guthrie, *Weavers* SBag & Gr H, *Flatt & Scruggs* Changing Times *& Peter Paul & Mary* Movin. *In* SO! *4:7, 44:4 &* Reprints *#1,* WHATFG, Am Fav Bal, Carry It On, *Weavers* SB *&* Children's S for a Friendly Planet. OA23

What Did You Learn in School Today?

What did you learn in school today
Dear little child of mine? (repeat)
I learned that Washington never told a lie
I learned that soldiers seldom die
I learned that everybody's free
And that's what the teacher said to me
That's what I learned in school today
That's what I learned in school

C - / - G / C - / CG C // F C / (4x) // C - / CG C

What ... ? / I learned that policemen are my friends
I learned that justice never ends
I learned that murderers die for their crimes
Even if we make a mistake sometimes / **That's ...**

... I learned our government must be strong
It's always right & never wrong
Our leaders are the finest men
And we elect them again & again...

... I learned that war is not so bad
I learned about the great ones we have had
We fought in Germany & in France
And someday I might get my chance ...

... I learned that boys grow into men
Fly up to the moon & back again
That little girls to mommies grow
To stay at home & cook & sew ...

... I learned that Columbus looked for land
For Isabella & Ferdinand
To India he was looking for a way
Til he bumped right into the USA ...

... I learned that Wash. couldn't chew steak
For fear his wooden false teeth might break
He rowed across the Delaware
And he caught the British in their underwear ...

... I learned & I learned & I learned some more
Til my eyes got red & my brain got sore
I wander the halls in a state of shock
But it all gets better at 3 o'clock...

— Tom Paxton (last v. John Braxton)

 v. 5, 6 & 7 written by Tom Paxton at the publisher's request for use in school settings. On his Ramblin Boy *& Pete Seeger* We Shall Overcome. *In* SO! *13:4 &* Reprints *#7 &* S that Changed the World. OA24

Your Flag Decal Won't Get You into Heaven Anymore

While digesting Readers' Digest in the back of a dirty bookstore
A plastic flag with gum on the back fell out on the floor
Well I picked it up & I ran outside & slapped it on my window shield
And if I could see old Betsy Ross, I'd tell her how good I feel

D - G - / A - - D / - - - G / A - - D

But your flag decal won't get you into heaven anymore
They're already overcrowded from your dirty little war
And Jesus don't like killing, no matter what the reason's for
And your flag decal won't get you into heaven anymore

G - D - / A - D - / G - D - / A - - D

Well, I went to the bank this morning & the teller said to me
If you join our Christmas club, we'll give you 10 of them flags for free
Well I didn't mess around a bit, I took him up on what he said
And I stuck them flags all over my car & one on my wife's forehead

Well I got my windowshield so filled with flags I couldn't see
So I ran the car upside a curb & right into a tree
By the time they got a doctor down, I was already dead
And I'll never understand why the man standing in the pearly gate said:

(last chorus: ... We're **already overcrowded ...)**

— John Prine

 On his John Prine. *In* SO! *20:6 & 44:4.* OA25

Chapters which include many other songs on the USA include: CITY, FARM & PRAIRIE, FREEDOM, and MOUNTAIN VOICES.

See also: "All Clear in Harrisburg" (ECO) "The Wild West Is Where I Want to Be" (FUN) "Sweet Sunny South" (HOME) "Rolling Mills of NJ" (OUT) "I Ain't Marchin Any More," "I Feel Like I'm Fixin to Die," "Two Brothers," "With God on Our Side" (PEACE) "I'm Changing My Name to Chrysler," "Do-Re-Mi" (RICH) "Pity Mr Morgan," "O Joy Upon This Earth" (ROUNDS) "Two Good Arms," "Wasn't That a Time" (STRUG) "City of New Orleans" (TRAV), "Same Boat Now" (UNITY) "Amelia Earhardt," "Lucretia Mott" (WOMEN) "Forty Hour Week" & "Taft-Hartley" (WORK).

Songs on Native Americans outside this section include: "Men of the Fields" (FARM) "Piney Wood Home" (HOME) "Seneca Canoe Song/Kayowajineh" (OUT) "I Circle Around" (SACR).

For songs on other *parts of the Americas, see the SPANISH listing in the Cultures Index. Also: "Day-o" (FARM) "Jamaica Farewell," "Nova Scotia Farewell," "Run Come See" (SEA) "It Could Have Been Me," "Victor Jara," "You Can Get It If You Really Want" (STRUG) {Un} "Canadien Errant" (TRAV) & "Nicolia" (WORK). Canadian listings in the Artists Index include Grit Laskin, Ian & Sylvia, Anna McGarrigle, Raffi, Stan Rogers & Buffy Sainte-Marie.*

The songs in this section are ballads, carols & other traditional songs derived (at least originally) from England, Scotland or Ireland. All are in the public domain unless otherwise noted.

Arthur McBride

O me & me cousin, one Arthur McBride
As we went a-walking down by the seaside
Now mark what did follow & what did betide
For it bein' on Christmas morning

C - - - / F Am Dm F / C - - - / - Am G -

All for recreation we went on a tramp
And we met Sgt. Nipper & Corp. Cramp
And the little wee drummer who roused up the camp
With his rowdy dow dow in the morning

Indented verses: / " / " / " / C Am G C

"Good morning, good morning" the sgt. did cry
"And the same to you gentlemen" we did reply
Intending no harm but meaning for to pass by
For it bein' on Christmas mornin'

But says he "My fine fellows, if you would enlist
It's 10 guineas of gold I'll slip in your fists
And a crown in the bargain for to kick up the dust
And drink the king's health in the mornin'

"For a soldier he leads a very fine life
And he always is blessed with a charmin' young wife
And he pays all his debts without sorrow or strife
And always is pleasant & charmin'

For a soldier he always is decent & clean
In the finest of clothin' he's constantly seen
While other poor fellows go dirty & mean
And sup on thin gruel in the mornin'"

"But" says Arthur "I would not be proud of your clothes
For you've only the lend of them, as I suppose
And you dare not remove them one night, for you know
You're sure to be flogged in the mornin'

And altho' that we are both single & free
We take great delight in our own company
And we have no desires strange faces to see
Altho' that your offers are charmin'

And we have no desire to take your advance
All hazards & fortunes we barter on chance
Besides you would no scruples but to send us to France
Where we'd sure to be shot in the mornin'"

"But, oh no" said the sgt. "I'll have no such chat
And neither will I take it from spalpeen nor brat
For if you insult me with more words like that
I'll cut off your heads in the mornin'"

And then Arthur & I, we took on the odds
And they hardly had time for to draw their own blades
When a trusty shillelagh came over their heads
And bade them take that as fair warning!

And the little wee drummer, we flattened his pow
And we made a football of his rowdy-dow-dow
Flung it in the tide for to rock & to roll
And bade it a tedious returnin'

And the old rusty rapiers that hung by their sides
We flung them as far as we could in the tide
"And the devil go with you" cried Arthur McBride
"For spoilin our walk in the mornin'"

And we have no money to put in their cracks
And we paid no respect to their two bloody backs
For we lathered them there like a pair of wet sacks
And left them for dead in the mornin'

And so to conclude & to finish disputes
We obligingly asked them if they'd like some recruits
For we were the lads that would give them hard clouts
And bade them look sharp in the mornin'

— Irish: 1st pub P.W. Joyce *Old Irish FM & S*, **1908**
This version is off an album by Andy Irvine & Paul Brady (Mulligan). Other versions on Planxty *(Shanachie), Martin Carthy* Prince Heathen, *Bluestein Fam* Travelin Blues *& Kevin Roth* High on a Mtn. *In* FS in England. ©B02

Barbara Allen

In Scarlet Town where I was born
There was a fair maid dwelling
Made many a youth cry well a-day
Her name was Barbara Allen

G C / Am G / F C / G C

It was in the merry month of May
When green buds they were swelling
Sweet William came from the west country
And he courted Barbara Allen

He sent his servant unto her
To the place where she was dwelling
Said my master's sick, bids me call for you
If your name be Barbara Allen

Well slowly, slowly got she up
And slowly went she nigh him
But all she said as she passed his bed
"Young man I think you're dying"

"O yes, I'm sick, & very sick
And death is in me dwellin'
Unless I have the love of one
The love of Barbara Allen"

"O don't you remember in yonder town
When we were at the tavern?
You gave a health to the ladies round
And you slighted Barbara Allen!

"O yes, I remember in yonder town
When we were at the tavern
I gave a health to the ladies round
Gave my heart to Barbara Allen"

Then lightly tripped she down the stairs
She heard those church bells tolling
And each bell seemed to say as it tolled
"Hard-hearted Barbara Allen"

O mother, mother, go make my bed
And make it long & narrow
Sweet William died for me today
I'll die for him tomorrow"

They buried Barbara in the old church yard
They buried sweet William nigh her
Out of his grave grew a red, red rose
And out of hers a briar

They grew & grew up the old church wall
Til they could grow no higher
And at the top twined in a lovers' knot
The red rose & the briar

— Child #84

Earliest appearance in print, 1740. Bronson, in his Trad Tunes of the Child Ballads, *gives 198 versions. 29 versions on the LP record* Versions & Variants of Barbara Allen *(Library of Congress, AAFSL54). Samuel Pepys wrote in his 17th Century diary: "Heard this evening the delightful new Scottish song, Barbara Ellen." Prob it is the most widespread old world ballad in the US - of course, everyone knows a different version & swears it is "the real one." On Baez* Bal B, *Ewan MacColl* Manchester's Angel *(Tradition), his & Peggy Seeger's* Cold Snap *(Folkways 8765), Pete Seeger* Am Fav Bals V2, God Bless the Grass, WHATFG *&* World Of, *John Jacob Niles* F Balladeer, *New Lost City Ramblers* Old Timey S for Children *&* 20th Anniv Conc, *Jean Ritchie* Br Trad Bal, *Art Garfunkel* Angel Clare *& Tom Rush* Blues S. *In* Baez SB *& A Lomax* FS of NAm. OB03

Black Is the Color

Black **(3x)** is the color of my true love's hair
Her lips are like something rosy fair
The prettiest face & the neatest hands
I love the ground whereon she stands

Am - Em Am / - - Dm - / F G Am - / - - Dm -

I know my love & well she knows
I love the grass whereon she goes
If she on earth no more I see
My life will quickly fade away

I now go to Clyde to mourn & weep
But satisfied I never can sleep
I'll write to you in a few short lines
I'll suffer death 10,000 times

Winter's past & the leaves now again are green
The time has passed that we have seen
But still I hope the time will come
When you & I will be as one

— collected, arr & adap by John Jacob Niles

 — Lomax says this song is an Am reworking of Br materials. On Mike Seeger M fr the True Vine, *Baez* Bal B, *Nina Simone* Wild is the Wind, *J Ritchie album (EKL125), Pete Seeger* Am Fav Bal V2, *Guy Carawan alb (FG3548) & on his* FS Sat Night *(KL1110). In* SO! *9:1 &* Reprints *#5, A Lomax* FS of NAm, Joan Baez SB, *Sharp* Eng FS fr the S Appalach V2 FS, EncyV1, *Readers Dig* Fam SB, Abecedary of FS *&* FB of Love Songs. OB04

Blow the Candles Out

When I was 'prenticed in London I went to see my dear
The fires were all burning, the moon shone bright & clear
I rapped upon her window to ease her of her pain
She rose to let me in, then she barred the door again

DmC Dm DmC DmAm / DmC Dm DmC Dm

DmC F Dm Am / " /

I like your well behaviour & thus I often say
I cannot rest contented whilst you are far away
The roads they are so muddy, we cannot gang about
So roll me in your arms love & **blow the candles out**

Your father & your mother in yonder room do lie
A-huggin' one another, so why not you & I
A-huggin' one another without a fear or doubt
So roll me in your arms love & **blow...**

And if we prove successful love, then name it after me
Keep it neat & kiss it sweet & daff it on your knee
When my 3 years are ended, my time it will be out
Then I will double my indebtedness by blowing...

In SO! *7:1 &* Reprints *#1, A Lomax* FS of NAm, SFest, Coffeehse SB, Abecedary of FS, *Bikel* FS & Footnotes *&* FS EncyV1. OB05

Brennan on the Moor

'Tis of a brave young highwayman this story I will tell
His name was Willie Brennan & in Ireland he did dwell
It was on the Kilwood mountain he commenced his wild career
And many a wealthy noble man before him shook with fear
It was **Brennan on the Moor, Brennan on the Moor**
Bold brave & undaunted was young Brennan on the moor

A - D A / / / D - A AE // A - - - / D A D A

One day upon the highway as Willie he went down
He met the Mayor of Cashiell a mile outside the town
The mayor he knew his features & he said "Young man" said he
"Your name is Willie Brennan, you must come along with me"
And it's Brennan...

Now Brennan's wife had gone to town provisions for to buy
And when she saw her Willie she commenced to weep & cry
Said "Hand to me that tenpenny." As soon as Willie spoke
She handed him a blunderbuss from underneath her cloak

Now Brennan got his blunderbuss, my story I'll unfold
He caused the mayor to tremble & to deliver up his gold
5000 pounds were offered for his apprehension there
But Brennan & the peddler to the mountain did repair

Now Brennan is an outlaw all on some mountain high
With infantry & cavalry to take him they did try
But he laughed at them & he scorned at them until it was said
By a false-hearted woman he was cruelly betrayed

They hanged Brennan at the crossroads, in chains he swung & died
But still they say that in the night some do see him ride
They see him with his blunderbuss in the midnight chill
Along, along the King's highway rides Willie Brennan still

Tune coll. ca. 1860 by P.W. Joyce, pub. 1908 in his Old Irish Folk M & S *The Kilworth Mtns are betw Counties Cork & Tipperary. Brennan was executed at Clonmel in abt 1846. Recorded by the Clancy Bros (TLF1042). In* Burl Ives SB *& on his* S of the Colonies. *A field recording is on* Wolf River S *(FM4001). In* SO! *12:1 &* Reprints *#5,* FiresB of FS, Golden Ency of FS *&* 1001 Jumbo S. OB06

The Broom of the Cowdenknowes

How blithe each morn was I ta' see
My lass come o'er the hill
She skipped the burn & ran ta' me
I met her wi' good will

A - - - / - - D E / A - - - / D - E -

O the broom, the bonny, bonny broom
The broom o' the Cowdenknowes!
Fain would I be in the north country
Herding her father's ewes [pron: "yows"]

We neither herded ewes nor lamb
While the flock near us lay
She gathered in the sheep at night
And cheered me all the day

Hard fate that I should banished be
Gone way o'er hill & moor
Because I loved the fairest lass
That ever yet was born

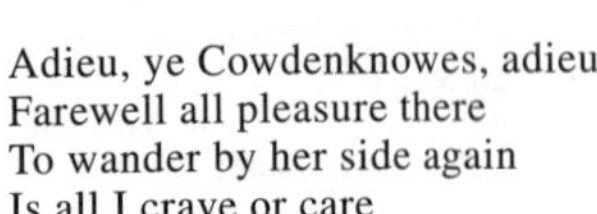

Adieu, ye Cowdenknowes, adieu
Farewell all pleasure there
To wander by her side again
Is all I crave or care

— Scottish. Child #217

In SO! *31:1,* Bright Morning Stars *(WAS)* & Oxford Scot SB. *On Silly Wizard* Caledonia's Hardy Sons, Golden Golden & Best of, *Archie Fisher* Will Ye Gang Love *(Topic), Jean Redpath* A Fine S for Singing, *Paris Kern & Lisa Liske* Bread & Roses. *Also rec by Garnet Rogers.* ©B07

Cherry Tree Carol

When Joseph was an old man an old man was he
He married Virgin Mary the Queen of Galilee **(2x)**

(in 3/4) C - - G / F C - Am / F C CCG C

Joseph & Mary walked thru an orchard green
There were berries & cherries as thick as might be seen...

And up spoke Virgin Mary so meek & so mild
Joseph gather me some cherries for I am with child

Then Joseph flew in anger, in anger flew he
"Let the father of the baby gather cherries for thee"

Then up spoke baby Jesus from in Mary's womb
"Bend down, thou tallest cherry, that my mother might have some"

And bent down the tallest branch til it touched Mary's hand
Cried she "O look thou Joseph, I have cherries by command!"

Then Joseph took Mary all on his right knee:
"O what have I done, Lord? Have mercy on me"

Then Joseph took Mary all on his left knee:
"O tell me, little baby, when your birthday will be?"

"On the 6th day of January, my birthday will be
And the stars in the firmament shall twinkle with glee"

— Child #54

Based on the book of Pseudo-Matthew, in the Apocrypha. In areas of Appalachia Jan 6 is thought of as "Old Christmas" & was celebrated on that day a couple of generations back: the different date can be traced to the change to our modern western calendar a couple of centuries ago. On Roberts & Barrand Nowell Sing We Clear, Christmas Revels & Wassail Wassail, *Pete Seeger* Am FS for Children, *Nancy Raven* S for the Holiday, *Bluestein Fam* Br Trad Bal, *J.E. Mainer's* V 10 *& JJ Niles* Folk Balladeer. *In* SFest, Am FS for Children, Baez SB, Abecedary of FS, *Sharp* FS fr the S Appalach *&* FS EncyV1. ©B08

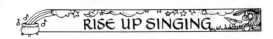

A Child This Day

A child this day is born, a child of high renown
Most worthy of a sceptre, a sceptre & a crown
Nowell **(3x)**, nowell sing all we may
Because the King of all kings was born this blessèd day

A E D E / AD A AE A :||

These tidings shepherds heard in field watching their fold
Were by an angel unto them that night reveal'd & told

To whom the angel spoke saying "Be not afraid
Be glad, poor silly shepherds, why are you so dismayed?

"For lo! I bring you tidings of gladness & of mirth
Which cometh to all people by this holy infant's birth

Then was there with the angel an host incontinent
Of heavenly bright soldiers which from the Highest was sent

Lauding the Lord our God & his celestial King
All glory be in paradise, this heavenly host did sing:

And as the angel told them, so to them did appear
They found the young child Jesus Christ with Mary, his mother dear

— from William Sandys' ***Christmas Carols*** **, 1833 (West of England)**

In Oxford B of Carols *& on Roberts & Barrand* Nowell Sing We Clear. ©B09

Come All Ye Fair and Tender Ladies

Come all ye fair & tender ladies
Be careful how you court young men
They're like the stars of a summer's morning
They'll first appear & then they're gone

(in G) Am D G - / Am D C D / G D G - / C - Am D

If I'd ha' known before I courted
I never would have courted none
I'd have locked my heart in a box of golden
And fastened up it with a silver pin

I wish I were some little sparrow
And I had wings & I could fly
I'd fly straightway to my false true lover
And when he's talking I'll be nigh
[**or:** And when he'd speak I would deny]

But I am not a little sparrow
I have no wings, neither can I fly
So I'll sit down here to weep in sorrow
And try to pass my troubles by

O don't you remember our days of courting
When your head lay upon my breast
You could make me believe by the falling of your arm
That the sun rose in the west

— coll 1916 by Cecil Sharp in Kentucky

1st pub in his Eng FS in the S Appalach, *1917. In his 1932 ed he lists 18 versions. In* SO! *4:6 &* Reprints *#3,* Am Fav Bal, *WHATFG, Lomax* FS USA *&* FS of NAm, Baez SB *&* FS EncV1. *On Baez* V Early *&* Love S, Van Ronk, *M McCaslin's* Life & Time, *Pete Seeger* Darling Corey *(FA2003), Happy Traum* Relax Your Mind, *B Sainte-Marie* Many a Mile, *Ian & Sylvia* So Much for Dreaming, *E Von Schmidt* 2nd Night, 3rd Row, *J Ritchie* Time for Singing *&* Best of, *&* SO! *36:1.* ©B10

The Coventry Carol

Lully, lullay, thou little tiny child
By by, lully lullay:
Lullay, thou little tiny child
By by, lully lullay

Em - Am B7 / Em AmB7 Em - / D - F#m B7 / Em AmB7 E -

O sisters too, how may we do
For to preserve this day
This poor youngling for whom we do sing
By by, lully lullay?

Herod the King in his raging
Charg è d he hath this day
His men of might in his own sight
All children young to slay

Then woe is me poor child for thee
And ever mourn & say
For thy parting nor say nor sing
By by, lully lullay!

— w: Robert Croo, 1534 — m: in 1591 manuscript

Part of the Pageant of the Shearmen & Tailors fr 15th c. The Coventry plays were witnessed by Richard III & Henry VII. On Roberts & Barrand Nowell Sing We Clear *(Front Hall), Nancy Raven* S for the Holiday, *Mary Zikos* Z & *Denver* Rocky Mtn High. *In* Oxford B of Carols & FiresB of FS. **OB11**

The Cutty Wren

"O where are you going?" **said Milder* to Malder**
[**pron.** "Mill-der"]
"O we may not tell you" **said Festle to Fose**
"We're off to the woods" **said John the Red Nose (2x)**

D C D C / D C D Am / D Am C - / D C DDC D

"What will you do there?" **said Milder...** **(in 3/4)**
"O we may not tell you" **said Festle...**
"We'll shoot the Cutty Wren" **said John... (2x)**

How will you shoot her?
O we may not tell you
With bows & with arrows

That will not do
O what will do then?
Big guns & big cannon

How will you bring her home?
O we may not tell you
On 4 strong men's shoulders

That will not do
O what will do then?
Big carts & big wagons

How will you cut her up?
O we may not tell you
With knives & with forks

That will not do
O what will do then?
Big hatchets & cleavers

Who'll get the spare ribs?
O we may not tell you
We'll give it all to the poor!

Words related to pre-Christian ceremony of hunting the wren, now done on St.Stephen's day, Dec.26. Also thought to be rel. to peasant uprisings in medieval times. In SO! *4:1* & Reprints *#5*, S of Work & Protest, & FS Ency V1. *On Ian & Sylvia* So Much for Dreaming & Gr Hits, *Robts & Barrand* 2nd Nowell *(FHR026), Holly Tannen* Invocation *(Kicking Mule), & on Rich Kirby & Michael Kline* They Can't Put It Back *(words adapt to strip mining struggle).* **OB12**

Geordie

As I walked out over London bridge
One misty morning early
I overheard a fair pretty maid
Was lamenting for her Geordie

Em D C Em / G - D - / Em G D Bm / C G B7 Em

Ah, my Geordie will be hanged in a golden chain
Tis not the chain of many
He was born of king's royal breed
And lost to a virtuous lady

Go bridle me my milk white steed
Go bridle me my pony
I will ride to London's court
To plead for the life of Geordie

Ah, my Geordie never stole nor cow nor calf
He never hurted any
Stole 16 of the king's royal deer
And he sold them in Bohenny

Two pretty babies have I born
The third lies in my body
I'd freely part with them every one
If you'd spare the life of Geordie

The judge looked over his left shoulder
He said fair maid I'm sorry
He said fair maid you must be gone
For I cannot pardon Geordie

Ah my Geordie will be hanged in a golden chain
Tis not the chain of many
Stole 16 of the king's royal deer
And he sold them in Bohenny

— English broadside ballad from the 18th century, Child #209

SO! *13:3* & Rep. *#7*, Baez SB, FS EncyV1 *& Sharp* Eng FS of the S App. *On E MacColl* Eng & Scottish Bal V2 *(FG3510), M Carthy* Crown of Horn, *A M Muir* So Goes My Heart *(FolkLeg)*, Oisin, *& Baez* 1st 10 Yrs, *Maddy Prior & June Tabor* The Silly Sisters. **OB13**

The Great Silkie

An earthly nourris *[nurse]* sits & sings
And aye she sings ba lilly wean
And little ken I my bairn's father
Far less the land that he staps *[steps]* in

D C - D / / G D C D / Em - C D

Then in staps he to her bed fit
And a grumbly guest I'm sure was he
Saying "Here am I, thy bairn's faither
Altho' I be not comely

I am a man upon the land
I am a silkie on the sea
And when I'm far & far frae land
My home it is in Sule Skerrie"

"It was na weel" quo the maiden fair
"It was na weel" indeed quo she
"That the great silkie from Sule Skerry
Should hae come & aught a bairn ta me"

Then he has ta'en a purse of gold
And he has pat it upon her knee
Saying "Gie to me my little young son
And take thee up thy nourris fee

And it shall come to pass on a summer's day
When the sun shines bright on every stane *[stone]*
I'll come & fetch my little young son
And teach him for to swim the faem *[foam]*

And thou shall marry a gunner good
And a right fine gunner I'm sure he'll be
And the very first shot that e'er he shoots
Will kill both my young son & me"

— w: Child Ballad #113 — m: (chords above) James Waters

Musical arr.© 1966 Folk Legacy Records. All rights reserved. Used by permission. — aka: "Silkie." A silkie is a mythological creature who can change back & forth betw being seal & human. In SO! *11:1* & Repr. *#5*, Baez SB, FS EncyV1, Golden Ency of FS, Coffeehse SB, *Sargent & Kitteridge* Eng & Scottish Pop Bal, & FS Abecedary. *On Ray Fisher* The Bonny Birdie *(Leader), Lui Collins* Made in New E., Judy Collins *& Baez* Bal B. **OB14**

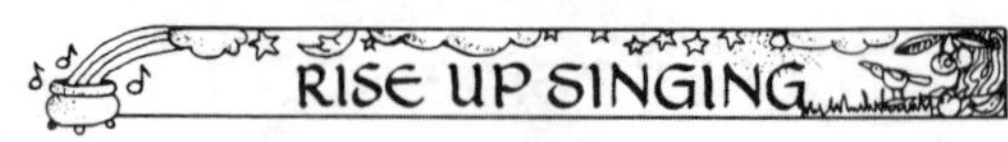

Green Grow the Rushes

I'll sing you one-o, **green grow the rushes-o**
What is your one-o?
One is one & all alone & evermore shall be

G - GD G / - - // G C D G

I'll sing you two-o, **green...**
What is your two-o?
2, 2 the lily white boys, clothéd all in green-o
One is one & all alone...

/ " / " // G C A D / G C D G

3, 3 the rivals

G D Em D

4 for the Gospel makers
5 for the symbols at your door
6 for the 6 proud walkers
7 for the 7 stars in the sky
8 for the April rainers
9 for the 9 bright shiners
10 for the 10 Commandments
11 for the 11 went up to heaven
12 for the 12 Apostles

(alternate verses:)
G - / D G / etc.

1st printed in Broadwood & Maitland English Country S, *(1893) On Robts & Barrand* 2nd Nowell *(FHR26). In* FiresB of FS, SFest, FS EncyV1, Joyful singing *(WAS)* & FS Abecedary. OB15

Holly and the Ivy

The holly & the ivy when they are both full grown
Of all the trees that are in the wood, the holly bears the crown
The rising of the sun & the running of the deer
The playing of the merry organ, sweet singing in the choir

(in 3/4) DDG D DDG A / D GDD DDA D :||

The holly bears a blossom as white as any flower
And Mary bore sweet Jesus Christ to be our sweet saviour

The holly bears a berry as read as any blood
And Mary bore sweet Jesus Christ to do poor sinners good

... a prickle as sharp as any thorn / ... on Christmas Day in the morn
... a bark as bitter as any gall / ... for to redeem us all

On Roberts & Barrand Nowell Sing We Clear *(FHR), Madeleine MacNeil* Holly & the Ivy, Anne Hills & Friends *(Hogeye 7),* Christmas Revels *(RC1078), & Linda Russell* Sing We All Merrily *&* On This Day Earth *(Hogeye). In* SO! *34:4,* Peoples SB & FS Abecedary. OB16

The Holly Bears a Berry

O the holly bears a berry as white as the milk
And Mary bore Jesus all wrappèd in silk
Mary bore Jesus, our saviour for to be
And the first tree in the greenwood it was the holly
Holly, holly - & the first tree in the...holly

(in 3/4) D - A D / // D - A Bm / 1st / Â D̂ D - A D

O the holly bears a berry that's green as the grass
And Mary bore Jesus who died on the cross

O the holly bears a berry as blood it is red
And Mary bore Jesus who died in our stead

O the holly bears a berry as black as the coal
And Mary bore Jesus who died for us all

— collected by John Greenway in Australia

Greenway taught the song to Rosalie Sorrels who helped spread it in this country. In SO! *12:5 &* Reprints #6, How Can We Keep fr Singing? & FS EncyV1. *On L Neustadt & the Angel Band* Shout for Joy & *Cambridge Singers* Xmas Day In The Morning. OB17

I Know Where I'm Going

I know where I'm going & I know who's going with me
I know who I love & my dear knows who I'll marry

(in C) C - - G / Em Am Dm G

I have stockings of silk & shoes of bright green leather
Combs to buckle my hair & a ring for every finger

O feather beds are soft & painted rooms are bonnie
But I would give them all for my handsome winsome Johnny

Some say he's black* but I say he's bonnie
Fairest of them all is my handsome winsome Johnny

***("black" probably means that Johnny's a gypsy)**

— fr Herbert Hughes *Irish Country Songs* **V1, 1909**

Song related to the Gypsy Laddie cycle. In Weavers SB, FiresB of Love S & FS EncyV1. *On Weavers* At Carnegie Hall, *J Collins* Maid of Const Sorrow *& Bellafonte* Returns to Carnegie Hall, *Ives* Wayfaring Stranger, *Odetta* My Eyes Have Seen *& Cambridge Singers* Lark In The Clean Air. OB18

Jock O' Hazeldean

Why weep ye by the tide Ladie, why weep ye by the tide?
I'll wed ye tae my youngest son & ye shall be his bride
And ye shall be his bride Ladie, sae comely to be seen
But aye she let the tears doon fa' for Jock o' Hazeldean

(in 3/4) C G Am G F Dm G - / C G F G F G C -
F - - - D - F - / " /

Now let this willfu' grief be done & dry that cheek sae pale
Young Frank is chief of Errington & laird o' Langley-dale
His step is first in peaceful ha', his sword in battle keen...

A chain of gold ye shall not lack nor braid to bind your hair
Nor mettled hound nor managed hawk nor palfrey fresh & fair
And you the foremost o' them a' shall ride our forest queen...

The kirk was deck'd at morningtide, the tapers glimmer'd fair
The priest & bridegroom wait the bride & dame & knight
were there
They sought her baith by bower & ha', the ladie was na' seen
She's o'er the Border & awa' wi' Jock o' Hazeldean

— Child #293 (aka: John of Hazelgreen)

In SO! *38:2. On D Gaughan* No More Forever *(Trailer), J McCormick* W Ireland, *P Herdman* Water Lilies, *Jon Wilcox* Close to Home *(SBR4210),* Fast Folk 3-9. OB19

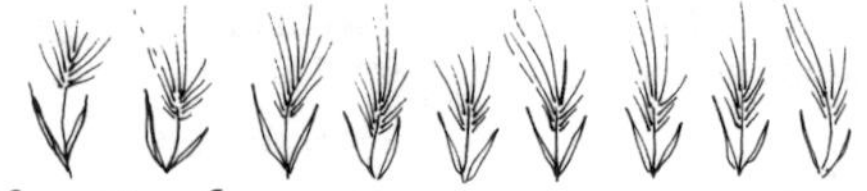

John Barleycorn

There was three men came out of the west
Their fortunes for to try
And these three men made a solemn vow
John Barleycorn should die
They plowed, they sowed, they harrowed him in
Threw clods upon his head
And these three men made a solemn vow
John Barleycorn was dead

(in Am)

D Am - - / F - Am - :|| C - Am - / Em D E - / 1st 2

They let him lie for a very long time
Til the rain from heav'n did fall
Then Little Sir John sprung up his head
And so amazed them all
They let him stand til midsummer
Til he grew both pale & wan
Then Little Sir John grew a long sharp beard
And so became a man

They hired men with the scythes so sharp
To cut him off at the knee
They rolled him & tied him about the waist
And used him barbarously
They hired men with the sharp pitchforks
To pierce him to the heart
And the loader he served him worse than that
For he tied him to a cart

They wheeled him around & around the field
Til they came unto a barn
And there they made a solemn mow
Of poor John Barleycorn
They hired men with the crab-tree sticks
To strip him skin from bone
And the miller he treated him worst of all
For he ground him between two stones

Here's little Sir John in a nut-brown bowl
And brandy in a glass
And Little Sir John in the nut-brown bowl
Proved the stronger man at last
For the huntsman, he can't hunt the fox
Nor loudly blow his horn
And the tinker can't mend kettles or pots
Without a little of the Barleycorn

Martin Carthy writes that this song is abt the cycle of seasons: It is based on the idea that the corn spirit is indestructible no matter what & alive in all things remotely touched by it. This version can be found on a Waterstons' album, Traffic's John Barleycorn *& in* Penguin B of FS. *Other versions are in SO! 32:3,* Bright Morning Stars *(WAS) &* Sing the Good Earth. *On M Carthy* Sweet Wivelsfield *& his* This is ..., *J Renbourn* Maid in Bedlam *&* Live in America, *Steeleye Span* Below the Salt, *J Roberts* Live at Holstein's, *Lou Killen* Old S, Old Friends, *& T Broadbent* Female Drummer. OB20

John Riley

Fair young maid all in a garden
Strange young man passerby
Said "Fair maid will you marry me?"
This then sir was her reply **(capo up)**

Am D Am - / /C - G - / Dm - Am -

"O no, kind sir, I cannot marry thee
For I've a love who sails all on the seas
He's been gone for 7 years
Still no man shall marry me"

"What if he's in some battle slain
Or drownded in the deep salt sea?
What if he's found another love
And he & his love both married be?"

"If he's in some battle slain
I will die when the moon doth wane
If he's drownded in the deep salt sea
I'll be true to his memory

And if he's found another love
And he & his love both married be
I wish them health & happiness
Where they dwell across the sea"

He picked her up all in his arms
And kisses gave her 1, 2, 3
Saying "Weep no more, my own true love
I am your long lost John Riley"

In SO! 13:3 & Reprints #8, Bells of Rhymney, *A Lomax* FS of NAm, FS EncyV1, FS N Am Sings, Baez SB *&* All Our Lives. *On Baez* Bal B, *Odetta* At Carnegie Hall, *Pete Seeger* God Bless the Grass *&* Darlin Corey, *Pat Sky* Harvest of Gentle Clang *& J Collins* Maid of Const Sorrow. OB21

The Keeper

The keeper would a-hunting go
And under his coat he carried a bow
All for to shoot at a merry little doe
Among the leaves so green-o

C - F C / /C - - G / C - G C

Jackie Boy? – Master – Sing ye well? – very well
Hey down, ho down, derry derry down
Among the leaves so green-o
To my hey down down – to my ho down down
Hey down, ho down, derry derry down
Among ...

C - - - / - - - G / C - G C :||

The 1st doe he shot at, he missed
The 2nd doe, he trimmed & kissed
The 3rd doe went where nobody wist / **Among ...**

The 4th doe she did cross the plain
The keeper fetched her back again
Where she is now she may remain / **...**

The 5th doe she did cross the brook
The keeper fetched her back with his crook
Where she is now you may go & look...

In SO! 2:7 *&* Reprints #5, Am Fav Bal, SFest, FiresB of Fun & Games, FS EncyV1, *&* FS Abecedary *(incl some addl bawdy v.). On Weavers* Trav On *& Pete Seeger* Am Fav Bal V2 *(FA2321).* OB22

Lakes of Ponchartrain

It was one fine March morning I bid New Orleans adieu
And took the road to Jackson Town my fortune to renew
I cursed all foreign money, no credit could I gain
Which filled my heart with longing for **the Lakes of Ponchetrain** **(capo up, in 3/4)**

G D C G Em C G - / - - Em D G - C - / / 1st

I stepped on board a RR car beneath the morning sun
And I rode the rails til evening & I laid me down again
All strangers they're no friends to me til a dark girl towards me came
And I fell in love with a Creole girl on **the Lakes...**

I said "Me pretty Creole girl, my money here's no good
If it weren't for the alligators I'd sleep out in the wood"
"You're welcome here kind stranger, our house is very plain
But we never turn a stranger out on..."

She took me into her mama's house & treated me right well
The hair upon her shoulders in jet black ringlets fell
To try to paint her beauty I'm sure t'would be in vain
So handsome was my Creole girl on...

I asked her would she marry me, she said that ne'er would be
For she had got a lover & he was far at sea
She said that she would wait for him & true she would remain
Til he returned to his Creole girl on...

So fair you well my bonnie old girl, I ne'er may see you no more
I'll ne'er forget your kindness in the cottage by the shore
And at every social gathering, a golden glass I'll drain
And I'll drink all health to the Creole girl on...

In Flanders et al: The New Green Mountain Songster *(1934). On Trapezoid* Now & Then, *Planxty* Collection *&* Cold Blows the Rainy Night, *Paul Brody album, Christy Moore* Time Has Come, Fast Folk *2-7, Carla Sciaky* To Meet You, *Huxtable, Christensen & Hood* Melancholy Babies *(FHR35).* OB23

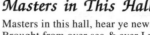

Mary Hamilton

Word is to the kitchen gone
And word is to the hall
And word is up to Madam the Queen
And that's the worst of all
That Mary Hamilton's borne a babe } **chords as lines 3 & 4**
To the highest Stuart of all

(in 3/4) C - F C / - - G - / F G C Am / C G C -

"Arise, arise, Mary Hamilton
Arise & tell to me
What thou hast done with thy wee babe
I saw and heard weep by thee?"

"I put him in a tiny boat
And cast him out to sea
That he might sink or he might swim
But he'd never come back to me"

"Arise, arise, Mary Hamilton
Arise & come with me
There is a wedding in Glasgow town
This night we'll go & see"

She put not on her robes of black
Nor on her robes of brown
But she put on her robes of white
To ride into Glasgow town

And as she rode into Glasgow town
The city for to see
The bailiff's wife & the provost's wife
Cried "Ach & alas for thee"

"Ah you need not weep for me" she cried
"You need not weep for me
For had I not slain my own wee babe
This death I would not dee

"Ah little did my mother think
When first she cradled me
The lands I was to travel in
And the death I was to dee

"Last night I washed the Queen's feet
And put the gold in her hair
And the only reward I find for this
The gallows to be my share

"Cast off, cast off my gown" she cried
"But let my petticoat be
And tie a napkin round my face
For the gallows I would not see"

Then by & come the King himself
And looked up with a pitiful eye [pron. "ee"]
"Come down, come down, Mary Hamilton
Tonight you'll dine with me"

"Ah hold your tongue, my sovereign liege
And let your folly be
For if you'd a mind to save my life
You'd never have shamed me here

"Last night there were four Marys
Tonight there'll be but three
There was Mary Beaton & Mary Seton
And Mary Carmichael & me"

— Child ballad 173

In SO! *11:5 &* Reprints *#5*, S of All Times *(WAS)*, FS EncyV1, Baez SB, *&* FS Abecedary. *On Baez 1st alb*, 1st 10 Yrs *&* Bal B, *Robin Roberts* Fair & Tender Ladies, *Peggy Seeger & E MacColl* Blood & Roses V4, *J Ritchie* The Most Dulcimer *(GR714)*, *JJ Niles* F Balladeer, *& McEwen Bros* Gr Scottish Bal. **OB24**

Masters in This Hall

Masters in this hall, hear ye news today
Brought from over sea & ever I you pray
Am - - Em / Am - Em Am

Nowell! (3x) Nowell sing we clear!
Holpen are all folk on earth, born is God's Son so dear
Nowell! (3x) Nowell sing we loud!
God today hath poor folk raised & cast a-down the proud
Am - - - / Dm Am E Am :||

Going o'er the hills thru the milkwhite snow
Heard I ewes bleat while the wind did blow

Shepherds many a one sat among the sheep
No man spake more word than they had been asleep

Quoth I "Fellows mine, why this guise sit ye?
Making but dull cheer, shepherds tho' ye be?

Shepherds should of right leap & dance & sing
Thus to see ye sit is a right strange thing"

Quoth these fellows then "To Bethlehem we go
To see a mighty lord lie in manger low"

"How name ye this lord, Shepherds?" then said I
"Very God" they said "come from heaven high"

Then to Bethlehem we went two & two
And in a sorry place heard the oxen low

Therein did we see a sweet & goodly may
And a fair old man, upon the straw she lay

And a little child on her arm had she
"Wot ye who this is?" said the hinds to me

Ox & ass him know kneeling on their knee
Wondrous joy had I this little babe to see

This is Christ the Lord, Masters be ye glad!
Christmas is come in & no folk should be sad

— w: William Morris — m: old French carol

Edmund Sedding learned the tune from the organist at Chartres Cathedral, introduced it to Morris, & published Morris' new words in his Ancient Christmas Carols *(1860). On Robts & Barrand* Nowell Sing We Clear *V1 & V3 (FHR 13 & 36),* Christmas Revels *(RC1078), Pete Seeger* Trad Christmas Carols *(FAS32311), &* Seth Austin *(Kicking Mule). In* SO! *11:5,* Oxford B of Carols, *&* FiresB of FS. **OB25**

Peggy-o

As we marched down to Fernario **(2x)**
Our captain fell in love with a lady like a dove
And the name she was called was pretty Peggy-o
D Bm G D / D - - A / G D - Bm / D Bm G D

Come go along with me, pretty Peggy-o **(2x)**
In coaches you shall ride with your true love by your side
Just as grand as any lady in the are-o

What would your mother think, pretty... **(2x)**
What...think for to hear the guineas clink
And the soldiers all are marching before ye-o

You're the man that I adore, handsome Willy-o **(2x)**
You're...adore but your fortune is too low
I'm afraid my mother would be angry-o

Come a-trippin down the stair, pretty... **(2x)**
Come...stair & tie up your yellow hair
Bid a last farewell to handsome Willy-o

If ever I return, pretty... this city I will burn
And destroy all the ladies in the are-o

Our captain, he is dead... & he died for a maid
And he's buried in the Louisiana Country-o

aka: "Pretty Peggy of Derby, The Bonnie Lass of Fyvie-o." In SO! *13:2 &* Reprints *#6*, FS EncyV1, *& Sharp* Eng FS of the So App v2. *On K Roth* Dulcimer Man. **OB26**

Rosebud in June

It's a rosebud in June & the violets in full bloom
And the small birds singing love songs on each spray

Dm - - Am / F - G A

We'll pipe & we'll sing, love, we'll dance in a ring, love
When each lad takes his lass, all on the green grass
And it's all to plow, where the fat oxen graze low
And the lads & the lasses do sheep shearing go

F - Dm A / Dm - - - / F - Dm A / Dm F A Dm

When we have all sheared, all our jolly, jolly sheep
What joy can be greater than to talk of their increase

For their flesh it is good, it's the best of all food
And their wool it will clothe us & keep our backs from the cold

It's the ewes & their lambs, it's the hogs & their rams
And the fat wethers too, they will make a fine show [pron. "shoe"]

— collected fr William King by Cecil Sharp in Somerset, 1904

aka: "The Sheep Shearing Song." On Steeleye Span Below the Salt . *In* SO! *37:1, Sharp & Manson* FS fr Somerset, *Mason* Nursery Rhymes & Country S, *Purslow* Marrow Bones & S for All Seasons. **OB27**

The Seven Joys of Mary

The first **good joy that Mary had it was the joy of** one
To see the blessèd Jesus Christ when he was first her son
When he was first her son, **good man, & blessèd may he be**
Both Father, Son & the Holy Ghost thru all eternity

D - A D/ /A - D DA / 1st /

The next good joy that Mary had it was the joy of two
To see her own son Jesus Christ to make the lame to go
To make the lame to go, **good man, & blessèd may he be**
Both Father, Son and Holy Ghost thru all eternity

3: **The next good joy that Mary had it was the joy of three**
To see her own son Jesus Christ to make the blind to see
4: ... to read the Bible o'er
5: ... to bring the dead alive
6: ... upon the Crucifix
7: ... to wear the crown of Heaven

aka: "Joys Seven." On Roberts & Barrand Nowell Sing We Clear *(FHR13). In* Oxford B of Carols, *A Lomax* FS of NAm, *Ives* SB, FS EncyV1, & FiresB of FS. **OB28**

Star of the County Down

Near Bambridge Town in the County Down
One morning last July
Down the green came a sweet colleen
And she smiled as she passed me by
She looked so sweet from her two bare feet
To the crown of her nut-brown hair
Such a winsome elf that I pinched myself
For to see I was really there

Em - C D / Em - D - / Em - C D / Em Am Em -

G - D - / " / " / " /

(chords as 2nd half of verse)
From Bantry Bay up to Derry Quay
And from Galway to Dublin Town
No maid I've seen like the brown colleen
That I met in the County Down

As she onward sped sure I scratched my head
And I looked with a feeling rare
And I says, says I to a passer-by
"Who's that maid with the nut-brown hair?"
He smiled at me & he says to me
"That's the gem of Ireland's crown
Young Rosie McCann from the banks of the Bann
She's the Star of the County Down"

At the harvest fair, she'll be surely there
So I'll dress in my Sunday clothes
With my shoes shined bright & my hat cocked right
For a smile from the nut-brown rose
No pipe I'll smoke, no horse I'll yoke
Til my plow is a rust-colored brown
Til smiling bright by my own firelight
Is the Star of the County Down

Irish. Same tune as "Dives & Lazarus," "The Banks of Newfoundland," & "Van Dieman's Land." Boreen is a lane or narrow road. On Scott Alarik *(Swallowtail), Kretzner & Leibowitz* Dulcimer fair, *Holly Tannen* Invocation, Fast Folk *3-9. In Lochlainn* More Irish Street Bal, *Edwards & Kelley* Coffeehse SB, *&* Wind that Shakes the Barley. **OB29** *in 4/4* **OB30** *in 3/4*

Sussex Mummers Carol

God bless the Master of this house
With happiness beside
Where-e'er his body rides or walks
His God must be his guide **(2x)**

D - A - / / G - D A / D - - A / DA Bm G D A D -

God bless the Mistress of this house
With gold chain round her breast
Where-e'er her body sleeps or wakes
Lord send her soul to rest **(2x)**

God bless your house, your children too
Your cattle & your store
The Lord increase you day by day
And send you more & more **(2x)**

— trad. carol coll by Lucy Broadwood

Sung by Christmas mummers of Horsham, in Sussex, in the late 1870s. Pub in her Sussex Carols, Eng Trad S & Carols *(Boosey & Co., 1908), & her* Christmas Carols for Children. *There are addl verses beginning "O mortal man, remember well," but the carol is cheerier in the shortened version given here, which is used in the Christmas Revels held each year in a number of cities in the Northeastern US. Also in* The Christmas Revels SB, Oxford B of Carols, Xmas Revels SB, *Bryant* Broadside Bal for Christmastyde, *& on* Christmas Revels *(RC1078), Percy Grainger* Plays Grainger. **OB31**

Thyme

Once I had a sprig of thyme
I thought it never would decay
Until a saucy sailor, he chanced upon my way
And he stole away my bonnie bunch of thyme

C G C - / - - Dm G / C C7 F G / C G C -

Thyme it is a precious thing
Thyme, brings all things to your mind
Thyme with all its labors, along with all its joys
And it's thyme, brings all things to an end

This sailor, he gave to me a rose
A rose that never would decay
He gave it to me, to keep me well minded
Of the night he stole my bonny thyme away

Come all you maidens, brisk & fair
All you who flourish in your prime
Beware & take care, & keep your garden fair
And let no man steal your bonny bunch of thyme

aka: "Sprig of Thyme." In SO! *21:1. On M Cooney* Singer of Old S, *Roberts & Barrand* Spencer Rover *(Swallowtail),* Van Ronk. **OB32**

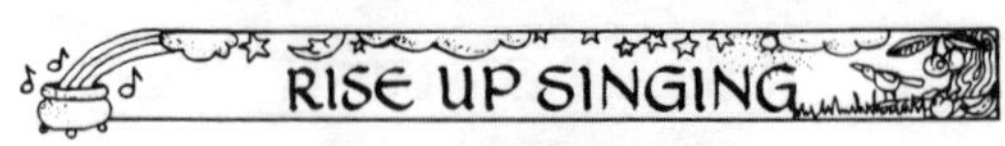

The Water Is Wide

The water is wide, I cannot cross over
And neither have I wings to fly
Build me a boat that can carry two
And both shall row my true love & I

D G D - / Bm Em A - / F#m - Bm G / A - D -

A ship there is & she sails the seas
She's laden deep as deep can be
But not so deep as the love I'm in
And I know not if I sink or swim

I leaned my back against a young oak
Thinkin' he were a trusty tree
But first he bended & then he broke
Thus did my love prove false to me

I thrust my hand into a soft bush
Thinking the sweetest flower to find
I pricked my finger unto the bone
And left the sweetest flower behind

O love is handsome & love is kind *[fine]*
Gay as a jewel when first it's new
But *[And]* love grows old & waxes cold *[bold]*
And fades away *[lights my life]* like the morning dew

O waly waly up the bank
And waly waly down the braes
And waly waly by yon burn side
Where me & my love were wont to gae

When sea sand turneth far inland
And mussels grow on every tree
When cockle shells turn silver bells
Then would I lose my love for thee

The seagulls wheel, they turn & dive
The mountain stands beside the sea
The world we know turns round & round
And all for them & you & me

— final verse by Pete Seeger *© 1993 Sanga Music, Inc.*

aka: "Waly, Waly." In SO! *9:1 &* Reprints *#3,* WHATFG, *Sharp* Eng FS of S App, FS EncyV1, *&* Baez SB. *On Pete Seeger* Pete, Sing-a-long Demonstration Concert, HARP, Am Fav Bal V2 *&* Now, *B Sainte-Marie* Little Wheel Spin, *K Bonoff* Restless Night, *Baez* V Early, *Ronnie Gilbert* The Spirit is Free, *Rory Block* High Heeled Blues, *Jackie Washington* V2, *John Gorka* WHATFG (S of Pete Seeger V1) *Fred Neil* Little Bit of Rain, *Beers family Golden Skein &* *Introducing, Bill Hinkley & Judy Larsen* Out in Our Meadow, Carolyn Hester *& Madeline MacNeil* Soon its Gonna Rain. OB33

Who's Gonna Shoe Your Pretty Little Foot?

Who's gonna shoe your pretty little foot?
Who's gonna glove your hand?
Who's gonna kiss your red ruby lips?
Who's gonna be your man?

C / F C / / G C

Papa can shoe my pretty little foot
Mama can glove my hand
Sister can kiss my ruby red lips
I don't need no man

I don't need no man, poor boy **(2x)**
Sister can kiss my red ruby lips
'Cause I don't need no man

This goes back at least to the 18th c. The title stanza is probably fr the "Lass of Rock Royal," Child #76. In SO! *6:4 &* Reprints*#2,* Here's to the Women, Am Fav Bal, *A Lomax* FS of NAm, Lib'd Woman's SB, FS EncyV1, *&* FiresB of Love S. *On Woody Guthrie* Poor Boy, *Pete Seeger* Am Fav Bal V2, Peggy Seeger & Tom Palen *& Blue Sky Boys* Presenting. OB34

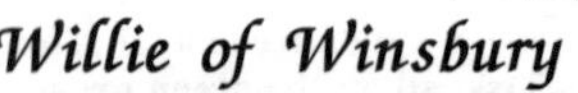

Willie of Winsbury

The king has been held a prisoner
And a prisoner long in Spain
And Willie o' the Winsbury
Has lain long with his daughter at home

Em - - D / Em Am C - / G Em G - / Em Bm C -

"What ails ye, what ails ye, my daughter Janet?
You look so pale & wan
O have you had any sore sickness
Or yet been sleeping with a man?"

"I have not had any sore sickness
Nor yet been lying with a man
But it is for you, my father dear
Abiding so long in Spain"

"Cast off, cast off, your berry brown gown
Stand naked upon the stone
That I may know you by your shape
If you be a maiden or no"

And she's cast off her berry brown gown
And she's standin on the stone
Her apron was low & her haunches were round
And her face was pale & wan

"O was it with duke or knight or lord
Or a man of wealth & fame
Or was it with one of my serving men
That's lately come out of Spain?"

"No, it was no lord, nor duke, nor knight
Nor yet with a servingman
But it was with Willie o' Winsbury
I could bide no longer alone"

And the king has called his merry men all
By thirty & by three
"Go, fetch me this Willie of Winsbury
For hang-ed he shall be!"

But when he was come the King before
He was clothed all in red silk
His hair was like the strands of gold
His skin was as pale as the milk

"And it is no wonder" said the King
"That my daughter's love you have won
For had I been a woman as I am a man
My bedfellow you would have been

And will you marry my daughter Janet
By the troth of your right hand?
O will you marry my daughter Janet
I will make you the Lord of my land"

"O yes I will marry your daughter Janet
By the troth of my right hand
Yes, I will marry your daughter Janet
But I'll not be the lord of your land"

And he's mounted her on his milk-white steed
And he's taken the dapple-grey
He has made her the lady of as much land
As she shall ride in a long summer's day

— Child Ballad 100

On Pentangle Solomon's Seal *&* Live, *J Renbourn* Faro Annie, *J McCormick* W. Islands. *In Sargent & Kitteridge* Eng & Scot Pop Bal, *G & M Polworth* FS fr the N, *Reeves* The Everlasting Circle, *& Karpeles* The Crystal Spring, B1. OB35 *includes "Wraggle Taggle Gypsies."*

Wraggle Taggle Gypsies

There were three gypsies a-come to my door
And downstairs ran this lady-o
One sang high and another sang low
And the other sang bonny bonny Biscay-o

Am - - - / - - Em - / - Am Em D / Am Em Am -

Then she pulled off her silk finished gown
And put on hose of leather-o
The ragged ragged rags about our door
And she's gone with **the wraggle taggle gypsies-o**

It was late last night when my lord came home
Inquiring for his lady-o
The servants said on every hand
"She's gone with **the wraggle...**"

"O saddle to me my milk-white steed
And go & fetch me my pony-o
That I may ride & seek my bride, who is gone with..."

O he rode high & he rode low
He rode through wood & copses too
Until he came to a wide open field
And there he espied his a-lady-o

"What makes you leave your house & land
What makes you leave your money-o
What makes you leave your new-wedded lord, to follow

"What care I for my house & land
What care I for my money-o
What care I for my new wedded lord, I'm off with..."

"Last night you slept on a goosefeather bed
With sheet turned down so bravely-o
Tonight you'll sleep in a cold open field, along with..."

"What care I for goosefeather bed
With the sheet turned down so bravely-o
For tonight I shall sleep in a cold open field
Along with the wraggle taggle gypsies-o!"

— Child Ballad #200

The "Gypsy Rover" is a modern rewriting of this ballad. Bob Franke's "Beggars to God" (GOOD) also draws on this ballad. SO! *4:7 &* Reprints#1, FiresB of FS, Liberated Woman's SB, S that Changed the World, All Our Lives, *&* FS EncyV1. *On* Planxty *& their* Collection. **OB35** *includes "Willie of Winsbury"*

The songs designated as "Child #..." were collected by Francis James Child in his classic Eng & Scottish Popular Ballads, *which appeared in a number of editions in the 19th c.*

Two other chapters which contain a number of trad Br Isles songs are: GOOD TIMES (mainly wassails & drinking songs) & SEA. In addition, see: "Be Thou My Vision," "Friendly Beasts" (FAITH) "Country Life" (FARM) "On Ilkley Moor," "Martin Said to His Man" (FUN) "Bridgit O'Malley," "Mairi's Wedding," "Red Is the Rose" (LOVE) "The Riddle Song," "Skye Boat Song" (LULL) "Pleasant & Delightful," "Loch Lomond," "Road to the Isles," "Wild Mtn Thyme" (OUT) "Mrs McGrath," "Johnny I Hardly Knew Ye" (PEACE) "Froggie Went a Courting," "Here's to Cheshire" (PLAY) "Kevin Barry," "MacPherson's Farewell," "Risin' of the Moon," "Roddy McCorley "(STRUG) & "Foggy Foggy Dew" (TIME).

Bottle of Wine

Bottle of wine, fruit of the vine
When you gonna let me get sober?
Leave me alone, let me go home
Let me go back & start over

C - - - / - - G C :||

Ramblin' round this dirty old town
Singin' for nickels & dimes
Time's gettin' rough, I ain't got enough
To buy a little bottle of wine

C G F C / C G C - :||

Little hotel, older than hell
Dark as the coal in a mine
Blankets are thin, I lay there & grin
I got a little bottle of wine

Pain in my head, bugs in my bed
Pants are so old that they shine
Out on the street, tell the people I meet
Won't you buy me a bottle of wine?

Preacher will preach, teacher will teach
Miner will dig in the mine
I ride the rods, trusting in God
Huggin' my bottle of wine

— Tom Paxton

 — On his Rambling Boy, Ain't That News & Anthology. *Also on J Collins* In Conc *& Doc & Merle Watson* Then & Now. *In* SO! *14:5 &* Reprints *#10.* **OC02**

Bourgeois Blues

Look-a-here people, listen to me
Don't try to find no home down in Washington DC
Lord it's a bourgeois town, ooh, it's a bourgeois town
I got the bourgeois blues, I'm gonna spread the news all around

C - / - - // F - C - / G - CF C

Me & Martha was standin' upstairs
I heard a white man say "Don't want no colored down there"

Home of the brave, land of the free
Don't want to be mistreated by no bourgeoisie

White folks in Washington, they know how
Throw a colored man a nickel just to see him bow

Tell all the colored folks to listen to me
Don't try to find no home now in Washington DC

— Huddie Ledbetter (edited w new addl material by Alan Lomax)

 — Leadbelly made the song in 1938 after he & some friends got kicked out of one hotel after another where the management couldn't stomach interracial parties. In his SB & on Easy Ridin. *In* SO! *14:1 &* Reprints *#8, and* Sing For Freedom. *On Pete Seeger* Sings Leadbelly *& Ry Cooder* Chicken Skin M. **OC03**

Chelsea Morning

Woke up, it was a Chelsea morning
And the first thing that I heard
Was a song outside my window
And the traffic wrote the words
It came ringing up like Christmas bells
And rapping up like pipes & drums
O won't you stay? we'll put on the day
And we'll wear it til the night comes

D9 - / D D9 / G Dmaj7 / Asus7 D
G Dmaj7 / Asus7 - - / D - / G D -

Woke up it was a Chelsea morning
And the first thing that I saw
Was the sun through yellow curtains
And a rainbow on my wall
Red, green & gold to welcome you
Crimson crystal beads to beckon
O won't you stay? we'll put on the day
There's a sun-show every second

(bridge)
Now the curtain opens on a portrait of today
And the streets are paved with passers-by
And pigeons fly & papers lie
Waiting to blow away

G Dmaj7 Asus7 D / G Dmaj7 / G - / - Asus7 -

Woke up it was a Chelsea morning
And the first thing that I knew
There was milk & toast & honey
And a bowl of oranges too
And the light poured in like butterscotch
And stuck to all my senses
O won't you stay? we'll put on the day
And we'll talk in present tenses

When the curtain closes & the rainbow runs away
I will bring you incense owls at night
By candlelight, by jewel light
If only you will stay (pretty baby won't you)
Wake up it's a Chelsea morning

Add at end: D9 - D -

— Joni Mitchell

 — On her Clouds *& in her* SB V1. *On Judy Collins* Living *& Dave Van Ronk* And the Hudson Dusters. *Joni tunes her guitar: D A D F♯ A D.* OC04

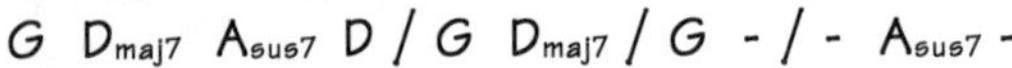

Cockles and Mussels

In Dublin's fair city where the girls are so pretty
'Twas there that I first met sweet Molly Malone
She wheeled her wheelbarrow **thru the streets broad & narrow**
Crying "cockles & mussels alive alive-o!"
Alive alive-o, alive alive-o
Crying "cockles & mussels alive alive-o"! (in 3/4)

D - G - / D - E A ‖: D - G Em / D - A D :‖

She was a fishmonger but sure 'twas no wonder
For so were her father & mother before
And they each wheeled their barrow **thru streets ...**

She died of a faver [= fever] & no one could save her
And that was the end of sweet Molly Malone
Her ghost wheels her barrow **thru ...**

— trad. (Irish)

On Burl Ives Women:Folk S About the Fair Sex, *in* Pocketful of S, Sing Together Children, FB of FS, 1004 FS, Abbecedary of FS, V Fav of the V Young. OC05

Dancing in the Street

Calling out around the world
Are you ready for a brand new beat?
Summer's here & the time is right
For dancin' in the street
They're dancin' in Chicago / Down in New Orleans
Up in New York City

D9 - / **(repeat 7x)**

All we need is music, sweet music
There'll be music everywhere
There'll be swinging & swaying & records playing
They're dancin' in the street
Oh it doesn't matter what you wear
Just as long as you are there
So come on every guy, grab a girl
Everywhere around the world
They'll be dancin', they're dancin' in the street

G - / - - / D9 - / - - / F♯ - / Bm - / Em - / G A / D9 - - -

This is an invitation across the nation
A chance for the folks to meet
There'll be laughin', singin', music swingin'
And dancin' in the street
Philadelphia PA / Baltimore & DC now
Don't forget the motor city

— William Stevenson, Marvin Gaye & Ivy Hunter

 In The Top 100 Motown Hits. OC06

Dirty Old Town

I found my love by a gasworks croft
Dreamed a dream by the old canal
Kissed my girl by the factory wall
Dirty old town, dirty old town

DDG D / GGA D / 1st / EmEmA D6

The clouds are drifting across the moon
Cats are prowling along the beat
Spring's a girl in the streets at night...

Heard a siren from the docks
Saw a train set the night on fire
Smelled the spring on the smoky wind...

I'm going to make a good sharp axe
Shining steel tempered in a fire
We'll chop you down like an old dead tree...

— Ewan MacColl

 — On his & Peggy Seeger Freeborn Man *& on his Blackthorne (1065) alb,* Jackie Washington, Bobby Clancy *& Ian Campbell Folk Group* Rights of Man. OC07

Downtown

When you're alone & life is making you lonely
You can always go – downtown
When you've got worries all the noise & the hurry
Seems to help I know – downtown
Linger on the sidewalks where the neon signs are pretty
Listen to the music of the traffic in the city
How can you lose?

G - C D / / / / G - C - / / Bm -

The lights are much brighter there
You can forget all your troubles forget all your cares
And go downtown where all the lights are bright
Downtown waiting for you tonight
Downtown it's gonna be all right now

C - - - / A - - - / G - C D / / G - C D G - - -

Don't hang around & let your troubles surround you
There are movie shows – downtown
Maybe you know some little places to go to
Where they never close – downtown
Listen to the rhythm of a gentle bossa nova
You'll be dancing with it too before the night is over
Happy again

— **Tony Hatch**

 — Rec by Petula Clark. In Gr S of the '60s. OC08

The Faucets Are Dripping

The faucets are dripping in old New York City
The faucets are dripping & o what a pity
The reservoir's drying because it's supplying
The faucets that drip in New York

(in 3/4) C - - - / F - C - / G - - - / - - C -

You can't ask the landlord to put in a washer
He'd rather you'd move than to put in a washer
The faucets are dripping, they sound in my ears
The tap in the bathroom's been running for years

/ " / " / " / G - - C

There's a wild streak of green in the sink in the kitchen
It comes from the rill trickling out of the plumbing
The streams from the mountains the pools from the lea
All run from my faucet & down to the sea

You can't ask the landlord to put in a washer
You can't ask the landlord to mend the old stairs
He takes in the rents & he lives in Miami
Where faucets don't drip & there's sun everywheres

The faucets are dripping, the landlord's content:
With every new tenant he raises the rent
The buildings can crumble the tenants can cry
There's a shortage of housing you'll live there or die

They're building some buildings & fine city centers
It's sure working hell with the low-income renters
They're jammed into rooms with the rat & the fly
Where the faucets all drip & the floor's never dry

— **Malvina Reynolds**

 — On her Another Country Heard fr *& in her* SB *& her* Little Boxes. *Also on* We Won't Move *(Folkways),* Broadside Singers, *Pete Seeger* God Bless the Grass *& in* Survival SB. OC09

Gee, Officer Krupke

Dear kindly Sgt. Krupke, you gotta understand
It's just our bringin' upke that gets us out of hand
Our mothers all are junkies, our fathers all are drunks
Golly Moses, natcherly we're punks!

A - B♭ - / - - E♭ - / - - A♭ Fm / Cdim - E A

Gee, Officer Krupke, we're very upset
We never had the love that ev'ry child oughta get
We ain't no delinquents, we're misunderstood
Deep down inside us there is good (there is good!)

D - A - / E - A - / Bm E A D / E - A -

There is good **(2x)** there is untapped good
Like inside the worst of us is good!

Dm - C - / G7 E7 A -

Cdim

Dear kindly Judge, your Honor, my parents treat me rough
With all their marijuana, they won't give me a puff
They didn't wanna have me, but somehow I was had
Leapin' lizards, that's why I'm so bad! (Right!)
Officer Krupke, you're really a square
This boy don't need a judge, he needs an analyst's care
It's just his neurosis that oughta be curbed
He's psychologic'ly disturbed (I'm disturbed!)
We're disturbed **(2x)** we're the most disturbed
Like we're psychologic'ly disturbed

My father is a bastard, my ma's an S.O.B.
My grandpa's always plastered, my grandma pushes tea
My sister wears a moustache, my brother wears a dress
Goodness gracious, that's why I'm a mess! (Yes!)
Officer Krupke, you're really a slob
This boy don't need a doctor just a good honest job
Society's played him a terrible trick
And sociologic'ly he's sick (I am sick!)
We are sick **(2x)** we are sick, sick, sick
Like we're sociologically sick

Dear kindly social worker, they say go earn a buck
Like be a soda jerker, which means like be a schmuck
It's not I'm antisocial, I'm only anti-work
Glory-osky, that's why I'm a jerk (Eek!)
Officer Krupke, you've done it again
This boy don't need a job, he needs a year in the pen
It ain't just a question of misunderstood
Deep down inside him, he's no good (I'm no good!)
We're no good **(2x)** we're no earthly good
Like the best of us is no damned good!

The trouble is he's crazy, the trouble is he drinks
The trouble is he's lazy, the trouble is he stinks
The trouble is he's growing, the trouble is he's grown!
Krupke, we got troubles of our own
Gee, Officer Krupke, we're down on our knees
'Cause no one wants a fellow with a social disease
Gee, Officer Krupke, what are we to do?
Gee, Officer Krupke, krup you!

(last line:) E - - A

— **w: Stephen Sondheim** — **m: Leonard Bernstein**

 — From their musical West Side Story. OC10

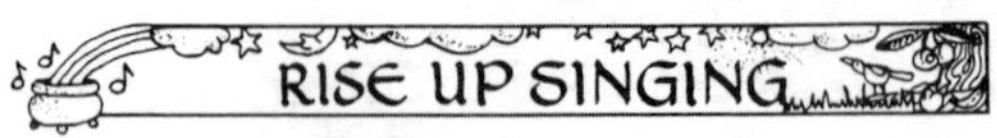

Heaven Help Us All

Heaven help the child who never had a home
Heaven help the girl who walks the streets alone
Heaven help the roses if the bombs begin to fall
Heaven help us all

CAm FDm / CAm FG / / CF C -

Heaven help the Black man if he struggles one more day
... White man if he turns his back away
... man who kicks the man who has to crawl / **Heaven ...**

Heaven help us all (2x)
Heaven help us, Lord, hear our call
When we call (2x) Heaven help us all!

FG C / / E Am / D G C -

... boy who won't reach 21
... man who gave that boy a gun
... people with their backs against the wall ...

Now I lay me down before I go to sleep
In a troubled world I pray the Lord to keep
Hatred from the mighty & the mighty from the small ...

— **Ronald Miller**

 — On Baez Blessed Are *& Stevie Wonder* Signed, Sealed, Delivered. OC11

Hot Time in the Old Town Tonight

When you hear them bells go ding ling ling
O then we all join round & sweetly you must sing
And when the verse is thru & the chorus all join in
There'll be a hot time in the old town tonight

D - - - / / / A - D -

Please, o please, o do not let me fall
O yes, & you're all mine & I love you best of all
And you must be my man or I'll have no man at all
There'll be a hot time in the old town tonight

— **w: Theodore A. Metz** — **m: Joe Hayden**

Orig a Blackface minstrel song. This became the "official" song of the 1898 Sp-Amer war. In Music at the Turn of the Century *(Am Herit), in* Life of the Party, Am Treas of Gold Oldies, S that Changed The World & Gold Era of Nost M V4. OC12

I Live in a City

I live in a city, yes I do (3x)
Made by human hands

D - - - / A7 - - - / D - Em - / A7 - D -

Black hands, white hands, yellow & brown
All together built this town
Black hands, white hands, yellow & brown
All together make the wheels go round

D - Em A / / / D - A D

Brown hands, yellow hands, white & black
Mined the coal & built the stack
Brown hands, yellow hands, white & black
Built the engine & laid the track

Black hands, brown hands, yellow & white
Built the buildings tall & bright
Black hands, brown hands, yellow & white
Filled them all with shining light

Black hands, white hands, brown & tan
Milled the flour & cleaned the pan
Black hands, white hands, brown & tan
The working woman & the working man

— **Malvina Reynolds**

 — On her Another County Heard From, Artichokes, Griddle Cakes & Other Good Things *& in her* Tweedles & Foodles for Young Noodles & Little Boxes. *In* SO! *5:4 & on Cathy Winter & Betsy Rose* As Strong as Anyone Can Be. OC13

Kansas City

(Intro:) I got to Kansas City on a Friday
By Satidy I larned a thing or two
For up to then I didn't have an idy
Of what the modren world was comin' to!
I counted 20 gas buggies goin' by theirsel's
Almost ev'ry time I tuck a walk
'Nen I put my ear to a Bell Telephone
And a strange womern started in to talk!

D - G - / A - D - :||: A D E A / E - A - :||

Evrythin's up to date in Kansas City
They've gone about as far as they c'n go
They went & built a skyscraper 7 stories high
About as high as a buildin' orta grow
Everythin's like a dream in Kansas City
It's better than a magic lantern show
Y' c'n turn the radiator on whenever you want some heat
With evry kind of comfort evry house is all complete
You c'n walk to privies in the rain & never wet your feet!
They've gone... (yes sir!) / **They've...**

D - - - / - - B7 - / E A D Bm / E - A - /
/ " / " / " / E A D Bm / Em - D B7
Em B7 Em - / G A D -

Evrythin's ... / They've ...
They got a big theayter they call a burleeque
Fer 50 cents you c'n see a dandy show
One of the gals was fat & pink & pretty
As round above as she was round below
I could swear she was padded from her shoulder to her heel
But later in the second act when she begun to peel
She proved that everythin' she had was absolutely real!
She went about as far as she could go (yes sir!) / She...

— **w: Oscar Hammerstein II** — **m: Richard Rodgers**

 — From their musical Oklahoma. OC14

The M.T.A. Song

Now let me tell you of a story 'bout a man named Charlie
On this tragic & fateful day
He put 10 cents in his pocket kissed his wife & family
Went to ride on the M.T.A.

G C / G D / G C / GD G

But did he ever return? No, he never returned
And his fate is still unlearned
He may ride forever 'neath the streets of Boston
He's the man who never returned

Charlie handed in his dime at the Kendall Square Station
And he changed for Jamaica Plain
When he got there the conductor told him "One more nickel!"
Charlie couldn't get off that train

Now all night long Charlie rides thru the tunnel
Saying "What will become of me?
How can I afford to see my sister in Chelsea
Or my cousin in Roxbury?"

Charlie's wife goes down to the Scollay Square Station
Every day at a quarter past two
And thru the open window she hands Charlie a sandwich
As the train comes rumblin' thru

Now you citizens of Boston, don't you think it is a scandal
That the people have to pay & pay?
Fight the fare increase, vote for Walter O'Brien
And get Charlie off the M.T.A.!

— w: Jacqueline Steiner & Bess Hawes

— m: trad. "Wreck of Old '97"

 — Written in 1948 as a protest against the proposed subway fare increase (fr 10¢ to 15¢!) & as a campaign song for the Progressive Party candidate for mayor, Walter O'Brien. (Under the proposed fare, riders would pay one fare on entering the subway & a 2nd on leaving.) In SO! *8:3, on Kingston Trio* Best of, 25 Yrs, College Conc *& on Country Gentlemen* Yesterday & Today V3. OC15

Morning Morgantown

When morning comes to Morgantown
The merchants roll their awnings down
The milk trucks make their morning rounds
In morning Morgantown
We'll rise up early with the sun
To ride the bus while everyone
Is yawning and the day is young / **In...**

A B7 / D A / / AD A :||

Morning Morgantown, buy your dreams a dollar down
Morning any town you name, morning's just the same

E DA A DA / F DA AD A

We'll find a table in the shade
And sip our tea & lemonade
And watch the morning on parade / **In ...**
Ladies in their rainbow fashions
Colored stop & go lights flashin'
We'll wink at total strangers passin' / **In ...**

I'd like to buy you everything
A wooden bird with painted wings
A window full of colored rings / **In ...**
But the only things I have to give
To make you smile to win you with
Are all the mornings still to live / **In ...**

— Joni Mitchell

 — On her Ladies of the Canyon *& in her* SB V1. OC16

Moscow Nights

Stillness in the grove, not a rustling sound
Softly shines the moon clear & bright
Dear, if you could know how I treasure so
This most beautiful Moscow night **(repeat last 2 lines)**

Am Dm E Am / C FG C B7E / Am - Dm -
Am E Am B7E / Am - Dm - / Am E Am -

Lazily the brook like a silv'ry stream
Ripples gently in the moonlight
And a song afar fades as in a dream
In the spell of this summer night ...

Dearest, why so sad, why the downcast eyes
And your lovely head bent so low?
O it's hard to speak & yet not to speak
Of the longing that my heart knows ...

Promise me my love as the dawn appears
And the darkness turns into light
That you'll cherish dear thru the passing years
This most beautiful Moscow night ...

Nye slishni v sadu dazhe shorokhi
Vsyo sdyes zamerlo do utra
Yesli b znali vi kak mne doroghi
Pod moskovniye vechera...

— w: M. Matusovsky (Russian), J.B.H.Silverman (English)
— m: V. Solovyov - Sedoy

Pron: a =ah, e =eh, i =ee, o =oh, u = oo (as in "food"). In SO! *11:1 &* Reprints #7 & FS EncyV1. *On Vladimir Troshin* Moscow Nights *(Monitor) and Ray Coniff* World of H. OC17

My Hometown

I was 8 years old & running with a dime in my hand
Into the bus stop to pick up a paper for my old man
I'd sit on his lap in that big old Buick and steer as we drove thru town
He'd tousle my hair & say "Son take a good look around:
This is your hometown" (4x)

(in D) D - GD A / - - DA G :|| **(3x)**

In '65 the tension was running high at my high school
There was lots of fights between the black & white, there was nothing you could do
Two cars at a light on a Saturday night, in a back seat there was a gun
Words were passed in a shotgun blast, troubled times had come to:
Your **hometown ...**

(bridge)
Now Main Street's whitewashed windows & vacant stores
Seems like there ain't nobody wants to come down here no more
They're closing down the textile mill across the RR tracks
Foreman says, "These jobs are going, boys, & they ain't coming back to / **Your ...**"

(in D) Bm - D - / / G - D - / G - D A

Last night me & Kate, we laid in bed, talkin' bout getting out
Packing up our bags, maybe heading south – I'm 35, we got a boy of our own now
Last night I sat him up behind the wheel & said "Son, take a good look around / This is **your hometown ...**"

— Bruce Springsteen

 On his Born in the USA. OC18

New York, New York

Start spreadin' the news, I'm leaving today _
I wanna be a part of it – New York, New York _
These vagabond shoes are longing to stray
And step around the heart of it – New York, New York
I wanna wake up in the city that doesn't sleep
To find I'm king of the hill, top of the heap

C - Dm G / C Am7 Dm7 G / 1st / C Cmaj7 C7 -
Fmaj7 Dm7 Am7 - / Em A7 Dm G

My little town blues are melting away
I'll make a brand new start of it in old New York
If I can make it there I'd make it anywhere
It's up to you, New York, New York

/ " / C Am7 Gm C7/F Dm7 C A7/DmEm Fmaj7G C -

(repeat v. 1 with last line:) To find I'm king of the hill, head of the list, cream of the crop, at the top of the heap

(repeat v. 2 with last line:) Come on, come thru, NY, NY!

— w: Fred Ebb — m: John Kander

 — Theme fr the motion picture New York, New York. *Rec by Frank Sinatra. In* 100 of the Gr Easy Listening Hits. OC19

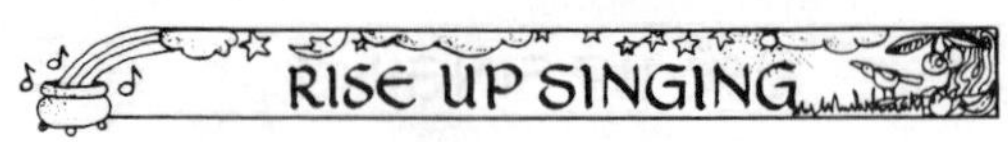

Penny Lane

In Penny Lane there is a barber showing photographs
Of ev'ry head that he's had the pleasure to know
And all the people that come & go stop & say hello

DBm EmA / DBm F / Dm B♭ A - **(capo up)**

On the corner is a banker & a motorcar
The little children laugh at him behind his back
And the banker never wears a "mac"
In the pouring rain, very strange

/ " / " /Dm B♭ A G

Penny Lane is in my ears & in my eyes
Wet beneath the blue suburban skies. I sit & meanwhile back:

D - G - / D - G A7

In Penny Lane there is a fireman with an hour glass
And in his pocket is a portrait of the queen
He likes to keep his fire engine clean
It's a clean machine

(2nd cho) Penny Lane is in my ears & in my eyes
Full of fish & finger pies in summer, **meanwhile back:**

In Penny Lane the barber shaves another customer
We see the barber sitting waiting for a trend
And then the fireman rushes in
From the pouring rain, very strange

— John Lennon & Paul McCartney

© 1967 Northern Songs Ltd. All rights administered by Blackwood Music Inc. under license from ATV Music (Maclen). All rights reserved. International copyright secured. Used by permission. — On the Beatles Magical Mystery Tour *&* Rarities 1967-70, *in* Club Date FakeB. **OC20**

Sidewalks of New York

Down in front of Casey's old brown wooden stoop
On a summer's evening we formed a merry group
Boys & girls together, we would sing & waltz
While Tony played the organ on the sidewalks of New York

(in 3/4) CG C F C/F C D G/ 1st /F CA DG C

Eastside, westside, all around the town
The gang played ring-a-rosy, London bridge is falling down
Boys & girls together, me & Mamie O'Rourke
We'd trip the light fantastic on the sidewalks of New York

C GC F C / F CA D G / CG C F C / 2nd

— James Blake & Charles Lawlor

Blake was a hat salesman who wrote these words at work after the musician shared his new tune with him in 1894. This was Al Smith's campaign song in 1928. In Fav S of the Early '90s, Fred Waring SB, Gr Legal FakeB, 120 Am S & Am Treas of Gold Oldies. **OC21**

Sounds of Silence

Hello darkness my old friend
I've come to talk to you again
Because a vision softly creeping
Left its seeds while I was sleeping
And the vision that was planted in my / Brain still remains
Within the sounds of silence

(Am -) G - - - / Am - - - / FC - - / FC -
F - - - / C - Am - / C - G - Am - - -

In restless dreams I walked alone
Narrow streets of cobblestone
'Neath the halo of a street lamp
I turned my collar to the cold & damp
When my eyes were stabbed by the flash of a neon
Light that split the night / & touched the sound of silence

And in the naked light I saw
10,000 people maybe more
People talking without speaking
People hearing without listening
People writing songs that voices never
Shared – no one dared / Disturb the sound of silence

"Fools" said I "You do not know
Silence like a cancer grows
Hear my words that I might teach you
Take my arms that I might reach you"
But my words like silent raindrops / Fell **(pause)**
And echoed in the well of silence

And the people bowed & prayed
To the neon god they'd made
And the sign flashed out its warning
In the words that it was forming
And the sign said "The words of the prophets are written on subway / Walls & tenement halls
And whisper in the sounds of silence"

— Paul Simon

© 1964 Paul Simon. All rights reserved. Used by permission. — In his S of *& in* Gr S of the '60s. *On his & Garfunkel's* Wed Morn 3am *& their* Sounds of ... **OC22**

Streets of London

Have you heard the old man in the closed down market
Kicking up the papers with his worn out shoes?
In his eyes you see no pride & held loosely at his side
Yesterday's paper telling yesterday's news

C G Am Em / F C D G / C G Am Em / F C G C

So how can you tell me you're lonely
And say for you that the sun don't shine?
Let me take you by the hand & lead you thru the streets of London
I'll show you something to make you change your mind

F Em G Am / D - G - / " / " /

Have you seen the old girl who walks the streets of London
Dirt in her hair & her clothes in rags?
She's no time for talking, she just keeps right on walking
Carrying her home in two carrier bags

In the all night cafe at a quarter past 11
Same old man sitting here on his own
Looking at the world over the rim of his teacup
Each tea lasts an hour & he wanders home alone

Have you seen the old man outside the seaman's mission
Memory fading with the medal ribbons that he wears?
In our winter city the rain cries a little pity
For one more forgotten hero & a world that doesn't care

— Ralph McTell

© 1970, 1971, 1976 Westminster Music Ltd, London, Eng. TRO - Essex Music International, Inc. New York, controls all publication rights for USA & Canada. Used by permission. — On his Streets of London *(Kicking Mule),* Spiral Staircase *(Transatlantic),* Ralph, Albert & Sydney *&* Best of. *Also on Liam Clancy* The Dutchman *&* Farewell to Tarwaithe, *Josh White Jr* Almost Alone, *Schooner Fare* Day of the Clipper *& Fred Holstein* Chicago & Other Ports. *In* SO! 36:4 *&* Club Date FakeB. **OC23**

Up on the Roof

When this old world starts getting me down
And people are just too much for me to take
I climb right up to the top of the stairs
And all my cares just drift right into space

(bridge 1:) On the roof the only place I know
Where you just have to wish to make it so, up on the roof

C Am / F - C - :|| F - - - / C Am Dm G

When I get home feeling tired & beat
I go up where the air is fresh & sweet
I get away from the hustling crowds
And all the rat race noise down in the street

(bridge 2:) At night the stars put on a show for free
And darling you can share it all with me, I keep telling you that

Right smack dab in the middle of town
I found a paradise that's troubleproof
And if this world starts getting you down
There's room enough for two up on the roof

— Gerry Goffin & Carole King

© 1962 Screen Gems-EMI Music, Inc. 6920 Sunset Blvd, Hollywood CA 90028. All rights reserved. Used by permission. — On her Writer, Laura Nyro Xmas & the Beads of Sweat *& recs by James Taylor & the Inkspots.* OC24

Other songs about city life: "He Played Real Good for Free" (CREAT) "Big Yellow Taxi" (ECO), "Simple Gifts/new verse" (FAITH) "Give My Regards to Broadway," "While Strollinig Thru the Park" (GOLD) "Ring Around the Rosy Rag," "Movin Day," "Tonight" (GOOD) "House of the Rising Sun," "I Think It's Gonna Rain," "San Francisco Bay Blues" (HARD) "The Boxer" (MEN) "Buckingham Palace," "Going to the Zoo" & "Wheels of the Bus" (PLAY), "Brother Can You Spare a Dime," "There But for Fortune" (RICH) "Chairs to Mend" (ROUND) "The Dutchman," "Hello in There," "Old Friends" (TIME) & "When I Needed a Neighbor" (UNITY). Also see the chapter on WORK.

La Bamba

Para bailar La Bamba (para bailar la Bamba)
Para bailar La Bamba se necesita
Una poca de gracia (una poca de gracia)
Una poca de gracia y otra cosita
Y arriba, y arriba (y arriba, y arriba)
Y arriba, y arriba por ti seré
Por ti seré, por ti seré
Bamba, bamba (3x)

DG A :|| **(10x)**

Yo no soy marinero (yo no soy marinero)
Yo no soy marinero, soy capitan
Soy capitan, soy capitan

— trad. (Mexican)

On rec by Richie Valens, Gr FSingers of the '60s, *Harry Belafonte* Return to Carnegie Hall, *Neil Diamond* Feel of, *Jose Feliciano* Newport FM Fest '64, *Mongo Santamaria* Gr H *& Jim Kweskin* What Ever Happened? *In* SO! *38-1,* 1001 Jumbo S & Golden Ency of FS. *Trans: In order to dance the Bamba one must have a little grace, a little grace & another little thing. And hurrah I will go, for you I will exist: Bamba / I'm not a sailor, I'm a captain.* OP02

La Bastringue

Mademoiselle, voulez-vous danser **La Bastringue (2x)?**
Mademoiselle, voulez-vous danser? La Bastringue va commencer **(instr:)**

D AD A D/D AD G AD//D C D GA D C D AD

Oui Monsieur, je veux bien danser La...
Oui...danser La Bastringue si vous voulez

Mademoiselle, il faut nous arrêter ...
Mlle ... vous allez vous fatiguer

Non, Monsieur, j'aime trop danser ...
... je suis prêt' à recommencer

Mademoiselle, je n' peux plus danser ...
... car j'en ai des cors aux pieds

— trad. (Quebecquois dance)

On Alan Mills & Jean Carrignan's Folkways album. Trans: Mlle, will you dance La B? La B is starting / Yes M, I'd love to dance La B if you would / Mlle, we need to stop: you're going to get tired / No, M, I love to dance La B. I'm ready to start over / Mlle, I can't dance any more because I have corns on my feet. OP03

Before They Close the Minstrel Show

The poster's peeling underneath last summer's morning glory vine
An old white hat & a stump of cigar & an empty bottle of wine

C - G7 - C - / - - G7 -

Lay me down, Carolina, lay me down
Don't want to wake up in the mornin' no more
Sing me one slow sad song for this one last old time
Before they close the minstrel show

C F C / - FC G - / C C7 F Dm / G - C -

Banjo's got a broken string, don't 'spect I'll get to fix it now
Won't be no more chance to sing, I'm rusty anyhow

The money & the crowd run out before we left the last town
This old show done played its run & rung the curtain down

Daddy Bones is dead I guess, you probably don't know or care
And Frank & Arch has gone away somewhere I don't know where

Don't know where I'll go from here, come to that I just don't care
Maybe I'll go to a better place & the minstrel show'll be there

— Bob Coltman

© 1971 Bob Coltman. Used by permission. — On his Before They Close the Minstrel Show *(MinstrelJD202) & on his Folk Legacy (46) album. Also on Ed Trickett* Telling Takes Me Home *(FSI-46) & in* SO! *22:4.* OP04

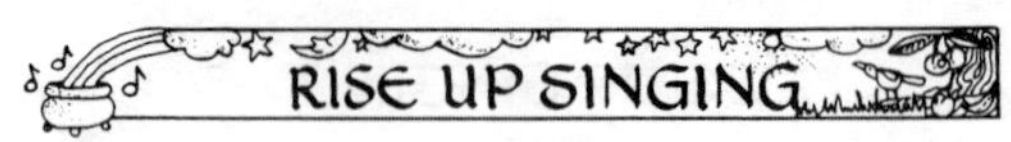

The Brand New Tennessee Waltz

Oh my, but you have a pretty face
You favor a girl that I knew
I imagine that she's still in Tennessee
And by God I should be there too
I've a sadness too sad to be true **(in 3/4)**

A - - - / D E A - / D - A - / E - A - / /

But I left Tennessee in a hurry, dear
The same way that I'm leavin' you
'Cause love is mainly just memories
And everyone's got him a few
So when I'm gone I'll be glad to love you

At the brand new Tennessee waltz
You're lit'rally waltzing on air
At the brand new Tennessee waltz
There ain't no tellin' who will be there

D - A - / - - E - / D - A - / - E A -

When I leave it'll be like I found you, love
Descending Victorian stairs
I'm feeling like one of your photographs
I'm trapped while I'm putting on airs
And getting even by asking "Who cares?"

So have all of your passionate violins
Play a tune for a Tennessee kid
Who's feeling like leaving another town
With no place to go if he did
'Cause they'll catch you wherever you're hid

— **Jesse Winchester**

 — On his Let the Rough Side Drag *&* Jesse Winchester, *Baez* Blessed Are, Gr H *&* Country Music Alb, *Colleen Peterson* Beginning to Feel Like Home, *Sam Cooke* The Legendary, *Bromberg* Demon in Disguise *& Stephane Grappelli & Vassar Clements* Together at Last *(FF). In* SO! *23:1 &* Reprints *#8.* OP05

Dancing at Whitsun

It's fifty long springtimes since she was a bride
And still you may see her at each Whitsuntide
In a dress of white linen & ribbons of green
As green as her memories of loving **(in 3/4)**

D - - A - / D Em - G A - / D A Bm A / D Em ADD D

The feet that were nimble tread carefully now
As gentle a measure as age will allow
Thru groves of white blossoms, by fields of young corn
As once she was pledged to her true love

The fields they stand empty, the hedges grow free
No young men to tend them, or pastures go seed
They are gone where the forests of oaks went before
And gone to be wasted in battle

Down from the green farmlands & from their loved ones
Marched husbands & brothers & fathers & sons
There's a fine roll of honor where the Maypole once stood
And the ladies go dancing at Whitsun

There's a straight row of houses in these latter days
All covering the downs where the sheep used to graze
There's a field of red poppies, a wreath from the Queen
But the ladies remember it's Whitsun
And the ladies go dancing at Whitsun

— **w: John Austin Marshall,**

— **m: trad English "The Week before Easter" & "I Once Loved a Lass"**

 — This song is abt Morris dancing. Traditionally these dances were only performed by the men in the particular Cotswolds village a given group of dances were identified with. In some villages where the male population was so decimated by WWI that a "side" of 6 men could not be formed, the women began doing the dances to keep the tradition alive. On Priscilla Herdman Water Lilies. *Tune:* Penguin B of Eng FS. OP06

Do Re Mi

(intro) Let's start at the very beginning
A very good place to start
When you read you begin with A, B, C
When you sing you begin with do re mi **(3x)**
The first 3 notes just happen to be
Do re mi (children:) do re mi
Do re mi fa so la ti -
(spoken: Come! I'll make it easier for you. Listen:)

G - / GD G / F C / FG C - - / G C / - - / - CG G

Doe – a deer, a female deer
Ray – a drop of golden sun
Me – a name I call myself
Far – a long, long way to run
Sew – a needle pulling thread
La – a note to follow "sew"
Tea – a drink with jam & bread
That will bring us back to Doe

C - / G - / C - / G - / C F / D G / E Am C7 / FGC

— **w: Oscar Hammerstein II** — **m: Richard Rodgers**

 — Fr their musical The Sound Of Music. *In* Readers Dig Fest of Pop S, Best Loved S of Am Stage, Gold Era Of Nost M V3 *& var Broadway SBs.* OP07

Fashioned in the Clay

When it seems like everyone is worried for themselves
Making plans for fallout shelters, stocking up the shelves
Living in the fast lane, staying high at night
Thinking that by accident we'll blow out all the lights

(capo up) G D C G / C G D - / 1st / C G D G

Look now at the potter whose wheel is spinning round
Shaping with her hands the past & future from the ground
Cups that will be filled & drunk so warm in wintertime
Plates & bowls for dinners served by candlelight with wine

And she believes, she believes [**later v:** he, they, we]
By her work it's so easy to see
That the future is more than the following day
It's fashioned securely in the clay

G - D - / Em C D - / Em C G C / G D G -

Now come see the farmer working in his fields
Hoping for the sun & rain to guarantee his yields
Like a seed the wind has blown to unfamiliar ground
He waits to see what fate will bring as each year rolls around

Elsewhere there are lovers in a warm embrace
Happy with their plans to carry on the human race
Now their baby cries & wonders if it's all alone
Soft the voices reassure, there'll always be a home

So if you had been worried that tomorrow wouldn't come
Look to see the ones whose lives are following the sun
And the hope that springs so clearly from the work they do
Will spread a little farther when it's found a place in you

— **Elmer Beal**

 — In the collection Elmer's Spring Bouquet *& on Bok, Muir & Trickett* Fashioned in the C;au *(Folk Legacy),* New Folk Favorites *(Hal Leonard).* OP08

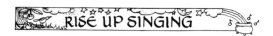

Guantanamera

Yo soy un hombre sincero, de donde crece la palma_**(2x)**
Y antes de morirme quiero echar mis versos de alma_

DEm A DEm A :|| **(3x)**

Guantanamera, guajira / Guantanamera (repeat)

G A / DEm A / / /

Mi verso es de un verde claro_y de un carmin encendido_**(2x)**
Mi verso es un ciervo herido_que busca en el monte amparo_

Con los pobres de la tierra quiero yo mi suerte echar_**(2x)**
El arroyo de la sierra_me complace mas que el mar_

— w: poem by José Marti adapted by Julian Orbon

— m: Jose Fernandez Dias (Joseito Fernandez) adapted by Pete Seeger & Julian Orbon

 — Marti was a Cuban poet & leader in several uprisings against Spanish colonial rule until his death in the insurrection of 1898. Trans: "I am a truthful man fr the land where palms grow. Before I die I want to share these poems of my soul/ My poems are clear green, they are flaming crimson, my poems are a wounded fawn searching thru the hills/ With the poor people of the earth I want to cast my lot. The coolness of the mtns pleases me more than the sea." On Pete Seeger We Shall Overcome, Gr Hits, World of, *HAPP, Baez* Gracias a La Vida *w/ Jackson Browne on* If I Had a S/S of Pete, *& Weavers* Travelling On, Reunion 1963, Gr H *& in their* SB. *In SO 13:1 & Reprints #6,* WHATFG, How Can We Keep fr Singing, Grtst Legal FakeB, FSEncyV1 *&* 1001 Jumbo S. **OP09**

He Played Real Good for Free

C#m

I slept last night in a good hotel
I went shopping today for jewels
The wind rushed around in the dirty town
And the children let out from the school
I was standing on a noisy corner
Waiting for the walking green
Across the street he stood & he played real good
On his clarinet for free

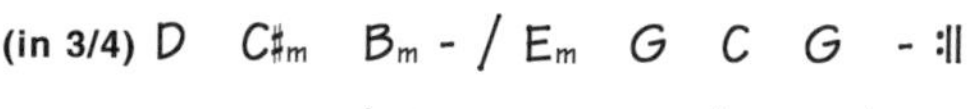

(in 3/4) D C#m Bm - / Em G C G - :||

Em Bm D - / G D A - / 1st 2 /

Me, I play for fortune
And those velvet curtain calls
I've got a black limousine & two gentlemen
Escorting me to the halls
And I play if you have the money
Or if you're a friend to me
But the one man band by the quick lunch stand
He was playin' real good for free

Nobody stopped to hear him
Tho' he played so sweet & high
They knew he had never been on their TV
So they passed his music by
I meant to go over & ask for a tune
Maybe put on a harmony
But I heard his refrain as the signal changed
He was playing real good for free

— Joni Mitchell

 — aka: "For free." On her Ladies of the Canyon *&* Miles of Aisles *& in her* SB V1. *On Buffy Sainte-Marie's* Quiet Places. **OP10**

Holly Ann

She is a weaver, thru her hands the bright thread travels
Blue green water, willows weeping, silver stars
She sings & sighs as the shuttle flies, like a Kerry dancer
Pink & purple, velvet red for a lover's bed

C - Dm - / F - C - :||

Living north of San Francisco
With a man who built his house
(or) Sometimes it's nice to be alone
She says it's peaceful in the country
(or) Where she's living
The lights of the Golden Gate will lead her home

Am Em F - / C G C - :||

She is a spinner, in her hands the wooden wheel turns
The wool around & around again
A gypsy from Bolinas sits & plays the mandolin
Faces smile in the firelight of a foggy night

(bridge, tune as in chorus)
You can see the bridges of the city
Hanging in the air by steel & stone
She says it's peaceful where she's living / **The lights ...**

She is a weaver, thru her hands the bright thread travels
Blue green water, willows weeping, silver stars
She is my sister, the baby born when I was older
Her hands are light, her hair as bright as the summer sun

— Judy Collins

 — Written for her sister. On her True Stories *&* First 15 yrs. **OP11**

I Could Have Danced All Night

Bed, bed, I couldn't go to bed
My head's too light to try to set it down
Sleep, Sleep, I couldn't sleep tonight
Not for all the jewels in the crown

(in G) D AmD / Am A7 / D6 - / Am CD G -

I could have danced all night **(2x)**
And still have begged for more
I could have spread my wings & done a thousand things
I've never done before
I'll never know what made it so exciting
Why all at once my heart took flight
I only know when he began to dance with me
I could have danced, danced, danced all night

G Gmaj7 - Em / G - Am7 - / Am Am (G#) - Am7 / Am - G - B7 F# B7 - / D A D - / G Gmaj7 Am C / EmAm C D G

— w: Alan Jay Lerner **— m: Frederick Loewe**

 — Fr their musical My Fair Lady. *On Julie Andrews* World of. **OP12**

Mama Don't Allow

1. **Mama don't 'low no** guitar pickin' **'round here (2x)**
I don't care what Mama don't 'low, gonna
pick my guitar **anyhow**
Mama don't 'low no guitar pickin' 'round here

D - - - / - - A - / D D7 G G7 / D A D -

2. **Mama don't 'low no** banjo playin' **'round here ...**
3. cigar smokin' *5. TV watchin'*
4. midnight ramblin' *6. candy eatin', etc.*

— trad. (US)

In SO! 8:1 & Reprints #5 & FiresB of Fun & Games. On Doc Watson Memories *(UA) & Ralph Stanley* Live at McClure VA *(SLP 1554/5). Si Kahn has written new words to this song: see Stevens* Don't Allow *in WORK.* **OP13**

CREATIVITY

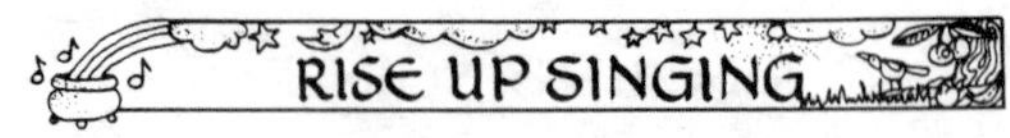

The Mandolin Man & His Secret

He came into town with his mandolin
Calling all the people & they came to him
He said I want to hear all that's pretty
He said I want to hear all that's nice **(in 6/8, capo up)**

G (D, E, F#, E) **(2x)** / / C (C, B, A, ABC) G (D, E, F#, E) / /

They laughed at him with his mandolin
They left him there with his funny grin

The children of the town then came to him
Magically called with his mandolin

They smiled at him with his mandolin
Their eyes like his were sparkling
<u>They</u> **said** d'<u>you</u> **want to hear ... pretty?** / They ... **nice?**
He said I want to hear all that's pretty / He ... nice

— **Donovan Leitch**

Mr. Bojangles

I knew a man Bojangles & he danced for you in worn out shoes
With silver hair, a ragged shirt & baggy pants, the old soft shoe
He jumped so high **(2x)**, then he lightly touched down

C ↓ F G / / F CE Am D9 G -

Mr. Bojangles (3x), dance!

Am G **(3x)** / C ↓ **(in 3/4)**

I met him in a cell in New Orleans, I was – down & out
He looked at me to be the eyes of age as he spoke right out
He talked of life **(2x)**, he laughed, slapped his leg a step

He said his name, Bojangles, then he danced a lick across the cell
He grabbed his pants a better stance, oh, he jumped up high, he clicked his heels
He let go a laugh **(2x)**, shook back his clothes all around

He danced for those at minstrel shows & county fairs throughout the South
He spoke with tears of 15 yrs how his dog & he traveled about
His dog up & died, he ... after 20 years he still grieved

He said "I dance now at ev'ry chance in honky tonks for drinks and tips
But most of the time I spend behind these county bars" he said "I drinks a bit"
He shook his head & as he ... I heard someone ask "Please:"

— **Jerry Jeff Walker**

My Old Man

My old man had a rounder's soul
He'd hear an old freight train & then he'd have to go
Said he'd been blessed with a gypsy bone
And that's the reason I guess that he's been cursed to roam

D Em / A D :||

He came thru town back before the war
Didn't even know what it was that he was lookin' for
He carried a tattered bag for his violin
Full of lots of songs of the places he'd been

He talked real easy & had a smilin' way
He could pass along to you when his fiddle played
Makin' people drop their cares & woes
To hum out loud those tunes that his fiddle bowed

Til the people there began to join the sound
And ev'ry one in town was laughin', singin' dancin' 'round
Like the fiddler's tunes were all they heard that night
Like some dream that says all the world is right

The fiddler's eye caught one beauty there
She had that rollin, flowin, golden kinda hair
Played for her as if she danced alone
He played his fav'rite songs, the ones he called his own

Til she alone was dancin' in the room
The only thing left movin' to that fiddler's tune
He played until she was the last to go
Then he stopped & packed his case, said he'd take her home

And all the nights that passed a child was born
And all the years that passed, love would keep them warm
And all their lives they'd share that dream come true
And all because she danced so well to his fiddle tunes

The train next mornin' blew a lonesome sound
As if she sang the blues of what she took from town
And all that I recall & said when I was young
Was no one else could really sing those sons he sung

— **Jerry Jeff Walker**

One Morning in May

One morning **(3x)** in May
I spied a fair couple a-making their way
One was a maiden so bright & so fair
And the other was a soldier & a brave volunteer

(in 3/4) I: A - E A / E A - - / D A - - / - - E A

"Good morning **(3x)** to thee
O where are you going, my pretty lady?"
"O I am a-going out walking to the banks of the sea
Just to see the waters gliding, **hear the nightingale sing"**

We had not been a-standing but a minute or two
When out from his knapsack a fiddle he drew
And the tune that he played made the valleys all ring
"Hark, hark" cried the lady **"hear ..."**

"Pretty lady, pretty lady, it's time to give o'er"
"O no, pretty soldier, please play one tune more
I'd rather hear your fiddle & the touch of one string
Than to see the waters gliding, **hear ...**

Pretty soldier, pretty soldier, will you marry me?"
"O no, pretty lady, that never can be
I've a wife in old London & children twice three
Two wives & the army's too many for me

I'll go back to London & stay there for a year
It's often I'll think of you, my little dear
If ever I return, 'twill be in the spring
Just to see the waters gliding, **hear ..."**

II: A G D A / - G D E / A F#m D A / A D E A

— **Jim Rooney & Bill Keith, based on trad. words**

Per Spelmann *(Peter the Fiddler)*

Per spelmann, han hadde ei einaste ku **(2x)**
Han bytte bort kua fekk fela igjen **(2x)**
"Du gamle, gode fiolin, du fiolin, du fela me!"

(in C) G C D G / / - C G - / - C G C // - - - - G C **(in 3/4)**

Old Peter the Fiddler had only one cow **(2x)**
He's traded her in for a violin now **(2x)**
"You dear old goodly violin, sweet violin, my fiddle friend!"

Per Spelmann played gently & his fiddle's sound **(2x)**
Made all the folks dance til they wept all around **(2x)**

"And tho I grow old as the earth is old now **(2x)**
I'll never swap my dear violin for a cow!" **(2x)**

– trad (Norwegian), Eng. Mary Byrne & Peter Blood
In Good Fellowship Songs *(World Around Songs).* OP18

Sarasponda

(Women:) Sarasponda **(3x)** retsetset! **(repeat)**
(Men: softly) Boomda, boomda ...

C - G C / // F C F C / G C G C

(Together:) Ahdoray-oh! Ahdoray-boomday-oh!
Ahdoray-boomday-retsetset, awsay-pawsay-oh

— trad. spinning song
The soft "boomda's" represent the "burr" of the spinning wheel. In Pocketful of S & FiresB of Fun & Games. OP19

Seventy-Six Trombones

76 trombones led the big parade
With a hundred & 10 cornets close at hand
They were followed by rows & rows of the finest virtuosos
The cream of every famous band
76 trombones caught the morning sun
With 110 cornets right behind
There were more than a thousand reeds springing up like weeds
There were horns of ev'ry shape & kind

(capo up) G - D - / - - G - / - G7 C A7 / [1.] D A D - :|| [2.] D - G -

(bridge) There were copper bottom tympani in horse platoons
Thundering **(2x)** all along the way
Double bell euphoniums & big bassoons
Each bassoon having his big, fat say
There were 50 mounted cannon in the battery
Thundering **(2x)** louder than before
Clarinets of ev'ry size & trumpeters who'd improvise
A full octave higher than the score

C FC G - / - B7 C - / - FC G - / D - GD G7
" / " / C FC F B7 / C G7 C D7

76 trombones led the big parade
When the order to march rang out loud & clear
Starting off with a big bang bong on a Chinese gong
By a big bang bonger at the rear
76 trombones hit the counterpoint
While 110 cornets played the air
Then I modestly took my place as the one & only bass
And I oompahed up & down the square
(sound of tuba: "buh, buh, buh ..." to last 4 lines above)

— Meredith Willson
 — Fr his musical The Music Man. *In Readers Dig* Pop S that Will Live, Best Loved S of Am People, *& var Broadway SBs.* OP20

Sur Le Pont d'Avignon

Sur le pont d'Avignon l'on y danse (2x)
Sur le pont d'Avignon l'on y danse tout en ronde

D A7 D A7 / D A7 D A7D

Les messieurs vont comme ci
Et puis vont comme ça

(slower) D AD / D AD

On the bridge at Avignon see them dancing (2x)
On the bridge ... see them dancing round & round

The gentlemen go this way
And again go that way

Additional verses:
les mesdames (the ladies), les enfants (the children), **etc.**

— trad. (French)
On Raffi Corner Grocery Store *& in his* Singable SB, *also in* V Fav S of the V Young. OP21

To Sing for You

When you're feelin' kinda lonesome in your mind
With a heartache followin' you so close behind
Call out to me as I ramble by, **I'll sing a song for you**
That's what I'm here to do: to sing for you

(in 3/4, capo up) D G D - / / G A G D / G D GD D

When the night has left you cold & feelin' sad
I will show you that it cannot be so bad
Forget the one who went & made you cry, **I'll ...**

When you feel you just can't make it anymore
With your head bowed down you're starin' at the floor
Search out to me with your weary eyes ...

Now everyone they have their work you know
And to find out mine you ain't got far to go
Call out to me with your weary eyes ...

— Donovan Leitch
 On his Pye History of Pop. OP22

Tumbalalaika

Shteyt a bokher un er trakht
Trakht un trakht a gantse nakht
Vemen tsu nemen un nit farshemen **(2x)**

(in 3/4) Am - - E / - - - Am / - - Dm Am / Dm E - Am

Tumbala, tumbala, tumbalalaika (2x)
Tumbalalaika, shpil balalaika
Tumbalalaika, frelakh zol zayn

Meydl, meydl, 'khvel ba dir fregn
Vos kon vaksn, vaksn on regn
Vos kon brenen un nit oyfheren
Vos kon beynken, veynen on treren

Narisher bokher, vos darfstu fregn
A shteyn kon vaksn, vaksn on regn
Libe kon brenen un nit oyfheren
A hartz kon beynken, veynen on treren

Hear my tale of a certain young man
Stayed up all night til he thought of a plan
He wanted a girl who would be his delight
A girl who was pretty, witty & bright

Tell me, my pretty one, tell if you know
What needs no rain & yet it can grow
Tell what can blossom, bloom thru the years
Tell what can yearn, cry without tears

O foolish boy, now surely you know
A stone needs no rain & yet it can grow
True love can blossom, bloom thru the years
And a heart when it yearns, cries without tears

— trad. (Yiddish), Eng trans. by Teddi Schwartz & Arthur Kevess
 — Shpil=play frehlakh zol zayn=let it be lively. Yiddish Riddle Song. In SO! 6:4, Israeli FS 1969, Treas of Jewish FS 1956, *Bikel* FS & Footnotes, Bells of Rhymney, FiresB of Love S, Treas of Jewish FS & FSEncyV1. OP23

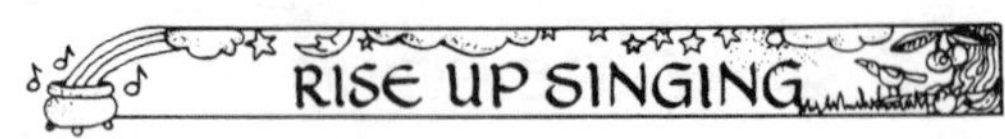

Tzena Tzena

Tzena **(4x)** habanot ur'ena Chayalim bamoshava
Alna **(4x)** alna tityarena mi ben Chayil ish tsava

Tzena **(2x)** habanot ur'ena Chayalim bamoshava
Alna **(2x)** alna tityarena mi ben Chayil ish tsava

Tzena **(2x)**, **(clap)** tzena **(3x)**, tzena **(2x)**, tzena **(4x)**
Tzena **(2x)**, **(clap)** tzena **(3x)**, tzena **(2x)**, tzena **(3x)**!

A D E A / // / // A D E - / A D E EA

— Issachav Miron, Julius Groissman, Yehiel Haggi

 — The 1st 2 verses should be sung as a round with both parts joining together for the 3rd v. The Hebrew words are abt all the people of the village coming out to dance all night with a gp of soldiers passing thru. On Hatikvah *(Tara T626),* Hava Nagila Festival *(T608),* Beautiful Israel *(T602), The Weavers* On Tour *& in their* SB. *In* SO! *1:2 &* Children's S for a Friendly Planet. OP24

Waltz Across Texas

When we waltz together my world's in disguise
A fairyland tale that's come true
And when you look at me with those stars in your eyes
I could **waltz across Texas with you**

(in 3/4) A - E - / - - A - :||

I could waltz across Texas with you in my arms
Waltz across Texas with you
Like a story book ending I'm lost in your charms
I could waltz across Texas with you

My trouble & heartaches are all up & gone
The moment you come into view
And with your hand in mine I could dance on & on / I could ...

Before I met you I never would dance
I never would dance, it is true
But now we're together I jumped at the chance / To ...

To you, John Barger, we make this request
There's one thing we want you to do
Just sing one more verse of the song we love best / To ...

— Quannah Talmadge ("Billy") Tubb

 — On Debby McClatchy Lady Luck. OP25

There are a number of songs on art, music, dance, etc. in the chapters on GOOD TIMES, GOLDEN OLDIES, & PLAY. In the latter, note that Raffi has written new words to "Old McDonald" & ""This Old Man that are about music-making.

Addl songs on this subject include: "Rosebud in June" (BALLAD) "Dancing in the Street" (CITY) "How Can I Keep fr Singing," "Lord of the Dance," "Shake These Bones," "Song of the Soul" (FAITH) "Buffalo Gals," "Iowa Waltz" (FARM) "Barnyard Dance," "Waltzing with Bears" (FUN) "Cook with Honey," "Food Glorious Food" (HOME) "Mairi's Wedding," "Roseville Fair" (LOVE) "Music Alone Shall Live" (ROUNDS) "Over My Head" (SPIRS) "MacPherson's Farewell," "Singing for Our Lives," "Victor Jara" (STRUG) "Homeward Bound" (TRAV) & "A Place in the Choir/All God's Critters, Sing Along" (UNITY).

Best Friend (The Unicorn Song)

When I was growing up, my best friend was a unicorn
The others smiled at me & called me crazy
But I was not upset by knowing I did not conform
I always thought their seeing must be hazy
The unicorn & I would while away the hours
Playing, dancing & romancing in the wildflowers & we'd sing

G D Em B7 / C G Dsus D :|| Em Am7 D Gmaj7 / Em A B7 - -

Seeing is believing in the things you see
Loving is believing in the ones you love (repeat)

C↓ Am7 G↑ G / Em↓ CG Am7 G :||

When I was 17, my best friend was the northern star
The others asked why was I always dreaming
But I did not reply, I found my thoughts were very far
Away from daily hurts & fears & scheming
The northern star & I would share our dreams together
Laughing, sighing, sometimes crying thru all kinds of weather, & we'd sing

And now that I am grown, my best friend lives inside of me
The others smile at me & call me crazy
But I am not upset, for long ago I found the key
I've always known their seeing must be hazy
My friend inside & I will while away the hours
Playing, dancing, & romancing in the wildflowers & we sing:

— Margie Adam

 — On (& in) her Songwriter. *On Ginni Clemens* Longtime Friends, *Peter, Paul & Mary* Reunion, *Josh White Jr.* Almost Done *& Kevin Roth* Living & Breathing Wind. OD02

Both Sides Now

Rows of floes of angel hair & ice cream castles in the air
And feather canyons everywhere, I've looked at clouds that way
But now they only block the sun they rain & snow on everyone
So many things I could have done, but clouds got in my way

G C - G - Bm C G / - C Am - C - D - :||

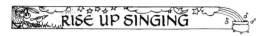

I've looked at clouds **from both sides now**
From up & down **& still somehow**
It's clouds' **illusions I recall**
I really don't know clouds **at all**

G - C G / C G C G / Bm C G C / G - Dsus - D - G - - -

Moons & Junes & ferriswheels, the dizzy dancing way you feel
As every fairytale comes real, I've looked at love that way
But now it's just another show, you leave them laughing when you go
And if you care don't let them know, don't give yourself away
I've looked at love ... **from** give & take ...

Tears & fears & feeling proud to say I love you right out loud
Dreams & schemes & circus crowds, I've looked at life that way
But now old friends are acting strange, they shake their heads, they say I've changed
Something's lost, but something's gained in living every day
I've looked at life ... win & lose ...

Daughter **(2x)** *don't you know, you're not the first to feel just so*
But let me say before I go, it's worth it anyway
Someday we may all be surprised, we'll wake & open up our eyes
And then we all will realize, the whole world feels this way
We've all been living upside down & turned around with love unfound
Until we turn & face the sun, yes all of us, everyone

— Joni Mitchell (new verse by Pete Seeger)

 — In her SB V1 *& on her* Clouds *&* Miles of Aisles. *In* Judy Collins SB *& on her* Wildflowers *&* First 15 yrs. *On* Pete Seeger World of *&* Young vs Old *&* Neil Diamond Love S *&* Gold. *In* SO! 18:6 *&* WHATFG. OD03

Brandy Tree

I go down to the Brandy Tree
And take my nose & tail with me
All for the world & the wind to see
And never come back no more

(capo up) Am Em / EmAm Em / F Em / FG Am

Down by the meadowmarsh, deep & wide
Tumble & tangle by my side
All for the westing wind to run
And slide in the summer rain

> Sun come follow my happy way
> Wind come walk beside me
> Moon on the mountain, go with me
> A wondrous way I know

C G / / Am Em / FG Am

I go down to the windy sea
And the little gray seal will play with me
Slide on the rock & dive in the bay
And sleep on the ledge at night

> But the seal don't try to tell me how
> To fish in the windy blue
> Seal's been fishing for a 1000 years
> And he knows that I have too

When the frog goes down to the mud to sleep
And the lamprey hides in the boulders deep
I take my nose & tail & go
A hundred thousand hills

> Sun come follow my happy way ...

Someday down by the Brandy Tree
I'll hear the Shepherd call for me
Call me to leave my happy ways
And the shining world I know

> Sun on the hill, come go with me
> My days have all been free
> The pipes come laughing down the wind
> And that's the way I go
> That's the way for me

C G / / Am Em / F G / FG A

— Gordon Bok

 — aka: "Otter's Song." On his Peter Kagan & the Wind *& in his* Time & the Flying Snow. OD04

Camelot

A law was made a distant moon ago here
July & August cannot be too hot
And there's a legal limit to the snow here in Camelot
The winter is forbidden til December
And exits March the 2nd on the dot
By order summer lingers through September in Camelot

DDmaj7 D / / A - D - / 1st / DE♭ D / A - F♯7 -

Camelot! Camelot! I know it sounds a bit bizarre
But in Camelot, Camelot, that's how conditions are
The rain may never fall til after sundown
By 8 the morning fog must disappear
In short, there's simply not a more congenial spot
For happ'ly ever aftering than here in Camelot

B - - - / D - EmA EmA /

DDmaj7 D / DE♭ D / AD F♯Bm / GGm D A D -

The winter ...
Camelot! Camelot! I know it gives a person pause
But in Camelot, Camelot, those are the legal laws
The snow may never slush upon the hillside
By 9PM the moonlight must appear / **In short ...**

— w: Alan Jay Lerner **— m: Fredrick Loewe**

 — Fr their musical Camelot. OD05

Come Take a Trip in My Airship

I once loved a sailor / Once a sailor loved me
He was not a sailor / Who sailed on the wide rolling sea
He sailed in an airship / Free as a bird on the wing
And every Sunday evening / He'd fly past my window & sing

(in 3/4) G - - - / Am - C - / D ↓ - - / G C G (D) :||

Come take a trip in my airship / Come let us sail to the stars
Come let us fly off to Venus / Come take a trip around Mars
No one will see when we're kissing,
No one will know when we spoon
Come take ... airship / & we'll visit the man in the moon

One night while sailing away from the crowds
We passed thru the Milky White Way
While idly drifting & watching the clouds,
He asked me if I'd name the day
Just by the dipper I gave him my heart
The sun shines on our honeymoon
We swore to each other we never would part
And we'd teach all the babies this tune

— George Evans & Ron Shields (1907)

aka: "The Airship." On Sally Rogers & Claudia Schmidt *Closing the Distance. In* Sally Rogers SB. OD06

Follow the Gleam

To knights in the days of old
Keeping vigil on mountain height
Came a vision of Holy Grail
And a voice thru the waiting night
Saying, "Follow, follow the gleam
Banners unfurled over the world
Follow, follow, follow the gleam
Of the chalice that is the Grail"

(in 3/4) D G D - / A - D - :||: G - D - / A - D - :||

And we who would serve the King [seek the Light]
And loyally Him obey [follow it on our way]
In the consecrate silence know
That the challenge still sounds today
Saying, "Follow, follow the gleam
Standards of worth over the earth
Follow, follow, follow the gleam
Of the light that shall bring the dawn"

— w: Helen Hill Miller **— m: Sallie Hume Douglas**

Written by a group of Bryn Mawr students for a song contest at a YWCA convention in Silver Bay, NY. In S of the Spirit & Treasury of Hymns. D07

Happiness Runs

Little pebble upon the sand
Now you're lying here in my hand
How many years have you been here?
Little human upon the sand
From where I'm lying here in your hand
You to me are but a passing breeze

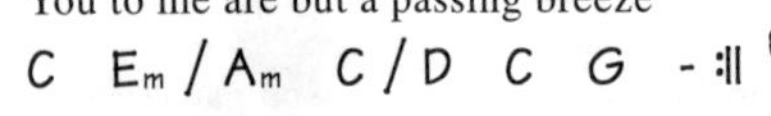

C Em / Am C / D C G - :||

The sun will always shine where you stand
Depending in which land
You may find yourself
Now you have my blessing, go your way

C F / / Em - / C F G -

1. La la la **(4x)** / La la la **(3x)** la **(repeat)**

FC GC :|| **(4x)**
(These verses can be sung as a round)

2. Happiness runs in a circular motion
   Thought is but a little boat upon the sea
   Everybody is a part of everything anyway
   You can have everything if you let yourself be
3. Happiness runs, happiness runs **(4x)**
4. Why-o? Because! **(4x)**
5. Da-dum, da-dum, da-dum-dee **(4x)**

— Donovan Leitch

© 1968 Donovan (Music) Ltd. All rights reserved. Used by permission of CPP Belwin Inc. aka: "The Pebble & the Man." On his Barbajagal & In Conc. *In Sol Webber* Rounds B. D08

If I Were a Featherbed

If I were a featherbed in your house so fine
I'd hold you in my arms each night, keep you warm in the wintertime

A AG A D / A - G A

If I were an old banjo, felt your fingers on my strings
I'd play the sweetest little song that a banjo e'er did sing

If I were a drop of rain that trickled down your chin
I'd run right up & kiss your lips & kiss them twice again

If I were a breath of wind on your cheeks as you walked by
I'd pick you up upon my back & teach you how to fly

If I were a hair ribbon & my color it was blue
I'd be ten times as beautiful, 'cause I'd be wearing you

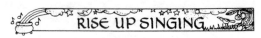

And if I were a big wool rug sitting in your front hall
I'd tickle your feet & make you laugh if you stepped on me at all

But I am not the wind or rain nor the rug in your front hall
And the whole world's countless loves can't match my love for you at all

— John McCutcheon (last v. adap. Cathy Fink)

© 1984 John McCutcheon. Pub by Appalsongs (ASCAP). Used by permission. — aka: "Featherbed." In his Water from Another Time SB. *On his & Si Kahn* Signs of the Times, *Sally Rogers & Howard Bursen* Satisfied Customers, *& rec by Cathy Fink.* D09

If It's Magic

If it's magic, then why can't it be everlasting?
Like the sun that always shines
Like the poets' endless rhyme
Like the galaxies in time

(freely) C G Am C D - / G C / DG Am / DG CF C

If it's pleasing, then why can't it be never leaving
Like the day that never fails
Like on seashores there are shells
Like the time that always tells?

(bridge)
It holds the key to every heart throughout the universe
It fills you up without a bite & quenches every thirst

F - Eb C / F - Eb Cmaj7 Cmaj7G

So, if it's special, then with it why aren't we as careful
As making sure we dress in style
Posing pictures with a smile
Keeping danger from a child?

So if it's magic, why can't we make it everlasting?
Like the lifetime of the sun
It will leave no heart undone
For there's enough for everyone

— Stevie Wonder

© 1975, 1976 Jobete Music Co. Inc. & Black Bull Music, Inc. International Copyright Secured. Made in USA. All rights reserved. Used by permission of CPP Belwin Inc. — On his S in the Key of Life. D10

Lavender's Blue

Lavender's blue, **dilly dilly,** lavender's green
When I am king, **dilly dilly,** you shall be queen
Who told you so, **dilly ...** who told you so?
'Twas my own heart ... that told me so

I: (in 3/4) C - F C / F C Dm G / C - F C / F C G C

Call up your men ... set them to work
Some with a rake ... some with a fork
Some to make hay ... some to thresh corn
While you & I ... keep ourselves warm

II: C - F - / C - G C :||

— trad. (English, 1st printed 1680 as "Diddle, Diddle")

In Sing Together Children, *Cole* FS of Eng, Ire, Scot & Wales, *J Tobitt* The Ditty Bag, Bright Morning Stars *(WAS) & T Glazer* Treas of FS. D11

Little Brown Dog (Autumn to May)

I buyed me a little dog, it's color it was brown
I learned him to whistle, sing, dance & run
His legs they were 14 yards long, his ears they were broad
Around the world in half a day & on him I could ride
Sing taddle-o day [**version II adds: sing Autumn to May**]

I: Em Bm Em D / / D G D G / D G Em Bm // Em C D -

I buyed me a little bull, about four inches high
Everybody feared him that ever heard him cry
When he begin to bellow, it made such a melodious sound
Til all the walls from London came a-tumbling to the ground

I buyed me a flock of sheep, I thought they were all wethers
Sometimes they yielded wool, sometimes they yielded feathers
I think mine are the best of sheep for yielding me increase
For every full & change of the moon they yield both lambs & geese

I buyed me a little box about four acres square
I filled it with guinea & silver so fair
O now I'm bound for Turkey, I'll travel like an ox
In my breeches pocket I'll carry my little box

I buyed me a little hen, all speckled gay & fair
I sat her on an oyster shell, she hatched me out a hair
The hair it sprang a handsome horse full 15 hands high
And him that tells a bigger tale would have to tell a lie

ll: F C F G/ /C AmG C Am/C AmEm F G//
CF G/Am AmF G - **(adap PP&M – capo up)**

— trad. (English)

These words (which are p.d.) can also be sung to the tune of Paul Stookey & Peter Yarrow's adaptation of this song, which is entitled "Autumn to May." Adapted chorus & PP&M chords above are © 1962 Pepamar Music Corp. Renewed 1991 Neworld Media Music Publishers & Silver Dawn Music All rights reserved. Used by permission. — In Ruth Crawford Seeger Animal FS for Children *& on Peggy Seeger* Animal FS ... *(FC7051). In* SO! *11:3 &* Reprints *#5, &* FSEncyV1. *On Judy Collins* Golden Apples, Jackie Washington *(VRS9110), &* Peter, Paul & Mary. OD12

Die Lorelei

Ich weiss nicht was soll es bedeuten, dass ich so traurig bin
Ein Märchen aus alten Zeiten, das kommt mir nicht aus dem Sinn
Die Luft is kühl und es dunkelt, und ruhig fliesst der Rhein
Der Gipfel des Berges funkelt im Abendsonnenschein

(in 3/4) AD AE AE A / / E EB7 EB7 E / **1st**

Die schönste Jungfrau sitzt dort oben wunderbar
Ihr gold'nes Geschmeide blitzt, sie kämmt ihr goldenes Haar
Sie kämmt es mit goldenem Kamme, und singt ein Lied dabei
Das hat eine wundersame, gewaltige Melodei

Den Schiffer im kleinen Schiffe, ergreift es mit wildem Weh
Er schaut nicht die Felsenriffe, er schaut nur hinauf in die Höh!
Ich glaube, die Wellen verschlingen am Ende Schiffer und Kahn
Und das hat met ihrem Singen, die Lorelei getan

— trad. (German)

Trans: (Varya Piper) "I know not the cause of my sorrow & yet it conquers me. An ancient tale floats fr nowhere into my memory. The air is cool at evening & calmly flows the Rhine. The crest of the hilltop glimmers as the last of the sun's rays shine/ The wondrously beautiful maiden is sitting above me there. Her golden bracelets flash as she combs her golden hair. She combs it w a comb of gold & sings a melody. It has the seeds of magic, the song she sings to me/ The passing sailor in his boat is seized by wild grief. His gaze is held by the hilltop, he sees not the threatening reef. The waves have swallowed him, I know, to keep him in their depths. The Lorelei w her magic song has lured him to his death." In SFest, Gambit B of Children's S, Golden Ency of FS, *&* 1001 Jumbo S. OD13

Michael from Mountains

Michael wakes you up with sweets
He takes you up streets & the rain comes down
Sidewalk markets locked up tight
And umbrellas bright on a gray background
There's oil in the puddles in taffeta patterns
That run down the drain
In colored arrangements that Michael will change
With a stick that he found

D - / Gm D :ll C - / B - / B♭ A / DEm D

Michael from mountains
Go where you will go to
Know that I will know you
Someday I may know you very well

Am - / G - / F♯m - / GBm EmF D -

Michael brings you to a park
He sings & it's dark when the clouds come by
Yellow slickers up on swings
Like puppets on strings hanging in the sky
They'll splash home to suppers in wall-papered kitchens
Their mothers will scold
But Michael will hold you to keep away cold
Til the sidewalks are dry

Michael leads you up the stairs
He needs you to care & you know you do
Cats come crying to the key
And dry you will be in a towel or two
There's rain in the window & sun in the painting
That smiles on the wall
You want to know all, but his mountains have called
So you never do

— Joni Mitchell

© 1967 Siquomb Publishing Corp. All rights reserved. Used by permission. — In her SB V1 *& on her* S to a Seagull *&* Miles of Aisles. *Also on Judy Collins* Wildflowers. OD14

Moonshadow

O I'm bein' followed by a moonshadow
Moonshadow, moonshadow
Leapin' and a hoppin' like a moonshadow
Moonshadow, moonshadow

C - - - / F G C - :ll

And if I ever lose my hands / Lose my plow, lose my lands
Yes, if I ever lose my hands / O, if –
I won't have to work no more

F C F C / F C F G / **1st** / F Dm C Am / Dm G C -

And if I ever lose my eyes / All my colors all run dry
Yes if I ever ... I won't have to cry no more

And if ever lose my legs / I won't moan & I won't beg
Yes if I ever ... I won't have to walk no more

And if I ever lose my mouth / All my teeth north & south
Yes if I ever ... I won't have to talk **(pause)**

(bridge) Did it take long to find me? I asked the faithful light
Yes, did it take long to find me & are you goin' to stay the night?

D - G - D - G - / /

— Cat Stevens

© Westbury Music Ltd., 56 Wigmore St, London W1H 9DG, UK. All rights reserved. Used by permission. On Teaser & Firecat *&* Gr H *& in his* SB. OD15

My Father

My father always promised us that we could live in France
We'd go boating on the Seine, & I would learn to dance
We lived in Ohio then, he worked in the mine
On his dreams like boats we knew, we sailed in time

(in 6/8) G ↓ CAm GD / G ↓ CAm D
Em A D ↓ / F ↓ C B♭ G (D)

All my sisters soon were gone to Denver & Cheyenne
Marrying their grownup dreams, the lilacs & the man
I stayed behind the youngest still, always danced alone
The colors of my father's dreams faded without a sound

I live in Paris now, my children dance & dream
Hearing the words of a miner's life in words they've never seen
I sail my memories on high like boats across the Seine
And watch the Paris sunset in my father's eyes again

— Judy Collins

© 1968 Rocky Mntn Natl Pk Publishing Co. Inc. (ASCAP) Admin. by Good Flavor Songs, Inc., 515 Madison Ave., 28th Flr, NY, NY 10022. Used by permission. In her SB *& on* Who Knows Where the Time Goes, 1st 15 yrs *&* Recollections. OD16

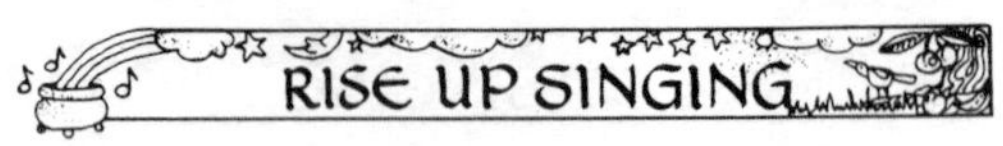

O Had I a Golden Thread

O had I a golden thread & needle so fine
I'd weave a magic strand of rainbow design,
Of rainbow design

D G D A / /G DA D -

In it I'd weave the bravery of women giving birth
In it I'd weave the innocence of children over all the earth,
Children of all earth

Far over the water I'd reach my magic band
To every city, thru ev'ry single land / Thru every land

Show my brothers & my sisters my rainbow design
Bind up this sorry world with hand & heart & mind / Hand ...

Far over the waters I'd reach my magic band
To every human being so they would understand / So ...

— **Pete Seeger**

 — On his Essential, Strangers & Cousins & Where Have all the Flowers. *In* SO! *8:4 &* Reprints *#2 &* Bells of Rhymney. OD17

Only a Song

If I were a bird, I'd fly round her window _
If I were a word, then she'd understand
If I were a dream, then I'd let her rest easy
And if I were a light, I'd lead her to land

(in 3/4) F - C - / /G - F - / G GF CF C

If I were the wind, then I'd tell her a story
And if I were the road, I'd help her along
And I'd flow thru her life if I were a river
But only a song, that's all I can give her

If I were a tree, then I'd be a willow
And she'd come to me & I'd be her pillow
And there we would be with the sun shining on us
A rose & a tree **(tacit)**

(instrumental 1st 2 lines)
And I'd flow thru her life if I were a river
But only a song, that's all I can give her

– **Bill Staines**

 On his Rodeo Rose *& in his* If I Were a Word. OD18

Over the Rainbow

Somewhere over the rainbow way up high
There's a land that I heard of once in a lullaby
Somewhere over the rainbow skies are blue
And the dreams that you dare to dream really do come true

C - Em - F - Em7 - / F Fm C A D7 G C - :||

(bridge) Someday I'll wish upon a star
And wake up where the clouds are far behind me
Where troubles melt like lemon drops
Away above the chimney tops, that's where you'll find me

C - / Dm G Am - F G / C - / Adim - Dm6 - Dm7 G

Somewhere over the rainbow bluebirds fly
Birds fly over the rainbow, why then, o why can't I?
(tag) If happy little bluebirds fly beyond the rainbow
Why o why can't I? *(Why not you & I?)*

C - Dm / G - C -

— **E Y Harburg & Harold Arlen (new final line: Pete Seeger)**

 — Fr their musical The Wizard of Oz. *On Kevin Roth* Lullabies. *In* Life of the Party, 100 of the Grtst Easy Listening Hits, Golden Era of Nost Music V1, & Those Wonderful Yrs. OD19

Rhymes and Reasons

So you speak to me of sadness & the coming of the winter
Fear that is within you now that seems to never end
And the dreams that have escaped you & a hope that you've forgotten
And you tell me that you need me now & you want to be my friend
And you wonder where we're going where's the rhyme & where's the reason
And it's you cannot accept it is here we must begin
To seek the wisdom of the children
And the graceful way of flowers in the wind

C G F C / Am C F G / 1st / Am C G -

F - C G / Am C G - / Dm - - - / C F G -

For the children & the flowers are my sisters & my brothers
Their laughter & their loveliness would clear a cloudy day
Like the music of the mountains & the colors of the rainbow
They're a promise of the future & a blessing for today

C G F C / Am C F G / 1st / Am C G C

Tho' the cities start to crumble & the towers fall around us
The sun is slowly fading & it's colder than the sea
It is written from the desert to the mountains they shall lead us
By the hand & by the heart & they will comfort you & me
In their innocence & trusting they will teach us to be free
(instrumental)

For the children & ... / ... clear a cloudy day
And the song that I am singing is a prayer to non-believers
Come & stand beside us, we can find a better way

— **John Denver**

 In John Denver SB *& on his* Rhymes & Reasons, Gr H & An Evening with. OD20

Rooty Toot Toot for the Moon

The whole kit & caboodle is in disrepair
There's nowhere to go if not here
Little captains & cuckoos from here to Timbuctoo
Are counting their dough in the mirror

(in 3/4) G (G, F#, E, G) / C (C, B A, G) / D - D7 - / G C D -

Singing rooty toot toot for the moon
It's the biggest star I've ever seen
It's a pearl of wisdom, a slice of green cheese
Burning just like kerosene (2x)

/ " / " / " / " / D - G -

He was just a young white kid trying to sing tough & black
With gravel & spit in his voice
He laughed at the things we do, the radio laughed too
I held up my arms to rejoice

So God bless motorcycles & far out heavy trifles
You know you can't memorize Zen
Hang your hat on your nose, don't hide in your clothes
Smile at someone, begin to begin

You know all of us are primates, some of us were classmates
Some of us were lovers in the fall
There were periods of blondness, periods of fondness
Periods that never came at all

— **Greg Brown (new verse Dick Pinney)**

 — On Lui Collins Baptism of Fire *& Michael Johnson* There is a Breeze. *In* SO! *30:1 &* New Folk Favs. OD21

Scarborough Fair

Are you going to Scarborough fair? **Parsley, sage, rosemary & thyme**
Remember me to one that lives there
For once she was a true love of mine (in 3/4)

I: Am - G Am / C Am D Em / Am C - G / Am G Em Am

Tell her to make me a cambric shirt, **parsley, sage ...**
Without any seam or fine needlework **& then she'll be ...**

Tell her to wash it in yonder dry well
Where water ne'er sprung nor drop of rain fell

Tell her to dry it on yonder thorn
Which never bore blossom since Adam was born

O will you find me an acre of land
Between the sea foam & the sea sand **or never be ...**

O will you plough it with a ram's horn
And sow it all over with one peppercorn? **& then she'll be ...**

O will you reap it with a sickle of leather
And tie it all up with a peacock's feather?

And when you have done & finished your work
Then come to me for your cambric shirt **& you shall be ...**

II: D A D A / D G Em A / 1st / G Em A D

— trad. (English: Child Ballad #2 "The Elfin Knight")
I=On Simon & Garfunkle Parsley Sage Rosemary & Thyme, *Ewan MacColl* Matching S, *Leo Kretzner & Jay Leibowitz* Dulcimer Fair, *John Renbourn* Lady & the Unicorn *& rec by Martin Carthy. In* SO! *12:5 &* Reprints *#6*, Fires B of FS=2, Golden Ency of FS, FSEncyV1, 1001 Jumbo S, Am Treas of Gold Oldies, S Am Sings, FM Gr H *& H* fr the Superstars. OD22

Sisters of Mercy

O the sisters of mercy they are not departed or gone
They were waiting for me when I thought that I just can't go on
They brought me their comfort & later they brought me their song
O I hope you run into them, you who've been trav'ling so long

(in 3/4) CF CG CF C / EmBm EmBm D - /

FC B♭Am G - / 1st /

Yes you who must leave eveything that you cannot control
It begins with your family & soon it comes round to your soul
I've been where you're hanging, I think I can see how you're pinned
When you're not feeling holy, your loneliness says that you've sinned

They lay down beside me, I made my confession to them
They touched both my eyes & I touched the dew on their hem
If your life is a leaf that the seasons tear off & condemn
They will bind you with love that is graceful & green as a stem

When I left they were sleeping, I hope you run into them soon
Don't turn on the lights, they can read your address by the moon
And it won't make me jealous if I learn that they sweetened your night
We weren't lovers like that & besides it would still be all right

— Leonard Cohen
On his S of *&* Best of. *Also on Judy Collins* Wildflowers. OD23

Suzanne

Suzanne takes you down to her place by the river
You can hear the boats go by, you can spend the night forever
And you know that she's half crazy & that's why you want to be there
And she feeds you tea & oranges that came all the way from China
And just when you want to tell her that you have no love to give her
She gets you on her wavelength & she lets the river answer
That you've always been her lover

G - / Am - / G - / Bm C / G - / Am - / G -
(Cohen's last 3 lines: G Am / G Am / G -)

And you want to travel with her & you want to travel blind
And you think you maybe trust her 'cause she's touched your perfect body
With her mind

Bm C / G Am / G -

And Jesus was a sailor when he walked upon the water
And he spent a long time watching from his lonely wooden tower
And when he knew for certain only drowning men could see him
He said all men shall be sailors then until the sea shall free them
But he himself was broken long before the sky would open
Forsaken almost human he sank beneath your wisdom like a stone
And you want to travel with him ... / ... 'cause he's ...

Suzanne takes your hand & she leads you to the river
She's wearing rags & feathers from Salvation Army counters
And the sun pours down like honey on our lady of the harbor
And she shows you where to look amid the garbage & the flowers
There are heroes in the seaweed, there are children in the morning
They are leaning out for love & they'll lean that way forever
While Suzanne holds her mirror
And you want to travel with her ...
...'cause you've touched her perfect body with your mind

— Leonard Cohen
On his S of & Best of, *Baez* Fr Every Stage & Carry It On, *Roberta Flack* Killing Me Softly, *Neil Diamond* Love S *& Judy Collins* In My Life. *Baez sings the chorus: "'cause she's touched you & she's moved you & she's kind." In* SO! *17:4.* OD24

The Swallow Song

Come wander quietly & listen to the wind
Come here & listen to the sky
Come walking high above the rolling of the sea
And watch the swallows as they fly

Em Em7 C B7 / Em ↓ B7 -
Am Em Am B7 / Am - B7 -

There is no sorrow like the murmur of their wings
There is no choir like their song
There is no power like the freedom of their flight
While the swallows roam alone

Do you hear the calling of a hundred thousand voice
Hear the echo in a stone
Do you hear the angry bells ringing in the night
Do you hear the swallows when they've flown?

And will the breezes blow the petals from your hand
And will some loving ease your pain
And will the silence strike confusion from your soul
And will the swallows come again?

— Richard Farina
On his & Mimi's Reflections on a Crystal Wind, Memories *&* Best of *& Holly Tannen* Invocation *(Kicking Mule 236). In* SO! *16:3.* OD25

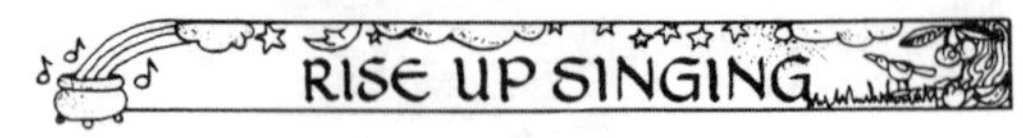

Violets of Dawn

Take me to the night I'm tipping
Topsy turvy turning upside down _ _
Hold me tight & whisper what you will
For there is no one here around
O you may singsong me sweet smiles
Regardless of the city's careless frown
Come watch the no colors fade blazing
Into petal sprays of violets of dawn

C Dm7 / C Dm7 (3x) :‖ F G / C Dm7 G - / 1st 2 /

In blindful wonderment's enchantment
You can lift my wings softly to flight
Your eyes are like swift fingers
Reaching out into the pockets of my night
O whirling twirling puppy warm
Before the flashing cloaks of darkness gone / **Come ...**

Some prince charming I'll be on two white steeds
To bring you dappled diamond crowns
And climb your towers sleeping beauty
'Fore you ever know I've left the ground
You can wear a cinderella-snow white-
Alice wonderlanded gown / **Come ...**

But if I seem to wander off in dreamlike looks
Please let me settle slowly
It's only me just staring out at you
A seeming stranger speaking holy
No I don't mean to wake you up
It's only loneliness just acoming on / **So let the ...**

Like shadows bursting into mist
Behind the echoes of this nonsense song
It's just a chasing whispering trail
Of secret steps - o see them laughing on
There's magic in the sleepiness
Of waking to a childish sounding yawn / **Come watch ...**

— **Eric Anderson**

 — On his 'Bout Changes 'n Things, Best of, Best S. *Also on* Gr FSingers of the 60s *&* *Rick Nelson* In Conc. ©D26

Walk Shepherdess Walk

Walk, Shepherdess, walk & I'll walk too
To find the ram with the ebony horn & the gold-footed ewe
The lamb with the fleece of silver, like summer sea foam
The wether with the crystal bell that leads them all home
So walk, Shepherdess, walk & I'll walk too
And if we never find them, I shan't care, shall you?

(in 3/4) CG Am FC G / CG AmD CG C :‖ (3x)

— **Eleanor Farjeon**

Reprinted by permission of Oxford University Press. In Let's All Sing & Bright Morning Stars *(WAS).* ©D27

There are more songs about fantasy & imagination in LULLABIES and PLAY. The chapter on HOPE consists basically of songs about people's dreams for a better world – or for a better life for themselves personally.

See also: "Great Silkie & Water is Wide/Waly Waly" (BALLAD) "Brother Sun/Sister Moon" (FAITH) "Oleanna," "Waltzing with Bears" (FUN) "There's a Long Long Trail" (GOLD), "Au Clair de la Lune" (GOOD) "Angel From Montgomery" (HARD) "Baby Tree" (HOME) "Since You Asked" (LOVE) "Mole in the Ground" (MTN) "Deep Blue Sea, Last Night I Had the Strangest Dream" (PEACE) "Big Rock Candy Mtn," "We Hate to See Them Go" (RICH) "Have You Seen the Ghost of John?," "O Joy Upon This Earth," "White Sands & Grey Sands" (ROUNDS) "A Capital Ship," "Come Fare Away," "Lord Franklin" (SEA) "Dona Dona" (STRUG) "Carolina in my Mind," "Sailing Down My Golden River" (TRAV) & "The Mill Was Made of Marble" (WORK).

ECOLOGY

Acres of Clams

I've lived all my life in this country
I love every flower & tree
I expect to live here til I'm 90
It's the nukes that must go & not me

(refrain) **It's the nukes that must go & not me (2x)**
I expect to live here til I'm 90
It's the nukes ... (use last 2 lines of each verse)

C - / - Am / C CF / CG C // C F / C Am / 3rd + 4th

I swallowed enough radiation
It's time I was standing my ground
So I'm joining that grand occupation
We're shutting that power plant down / We're

Now Seabrook, New Hampshire's a swell town
It's there that we're taking our stand
Don't sit home & wait for a meltdown
Come fight for your freedom & land ...

Now Seabrook is just the beginning
We'll soon have the nukes on the run
It's a fight that the people are winning
The fight for our place in the sun ...

We're seizing that land with a vision
Exposing the P.S.C.'s shams
As I sing of my happy condition
Surrounded by acres of clams ...

— **w: Charlie King** — **m: trad ("Old Rosin the Beau")**

 — The largest nonviolent occupation of a nuclear power plant construction site in this country was organized by a group called the Clamshell Alliance. On his Somebody's Story & For Our Children, Heal the Earth *(Leveler Records) & in SO! 27:1. For tune sources see: GOOD.* ©E01

All Clear in Harrisburg

You can return to your homes now, Citizens
You can come back to the nest
The nuclear episode is history now
It all turned out for the best
Pregnant women & pre-school kids
Can get off of the bus
And, of course, if you live down wind
You'll be hearing from us

C A7 / DG C / - A7 / D G
F C / F E7 / F CA7 / DG C

You just might glow in the dark, grow feathers just like a lark
Stand in the fountain & light up the park
What can I say? The chance is you may
Blow yourself & half of Pennsylvania away

G - / C - / G - / C GC

You can return to your homes now, Citizens
It was a terrible mess
There never really was a danger to you
It was the fault of the press
They made a mountain from a mole-hill again
They always do it somehow
Oh, by the way, I wouldn't eat that egg
Or drink the milk from that cow

You can come back to the town now, Citizens
The town is perfectly clean
And please believe us, you have nothing to fear
If now & then you turn green
Three Mile Island has your welfare at heart
And we're so glad you're alive
And we just want to provide cheap energy
For the ones who survive

— Tom Paxton

* — The worst nuclear accident to date in the US was at Three Mile Island, near Harrisburg, PA. On his* Paxton Report, *Nan Hoffman* A Thousand Cranes. *In* SO! *27:4.* OE02

Big Yellow Taxi

They paved paradise & put up a parking lot
With a pink hotel, a boutique & a swinging hot spot
Don't it always seem to go
That you don't know what you've got til it's gone
They paved paradise & put up a parking lot

(in G) C - G - / C D G - / - - C FG / C D G -

They took all the trees & put em in a tree museum
And they charged all the people a dollar & a half just to see 'em

Hey farmer, farmer, put away that DDT now
Give me spots on my apples but leave me the birds & the bees (please!)

Late last night I heard the screen door slam
And a big yellow taxi took away my old man

— Joni Mitchell

* — On her* Ladies of the Canyon *&* Miles of Aisles *& in her* SB V1. *Also on* Dylan. OE03

Community Power

They're taking away all our power
By bringing in nuclear plants
They talk of technology's flower
We'd rather give safety a chance
Power, power, community power is ours for free
Power, power, o bring back my power to me

A D A - / A B7 E - / A D A - / B7 E A -
A - D B7 / E - A - / A - B7 - / E - A -

There're fish washing up in the rivers
Pipes crack & the cancer rates rise
They can't find a dump for the garbage
It's trouble catastrophe-size

The companies can't get insurance
The dangers are so plain to see
How long can they lie to the public
About "public utility"?

But now folks are coming together
Control of our lives we demand
We think we might handle it better
Than experts in Washington-land

Some make this task their "occupation"
They're camping out, going to jail
While others work hard in the courtrooms
Combined effort never will fail

They're taking away all our power
By bringing in nuclear plants
Like doomsday machines they will tower
We'll stop 'em however we can (& meanwhile)

I've heard of some farms using windmills
And houses kept warm with chopped wood
And factories running on water-wheels
And the sun heating bathtubs real good!

— w: Joanna Cazden m: trad. ("My Bonnie")

* Written for Seabrook, NH, demonstrations.* OE04

Down on the Farm

1. Down on the farm we get up in the morning
Up in the morning early
We raise our voices to <u>the sun</u>
And tell the sun good morning, & howdy, & shanti!

D - - - / - - G A / C G D - / - C CD D, CD D, C G D -

2. **...We raise our voices to <u>the trees</u>**
3. the hills 4. each other, etc.

— Molly Scott

* — Shanti is a Hindi word meaning "peace". On her* Honor the Earth. *In* Children's S for a Friendly Planet. OE05

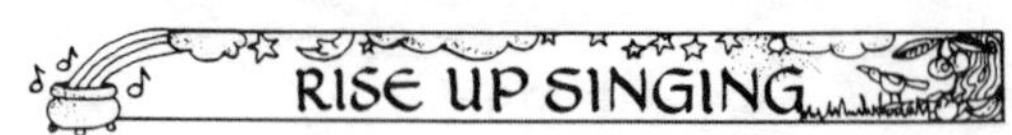

The Earth Is My Mother

The earth is my mother* she's good to me* (* = echo)
She gives me everything that I ever need*
Food on the table * the clothes I wear*
The sun & the water & the cool, fresh air*

C (C) Dm (Dm) / FC GC (FC GC) :||

The earth is my mother & my best friend, too
The great provider for me & you **(repeat)**

CEm FC / FC GC :||

Her ways are gentle, her life is strong
Living in tune like a beautiful song
There's only one thing she asks of me
I treat her as kindly as she treats me

— Carol Johnson

© Carol Johnson, Noeldner Music (BMI), All Rights Reserved. PO Box 6351, Grand Rapids MI 49506. Used by permission. — On her Might As Well Make It Love. *In* Children's S for a Friendly Planet. OE06

Eleckatricity and All

I love my longshoreman, I do, **mama**
I love that longshoreman, I do, **ha ha!**
We're bound to get marri'd but don't you tell pa
And we'll **have eleckatricity & all**
We'll **have eleckatricity & all**

(in 3/4) D - - - / A - - - / D - G - / D A D - / /

He held my hand, he did, **mama**
He held my hand, he did, **ha ha!**
He whispered & told me just how it would be
To **have eleckatricity & all (2x)**

We walked 'long the seashore, we did, mama / We ... **ha ha!**
He says we'll come walk here just about every day / When we ...

He combed my hair, he did ...
He says it will curl just like the waves on the sea / When ...

He hugged me real tight, he did ...
He told me he'd hug me both morning & night / When ...

I kissed his lips, I did ...
I told him I'd kiss him 'bout 6 dozen ways / When ...

I'm goin' to tell daddy, I am, **mama**
I'm goin' to tell daddy, right now, **ha ha!**
He's gonna rave & turn flipflops but I don't care
'Cause I'll **have eleckatricity & all!** / Gonna **have ...**

— Woody Guthrie

TRO © 1963 Ludlow Music, Inc. NY, NY. International copyright secured. Made in USA. All rights reserved incl public performance for profit. Used by permission. — Remember all the idealistic pipedreams about how all the world's problems would be solved by nuclear power a few years after the country's infatuation with electricity eased a bit? On & in his Roll On Columbia. SO! *12:2 & Reprints #8.* OE07

Garbage

Mr. Thompson calls the waiter, orders steak & baked potater
But he leaves the bone & gristle & he never eats the skins
Then the bus boy comes & takes it, with a cough contaminates it
As he puts it in a can with coffee grounds & sardine tins
Then the truck comes by on Friday & carts it all away
And a thousand trucks just like it are converging on the bay

Em - / - B7 / - - / - Em / B7 Em / Am D

Oh, garbage! (garbage 3x) Garbage! (garbage 3x)
We're filling up the sea **with garbage (garbage 3x)**
Garbage! (garbage 3x) Garbage! (garbage 3x)
What will we do when there's no place left to put all the **garbage?**

Em - / - B7 / - - / Em B7 Em -

Mr. Thompson starts his Cadillac & winds it up the freeway track
Leaving friends & neighbors in a hydrocarbon haze
He's joined by lots of smaller cars, all sending gases to the stars
Up there to form a seething cloud that hangs for 30 days
While the sun licks down into it with an ultraviolet tongue
And turns it into smog & then it settles in our lungs

(2nd cho) ...We're filling up the air **with garbage! ...**
What will we do when there's nothing left to breathe but ...?

Getting home & taking off his shoes, he settles down with the evening news
While the kids do homework with the TV in one ear
While Superman for the thousandth time sells talking dolls & conquers crime
Dutifully they learn the date of birth of Paul Revere
In the paper there's a piece about the mayor's middle name
And he gets it read in time to watch the All-Star bingo game

(3rd cho) ...We're filling up our minds **with garbage ...**
What will we do when there's nothing left to read & there's nothing left to need
There's nothing left to watch & there's nothing left to touch
There's nothing left to walk upon & nothing left to talk upon
And nothing left to see & nothing left to be but Garbage!

Em - / - B7 / - - / Em B7 - ||: B7 - :|| *B7 - Em

In Mr. Thompson's factory, they're making plastic Christmas trees
Complete with silver tinsel & a geodesic stand
The plastic's mixed in giant vats from some conglomeration that's been
Piped from deep within the earth or strip-mined from the land
And if you ask them questions, they say "Why don't you see?
It's absolutely needed for the ec-o-no-mee!"

Garbage! **(2x)** */ Their stocks & their bonds – all garbage!*
Garbage! **(2x)** */ What will they do when their system goes to smash, there's no value to their cash*
There's no money to be made, but there's a world to be repaid
Their kids will read in history books 'bout financiers & other crooks
And feudalism & slavery & nukes & all their knavery
To history's dustbin they're consigned, along with many other kinds of GARBAGE! **(* ad lib)**

— Bill Steele (new v. & last cho Pete Seeger & Mike Agranoff)

© 1969 William Steele. Copyright assigned 1992 to the Rainbow Collection Ltd., PO Box 300, Solebury PA 18963. All rights reserved. Used by permission. — On his Garbage *(Bay 202),* Peter Alsop, *& Guy Carawan* My Rhinoceros *& his* S of Struggle & Celeb. *On Pete Seeger* Banks of Marble, God Bless the Grass & Circles & Seasons, *Rozenshontz* Share It. *In* SO! *20:1,* Where Have All The Flowers Gone, *&* Survival SB. OE08

God Bless the Grass

God bless the grass that grows thru the crack
They roll the concrete over it to try & keep it back
The concrete gets tired of what it has to do
It breaks & it buckles & the grass grows thru
And God bless the grass

Am - AmE Am / E - AmE Am

C Am C Am / F Am CD E / Am E Am -

God bless the truth that fights toward the sun
They roll the lies over it & think that it is done
It moves thru the ground & reaches for the air
And after a while it is growing everywhere / **And ...**

God bless the grass that grows thru cement
It's green & it's tender & it's easily bent
But after a while it lifts up its head
For the grass is living & the stone is dead / **And ...**

God bless the grass that's gentle & low
Its roots they are deep & its will is to grow
And God bless the truth, the friend of the poor
And the wild grass growing at the poor man's door / **And ...**

— Malvina Reynolds

Honor the Earth

Look at her face, walk in her fields
Savor her mountains, her forests, her valleys
Tasting her winds, washed by her tides
Growing like flow'rs in her soil, in her water
Hear when she weeps! Hear with the heart
Tuned by our senses aware of time passing
Surely our flesh bleeds as she bleeds
Surely our bones are her dust, are her mountains
Honor the earth & each other (2x)

Am - - Dm / Dm6 - - E :|| Am Dm6 Am Dm / E7 - - -
/ " / " // Am Dm Am Dm6 / Am Dm Am - **(in 3/4)**

Locked in our cells of concrete & steel
Choked by the papers, the clutter, the chatter
Blindered by mind, harnessed by fears
Deaf to the cries & the calls of the mother
Hear her at last! Know what we are
Flesh that will die, but that death is no master
Cherish the earth, silence that sings
Touching the earth we give birth to the mother

— Molly Scott

Let It Be (Reynolds)

When you walk in the forest, let it be
There's a flower in the wood, let it be
There's a flower in the wood & it's innocent & good
By the stone where it stands let it be

F A Dm A / F A Dm - / F - A - / Bb - A -

Let it be, let it be
It's so lovely where it is, let it be
Tho' you want it for your own, if you take it from its place
It will not be what it was when you loved it where it stood in the wood

/ " / " / " / Bb - A - Dm -

Let it be, let it be
It's so lovely where it is, let it be
It's a thoughtful child, innocent & wild
By the stone, by the reed, let it bloom, let it seed, let it be!

— Malvina Reynolds

Little Blue Top

Round & round goes the little blue top
Whirling & turning with never a stop
Dappled with white, dappled with brown
The little blue top keeps a-turning around

D - G D / - - E A / D - G D / A - G D

O there's wild raging oceans & proud mountain chains
Green, peaceful valleys & wide grassy plains
Families of life that each setting contains
Dolphins & spiders & cattle & cranes

And there's red folk & white folk & yellow folk too
Black folk & brown folk to name just a few
Folks green with envy & others who're blue
And partners for all these & babies just new

O there's teachers & lawyers & medicine men
Places to go to & people who've been
Others who stay home & tend to the shop
And they whirl & turn on the little blue top

But there're some who are greedy & some who don't care
And they're fouling our rivers & pois'ning our air
If all of the rest of us don't make them stop
They might end the life on the little blue top

— Tony Hughes

My Rainbow Race

One blue sky above us, one ocean lapping all our shores
One earth so green & round, who could ask for more?
And because I love you, I'll give it one more try
To show my rainbow race it's too soon to die

G C D G / Em Am D G :||

Some people live like an ostrich
Bury their heads in the sand
Some hope that plastic dreams
Can unclench all those greedy hands

Some people want to take the easy way
Poisons, bombs, they think we need 'em
Don't you know you can't kill all the unbelievers?
There's no short cut to freedom

Go tell, go tell all the children
Go tell all the mothers & fathers too
Now's our last chance to learn to share
What's been given to me & you

— Pete Seeger

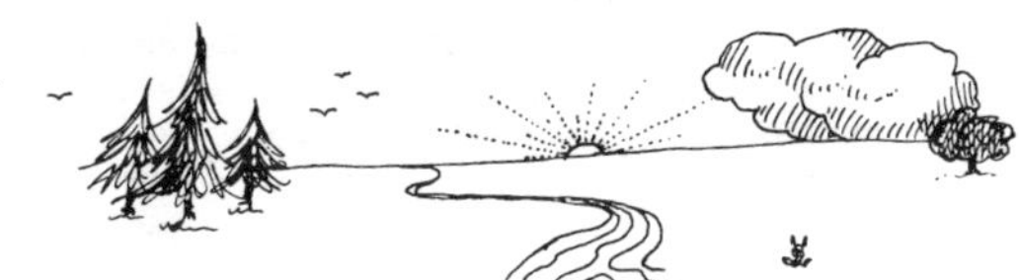

Now Is the Cool of the Day

1. **My Lord he said unto me**
Do you like my garden so fair
You may live in this garden if you keep the grasses green
And I'll return in the cool of the day

Am E A - / Em - A - / - - Em A / E7 - A -

Now is the cool of the day (2x)
O this earth is a garden, the garden of my Lord
And he walks in his garden in the cool of the day

Am E Am - / G - Am - / - - G Am / - - - - C - Am -

2. **My Lord ... / Do you like my** garden so pure?
You may ... if you keep the waters clean / **& I'll return ...**
3. pastures of green / feed all of my sheep
4. garden so free / keep the people free

— Jean Ritchie

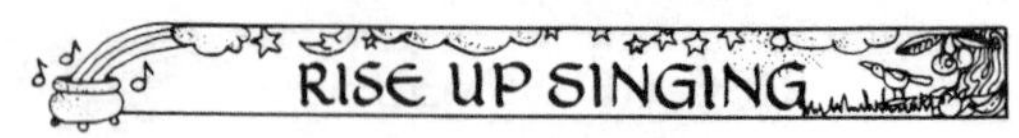

The People Are Scratching

Come fill up your glasses & set yourselves down
I'll tell you a story of somebody's town
It isn't too near & it's not far away
It's not a place where I'd want to stay
Now the people are scratching all over the street
Because the rabbits had nothing to eat

Am E / - Am / C G / C E // Am - Dm / E EAm

The winter came in with a cold icy blast
It killed off the flowers & killed off the grass
The rabbits were starving because of the freeze
They started eating the bark off the trees

The farmers said "This sort of thing just won't do
Our trees will be dead when the rabbits get thru
We'll have to poison the rabbits, it's clear
Or we'll have no crops to harvest next year"

So they bought the poison & spread it around
And soon dead rabbits began to be found
Dogs ate the rabbits & the farmers just said
"We'll poison those rabbits til the last dog is dead"

Up in the sky there were meat-eating fowls
The dead rabbits poisoned the hawks & the owls
Thousands of field mice the hawks used to chase
Were multiplying all over the place

The fields & the meadows were barren & brown
The mice got hungry & moved into town
The city folks took the farmers' advice
And all of them started to poison the mice

There were dead mice in all the apartments & flats
The cats ate the mice & the mice killed the cats
The smell was awful & I'm glad to say
I wasn't the man hired to haul them away

All thru the country & all thru the town
There wasn't a dog or a cat to be found
The fleas asked each other "Where can we stay?"
They've been on the people from then til this day

All you small creatures that live in this land
Stay clear of the man with the poisonous hand!
A few bales of hay might keep you alive
But he'll pay more to kill you than to let you survive

— w: Ernie Marrs, Harold Martin — m: Pete Seeger

— On Pete Seeger God Bless the Grass *& in* Survival SB. OE15

Pollution

If you visit American city
You will find it very pretty
Just two things of which you must beware
Don't drink the water & don't breathe the air!
Pollution **(2x)** – they got smog & sewage & mud
Turn on your tap & get hot & cold running crud

C G / - C / - F / C GC / Am G F E / F C G C

See the halibuts & the sturgeons
Being wiped out by detergeons
Fish gotta swim & birds gotta fly
But they don't last long if they try
Pollution **(2x)** – you can use the latest toothpaste
And then rinse your mouth with industrial waste

Just go out for a breath of air
And you'll be ready for Medicare
The city streets are really quite a thrill
If the hoods don't get you, the monoxide will
Pollution **(2x)** – wear a gas mask & a veil
Then you can breathe, long as you don't inhale

Lots of things there that you can drink
But stay away from the kitchen sink
Throw out your breakfast garbage & I've got a hunch
That the folks downstream will drink it for lunch
So go to the city, see the crazy people there
Like lambs to the slaughter, they're drinking the water
And breathing (cough) the air

C G / - C / C7 F / C GC / Am G F E
FEm CAm **(3x)** / Dm G C -

— Tom Lehrer

 On his That Was the Year That Was *& in his* Too Many S by. *In* Survival SB *&* SO! *35:4.* OE16

Power

Just give me the warm power of the sun
Give me the steady flow of a waterfall
Give me the spirit of living things as they return to clay
Just give me the restless power of the wind
Give me the comforting glow of a wood fire
But won't you take all your atomic poison power away

G Bm / Em D / AmBm CD G (D) :||

(bridge: same chords) Everybody needs some power I'm told
To shield them from the darkness & the cold
Some may seek a way to take control when it's bought & sold
I know that lives are at stake
Yours & mine & our descendants in time
There's so much to gain & so much to lose, everyone of us has to choose

(Last Line:) AmBm C D -

— John & Johanna Hall

 — On their No Nukes *(Muse) & Holly Near* Speed of Light. *In* SO! *29:4.* OE17

Roll to the River

And it's roll to the rivers that once shaped these sands
And it's roll to the river upon me
And it's fly to the waves that still pound these shores
And it's less than a mile to sea

(in C) C F C F / C - F G / C F C F / C G F G

I climbed the high hills to search for the sea
Took to the treetops in flight
Saw water in valleys where blueberries once grew
Watched red-tailed hawks soar out of sight

F - C F / G - F - / - G C F / C - F -

I watched as the houses spread over the plains
And I prayed for the sea to crash in
And the reasons they gave were so righteous & so grave
Don't they know that in the end no one can win?

I roamed the Great Plains where the juniper grows
And I climbed the morainal north shore
And I ran out to Wasque to catch the four tides
And rose high on the bluffs to see more & more & more

They call the land theirs, I call the land ours
For those who can care to walk free
How many houses can rise, how many roads can scrape thru
Before we drive into the sea?

These times come by hard, there's no need to explain
One look in your eyes and I know
We've seen the green hills and we've watched the plains bare
And we've known the sands covered with snow

— Cindy Kallet

 On her Working on Wings. SO! *35:4.* OE18

Sailing Up, Sailing Down

1. Sailing up (sailing up), sailing down (sailing down)
Up (down), down (up!) **– up & down the river**
Sailing on – stopping all along the way
The river may be dirty now but it's getting cleaner every day

C - / - - / F - C - / G F C (G)

2. People come (people come), people go (people go)
Come (go), go (come) **– up & down the river, sailing on ...**
3. Garbage here, garbage there / Here (there), there (here) ...
4. Catching fish, catching hell / Hell (fish), fish (hell!) ...
Make up your own verses! Here are some Pete Seeger uses:
5. Singing here, singing there 6. Some are young, some are old

— w: Lorre Wyatt
— m: Jimmy Reed ("Baby, What Ya Want Me to Do?")

Lyrics © 1973 Roots & Branches Music, PO Box 369, Greenfield MA 01302. Used by permission. — On Pete Seeger & Arlo Guthrie Precious Friend, *the 1st Clearwater album.* OE19

Solar Carol

See the sun how bright it shines on the nations of the earth
All who share this thing called life celebrate each day's rebirth
So-o-olar power, inexpensive energy (2x)

D - A D (2x) / // D G - A D G A - DA DG D A / 3rd above / DA DG D A D -

Brother river, so you hear how the valley calls you down
Send your rushing waters near, let the joyful hills resound
Sister wind we've heard on high sweetly singing o'er the plain
And the windmills in reply echoing their glad refrain
How we love complexity when the answer's rather plain
Join the sun in jubilee, sing with us this joyous strain

— w: Adam Auster, Court Dorsey, Charlie King, Marcia Taylor
— m: "Angels We Have Heard on High"

© 1980 Authors. Used by permission. On Bright Morning Star Arisin'. OE20

There'll Come a Time

There'll come a time the smog will be so thick
We'll all have to walk with a long white walking stick
But we won't walk anyhow, we'll go by air
And the helicopters will be so thick we won't get anywhere
There'll come a time, believe me son
And when that day is here, I will be gone

(in A) D - A - / E - A - :|| (3x)

Such adulteration will have hit the food
You'll throw way the contents & eat the carton if you want anything good
And women will live on synthetic meals
And they'll all be as slender as synthetic eels
There'll come a time the kids will be so smart
They'll be able to recite their own psychoanalysis by heart
And they'll all be scientists by the time they're 10
And thank the Lord I won't have any children then
The cities will be so overpopulated
We'll all be buried from the apt. house where we were created
And if you take a trip to the country somewhere
You'll have to be inoculated against fresh air
There'll come a time we'll lose our walking feet
And food will all be predigested so we won't have to eat
And children will be made in test-tubes, so we won't have to wed
And thank God by that time I will be dead

(last cho) There'll come a time, won't you be proud?
And by that time I'll be playing an unamplified harp
On an 18th century cloud

D - A - / E - - / - A -

— Malvina Reynolds

© 1959 Schroder Music Co. (ASCAP) Used by permission. On her Another Country & Malv Reynolds. *In her* SB, *her* Little Boxes, & SO! *36:3.* OE21

This Old Earth

Fragments of another sunset, ashes of another dawn
Drowned in time's immortal ocean, all too soon we may be gone

C Dm F C / Em Am F G

This old earth has seen a lot of living
This old earth: the stories she could tell
But this old earth is finished with the giving
This old earth we used so well

Am Em / F C / Dm Am / G F (in C)

Now the playground stands deserted in the yellow afternoon
And the cotton-candy children have all gone home too soon
And the tree of knowledge trembles
For the fruit was ours before
Will we be like Eden's lovers
Driven from the garden's door?

So, what can it take from nature & what must it take from man
For the future generations to save the sky, the sea, the land?
This old earth has seen a lot of living ...

So, ask your child what really matters & ask your friend what he will do
And ask the leaders you've elected but the answer lies with you
This old earth has seen a lot of living
This old earth we've used from end to end
Now it's time for mankind *[our kind]* to start giving
This old earth could use a friend

— Bob Zentz

© Folk-Legacy Records, Inc. Used by permission. On his Mirrors & Changes *& Magpie* Living Planet *(w/altered words entitled "This Old Bay").* OE22

Waydy Bug & Wittle Woim

I'm a wittle bitty woim, cwalling in da gwound
Twying to be good, making not a sound
Hiding from da boids, hiding from da toads
Doing what I can to see da garden gwoes

C - - - / Dm G Dm G / 1st / Dm G Dm G C

Pwease be nice to us woims
Cuz we nebba did nobody any hoim
Wurn to wuv all us woims
Cuz we woosen up da zoil & eat da geoims

F - C - / - - D G / F - C - / G - C -

I'm a pretty lady bug, crawlin' on a limb
Eating other bugs that chew on flower stems
Chasin' after grubs & mites & flies & pests
Until I eat a few, you won't see me rest
Please be good to lady bugs
Don't play rough or squeeze us with your finger hugs
We're your friends, please be kind
And we'll live to eat the varmints on the vine

Please don't take us home & put us in a jar
We'd be lonesome all alone, that's not what we are for
We like to work all day, so please show some respect
If you take us in to play, we'll become a nervous wreck
Be our friends, we love you
Come & see us for a minute or two
We won't last on your shelf
Mother nature put us here so we could help
(tag:) From waydy bug 'n wittle woim "goodbye!"

— Stephen Sedberry

© 1978, 1984 Stephen Sedbery. Used by permission. On his Kidsongs V1 *& in his* Songletter #21 *(c/o PO Box 11130, Birmingham, AL 35202.)* OE23

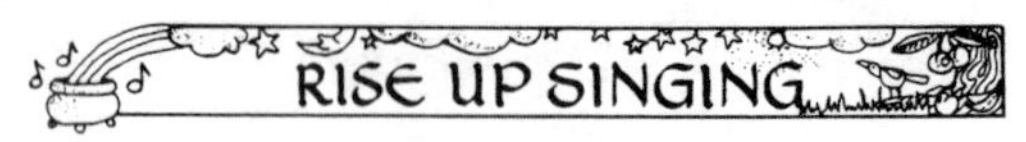

We Are All One Planet

We are all one planet, all one people of Earth
All one planet sharing our living, our dying, our birth
And we won't stand by watching her die
Hearing her cry & deny, we live as she lives, we die as she dies

(in 3/4) C - - Dm / - - - GC/F Dm Em Am/Dm - - G

So many ways to divide us, so many ways to build bound'ries and walls
Systems we set up to hide us, neighborhoods, nations ignoring the call
Of the beings who live outside of the bound'ries
Inside of the skins that are different from ours
Creatures whose eyes reflect the same skies & watch the same stars

/ " / " / F Dm / Em A7 / Dm G

So many ways to hurt & not heal
To speak & not listen, to act & not feel
And too little time to be simple & see
The circle includes every bird, every tree, every you, every me

DmAm **(2x)** // Dm - / - - G

Think of the things we love
Remember the ones we love
Open our minds, our hearts & our hands
And trust when we don't understand

C Am / AmE A / Dm - / - G

— Molly Scott

 Written for the 1st Women's Pentagon Action. "I was inspired by a vision of merging spiritual understanding with political means to create change from the inside out. I still am" — MS. On her We Are All ... *(Sumitra). Chorus is on* Peace Gathering S *(NSL).* OE24

What Have They Done to the Rain

Just a little rain falling all around
The grass lifts its head to the heavenly sound
Just a little rain, just a little rain
What have they done to the rain?

G - C G / Bm D G - / Em - Bm - / C - D -

Just a little boy standing in the rain
The gentle rain that falls for years
And the grass is gone, the boy disappears
And rain keeps falling like helpless tears / And what ...?

/ " / Bm AmB7 Em - / C - Bm - / Am D G E7 /

Just a little breeze out of the sky / Am Am7 D -
The leaves pat their hands as the breeze blows by
Just a little breeze with some smoke in its eye / And what ...?

— Malvina Reynolds

 — In her SB *and* Little Boxes *& on her* Held Over *&* Sings the Truth. *In* SO! *13:1 &* Reprints #6, Here's to the Women, S That Changed the World, *&* Survival SB. *On* Joan Baez *& her* In Conc *& in her* SB. *Also rec by Cris Williamson (Avanti), The Searchers, Marianne Faithful, & Pete King.* OE25

A good collection of environmental songs which has sadly gone out of print, it seems, is Jim Morse & Nancy Matthews, Survival SB, Sierra Club, 1971. Maybe you can still get copies from some Sierra Club branches?

There are a number of songs about the environment & nature in FARM & PRAIRIE, HOPE, MOUNTAIN VOICES (struggles against strip mining) and OUTDOORS (songs about hiking, hymns about nature, etc.) There is a special "animal songs" index at the end of PLAY.

Other songs include: "All I Really Need" (HOME), "Baby Beluga" (PLAY), "One Bottle of Pop" (ROUNDS), "He's Got the Whole World" (SPIRS), & "A Place in the Choir" (UNITY).

All I Ask of You

All I ask of you is forever to remember me as loving you
Deep the joy of being together in one heart
And for me that's just where it is

D (D, C#, B, A) G A D - // D E A D / Em - A -

As we make our way thru all the joys & pains
Can we find our younger, truer selves?

Someone will be calling you to be there for a while
Can you hear their cry from deep within?

Laughter, joy & presence, the only gifts you are
Have you time? I'd like to be with you

Persons come into the fiber of our lives
And then their shadow fades & disappears

— Gregory Norbert, O.S.B.

 Fr the Weston Priory album Listen. OF02

Babylon Is Fallen

Hail the day so long expected, hail the year of full release
Zion's walls are now erected & her watchmen publish peace
Thru our Shiloh's wide dominion, hear the trumpet loudly roar
Babylon is fallen (3x) Babylon is fallen to rise no more

Dm - C FC Dm - C Dm / /
Dm F Bb Dm F Dm C Dm // 1st /

All her merchants stand with wonder, what is this that comes to pass?
Murmr'ing like the distant thunder, crying "O alas, alas"
Swell the sound ye kings & nobles, priest & people, rich & poor
Babylon is fallen (3x) Babylon is fallen to rise no more

Blow the trumpet in Mt. Zion, Christ shall come the second time
Ruling with a rod of iron, all who now as foes combine
Babel's garments we've rejected & our fellowship is o'er ...

— trad. (US, early 19th c.)

From Christian Harmony *(one of the main texts used in traditional "shape-note" singing) & on Roberts and Barrand* Spencer The Rover *(ST-1).* OF03

Be Thou My Vision

Be thou my vision, O Lord of my heart
Naught be all else to me save that thou art
Thou my best thought, by day or by night
Waking or sleeping, thy presence my light

(in 3/4) D GAA BmBmA D / A EmDD GDD A
G GDD D GGA / D GDD G D

Be thou my wisdom & thou my true word
I ever with thee & thou with me, Lord
Thou my great Father, I thy true son
High king of heaven, my victory won

Riches I need not, nor man's empty praise
Thou mine inheritance, now & always
Thou & thou only, first in my heart
High king of heaven, my treasure thou art

High king of heaven, my victory won
May I reach heaven's joys, O bright heaven's Sun
Heart of my own heart, whatever befall
Still be my vision, O ruler of all

— w: Ancient Irish, trans Mary E Byrne (1880-1931), versified Eleanor Hull (1860-1935) — m: "Slane" (trad. Irish)
In many hymnals, some w/different tune by Leroy Campbell, 1929. ⊙F04

Brightest and Best

Hail the blest morn! See the Great Mediator
Down from the regions of glory descend!
Shepherds, go worship the babe in the manger
Lo, for a guard the bright angels attend

D - C D / - - A D :||

Brightest & best of the sons of the morning
Dawn on our darkness & lend us thine aid
Star of the East the horizon adorning
Guide where our infant Redeemer is laid

D - G D / - - G A / D - C D / - - A D

Cold on his cradle the dewdrops are shining
Low lies his head with the beasts of the stall
Angels adore him in slumber reclining
Maker & monarch & saviour of all

Say shall we yield him in costly devotion
Odors of Edom & offerings divine
Gems from the mountain & pearls from the ocean
Myrrh from the forest or gold from the mine?

Vainly we offer each ample oblation
Vainly with gifts would His favor secure
Richer by far is the heart's adoration
Dearer to God are the prayers of the poor

— w: Reginald Heber, 1811
aka: "Star of the East." The music in most hymnals is by James P. Harding, 1892, but another tune (for which chords are given above) is popular in Appalachia & can be found in Southern Harmony, FS NAm Sings *& on J Couza* Brightest & Best, *J McCutcheon* Winter Solstice *(Rounder) & J Ritchie* Sweet Rivers *(June Appal 37)* , Ritchie Fam & *Roberts & Barrand* Nowell We Sing Clear Vol 3. *In Christmas Revels SB & Worship in Song.* ⊙F05

Bring a Torch, Jeanette Isabella

Bring a torch, Jeanette Isabella
Bring a torch & quickly run
Christ is born, good folk of the village
Christ is born & Mary's calling
Ah! ah! beautiful is the mother
Ah! ah! beautiful is her son

D - Em A / D - A D / - - - A /
G D - Em A // Bm A D A D / /

Quiet all nor waken Jesus
Quiet all & whisper low
Silence all & gather around him
Talk & noise might waken Jesus
Hush! hush! quietly now he slumbers / ... he sleeps

Softly creep in the little rude stable
Softly just for one moment come
Catch one glimpse of the tiny child Jesus
Tender his brow, his cheeks are rosy
Hush! hush! quietly now he slumbers / ... he sleeps

Un flambeau, Jeanette Isabelle
Un flambeau, courons au berceau
C'est Jésu, bonnes gens du hameau
Le Christ est né, Marie appelle
Ah **(3x)** que la mére est belle / ... que l'enfant est beau

C'est un tort quand l'enfant sommeille
C'est un tort de crier si fort
Taissez vous l'un et l'autre d'abord
Au moindre bruit Jésu s'éveille
Chut **(3x)** qu'il dort à merveille / ... voyez comme il dort

Doucement dans l'étable close
Doucement venez un moment
Approchez, que Jesu est charmant
Comme il est blanc, comme il est rose
Do **(3x)** que l'enfant répose / ... qu'il rit en dormant

— French carol attrib to Nicola Saboly (1614-1675)
The custom of bringing torches to the manger goes back to the middle ages, and of using torches for the midwinter festival even farther back (for example the Jewish festival of lights.) In S of the Spirit, Christmas Carols fr Many Countries, & Pilgrim Hymnal. ⊙F06

Bringing in the Sheaves 

Sowing in the morning, sowing seeds of kindness
Sowing in the noontide & the dewy eves
Waiting for the harvest & the time of reaping
We shall come rejoicing, bringing in the sheaves
Bringing in the sheaves (2x) / We shall... (repeat)

A - D - / A - B7 E / A - D - / A - E A //
A - D A / A - B7 E / A - D A / A - E A

Sowing in the sunshine, sowing in the shadows
Fearing neither clouds nor winter's chilling breeze
By & by the harvest & the labor ended / **We shall ...**

Going forth with weeping, sowing for the Master
Tho the loss sustained our spirit often grieves
When our weeping's over, He will bid us welcome / **We ...**

— w: Knowles Shaw — m: George A. Minor
Based on Psalm 126. In Am Heritage SB, 1001 Jumbo S *& hymnals.* ⊙F07

Brother James' Air

The Lord's my shepherd, I'll not want, he makes me down to lie
In pastures green he leadeth me, the quiet waters by
He leadeth me, he leadeth me, the quiet waters by

(C) C-- FEmDm C-G C-/ /(G) CAmG **(2x)** CF- C-

My soul he doth restore again & me to walk doth make
Within the paths of blessedness, e'en for his own name's sake **(2x)**

Yea, tho' I pass thru shadowed vale yet will I fear no ill
For thou art with me & thy rod & staff me comfort still
Thy rod & staff me comfort still, me comfort still

My table thou has furnishèd in presence of my foes
My head with oil thou dost anoint & my cup overflows **(2x)**

Goodness & mercy all my days will surely follow me
And in my father's heart alway my dwelling place shall be
And in my heart forever more thy dwelling place shall be

— w: 23rd Psalm (Edinburgh Psalter, 1650) (in 3/4)
— m: James Leith Macbeth Bain (1840-1925)
To degenderize change each "he" to "thou" (... thou makest me down to lie ... thou leadest me, etc.). In Quaker SB *& many hymnals.* ⊙F08

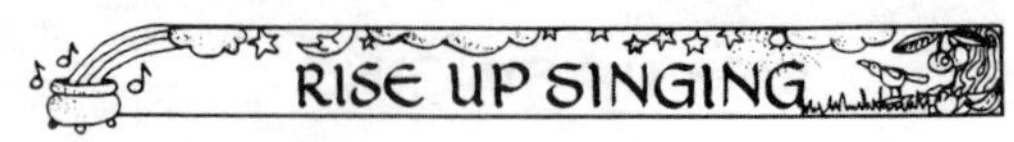

Brother Sun, Sister Moon

Brother Sun & Sister Moon
I seldom see you, seldom hear your tune
Pre-occupied with selfish misery

C - FG C / Am Em FG C / /

Brother Wind & Sister Air
Open my eyes to visions pure & fair
That I may see the glory around me

(bridge) I am God's creature, of God I am a part
I feel a love awakening my heart

F Em FG C / F Em B♭ G

Brother Sun & Sister Moon
I now do see you, I can hear your tune
So much in love with all that I survey

— Donovan Leitch

 — Fr the movie Brother Sun, Sister Moon *(about St. Francis).* OF09

Day By Day

Day by day, day by day
O dear Lord, three things I pray:
To see thee more clearly, love thee more dearly
Follow thee more nearly, day by day

Cmaj7 Dmaj7 **(2x)** / Fmaj7 Em Dmaj7 -
Bm E **(2x)** / Am D Gmaj7 -

— Stephen Schwartz

 — Fr his musical Godspell. *Words are adapted only slightly from a much older song by St. Richard of Chichester (1197-1253). On Percy Faith* Day By Day, *Judy Collins* Trust Your Heart, *5th Dimension* Living Together *& Andy Williams* Alone Again. *In Broadway SBs.* OF10

Dayenu

Ilu hotsi, hotsi onu
Hotsi onu mi Mitsrayim **(2x)** / Dayenu
Da-Dayenu (3x) / Dayenu (3x) (repeat)

C - / - - / CG CG / CG C ||: C G - C - G / - C :||

Ilu nosan, nosan lanu
Nosan lanu et Hashabat **(2x)** / Dayenu

Ilu nosan, nosan lanu
Nosan lanu et Hatora **(2x)** / Dayenu

Had He led us out of Egypt / Only led us out of Egypt
Had He led us out of Egypt / Dayenu

Had He given us the Sabbath / Only given us the Sabbath
Had He given us the Sabbath / Dayeynu

Had He given us the tora / Only given us the tora
Had He given us the tora / Dayeynu

— trad. (Hebrew Passover Song) Eng: Teddi Schwartz & Arthur Kevess

 — Dayenu: It would have been enough. In SO! 1:11 Teddi Schwartz' Tumbalalaika & 14 Other Jewish S, *V Pasternak's* Holidays in S *& his* Israel in S *(Tara),* Harv of Jewish S, *&* Gr Legal FakeB. OF11

Dear Lord and Father of Mankind

Dear Lord & Father of mankind *[Dear God, Creator of our kind]*
Forgive our foolish ways
Reclothe us in our rightful mind
In purer lives thy service find
In deeper rev'rence, praise

C - - DF / C Am G - / C - E7 F
F DmD G C / F - C -

In simple trust like theirs who heard
Beside the Syrian sea
The gracious calling of the Lord
Let us, like them, without a word
Rise up & follow thee
    O Sabbath rest by Galilee!
    O calm of hills above
    Where Jesus knelt to share with thee
    The silence of eternity
    Interpreted by love
Drop thy still dews of quietness
Til all our strivings cease
Take from our souls the strain & stress
And let our ordered lives confess
The beauty of thy peace
    Breathe thru the heats of our desire
    Thy coolness & thy balm
    Let sense be dumb, let flesh retire
    Speak thru the earthquake, wind & fire
    O still, small voice of calm

— w: John G. Whittier, 1872 — m: Frederick C. Maker, 1887 ("Rest")

In Joyful Singing *(WAS),* Quaker SB *(incl alt melody) & many hymnals.* OF12

Demos Gracias *(Let Us Give Thanks)*

Demos gracias al Señor, demos gracias
Demos gracias por su amor (repeat)

A - / E A :||

Por las mañanas las aves cantan
Las alabanzas del Cristo el Salvador
¿Y tu amigo, porque no cantas
Las alabanzas del Cristo el Salvador?

D A / E A :||

(2nd v. same but ending:) ... alabanzas a Dios el Creador

— trad. (Latin American folksong)

Trans.:Let us give thanks to the Lord for his love/In the morning the birds sing the praises of Christ, the Savior. And you, friend, why don't you sing praises to Christ / ... to God, the Creator? In Let Our Lives Sing / ¡Que Canten Nuestras Vidas! (WGYF SB). OF13

Eli, Eli *(Halicha L'Kesariya)*

Eli, Eli, shelo yigamer l'olam
Hachol v'hayam rishrush shel hamayim
B'rak hashamayim t'filat haadam **(repeat last 2 lines)**

(in Em) B7 Em AmB7 Em / - B7 Em Am
G Am EmC B7 / - Em B7 EmC / Am Em B7 Em

My God, my God, I pray that these things never end
The sand & the sea, the rush of the waters
The crash of the heavens, the prayer of my heart / The sand ...

Ilahi, Ilahi, ala yazul liladad
Aramlu walbahru hadiru'l miyahi
Wabarku sama'i salatu'l insan / Aramlu ...

— w: Hana Senesh (Hebrew) — m: David Zehavi

 — Hana, a paratrooper who saved many Jews in Europe during WWII wrote these words: "When I feel like my world is falling apart, I look up at the sky & somehow feel comforted in seeing that it is still there." She was killed by the Nazis. May her prayer never end. The 3rd v. is the Arabic translation. In Treasury of Jewish S, Harvest of Jewish S *& SO! 36:2.* OF14

Eliyahu

Eliyahu Hanavi, Eliyahu Hatishbi
Eliyahu Eliyahu Eliyahu ha-Giladi
Bimheira v'yameinu, yavo eilenu
Im Mashiach ben David, Im Mashiach ben David

Em B7Em - Em DG - / Em Am B7Em -
D - B7 B7Em - / /

— trad. (Hebrew folktune)
Eng: "Elijah the prophet, the Tishbite, the Gilendite, may he soon come to us with the Messiah, son of David." A song of redemption focusing on Elijah as harbinger of the Messiah, sung at Havdalah (ceremony separating the sabbath fr the rest of the wk) & during the seder. In V Pasternak Holidays in S *(Tara),* The S We Sing, More S We Sing, New Jewish SB, Holiday S for Limor, Harv of Jewish S. OF15

Fairest Lord Jesus

Fairest Lord Jesus, ruler of all nature
O thou of God & man the son
Thee will I cherish, thee will I honor
Thou, my soul's glory, joy & crown

DBm AD (2x) / DG D GD A
D B7Em Em AD / DG DA D -

Fair are the meadows, fairer still the woodlands
Robed in the blooming garb of spring
Jesus is fairer, Jesus is purer
Who makes the woeful heart to sing

Fair is the sunshine, fairer still the moonlight
And all the twinkling starry host
Jesus shines brighter, Jesus shines purer
Than all the angels heav'n can boast

— w: German, 17th c. ("Schonster Herr Jesu")
— m: Silesian, fr Schlesischen Volkslieder OF16

Friendly Beasts

Jesus, our brother, strong & good
Was humbly born in a stable rude
And the friendly beasts around him stood
Jesus, our brother, strong & good

(in 3/4) D - A D / - G A D / - G D Bm / D - A D

"I" said the donkey, shaggy & brown
"I carried his mother up hill & down
I carried her safely to Bethlehem town"
"I" said the donkey, shaggy & brown

"I" said the cow all white & red
"I gave him my manger for his bed
I gave him my hay to pillow his head"
"I" said the cow all white & red

"I" said the sheep with curly horn
"I gave him my wool for his blanket warm
He wore my coat on Christmas morn"
"I" said the sheep with curly horn

"I" said the camel, all yellow & black
"Over the desert upon my back
I brought him a gift in the Wise man's pack"
"I" said the camel, all yellow & black

"I" said the dove from the rafters high
"I cooed him to sleep that he should not cry
We cooed him to sleep, my mate & I"
"I" said the dove from the rafters high

Thus every beast by some good spell
In the stable dark was glad to tell
Of the gift he gave Immanuel
The gift he gave Immanuel

— w: anon. m: 12th century
aka: "Jesus Our Brother, Strong & Good." In Friends Hymnal. OF17

George Fox

There's a light that was shining when the world began
There's a light that is shining in the heart of a man
[in each woman & man]
There's a light that is shining in the Turk & the Jew
And a light that is shining, friend, in me & in you

C - C - / F G F C :||

(orig cho) Old leather britches, shaggy shaggy locks (2x)
In your old leather britches & your shaggy shaggy locks
You are pulling down the pillars of the world, George Fox!

(new cho) *Walk in the light wherever you may be* (2x)
In my old leather britches & my shaggy shaggy locks
I am walking in the glory of the Light, said Fox!

C Am F G / / C G CF C / /

With a book & a steeple & a bell & a key
They would bind it forever, but they can't, said he
O the book it will perish & the steeple will fall
But the light will be shining at the end of it all

"If we give you a pistol, will you fight for the Lord?"
"But you can't kill the devil with a gun or a sword"
"Will you swear on the Bible?" "I will not!" said he
"For the Truth is more holy than *[as holy as]* the book to me"

"There's an ocean of darkness & I drown in the night
Til I came thru the darkness to the ocean of light
You can lock me in prison but the Light will be free*
And I'll walk in the glory of the Light" said he
* *[The Light is forever & the Light it is free]*

— Sydney Carter
© 1964, 1974 Stainer & Bell Ltd. Used by permission of Galaxy Music Corp, NY, NY, sole U.S. agent. *— aka: "The George Fox Song." George Fox (1624-91) was the fiery charismatic founder of Quakerism. (He would probably upset most Friends Mtgs. today if he showed up in their midst!) On* Lovely in the Dances: S of Sydney Carter. *In his* Green Print for S, S of Sydney Carter in the Present Tense Bk 1, Worship in S & Quaker SB. *On* County Down *& Recollection* Present Tense: S of Sydney Carter. OF18

Healing River

O healing river send down your waters
Send down your waters upon this land
O healing river send down your waters
To wash the blood from off the sand

GC GD (2x) / G A DA D - /
GC GB7 Em A / GEm AmD GC GD

This land is thirsting, this land is parching
No seed is growing in the barren ground
This land is thirsting, this land is parching
O healing river, send your waters down

last line 2nd v: GEm AmD GC GB7

(bridge) Let the seed of freedom awake & flourish
Let the deep roots nourish, let the tall stalk rise
O seed of freedom awake & flourish
Proud leaves uncurling unto the skies

Em - B7 - / Em - EmA DA D / → 3rd & 4th of 1st verse

— Fred Hellerman & Fran Minkoff
© 1964 Appleseed Music Inc. All rights reserved. Used by permission. *— On Pete Seeger* I Can See A New Day. *In* SO! *15:4 &* Reprints *#10 &* A Time for Singing. OF19

FAITH

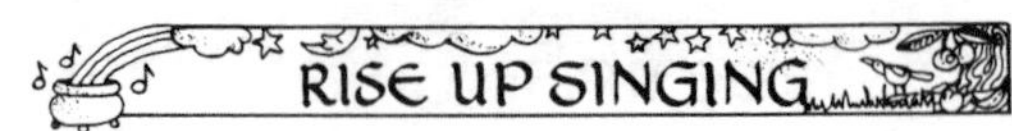

Holy Ground

This is holy ground, we're standing on holy ground
For the Lord is present & where He* *[God]* is is holy **(repeat)**

C - F - / C - G - / C - F - / C G F C

These are holy hands, He's given us holy hands
He works thru us & so these hands are holy

These are holy lips, He's given us holy lips
He speaks thru us & so these lips are holy

These are holy times, we're living in holy times
God loves thru us & so these times are holy

— Christopher Beatty (new v. Anne Patterson)

**Degenderize by substituting the word "God" for "He" thru out the song. © 1982 Birdwing Music (a division of Sparrow Corp.) & BMG Songs Inc../Cherry Lane Music Publishing Co, Inc. All rights admin. by BMG Songs, Inc. All rights reserved. International copyright secured. Used by permission. — In Michael Talbot's* S for Worship & Praise, Prayer & Worship *(Birdwing Music).* OF20

How Can I Keep from Singing

My life flows on in endless song above earth's lamentation
I hear the real tho' far-off hymn that hails a new creation
Thru all the tumult & the strife I hear that music ringing
It sounds an echo in my soul, **how can I keep from singing?**

(in 3/4) D G D A / D G DAA D
D - - - / D GDD (or just G) DAA D

What tho' the tempest loudly roars, I hear the truth, it liveth
What tho' the darkness round me close, songs in the night it giveth
No storm can shake my inmost calm while to that rock I'm clinging
Since Love is Lord of heaven & earth, **how can I keep ... ?**

When tyrants tremble sick with fear & hear their death knells [as they hear the bells of freedom] ringing
When friends rejoice both far & near, ***how ...***
In prison cell & dungeon vile our thoughts to them are winging
When friends by shame are undefiled, ***how ...***

I lift my eyes, the cloud grows thin, I see the blue above it
And day by day this pathway clears, since first I learned to love it
The peace of God restores my soul, a fountain ever springing
All things are mine since I am loved, **how ...**

— w: Anne Warner, 1864 (v3. Doris Plenn) — m: Rev. R. Lowry

This version © 1957 (renewed) Sanga Music Inc. All rights reserved. Used by permission. — This is not an old "Quaker" hymn , thou it certainly dates from at least 1864. It is popular in Iredell Co., North Carolina. Plenn wrote the new verse when friends were imprisoned during the McCarthy period. In SO! 7:1, Reprints #8, How Can We Keep ... , S of the Spirit, Quaker SB, & FSEncy V2. *In Pete Seeger's* Bells of Rhymney, *and on his* I Can See a New Day & Prec Friend *(w/A Guthrie). On J McCutcheon* How Can I ..., *Bok Muir & Trickett* Turning Toward the Morning & Simple Gifts for the Dulcimer. OF21

I Will Arise and Go to Jesus

Come now fount of every blessing
Tune my heart to sing thy praise
Streams of mercy never ceasing
Call for songs of loudest praise **(in G)**

C G - CG / G CG CD G / - - - D CG / C G - C

I will arise & go to Jesus
He will embrace me in his arms
In the arms of my dear Saviour
O there are 10,000 charms

Teach me some melodious song
As sung by flaming tongues above
Praise the mount I'm fixed upon it
Songs of thy redeeming love

Here I'll raise my songs in praises
Hither by thy help I'm come
And I hope by thy good pleasure
Safely to arrive at home

— w: Robert Robinson, England ca. 1740 — m: trad. hymn

This arr © 1987 Happy Valley Music Ltd. Used by permission. — aka: "Come Thou Fount, I Shall Arise ..." Based on Psalm 15. Chorus may be a later Amer addition. On Trapezoid 3 Forks of Cheat, *J McCutcheon* Step by Step & Sharon Mtn Harmony *(FolkLegacy).* OF22

I Will Bow and Be Simple

I will bow & be simple, I will bow & be free
I will bow & be humble, yea bow like the willow tree **(repeat)**
I will bow this is the token, I will wear the easy yoke
I will bow & be broken, yea I'll fall upon the rock **(repeat)**

C - F - / C - F C :‖: C G Am Em / F C F C :‖

— trad. (Shaker)

A "bowing song" from the North Family, New Labanon, KY, 1847. In Andrews The Gift to be Simple, *Sturm* The Shaker Gift of Song, *& on Molly Scott* Honor the Earth. OF23

I Wonder as I Wander

I wonder as I wander out under the sky
How Jesus our savior did come for to die
For poor orn'ry people like you & like I
I wonder as I wander out under the sky

Am Dm Am E / Am Dm Em Am /
Am Dm - A7 / Am Dm Am Dm

When Mary birthed Jesus 'twas in a cow's stall
With wise men & farmers & shepherds & all
But high from the heavens a star's light did fall
And the promise of ages it then did recall

If Jesus had wanted for any wee thing
A star in the sky or a bird on the wing
Or all of God's angels in heav'n for to sing
He surely could have it 'cause he was the King

— collected & arranged by John Jacob Niles

© 1934 by G. Schirmer Music Inc. Copyright renewed. All rights reserved. Used by permission. — On his Sings FS & Best of, *J Baez* Noel, *Anne Hills & Friends* On This Day Earth Shall Ring *& Burl Ives* FS Dramatic & Humorous. *In* S of the Spirit, FS NAm Sings & S of the Hill Folk. OF24

Lift Me Gentle Lord

Lift me gentle, Lord, the stormy winds are blowing
Lift ... the night is dark & wild
Lift ... I don't know where I'm going
... I want to be thy child

Am - - Dm / - - - Am / - - - Dm / - - Em Am

Lift ... my heart is tired of danger
... I've been too long alone
... too long I've been a stranger / ... & take me for thy own

Am Em Am Em / Am Em AmEm Am / " / " /

— Deborah Haines

© 1988 Deborah Haines. Used by permission. OF25

Light One Candle

Light one candle for the Maccabee children
With thanks that their light didn't die
Light ... for the pain they endured
When their right to exist was denied
... for the terrible sacrifice / Justice & freedom demand, but
... for wisdom to know / When the peacemaker's time is at hand

G - Em - / / C - - - / - - B7 -
Em - G - / C - A - / G Em G Em / C D G B7

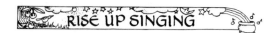

Don't let the light go out
It's lasted for so many years
Don't let the light go out
Let it shine thru our love & our tears

E - Am - / D - G B7 / E - Am - / D- G -

Light ... for the strength that we need
To never become our own foe
... for those who are suff'ring
The pain we learned so long ago
... for all we believe in / That anger won't tear us apart &
... to bring us together / With peace as the song in our heart

What is the mem'ry that's valued so highly
That we keep it alive in that flame?
What's the commitment to those who have died
When we cry out they've not died in vain?
Have we come this far always believing
That justice would somehow prevail?
This is the burden & this is the promise
And this is why we will not fail

— Peter Yarrow

© 1983 Silver Dawn Music (ASCAP). Used by permission. On Peter Paul & Mary No Easy Walk To Freedom. *In* Shofar *(Dec. '84), Kislev/Tevet 5745.* OF26

Lone Wild Bird

The lone wild bird in lofty flight
Is still with thee nor leaves thy sight
And I am thine, I rest in thee
Great spirit come & rest in me

C Dm Em Am /F Dm G C / - - - Am / F Dm G C

The ends of the earth are in thy hands
The sea's dark deep & no man's land / **And I am thine ...**

— w: Henry Richard McFadyen
— m: Cwnafon / Philip James 1927

Setting (chords) © 1968 Augsburg Publishing House. Used by permission. — In The Hymnbook (United Presbyt. Ch.) & in *12 FS* & *Spirituals.* OF27

Lonesome Valley

Jesus walked that lonesome valley
He had to walk it by himself
O nobody else could walk it for Him
He had to walk it by himself

D - G - / D - A - / D D7 G - / D G D -

You must go & stand your trial
You have to stand it by yourself
O nobody else can stand it for you
You have to stand it by yourself

We must walk that lonesome valley
We must walk it by ourselves
Nobody else can walk it for us
We have to walk it by ourselves

— Trad ("White Spiritual")

In Gladys Johnson White Spirituals fr the So Appalachs, Friends Hymnal & Singing America. *Baez* V Early, *Carter Fam* The Famous, *Mary Faith Rhoads & John Pearse* Together.

You gotta walk that lonesome valley
You gotta walk it by yourself
Nobody here can walk it for you
You gotta walk it by yourself

D - G D / A - D - / G - D - / - A D -

Some people say that John was a Baptist
Some folks say he was a Jew
But your holy scripture tells you
That he was a preacher too

Daniel was a Bible hero
Was a prophet brave & true
In a den of hungry lions
Proved what faith can do for you

Samson when he was out walking
Killed a lion with his hands
But it took a pretty woman
To show Samson was a lamb

There's a road that leads to glory
Thru a valley far away
Nobody else can walk it for you
They can only point the way

Mammy & daddy loves you dearly
Sister does & brother too
They may beg you to go with them
But they cannot go for you

I'm gonna walk that lonesome valley
I'm gonna walk it by myself
Don't want nobody to walk it for me
I'm gonna walk it by myself

Now tho' the road be rough & rocky
And the hills be steep & high
We can sing as we go marching
And we'll win that one big union by & by

— new words & music adaptation Woody Guthrie

Guthrie version TRO © 1963, 1977 Ludlow Music, Inc, NY, NY. International copyright secured. Made in the USA. All rights reserved incl. public performance for profit. Used by permission. On his Hard Trav & Lib. of Cong, *Pete Seeger & Arlo Guthrie* Together *& in* 50 Yrs of Country M. *Woody used this melody for his song "You Gotta Go Down & Join the Union" (See WORK p. 261).* OF28

Lord of the Dance

I danced in the morning when the world was begun
And I danced in the moon & the stars & the sun
And I came down from heaven & I danced on the earth
At Bethlehem I had my birth

D - - - / A - - - / D - - - / A - G D

Dance, dance wherever you may be
I am the Lord of the Dance said he
And I'll lead you all wherever you may be
And I'll lead you all in the dance, said he

D - - - / - - A - / D - - - / A - G D

I danced for the scribe & the pharisee
But they would not dance & they would not follow me
I danced for the fishermen, for James & John
They came with me & the dance went on

I danced on the Sabbath & I cured the lame
The holy people said it was a shame
They whipped & they stripped & they hung me high
And they left me there on a Cross to die

I danced on a Friday when the sky turned black
It's hard to dance with the devil on your back
They buried my body & they thought I was gone
But I am the dance & I still go on

They cut me down but I leaped up high
For I am the dance that can never, never die
I'll live in you if you'll live in me
For I am the Lord of the Dance, said he!

— w: Sydney Carter — m: Shaker hymn ("Simple Gifts")

© 1963 Galliard, Ltd. Used by permission of Galaxy Music Corp., NY, NY, sole U.S. agent. — In his Green Print for S. *On* Lovely in the Dances: S of Sydney Carter, *J Robts & T Barrand* 2nd Nowell *(FHR26),* Bobby Clancy *(Talbot Prods), Martin Carthy* This Is, & Christmas Revels *(Revel1078). In* Worship in S, Quaker SB & A Time for Singing. OF29

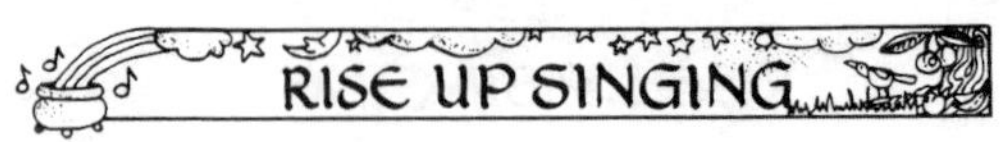

May the Light of Love

As we come around to take our places at the table
A moment to remember & reflect upon our wealth
Here's to loving friends & family, here's to being able
To gather here together in good company & health

D - A - / D G A D :‖ **(1st verse only)**

May we be released from all those feelings that would harm us
May we have the will to give them up & get them gone, for
Heavy are the satchels full of anger & false promises
May we have the strength to put them down

D - A - / D G A G / D - A - / D A G D

May the light of love be shining deep within your spirit
May the torch of mercy clear the path & show the way
May the horn of plenty sound so everyone can hear it
May the light of love be with you every day

A - G D / F#m G Em A / D - A Bm / Em A D -

May we wish the best for everyone that we encounter
May we swallow pride & may we do away with fear, for it's
Only what we do not know that we have grown afraid of
And only what we do not choose to hear

As we bless our daily bread & drink our day's libation
May we be reminded of the lost & wayward soul
The hungry & the homeless that we have in every nation
May we fill each empty cup & bowl

(last v. – tune as chorus)
May nothing ever come between or threaten to divide us
May we never take for granted all the gifts that we receive
Being ever mindful of the Unseen Hands that guide us
And the miracles that cause us to believe

— David Roth

© 1986 David Roth (ASCAP). Used by permission. — On his May the Light *(c/o Maythelight Music, PO Box 1174, Old Chelsea Station, New York NY 10011), on Anne Hills* Woman of a Calm Heart *(FF) & in* SO! *33:2.* OF30

Mi Y'malel *(Who Can Retell?)*

(round) 1) Mi y'malel g'vurot Yisrael 2) Otan mi yimne?
Hen b'ekhol dor yakum hagibor, go-el ha-am
Sh'ma! Bayamim ha-hem baz'man hazzeh
Makkabi moshi-a ufodeh
Uv'yamenu kol am Yisrael
Yitached, yakum veyiga-el

round: 1. D - **2.** - - / - - - - // Am A Dm E Am A
Dm E Am A / Dm E A Am / F E Am A

Who can retell the things that befell us? Who can count them?
In every age a hero or sage came to our aid

Sh'ma! On this very day so long ago
Brave Maccabee arose to smite the foe
And we today must be like Maccabee
And all unite to keep our people free

— trad. (Hebrew Chanukah song) Eng: Sam Hinton

In SO! *1:7 & 34:4,* The S We Sing, Fireside B of FS, FSEncy V1, New Jewish SB. OF31

Mo'oz Tzur *(Rock of Ages)*

Mo'oz tzur y'shuosi / L'cho noe I'shabeyah
Tikon bes t'filosi / V'shom todo n'za beyah
L'yeshto hinmat beyah / Mitzor ham'nabeyah
Oz egmore, b'shir mizmor / Hanukkas hamiz beyah
Oz egmore ... / Hanukkas ... beyah

D DG DA D / DG A DA D :‖ D G D -
Bm G A - / D - A - / D G A - / D G A D

Rock of ages, let our song / Praise thy saving power
Thou, amidst the raging foe / Wast our sheltering tower
Furious they assailed us / But thine arm availed us
And thy word broke their sword / When our own strength failed us

Children of the martyr race / Whether free or fettered
Raise the echoes of the song / Where you may be scattered
Yours the message cheering / That the time is nearing
Which will see all men free / Tyrants disappearing

— Hebrew: trad. (Hanukah song) Eng: v1 trad., v2 Sam Hinton

This is a Hanukah song, usually sung after the lighting of the menorah. In Coopersmith The S We Sing, SO! *36:3,* Holidays in S, New Jewish SB, Songs We Sing, *Botsford* Universal FSster, Harv of Jewish S & S that Changed the World. *On* S for Hanukah, Chanukah S Parade & Hanukkah S for Children. *In* SO! *36:3.* OF32

More Love

More love, more love, the heavens are blessing
The angels are calling, o Zion, more love **(repeat)**
If ye love not each other in daily communion
How can ye love God, whom ye have not seen? **(repeat)**

D - G D / - - A D :‖: D - - - / - - A D :‖

More love, more love, alone by its power
The world we will conquer, for true love is God **(repeat)**
If ye love one another, then God dwelleth within you
And ye are made strong to live by God's word **(repeat)**

— trad. (Shaker, 1870's)

Fr the Shaker Village, Canterbury, NH. In Andrews The Gift to be Simple & S of the Spirit. *On Molly Scott* Honor the Earth *& on Linda Worster & Pat McKernon* River Of Light. OF33

My Faith It Is an Oaken Staff

My faith it is an oaken staff, the traveler's well-loved aid
My faith it is a weapon stout, the soldier's trusted blade
I'll travel on & still be stirred by silent thought or social word
By all my perils undeterred, a soldier pilgrim staid

G - - - / - - A D / G - C - / G - D G

I have a Guide & in his steps, when travelers have trod
Whether beneath was flinty rock or yielding grassy sod
They cared not but with force unspent, unmoved by pain they onward went
Unstayed by pleasures til they bent their zealous course to God

My faith it is an oaken staff, o let me on it lean
My faith it is a trusty sword, may falsehood find it keen!
Thy spirit, Lord, to me impart, o make me what thou ever art
Of patient & courageous heart as all true saints have been

— w: Thomas T. Lynch (1818-71) — m: trad. (Swiss) OF34

Now Let Us Sing

Now let us sing (sing til the pow'r of the Lord comes down) **(2x)**
Lift up your voice (lift ...), be not afraid (be ...)
Now let us sing til the pow'r of the Lord comes down!

G - - - / - - A D / G - C - / G - D G

(Make up new v:) Now let us shout (shout til the power ...)
Now let us clap ...
1. *Now let us work (work til ...) / Roll up your sleeves ...*
2. *... dance / Kick up your heels ...*
3. *... pray / Fall on your knees ...*
4. *... wait / Lift up your face ...*

— A.B. Windom (new v. by Anne & Charlotte Wright)

©1948 A.B. Windom Studio. All rights reserved. — aka: "Sing til...," "Let Us Sing til ..." On Linda Worster & Pat McKernon River of Light. *In* S of the Spirit, *G & C Carawan* We Shall Overcome *& R Shull* CFO Songs, *and in* Sing For Freedom *(as "Sing Til the Power ...").* OF35

O Come, Emmanuel

O come, o come, Emmanuel
And ransom captive Israel
That mourns in lonely exile here
Until the Son of God appear

Rejoice! Rejoice! Emmanuel
Shall come to thee, O Israel!

Em G Am D G / G C Am EmBm Em /

Am Em C DA D / - G Am D G // D - Bm - AmD Em / 2nd

O come thou Dayspring, come & cheer
Our spirits by thine advent here
Disperse the gloomy clouds of night
And death's dark shadows put to flight

O come, thou Wisdom from on high
And order all things, far & nigh
To us the path of knowledge show
And cause us in her ways to go

O come, Desire of nations, bind
All peoples in one heart & mind
Bid envy, strife & quarrels cease
Fill the whole world with heaven's peace

(Orig. Latin)
Veni, veni Emmanuel / Captivum solve Israel
Qui gemit in exsilio / Privatus Dei Filio
Gaude, gaude, Emmanuel / Nascetur pro te Israel.

— w: 9th c. Latin, v 1 & 2 trans. John M. Neale, 1811, v 3 & 4 Henry Sloane Coffin, 1909
— m: adapt. by Thomas Helmore (1811-90)
On Reilly & Maloney Christmas Album *(FR1906), J Baez* V2 *& Sylvia Woods* 3 Harps for Xmas. OF36

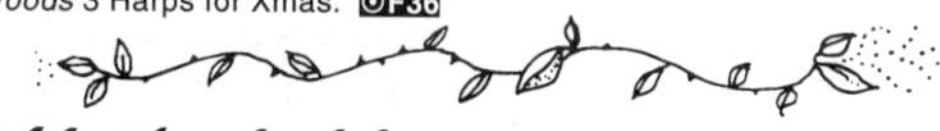

Old Hundredth

All people that on earth do dwell
Sing to the Lord with cheerful voice
Him serve with fear, His praise forth tell
Come ye before Him & rejoice

I: D - A G D D A D - / D - - A Bm G D A -

D A D A D G A Bm - / D - - A G D A D -

The Lord, ye know, is God indeed
Without our aid He did us make
We are His flock, He doth us feed
And for His sheep He doth us take

O enter then His gates with praise
Approach with joy His courts unto
Praise, laud, & bless His name always
For it is seemly so to do

For why? the Lord our God is good
His mercy is forever sure
His truth at all times firmly stood
And shall from age to age endure

Praise God, from whom all blessings flow
Praise Him all creatures here below
Praise Him above, ye heav'nly host
Praise Father, Son & Holy Ghost

II: D DA GD D A D - / - - AD G D A -

D AD AD G A D - / D DBm Em D A D -

— w: attr. to William Kethe, 1561;
— m: Louis Bourgeois, 1551 (Geneva Psalter)
aka: "The Doxology." Paraphrase of Psalm 100. In hymnals.

All people that on earth do dwell
Sing out for peace 'tween heav'n & hell
'Tween East & West & low & high
Sing! peace on earth & sea & sky

Old Hundred you've served many years
To sing one people's hopes & fears
But we've new verses for you now
Sing peace between the earth & plow

Sing peace between the grass & trees
Between the continents & the seas
Between the lion & the lamb
Between young Ivan & young Sam

Between the white, black, red & brown
Between the wilderness & town
Sing peace between the near & far
'Tween Allah & the six-pointed star

The fish that swim, the birds that fly
The deepest seas, the stars on high
Bear witness now that you & I
Sing! Peace on earth & sea & sky

Old Hundred, please don't think us wrong
For adding verses to your song
Sing peace between the old & young
'Tween every faith & every tongue

— new words by Pete Seeger
 — Seeger uses the 2nd version of chords & calls this "Old Hundred." For 4-part harmony arrangement by Pete see SO! *31:4 and* Where Have All The Flowers Gone. OF37

Peace of the River

Peace I ask of thee, o river – peace, peace, peace
When I learn to live serenely, cares will cease
From the hills I gather courage, visions of the day to be
Strength to lead & faith to follow, all are given unto me
Peace I ask of thee, o river – peace, peace, peace

C G AmG C / / F C G C / / 1st

Orig printed in The Ditty Bag by Janet E. Tobitt. Used by permission of Girl Scouts of the U.S.A. — Fr Isaiah 48:18. In Joyful Singing, Pocketful of S *(WAS),* Sfest. OF38

Prayer of St. Francis

Make me a channel of your peace
Where there is hatred let me bring your love
Where there is injury your pardon, Lord
And where there's doubt, true faith in you

D - - - / - - A - / - - - - / - DA D -

Make me a channel of your peace
Where there's despair in life, let me bring hope
Where there is darkness, only light
And where there's sadness ever joy

(bridge) O Master grant that I may never seek
So much to be consoled as to console
To be understood as to understand
To be loved as to love with all my soul

G - D - / A - D - / 1st / E - A -

Make me a channel of your peace
It is in pardoning that we are pardoned
In giving to all men that we receive
And in dying that we're born to eternal life

— Sebastian Temple
Dedicated to Mrs. Frances Tracey. © 1967. Reprinted with permission. Franciscan Communications, Los Angeles, CA 90015. — In S of the Spirit, S of Praise V2 *and* Praise the Name of Jesus *(Word of God, Ann Arbor MI) &* Quaker SB. OF39

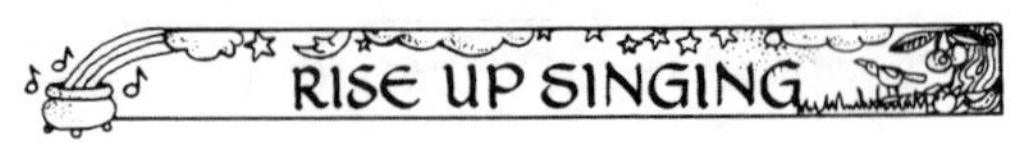

Sabbath Prayer

May the Lord protect & defend you
May he always shield you from shame
May you come to be in Yisrael a shining name

Em A7 Em A7 / / Em A7 Em A7 D - B7 -

May you be like Ruth & like Esther
May you be deserving of praise
Strengthen them o Lord & keep them from the stranger's ways

/ " / / Em A7 Em A7 D - - -

(bridge) May God bless you & grant you long lives
May the Lord fulfill our Sabbath prayer for you
May God make you good mothers & wives
May he send you husbands who will care for you

D - - - / C - D - / - - - - / C - B7 -

May the Lord protect & defend you
May the Lord preserve you from pain
Favor them o Lord with happiness & peace
O hear our Sabbath prayer, amen!

— w: Sheldon Harnick — m: Jerry Bock

 Fr their musical Fiddler on the Roof. OF40

Shake These Bones

I'll show you what I'm feelin', Lord, anyday
I'll shake these bones & shout & sing my life away
I'll shake these bones & I will shout & sing my life away
It won't be long before these bones turn to clay

G Em DG / G Em EmG / G Em C D / C G CD

G Em DG **(better as a capella)**

I'll tell you what I'm thinkin', Lord, anytime
I'll tell you lies, I'll tell you dreams that you won't mind
I'll tell you lies, I'll ... dreams, I know that you won't mind
There's something there that's out of reach I will find

I'll tell you what I'm seein', Lord, ev'rywhere
It may be only a small part of what is there
It may be only a small part of what is really there
But I'll stumble like the blind man, Lord, without fear

I'll tell you what I'm hearin', Lord, all the time
I'm hearin' songs & melodies in my mind
I'm hearin' songs & melodies but when they're out of mind
I'll hear the sweetest peace of all, left behind

I'll show you how I'm livin', Lord, every day
I may not fall down on my knees & start to pray
I may not fall down on my knees or worship you or pray
But there's reverence in my laughter, Lord, anyway

I'll show you who I'm lovin', Lord, in the night
And when the door is open, Lord, & filled with light
And when the door is open, Lord, & filled with the morning light
We'll hear the child that calls for us out of sight

I'll show you who I'm lovin', Lord, in the day
And to my fellow people, Lord, these words I'll say
And to all my fellow people, Lord, these loving words I'll say
And I'll shake these bones & shout & sing my life away!

— Malcolm Dalglish

 On his & Grey Larson's First of Autumn. OF41

Simple Gifts

'Tis the gift to be simple, 'tis the gift to be free
'Tis the gift to come down where we ought to be
And when we find ourselves in the place just right
'Twill be in the valley of love & delight

When true simplicity is gained
To bow & to bend we shan't be ashamed
To turn, turn will be our delight
Til by turning, turning we come 'round right

D - / A - / A GD // DA D / - A / D - / A GD

The earth is the Lord's & the fullness thereof
Its streets, its slums, as well as stars above
Salvation is here where we laugh, where we cry
Where we seek & love, where we live & die

When the true liberty is found
By fear & by hate we will no more be bound
In love & in life we will find a new birth
In peace & in freedom redeem the earth

— trad. (Shaker), new v. Victor Ferkiss & Landon Dowdey

The Shakers were the most successful of the many 19th c. communitarian movements. This song was sung throughout the Shaker communities & appears in many pre-Cival War manuscripts. In Andrews The Gift to be Simple *& Sturm* The Gift of Shaker S. *On Univ of KY Choristers* Music of the Shakers *(Pleiades), Judy Collins* Whales & Nightingales, *Bright Morning Star* Arisin', *C Winter & B Rose* As Strong As Anyone Can Be, *Devilish Merry* The Ghost of His Former Self, *S Stark* Rainbow People, *Kretzner & Leibowitz* Dulcimer Fair, *C Hester* Simply, *E & B Beers* Seasons of Peace, *B Bowers* View fr Home & Golden Ring *(Folk-Legacy FSI-16). In* SO! *37:3.* OF42

Sing and Rejoice

Sing & rejoice, ye children of the Day & of the Light (2x)
For the Lord God is at work (3x) in this thick night
In this thick night of darkness (3x) that may be felt
In this thick night ... that may be felt (repeat: 1st 2 lines)

D - G D / - - E A / D D7 G E7 D GA D -
G E7 DF# Bm Em G A - / Em G A - / **as above**

1. Truth doth flourish, flourish as the rose
   Lilies do grow, do grow among the thorns
   And the plants do grow atop the hills
   Upon them the lambs do skip & play

G D Em - / Bm Em A - :||

2. Never heed the tempests nor the storms
   Never heed the floods nor heed the rains
   For the Seed Christ is over all
   Over all the seed Christ doth reign

— William Guthe

 — Lyrics based on a 1663 epistle by George Fox. In (& on) Go Cheerfully *(FUM).* OF43

Song of the Soul

(intro) Open mine eyes that I may see
Glimpses of truth thou hast for me
Open mine eyes, illumine me / Spirit divine

A E / - A / - D / E A

"Love of my life" I am crying
I am not dying, I am dancing
Dancing along in the madness
There is no sadness, only a song of the soul

A ED / E DE / A ED / E A

And we'll sing this song, why don't you sing along?
And we can sing for a long, long time (repeat)

E - AD A / D E D A / 1st / D E A -

What do you do for your living?
Are you forgiving, giving shelter?
Follow your heart, love will find you
Truth will unbind you, sing out a song of the soul

Come to your life like a warrior
Nothing will bore you, you can be happy
Let the light in, it will heal you
And you can feel you, sing out a song of the soul

— **Cris Williamson**

© Bird Ankle Music. Used by permission. — Intro is from a hymn by Clara Scott. On her Changer & the Changed. *In her* SB *&* SO! *32:1.* OF44

Take These Hands

Take these hands, turn them into light beams
Take these feet, turn them into your shoes
Take this life, make it everything it might be
Give me courage walking in the dark, o help me choose a lighted path

D - / A D / G- / DA G D

May my back be the wings of a dove
May my knees learn to bend
May my heart know the depth of your love
And may this love never end

Bm E / / / Bm EA

May my ears take pleasure in silence
May my mind learn to feel
May my eyes come to recognize
The shape & the contour of the real

— **Patricia McKernon**

© 1983 Intermodal Music, PO Box 8828 Minneapolis MN 55408. Used by permission. — On her New Moon *& her and Linda Worster* River of Light. OF45

Wear it as Long as You Can

Will Penn said to George Fox "Oh what should I do?
Can I wear this sword while I serve my God too?"
George Fox said to Will Penn "You'll know when you're thru
Just wear it, use it, but don't you abuse it
Just wear it as long as you can"

G - - - / D7 - - G / - - - - / D7 G D7 G / D7 G -

"And what about words, can I speak without care?"
"Well, words can be tricky, so say what you dare
It's Spirit that calls us more clearly than words
So hear them, use them, but don't you abuse them
Just wear them as long as you can"

"And what about money, oh, what is my role?
Can I live in comfort while others go cold?"
"Just realize money is not yours to hold
Just make it, use it, but don't you abuse it / **Just wear it ...**

"And what about love, must I give that up, too?"
"What's great about love is it grows as you do
So spend love quite freely & watch it return
Just share it, use it, but don't you abuse it" / **Just wear it ...**

— **Barbara Mays**

© 1981 Barbara Mays. Used by perm. — Based on a famous interchange between Penn, the wealthy founder of Pennsylvania, & Fox, the founder of Quakerism, on whether it was ethical to wear a ceremonial sword as a pacifist. In (& on) Go Cheerfully *(FUM).* OF46

The Wedding Banquet

I cannot come **(2x)** to the banquet, don't trouble me now
I have married a wife, I have bought me a cow
I have fields & commitments that cost a pretty sum
Pray, hold me excused, I cannot come

D G D / A D / G D / A D ||: **verse:** G D / A D :||

A certain man held a feast on his fine estate in town
He laid a festive table & wore a wedding gown
He sent invitations to his neighbors far & wide
But when the meal was ready, each of them replied:

The master rose up in anger, called his servants by name
Said "Go into the town, fetch the blind & the lame
Fetch the peasant & the pauper for this I have willed
My banquet must be crowded & my table must be filled"

When all the poor had assembled there was still room to spare
So the master demanded, "Go search ev'ry where
To the highways & the byways & force them to come in
My table must be filled before the banquet can begin"

Now God has written a lesson for the rest of our kind:
If we're slow in responding He may leave us behind
He's preparing a banquet for that great & glorious day
When the Lord & master calls us, be certain not to say:

— **Sr. Miriam Therese Winter**

© 1965 Medical Mission Sisters, Phila. PA. Used by permission. From Joy Is Like the Rain *(album & SB).* OF47

Wondrous Love

What wondrous love is this, o my soul, o my soul!
What wondrous love is this, o my soul
What wondrous love is this that caused the Lord of bliss
To bear the dreadful curse for my soul, for my soul
To bear the dreadful curse for my soul

DmC DmC Dm C / Am FC Dm - /
F G Am Dm / **1st 2**

When I was sinking down, sinking down, sinking down
When I was sinking down, sinking down
When I was sinking down beneath God's righteous frown
Christ laid aside His crown for my soul, for my soul
Christ laid aside His crown for my soul

To God & to the Lamb, I will sing ...
To God & to the Lamb who is the great I Am
While millions join the theme, I will sing ...

And when from death I'm free I'll sing on ...
And when from death I'm free I'll sing & joyful be
Throughout eternity I'll sing on ...

— **trad. (early US)**

Some sources attribute to Rev. Alex Means. In George Pullen Jackson Spiritual FS of Early America, SO! *16:1,* The Orig Sacred Harp, S of the Spirit, *&* Best Loved S of the Am People. *On J Ritchie* None But One *(SA75301),* *Christmas Revels* Wassail Wassail *(RC 1082) & Coop 2-6.* OF48

Other religious songs can be found in the following chapters: GOSPEL (mainly composed songs springing out of Revival movements), HOPE (aspirations for a better world), LULLABIES, OUTDOORS (hymns about nature), SACRED ROUNDS & CHANTS (incl. very short or repetitive hymns/spiritual songs useful in helping to gather a group into a sense of God's presence), and SPIRITUALS (trad. Black hymns mainly derived from the period of slavery). Also see the Holidays Index and the Cultures Index listings for Jewish Song, Quakers, & Shakers.

Individual songs include: "Follow the Gleam" (DREAM); "Now is the Cool of the Day" (ECO); "Lift Every Voice," "Rivers of Babylon" (FREE); "Wayfaring Stranger" (HARD); "Bright Morning Stars" (MTN); "The Rich Man & the Poor Man (Story of Lazarus)," "Hymn for Nations," "Peace in the Valley," "Song of Peace" (PEACE); "Tramp on the Street" (RICH); "Because All Men Are Brothers (Bach chorale)," "In Christ There Is No East Nor West," "When All Thy Names Are One," "When I Needed a Neighbor" (UNITY); "Good Old Dora," "Sara's Circle," "Sister" (on evangelist Aimee McPherson), & "Testimony" (WOMEN).

Songs are traditional U.S. cowboy songs where not otherwise credited.

Applepicker's Reel

Hey, ho, makes you feel so fine
Looking out across the orchard in the bright sunshine
Hey, ho, you feel so free
Standing in the top of an apple tree!

D G / A D :||

Up in the morning, before the sun
I don't get home until the day is done
My pick-sack's heavy & my shoulder's sore
But I'll be back tomorrow to pick some more

Start at the bottom & you pick 'em from the ground
And you pick that tree clean all the way around
Then you set your ladder & you climb up high
And you're looking thru the leaves at the clear blue sky

Three-legged ladder, wobbly as hell
Reaching for an apple – whoa! I almost fell
Got a 20-pound sack hanging 'round my neck
And there's three more apples that I can't quite get!

They come in green & yellow & red
You eat them in the morning & before you go to bed
You can play catch if you throw 'em up high
Oops! Squish! Apple Pie!

Hey, ho, you feel so funny
Walkin' thru a town when you got no money
Hey ho, makes you feel so free / Standing in the top ...

Hey, ho, makes you feel so down
Pickin' up the windfalls crawling on the ground / **Hey ...**

Hey, ho, you lose your mind
If we sing this song about a hundred times / **Hey ...**

— Larry Hanks

© 1967 Larry Hanks. All rights reserved. Used by permission. *— "I worked picking apples only a few weeks in the Fall of '66, near Sebastopol. It was hard work for me but remained fresh, a joyful exercise." — LH. On his* Berkeley Farm *(Folkways 2436), M Cooney* The Cheese Stands Alone *(FolkLeg), F Petric* Sing A Song *& G Carawan* The Telling Takes Me Home. *In* V Favs of the V Young, Bright Morning Stars *(both WAS)* & Rainy Day SB. OM02

Buffalo Gals

As I was walking down the street **(3x)**
A pretty girl I chanced to meet under the silvery moon
Buffalo gals won't you come out tonight **(3x)**
Buffalo gals won't you ... & dance by the light of the moon

D - A D / // G D A D / /

I asked her if she'd stop & talk **(3x)**
Her feet covered up the whole sidewalk, she was fair to view

I asked her if she'd be my wife **(3x)**
Then I'd be happy all my life if she'd marry me

O I danced with the dolly with a hole in her stocking
And her feet kept a-rocking & her knees kept a-knocking
O I danced with the dolly with a hole in her stocking
And we danced by the light of the moon

Orig published in 1880s & later in Heart S *(1909) & B.A. Botkin* Am Play Party S & Treas of Am S. *On (& in) Pete Seeger* Am Fav Bals V1 *(Folkways 2320). On G Carawan* Songs With, *C Fink* Grandma's Patchwork Quilt *(AmMelody), W Guthrie* Sings FS V2, *E Weissburg* Banjo & Bluegrass, *Ives* S of the Frontier, *& soundtrack for* Deliverance. *In* SFest & FSEncyV1. OM03

Ca' the Ewes

Ca' the ewes to the knowes, ca' them where the heather grows
Ca' them where the burnie rows, my bonnie dearie

Am G Em D / Em G AmBm Em

Hark the mavis evenin' song soundin' Cluden's woods amang
Then a-foldin' let us gang, my bonnie dearie

We'll gae doon by Cluden side thru the hazels spreading wide
O'er the waves that sweetly glide to the moon sae clearly

Fair & lovely as thou art, thou hast stol'n my very heart
I can die but canna part, my bonnie dearie

— w: Robert Burns **— m: trad. (Scottish)**

Pron: ewes as yows, knowes as nows. Trans: Ca' = call, knowes = knolls, burnie = brooklet, rows = rolls, afolding = to sheep folding, lift = sky. On Gordon Bok *(FT3016), L Killen* Old S, Old Friends. *In* Fires B of Love S & Oxford Scottish SB. OM04

Country Life

O I like to rise when the sun she rises
Early in the morning
I like to hear them small birds singing
Merrily upon their lay-land
And hurrah for the life of a country boy
And to ramble in the new mown hay

A - D E / / / / / G D A D / A E A -

In the spring we sow, in the harvest mow
And that's how the seasons around they go
But of all the times if choose I may
It's to ramble in the new mown hay

A - D E / / / / A E A -

In the winter when the sky is gray
We edge & ditch our life away
But in the summer when the sun shines gay
We go rambling in the new mown hay

— trad. (English)

In Sing the Good Earth *&* V Favs of the V Young *(both WAS). On The Watersons* For Pence and Spicy Ale *(Antilles). In* SO! *35:4 &* Bright Morning Stars *(WAS).* OM05

Day-O (Banana Boat Song)

Day-o, me say day-o - daylight come & me wan' go home (2x)

G CG G DG / /

Work all night til the mornin' come – daylight come & me ...
Stack banana til the mornin' come – daylight ...
Come, Mr. Tallyman, tally me banana – daylight ...
Me say, come, Mr. Tallyman ... – daylight ...
Lift 6 hand, 7 hand, 8 hand bunch ...
Me say, 6 hand ...

G - - DG :||: (3rd + 4th lines) G D G DG :||

A beautiful bunch o' ripe banana ... **(2x)**
Lift 6 hand, 7 hand, 8 hand bunch ... / Me say, 6 hand ...

— Erik Darling, Bob Carey & Alan Arkin

© 1957 Edward B. Marks Music Co. Copyright renewed. International copyright secured. Made in USA. All rights reserved. Used by permission. *— Based on traditional Trinidad material & popularized by Harry Belafonte. On Raffi* Baby Beluga *& in his 2nd SB. On Enoch Light* Far Away. *In* Best Fake B Ever. *Used in film* Beetlejuice. OM06

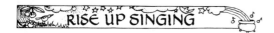

Deportees (Plane Wreck at Los Gatos)

The crops are all in & the peaches are rotting
The oranges piled in their creosote dumps
You're flying them back to the Mexican border
To pay all their money to wade back again

(in 3/4) D - G D / / G - D - / - - G D

Good-bye to my Juan, good-bye, Rosalita
Adios mis amigos, Jésus y Maria
You won't have a name when you ride the big airplane
All they will call you will be deportees

G - D - / A - D - / G - D - / - - G - D - - -

My father's own father, he waded that river
They took all the money he made in his life
My brothers & sisters come working the fruit trees
And they rode the trucks til they took down & died

Some of us are illegal & some are not wanted
Our work contract's out & we have to move on
600 miles to that Mexican border
They chase us like outlaws, like rustlers, like thieves

We died in your hills, we died in your deserts
We died in your valleys & died on your plains
We died 'neath your trees & we died in your bushes
Both sides of the river, we died just the same

The sky plane caught fire over Los Gatos canyon
A fireball of lightning, & shook all our hills
Who are these friends, all scattered like dry leaves?
The radio says they are just deportees

Is this the best way we can grow our big orchards?
Is this the best way we can grow our good fruit?
To fall like dry leaves to rot on my topsoil
And be called by no name except deportees?

— w: Woody Guthrie — m: Martin Hoffman

© 1961 & 1963 Ludlow Music, Inc, NY, NY. Internat'l copyright secured. Made in USA. All rights reserved incl. pub. performance for profit. Used by permission. — On Guthrie's Hard Trav & Gr S *& in his SB. In* SO! *9:1 & 28:3,* Reprints #4 *&* Carry It On. *On J Collins #3, Priscilla Herdman* Seasons of Change *(FF), Sweet Honey in the Rock* The Other Side, *Pete Seeger* Sings Woody Guthrie, *Christy Moore* Spirit of Freedom, *&* Tribute to Guthrie, pts 1&2. OM07

Desperado

Desperado, why don't you come to your senses
You been out riding fences for so long now
O you're a hard one but I know that you got your reasons
These things that are pleasin' you will hurt you somehow

C C7 F Dm / C Am D G / 1st / C Am G C

Don't you draw the queen of diamonds, boy
She'll beat you if she's able
You know the queen of hearts is always your best bet
Now it seems to me some fine things
Have been laid upon your table
But you only want the ones that you can't get

F G / C - / Am Dm C - / F G / C Am / D - G -

Desperado, you know you ain't gettin' younger
Your pain & your hunger they're driving you home
And freedom, o freedom, that's just some people talkin'
Your prison is walking thru this world all alone

Don't your feet get cold in the winter time
The sky won't snow & the sun won't shine
It's hard to tell the night time from the day
You're losing all your highs & lows
Ain't it funny how the feeling goes / Away

Desperado, why don't you come to your senses
Come down from your fences open the gate
It may be raining but there's a rainbow above you
You better let somebody love you **(3x)** before it's too late

C C7 F Dm / C Am D G / 1st /
C C7 F Dm C Am DmG C

— Don Henley & Glenn Frey

© 1973 Cass County Music & Red Cloud Music. All rights reserved. Used by permission. — On L Ronstadt Don't Cry Now *&* Gr H, *J Collins* Hard Times for Lovers *& rec by Eagles. In* SO! *1:12,* All the Best Contemp H *&* Gr Legal FakeB. OM08

Djankoye (Hey Zhankoye)

Az man fort kine Sevastopol, is nit veit fun Simfereopol
Dortn iz a stantziye faron
Ver darf zuchen naiye glikken, s'iz a stantziye an antikel
In Djankoye, Djan, djan, djan

Em - AAm Em / Em AmB7 Em - :||

Hey Djan, hey Djankoye, hey Djanvili, hey Djankoye
Hey Djankoye, Djan, djan, djan **(repeat)**

Am D G - / Em AmB7 Em - :||

If you go from Sevastopol on the road to Simfereopol
Just you go a little further on
There you'll find a RR depot, known quite well to all the people
Called Djankoye, Djan, djan, djan

There's Abrrasha runs the tractor, grandma runs the cream extractor
While we work we can all sing our songs
Who says that Jews cannot be farmers?
Spit in his eye who would so harm us
Tell him of Djankoye, Djan

— trad. (Soviet-Yiddish) Eng. w: Pete Seeger

© 1947 (renewed) Stormking Music Inc. All rights reserved. Used by permission. — aka: "Hey Zhankoye." As collected by Ruth Rubin. In Bells of Rhymney, FSEncy V1, Peoples SB, Treasury of Jewish FS *(as "Azmen ..."), R Rubin* Jewish FS *(as "Zhan ..."), &* Fav Hebrew S. OM09

Down on the American Farm

First you run down to the bank & you get yourself a loan
For $80,000 cash you can drive that tractor home
You can drive all night, you can drive all day
You can drive over anything gettin' in your way
And you ain't got a worry til the pay-back day
Down on the American Farm

G - C G / - D G - ||: G - - - :|| 1st 2

So you get some stuff & you spread it around
To keep the bugs & the animals down
And you spray it on the crops & you pump it on the ground
But the bugs get bigger & attack the folks in town
You can spray all day, you can spray all night
But the bugs get bigger & they ain't afraid to fight
You can drive all night, you can drive all day
You can drive over anything gettin' in your way
And you still ain't got a worry til the pay-back day / **Down ...**

Pretty soon the crops come up & you goes to cut 'em down
You put some in a pickup truck & you hauls it all to town
But the more you grow, the more you spend
The less it's worth to the market in the end
You can spray all day ...
But the bugs get bigger ...
You can drive all night ...
You can drive over anything ...
Now it's drivin' you crazy cuz you can't afford to stay
Down on the American Farm

— w: Arlo Guthrie — m: trad

© 1988 by Arloco Music Inc. All rights reserved. Used by permission. — The tune is derived fr "Old MacDonald," "Uncle Sam's Farm" & "Down On Penny's Farm." OM10

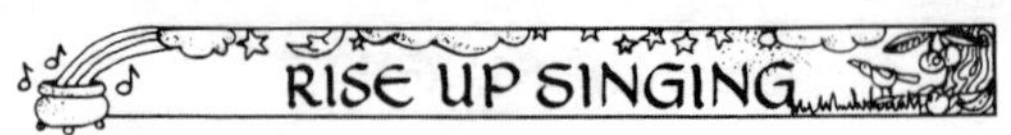

Eleven Cent Cotton

'Leven cent cotton, forty cent meat
How in the world can a poor man eat?
Pray for the sunshine, what you get is rain
Things gettin' worse, drivin' us insane
Built a nice house, painted it brown
Lightnin' came along & burnt it down
No use talkin', any man's beat
With eleven cent cotton & forty cent meat

A - D A / D A B7 E / A - D A / - - E A
D - A - / B7 - E - // " / " /

'Leven cent cotton, forty cent meat
Keep gettin' thinner cuz we don't eat
Tried to raise peas, tried to raise beans
All we can raise is turnip greens
No corn in the crib, no chicks in the yard
No meat in the smoke house, no tubs full of lard / **No use ...**

'Leven cent cotton, forty cent meat
How in the world can a poor man eat?
Our clothes worn out, shoes run down
Old slouch hat with a hole in the crown
Poor gettin' poorer all around here
Kids comin' regular ev'ry year / **No use ...**

'Leven cent ... / How in the world ...
Mule's in the barn, no crops laid by
Corn crib empty & the cow's gone dry
Well water's low, nearly out of sight
Can't take a bath on a Saturday night / **No use ...**

— Bob Miller & Erma Derner

 — On Pete Seeger Industrial Ballads, *JE Mainer* V 3, *& Uncle Dave Macon* Laugh Your Blues Away. *In* S Work & Protest & Fires B of Am S. OM11

Farmer

I am a farmer, been one all my life
Call me a farmer, not a farmer's wife
The plough & hoe left their patterns on my hand
And now they tell me this is not my land

(in C) G F C - / G F G - / Am - Em - / F Dm G -

We raised two children, they are farmers too
A crop & garden every year we grew
Two hundred acres ain't no easy haul
But it's a good life, no regrets at all

When Joe turned fifty, back was actin' up
We three took over, so's he could rest up
My Joe was buried where his daddy lies
And soon some men came, askin' for my price

I said "I live here, here I'm gonna stay
What makes you think I wanna move away?"
They smiled really sly, said "Now your farmer's dead
The farm ain't yours til you pay the overhead"

I know we women ain't been in the know
But we're no fools as far as farming goes
The crop don't know no woman's work or man's
There ain't no law can take me from my land

'Cause I'm a farmer, been one all my life
Call me a farmer, not a farmer's wife
The plough & hoe left their patterns on my hand
No one can tell me this is not my land
This is my land!

— Kristin Lems (ending) F Dm G / - C - - -

 — On her Oh Mama! *& in* Here's to the Women. OM12

The Farmer Is the Man

When the farmer comes to town with his wagon broken down
O the farmer is the man *[one]* **who feeds them all**
If you'll only look & see I think you will agree
That the farmer is the man *[one]* **who feeds them all**

D - - - / - A D - :||

The farmer is the man *[one]*, **the farmer is the man** *[one]*
Lives on credit til the fall
Then they take him *['em]* by the hand & they lead him
['em] from the land
And the middleman's the one who gets it all

D - - - / - - A - / D - - - / - A D -

O the lawyer hangs around while the butcher cuts a pound, but ...
And the preacher & the cook go a-strolling by the brook, but ...

(2nd cho) The farmer is the man *[one]* **... / ... til the fall**
With the interest rate so high, it's a wonder he don't die
For the mortgage man's the one who gets it all

When the banker says he's broke & the merchant's up in smoke
They forget that it's the farmer feeds them all
It would put them to the test if the farmer took a rest
Then they'd know that it's the farmer feeds them all

(3rd cho) The farmer ... / ... fall
And his pants are wearing thin, his condition it's a sin
He forgot that he's the one who feed us all
[With the taxes out of hand, they are forced to sell their land
And so we get a thousand shopping malls]

— anon. (US, 1870s, adap w/new last cho Pete Seeger)

"The Farmer Is the Man" was popular w/Midwestern farmers at the time of the Farmer's Alliance, the Greenback Party & the founding of the Grange. On Pete Seeger Industrial Ballads & S for Young People, *& JE Mainer* V 14. *In* S Work & Protest, *Lomax* FS of NA, Am Fav Bal, The Peoples SB, Sing the Good Earth *(WAS)*, Carry It On, Childrens S for a Friendly Planet & FSEncy V2. *In SO! 36:2.* OM13

The Field Behind the Plow

Watch the field behind the plow turn to straight dark rows
Feel the trickle in your clothes, blow the dust cake from your nose
Hear the tractor's steady roar, oh you can't stop now
There's a quarter section more or less to go

(capo up) G - DC G / C D Am D / 1st / Am D G -

And it figures that the rain keeps its own sweet time
You can watch it come for miles, but you guess you've got a while
So ease the throttle out a hair, every rod's a gain
And there's victory in every quarter mile

(bridge #1)
Poor old Kuzyk down the road
The heartache, hail & hoppers brought him down
He gave it up & went to town
And Emmett Pierce the other day
Took a heart attack & died at forty-two
You could see it coming on 'cause he worked as hard as you

D - / C - G / - D - / - - / C - G / - D - C -

In an hour, maybe more, you'll be wet clear thru
The air is cooler now, pull your hat-brim further down
And watch the field behind the plow turn to straight dark rows
Put another season's promise in the ground

(bridge #2)
And if the harvest's any good
The money just might cover all the loans
You've mortgaged all you own
Buy the kids a winter coat
Take the wife back East for Christmas if you can
All summer she hangs on when you're so tied to the land

For the good times come & go, but at least there's rain
So this won't be barren ground when September rolls around
So watch the field behind the plow turn to straight dark rows
Put another season's promise in the ground

— **Stan Rogers**

© 1981 Fogarty's Cove Music, Inc. (PRO CANADA). All rights reserved. Used by permission. *— On his* Northwest Passage *& in* S fr Fogarty's Cove. *On Priscilla Herdman* Seasons of Change *(FF309) & Jerry Rau* Gypsy Roving Yrs. *In* SO! *37:1 &* New Folk Songs. OM14

Garden Song

Inch by inch, row by row
Gonna make this garden grow
All you need is a rake & a hoe *[Gonna mulch it deep & low]*
And a piece of fertile ground *[Gonna make it fertile ground]*
Inch by inch, row by row
Someone *[Please]* **bless these seeds I sow**
Someone warm them from below *[Please keep them safe below]*
Til the rains come tumbling down

D - GD/G AD-/G A DBm/C G CD/E - A - :||E A D-

Pulling weeds, picking stones
We are made of dreams & bones
Need a place to call my own for the time is near at hand
Grain for grain, sun & rain
Find my way thru nature's chain
Tune my body & my brain to the music of the land

Plant your rows straight & long
Temper them with prayer & song
Mother earth will make you strong if you give her love & care
An old crow watching hungrily
From his perch in yonder tree
In my garden I'm as free as that feathered thief up there!

— **Dave Mallet (alt cho Pete Seeger)**

© 1975, 1978 Cherry Lane Music Publishing Co. Inc. All rights reserved. Used by permission. *— On his* Dave Mallet *(New World Media, S Blue Hill, ME 04615), Pete Seeger* Circles & Seasons *&* Prec Friend *(w/A Guthrie),* John Denver, *Guy Carawan* Jubilee *(June Appal 29), S Stark* Rainbow People, *Rosenhonz* Tickles You *(RS) & Tom Smith* Chip Off the New Block *(GW1005). In* SO! *26:6 &* New Folk Favs. OM15

(Parody) *The Anti-Garden Song*

Slug by slug, weed by weed
My garden's got me really teed
All the insects love to feed upon my tomato plants
Sunburned face, scratched-up knees
My kitchen's choked with zucchinis
I'm shopping at the A & P next time I get a chance

The crabgrass grows, the ragweed thrives
The broccoli has long since died
The only things still left alive are some radishes & beans
My carrot plants are dead & gone
Hear the rabbits sing a happy song
Until you've weeded all day long you don't know what boredom means

You get up early, work til late
Watch moles & mice get overweight
They eat their dinners on a plate from the hard work you have done
As ye sow, so shall ye reap
But I smell like a compost heap
I'm gonna get that lousy creep who said gardening was fun

— **new w: Eric Kilburn — m: Dave Mallet ("The Garden Song")**

Words © 1982 Eric Kilburn. Used by permission. *On his* Carryin' On.

Garnening

O, my friends, it's springtime again
Buds are swelling on every limb
The peepers do call, small birds do sing
And my thoughts return to gardening

(better a capella)

D - A D / A Bm A Bm / A - - D / A - F#m Bm

Gardening is a very fine art
Bear well in mind before you start
Lay up your ax, your saw blade also
And take down your spade, your rake & your hoe

Polish your hoe til the blade it does shine
Likewise your rake & sharpen each tine
Dress up your spade with a light coat of oil
Then you are ready to prepare your soil

Prepare your soil with a good free will
Bear well in mind what you may till
Some compost & lime are all you need
Then you are ready to plant your seed

Plant your seed but none too soon
Bear well in mind the phase of the moon
Set out the fruit the roots & the grain
And hope it all sprouts in the cool early rain

If the cool early rain don't drown you out
The first hot spell will bring on a drought
The midsummer sun is hotter than hell
Mulch down your rows & you water them well

Water them down well & thin them also
Beware of weeds & beetles & crows
If you work every day then little is lost
Just hope it all ripens before the first frost

The first frost will come as sure as sin
Then you must hasten to gather it in
By cartloads & bushels, by pecks & by quarts
Your harvest of fruits & grains of all sorts

All sorts of peaches & apples & wheat
Oat & rye & strawberries sweet
Squashes & melons with colorful rinds
Your harvest of vegetable roots of all kinds

All kinds of turnips & carrots & beets
Potatoes, tomatoes & strong smelling leeks
Cabbage & corn, the beans & the hay
Then you must carefully store it away

Away in the cellars & lofts & bins
Make cider & kraut, pickles & gin
If you do it all well then you'll not go wrong
You will have plenty for all winter long

All winter long while the cold winds blow
Take down your saw & woodcutting go
If you're well fed & warm be well-content then
Til warm weather comes & you say to your friends
O my friends, it's springtime again ...

— **Dillon Bustin**

© 1983 Dillon Bustin, Moonbow Music. Used by permission. *— On his* Almanac *& rec by Metamora. In* SO! *30:2 &* Bright Morning Stars *(WAS).* OM16

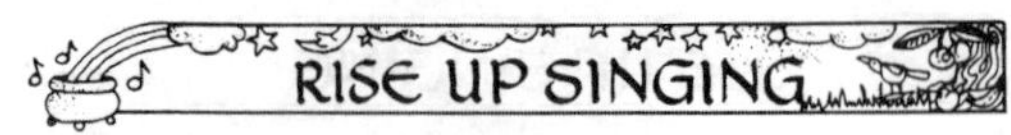

Git Along, Little Doggies

As I was a-walking one morning for pleasure
I spied a cowpuncher all riding along
His hat was throwed back & his spurs was a-jinglin'
As he approached me a-singin' this song:

(in 3/4) C F G7 C / / / /

Whoopee ti yi yo, git along, little dogies
It's your misfortune & none of my own
Whoopee ti yi yo, git along, little dogies
For you know Wyoming will be your new home

G - C - / / C F G7 C / /

Early in the spring we round up the dogies
Mark 'em & brand 'em & bob off their tails
Drive up our horses, load up the chuck-wagon
Then throw the dogies out on the trail

It's whoopin' & yellin' & a-drivin' them dogies
O how I wish that you would go on
It's a-whoopin' & punchin' & go on-a little dogies
For you know Wyoming is to be your new home

Some boys goes up the trail for pleasure
But that's where they get it most awfully wrong
For you haven't any idea the trouble they give us
While we go driving them along
When the night comes on & we hold them on the bed-ground

These little dogies that roll on so slow
Round up the herd & cut out the strays
And roll the little dogies that never rolled before

Your mother she was raised way down in Texas
Where the jimson weed & sand-burrs grow
Now we'll fix you up on prickly pear & cholla
Til you're ready for the trail to Idaho

— coll, adap, & arr. by John A. Lomax & Alan Lomax

TRO © 1934 (renewed 1962) Ludlow Music, Inc, NY, NY. Internat'l copyright secured. Made in USA. All rights reserved incl. pub. performance for profit. Used by permission. *— aka: "Whoopie-ti-yi-yo" & "Little Dogies." Probably originated in Ireland, as "The Old Man Rocking The Cradle" & paraphrased by some unknown cowhand. In SO! 14:5,* FSEncy V1, *Lomax* FS of NAm, FiresB of FS & SFest. *On Pete Seeger* Darlin' Corey, *Riders in the Sky* Saddle Pals, *W Guthrie* Sings FS V2, *Bill Oliver* Better Things To Do, *Peter La Faye* Sings of the Cowboys *(FA2533), D Bromberg* How Late'll Ya Play, *Ives* S of the Frontier & FS Dramatic & Humorous. OM17

Home on the Range

O give me a home where the buffalo roam
Where the deer & the antelope play
Where seldom is heard a discouraging word
And the skies are not cloudy all day

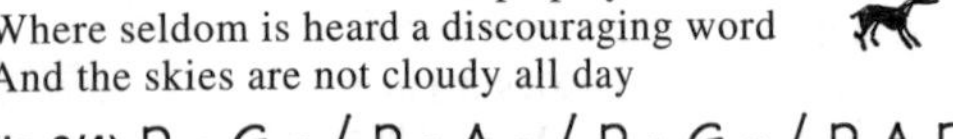

(in 3/4) D - G - / D - A - / D - G - / D A D -

Home, home on the range
Where the deer & the antelope play
Where seldom is heard a discouraging word
And the skies are not cloudy all day

D A D - / Bm E A - / " / " /

Where the air is so pure & the zephyrs so free
And the breezes so balmy & light
That I would not exchange my home on the range
For all of the cities so bright

How often at night when the heavens are bright
With the light of the glittering stars
I stand there amazed & I ask as I gaze
Does their glory exceed that of ours?

There were a number of disputes & lawsuits over authorship of this song in 19th c. The probable authors are Brewster Higley & Dan Kelly. On Pete Seeger Am Fav Bal V2 *(FA2320) & J Denver* Rocky Mtn Holiday. *In* Am Fav Bal *&* FSEncy V1. OM18

I Ride an Old Paint

I ride an old paint, I lead an old Dan
I'm goin' to Montan for to throw the hoolihan
They feed in the coolies, they water in the draw
Their tails are all matted, their backs are all raw

Ride around, little dogies, ride around them slow
For the fiery & snuffy are rarin' to go

(in 3/4) G - - - / D - G - / / // / /

I've worked in the town & I've worked on the farm
And all I got is this muscle in my arm
Got a blister on my foot & a callus in my hand
But I'll be a cowpuncher as long as I can

Old Bill Jones had two daughters & a song
One went to Denver & the other went wrong
His wife she died in a poolroom fight
And still he keeps singin' from morning to night

O when I die, take my saddle from the wall
Put it on my pony, lead him out of his stall
Tie my bones to his back, turn our faces to the west
And we'll ride the prairies that we love the best

Fr the collection of M P Larkin. In SO! *3:7,* Am Fav Bal & FSEncy V1. *On (& in) Pete Seeger* Am Fav Ballads V1. *On W Guthrie* Poor Boy, *Ives* S of the Frontier & More FS, *& Peter La Farge* Sings of the Cowboys. OM19

The Iowa Waltz

Home in the midst of the corn, in the middle of the USA
Here's where I was born, here's where I'm going to stay

(in 3/4) DD♭ DG D A / DD♭ DG DA D

Iowa, Iowa, winter spring summer & fall
Come & see, come dance with me to the beautiful Iowa Waltz

G D E A / " /

We take care of our old, take care of our young & make hay while the sun shines
Growing our crops & singing our songs from planting until harvest time

— Greg Brown

© 1981 Brownstreet Music. Used by permission. *On his* Iowa Waltz. OM20

Mammas, Don't Let Your Babies Grow Up To Be Cowboys

Cowboys ain't easy to love & they're harder to hold
They'd rather give you a song than diamonds or gold
Lone star belt buckles & old faded Levis and each night begins a new day
If you don't understand him & he don't die young he'll probably just ride away

(in 3/4) D - G - / A - D - / - - G - / A - - D

Mammas, don't let your babies grow up to be cowboys
Don't let 'em pick guitars & drive them old trucks let 'em be doctors & lawyers & such
Mammas, don't let your babies grow up to be cowboys
They'll never stay home & they're always alone even with someone they love

D - G - / A - - D :||

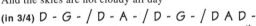

Cowboys like smokey old poolrooms & clear mountain mornings
Little warm puppies & children & girls of the night
Them that don't know him won't like him & them that do, sometimes won't know how to take him
He ain't wrong, he's just different & his pride won't let him do things that make you think he's right

— **Ed & Patsy Bruce**

© 1975 Tree Publishing Co., Inc, 8 Music Square West, Nashville TN 37203. Internat'l copyright secured. Made in USA. All rights reserved. Used by permission. — On Waylon Jennings' Gr H & Waylon & Willy & *rec by Electric Horsemen. In* Ult Country FakeB, Golden Ency of S, Top 100 Movie Themes & Best Fake B Ever. OM21

Men of the Fields

Men of the hills, men of the valley
Men *[women]* of the season & the soil
Strong hearts & hands molding the land
All over earth they toil

C - FC GC / F G C A / Dm G C Am / F Dm G -

Down in the fields, nine in the morning
Day's work three hours done
Care for the cows, care for the corn
Care for the land we need

God moves the sun, noon brings the weary man *[ones]*
Home to his *[their]* table & his grace
Bow on our knees, thankful that these
Days are our very own

Life means our work, home means our children
Love means each other every day
Hope for the best, pray for the rest
All over earth they toil

— **Buffy Sainte-Marie**

© 1965 Gypsy Boy Music. Used by permission. On her Little Wheel Spin & Spin. OM22

The Migrant Song

Up from El Centro & San Bernadino
From Bakersfield, Fresno, Madera, Merced
Salinas & Stockton, up to Sacramento
Santa Rosa & Red Bluff & on back again
One hundred thousand men, women & children
They flow on the highways, the old & the young
In an unending cycle of sowing & reaping
The long valley's labor can never be done

D - G - / D - A - :|| 4x

And see how the land
Yields up her treasure
To man's patient hand

G A D - / / /

Up in the morning an hour before dawning
They're stretching & yawning, rubbing sleep from their eyes
With the last stars still quivering in the morning breeze shivering
The sun is just lighting the easternmost skies
Soon in the big open trucks they will travel
Crammed in together, crowded like cattle
Over pavement, over gravel, over dirt roll the wheels
Out to the orchards, the vineyards, the fields

Soon in the long rows the swift hands are toiling
In the day's growing heat, in the dusty row's boiling
The sun presses down like a hot, heavy hand
At the backs of the laborers working the land
In the shade of the oak trees by the side of the field rows
Dirty & shoeless the young children play
While fathers & mothers, older sisters & brothers
Toil on their knees in the heat of the day

Down from the highway come men in brown uniforms
Questioning, checking & searching & soon
One or two whose papers are not in order
Are gone from the crew in the hot afternoon
When the sun has descended & the long day has ended
It's back to the trucks wiping sweat from their eyes
Tired & weary & covered all over
With fruit juice & brown dust, with sweat & black flies

When there's crops in the field rows & grapes in the vineyards
When the limbs in the orchards bow down to the ground
There's food on the table, there's clothes for the children
There's singing & dancing, there's joy all around
But with skies grey as iron & icy winds whistling
And frost in the field & no work to be found
Thru cold nights they huddle & hunger & struggle
Til spring brings back sweetness & life to the ground

— **Peter Krug**

© Peter Krug. Used by permission. — "I originally wrote this song in a farm labor barracks in Cloverdale, CA, in October 1964 when I was 21 yrs old. The melody was based on a tune I heard on a Spanish language radio station before dawn on the day described in the song. All the sights & actions described actually happened that day, incl the INS raid." — PK. In SO! 21:3 & on Jon Wilcox Stages of My Life & The Time Will Come *(Broadside).* OM23

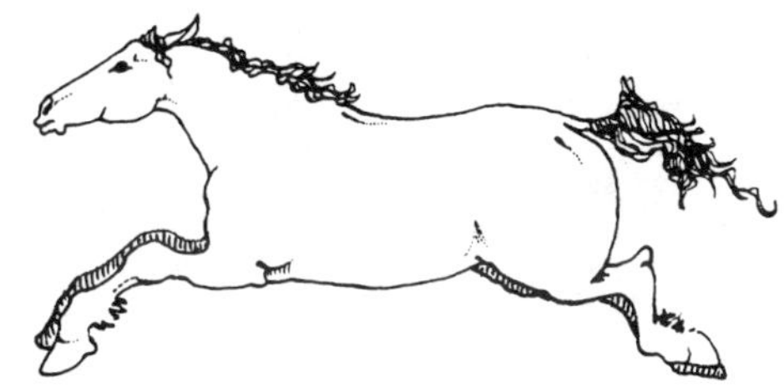

My Sweet Wyoming Home

There's a silence on the prairie that a man *[you just]* can't help but feel
There's a shadow growing longer now a-nipping at my heels
I know that soon that old four-lane that runs beneath my wheels
Will take me **home to my sweet Wyoming home**

C - F - / G - FG C / - G Am - / Dm G C -

I headed down the road last summer with a few old friends of mine
They all hit the money, Lord, I didn't make a dime
The entrance fees they took my dough, the traveling took my time
And I'm headed **home to my ...**

Watch the moon, it's smiling in the sky
And hum a tune, a prairie lullabye
Peaceful wind & old coyote's cry
A song of home, my sweet Wyoming home

C - FEm Dm / G - F C / 1st / G - C -

(bridge) The rounders they all wish you luck when they know you're in a jam
But your money's riding on the bull & he don't give a damn

F - C - / F Am G -

There's the show in all the cities but cities turn your heart to clay
It takes all a man *[that you]* can muster just to try & get away
The songs I'm used to hearing ain't the kind the jukebox plays
And I'm headed **home ...**

And now I've always loved the riding, there ain't nothing quite the same
And another year may bring the luck, the winning of the game
But there's a magpie on a fence rail & he's calling out my name And he calls me **home ...**

— **Bill Staines**

© Folk Legacy Records. Used by permission. — On his Just Play One More *(Folk Legacy) &* Miles *(Mineral River). In his* If I Were A Word & SO! *30:4.* OM24

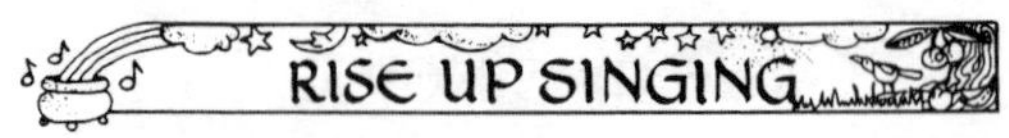

Oats, Peas, Beans and Barley

Oats, peas, beans & barley grow **(2x)**
Do you or I or anyone know
How oats, peas, beans & barley grow?

D - / G A / D - / A D

First the farmer sows the seed
Then he stands & takes his ease
He stamps his foot & claps his hands
And turns around to view the land!

This is a game song; the game & the song were known in 14th c. France & in many other European countries — but not in England. On Raffi Baby Beluga *& in his* Baby Beluga SB *&* 2nd SB. *In* Sing the Good Earth *&* Fireside B of Children's S. OM25

Oklahoma

O-klahoma, where the wind comes sweepin' down the plain
And the wavin' wheat can sure smell sweet
When the wind comes right behind the rain
O-klahoma, every night my honey lamb & I
Sit alone & talk & watch a hawk
Makin' lazy circles in the sky

C - - - G - - - / C - F Fm / C A D G
/ " / " / C G C -

We know we belong to the land
And the land we belong to is grand!
And when we say "Yeeow!
A-yip-i-o-ee-ay!"
We're only sayin' "You're doin' fine, Oklahoma
Oklahoma – OK!"

F - C - / G D G - / C - - -
D - - - / C E Am D / C G C -

— w: Oscar Hammerstein II — m: Richard Rodgers

 — Fr their musical Oklahoma. In Broadway Deluxe SB. OM26

Ol' Texas

I'm going to leave old Texas now
They've no more use for the long-horned cow
They've plowed & fenced my cattle range
And the people there are all so strange

D - - - / A G D - :||

I'll take my horse, I'll take my rope
And I'll hit the trail upon a lope
I'll bid Adios to the Alamo
And I'll turn my head toward Mexico

In Fires B of Am S, SFest *&* Pocketful of S *(WAS).* OM27

Old Chisholm Trail

Well, come along boys & listen to my tale
I'll tell you of my troubles on the old Chisholm Trail
Come a ti yi yippi yappi yay, yappi yay
Come a ti yi yippi yappi yay

D - - - / A7 - D - // / /

Two dollar hoss & a forty dollar saddle
And I'm goin' to punchin' Texas cattle / **Come a ...**

> I can ride any hoss in the wild & woolly West
> I can ride him, I can rope him, I can make him do his best

Old Ben Bolt was a blamed good boss
But he'd go to see the girls on a sore-backed hoss

> Woke up one morn on the Chisholm Trail
> With a horse between my legs & cow by the tail

O it's bacon & beans 'most every day
I'd as soon be a-eatin' prairie hay

> It's cloudy in the west, & it looks like rain
> And my damned old slicker's in the wagon again

It's raining like hell & it's gettin' mighty cold
And those long-horned sons-o'guns are gettin' hard to hold

> I herded & I hollered & I done very well
> Til the boss said "Boys, just let 'em go to hell"

I hunted up my boss to draw my roll
He figgered me out nine dollars in the hole

> Goin' to sell my hoss, goin' to sell my saddle
> Goin' to tell my boss where to go with his cattle

Goin' back to town to draw my money
Goin' back home to see my honey

> No more a cow puncher to sleep at my ease
> Mid the crawlin' of the lice & the bitin' of the fleas

With my knees in the saddle & my seat in the sky
I'll quit punching cows in the sweet by & by

Jesse Chisolm was a half Cherokee trader who started a trading post in Kansas in 1866. The trail itself ran fr West Texas to Abilene, Kansas. 1st appeared in Thorp S of the Cowboys, 1908. *On Spider John Koerner* Nobody Knows the Trouble, *J Warner & J Davis* Oldtime S for Kids *& P LaFarge* Sings of the Cowboys. *In* S of Work & Protest, FiresB of Am S, FSEncy V1, *Lomax* FS of NAm *&* SFest. OM28

Pastures of Plenty

It's a mighty hard row that my poor hands have hoed
My poor feet have traveled a hot dusty road
Out of your dust bowl & westward we rolled
And your desert was hot & your mountain was cold

Em - - - / G - - - / / Em - - -

I've worked in your orchards of peaches & prunes
Slept on the ground in the light of the moon
On the edge of your city you've seen us & then
We come with the dust & we go with the wind

California, Arizona, I make all your crops
And it's north up to Oregon to gather your hops
Dig the beets from your ground, cut the grapes from your vines
To set on your tables your light sparkling wine

Green pastures of plenty from dry desert ground
From the Grand Coulee Dam where the water runs down
Every state in this Union us migrants have been
We work in your fight & we'll fight til we win

Well, it's always we ramble, that river & I
All along your green valley I'll work til I die
My land I'll defend with my life, if it be
'Cause my pastures of plenty must always be free
[These lands I will fight for with all that I can
Til these pastures of plenty are in our own hands]

— Woody Guthrie

 — The tune is Guthrie's skillful reworking of "Pretty Polly". In his SB & on Bound for Glory, Orig Recordings, Hard Trav, Gr S 1940-46, This Land, Bonneville Dam. *On Weavers* Trav On, *H Near & R Gilbert* Lifeline, *D Van Ronk* Somebody Else *&* Just Dave, *& on* Tribute to Woody, pt 1. *In* SO! *7:2 &* Reprints #2, Carry It On *&* Bells of Rhymney. OM29

Pick a Bale o' Cotton

1. Gonna jump down, turn around, pick a bale o'cotton
   Gonna jump down, turn around, to pick a bale a day **(repeat)**

O Lordy *[Julie]*, **pick a bale o'cotton**
O Lordy *[Julie]*, **pick a bale a day (repeat)**

G - - D / G - D G :|| **(4x)**

2. Gonna get on my knees & pick ...
3. Gonna jump, jump, jump down, pick ...
   Gonna jump down, turn around ...
4. Me & my gal gonna pick ...
5. Me & my buddy gonna ...
6. I b'lieve to my soul I can ...
7. Went to Corsicana to ...
8. Gonna pick-a pick-a pick-a pick-a pick a bale o'cotton
   Gonna pick-a pick-a pick-a pick-a pick a bale a day
   Gonna pick-a pick-a pick-a pick-a pick a bale o'cotton
   We're gonna jump down turn around pick a bale a day

— Huddie Ledbetter

TRO © 1936 & renewed 1964 Folkways Music Publishers Inc, NY, NY. Internatl copyright secured. Made in USA. All rights reserved incl pub performance for profit. Used by permission. — Coll & adap by John A. Lomax & Alan Lomax. "A good work song makes the long day seem shorter. In the fields this was sung medium slowly. Leadbelly made a party song out of it by speeding it up & adding guitar" — PS. On Pete Seeger Sings Leadbelly *&* At Carnegie Hall. *On Mike & Peggy Seeger* Am FS for Children *(Rounder), Raffi* Corner Grocery Store *& recs by Bellafonte & Leadbelly. In* SO! *3:1 &* Reprints #2, Am Fav Bal, FiresB of Am S, Negro FS as Sung by Leadbelly *&* FSEncy V2. OM30

Plegaria a un Labrador

Levántate y mira la montaña
De donde viene el viento, el sol y el agua
Tú que manejas el curso de los ríos
Tú que sembrado el vuelo de tu alma

Am Dm - Am / / Am G E Am / /

Levántate y mírate las manos
Para crecer estréchala a tu hermano
Juntos iremos, unidos en la sangre
Hoy es el tiempo que puede ser mañana

Líbranos de aquel que nos domina en la miseria_ _ _
Tráenos tu reino de justicia_e igualdad_ _ _
Sopla como el viento la flor de la quebrada
Limpia como el fuego el cañón de mi fusil

Dmaj7 - - - A - - - / / C G D A / /

Hágase por fin tu voluntad aquá en la tierra
Danos tu fuerza y valor al combatir
Sopla como el viento ... quebrada / Limpia ... fusil

Levántate y mírate las manos
Para crecer estréchala a tu hermano*[a]*
Juntos iremos, unidos en la sangre
¡Ahora y en la hora de nuestra muerte Amén!

— Victor Jara

© 1971 & 1976 Editorial Lagos, Buenos Aires, Argentina. TRO - Essex Music International, Inc, NY, controls all publication rights for the USA & Canada. International copyright secured. Made in USA. All rights reserved incl pub performance for profit. Used by permission. — Written as a plea to Chile's farm laborers to join with urban workers in taking their tools & lives into their own hands. Jara was a leader in the peoples song movement in Chile closely allied with Salvador Allende. Jara was murdered in the brutal military coup overthrowing the elected Allende govt. (Eng. Translation by Herbert Kretzner: "Stand up & see the power of the mountain / Source of the sun, of water & the wild wind / You who can harness the rush of mighty rivers / You who can gather the harvest of your soul // Stand up & see the hands with which you labor / Reach out to hold your brother's hand in your hand / Growing together by ties of earth united / Knowing together the future can be now // Yea, deliver us, deliver us from those who command us / Teach us the strength to take our share of the sun / Blow like the high wind thru wild mountain flowers / Cleansing like flame the barrel of my gun // Give us this day a world where no man is master / Our kingdom come on earth, let our will be done / Blow like the high wind thru ... flowers / Cleansing ... gun // Stand up & see the power of the mountain / Reach out to hold your sister's hand in your hand / Growing together by ties of earth united. / Now & in the hour of our death, amen!") See also "Victor Jara" in CREAT & "It Could Have Been Me" in STRUG. In SO! *23:3. On* Victor Jara *(Monitor), Quilapayun (Rounder), Judy Collins* Bread & Roses, NW Regional Folk Fest V2 *&* Lucha Means Struggle. OM31

Prairie in the Sky

I ride a big blue roan, I carry all I own
In the pouches of my saddle bags with my bedroll tied behind

(in F) C F C F / C F C F -

There's a prairie in the sky, I'll find it by & by
Hills of brown & yellow to make a soul unwind

Let the music take me home to where a heart may roam
Beside me til the day is done & the sun has settled low

Leave the ponies to run free far as the eye can see
I'd ride the range forever to see them once again

Let the wild flying things soar above on their wings
And the stars fill up the night sky & the moon light up the plain

— Mary McCaslin

© 1976 Folklore Music (ASCAP). Used by permission. On her Prairie in the Sky. OM32

Red River Valley

From this valley they say you are going
We will miss your bright eyes & sweet smile
For they say you are taking the sunshine
Which has brightened our pathway a while

E B7 E - / - - B7 - / E E7 A - / B7 - E -

Come & sit by my side if you love me
Do not hasten to bid me adieu
But remember the Red River Valley
And the one who has loved you so true

Won't you think of the valley you're leaving
O how lonely, how sad it will be?
O think of the fond heart you're breaking
And the grief you are causing to me

As you go to your home by the ocean
May you never forget those sweet hours
That we spent in the Red River Valley
And the love we exchanged 'mid the flowers

A popular song that evolved into a folksong. James Kerrigan wrote a sentimental piece "In the Bright Mohawk Valley" in 1896. Pioneers heading west picked up the song, simplified it & changed the locale to the Texas panhandle. In FiresB of FS, SFest, FSEncy V1 *&* Rdrs Dig Fam SB. OM33

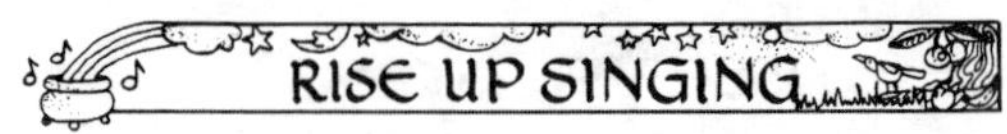

Roll On, Columbia

Roll on, Columbia, roll on (2x)
Your power is turning our darkness to dawn
So roll on, Columbia, roll on!

(in 3/4) G D / - G / G C / D G

Green Douglas firs where the waters cut thru
Down her wild mountains & canyons she flew
Canadian Northwest to the ocean, so blue
Roll on, Columbia, roll on

Other great rivers add power to you
Yakima, Snake & the Klickitat too
Sandy Willamette & Hood River too / **Roll on ...**

Tom Jefferson's vision would not let him rest
An empire he saw in the Pacific Northwest
Sent Lewis & Clark & they did the rest / **Roll ...**

It's there on your banks that we fought many a fight
Sheridan's boys in the blockhouse that night
They saw us in death but never in flight / **Roll ...**

At Bonneville now there are ships in the locks
The waters have risen & cleared all the rocks
Shiploads of plenty will steam past the docks / **So roll ...**

And on up the river is Grand Coulee Dam
The mightiest thing ever built by a man
To run the great factories & water the land / **It's roll ...**

These mighty men labored by day & by night
Matching their strength 'gainst the river's wild flight
Thru rapids & falls they won the hard fight / **Roll on ...**

— w: Woody Guthrie
— m: based on "Goodnight Irene" by Huddie Ledbetter & John Lomax

© 1936 (renewed 1964), 1957 (renewed 1985) & 1963 Ludlow Music, Inc. NY, NY. International copyright secured. Made in USA. All rights reserved including public performance for profit. Used by permission. *— A uniquely creative moment in US history was the decision of the Bonneville Power Admin to hire Woody as a "research asst" in 1940 leading to the creation of a batch of songs. On his* Hard Trav & Gr S, *Pete Seeger* Gazette & Sings Guthrie, *Weavers* Reunion at Carnegie Hall, pt2, & Tribute to Guthrie, pt2. *In* SO! *5:3 &* Reprints *#3, J Lomax* FS of NAm *&* Bells of Rhymney. OM34

So Long It's Been Good to Know Yuh

I've sung this song, but I'll sing it again
Of the place that I lived on the wild, windy plains
In the month called April, the county called Gray
And here's what all of the people there say

(in 3/4) C - G - / / C - F - / C - G C

So long, it's been good to know yuh (3x)
This dusty old dust is a-getting my home
And I've got to be drifting along

C - - - / G - - C / - - F - / C - G - - / - - C -

A dust storm hit, it hit like thunder
It dusted us over & it covered us under
Blocked out the traffic & blocked out the sun
Straight for home all the people did run

The sweethearts sat in the dark & they sparked
They hugged & kissed in that dusty old dark
They sighed & cried, hugged & kissed
Instead of marriage they talked like this: Honey:

I walked down the street to the grocery store
It was crowded with people both rich & both poor
I asked the man how his butter was sold
He said "One pound of butter for two pounds of gold", I said:

Now the telephone rang & it jumped off the wall
That was the preacher a-makin' his call
He said "Kind friend, this may be the end
You've got your last chance of salvation of sin

The churches was jammed & the churches was packed
And that dusty old dust storm blowed so black
The preacher could not read a word of his text
And he folded his specs & he took up collection, said:

— Woody Guthrie

TRO © 1940 (Renewed 1968), 1950 (renewed 1978) & 1963 Folkways Music Publishers, Inc. NY, NY. International copyright secured. All rights reserved incl. public performance for profit. Used by permission. *— aka: "Dusty Old Dust." One of Guthrie's great dustbowl ballads. In his SB & on his* Orig Recording 1940-46, Gr S, Lib. of Cong & We Ain't Down Yet. *On* Tribute to Woody, pt1. *On (& in) Pete Seeger* Am Fav Bal V2 *(FA2320) &* Sings W Guthrie. *On Weavers* On Tour & Gr H *& in their SB. On Jack Elliott* Talking Woody & Sings the S of Guthrie. *In* S Work & Protest, Carry It On, Childrens S for a Friendly Planet. OM35

Someday Soon

There's a young man that I know, his age is 21
He comes from down in southern Colorado
Just out of the service & he's looking for some fun
Someday soon I'm going with him, someday soon

↓G C G / Bm - C D / 1st / Am D G -

My parents cannot stand him cause he rides the rodeo
My father says that he will leave me crying
I would follow him right down the toughest road I know
Someday soon ...

And when he comes to call my pa ain't got a good word to say
Guess it's 'cause he's just as wild in his younger days

D - C G / Em - A D -

So blow you old blue norther, blow my love to me
He's driving in tonight from California
He loves his damned old rodeo as much as he loves me ...

— Ian Tyson

©1963 Warner Bros. Music ASCAP. All rights reserved. Used by permission. *— "Blue Norther" is a cold wind. On J Collins* Who Knows Where the Time Goes & Colors of the Day *& rec by Ian & Sylvia.* OM36

Streets of Laredo (The Cowboy's Lament)

As I walked out in the streets of Laredo
As I walked out in Laredo one day
I spied a poor cowboy wrapped up in white linen
Wrapped up in white linen as cold as the clay

(in 3/4 – capo up) D A D A / / / D Em A D

"I see by your outfit that you are a cowboy"
These words he did say as I boldly stepped by
"Come sit down beside me & hear my sad story
I am shot in the breast & I know I must die

My friends & relations they live in the Nation
They know not where their boy has gone
He first came to Texas & hired to a ranchman
O I'm a young cowboy & I know I've done wrong

It was once in the saddle I used to go dashing
It was once in the saddle I used to go gay
First to the dram-house & then to the card-house
Got shot in the breast & I am dying today

Get six jolly cowboys to carry my coffin
Get six pretty maidens to bear up my pall
Put bunches of roses all over my coffin
Roses to deaden the clods as they fall

O beat the drum slowly & play the fife lowly
Play the dead march as you carry me on
Take me out to the graveyard and throw the sod o'er me
For I'm a young cowboy & I know I've done wrong

Go bring me a cup, a cup of cold water
To cool my parched lips" the cowboy then said
But 'ere I returned the spirit had left him
And gone to its maker: the cowboy was dead

We beat the drum slowly & played the fife lowly
And bitterly wept as we bore him along
For we all loved our comrade so brave, young & handsome
We all loved the cowboy altho' he'd done wrong

— coll, adap & arr by John A. Lomax & Alan Lomax

TRO © 1938 (renewed 1966) Ludlow Music, Inc., NY, NY. International copyright secured. Made in USA. All rights reserved incl. public performance for profit. Used by permission. *— aka: "The Cowboy's Lament." Based on the 18th c. British broadside "The Unfortunate Rake." Some people use bldface as chorus. On Baez* V Early, *Willie Nelson* Country Winners, *P LaFarge* Sings of the Cowboys", *Pete Seeger* W Voices Together We Sing *(FA2452), & Ives* S of Expanding Am, Wayfaring Stranger" & Bals & FS V2. *In Lomax* Cowboy S & FS of NAm, SFest, Am Fav Bal, & FSEncy V1. OM37

Time's a Gettin' Hard

Times a-getting hard, boys, money's getting scarce
If time's don't get no better, boys, gonna leave this place
Take my true love by the hand, lead her through the town
Saying good-bye to ev'ryone, good-bye to ev'ryone

D Em A D / / / /

Take my Bible from the bed, shotgun from the wall
Take Old Sal & hitch her up, the wagon for to haul
Pile the chairs & beds up high, let nothing drag the ground
Sal can pull & we can push, we're bound to leave this town

Made a crop a year ago, it withered to the ground
Tried to get some credit but the banker turned me down
Goin' to Californ-i-ay, where everything is green
Goin' to have the best farm that you have ever seen

— new w & new music arr by Lee Hays

TRO © 1950 & renewed 1977 Folkways Music Publishers Inc., NY, NY. International copyright secured. Made in USA. All rights reserved incl. public performance for profit. Used by permission. *— In* Weavers SB & FSEncy V2. *On Pete Seeger* Time's a Gettin Hard & *Kevin Roth* Somebody Give Me Direction. OM38

Zum Gali Gali

Chant (continues during verses below)
Zum gali gali gali, zum gali gali (2x)

Em - Am Em / etc.

Hechalutz le'man avodah / Avodah le'man hechalutz
Avodah le'man hechalutz / Hechalutz le'man avodah

Hechalutz le'man hab'tulah / Hab'tulah le'man hechalutz
Hab'tulah le'man hechalutz / Hechalutz le'man hab'tulah

— trad. (Israeli)

Eng. trans: The pioneer is for his work, work is for the pioneer. The pioneer is for his friend. On Hebrew Playsongs *(Tara) & in* S Work & Protest, Peoples SB, Joyful Singing & Sing Together Children *(WAS)*, FSEncy V1, FiresB of Fun & Games, & Fav Hebrew S. OM39

For other songs about farming see: "Rosebud in June" (BAL); "Fashioned in the Clay" (CREAT); "Down on the Farm" (ECO); "Old Settler Song" (GOOD); "All the Weary Mothers" & "Faith of Man" (HOPE); "Barnyard Dance" (FUN); "Lovely Agnes" (LOVE); "When I First Came to this Land" (PLAY); "Banks of Marble" & "Waltzing Mathilda" (RICH); "Gone Gonna Rise Again" (TIME); and "Gallo Song" (WORK).

For other songs about the Western US & Canada see: "Wild West Is Where I Want to Be" (FUN); "Spanish Is The Loving Tongue" (LOVE); "Sweet Baby James" (LULL); "They Call the Wind Maria" (OUT); "Goodnight Loving Trail" (TIME); and "Four Strong Winds" (TRAV). For songs about Native Americans see AMERICA.

Ain't Gonna Let Nobody Turn Me Round!

Ain't gonna let nobody **turn me around**
Turn me around! (2x)
Ain't gonna let nobody **turn me around**
I'm gonna keep on a-walkin', keep on a-talkin'
Marchin' down to freedom's land

Dm - / A Dm / - - / A - / - Dm

Ain't gonna let segregation turn me around ...
(addl v:) no police, no jail cell, no killin's, no despair, etc.
(or use someone's name, eg.:) Ain't gonna let Sheriff ...

— the Albany (GA) Movement

In SO! 14:1, Sing For Freedom, Everybody Says Freedom & We Shall Overcome. *On Carawan* S of Strug & Celeb. OJ01

Ain't You Got a Right?

Ain't you got a right (ain't you got a right) **(3x)**
To the tree of life (to the tree of life)?

(D) Em A / D - / Em AG / D -

You can tell all my sisters (you can tell ...)
You can tell all of my brothers (you can tell ...)
You can tell it to the world (tell it to ...)
'Bout **the tree of life** ('bout **the tree** ...)

We come from a distance (come from ...) **(2x)**
And we got a right (& we ...) / **To the tree of life (to** ...)

So rocky was the road (rocky was ...)
And dangerous the journey (& dangerous ...)
But we got a right (but we ...) / **To the** ...

Our lives will be sweeter (yours & mine & our children's)
Lives will be sweeter (lives...)
'Cause we got a right (we got...) / **To the tree of life**

— Guy Carawan (adap Luci Murphy)

© 1965, 1985 Stormking Music Inc. All rights reserved. Used by permission. *— The title is from an old John's Island, SC, chant. On his* S of Strug & Celeb *FF). In SO! 15:6,* Reprints *#10,* & How Can We keep fr Singing. OJ02

Biko

Biko! **(3x)**
Here comes Stephen Biko, walking down the waters
Hey, hey! whatcha gonna do with Biko? Biko! Biko!

A - - / - GA A GA / A - GA GA GA

Waters of fear & hatred, waters of starving babies / **Hey ...**
Come all the way from Capetown to Wilmington, N.C. / **Hey ...**
You can break one human body, I see 10,000 Biko's / **Hey ...**

— Bernice Johnson Reagon

© Songtalk Publishing Co. All rights reserved. Used by permission. *— About the South African Black leader murdered while in police custody. The Rev. Ben Chavez & 7 other leading civil rights leaders were framed, tried & imprisoned on trumped-up charges in Wilmington, NC, but eventually freed after years of international protests. In her* Composition One. *On Sweet Honey in the Rock* Good News *(FF)* & *H Near & R Gilbert* Lifeline. OJ03

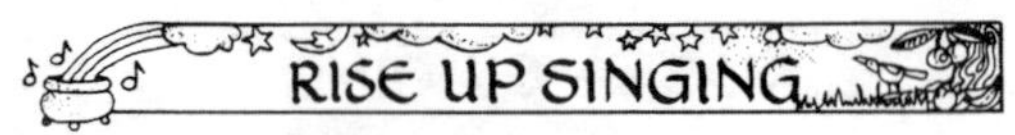

Birmingham Sunday

Come round by my side & I'll sing you a song
I'll sing it so softly, it'll do no one wrong
On Birmingham Sunday the blood ran like wine
And the choirs kept singing of Freedom

(in 3/4)
E - - A / E - D E B7 / E B7 E - / D - E - -

That cold autumn morning no eyes saw the sun
And Addie Mae Collins, her number was "one"
At an old Baptist church there was no need to run
And the choirs kept singing ...
  The clouds they were grey & the autumn winds blew
  And Denise McNair brought the number to "two"
  The falcon of death was a creature they knew / **And the ...**
The church it was crowded, but no one could see
That Cynthia Wesley's dark number was "three"
Her prayers & her feelings would shame you & me ...
  Young Carol Robertson entered the door
  And the number her killers had given was "four"
  She asked for a blessing but asked for no more ...
On Birmingham Sunday a noise shook the ground
And the people all over the earth turned around
For no one recalled a more cowardly sound ...
  The men in the forest they once asked of me
  How many black berries grew in the Blue Sea
  And I asked them right back with a tear in my eye
  How many dark ships in the forest?
The Sunday has come & the Sunday has gone
And I can't do much more than to sing you a song
I'll sing it so softly, it'll do no one wrong
And the choirs kept singing of Freedom

— w: Richard Fariña — m: trad. (English "I Loved a Lass")

© 1964 Vogue Music (c/o The Welk Music Group, Santa Monica CA 90401). International copyright secured. All rights reserved. Used by permission. — Whites who felt threatened by the civil rights movement in Birmingham, AL, exploded a bomb during a Black church service in 1963, killing 4 children. In SO! *15:5,* Reprints *#10,* SFF & ESF. *On Baez* Contemp Bal B & Bright Morning Star Alive *in the USA.* OJ04

Black and White

The ink is black, the page is white
Together we learn to read & write, to read & write
And now a child can understand
This is the law of all the land, all the land
The ink is black ... **(repeat first 2 lines)**

D A D A / D G - A - D - - - / A - D -
A - G A AGA - - / 1st 2 /

Their robes were black, the heads were white
The schoolhouse doors were closed so tight, were closed ...
Nine judges all set down their names
To end the years & years of shame, years of shame / Their ...
  The slate is black, the chalk is white
  The words stand out so clear & bright, so clear & bright
  And now at last we plainly see
  The alphabet of Liberty, Liberty! / The slate ...
A child is black, a child is white
The whole world looks upon the sight, a beautiful sight
For very well the whole world knows
This is the way that freedom grows, freedom ... / A child ...
  The world is black, the world is white
  It turns by day & turns by night, it turns by night
  It turns so each & everyone
  Can take their stations in the sun, in... / The world...

— w: David Arkin — m: Earl Robinson

© 1956 (renewed) Templeton Publishing Co, Inc, a division of Shawnee Press, Inc. International copyright secured. All rights reserved. Used by permission. — In SO! 6:1 & Reprints #1. *On Robinson* Alive & Well *(Aspen) &* Walk in the Sun *(FA2324), E MacColl & Peggy Seeger* Contemp S *(FW8736) & rec by 3 Dog Night.* OJ05

Follow the Drinkin' Gourd

Follow the drinkin' gourd! (2x)
For the old man is a-waitin' for to carry you to freedom
If you follow the drinkin' gourd

Em A Em - / / G D Em Bm / Em Bm Em -

When the sun comes up & the first quail calls / **Follow ...**
For the old man is a-waitin' for to carry you ... / **Follow ...**

Em - - - / / " / " /

The river bank will make a mighty good road
The dead trees will show you the way
Left foot, peg foot, travelin' on ... / **Follow ...**

The river ends between two hills / **Follow ...**
There's another river on the other side ... / **Follow ...**

— trad. (arr. by Lee Hays & the Weavers)

TRO © 1951 & renewed 1979 Folkways Music Publishers Inc., NY, NY. International copyright secured. Made in USA. All rights reserved incl. public performance for profit. Used by permission. — This song is an adaptation of the traditional spiritual "Follow the Risen Lord," which Lee Hays learned from his "Auntie Laura." It includes the type of instructions that were given to runaway slaves for reaching freedom in Canada — above all, of course, to keep heading toward the "drinking gourd" (the Big Dipper). On Sparky Rucker Heroes & Hard Times *(SIF1032), Pete Seeger* I Can See a New Day & 50 Sail, *Weavers* At Carnegie Hall & Gr H, *Bright Morning Star* Arisin, *Kim & Reggie Harris* M & the Undergrd RR *& Shays Rebellion* Daniel Shay's Hwy. *In Weavers* SB, S of the Spirit, Carry It On, Here's to the Women & Childrens S for a Friendly Planet. OJ06

Freedom Is a Constant Struggle

1. **They say that freedom is a <u>constant struggle</u> (3x)**
   O Lord we've struggled so long we must be free, we must be free!

Em - - - / Am - Em - / Em - - - / B7 - - Em

2. **They say that freedom is a** constant seeking ...
3. **They say that freedom is a** long, long journey ...

— Roberta Slavitt

© 1965 Stormking Music Inc. All rights reserved. Used by permission. — In SO! *14:6,* Reprints *#9*, FSEncyV1, SFF & ESF. *On* Broadside Singers. OJ07

Go Down, Moses

When Israel was in Egypt's land – **"Let my people go!"**
Oppressed so hard they could not stand – **"Let my people go!"**

EmB7 Em (2x) / EmB7 EmC EmB7 Em

Go down, Moses, way down in Egypt's land
Tell ol' Pharoah to let my people go!

Em Am EmB7 EmC / Em Bm EmB7 Em

"Thus saith the Lord" bold Moses said – **"Let ...**
If not I'll smite your firstborn dead – **Let ..."**

No more shall they in bondage toil ...
Let them come out with Egypt's spoil ...

We need not always weep & mourn ...
And wear these slavery chains forlorn ...

Your foes shall not forever stand ...
You shall possess your own good land ...

O let us all from bondage flee ...
And soon may all the earth be free ...

— trad. ("Spiritual")

Pub in Relig FS of the Negro *(Hampton Institute, 1874). On Kim & Reggie Harris* Music & the Undergrd RR, *Ralph Stanley* Snow Covered Mound *(Rebel 1613) & Paul Robeson* Carnegie Hall Conc V2 *(Vang). In* S of Work & Protest, Peoples SB, SFest, S of the Spirit, FiresB of FS, Childrens S for a Friendly Planet, SFF & ESF. OJ08

Hallelujah, I'm a Travelin'

Stand up & rejoice, a great day is here
We are fighting Jim Crow & the vict'ry is near
Hallelujah, I'm a travelin', hallelujah ain't it fine?
Hallelujah, I'm a travelin' down freedom's main line!

E - - - / - - B7 - // E - - B7 / E A B7 E

I read in the news, the Supreme Court has said
"Listen here, Mr. Jim Crow, it's time you was dead ...

The judges declared in Washington town
"You white folks must take that old Jim Crow sign down" ...

I'm paying my fare on the Greyhound Bus line
I'm riding the front seat to Nashville this time ...

Columbia's the gem of the ocean they say
We're fighting Jim Crow in Columbia today ...

I hate Jim Crow & Jim Crow hates me
And that's why I'm fighting for my liberty ...

— w: anon. (4th v. James Foreman ca. 1960)

— m: "Hallelujah, I'm a Bum" (in turn adap fr an old hymn)

© 1947 Sing Out Corp. All rights reserved. — Written by a southern Black farmer, who had to remain anonymous during the freedom struggle & trials in Columbia, TN, 1946. Orig pub in the Peoples Songs *(*Sing Out!*'s predecessor in the late '40s). In* Peoples SB, Hootenany SB, SFF & ESF. *For tune sources see RICH.* OJ09

Harriet Tubman

One night I dreamed I was in slavery
'Bout 1850 was the time
Sorrow was the only sign
Nothing about to ease my mind
Out of the night appeared a lady
Leading a distant pilgrim band
"First Mate!" she cried pointing her hand
"Make room aboard for this young woman"

Em - - - / C - CD Em / G - - B7 / 2nd /

Come on up, I got a life line
Come on up to this train of mine (repeat 1st two lines)
She said her name was Harriet Tubman
And she drove for the Underground Railroad

/ " / " :|| D - C - / G - D - - Em - -

Hundreds of miles we traveled onward
Gathering slaves from town to town
Seeking every lost & found
Setting those free that once were bound
Somehow my heart was growing weaker
I fell by the wayside sinking sand
Firmly did this lady stand
Lifted me up & took my hand

Then I awoke, no more I faltered
Finding new strength in paths we're shown
Sisters & brothers fleeing their homes
Their history, their people, all they've known
And they are fleeing their homes in Guatemala
Chile, Brazil, El Salvador
Fleeing from the prisons & war
Thru the night & thru Mexico to our door
Will we sing come on up ...?

— Walter Robinson (new v. John McCutcheon)

© 1980 Shawnee Press, Inc. International copyright secured. All rights reserved. Used by permission. — On Bright Morning Star Arisin, *J McCutcheon* Gonna Rise Again *(Rounder), H Near & R Gilbert* Lifeline *(Redwood), Kim & Reggie Harris* Music & the Undergrd RR, *Jasmine* Wild Strings *& Kate Taylor (Columbia). In SO! 30:2,* Here's to the Women, Childrens S for a Friendly Planet *and in/on* Carry It On. OJ10

Hold On (Keep Your Eyes on the Prize)

Paul & Silas were bound in jail
Had no money for to go their bail
Keep your eyes on the prize, hold on

Dm - / DmC Dm / - DmC DmC Dm /

Hold on, hold on!
Keep your eyes on the prize, hold on!

C - Dm - / " /

Paul & Silas began to shout
The jail doors opened & they walked out / **Keep ...**

The only thing that we did wrong
Was stayin' in the wilderness too long ...

The only thing that we did right
Was the day we begun to fight ...

Ain't but one chain that we can stand
That's the chain of a hand in a hand ...

Freedom's name is mighty sweet
Black & white are gonna meet ...

We've fought jail & violence too
And God's love has seen us thru ...

Got my hand on the freedom plow
Wouldn't take nothin' for my journey now ...

— Alice Wine

Orig "Keep your hand on the plow ..." On Odetta The Essential *&* At Carnegie Hall *& Pete Seeger* Sing Out w/Pete *&* Wimoweh. *In* We Shall Overcome, S of the Spirit, SFF & ESF. OJ11

I'm on My Way

I'm on my way (I'm ...) to the freedom land (to ...) **(3x)**
I'm on my way, Great God, I'm on my way

D - A - / - - D - / - D7 G - / D A D -

I asked my sister to go with me **(3x)** / **I'm on my way ...**
If she says no, I'll go anyhow ...
I asked my boss to let me go ...
If he says no, I'll go anyhow ...
If you can't go, don't hinder me ...
If you won't go, let your children go ...
I'm on my way & I won't turn back ...

In Bells of Rhymney, FSEncyV2, S That Changed the World, People's SB, SFF & ESF. *On Pete Seeger* We Shall Overcome, Sing Out w/Pete, Winoweh & Sampler, *Arlington St Women's Caucus* Honor Thy Womanself *& Odetta* Bals & Blues. OJ12

FREEDOM

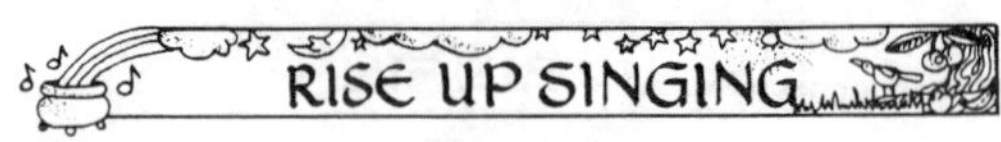

If Rosa Parks Can Go to Jail

If Rosa Parks **can go to jail, then I can do it too (2x)**
Please everybody send my mail care of the D.C. City Jail
If Rosa Parks can go to jail, then I can do it too

C A7 DG C / - A7 D G / C C7 F D7 / 1st

(Other v: substitute) Dolores Huertes, Mother Jones, etc.

— **Peter & Steve Jones**

© 1984 Peter & Steve Jones. Used by permission. — A 43-yr-old Black woman, Rosa Parks, sparked the great Birmingham bus boycott, a pivotal event in the freedom movement, when she refused to go back to the segregated Black section at the rear of the bus. Dolores Huertes is a leader of the United Farmworkers Union. Mother Jones was an organizer for the miners union. On their Clouds. OJ13

If You Miss Me from the Back of the Bus

If you miss me from the back of the bus
And you can't find me nowhere
Come on up to the front of the bus
I'll be ridin' up there **(3x)**
Come on up to the front of the bus
I'll be ridin' up there

D A / - D / G D / D A D :||

If you miss me from Jackson State
And you can't find me nowhere
Come on over to Ole Miss
I'll be studyin' over there **(3x)** / Come on over ...

If you miss me from the cotton fields / **And you can't ...**
Come on down to the court house
I'll be votin' right there ...

If you miss me from Thrifty Drug Store / **And ...**
Come on over to Woolworth's
'Cause I'll be sittin' in there ...

If you miss me from the picket line / **And ...**
Come on down to the jailhouse
I'll be roomin' down there ...

If you miss me from the Mississippi River / **And ...**
Come on down to the municipal plunge
'Cause I'll be swimmin' in there ...

If you miss me from the front of the bus / **And ...**
Come on up to the driver's seat
I'll be drivin' up there ...

— **w: Charles Neblett (& others)**
— **m: trad ("O Mary Don't You Weep")**

© 1962 Sanga Music Inc. All rights reserved. Used by permission. — On Pete Seeger We Shall Overcome. *In* Peoples SB, We Shall Overcome, SFF, *&* ESF. OJ14

It Isn't Nice

It isn't nice to block the doorway
It isn't nice to go to jail
There are nicer ways to do it
But the nice ways always fail
It isn't nice, it isn't nice
You told us once, you told us twice
But if that is Freedom's price
We don't mind (no, no, no!)

I: G - / D - :|| G Em / Am D :|| GC GD / G -
II: C Am / F G :|| 3x F G * / C Am F G

(* repeat 2x on last verse)

It isn't nice to carry banners
Or to sit in on the floor
Or to shout our cry of Freedom
At the hotel or the store
It isn't nice, it isn't nice
You told us once, you told us twice / **But if that ...**

61 have tried negotiations
And three-person picket lines
Mr. Charlie didn't see us
And he might as well be blind
Now our new ways aren't *[so]* nice
When we deal with men of ice / **But if ...**

How about those years of lynchings
And the shot in Evers' back?
Did you say it wasn't proper
Did you stand out on the track?
You were quiet just like mice
Now you say *[that]* we aren't nice / **But if ...**

It isn't nice to block the doorway
It isn't nice to go to jail
There are nicer ways to do it
But the nice ways always fail
It isn't nice, it isn't nice
You told us once, you told us twice
But thanks *[Well thank you buddy]* for your advice
'Cause if that is Freedom's price ...

— **Malvina Reynolds (2nd m setting: Barbara Dane & Judy Collins)**

© 1964 Schroder Music (ASCAP) Berkeley CA 94704. Used by permission. — In her SB & on Malvina Reynolds *(CFS 5100), &* Sings the Truth. *In* SO! *14:6,* Reprints *#9,* S That Changed the World, SFF, *&* ESF. *On* Judy Collins *& Jackie Washington* At Club 47. OJ15

John Brown's Body

1. John Brown's body lies a-mouldrin' in the grave **(3x)**
   But his soul goes marchin' on

Glory, glory hallelujah (3x)
His soul goes marchin' on

G - - - / C - G - / - - B7 Em / C D G - :||

2. John Brown died to put an end to slavery **(3x) / But his ...**
3. He captured Harper's Ferry with his 19 men so true
   He frightened Old Virginny til she trembled thru & thru
   They hung him for a traitor, they themselves the traitor crew
   But his ...
4. The stars above in heaven are looking kindly down **(3x)**
   On the grave of old John Brown

— **trad. (US)**

The popular Civil War song "Battle Hymn of the Republic" was set to this tune. John Brown was a deeply religious abolitionist leader from Kansas who came to Virginia to distribute the arms from the arsenal at Harper's Ferry to slaves in the area. The plan was aborted & Brown was hung for treason. In SO! *36:3,* S of Work & Protest, Am Fav Bals, FSEncyV2, *&* People's SB. *On Pete Seeger* Dangerous Songs *& his* Am Fav Bal V3 *(Folkways 2322) &* S of the Civil War *(FH5717). On Burl Ives* S of North & South *& on* Essential *Paul Robeson (VSD 57/58).* OJ16

Lift Every Voice and Sing!

Lift ev'ry voice & sing, til earth & heaven ring
Ring with the harmonies of liberty
Let our rejoicing rise, high as the list'ning skies
Let it resound loud as the rolling sea

(capo up) CE Am AmE Am / DmE F C G
CE A7 DmE F / C G C -

Sing a song full of the faith that the dark past has taught us
Sing a song full of the hope that the present has brought us
Facing the rising sun of our new day begun
Let us march on til victory is won

C Am - CG / C A♭ - C G / **3rd + 4th as above** /

Stony the road we trod, bitter the chast'ning rod
Felt in the days when hope unborn had died
Yet with a steady beat, have not our weary feet
Come to the place for which our fathers sighed?

We have come over a way that with tears has been watered
We have come, treading our path thru the blood of the slaughtered
Out of the gloomy past til now we stand at last
Where the white gleam of our bright star is cast

God of our weary years, God of our silent tears
Thou who hast brought us thus far on our way
Thou who hast by thy might led us into the light
Keep us forever in the path, we pray
    Lest our feet stray from the places, our God, where we met thee
    Lest our hearts, drunk with the wine of the world, we forget thee
    Shadowed beneath thy hand may we forever stand
    True to our God, true to our native land

Let us keep onward still, keep our resolve until
We achieve brotherhood *[unity]* for all mankind *[womankind]*
Look to the rising sun, new work each day is begun
Daily we strive til we true freedom find
    Save our hope that we so long & so dearly did cherish
    Lest our hearts weary with cruel disillusion should perish
    Stretch forth a loving hand, you who in power stand
    Lose not our faith, lose not our native land

— w: James Weldon Johnson (v.4 Henrietta McKee)

— m: J. Rosamund Johnson

 — aka: "The Black National Anthem." In many hymnals, How Can We Keep Fr Singing, Peoples SB *&* Carry It On. OJ17

Man Come into Egypt

There is a man come into Egypt & Moses is his name
When he saw the grief upon us in his heart there burned a flame
    In his heart there burned a flame, o Lord, in his heart ...
    When he saw the grief upon us in his heart ... flame

Am D FE AmA7 / Dm - DmF CE
AmD GE AmF E / Am D FE Am

There is a man come into Egypt, his eyes are full of light
Like the sun come up in Egypt, come to drive away the night
    Come to drive away ... **(2x)** / Like the sun ...

There is a man come into Egypt, he's come for you & me
On his lips a word is singing & the word is liberty...

There is a man come into Egypt to stir the souls of men
We will follow him to freedom, never wear those chains again...

— Fred Hellerman & Fran Minkoff

 On Peter Paul & Mary Moving. OJ18

Michael Row the Boat Ashore

Michael row the boat ashore, hallelujah (2x)

C - F C / Em Dm CG C

1. Sister help to trim the sail, **hallelujah (2x)**
2. River Jordan is chilly & cold ...
   Chills the body but not the soul ...
3. Jordan's river is deep & wide ...
   Milk & honey *[Get my freedom]* on the other side ...
4. Michael's boat is a music boat ...
   If you stop singing, then it can't float ...

— trad. ("Spiritual")

Michael is the archangel. In Slave S of the US *(1867),* SO! *6:1,* Reprints #1, FSEncyV2, Am Fav Bals, S of the Spirit, *&* ESF. *On Pete Seeger* With Voices Together We Sing *(FA2452),* Sing Out w/ & Now *& Weavers* Gr H. OJ19

No Easy Walk to Freedom

Brother Martin was walkin' with me
And ev'ry step I heard liberty
Tho' he's fallen, come a million behind
Glory hallelujah, gonna make it this time

(in C, capo up) C E7 / Am E7 / F CA / D7 G

No easy walk to freedom (2x)
Keep on walkin' & you shall be free
That's how we're gonna make history
(last time add:) You & me!

C E7 / Am C7 / F CA / D7 G / last cho add: CF C

Cross the ocean, blood runnin' warm
I feel it comin' now, a thunderin' storm
Just like we lived it, you know that it's true
Nelson Mandela, now we're walkin' with you

In our land not so long ago
We lived the struggle & that's how we know
Slav'ry abolished, comin' freedom's call
Keep on walkin' & apartheid will fall

Bread for the body there's got to be
But the soul will die without liberty
Pray for the day when the struggle is past
Freedom for all, free at last, free at last!

— Peter Yarrow & Margie Tabankin

 Nelson Mandela, the leader of the African National Congress, was a political prisoner in South African prisons for decades. On Peter, Paul & Mary No Easy Walk *(Gold Castle) & in* SO! *32:4.* OJ20

No More Auction Block

1. No more auction block for me, **no more, no more**
   No more auction block for me, **many thousand gone**

DG D - A / DG DBm EmA D

2. No more driver's lash for me ...
3. No more pint of salt for me ...

— trad. ("Spiritual")

aka: "Many Thousand Gone." On Kim & Reggie Harris Music & the Undergrd RR, *Phil Ochs* At Carnegie Hall *& Odetta* At Carnegie Hall *& rec by Paul Robeson. On* Songs of the Working People *(FF 483) by Pete Seeger, Earl Robinson, Odetta, Ronnie Gilbert, Tommy Makem & others. In* SO! *24:6, Lomax* FS of NAm *&* Wade in the Water, S of Work & Protest, FiresB of FS, Treasury of FS, Children's S for a Friendly Planet *&* FS NAm Sings. OJ21

O Freedom

O freedom, o freedom
O freedom **over me!**
And before I'd be a slave I'll be buried in my grave
And go home to my Lord & be free

D - A D / - - A - / D D7 G - / D A D -

No more killin's **(3x) over me ...**
No more fear ...
No more hunger ...
There'll be joy ...
There'll be singing ...
There'll be peace ...

— trad. (adapted by SNCC)

On Odetta & on her Bals & Blues, *Baez* Recently, *Pete Seeger* We Shall Overcome *& Sparky Rucker* Bound to Sing the Blues. *In* SO! *36:1,* S of Work & Protest, People's SB, S of the Spirit, Carry It On, Children's S for a Friendly Planet, SFF, *&* ESF. OJ22

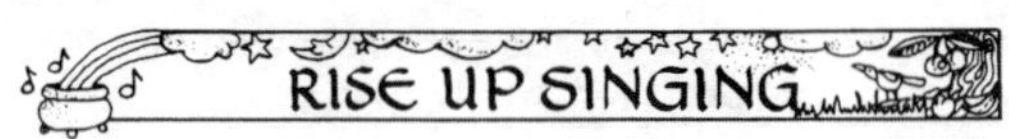

O Mary Don't You Weep

If I could I surely would
Stand on the rock where Moses stood
Pharoah's army got drownded
O Mary don't you weep

D A / - D / G D / DA D

O Mary don't you weep don't you mourn (2x)
Pharoah's army got drownded / O Mary don't you weep!

Moses stood on the Red Sea Shore
Smotin' the water with a two by four / **Pharoah's army ...**

The Lord told Moses what to do
To lead those Hebrew children thru ...

God gave Noah the rainbow sign
No more water but fire next time ...

Mary wore three links of chain
Every link was Freedom's name ...

When I get to Heaven, gonna sing & shout
Nobody up there to put me out! ...

One of these mornings, it won't be long
You're gonna call my name, but I'll be gone ...

One of these days 'bout 12 o'clock
This old world's gonna reel & rock ...

One of these days in the middle of the night
People gonna rise & set things right ...

Fr the book of Exodus. On Pete Seeger Am Fav Bal V3 *(FA2322) & his* Sing Out w/, *& Mississippi John Hurt* Worried Blues. *In* Am Fav Ballads, People's SB, S of Spirit, FSEncy V2, & SFF. **OJ23**

Rivers of Babylon

By the rivers of Babylon, there we sat down
And there we wept when we remember Zion
There the wicked carry us away captivity,
require of us a song
How can we sing King Alfa's *[the Lord's]* song
in a strange land?

D - - - / A - D - / - - G D / - - A D

(bridge) Let the words of my mouth & the meditation of my heart
Be acceptable in thy sight over I *[here tonight]*

D A D A / D A D -

— Brent Dowe & Trevor McNaughton

 — aka: "By the ..." Fr Psalm 137. Orig recording by the Reggae gp The Melodians. *Also on Jimmy Cliff* The Harder They Come, *Sweet Honey in the Rock* Feel Something Drawing Me On *(FF 375), Delaware Water Gap* Fr the Rivers of Babylon *& Linda Ronstadt* Hasten Down the Wind. *In* SO! *23:6* & Worship in Song: A Hymnal for Friends. **OJ24**

This Little Light

This little light of mine, **I'm gonna let it shine (3x)**
Let it shine, let it shine, let it shine!

D - - - / G - - D / - - F♯ Bm / D A DG D

All around the town, **I'm gonna let it shine ...**
Everywhere that I may go ...
In my daily work ...
For the poor & hungry folk ...
Free of fear & hatred ...
Trustin' in the Lord ...
Building a new world ...
Put it under a bushel – No! ...
Ain't nobody gonna "whoof" it out ...

(longer verses with different melody: can be used as "bridges")
On Monday He gave me the gift of love
On Tuesday peace came from above
On Wednesday told me to have more faith
On Thursday gave me a little more grace
On Friday told me to watch & pray
On Saturday told me what to say
On Sunday gave me power divine
Just to let my little light shine

D - / G - / D - / E A / D - / G7 - / D B7 / EA D

The light that shines is the light of love
Lights the darkness from above
It shines on me & it shines on you
Shows what the power of love can do
I'm gonna shine my light both far & near
I'm gonna shine my light both bright & clear
If there's a dark corner in this land
I'm gonna let my little light shine!

Some say "It's dark, we cannot see"
But love lights up the world for me
Some say "Turn around & just go hide"
But we have the power to change the tide
Some call life a sad old story
But we see a world that's bound for glory
The real power is yours & mine
So let your little light shine!

— trad. ("gospel song")

Guy Carawan, Pete Seeger, Frank Hamilton, Joe Glazer & others helped create the longer verses. aka: "Let My Little Light Shine." In SO! *5:2* & Reprints #2 & Bells of Rhymney, Children's S for a Friendly Planet, FSEncyV2, We Shall Overcome, Hootenany SB, SFF & ESF. *On Odetta* Sings FS, *Carawan* My Rhinoceros *(GW1023) & Rosenshonz* Rock & Roll Teddybear. *On Raffi* Rise & Shine *& in his 2nd SB.* **OJ25**

Wade in the Water

Wade in the water, wade in the water, children
Wade in the water, God's gonna trouble the water!

Dm - - - / - - - ADm **verse:** ||: Dm - / - ADm :||

1. **Who are those children there dressed in** red?
   God's gonna trouble the waters
   Must be the children that Moses led / **God's ...**
2. white / Must be the people getting ready for the fight
3. blue / Must be the people gonna see this thru
4. black / Must be the hypocrites turning back
5. *He spoke & divided the sea in 2 / **God's gonna ...***
   *Allowing all his people to pass on thru / **God's ...***
6. *He spoke & the water flowed back again ...*
   And drowned the oppressors pursuing them ...
7. *The enemy's great but my Captain's strong ...*
   I'm marchin' to the City & the road ain't long ...

— trad. ("Spiritual" — new v. Paul Ashton)

New v. *On Carter Fam* Their Last Recording. *In* SO! *2:3,* Lift Every Voice, FSEncyV2, *Lomax* FS of NAm, Hootenany SB, 1004 FS, & SFF. **OJ26**

We Shall Overcome

We shall overcome, we shall overcome
We shall overcome some day
O deep in my heart, I do believe
We shall overcome some day!

C F C - **(2x)** / C FG Am D G D G -
C F C - F G Am - / C F C G C F C -

We are not afraid **(3x)** today! ...
We shall stand together **(3x)** someday ...
The truth will make us free ...
The Lord will see us thru ...
We shall be like Him ...
We shall live in peace ...

The whole wide world around ...
We are not alone ...
We'll walk hand in hand ...
Black & white together ...
We shall all be free ...

— **musical & lyrical adap. by Zilphia Horton, Frank Hamilton, Guy Carawan & Pete Seeger. Inspired by African American Gospel Singing, members of the Food & Tobacco Workers Union, Charleston, SC & the southern Civil Rights Movement.**

 — Taught by two Black union members to Horton in Charleston in 1946. Modified by Freedom riders & sit-in demonstrators in the early '60s. One of many songs that's gone from being gospel to union to civil rights to anti-war in thrust. In SO! *11:2 &* Reprints #6, Bells of Rhymney, S of Work & Protest, Carry It On, Children's S for a Friendly Planet, How Can We Keep Fr Singing, SFF, & ESF. *On Pete Seeger* We Shall Overcome, *Joan Baez* In Conc & *Guy Carawan* S of Strug & Celeb. OJ27

Woke Up This Morning

1. Woke up this morning with my mind (my mind it was) stayed on freedom **(3x)**

Hallelu, hallelu, hallelujah!

G - - - / C - - G / - - GB7 Em / G D C G

(bridge) Walk **(6x)** with my mind on freedom **(repeat)**
Ah – walk walk walk walk

G - - G7 / C7 - G - / D7 C7 G -

2. Ain't no harm to keep your mind (in keepin' it) stayed on freedom **(3x)** / **Hallelu ...**
3. Walkin' & talkin' with my mind ...
4. Singin' & prayin' with my mind ...

— **Rev. Osby of Aurora, IL (addl lyrics Robert Zellner)**

 — In SO! 12:5 & Reprints #6. In SFF, We Shall Overcome, S That Changed the World, FSEncyV1. *On* Trav On w/the Weavers *& their* Reunion 1963. OJ28

Sing Out! has reissued the only two exhaustive collections of Southern U.S. Freedom Movement songs, namely Guy & Candie Carawan's We Shall Overcome! *and their* Freedom Is A Constant Struggle. *These two books have been combined in a single collection entitled* Sing For Freedom: Songs Of The Civil Rights Movement *(available from Sing Out! or at finer book stores). In addition, Norton has published Pete Seeger & Bob Reiser's new book* Everybody Says Freedom *– which includes several dozen freedom songs along with first-hand accounts by participants in the movement. Many of the songs in this chapter are also on* I'm Gonna Let it Shine *(Round River Records).*

A majority of these songs are originally derived from Black Spirituals, some having been used at an earlier stage as union songs. Many of the other songs in SPIRITUALS have also been used by the Freedom Movement (eg. "Free at Last," "Over My Head," "I'm Gonna Do What the Spirit Says").

Other songs in the book that relate to racism & Afro-American experiences include: "Bourgeois Blues," "Dancing in the Street" (written at the time of the 1968 urban riots), "Heaven Help Us All" & "I Live in a City" (CITY); "Carry It On" (PEACE); "Asikatali," "Once to Every Man & Nation" (STRUG); "Because All Men Are Brothers," "Color Song" & "Same Boat Now" (UNITY); "Lucretia Mott" (WOMEN); & "We Shall Not Be Moved" (WORK). There is a special index of prison songs at the end of HARD TIMES & BLUES.

All the Good People

This is a song for all the good people
All the good people who touched up my life
This is a song for all the good people
People I'm thankin' my stars for tonight

A E D A / D A D E / A E D A / D A D A

This is a song for all the good women
Who knew what I needed was somethin' they had
Food on the table, a heart that was able
Able to keep me just this side of sad

This is a song for all the good fellows
Who shared up my time, some good & some bad
We drank in the kitchen & held no competition
Each knowing the other was a good friend to have

This is a song for all the good people
All the good people that touched up my life
Some helped in small ways, some helped in hallways
And some always told me you're doin' all right

This is a song I sing for my lady
For my lady that puts up with me
My ramblin' & roamin', my late night come homin'
She is the sunshine that flows down on me

This is a verse for the pickers & singers
Whose tunes & whose voices have blended with mine
On backsteps & stages, for love & for wages
It's one kind of givin' & some kinda fine

— **Ken Hicks**

 "The last verse was a gift from Folk Legacy singer/songwriter Joan Sprung. It's very natural for the singers to modify & add to 'All the Good People' & if it winds up being the longest song ever written that will be just dandy fine with me!" — KH. In SO! *32:3. On* Fred Holstein *(Holstein 001).* OK01

Bring Me a Rose

Bring me a rose in the wintertime **when it's hard to find**
Bring me a rose in the wintertime, **I've got** roses **on my mind**
A rose **is sweet most anytime & yet**
Bring me a rose in the wintertime: **it's so easy to forget**

C - - F / C - F G / C - - F / C - F G C

2. Bring me a friend when I'm far from home **when it's ...**
   Bring me a friend ... **I've got** friendship **on my mind**
   A friend **is sweet most anytime & yet**
   Bring me a friend when I'm far from home: **it's so easy ...**
3. Bring me a smile when I'm all alone ... / I've got smiles ...
4. Bring me a kiss when my child is grown ... / kisses
5. Bring me some love in my autumn years ... / loving
6. Bring me some peace when there's talk of war ... / peace

— **Ernie Sheldon**

 On Joe Wise Sweet Water *& rec by the Limelighters.* OK02

Fire and Rain

Just yesterday morning they let me know you were gone
Suzanne, the plans they made put an end to you
I walked out this morning & I wrote down this song
I just can't remember who to send it to

C Dm F C / - Dm F - :||

I've seen fire & I've seen rain
I've seen sunny days that I thought would never end
I've seen lonely times when I could not find a friend
But I always thought I'd see you again

F G C - / / / F - C -

Won't you look down upon me, Jesus, you've got to help me make a stand
You've just got to see me thru another day
My body's aching & my time is at hand
And I just won't make it any other way

Now I'm walking my mind to an easy time, my back turned towards the sun
Lord knows when the cold wind blows, it'll turn your head around
There's hours of time in the telephone line to talk about things to come
Sweet dreams & flying machines in pieces on the ground

— **James Taylor**

 — On his Sweet Baby James & Gr H, *John Denver* Poems, Prayers & Promises, *Cher* Gypsy Tramps *& rec by Richie Havens. In* Best of the '70s & FM Gr H. OK03

Getting to Know You

(intro) It's a very ancient saying but a true & honest thought
That if you become a teacher, by your pupils you'll be taught
As a teacher I've been learning (you'll forgive me if I boast)
And I've now become an expert on the subject I like most
(spoken:) Getting to know you

G D Em - / Bm - Em G7 /
C Cmaj7 G E7 / Em A7 Am C / D7 -

Getting to know you, getting to know all about you
Getting to like you, getting to hope you like me
Getting to know you, putting it my way, but nicely
You are precisely my cup of tea

G - Am D7 / - - G - / - - C - / A7 - Am D7

Getting to know you, getting to feel free & easy
When I am with you, getting to know what to say
Haven't you noticed? Suddenly I'm bright & breezy, because of
All the beautiful & new things I'm learning about you
Day by day

/ " / " / C D7 G C /
G AmD Em A7 / Am D G -

— **w: Oscar Hammerstein II** — **m: Richard Rodgers**

 — Fr their musical The King & I. *In* Readers Dig Festival of Pop S *&* Broadway Sbs. OK04

The Hug

Dan Murrow is a mighty friendly man
He's big & round like a bear
He hugs his friends & his friends hug him
Anytime, anywhere
His patients would come for therapy
To drive their blues away
And sooner or later they'd feel alot better
'Cause this is what he'd say:

C - / FGC / - - / D G / C Em / Dm C / - F / G C

I want a hug when we say hello
I want a hug when it's time to go
I want a hug 'cause I want you to know
I'm awfully fond of you
I want a hug, what a wonderful feeling
I want a hug to feel you squeezing
I want a hug, it certainly feels
Like the natural thing to do

C - / F - / G - / - C :||

But when the head of the hospital heard about it
He got all annoyed
'Cause hugging is sexual sublimation
According to Dr. Freud
You can beat 'em down, you can hide 'em away
You can keep 'em quiet with drugs
You can strap 'em & zap 'em with electroshock
But you better not give 'em a hug

So the boss says "Dan, clean out your desk
Your conduct is lax & lewd
Any deviation from the standard medical
Practice can get us sued"
Dan don't feel too bad for himself
He's really kind of proud
But he's sorry for the people who are locked away
Where hugging ain't allowed

— **Fred Small**

 — In his Breaking Fr The Line. *On his* Love's Gonna Carry Us *& Peter Alsop* Fan Club Favs. OK05

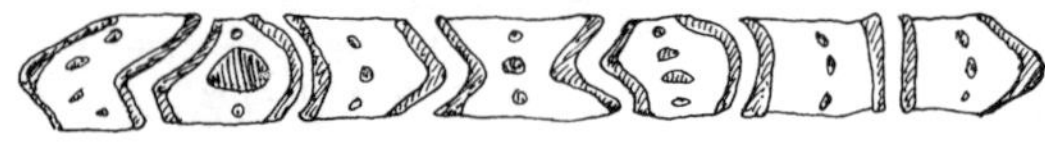

Hymn Song

I believe if I lived my life again
I'd still be here with you (repeat)

D G D - / A - D - :||

You know I think if Lady Luck was blind
That old sun would never shine
You know I think if Death really held a knife
We'd all be beggars of life

Sometimes I wish that I could close my eyes
To some things I don't want to see
Still I believe if you lived your life again
You'd still be here with me

I'll never see the ending of my mind
Everything will have a time
Why should I ask for things that I don't need
Or pretty lies to hide my greed?

— **Utah Phillips**

 — In his Starlight on the Rails. On E Trickett Gently Down the Streams of Time, *J Ringer* Waitin for the Hard Times. OK06

It's All Right to Cry

It's all right to cry, crying gets the sad out of you
It's all right to cry, it might make you feel better

C F - G / C F G C

Raindrops from your eyes, taking all the mad out of you
It's just fine to cry, it might make you feel better

(bridge)
It's all right to feel things tho' the feelings may be strange
Feeling are such real things & they change & change & change
Sad & grumpy, down in the dumpy, snuggly huggly, mean & ugly
Slippy slappy, hippy happy, change & change & change!

F C F C / F C FDm G / C - F - / G - - C

It's all right to know, feelings come & feelings go
And it's all right to cry, it might make you feel better

— **Carol Hall**

© Free to Be Foundation, Inc. in cooperation with the Ms. Foundation for Women, Inc. Used by permission. On Free To Be You & Me. OK07

Lean on Me

Sometime, in our lives
We all have pain, we all have sorrow
But, if we are wise
We know there's always tomorrow

D (↑) G (↓) / D (↑) A - - -/ 1st /D - - - A - D -

Lean on me, when you're not strong
And I'll be your friend, I'll help you carry on
For, it won't be long
Til I'm gonna need somebody to lean on

Please swallow your pride
If I have things you need to borrow
For no one can fill
Those of your needs that you won't let show

(bridge) You just call on me brother when you need a hand
We all need somebody to lean on
I might just have a problem that you'll understand
We all need somebody to lean on

D - - - - - - - / - - - - A - D - :||

If there is a load
You have to bear, that you can't carry
I'm right up the road
I'll share your load if you just call me

D (↑) = D - - EmF#m G (↓) = G - - F#mEm

— **Bill Withers**

© 1972 Interior Music (BMI). All rights reserved. International copyright secured. Used by permission. — On Club Nouveau Life Love & Pain. *In* Platinum '87. OK08

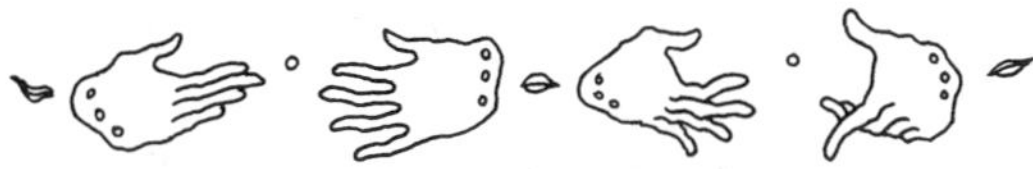

Long Time Friends

Well I'm looking for some long time friends
I'm looking for some long time friends
Life's a long & twisted road, many curves & unseen bends
So I'm looking for some long time friends

D A D - / - G A - / G D G A / D A D -

Good friends tend to slip out of your reach
If you walk too tall & keep too straight a path
With your eyes so far ahead that you can't see by your side
You'll never see your long time friends

There are women that I hold close to my heart
And men I hope will always be part of my life
You've got to know each heart is real & each life can touch your own
And this world will be your long time home

It's a wide world with many ways to live
Many ways to love & ways to give
I'm not so sure I want to find just one soul to blend with mine
So I'm looking for some long time friends

— **Cathy Winter**

© 1975 Cathy Winter. Used by permission. With Betsy Rose on Sweet Sorcery *(Origami) & their* As Strong As Anyone Can Be *(GentleWind). On Ginni Clemmens* Long Time ... *(OpenDoor). In* All Our Lives. OK09

Moon River

Moon river, wider than a mile
I'm crossing you in style some day
Old dream-maker, you heart breaker
Wherever you're goin', I'm goin' your way

G Em C G / C G A B7 / Em G C F / Em Em7 A Am

Two drifters, off to see the world **(in 3/4)**
There's such a lot of world to see
We're after the same rainbow's end
Waitin' round the bend, my huckleberry friend
Moon river & me

/ " / " / Em Em7 A C G / C G C G / Em Am C G

— **Johnny Mercer & Henry Mancini**

© 1961 Famous Music Co. 1 Gulf & Western Plaza, NY, NY 10023. International copyright secured. Made in USA. All rights reserved. Used by permission of CPP Belwin Inc. — Fr Breakfast at Tiffany's. *On Mantovani* Gr H, *Trini Lopez* Love Alb, *Roger Williams* Gold H, *Henry Mancini* Best of, *Ray Coniff* World of H *& Andy Williams* Gr H. *In* Readers Dig Treasury of Best Loved S, Worlds Best-loved S of the '60s, 101 Of The Gr Nost S & Top 100 Movie Themes. OK10

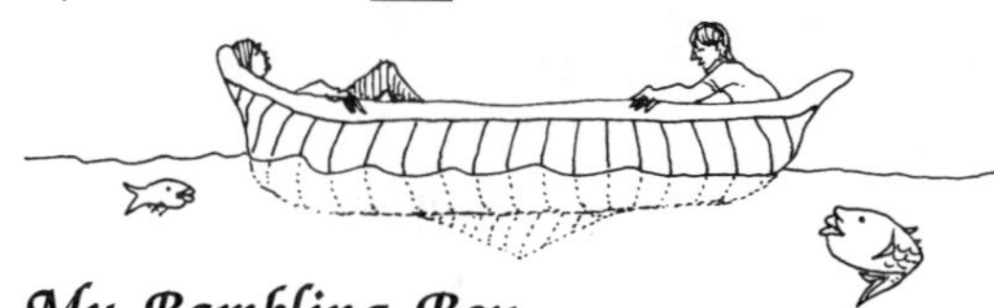

My Rambling Boy

He was a man & a friend always
He stuck with me in the hard old days
He never cared if I had no dough
We rambled round in the rain & snow

(in A) E - A - / / A D A - / E - A -

And here's to you my ramblin' boy
May all your ramblin' bring you joy (repeat)

A D A - / E - A - :||

In Tulsa town we chanced to stray
We thought we'd try to work one day
The boss says he had room for one
Says my old pal "We'd rather bum!"

Late one night in a jungle camp
The weather it was cold & damp
He got the chills, & he got 'em bad
They took the only friend I had

He left me there to ramble on
My ramblin' pal is dead & gone
If when we die we go somewhere
I'll bet you a dollar he's ramblin' there

— **Tom Paxton**

© 1963 by Cherry Lane Music Publishing Co., Inc. All rights reserved. — On (& in) his Rambling Boy. *In Judy Collins* SB *& on her* Conc. *On Country Gentlemen* New Look New Sound, *Weavers* Reunion 1963, Gr FSingers of the '60s *& Patrick Sky* Thru a Window. *In* SO! *13:4 &* Reprints *#7.* OK11

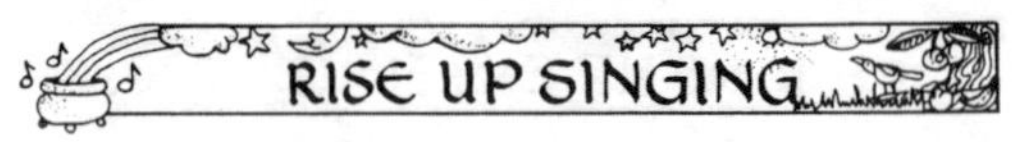

Pack Up Your Sorrows

No use crying, talking to a stranger
Naming the sorrows you've seen
Too many sad times, too many bad times
Nobody knows what you mean

C - F - / C - G - / C - F - / C G C -

But if somehow you could pack up your sorrows
And give them all to me
You would lose them I know how to use them
Give them all to me

No use rambling, walking in the shadows
Trailing a wandering star
No one beside you, no one to guide you
And nobody knows where you are

No use gambling, running in the darkness
Looking for a spirit that's free
Too many wrong times, too many long times
Nobody knows what you see

No use roaming, lying by the roadside
Seeking a satisfied mind
Too many highways, too many byways
And nobody's walking behind

— Richard Fariña & Pauline Marden

 — With Mimi on their Celebs for a Gray Day, Best of & Memories. *On P,P&M* Alb, & Gr FSingers of the '60s. *In SO! 16:1 & Reprints #10.* OK12

People Like You

Old fighter, you sure took it on the chin
Where'd you ever get the strength to stand
Never giving up or giving in
You know that I just want to shake your hand, because
People like you help people like me go on, go on (2x)

D G A D / / G D A / D G A D A // D - - A / /

Old battler, with a scar for every town
Thought you were no better than the rest
You wore your colors every way but down
All you ever gave us was your best, but you know that:

Old dreamer, with a world in every thought
Where'd you get the vision to keep on
You sure gave back as good as what you got
I hope that when my time is almost gone, they'll say that:
People like me helped **people like** you **go on, go on (2x)**
Because **people like you help people like me ...**

— Si Kahn

 — On his Home, *Ed Trickett* People Like You, *Nan Hoffman* A Thousand Cranes, *Charlie King* Two Good Arms. OK13

Precious Friend

E♭7

Just when I thought / All was lost, you changed my mind
You gave me hope (not just the old soft soap)
You showed that we could learn to share in time
(you & me & Rockefeller)
I'll keep plugging on / Your face will shine thru all our tears
And when we sing another little victory song
Precious friend, you will be there (singing in harmony)
Precious friend, you will be there

G D7E♭7 G - / C - G - / G D7E♭7 G Em / A7 - D7 - / " / C - F - / C A G E / A D G E / A D G C G

— Pete Seeger

 — On his Banks of Marble *& his* Prec Friend *(w/Arlo Guthrie). On Bright Morning Star* Live in the US *& in* SO! *31:1.* OK14

Song for Judith (Open the Door)

Sometimes I remember the old days
When the world was filled with sorrow
You might have thought I was living, but I was all alone
In my heart the rain was falling
The wind blew, the night was calling
Come back, come back I'm all you've ever known

A - / E - / D - A - :||

Open the door & come on in
I'm so glad to see you my friend(s)
You're like a rainbow (rainbows) **coming around the bend**
And when I see you happy
Well it sets my heart free
I'd like to be as good a friend to you as you are to me

E - / D DA / D A E - / D A / - DA / E - DA DA

There were friends who could always see me
Thru the haze their smiles would reach me
Saying OK, saying goodbye, saying hello
Soon I knew what I was after
Was life & love, tears & laughter
Hello my good friend, hello my darling, what do you know?

I used to think it was only me
Living alone not feeling free
To be alive **(pause)** to be your friend
Now I know we all have stormy weather
The sun shines thru when we're together
I'll be your friend right thru to the end

— Judy Collins

 aka: "Open the Door." On her Living. OK15

Tell Me I'm Lovely When I Cry

Tell me I'm lovely when I cry
That my tears add a sparkle, a softness in my eyes
That it's all right, it's OK
And you love me just that way

G C G - / Am D DC G / - - Bm - / D G -

Tell me I'm lovely when I'm tired
That my work means a lot, that you know how hard I've tried
That it's all right ...

Tell me it's fine when I'm annoyed
That you know that I'm low & I'm hurting down inside ...

Tell me when I'm fearful in the night
That you're there & you care & you'll hold me very tight ...

When I'm caught up in trouble, set me free
Won't you help me to see all the loveliness in me? ...

— Mary Dart

 In her S About People. OK16

That's What Friends Are For

And I never thought I would feel this way
And as far as I'm concerned, I'm glad I got the chance to say
That I do believe I love you
And if I should ever go away
Well then close your eyes & try to feel the way we do today
(And then if you can remember)

Cmaj7 Em7 Am7 Dm7 / - - E7 Am7 / Fmaj7 Dm7
/ " / " / Fmaj7 Dm7 G7

Keep smiling, keep shining, knowing you can always count on
Me, for sure – that's what friends are for
For good times, for bad times, I'll be on your side forever
More – that's what friends are for

Cmaj7 - Fmaj7 Fmaj7G / Em7 Am7 Fmaj7 Dm7G
Cmaj7 Em Bb A / Dm - G7sus4 -

And I never thought I would feel this way
Well you came & opened me & now there's so much I can see
And so by the way I thank you / And then for the times we're apart
Well then close your eyes & know these words are coming from my heart / **And then if you can ...**

— Burt Bacharach & Carole Bayer Sager

 — The anthem of the movement to support AIDS victims. On Dione Warwick Friends & in Platinum '88. OK17

To Try for the Sun

We stood in the windy city
The gypsy boy & I
We laughed & we sang in the moonlight
With the rain droppin' tears in our eyes

C - G - / F G C - :||

And who's gonna be the one
To say it was no good what we done?
I dare a man to say that I'm too young
For I'm goin' to try for the sun

F G C - / / / /

We huddled in a derelict building
And when he thought that I was asleep
He threw his full coat 'round my shoulder
And shivered there beside me in a heap

We sang & cracked the air with our laughter
Our breath turned to mist in the cold
Our ages put together counted thirty
But our eyes told the dawn that we were old

Mirror, mirror, hangin' in the sky
Please look down see what's happenin' here below
I stand here singin' to the flowers
So very few people really know

— Donovan Leitch

 On his Fairytale, Like It Is & Real. OK18

What Do I Do

What do I do when my sister is crying
What do I do? I don't know what to say
You take your sister in your arms & you hug her **(2x)**

C - G C / FG Am (2x) / FG Am G C / /

What do I do when my brother is crying ... / What do ... say
You take your brother in your arms & you hug him **(2x)**

[You can then substitute "friend," "father," etc.]

What do I do when the whole world **is crying? / What do ... say**
You take the world into your heart & you love us **(2x)**

What do I do when I am crying? ... / What do ... say
You go deep into your heart, Love will find you **(2x)**

What do I do when I am crying? ... / What do ... say
Well, you can climb into my arms & I'll hug you
Yes, you can climb into my arms & I'll hold you
Yes, you can climb into my arms because I love you

— Ruth Pelham

 On her Under One Sky (Gentle Wind). OK19

With a Little Help from My Friends

What would you do if I sang out of tune?
Would you stand up & walk out on me?
Lend me your ears & I'll sing you a song
And I'll try not to sing out of key

D - Em - / A - D - :||

O I get by with a little help from my friends
O I get high with a little help from my friends
I'm gonna try with a little help from my friends

C G D - / / /

What do I do when my love is away?
Does it worry you to be alone?
How do I feel by the end of the day?
Are you sad because you're on your own? / No, **I get by ...**

(bridge) Do you need anybody? I need somebody to love
Could it be anybody? I want somebody to love

Bm - E - D C G - / /

Would you believe in a love at first sight?
Yes I'm certain that it happens all the time
What do you see when you turn out the light?
I can't tell you but I know it's mine

(last cho) O I get by... / O I get high... / I'm gonna try...
With a little help from my friends

C G D - / / C - G - / F - G - D - - -

— John Lennon & Paul McCartney

 — On Beatles Sgt Pepper & '67-'70, Joe Cocker With A Little ..., & Richie Havens 1963. In Club Date Fake B. OK20

You Are the Sunshine of My Life

You are the sunshine of my life
That's why I'll always be around
You are the apple of my eye
Forever you'll stay in my heart

(capo up) C Dm7 Em C / Dm7 - C Dm7 :||

I feel like this is the beginning
Tho' I've loved you for a million years
And if I thought our love was ending
I'd find myself drowning in my own tears

C Dm7 Cmaj7 Dm7 / Cmaj7 F E7 - / A DE Am - / D - G -

You must have known that I was lonely
Because you came to my rescue
And I know this must be heaven
How could so much love be inside of you?

— Stevie Wonder

 — Written for his sister after she nursed him back to health. On his Talking B & Orig Musiquarium 1 & in his Gr H. On 25 #1 H (Motown) & in The Top 100 Motown H. OK21

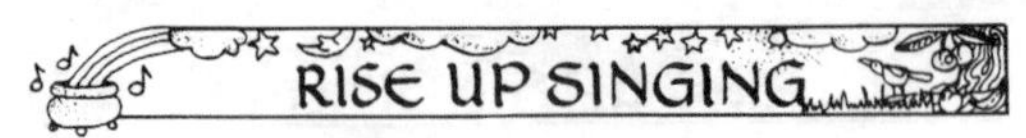

You've Got a Friend

When you're down & troubled & you need some loving care
And nothin', nothin' is goin' right
Close your eyes & think of me & soon I will be there
To brighten up even your darkest night

Am E AmE Am / F G C - /

E - AmE Am / F Em DmG DmG

You just call out my name & you know wherever I am
I'll come running to see you again
Winter, spring, summer or fall, all you have to do is call
And I'll be there: you've got a friend

C - F - / C - Dm - / C Em F Dm / F Dm C -

If the sky above you grows dark & full of clouds
And that old north wind begins to blow
Keep your head together & call my name out loud
Soon you'll hear me knockin' at your door

(bridge) Ain't it good to know that you've got a friend
When people can be so cold
They'll hurt you & they'll desert you
And take your soul if you let them
O but don't you let them

F - / C Em / F Fm / Am D / Dm G

— Carole King

 — On her Tapestry, *on James Taylor* Mud Slide Slim & Something in the Way She Feels, *Roberta Flack* Best Of, *& R Flack & D Hathaway* Best Of. *In Gr Legal Fake B.* OK22

For related songs, see GOOD TIMES, HOME & FAMILY, LOVE, and UNITY. See also: "Sidewalks of New York" (CITY); "Heart of My Heart" (GOLD); "What a Friend We Have in Jesus" (GOSP); "Make New Friends" (ROUNDS); "The Activity Room," "Auld Lang Syne" & "Old Friends" (TIME).

FUNNY SONGS

Anne Boleyn

(intro) O in the tower of London large as life
The ghost of Anne Boleyn walks, they declare
For Anne Boleyn was once King Henry's wife
Until he had the axman bob her hair
O yes he done her wrong long years ago
And she comes back each night to tell him so

Am - - - / E - Am - :|| E Dm Am - / Dm - E -

With her head (head!) **tucked** (tucked!) **underneath her arm**
She walks the bloody tower
With her head (head!) **tucked** (tucked!) **underneath her arm**
At the midnight hour

Am - - - / / Dm - Am - / B7 - E -

She's going to find King Henry, she's giving him whatfor
Gadzook she's going to tell him off for having spilled her gore
And just in case the axman wants to give her an encore
She's got **her head tucked underneath her arm**

Am - E Am / / E Dm Am Dm / E - Am -

Along the drafty corridors for miles & miles she goes
She sometimes catches cold, poor thing, it's cold there when it blows
And it's awfully awkward for the queen when she has to blow her nose / With **her ...**

(as intro) Now sometimes old King Henry throws a spread
For all his pals & gals, the ghostly crew
The axman carves the joints & cuts the bread
When in walks Anne Boleyn to spoil the "do"
She holds her head up with a wild war whoop
And Henry cries "Don't drop it in the soup!"

One day she found Henry, he was in the castle bar
"Are you Jane Seymour, Anne Boleyn or Katherine Parr
Now how the heck am I to know just who you are?
You got your head tucked underneath your arm!"

The sentries think that it's a football that she carries in
And when they see her they all shout "Is Army going to win?"
For they think that it's Red Grange instead of poor old Anne Boleyn
With her head tucked underneath her arm

— R. P. Weston & Bert Lee

This is an English Music Hall composition. On Jim Kweskin Lives Again, *Caryl P Weiss* With Her Head ... *& Clancy Bros* Live. *Also rec by Shelley Posen, Oscar Brand, Alan Arkin & the Kingston Trio. In* SO! 37:3 & FS Abecedary. OD28

Away with Rum

We're coming, we're coming our brave little band
On the right side of temperance we now take our stand
We don't use tobacco because we do think
That the people who use it are liable to drink

D - A7 D / / A7 D A7 D / - - A7 D

Away, away with rum by gum
With rum by gum, with rum by gum
Away, away with rum by gum
That's the song of the Salvation Army

D - - - / A7 - D - :||

We never eat cookies because they have yeast
And one little bite turns a man to a beast
O can you imagine a sadder disgrace
Than a man in the gutter with crumbs on his face?

We never eat fruitcake because it has rum
And one little slice puts a man on the bum
O can you imagine a sorrier sight
Than a man eating fruitcake until he gets tight?

We never drink water – they put it in gin
And one little sip & a man starts to grin
O can you imagine a sorrier plight
Than a man drinking water until he gets tight?

We never drink tea for they mix it with wine
And one little drink turns a man to a swine
O can you imagine a sorrier sight
Than a man drinking tea & singing all night?

On Theodore Bikel FSinger's Choice *& rec by Judy Henske (Elektra 231). In* SO! *11:2* & Reprints #5, FSEncyV2, S for Pickin & Singin & FiresB of Fun & Games. *Rec by the Chad Mitchel Trio (KL-1262).* OD29

Barnyard Dance

It was late one night in the pale moonlight
And all the vegetables went on a spree
They put out a sign that said "Dancin' at Nine"
And all the admission was free

F C F C / D G C - / 1st / D - G -

It was peas & beans, cabbage & greens
Well it was the biggest sight you've ever seen
And when old man cucumber struck up his number
You oughta heard the vegetables scream

/ " / " / D - - - / G - - -

Well the little turnip top did the backwards flop
The cabbage tried to shimmy & it could not stop
Little red beet she took his feet
And the watermelon dived with the cockeyed beat

A - - - / D - - - / G - - - / C - - -

Little tomato, agitator
Shook the shimmy with the sweet potato
And old man garlic dropped dead with the colic
Down at the barnyard dance – this mornin'!
Down at the barnyard dance

/ " / " / F D C A / D G C A / D G C -

— Carl Martin

© Flying Fish Music (BMI). Used by permission. — In SO! *27:5. On Martin, Bogan & Armstrong* Barnyard Dance *(Rounder), Wry Straw* Earth to Heaven *(JA28), Steve Goodman* Somebody Else's Troubles, *Geo Turman* One Thing for Certain, *Jim Couza* Friends & Neighbors, *B Hinkley & J Larson* Out In Our Meadow, *John McCutcheon* Mail Myself ..., *& Delaware Water Gap* Stringband Music. OD30

Be Kind to Your Web-Footed Friends

Be kind to your web-footed friends
For a duck may be somebody's mother
Be kind to the denizen*[s]* of the swamp
He's a dilly thru & thru *[Where the weather is very, very dahmp]*
Now you may think that this is the end
Well it is

C - - - / - - G - / - - - - / C F G - / C - - - / - -

— w: unknown — m: "Stars & Stripes Forever." OD31

Buffalo Boy

1. When are we gonna get married, married, married?
When are we gonna get married, **dear old Buffalo Boy?**

D - A7 D / /

2. I guess we'll marry in a week, a week, a week
I guess we'll marry in a week, that is, **if the weather be good**
3. How're you gonna come to the wedding ...?
How're you gonna come to the wedding, **dear old Buffalo Boy?**
4. I guess I'll come in my ox-cart ...
I guess ... ox-cart, that is, **if the weather be good**
5. Why don't you come in your buggy ... **dear old ...?**
6. My ox won't fit in the buggy ... not even **if the weather ...**
7. Who you gonna bring to the wedding ... **dear old ...?**
8. I guess I'll bring my children ... that is, **if the weather ...**
9. I didn't know you had no children! ... **dear old ...**
10. O yes, I have 5 children ... maybe six **if the weather ...**
11. There ain't gonna be no wedding ... not even **if the ...**

— trad. (US)

In SO! *7:4 &* Reprints *#1,* FS & Footnotes, FS B of Fun & Games, FS Abecedary, S for Pickin & Singing, Hootenanny SB *&* FSEncyV1. OD32

The Cat Came Back

Old Mr. Johnson had troubles of his own
He had a yellow cat which wouldn't leave its home
He tried & he tried to give the cat away
He gave it to a man going far, far away

Em D C B7 / / / /

But the cat came back the very next day
The cat came back, they thought he was a goner
But the cat came back, it just couldn't stay / Awa-ay

The man around the corner swore he'd kill the cat on sight
He loaded up his shotgun with nails & dynamite
He waited & he waited for the cat to come around
97 pieces of the man is all they found

He gave it to fisherman with a dollar note
Told him for to take it up the river in a boat
They tied a rope around its neck, it must have weighed a pound
But they had to drag the river for the fisherman was drowned

He gave it to a man going up in a balloon
He told him for to take it to the man in the moon
The balloon came down about 90 miles away
And where he is now I dare not say

He gave it to a man goin' way out west
Told him for to take it to the one he loved the best
First the train hit the curve, then it jumped the rail
Not a soul was left behind to tell the gruesome tale

The atom bomb fell one bright summer day
Then they dropped the H-Bomb the very same way
Russia went, England went & then the U.S.A.
The human race was finished without a chance to pray

— Harry S. Miller (with later folk additions)

Miller was a late 19th c. popular composer specializing in minstrel shows. This composite is Ethel Raim's. In SO! *9:2 &* Reprints *#7,* FS Abecedary, Fav S of the '90s, Read 'em & Weep *& Roxanne & Dan Keding* In Came That Rooster *(TR 8101).* OD33

A Chat with Your Mom

O the pirates with their fetid galleons, daggers in their skivvies
With infected tattooed fingers on a blunderbuss or two
Signs of scurvy in their eyes & only mermaids on their minds
It's from them I would expect to hear the F-word, not from you

Dm C Bb A7 / / Gm Dm C Dm / - - Gm A7

We sit down to have a chat, it's F-word this & F-word that
I can't control how you young people talk to one another
But I don't want to hear you use that F-word with your mother

DA (4x) / GA DA D A / DA (3x) D

And the lumberjacks from Kodiak vacationing in Anchorage
Enchanted with their pine tar soap & caribou shampoo
With 7 weeks of back pay in their aromatic woolens / **It's ...**

There are militant survivalists with Gucci bandoleros
Taking tacky khaki walkie talkies to their rendezvous
Trading all the latest armor-piercing ammo information / **It's ...**

There are jocks who think that God himself is drooling in the bleachers
In a cold November downpour with a belly full of brew
Whose entire grasp of heaven has a lot to do with football ...

There's unsavory musicians with their filthy pinko lyrics
Who destroy the social fabric & enjoy it when they do
With their groupies & addictions & their poor heartbroken parents / **It's from them ...**

— Lou & Peter Berryman

© 1984 Lou & Peter Berryman. Used by permission. — On their So Comfortable *(CR300) & in* The Berryman SB *(both available fr the authors c/o Box 3452, Madison WI 53704.) In* SO! *30:4.* OD34

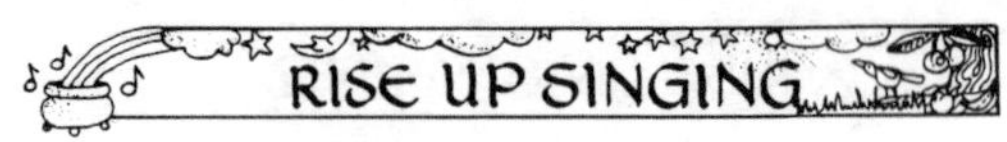

Clementine

In a cavern, in a canyon, excavating for a mine
Dwelt a miner, '49-er, & his daughter Clementine

(in 3/4) D - - A7 / - D A7 D

O my darling (3x) Clementine
You are lost & gone forever, dreadful sorry, Clementine

Light she was & like a fairy & her shoes were number nine
Herring boxes without topses, sandals were for Clementine

Drove she ducklings to the water every morning just at nine
Stubbed her toe against a splinter, fell into the foaming brine

Ruby lips above the water, blowing bubbles soft & fine
But alas! I was no swimmer, so I lost my Clementine

In a churchyard near the canyon where the myrtle doth entwine
There grow roses & other posies, fertilized by Clementine

Then the miner, '49-er, soon began to peak & pine
Thought he oughter jine his daughter, now he's with his Clementine

In my dreams she still doth haunt me, robed in garments soaked with brine
Tho' in life I used to hug her, now she's dead I draw the line

Now ye Boy Scouts, heed the warning to this tragic tale of mine
Artificial respiration would have saved my Clementine

How I missed her **(2x)** how I missed my Clementine
Til I kissed her little sister & forgot my Clementine

— trad. (US)

On (& in) Pete Seeger Am Fav Bals *(FA2322). In* FiresB of FS, FS Abecedary, S for Pickin & Singin, Fred Waring SB, FSEncyV1, Bestloved S of the Am People, FiresB of Fun & Games *& Weavers* On Tour *(CVM 73116).* ⊙D35

Eddystone Light

Me father was the keeper of the Eddystone light
And he slept with a mermaid one fine night
From this union there came three
A porpoise & a porgy & the other was me!
Yo ho ho, the wind blows free
O for a life on the rolling sea!

(TD ↑ 3) A - - - / D E A - :|| Bm - E - / - - A -

One dark night, as I was a-trimming of the glim
Singing a verse from the evening hymn
A voice from the starboard shouted "Ahoy!"
And there was my mother, a-sitting on a buoy. / **Yo ho ho ...**

"O where are the rest of my children three?"
My mother then she asked of me
"One was exhibited as a talking fish
The other was served from a chafing dish" / **Yo ho ho ...**

Then the phosphorous flashed in her seaweed hair
I looked again, & my mother wasn't there
But her voice came echoing back from the night
"To Hell with the keeper of the Eddystone Light!" / **Yo ho ho ...**

(Parody) *Keeper of the London Zoo*

My father was the keeper of the London Zoo
And he slept one night with a kangaroo
From this union there came three
A wallaby & a wombat & the other was me
The monkeys chatter the whole night thru
O for the life in the London Zoo

I went to a carnival one fine night
Went into a tent to see a fight
And as the bell went ting-a-ling
I saw my mother standing in the ring / **The monkeys ...**

"What has become of my children three?"
My mother then, she asked of me
"One was employed as a pogo stick
And the other was given a bishopric"

Her chin connected with a flashing right
When I looked again she was out like a light
I heard her mutter as she came to
"To Hell with the keeper of the London Zoo"

aka: "Keeper of the Eddystone Light." On Burl Ives S Of The Sea & Bal & FS V1, *& Weavers* Trav On. *In* SFest, Hootenanny SB, FS Abecedary & S for Pickin & Singin. ⊙D36

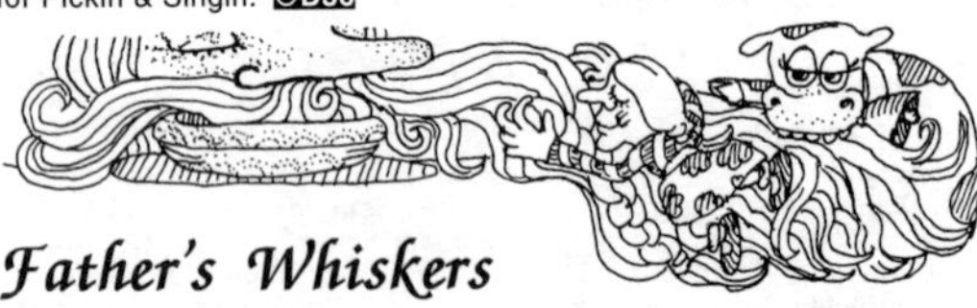

Father's Whiskers

We have a dear old father, to whom we dearly pray
He has a set of whiskers, they're always in the way
O they're always in the way, the cows eat them for hay
They hide the dirt on Father's shirt, they're always in the way

G - A7 - / D7 - - G :||

We have a dear old mother, with him at night she sleeps
She wakes up in the morning, eating shredded wheat

We have a dear old brother, he has a Ford machine
He uses Father's whiskers to strain the gasoline

We have a dear old sister, it really is a laugh
She sprinkles Father's whiskers as bath salts in her bath

Father has a son, his name is Sonny Jim
He wants to grow some whiskers but Father won't let him

Father has a daughter, her name is Ella-Mae
She climbs up Father's whiskers & braids them all the way

Around the supper table, we make a merry group
Until dear Father's whiskers get tangled in the soup

Father fought in Flanders, he wasn't killed, you see
His whiskers looked like bushes & fooled the enemy

When Father goes in swimming, no bathing suit for him
He ties his whiskers round his waist & gaily plunges in

Father went out sailing, the wind blew down the mast
He hoisted up his whiskers & never went so fast

Father, in a tavern, he likes his lager beer
He pins a pretzel on his nose to keep his whiskers clear

Father went out chopping, he struck a mighty blow
He pinned down all his whiskers, now hear those cuss words flow

Father went out skiing, he thought he'd try a schuss
He caught his whiskers on his skis & landed on his puss

— trad.

In Sfest. ⊙D37

The Hippopotamus Song

A bold Hippopotamus was standing one day
On the banks of the cool Shalimar
He gazed at the bottom as it peacefully lay
By the light of the evening star
Away on the hill top sat combing her hair
His fair Hippopotamine maid
The Hippopotamus was no ignoramus
And sang her this sweet serenade **(in 3/4)**

G - Am D / Em A D - / G - Am B7 / Em A D -
Am Em F E / F E Am D / G D G D / Am A7 D -

Mud! mud! glorious mud!
Nothing quite like it for cooling the blood
So, follow me, follow, down to the hollow
And there let us wallow in glorious mud

G - Am D / G Em A D / G - Am - / C G Am D G -

The fair Hippopotama he aimed to entice
From her seat on the hilltop above
As she hadn't got a ma to give her advice
Came tiptoeing down to her love
Like thunder the forest reechoed the sound
Of the song that they sang as they met
His inamorata adjusted her garter
And lifted her voice in duet

Now more Hippopotami began to convene
On the banks of that river so wide
I wonder now what am I to say of the scene
That ensued by the Shalimar side
They dived all at once with an ear-splitting splosh
Then rose to the surface again
A regular army of Hippopotami
All singing this haunting refrain

— Michael Flanders & Donald Swann

 In their S of ... *(St Martin's Press).* D38

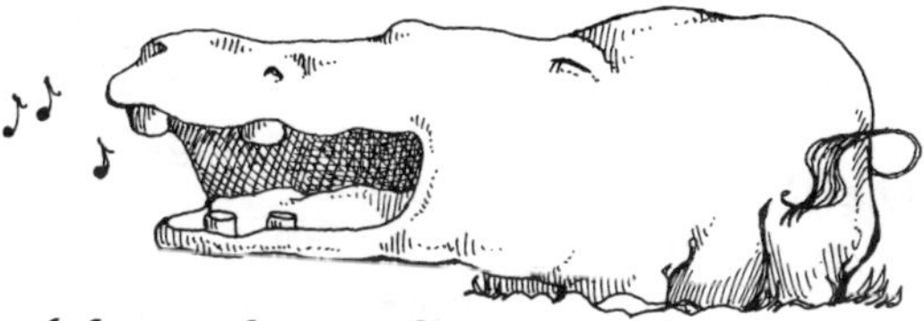

Hole in the Bucket

1. There's a hole in the bucket, **dear Liza, dear Liza**
There's a hole in the bucket, **dear Liza**, there's a hole

(in 3/4) D G - - / D G GGA D

2. Then fix it, **dear Willy, dear Willy, dear Willy**
Then fix it, **dear Willy, dear Willy**, then fix it!
3. With what shall I fix it, **dear Liza, dear Liza**?
With what shal I fix it, **dear Liza**, with what?
4. With straw, **dear Willy, dear Willy, dear Willy**
With straw, **dear Willy, dear Willy**, With straw.

Dear Liza verses:	**Dear Willy verses:**
5. But how shall I cut it ...?	6. With a knife ...!
7. But the knife is too dull ...?	8. Then sharpen it ...!
9. With what shall I sharpen it ...?	10. With a stone ...!
11. But the stone is too dry ...	12. Then wet it ...
13. With what shall I wet it ...?	14. With water ...
15. With what shall I fetch it ...?	16. In a bucket ...!
17. There's a hole in the bucket ...	

— trad. (orig a German song "Liebe Heinrich")

On Faith Petric Sing a S Sing Along *(Gentle winds 1015), Oscar Brand* Laughing Am *& Ives* Cheers. *On (& in) Pete Seeger* Am Fav Bal V4. *In* SO! *12:1,* Joyful Singing *&* FiresB Of Fun & Games. D39

I Wish They'd Do it Now

I was born of Geordie parents, one day when I was young
That's how the Geordie dialect became me native tongue
That I was a pretty baby, my mother she did vow
The girls all ran to kiss me, well **I wish they'd do it now**
O I wish they'd do it now (2x)
I've got itches in my britches & I wish they'd do it now

G - - - / C G A D ||: G - - - / C G D G :||

When I was only six months old, the girls would handle me
They'd hug me to their bosoms & they'd dance me on their knee
They'd rock me in the cradle, & if I made a row
They'd tickle me, they'd cuddle me, **I wish ...**

At 16 months as fine a lad as ever could be seen
The lasses they would follow me, right down to the green
They'd make a chain of buttercups & drop it round me brow
Then they'd roll me in the clover, well **I wish ...**

The East-end girls would call for me to swim when it was mild
Down to the river we would go, to splash about a while
They would throw the water over me & dip me like a ewe*
Then they'd rub me nice all over, well **I ...** *[*pron. "yowe"]*

It's awful lonely for a lad, to lead a single life
I think I'll go to the dance tonight & try & find a wife
Me fortune is six brindle pigs, likewise one big fat sow
There'll be plenty love & bacon for the girl who'll have me now
(last cho:) For the girl who'll have me now (2x)
There'll be plenty love & bacon for the girl who'll ...

— C.P.Hyland, 1879 (adapted)

Orig an imitation Irish song (see his I Wish They'd Do It Now Songster*) but much altered by the folk process. This version rec by Eng singer Bob Davenport. In* SO! *20:5,* How Can We Keep fr Singing *& on Roberts & Barrand* Spencer Rover *(ST 1).* D40

I'm My Own Grandpa

Now many many years ago when I was twenty-three
I was married to a widow who was pretty as can be
This widow had a grown-up daughter who had hair of red
My father fell in love with her & soon they too were wed

C - G7 - / - - C - / - C7 F - / D7 - G -

O I'm my own grandpa / I'm my own grandpa
It sounds funny I know, but it really is so
O I'm my own grandpa

C CG C - / F FD G - / C C7 F D / C CG C -

This made my dad my son-in-law & changed my very life
My daughter was my mother 'cause she was my father's wife
To complicate the matter even though it brought me joy
I soon became the father of a bouncing baby boy

My little baby then became a brother-in-law to Dad
And so became my uncle, though it made me very sad
For if he was my uncle, then that also made him brother
Of the widow's grown-up daughter who was also my stepmother

Father's wife then had a son who kept them on the run
And he became my grandchild, for he was my daughter's son
My wife is now my mother's mother & it makes me blue
Because altho' she is my wife, she's my grandmother too

Now if my wife is my grandmother, then I'm her grandchild
And every time I think of it, it nearly drives me wild
For now I have become the strangest case I ever saw
As husband of my grandmother, I am my own grandpa

— Dwight Latham & Moe Jaffe

 – In SO! *31:3 & on Michael Cooney* Pure & Unsweetened, *Ray Owen* Well Wasted Afternoons *(PoliceRecs), Reid Miller* Storytelling Minstrel *& rec by Richie Havens.* D41

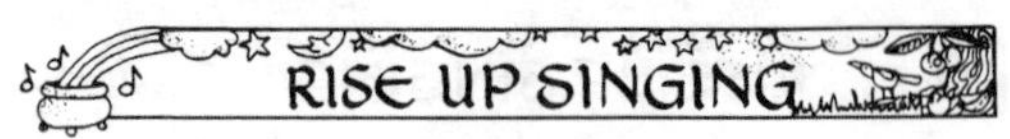

The Irish Ballad

About a maid I'll sing a song, **sing rickety-tickety-tin**
About a maid I'll sing a song who didn't have her family long
Not only did she do them wrong
She did ev'ryone of them in, them in
She did ev'ryone of them in

Dm - DmGm Dm / Gm Dm DmC Dm /
DmGm DmGm / DmC Dm C / DmC Dm

One morning in a fit of pique, **sing ...**
One morning ... she drowned her father in the creek
The water tasted bad for a week
And we had to make do with gin, with gin / We had ...

Her mother she could never stand, **sing ...**
Her mother ... & so a cyanide soup she planned
The mother died with the spoon in her hand
And her face in a hideous grin, a grin / Her face ...

She set her sister's hair on fire, **sing ...**
She set ... & as the smoke & flame rose high'r
Danced around the funeral pyre
Playing a violin, -olin / Playing ...

She weighted her brother down with stones, **sing ...**
She weighted ... & sent him off to Davy Jones
All they ever found were some bones
And occasional pieces of skin, of skin / Occasional ...

One day when she had nothing to do, **sing ...**
One day ... she cut her baby brother in two
And served him up as an Irish stew
And invited the neighbors in, -bors in / & invited ...

And when at last the police came by, **sing ...**
And when ... her little pranks she did not deny
To do so she would have had to lie!
And lying, she knew, was a sin, a sin ... / & lying ...

My tragic tale I won't prolong, **sing ...**
My tragic ..., & if you do not enjoy my song
You've yourselves to blame if it's too long
You should never have let me begin ...

— Tom Lehrer

© 1952 Tom Lehrer. Copyright renewed. Used by permission. — In his Too Many S by *& on his* S by. *In* FiresB of Fun & Games. D42

John Jacob Jingleheimer Schmidt

John Jacob Jingleheimer Schmidt / That's my name too
Whenever I go out, the people always shout
"There goes John Jacob Jingleheimer Schmidt!" – la (7x)

D A / - D / - G / A D

— trad. (US)

In Sfest. D43

Junk Food Junkie

Well you know I love that organic cookin', I always ask for more
They call me Mr. Natural on down to the health food store
I only eat good sea-salt, white sugar don't touch my lips
And my friends is always beggin' me to take 'em on macrobiotic trips
But at night I take out my strongbox that I keep under lock & key
And I take it off to my closet where nobody else can see
I open that lid so slowly, take a peek up North & South
Then I pull out a Hostess Twinkie & I pop it in my mouth!

C - F C / - A D G / C - F C / C A DG C
Am - Dm Am / - - E - / 1st / C A DG C

In the daytime I'm Mr. Natural, just as healthy as I can be
But at night I'm a junkfood junkie, good Lord have pity on me! F C G C / - Am E Am

Well at lunch time you can always find me at the whole earth Vitamin Bar
Just sucking on my plain white yogurt from a hand thrown pottery jar
And sippin' little hand-pressed cider with a carrot stick for dessert
And wipin' my face in a natural way on the sleeve of my peasant shirt!
But when that clock strikes midnight & I'm all by myself
I work that combination on my secret hide-away shelf
I pull out some Fritos corn chips, DrPepper & an Old Moon Pie
And I sit back in glorious expectations of a genuine junkfood high

My friends down at the commune, they think I'm pretty neat
I don't know nothin' 'bout arts & crafts but I give 'em all somethin' to eat
I'm a friend to old Euell Gibbons & I only eat homegrown spice
I got a John Keats autograph Grecian Urn filled up with my brown rice
O but lately I've been spotted with a Big Mac on my breath
Stumblin' into a Col. Sanders with a face as white as death
I'm afraid some day they'll find me just stretched out on my bed
With a handful of Pringle's potato chips & a DingDong by my head!

— Larry Groce

© 1975 Peaceable Kingdom Music Publishing (ASCAP). All rights reserved. Used by permission. – On his Junk Food Junkie *& on* Peter Alsop. D44

Martin Said to His Man

Martin said to his man, **fie, man, fie!**
Martin said to his man, **who's the fool now?**
Martin said to his man, fill thou the cup & I the can
Thou hast well drunken, man, who's the fool now?

G - - - / D C Am D / G D G D / C - D G

I saw the man in the moon, **fie ...** / I saw ... **who's ...?**
I saw the man in the moon, clouting of St. Peter's Shoon
Thou hast well drunken, man, who's the fool now?

I saw the goose ring the hog / saw the snail bite the dog
I saw the hare chase the hound / 20 miles above the ground
I saw the mouse chase the cat / saw the cheese eat the rat
I saw a flea heave a tree / 20 miles out to sea
I saw a maid milk a bull / at every pull a bucketful

— trad. (English)

A drinking song popular in Shakespeare's time, the earliest printed version fr 1588. cf. "Fooba Wooba John." On J Roberts & T Barrand Spencer Rover *(Swallowtail). In* SO! 20:6, Eng Dance & S & How Can We Keep fr Singing. D45

The Merry Minuet

They're rioting in Africa **(whistle)**
They're starving in Spain **(whistle)**
There's hurricanes in Florida **(whistle)**
And Texas needs rain **(whistle)** **(in 3/4)**

G - GGD G / C G CCD G / 1st / CCD G **(2x)**

The whole world is festering with unhappy souls
The French hate the Germans, the Germans hate the Poles
Italians hate Yugoslavs, South Africans hate the Dutch
And I don't like anybody very much

G C A D / C G A D / G C A D / C GGD G -

But we can be tranquil & thankful & proud
For man's been endowed with a mushroom-shaped cloud
And we know for certain that some lucky day
Someone will set the spark off & we will all be blown away

/ " / " / " / C G CCD G

They're rioting in Africa **(whistle)**
There's strife in Iran **(whistle)**
What nature doesn't do to us **(whistle)**
Will be done by our fellow man

— Sheldon Harnick

© 1958 Alley Music corporation & Trio Music Company, Inc. Copyright renewed. All rights administered by Hudson Bay Music Inc. All rights reserved. Used by permission. — On Kingston Trio Best of. *On Tom Lehrer* That Was the Yr That Was. D46

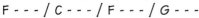

Multiple Relationship Blues

I love Peggy & George & you, you love me & Bob & Sue
Peggy loves George & Sal & Ralph, Helen wants Bob all for herself
You know we got the multiple relationship blues
Multiple (16x) / Multiple relationships!

C Am F G / / / // C Am F G (2x) C F C -

I was pacing up the floor (much uptight)
Deciding who to be with (to spend the night)
It's so hard to have to choose between the four of you
(Who will it be, maybe him or her or me)

(bridge) We love each other, it's plain to see
(Why did she choose him instead of me?)
I love you all, about the same
(I wish you'd stop calling me by his name)

F - - - / C - - - / F - - - / G - - -

I met someone new to love (o hurray!)
I know you will like him so (go away!)
Let's spend some time together soon perhaps in early June
(He & I we're very happy together)

— new words by Michael Zwell — m: "Silhouettes"
 OD47

Old Time Religion

Give me that old time religion (3x)
And that's good enough for me

(TD ↑ 3) E - / B7 E / - A / EB7 E

We will pray to Aphrodite
Even tho' she's rather flighty
And they say she wears no nightie **& that's ...**

We will pray with those Egyptians
Build pyramids to put our crypts in
Cover subways with inscriptions **& that's ...**

O-old Odin we will follow
And in fighting we will wallow
Til we wind up in Valhalla **& that's ...**

Let me follow dear old Buddha / For there is nobody cuter
He comes in plaster, wood, or pewter ...

We will pray with Zarathustra / Pray just like we useta
I'm a Zarathustra booster ...

We will pray with those old Druids
They drink fermented fluids
Waltzing naked thru the woo-ids ...

Hare Krishna gets a laugh on
When he sees me dressed in saffron
With my hair that's only half on ...

I'll arise at early morning
When my Lord *[the sun]* gives me the warning
That the solar age is dawning **& that's ...**

— new words & music adap by anon. filk singers & Pete Seeger
© 1993 Sanga Music Inc. Used by permission. Filk Singers are science fiction fans that enjoy writing folk music parodies. On his & Arlo Guthrie's Precious Friend. *For original version & tune sources see p. 211 in SPIRITUALS.* OD48

Oleanna

O to be in Oleanna! That's where I'd rather be
Than be bound in Norway & drag the chains of slavery
Ole-Oleanna (2x) / Ole- (5x) Oleanna

D - G D / A D A D :||

In Oleanna land is free, the wheat & corn just plant themselves
Then grow a good four feet a day, while on your bed you rest yourself

Beer as sweet as Munchener springs fr the ground & flows away
The cows all like to milk themselves & hens lay eggs ten times a day

Little roasted piggies just rush about the city streets
Inquiring so politely if a slice of ham you'd like to eat

Aye, if you'd begin to live, to Oleanna you must go
The poorest wretch in Norway becomes a Duke in a year or so

— Eng Pete Seeger (based on a trad. Norwegian song)
TRO © 1958 & renewed 1986 Ludlow Music Inc. NY NY. International copyright secured. All rights reserved including public performance for profit. Used by permission. — Oleanna was one of the many Utopian communities which sprang up in the US in the mid 19th c. This one was founded by the famous Norwegian violinist Ole Bull. This song is an ironic response to high flown advertising for the new commune. In SO! *5:2 & Reprints #2,* Hootenanny SB, *Ives* FS & Footnotes *& Pete Seeger* With Voices Together We Sing *(FA 2452). Rec by the Kingston Trio.* OD49

On Ilkley Moor Bah T'at

1. Whear 'ast tha been sin' I saw thee? (I saw thee)
On Ilkley Moor bah t'at
Whear 'ast tha been sin' I saw thee? (2x)

G - - - / - - D - / - - G - / A - D -

On Ilkley Moor bah t'at (bah t'at) on Ilkley Moor bah t'at
On Ilkley Moor bah t'at!

G - - GC / Am D G -

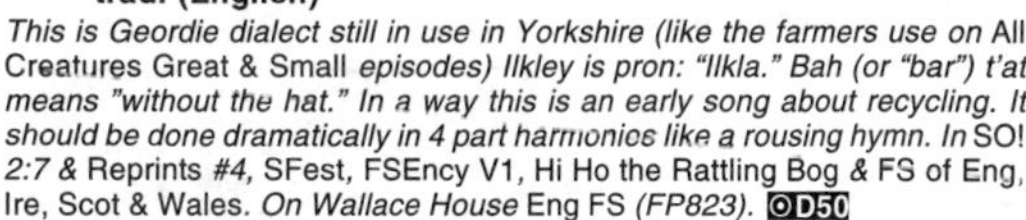

2. Tha's been a-coortin' Mary Jane
3. Tha'll go an' get thee death o' cowld
4. Then we shall ha' to bury thee
5. Then t'worms'll cum an' et thee oop
6. Then t'doox'll cum an' et oop t'worms
7. Then us'll cum an' et oop t'doox
8. Then us'll all 'ave etten thee
9. That's whear we'll get our owen back

— trad. (English)
This is Geordie dialect still in use in Yorkshire (like the farmers use on All Creatures Great & Small *episodes) Ilkley is pron: "Ilkla." Bah (or "bar") t'at means "without the hat." In a way this is an early song about recycling. It should be done dramatically in 4 part harmonies like a rousing hymn. In* SO! *2:7 & Reprints #4,* SFest, FSEncy V1, Hi Ho the Rattling Bog *&* FS of Eng, Ire, Scot & Wales. *On Wallace House* Eng FS *(FP823).* OD50

The Preacher Went Down

1. O the preacher went down (O the preacher ...)
To the cellar to pray (to ...)
He found a jug *[book]* (...)
And he stayed all day (...)
O the preacher went down to the cellar to pray,
He found a jug & he stayed all day
I ain't a-gonna grieve my Lord no more (4x)

D - / GD GD / A - / D - ||: G - / D - / A - D - :||

2. O you can't get to heaven ... on roller skates ...
Cuz you'd roll right by ... those pearly gates ...
3. O you can't get to heaven in a rocking chair
Cuz the Lord don't want no lazybones there
4. O you can't get to heaven in a limousine
Cuz the Lord don't sell no gasoline
5. O you can't get to heaven in ________'s old car
Cuz the darned old thing won't go that far
6. O you can't get to heaven in a birch canoe
Cuz you'd need to paddle til you're black & blue
7. O you can't get to heaven on a pair of skis
Cuz you'll shuss right thru St Peter's knees
8. You can't chew terbaccy on the golden shore
Cuz the Lord ain't got no cuspidor
9. O you can't get to heaven with powder & paint
Cuz it makes you look like what you ain't
10. That's all there is & there ain't no more
St Peter said & he closed the door

— trad. (adapted from a Black Spiritual)
aka: "Ain't Gonna Grieve." In SFest, S for Pickin & Singing, Fred Waring SB, *&* FiresB of Fun & Games. OD51

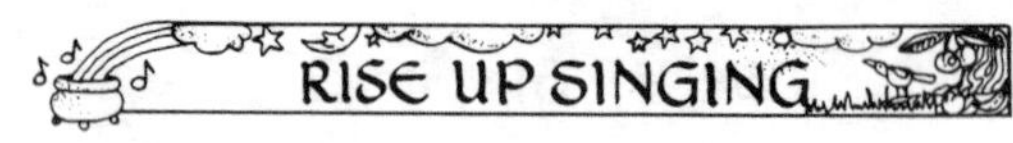

Rooster Song

We had a chicken, no eggs would she lay **(2x)**
My wife said "Honey, we're losing money
We've got a chicken, no eggs will she lay"
One day a rooster came into our yard
And caught that chicken right off her guard
She's laying eggs now **just like** she **used to**
Ever since that rooster came into our yard (repeat)

D A / - D :‖ (3x) G D / A D :‖

We had a moo cow, no milk would she give **(2x)**
My wife ... / We've got a moo cow ...
One day that rooster came into our yard
And caught that moo cow right off her guard
She's laying eggnog **just like** she **used to / Ever ...**

We had a gas pump, no gas would it give **(2x)**
My wife ... / We've got a gas pump ...
One day that rooster came into our yard
And caught that gas pump right off its guard
It's giving shell gas **just like** it **used to / Ever ...**

We had a gum tree, no gum would it give **(2x)**
My wife ... / We've got a gum tree ...
One day that rooster staggered into our yard
And caught that gum tree right off its guard
It's giving chicklets **just like** it **used to / Ever ...**

We had a rooster, no love would it give **(2x)**
My wife ... / We've got a rooster ...
One day a rooster came into our yard
And caught my rooster right off of his guard
He's laying hens now **just like** he **used to / Ever ...**

— trad. (US)

On Kevin Roth Collection *& Roxanne & Dan Keding* In Came That Rooster. D52

Squalor

In the squalor of her awful little shack she sat
With her grungy cat & her parakeet
With rats a-runnin' round the size of caribou
Playing peek-a-boo with her filthy feet
Eatin' donuts with a spoon & drinkin' Ovaltine
Thru a scum of green floating leisurely
In a coffee cup of plastic from the Sally Ann
Shaking in her hand out of misery

Dm - / A Dm :‖ (4x)

And it's all because she (he, they) **didn't eat her vegetables (3x)**
As a kid _ / Or maybe didn't chew 'em properly,
if she (he, they) **did**

G D / / / A - / - - D -

Her brother slept behind the shack without a bed
With his battered head resting on his knee
As the roaches & the traffic sang a lullabye
The water pipes would sigh a little harmony
With the stogies he had found wrapped up in cellophane
To keep out the rain when the night was through
He would stumble down the alley pickin' junk sometimes
Or try to beg for dimes on the avenue

Her mother as a seamstress never brought in much
'Cause she'd lost her touch in a Codeine haze
Now she staggers in a stupor thru the city streets
Wrapped in ratty sheets from her sewing days
Her crazy little face is hidden in the shade
Of a hat she made from a cardboard box
The hair beneath her hat is so in need of care
It doesn't look like hair it looks like dirty socks

Her uncle'd come to see her in his tattered clothes
With a runny nose & a pint of wine
And a bucket full of bullheads he had caught that day
On Monona Bay with a hand held line
She would spread a little blanket on the apple crate
Where they always ate when they had the food
They would eat & they would drink & when the grub
was gone
They would carry on if they were in the mood

— Peter Berryman

 On Peter & Lou Berryman (no relation) *& in* The Berryman Berryman SB. D53

Traveling Man

Folks, I want to tell you 'bout a man named Bloom
He come from down in New Orleans
And made his living stealing chickens
And anything he could see
That popeyed man could run so fast
That his feet wouldn't stay in the road
And if a freight train passed, no matter how fast
He could always get on board

D - / G7 D / [1.] - Bm / E A :‖ [2.] G D / EA D

He was a travelling man
Certainly was a travelling man
He was the most travellin'est man
There ever was in the land
He travelled East, he travelled West
Was known for miles around
And he never got caught & he never got whupped
Til the police shot him down

Well the police shot him with a rifle
And the bullet went thru his head
The folks was comin' from miles around
Just to see if that boy was dead
Telegrammed down south where his mama lived
She was all upset with tears
She walked up & opened the coffin lid
But that fool had disappeared

Now Bloom was on the Titantic Ship
When it was sinking low
He was standing outside the railing
And he had his head hung low
Well the people who saw him jump overboard
Said "Get a load of that crazy fool!"
But just 45 minutes after that
He was shooting craps in Liverpool

Now the police caught that Bloom at last
They had him up to hang one day
The judge leaned over, said "My good man
Do you have any last words to say?"
He asked the courtroom to bow their heads
To bow their heads in prayer
Then he crossed one leg & winked one eye
And vanished straight up in the air

Well Bloom went down to the spring one day
To fetch himself a pail of water
The distance this rascal had to traverse
Was approximately three miles & a quarter
Now he filled up the bucket & started back
Then he stumbled & fell down
He ran back to the house, grabbed another bucket
And caught the water b'fore it hit the ground

— Pink Anderson

 — In SO! 22:3. On David Bromberg Bandit In a Bathing Suit, *Roy Bookbinder* Travelin' Man & Going Back to Tampa, *Doc & Merle Watson* Bal fr Deep Gap *& Bob Bovee* Roundup. *Bookbinder learned the song fr Anderson. Watson says he learned it fr the blues singer Luke Jordan.* D54

Waltzing With Bears

I went to his room in the middle of the night
I crept to his side & I turned on the light
And to my surprise he was nowhere in sight
'Cause my Uncle Walter goes waltzing at night

G - C G / D - - G / G - C G / C G D G

He goes wa-wa-wa waltzing waltzing with bears
Raggy bears, baggy bears, shaggy bears too
There's nothing on earth Uncle Walter won't do
So he can go waltzing, wa-wa-wa waltzing
Wa-wa-wa waltzing go waltzing with bears

/ " / D - G - / " / C G C G / C G D G

We bought Uncle Walter a new coat to wear
But when he came home it was covered with hair
And lately I've noticed several new tears
I'm sure Uncle Walter's been waltzing with bears

We told Uncle Walter that he should be good
And do all the things we said that he should
But I know he would rather be off in the woods
I'm afraid we'll lose Uncle Walter for good

We begged & we pleaded, oh please won't you stay
And managed to keep him home for a day
But the bears all barged in & they took him away
Now he's dancing with pandas & he won't understand us
And the bears all demand at least one dance a day

G - C G / D - - G / 1st / C G C G / C G D G

— orig. concept & chorus: w: Dr. Seuss m: Eugene Poddany
— adaption of cho. & new verses: Dale Marxen

© 1967 Dr. Seuss & Eugene Poddany. Reprinted by permission of Random House, Inc. The original version of this song entitled "My Uncle Walter Waltzes With Bears" appeared in The Cat in the Hat Songbook. *The author of the above adaptation claims it is an original composition © 1986 Dale Marxen, Tomorrow Music, PO Box 165, Madison, WI 53701. On Robbie Clement* Magic Place, *Bok Muir & Trickett* Minneapolis Conc, *& Prisc. Herdman* Stardreamer. *Also in* New Folk Favs *(Hal Leonard).* D55

The Wild West Is Where I Want to Be

Along the trail you'll find me lopin'
Where the spaces are wide open
In the land of the old A.E.C.
Where the scenery's attractive
And the air is radioactive
Oh, the wild west is where I want to be

D - / G - / D - A - / D - / G D / - A D -

'Mid the sagebrush & the cactus
I'll watch the fellers practice
Droppin' bombs through the clean desert breeze
I'll have on my sombrero
And of course I'll wear a pair o'
Levis over my lead B.V.D.'s

(bridge) I will leave the city's rush,
Leave the fancy & the plush
Leave the snow & leave the slush & the crowds
I will seek the desert's hush
Where the scenery is lush
How I long to see the mushroom clouds

G - / D - / A - D - / G - / D - / E - A -

'Mid the yuccas & the thistles
I'll watch the guided missiles
While the old F.B.I. watches me
Yes, I'll soon make my appearance
(Soon as I can get my clearance)
'Cause the wild west is where I want to be

— Tom Lehrer

© 1953 Tom Lehrer. Copyright renewed.Used by permission. — aka: "AEC Song." In his Too Many S by ... *& on Pete Seeger* Gazette. *In* SO! *4:1.* D56

There are many humorous songs in PLAY and in ROUNDS. Others include: "Be Prepared," "Your Flag Decal" (AMER); "Gee, Officer Krupke," "MTA" (CITY); "Garbage," "Pollution" (ECOLOGY); "Garden Song" (parody) (FARM); "After the Ball Is Over" (parody), "I Want a Girl" (parody), "Whiffenpoof" (GOLDEN); "Ring Around The Rosy Rag," "Vive l'Amour" (parody) (GOOD); "S-A-V-E-D" (GOSPEL); "Hang on the Bell, Nellie" (HARD); "Be Kind to Your Parents," "No No No" (HOME); "Frozen Logger," "Government by Horseback," "It's Only a Wee Wee," (MEN); "Mountain Dew" (MTN) "Pleasant & Delightful" (parody), "Rollings Hills of the Border" (parody) (OUTDOORS); "Andorra," "Draft Dodger Rag," "I-Feel-Like-I'm-Fixin'-to-Die," "We Hate to See them Go," "What If the Russians Don't Come," "Willing Conscript" (PEACE); "I'm Changing My Name to Chrysler," "Man Who Waters the Workers Beer" (RICH), "Capital Ship," "Ship Titanic" (SEA); "Get Up & Go" (TIME); "Er-i-ee," "Motorcycle Song" (TRAVEL); "God's Gift to Woman," "I.P.D.," "There Was a Young Woman," "We Don't Need the Men" (WOMEN); "Coffee," "Gallo Song," "White Collar Holler" (WORK).

After the Ball

After the ball is over, after the break of morn
After the dancers' leaving, after the stars are gone
Many a heart is aching, if you could read them all
Many the hopes that have vanished, after the ball

D - - A / A7 - - D / - - B7 E / A D EA D

After the ball was over, Maggie took out her glass eye
Put her wooden leg in the corner, hung her wig out to dry
Put her false teeth in some water, hung her wax ear on the wall
There was nothing left of Maggie, after the ball

— Charles K. Harris (parody source: Louis Halpern)

On J Morris & W Balcom After the Ball, *Lenny Dee* S Everybody Knows *& Lincoln Ctr Series* Show Boat. *In* FiresB of Am S, Bestloved S of the Am People, *The* S We Sang, Fav S of the '90s, 100 S of Nost, Read 'Em & Weep, Fred Waring SB, Gr Legal FakeB, Life of the Party. A27

Alexander's Ragtime Band

Come on & hear **(2x)** Alexander's Ragtime Band!
Come on & hear **(2x)**, it's the best band in the land!
They can play a bugle call like you never heard before, so natural that you want to go to war
That's just the bestest band what am, Honey Lamb!
Come on along **(2x)**, let me take you by the hand
Up to the man **(2x)** who's the leader of the band
And if you want to hear the Swanee River played in ragtime
Come on & hear **(2x)** Alexander's Ragtime Band

Ddim

D - DA D / G - - - / D - - - / E7 - A7 -
/ " / " / D D7 G Ddim / D - GA D

— Irving Berlin, 1911

On Julie Andrews World of, *Boston Pops* Fiedler in Rags, *Ray Charles* Genius of, *Al Jolson/Bing Crosby* Immortal Al Jolson, *Ethel Merman* Merman Sings Merman *& Lawrence Welk* Best of. A28

The Band Played On

Casey would waltz with a strawberry blond
And the Band played on
He'd glide cross the floor with the girl he adored
And the Band played on
But his brain was so loaded it nearly exploded
The poor girl would shake with alarm
He'd ne'er leave the girl with the strawberry curls
And the ...

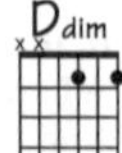

(in 3/4) D - - - / A - - - / - - - - / D - - -
D A7 D7 G / - - Em - / - Ddim D Bm / E A D -

— w: Charles B. Ward, 1895 — m: John F. Palmer
On Bill & Taffy Aces, *G Lombardo* Gr H & Best of, *& rec by Roto Rooter. In* S We Sang, Fav S of the '90s, Flashes of Merriment, Best Loved S of the Am People, 100 S of Nost, Read 'Em & Weep, Gr Legal FakeB, Life of the Party, S for the Rotary Club *&* Am Treas of Gold Oldies. OA29

Believe Me If All Those Endearing Young Charms

Believe me if all those endearing young charms
Which I gaze on so fondly today
Were to change by tomorrow & flee from my arms
Like fairy gifts fading away
Thou wouldst still be adored as this moment thou art
Let thy loveliness fade as it will
And around the dear ruin each wish of my heart
Would entwine itself verdantly still

C C7 F - / C G C G / C C7 F - / C G C -
/ " / C Dm E G7 / " / C G C -

It is not that while beauty & youth are thine own
And thy cheeks unprofaned by a tear
That the fervor & faith of a soul can be known
To which time will but make thee more dear
No the heart that has truly loved never forgets
But as truly lives on to the close
As the sunflower turns on her God when he sets
The same look which she turned when he rose

— w: Thomas Moore, 1808 — m: trad.
On Kenneth McKellar S of Ireland *& Frank Patterson* My Dear Native Land. *In* FiresB of Am S, S We Sang, FSEncy v1, Joyful Singing *WAS)*, Grtst Legal FakeB, S Am Sings *&* S that Reach the Heart. OA30

Bill Bailey

"Won't you come home, Bill Bailey, won't you come home?"
She moans the whole night long
"I'll do the cookin', darlin', I'll pay the rent
I know I've done you wrong
'Member that rainy evening that I drove you out
With nothing but a fine tooth comb?
I know I'm to blame, well ain't that a shame?
Bill Bailey, won't you please come home!"

D -/- A /- -/- D/- -/- G/GDdim DB7/EA D

— Hughie Cannon, 1902
Bill Bailey was a vaudeville actor locked out of his apt by his wife. His friend Cannon lent him money for a hotel rm & with this ragtime song he assured his friend his wife would want him back. On Jim Kweskin What Ever Happened to Those *& in* Am Treas of Gold Oldies, Life of the Party, Best Loved S of the Am People, S Am Sings, 101 of the Gr Nost S *&* S Along w/World's Fav FS. OA31

Blue Moon

Blue Moon, you saw me standing alone
Without a dream in my heart, without a love of my own
Blue Moon, you knew just what I was there for
You heard me saying a prayer for, someone I really could care for

C Am Dm G **(2x)** / C Am Dm F [1. C Am Dm G :|| [2. C F C -

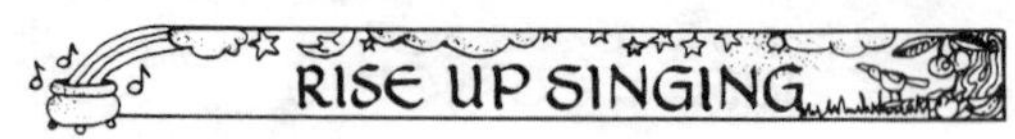

(bridge) And then there suddenly appeared before me
The only one my arms will ever hold
I heard somebody whisper "Please adore me"
And when I looked, the moon had turned to gold!

Dm7 G C - / / Fm B♭ E♭ - / G D G -

Blue Moon! Now I'm no longer alone
Without a dream in my heart, without a love of my own

— w: Richard Rodgers — m: Lorenz Hart
 – Rec by Shanana & on Dylan Self Portrait. *In* Rodgers & Hart SB, Readers Dig Treas of Bestloved S, Gold Standards of the 1900s, Life of the Party, 101 of Gr Nost S, Gold Era of Nost M V1 *&* Those Wonderful Yrs. OA32

By the Light of the Silvery Moon

(intro) Place: Park. Scene: Dark
Silver moon is shining o'er the trees
Cast: two – me, you
Sound of kisses floating on the breeze
Act One begun: Dialog – "Where would you like to spoon?"
My cue with you: "Underneath the silv'ry moon"

G -/- D7/- -/Am7 G/- - - B7/EA DBm EA D

By the light of the silvery moon
I want to spoon, to my honey I'll croon love's tune
Honey Moon, keep a-shining in June
Your silv'ry beams will bring love's dreams, we'll be cuddling
Soon, by the silvery moon

G - A7 - / D - G D / G - CE Am / GC G / GE AD G -

— w: Edward Madden — m: Gus Edwards
Introduced in 1909 by child singer Georgie Price, planted in theater audiences as part of Gus Edwards' vaudeville sketch "School Boys & Girls." On Julie Andrews World of *& in* Readers Dig Fam SB & Gr Legal FakeB. OA33

Daisy Bell

Daisy, Daisy, give me your answer, do!
I'm half crazy, all for the love of you!
It won't be a stylish marriage, I can't afford a carriage
But you'll look sweet upon the seat of a bicycle built for two

D - G D / A D E A / - D DG D / DA **(3x)** D

Harry, Harry, here is your answer true
I'll not marry all for the likes of you
If you can't afford a carriage, there won't be any marriage
And I'll be switched if I'll be hitched on a bicycle built for two

— Harry Dacre, 1892 (2nd v. anon.)
In Cub Scout SB, Goodtimes SB, FiresB of Am S, S We Sang, SFest, Fav S of the '90s, 120 Am S, Life of the Party, Bestloved S of the Am People, Am Treas of Gold Oldies, Fred Waring SB, *&* S for the Rotary Club. OA34

Down by the Old Mill Stream

Down by the old mill stream where I first met you
With your eyes so blue, dressed in gingham too
It was there I knew that you loved me true
You were 16, my village queen, down by the old mill stream

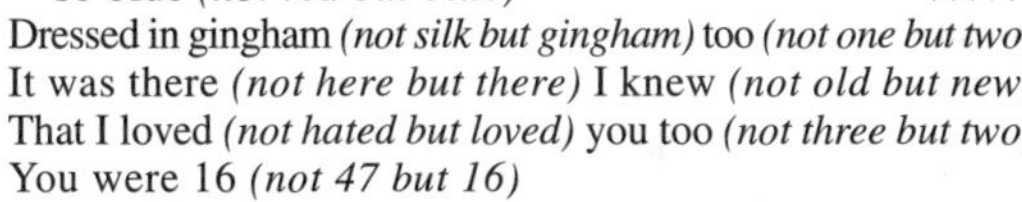

(TD ↑ 5)

Down by the old *(not the new but the old)*
mill stream *(not the river but the stream)*
Where I first *(not second but the first)*
met you *(not me but you)*
With your eyes *(not your nose but your eyes)*
so blue *(not red but blue)*
Dressed in gingham *(not silk but gingham)* too *(not one but two)*
It was there *(not here but there)* I knew *(not old but new)*
That I loved *(not hated but loved)* you too *(not three but two)*
You were 16 *(not 47 but 16)*
the village queen *(not king but queen)*
Down by the old *(not the new ...)* millstream

Cdim

— Tell Taylor, 1910

On Denver Rocky Mtn Holiday *& in* Readers Dig Fest of Pop S, 120 Am S, Life of the Party & FiresB of Fun & Games. A35

Dream a Little Dream of Me

Stars shining bright above you
Night breezes seem to whisper "I love you"
Birds singing in the sycamore tree
"Dream a little dream of me"
Say "nightie-night" & kiss me
Just hold me tight & tell me you'll miss me
While I'm alone & blue as can be
Dream a little dream of me

C♯m7

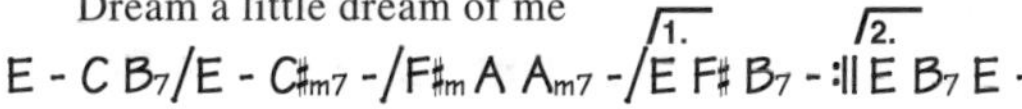

(bridge) Stars fading but I linger on dear
Still craving your kiss
I'm longing to linger til dawn, dear
Just saying this:

C Am7 G7 - / / / C - B7 -

Sweet dreams til sunbeams find you
Sweet dreams that leave all worries behind you
But in your dreams whatever they be
Dream a little dream of me

— w: Gus Kahn — m: Wilbur Schwandt & Fabian Andree

 – On Mamas & Papas Best of, Lullabye Magic V2 *(DiscoveryMusic), Wayne King* & His Orch *& rec by Kate Smith. In* Those Were the Days, These Are the S & Readers Dig Fest of Pop S. A36

Fly Me to the Moon

Fly me to the moon & let me play among the stars
Let me see what spring is like on Jupiter & Mars
In other words – hold my hand!
In other words – darling, kiss me!
Fill my heart with song & let me sing forever more
You are all I long for all I worship & adore
In other words – please be true!
In other words – I love you!

(in 3/4) Am7 Dm7 G Cmaj7 / F Dm E Am /
Dm G C A7 / Dm G C - :||

— Bart Howard

 – In Readers Dig Fest of Pop S, Those Were the Days, These Were the S, Spectacular H for Guitar, Club Date FakeB, Golden Era of Nost M V3 & 101 of the Gr Nost S. A37

For Me and My Gal

The bells are ringing **for me & my gal**
The folks are singing **for me & ...**
Everybody's been knowing to a wedding they're going
And for weeks they've been sewing, every Susie & Sal!
They're congregating **for ...**
The parson's waiting **for ...**
And some day there's gonna be a little home for two or three or four or more
In Loveland, **for ...!**

E♭7

(in G) D7 G / / B7 Em / A7 D7
/ " / D7 B7 / G CE♭7 / D7 G

— w: Edgar Leslie & E. Ray Goetz — m: George W. Meyer

 – In 100 S of Nost, Gr Legal FakeB, Gold Era of Nost M V2, Readers Dig Treas of Bestloved S & Bestloved S of Am People. A38

Give My Regards to Broadway

Give my regards to Broadway, remember me to Herald Square
Tell all the gang at 42nd street that I will soon be there
Whisper of how I'm yearning to mingle with the oldtime throng
Give my regards to old Broadway & say that I'll be there ere long!

G CD7 CD7 G / - D7 EmA7 D7
/ " / E7 Am GD7 G

— George M. Cohan, 1904

In Fav S of the '90s, 100 S of Nost, Fred Waring SB, 120 Am S, Life of the Party, Bestloved S of the Am People, Am Treas of Gold Oldies, S Am Sings & S for the Rotary Club. A39

Heart of My Heart

"Heart of My Heart," I love that melody
"Heart of My Heart" brings back a memory
When we were kids on the corner of the street
We were rough & ready guys but o! how we could harmonize
"Heart of My Heart" meant friends were dearer then
Too bad we had to part
I know a tear would glisten if once more I could listen
To that gang that sang "Heart of My Heart"

G D / - G / E A / - D / G D / - B7 / E A / A D G

— Ben Ryan

 — aka: "The Gang that Sang ..." In Bert Hill SB, Fav S of the '90s, Am Treas of Gold Oldies & Those Wonderful Yrs. A40

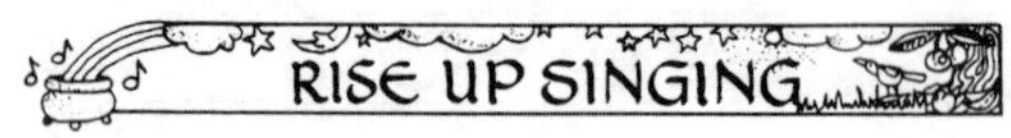

I Get a Kick out of You

I get no kick from champagne
Mere alcohol doesn't thrill me at all
So tell me why should it be true
That I get a kick out of you?

Some get a kick from cocaine
I'm sure that if I had even one sniff
It would bore me terrifically too
Yet I get a kick out of you

(interlude) I get a kick every time I see
You're standing there before me
I get a kick tho it's clear to me
You obviously don't adore me

D7 G C - / Bm - D7 B7 / Em - Am6 - / E7 - Em A7

I get no kick in a plane
Flying too high with some guy in the sky
Is my idea of nothing to do
Yet I get a kick out of you

Em A7 D F#m / / Em A7 B7 - / Em A7 D -

— Cole Porter

 – 1st sung in 1934 by Ethel Merman in Porter's musical Anything Goes. *On Country Gentlemen* Yesterday & Today *& in* Gr Legal FakeB, Readers Dig Fam SB & Broadway SBs. ©A41

I Want a Girl Just like the Girl

I want a girl just like the girl that married dear old dad
She was a pearl & the only girl that daddy ever had
A dear old fashioned girl with heart so true
One who'd love nobody else but you
I want a girl just like the girl that married dear old dad

G C GD7 G/C G A7 D7/G B7/Em B7D7/ 1st

— w: William Dillon — m: Harry Von Tilzer, 1911

Von Tilzer, who is credited with having invented the term "Tin Pan Alley" is one of the most prolific popular songwriters of all time. He was also one of the 1st songwriters to start his own publishing co. In Readers Dig Pop S That Will Live Forever. ©A42

I'm Looking over a Four Leaf Clover

I'm looking over a four leaf clover
That I overlooked before
One leaf is sunshine, the second is rain
3rd is the roses that grow in the lane
You know there's no need explaining the one remaining
Is someone that I adore / I'm looking over ...

G - - - / A7 - - - / D7 - Em E7 / A - D7 - /
/ " / " / C Cm Bm E7 /A7 D7 G -

— w: Mort Dixon — m: Mort Dixon & Harry Woods

 — In Gr Legal FakeB & Best S of the '20s & '30s. ©A43

I'm Sitting on Top of the World

Don't want any millions, I'm getting my share
I've only got one suit, that's all I can wear
A bundle of money won't make you feel gay
A sweet little honey is making me say:

D - Am B7 / E7 A D - / G - D - / Bm E7 A -

I'm sitting on top of the world
Just rolling along (2x)
I'm quitting the blues of the world
Just singing a song (2x) (glory hallelujah!)
I just phoned the Parson "Hey Par get ready to call"
Just like Humpty Dumpty, I'm going to fall
I'm sitting on top of the world / Just rolling along (2x)

D G D -/E7 A7 D - :|| G - D -/Bm B7 E A/ 1st 2

Some people have diamonds & beautiful pearls
While others have children, just kiddies with curls
Keep all your fortunes, keep all of your fame
I just found a sweetie, who's changing her name

— w: Lewis & Young m: Ray Henderson

 — In Those Wonderful Yrs. ©A44

In a Little Spanish Town

In a little Spanish town 'twas on a night like this
Stars were peek-a-booing down, 'twas on a night like this
I whispered "Be true to me" & she sighed "Si, si"
Many skies have turned to gray because we're far apart
Many moons have passed away & still she's in my heart
We made a promise & sealed it with a kiss
In a little Spanish town 'twas on a night like this

D A / - D :|| D A / F#7 B7 / - E7 / DA D
(in 3/4)

— Sam Lewis, Joe Young & Mabel Wayne

 – aka: "'Twas on a Night Like This." In Life of the Party, Golden Era of Nost M V. ©A45

In the Good Old Summertime

In the good old summertime, in the good old summertime
Strolling down the shady lane, with your baby mine
You hold her hand & she holds yours and that's a very good sign
That she's your tootsey wootsey in the good old summertime

G - C G / - - A7 D7 / G - C G / G GEm AD G
(in 3/4)

— w: Ren Shields & Charles B. Lawlor
— m: George Evans & James W. Blake

Evans remarked "There's nothing like the good old summertime" one warm evening in 1902 w/his partner Shields. Shields turned up with the completed lyric a few days later. Makes a nice duet with "Sidewalks of NY." In Golden Era of Nost M V3, S Am S, 100 S of Nost, Bestloved S of the Am People, Gr Legal FakeB, Am Treas of Gold Oldies & M at the Turn of the Century. ©A46

It's a Long, Long Way to Tipperary

It's a long way to Tipperary, it's a long way to go
It's a long way to Tipperary to the sweetest girl I know!
Goodbye, Piccadilly, farewell Leicester Square
It's a long, long way to Tipperary, but my heart's right there!

G - C G / - - A7 D7 / G - C B7 / G CG GD G

— Jack Judge & Harry Williams

Before the US entered WWI, Americans were singing songs like "I Didn't Raise My Son to Be a Soldier" & "Don't Take My Darling Boy Away" but after 1917 they picked up the songs the English had been singing like "Keep the Home Fires Burning" & "Pack up Your Troubles." Judge & Willims were English music hall performers who wrote the song in 1912 as a love ballad which the Br soldiers quickly adapted as a marching tune. In Readers Dig Fest of Pop S. ©A47

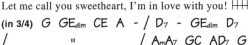

Java Jive

I love coffee, I love tea / I love the Java Jive & it loves me
Coffee & tea & jivin' & me / A cup **(5x)**

D Fdim Em A / - - D - / - D7 G Gm / D A D -

I love Java sweet & hot
Whoops, Mr. Moto, I'm a coffee pot
Shoot me the pot & I'll pour me a shot / **A cup ...**
(bridge #1) Slip me a slug from that wonderful mug
And I'll cut a rug til I'm snug in a jug
A slice of onion on a raw one,
Draw one – waiter, percolator! **(to v.1)**

G7 - - - / D - - - / - - A7 - / - - - -

Fdim

Boston beans, soy beans
I said green beans, cabbage & greens
O I'm not keen about a bean
Unless it is a chili chili bean, boys **(to v.2)**
(bridge #2) Slip me a slug from that wonderful mug
And I'll cut a rug 'til I'm snug in a jug
Drop your nickel in my pot, Joe, takin' it slow
Waiter, waiter, percolator! **(to v.1)**

— w: Milton Drake — m: Ben Oakland

 – On Manhattan Transfer Best of *& Jim Kweskin* Lives Again. *In* Gr Legal FakeB. A48

Keep the Home Fires Burning

**Keep the home fires burning while your hearts are yearning
Tho' your lads are far away, they dream of home
There's a silver lining, 'neath the dark clouds shining
Turn the lining inside out til the boys come home**

C G Am Em / F C D G / 1st / F C CG C

They were summoned from the hillside, they were called in from the glen
And the country found them ready at the stirring call for men
Let no tears add to their hardship as the soldiers march along
And altho' your hearts are breaking, make them sing this cheery song:

CF C AmF C / GC DC GD G
/ " / Em A7 G D G -

Overseas they came a-bleeding, help a nation in distress
So we gave our glorious laddies, honor bade us do no less
For no gallant son of freedom to a tyrant's yolk should bend
And a noble heart must answer to the sacred call of "friend"

— Ivor Novello & Lena Guilbert Ford

 — aka: "'Til the Boys Come Home." On Red Clay Ramblers Stolen Love. A49

Let Me Call You Sweetheart

Edim

Let me call you sweetheart, I'm in love with you
Let me hear you whisper that you love me too
Keep the love light glowing in your eyes so true
Let me call you sweetheart, I'm in love with you!

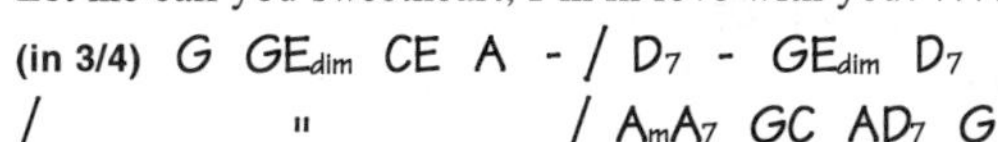

(in 3/4) G GEdim CE A - / D7 - GEdim D7
/ " / AmA7 GC AD7 G

Let me call you Lizzie, I'm in debt for you
Let me hear you rattle as you used to do
Keep your headlights burning & your tail-lights too
Let me call you sweetheart, I'm in debt for you!

— w: Beth Slater Whitson — m: Leo Friedman, 1910

Friedman & Whitson sold their 1st collaboration Meet Me Tonight in Dreamland *for a small outright fee only to watch it go on & sell 2 mill. copies of sheet music. They were wiser the next time & gained a share of the profits on the 5 mill. copies this tune sold. In* Fred Waring SB, Gr Legal FakeB, S Am Sings, Readers Dig Treas of Bestloved S & S for the Rotary Club. A50

The Man on the Flying Trapeze

Once I was happy but now I'm forlorn
Like an old coat that is tatter'd & torn
I'm left in this wide world to fret & to mourn
Betray'd by a maid in her teens
Now this girl that I lov'd, she was handsome
And I tried all I knew, her to please
But I never could please her a quarter as well
As the Man on the Flying Trapeze! Whoa!

G C / D7 G :|| Em B7 / / Em EmB7 / Em B7 D7

**He flies thru the air with the greatest of ease
This daring young man on the flying trapeze
His movements are graceful, all girls he does please
And my love he's purloined away**

G C / D7 G :||

Now the young man by name was Señor Boni Slang
Tall big & handsome, as well made as Chang
Where'er he appeared, how the hall loudly rang
With ovations from all people there
He'd smile from the bar on the people below
And one night he smiled on my love
She blew him a kiss & she hollered "Bravo!
As he hung by his nose up above! Whoa!

Her father & mother were both on my side
And tried very hard to make her my bride
Her father, he sighed & her mother, she cried
To see her throw herself away
'Twas all no avail she went there ev'ry night
And threw her bouquets on the stage
Which caused him to meet her, how he ran me down
To tell it would take a whole page

One night I as usual went to her dear home
And found there her mother & father alone
I asked for my love & soon 'twas made known
To my horror that she'd run away
Without any trousseau she fled in the night
With him with the greatest of ease
He'd lowered her down from a two-story height
To the ground on his flying trapeze

Some months after that I went into a hall
To my surprise found there on the wall
A bill in red letters which did my heart gall
That she was appearing with him
He'd taught her gymnastics & dressed her in tights
To help him to live at his ease
He'd made her assume a masculine name
And now she goes on the trapeze

(last cho) She floats thru the air with the greatest of ease
You'd think her a man on the flying trapeze
She does all the work while he takes his ease
And that's what's become of my love

— unknown

Sung by the Singing Clowns in the small circuses before the Civil War. Some attribute to Walter O'Keefe. In Bill Hardey's S of the Gay '90s, FiresB of Fav Am S, S We S, 100 S of Nost, Read 'Em & Weep, Grtst Legal FakeB, Best Loved S of Am People *&* 1001 Jumbo S. A51

My Blue Heaven

When Whippoorwills call & evening is nigh
I hurry to my blue heaven
A turn to the right, a little white light
Will lead you to my blue heaven
You'll see a smiling face, a fireplace, a cozy room
A little nest that's nestled where the roses bloom
Just Molly & me & Baby makes three
We're happy in my blue heaven **(capo up)**

G - - GE/A D G - :|| C E Am -/D - G D7/1st 2

— w: George Whiting — m: Walter Donaldson

 — In 1927 the yr Berlin's Blue Skies was published Gene Austin's rec of this song became the hit of the century w/around 12 million copies sold. On Duane Eddy Vintage Yrs *& rec by Fats Domino. In* Readers Dig Treas of Bestloved S, Gr Legal FakeB, Life of the Party, Golden Era of Nost M V1, 101 of the Gr Nost S *&* Those Wonderful Yrs. A52

Pack up Your Troubles

Pack up your troubles in your old kit bag
And smile, smile, smile
While you've a lucifer to light your fag
Smile, boys, that's the style
What's the use of worryin'?
It never was worthwhile - so-o-o / Pack ...

G -/C G/G -/A D/G D/CG D/G GC/GD G

— w: George Asaf m: Felix Powell

 A53

Put on Your Old Grey Bonnet

Put on your old gray bonnet with the blue ribbons on it
And we'll hitch old Dobbin to the shay
And thru fields of clover we'll drive up to Dover
On our golden wedding day!

G - C - / G - A D / G - C G / G D G -

— w: Stanley Murphy — m: Percy Weinrich, 1909

In Fred Waring SB *&* Gr Legal FakeB. A54

Shine on, Harvest Moon

The night was mighty dark & you could hardly see
'Cause the moon refused to shine
Couple sitting underneath the willow tree
For love they pined
The little maid was kinda 'fraid of darkness
So she said "I guess I'll go"
Boy began to sigh, looked up at the sky
And told the moon his little tale of woe:

Bm - / - F# / 1st / E7 A7 / - - / D -
E7 - / - A7

Shine on, shine, on harvest moon, up in the sky
I ain't had no lovin' since January, February, June or July
Snow time ain't no time to stay outdoors & spoon
So shine on, shine on, harvest moon, for me & my gal

B7 - E7 - / A7 - D - / 1st / A7 - DG7 D

— w: Jack Norworth — m: Nora Bayes-Norworth

 (US copyrights expire after 75 years but the rules are different in Canada.) — This Vaudeville couple who insisted on being billed as "the Stage's Happiest Couple were divorced in 1913. Oh well ... In Readers Dig Pop S That Will Live Forever *&* M at the Turn of the Century. A55

Tea for Two

C#m Emaj7

Picture you upon my knee
Just tea for two & two for tea
Just me for you & you for me alone
Nobody near us to see us or hear us
No friends or relations on weekend vacations
We won't have it known, dear, that we own a telephone, dear

Dm7 G7 (2x) / Cmaj7 Am7 (2x) / Dm7 G7 (2x) C - - -
F#m B7 (2x) / Emaj7 C#m (2x) / F#m B7 (2x) E - G7 -

Day will break & you'll awake **(in C – capo up)**
And start to bake a sugar cake
For me to take for all the boys to see
We will raise a family / A boy for you, a girl for me
O can't you see how happy we would be?

Dm7 G7 (2x) / Cmaj7 Am7 (2x) / Dm7 G7 (2x) A7 - - -
Dm Em Dm A / Edim Dm Fm - / Dm7 G7 (2x) C - - -

— w: Irving Caesar — m: Vincent Youmans

 — Fr their musical No No Nanette. *In* Broadway SB, Readers Dig Fam SB, Best Loved S of Am People, The Gr Legal FakeB *&* Best S of the '20s & '30s. A56

There's a Long, Long Trail

There's a long, long trail a-winding
Into the land of my dreams
Where the nightingales are singing
And a white moon beams
There's a long, long night of waiting
Until my dreams all come true
Til the day when I'll be going
Down that long, long trail with you

G - / C G / C G / A D
/ " / C B7 / " / AD G

(parody: sung by the Boy Scouts in the 1920s)
There's a long, long nail a-grinding into the heel of my shoe
And it feels as if it were stuck in about a mile or two
And when this hike is over then I will give one glad shout
And sit down by the roadside & I'll pull that darn nail out!

— w: Stoddard King — m: Zo Elliott

 — 1st written by 2 Yale undergrads as a sentimental piece for a fraternity banquet in 1913, but first published in England & quickly picked up by Br soldiers going to war. In Bert Hill S for Happy Singing, Readers Dig Fam SB, *&* The Legal FakeB. A57

The Trail of the Lonesome Pine

In the Blue Ridge Mountains of Virginia
On the Trail of the Lonesome Pine
In the pale moonshine, our hearts entwine
Where she carved her name & I carved mine
O! June, like the mountains I'm blue
Like the pines, I am lonesome for you
As I sit repining in Virginia
On the Trail of the Lonesome Pine

GE A7 / D7 G / 1st / A7 D7 / G - / Am CB7 / 1st 2

— w: Ballard MacDonald m: Harry Carroll

In Legal FakeB. A58

Two Sleepy People

Here we are, out of cigarettes
Holding hands & yawning, look how late it gets
Two sleepy people, by dawn's early light
And too much in love to say "Good night"

C B7 Dm7 G7 / C Cmaj7 Dm7 Dm7G
Cmaj7 A7 Dm Fm / [1.] C D7 Dm7 G :|| [2. + 3.] C DG C -

Here we are, in the cozy chair
Picking on a wishbone from the Frigidaire
Two sleepy people with nothing to say
And too much in love to break away

(bridge)
Do you remember the nights we used to linger in the hall?
Father didn't like you at all
Do you remember the reason why we married in the fall?
To rent this little nest & get a bit of rest

F G CG C / AmE Am F G / C G C A7 / D7 - Dm G

Well, here we are, just about the same
Foggy little fella, drowsy little dame
Two sleepy people, by dawn's early light
And too much in love to say "good night"

— w: Frank Loesser — m: Hoagy Carmichael
 In 101 of the Gr Nost S. ⓄA59

Wait Til the Sun Shines, Nellie

Wait til the sun shines, Nellie
When the clouds go drifting by *[the gray skies turn to blue]*
We will be happy, Nellie *[You know I love you, Nellie]*
Don't you sigh *[Deed I do]*
Down lover's lane we'll wander *[We'll face the years together]*
Sweethearts you & I, so won't you
Wait til the sun shines, Nellie
Bye & bye

G CG / D G / C GE / A7 D7
/ " / D7 B7 / CE7 A7 / GD7 G

— w: Andrew Sterling — m: Harry Von Tilzer
In Readers Dig Treas of Bestlovd S, Fav S of the '90s, 100 S of Nost, Read 'Em & Weep, Fred Waring SB, 120 Am S, Life of the Party, Best Loved S of Am People, 1001 Jumbo S, Am Trea of Gold Oldies *&* S for the Rotary Club. ⓄA60

When Irish Eyes Are Smiling

When Irish eyes are smiling, sure it's like a morn in spring
In the lilt of Irish laughter you can hear the angels sing
When Irish hearts are happy, all the world seems bright & gay
And when Irish eyes are smiling sure they steal your heart away

(in 3/4) C - F C / F C D7 G / 1st / F CA7 DG C

— w: Chauncey Olcott & George Graff, Jr m: Ernest R. Ball
Fr the 1912 musical play The Isle of Dreams. *In* Readers Dig Fam SB, S for the Rotary Club, The Legal FakeB *&* 31 S & 3 Cheers for the Irish. ⓄA61

When You Wore a Tulip

When you wore a tulip, a sweet yellow tulip
And I wore a big, red rose
When you caressed me, 'twas then heaven blessed me
What a blessing no one knows
You made life cheery when you called me "dearie"
'Twas down where the blue grass grows
Your lips were sweeter than julep, when you wore that tulip
And I wore a big, red rose

G - / C G / C GE / A D / G - / C B7 / E A / AD G

— w: Jack Mahoney — m: Percy Wenrich
 — In Life of the Party & Golden Era of Nost M V2. ⓄA62

The Whiffenpoof Song

To the tables down at Morrie's, to the place where Louie dwells
To the dear old Temple Bar we love so well
See the Whiffenpoofs assembled, with their glasses raised on high
And the magic of their singing casts its spell
O the magic of their singing all the songs we love so well
"Shall I Wasting" & "Mavourneen" & the rest
We will serenade our Louie while life & voice shall last
Then we'll pass & be forgotten with the rest

C G7 / - C :|| **3x** CC7 FFm / CG7 C **(4/4 → 3/4)**

We're poor little lambs who have lost our way "Baa, baa, baa"
We're little black sheep who have gone astray "Baa, baa, baa"
Gentlemen songsters out on a spree, doomed from here to eternity
Lord have mercy on such as we "Baa, baa, baa"

C G DmG C / / Am Dm G Cmaj7 / A Dm DmG C

— Meade Minigerode & George S. Pomeroy, Tod B. Galloway
 — This Yale classic was prob orig written by a Harvard man, Guy Scull, who freely adapted a Kipling poem "Gentlemen Rankers." The song was adapted in 1909 by Minnigerode et al, who were members of The Whiffenpoofs, an offshoot of the Yale Glee Club. The song was further adapted by Yale grad Rudy Vallee for his radio show in 1935. In Bert Hill SB, Readers Dig Treas of Bestlovd S, Life of the Party, Gold Era of Nost M V1 *&* Those Wonderful Yrs. ⓄA63

While Strolling Through the Park

While strolling thru the park one day
All in the merry month of May
A roguish pair of eyes they took me by surprise
In a moment my poor heart they stole away!

G CE7 / A7 D7 / G CA7 / D7 G

(bridge) O a sunny smile was all she gave to me (whistle)
And of course we were as happy as could be (whistle)

B7 Em B7 Em / A7 D7 A7 D7

So neatly I raised my hat
And made a polite remark
I never shall forget that lovely afternoon
When I met her at the fountain in the park

We linger'd there beneath the trees
Her voice was like the fragrant breeze
We talked of happy love til the stars above
When her loving "yes" she gave my heart to please

— Ed Haley
Orig title "The Fountain in the Park." In The Fred Waring SB, Fav S of the '90s, Read 'Em & Weep, 120 Am S, Life of the Party, Best Loved S of Am People, 1001 Jumbo S *&* Am Treas of Gold Oldies. ⓄA64

You Are My Sunshine

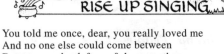

The other night, dear, as I lay sleeping
I dreamed I held you in my arms
When I awoke, dear, I was mistaken
And I hung my head & cried

D - - - / G - D - / / D A D -

You are my sunshine, my only sunshine
You make me happy when skies are gray
You'll never know, dear, how much I love you
Please don't take my sunshine away

I'll always love you & make you happy
If you will only say the same
But if you leave me to love another
You'll regret it all someday

You told me once, dear, you really loved me
And no one else could come between
But now you've left me & love another
You have shattered all my dreams

— Jimmie Davis & Charles Mitchell

 — On Paul Strausman Camels Cats & Rainbows *& J Kweskin* Lives Again. *In* Readers Dig Fest of Pop S, & 101 Of The Gr Nostalgia S. OA65

Other old popular songs in the book include: "Take Me Out to the Ballgame" (AMER); "Sidewalks of New York," "Hot Time" & "New York, New York" (CITY); "Come Take a Trip in My Airship" (DREAM); "Home on the Range" (FARM); "Moon River" (FRIEND); "Anne Boleyn" (FUNNY); "Hey Look Me Over," "I've Got Sixpence" & "There is a Tavern" (GOOD); "Hang on the Bell, Nellie" (HARD); "Spanish is the Loving Tongue" (LOVE); "Kentucky Babe" (LULL); "I Didn't Raise My Boy to be a Soldier" (PEACE); "Grandfather's Clock" (TIME) "Beware, O Take Care" (WOMEN). See also the Musicals Index.

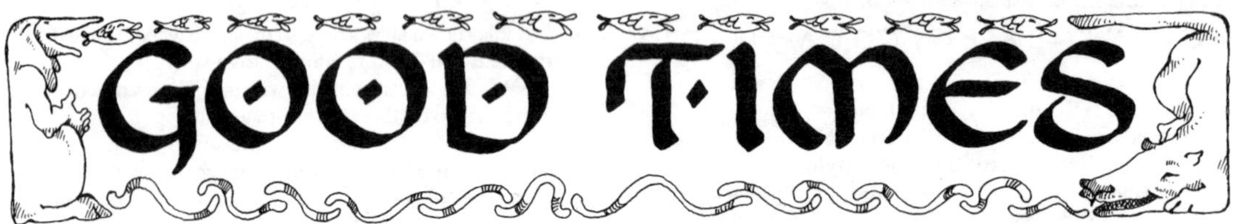

After Hours

In by the side door no stir
No need to worry, Kate, the coast is clear
We can make a little music for the night is ours
And it'll sound a little sweeter after hours

D - A D / G D - A / / G D A D

After hours really let your hair down
After hours with the lights low
Forget about your trouble & the boys in blue *[morning blues]*
Put up another round (2x)

D G - D / - G D G A / G D - G / G A D **(2x)**

Paddy sing a song like a good man
Sing it in your own way like only you can
You can give it all your feeling now the floor is yours
And it'll sound a little sweeter after hours

Out in the bright light of dawning
Street seems strange in the early morning
I never heard the birds sing like this before
They sure sound a little sweeter after hours

— Charlie McGettigan

Lyrics reprinted by kind permission of the original publisher, Helmar Music Publishing, 5 Lombard St, East, Dublin 2, Ireland, (p) & © 1986. — On his S of the Night *& Battlefield Band* On the Rise. OS02

Au Claire De La Lune

Au claire de la lune, mon ami Pierrot
Prête-moi ta plume pour écrire un mot
Ma chandelle est morte, je n'ai plus de feu
Ouvre-moi ta porte pour l'amour de Dieu

G GD GD G / / Am - A D / 1st /

Au clair de la lune Pierrot répondit
"Je n'ai pas de plume, je suis dans mon lit
Va chez la voisine, je crois qu'elle y est
Car dans sa cuisine on bat le briquet"

Au clair de la lune s'en fut Arlequin
Frapper chez la brune, elle répond soudain
"Qui frappe de la sorte?" Il dit à son tour
"Ouvrez votre porte, pour le dieu d'amour!"

Au clair de la lune on n'y voit qu'un peu
On chercha la plume, on chercha du feu
En cherchant d'la sorte je n'sais c'qu'on trouva
Mais je sais qu'la porte sur eux se ferma

"At thy door I'm knocking, by the pale moonlight
Lend a pen, I pray thee, I've a word to write
Guttered is my candle, my fire burns no more
For the love of heaven, open up the door!"

Pierrot cried in answer by the pale moonlight
"In my bed I'm lying, late & chill at night
Yonder at my neighbor's, someone is astir
Fire is freshly kindled, get a light from her"

To the neighbor's house then, by the pale moonlight
Goes our gentle Lubin to beg a pen to write
"Who knocks there so softly?" calls a voice above
"Open wide your door now for the God of Love!"

Seek they pen & candle by the pale moonlight
They can see so little since dark is now the night
What they find while seeking, that is not revealed
All behind her door is carefully concealed

"Underneath the moonlight, Pete my dearest friend
Help me out this once, pal. Won't you lend your pen?
My electric's out & so I have no light
For the love of God, Pete, open up tonight"

Underneath the moonlight, Peter he replied
"I ain't got no pen, Harl, I'm in bed – Good night!
Go bother my neighbor, I'm sure that she's there
Warmin' up her wood stove, by the kitchen stair"

Underneath the moonlight, Harlequin stayed out
Knocked at the brunette's house, then he heard her shout
"Who is out there knocking?" "Me," said Harlequin
"For the God of love, dear, please let me come in"

Underneath the moonlight, one can just discern
Someone hunting pens, someone a light to burn
Looking for these things, I don't know what they'll find
But I know the door closed. And then? Nevermind!

— Charles Fonteyn Manney & J.B. Lully
— 1st Eng: anon. 2nd: Dorothy H. Patterson

New trans. © 1988 Dorothy H. Patterson. Used by permission. — In SO! 26:6, FiresB of FS, FSEncyV1, Baby's SB, Sing Together, Savez-vous Planter les Choux,*&* Readers Dig Fest of Pop S. OS03

Auprès de Ma Blonde

Au jardin de mon pêre les lauriers sont fleuris **(2x)**
Tous les oiseaux du monde s'en vont y fair' leurs nids
Auprès de ma blonde, qu'il fait bon, fait bon, fait bon
Auprès de ma blonde, qu'il fait bon dormir

D - DG D / / G - A7 D // DA D A D / /

La caill', la tourterelle et la jolie perdrix **(2x)**
Et ma jolie colombe qui chante jour et nuit / **Auprès ...**

Qui chante pour les filles, qui n'ont pas de mari **(2x)**
Pour moi, ne chante guère, car j'en ai un joli ...

Dites-nous donc, la belle, où donc est vot' mari? **(2x)**
Il est dans la Hollande, les Hollandais l'ont pris ...

Que donneriez-vous, belle, pour avoir votre ami? **(2x)**
Je donnerais Versailles, Paris et Saint-Denis ...

Je donnerais Versailles, Paris et Saint-Denis **(2x)**
Les tours de Notre-Dame et l'clocher d'mon pays ...

— trad. (French)
In SFest *&* FiresB of Am S. S04

Beggars to God

The song of Gypsy Davy rang delighted thru the night
The wise & foolish virgin kept her candle burning bright
Rise up my young & foolish one & follow if you can
There'll be no need for candles in the arms of such a man

(in 3/4) D C GC D / G F♯m EmF♯m GA
/ " / G F♯m EmC D

Make love to each other, be free with each other
Be prisoners of love til you lie in the sod
Be friends to each other, forgive one another
See God in each other: be beggars to God

D C / EmF♯m GA / 1st / Em AD D

The night was cold & dark & wet as they wandered on alone
The sky became their canopy, the earth became their throne
And as their raiment ran to rags, they thought it nothing wrong
For earth & sky are robe enough when you sing the Gypsies' song

They sang & played the Gypsies' song wherever they were sent
To some it seemed a dancing tune – to some, a sad lament
But in ev'ry heart that heard them true a tear became a smile
And a pauper or a prince became a Gypsy for a while

— Robert J. Franke
© 1983 Telephone Pole Music Pub. Co. (BMI) Used by permission. – On his For Real *& Sally Rogers & Howard Bursen* Satisfied Customers. S05

The Boar's Head Carol

The boar's head in hand bear I
Bedecked with bays & rosemary
And I pray you my masters, be merry
Quot estis in convivio
Caput apri defero / Redens laudes Domino

C - G C / F - G C :|| C G F C / F - G C

The boar's head as I understand
Is the rarest dish in all this land
Which thus bedecked with a gay garland
Let us *servire cantico /* ***Caput apri defero...***

Our steward hath provided this
In honour of the King of bliss
Which on this day to be servèd is
In reginensi atrio / ***Caput...***

— trad. (English) Queen's College (Oxford U.) version.
Transl of Latin: Quot ... = So many as are in the feast / Caput ... = The boar's head I bring, giving praises to the Lord / servire ... = serve with a song / In reginensi ... = In the Queen's hall. In Oxford B of Carols, FiresB of Birds & Beasts. *On* Xmas Revels *(RevelsRec).* S06

Chevaliers de la Table Ronde

Chevaliers de la table ronde
Goutons voir si le vin est bon **(repeat)**

Goutons voir, **oui, oui, oui**
Goutons voir, **non, non, non**
Goutons voir si le vin est bon **(repeat fr 3rd line)**

D-- ---/A-- D-- :||: G---/D---/A-- D-- :||
(in 3/4 & 4/4)

S'il est bon, s'il est agr,able
J'en boirai jusqu'à mon plaisir **(repeat)**

J'en boirai, oui, oui, oui / J'en boirai, **non ...**
J'en boirai jusqu'à mon plaisir **(repeat)**

J'en boirai cinq ou six bouteilles
Une femme sur les genoux ... / Une fem', **oui, oui ...**

Toc, toc, toc, qui frappe à la porte?
J'crois bien que c'est le mari ... / J'crois bien ...

Si c'est lui, que le diabl' l'emporte
Car il vient troubler mon plaisir ... / Car il vient ...

Quand je meurs je veux qu'on m'interre
Dans une cave où il y a du bon vin ... / Dans un' cave ...

Et les quatre plus grands ivrognes
Porteront les quat' coins du drap ... / Porteront ...

Les deux pieds contre la muraille
Et la têt' sous le robinet ... / Et la têt' ...

Sur ma tombe je veux qu'on inscrive
"Ici gît le roi des buveurs" ... / Ici gît ...

La morale de cette histoire
C'est à boire avant de mourir ... / C'est à boire ...

— trad. (French)
In SO! *11:2 &* Reprints #12, How Can We Keep fr Singing *&* SFest. *Eng. transl: "Knights of the round table, let's see if the wine is good / If it's good stuff, I will drink as much as I want / I'll drink down 5 or 6 bottles with a girl sitting on my knees / Who's that rapping on the door: I guess it's her husband / If it is, the devil take him for messing up my fun / When I die, bury me in a cave full of good wine / Let the world's 4 biggest drunkards carry me in my shroud / With my 2 feet against the wall & my head under the tap / On my tombstone write: here lies the king of drinkers / The moral of this story is: Drink before you die!"* S07

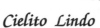

Cielito Lindo

De la Sierra Morena, Cielito Lindo, vienen bajando
Un par de ojitos negros, Cielito Lindo, de contrabando
Ay, ay, ay, ay, canta y no llores
Porque cantando se alegran, Cielito Lindo, los corazones

(in 3/4) AE AE A E / - - - A // A D E A / - E - A

Una flecha en el aire, Cielito Lindo, lanzo Cupido
Y como fué, jugando, Cielito Lindo, yo fuí el herido

El amor es un bicho, Cielito Lindo, que cuando pica
No se encuentra remedio, Cielito Lindo, en la botica

From Sierra Morena, Cielito Lindo, comes softly stealing
Laughing eyes, black & roguish, Cielito Lindo, beauty revealing
Ay, ay, ay, ay, sing, banish sorrow
To pass the hours lightly singing, Cielito Lindo gladdens the morrow

In the air brightly flashing, Cielito Lindo, flies Cupid's feather
In my heart it is striking, Cielito Lindo, wounding forever

— trad. (Mexican - Eng. anon.)
On (& in) Pete Seeger Am Fav Bals V1, *Jim Kweskin* Lives Again *&* Side by Side *& Orziba* Viva Mexico. *In* Holiday SB, El Toro Pinto, *Sandburg* Am SBag, Joyful Singing *(WAS),* FiresB of Love S, Treas of FS, FSEncy V1, 1001 Jumbo S *&* S Am Sings. S08

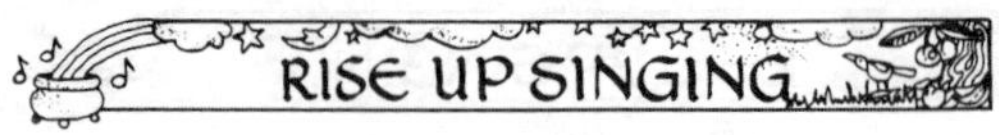

Everybody Loves Saturday Night

(orig Nigerian version) Bobo waro ferro Satodeh **(2x)**
Bobo waro **(4x)**, Bobo waro ferro Satodeh

D A7 D - / / D A (or G) D A7 / 1st

Eng: Ev'rybody loves Saturday night **(2x)**
Ev'rybody **(4x)**, ev'rybody loves Saturday night

It: Tutti ama sabato sera / Tutti ama ...
Yid: Yeder ener glächt [hot lieb] shabbas ba nacht
Fr: Tout le monde aime samedi soir
Ger: Eider Man hat dem Samstag Abend
Port: Todos gostan dos sabados a noite
Dan: Alle elsker Lordag asften
Norw: Alle elsker Lorday kveld
Sp: El sabado ama todo el mundo
(addl phonetic v:)
Czech: Kazdee mah rahd Saotoo vyécher
Dutch: Ledereen find Zaterdag avond fyn
Finnish: Yokinen rakastah lauwandai illtah
Hungarian: Mindenkee Serret sumbut Eshteh
Japanese: Dá re demo do yó bi gasukí
Lithuanian: Visih meelih soobatos vakarra
Mandarin: Ren ren shi huan li pai loo
Polish: Kazhdeh loobya sabaute vietcher
Rus: Vsyem nrávit soobohta vyecheram
Sierra Leone: Mawfay moni s'mah hah bekay
Singhalese: Samadana sanasurade vakarra
Slovenian: Kazhday lubee sobautu nautz

— adapted & arranged by Paul Campbell

Weavers arrangement TRO © 1953 (renewed 1981) Folkways Music Publishers, Inc., NY, NY. International copyright secured. Made in USA. All rights reserved incl. public performance for profit. Used by permission. *– The British imposed an early evening curfew in colonial Nigeria. Popular struggle got the curfew lifted at least on the most important evening of the week. This song was written to celebrate their victory & ongoing struggle for independence. In SO! 3:4,* How Can We Keep fr Singing, Children's S for a Friendly Planet, S that Changed the World, FSEncy V1 & S Am Sings. OS09

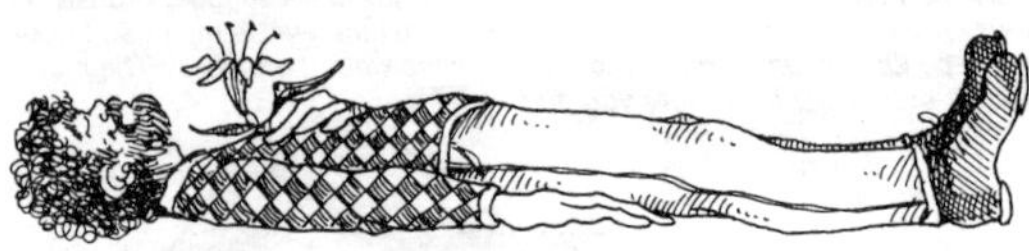

Finnegan's Wake

Tim Finnegan lived in Walkin Street
A gentle Irishman mighty odd
He'd a beautiful brogue so rich & sweet
And to rise in the world he carried a hod
  You see, he'd a sort o the tipp'lin' way
  With a love for the liquor poor Tim was born
  To help him on with his work each day
  He'd a "drop of the craythur" ev'ry morn

Am - / - G / Am - / - GC / C Am / / / F GC

Whack fol the da, now, dance to your partner
Welt the floor your trotters shake
Wasn't it the truth I told you
Lots of fun at Finnegan's Wake

Am AmEm / Am G / 1st / Am GC

One mornin' Tim was rather full
His head felt heavy which made him shake
He fell from a ladder & he broke his skull
And they carried him home his corpse to wake
  They rolled him up in a nice clean sheet
  And laid him out upon the bed
  A gallon of whisky at his feet
  And a barrel of porter at his head

His friends assembled at the Wake
And Mrs. Finnegan called for lunch
First they brought in tay & cake
Then pipes, tobacco & whisky punch
  Biddy O'Brien began to cry
  Such a nice clean corpse did you ever see?
  Tim Mavourneen why did you die?
  Arrah hold your gob, said Paddy McGhee

Then Maggie O'Connor took up the job
O Biddy, says she, you're wrong I'm sure
Biddy gave her a belt in the gob
And left her sprawling on the floor
  Then the war did soon engage
  'Twas woman to woman & man to man
  Shelalaigh law was all the rage
  And a row & a ruction soon began

Then Mickey Maloney raised his head
When a noggin of whisky flew at him
It missed & falling on the bed
The liquor scattered over Tim
  Tim revives, see how he rises
  Timothy rising from the bed
  Said "Whirl your whisky around like blazes
  Thanum an dial do you think I'm dead?"

— unknown

The music is a traditional Irish jig. The words were probably written in England as a stereotyped Irish satire for the Victorian stage. The Gaelic League objected to the song as anti-Irish, but it is a favorite of many Irish glad to laugh at themselves. Joyce used the song title satirically as the title for one of his greatest novels — using the not-so-dead Finnegan as a symbol for Ireland herself rising up. On Judy Small Reunion *&* The Clancy Brothers Come Fill Your Glass With Us *& in their* SB. *In* SO! *11:2 &* Reprints #5, Wind that Shakes the Barley, *Dubliners* SB, FSEncy V2 & Treas of Am S. OS10

Funiculi Funicula

Some think the world is made for fun & frolic
And so do I! And so do I!
Some think it well to be all melancholic
To pine & sigh, to pine & sigh
But I, I love to spend my time in singing
Some joyous song, some joyous song
To set the air with music bravely ringing
Is far from wrong, is far from wrong

C - - - CG / C CG C - :|| Em - - - EmB7
Em EmB7 Em - / G - - - GD / G GD G -

Harken! Harken! Music sounds afar! (2x)
Tralalala (4x) / Joy is everywhere – Funiculi funicula!

G - D G / - - D C / E Am E Am / F C G C

Ah me! 'Tis strange that some should take to sighing
And like it well, and like it well
For me, I have not thought it worth the trying
So cannot tell, so cannot tell
With laugh & dance & song the day soon passes
Full soon is gone, full soon is gone
For mirth was made for joyous lads & lasses
To call their own, to call their own

— Italian popular song

Written to commemorate the opening of a funicular RR to the top of Mt Vesuvius. In FiresB of FS, SFest, Gr Legal FakeB, FSEncyV1, 1001 Jumbo S & Singalong w/World's Fav FS. OS11

Gloucestershire Wassail

Wassail, wassail, all over the town
Our toast it is white & our ale it is brown
Our bowl it is made of the white maple tree
With the wassailing bowl we'll drink to thee

D - G A / G - D A / D - - A / D G A D

So here is to Cherry & to his right cheek
May God send our master a good piece of beef
And a good piece of beef that may we all see / **With the ...**

And here is to Dobbin & to his right eye
Pray God send our master a good Christmas pie
And a good Christmas pie that may we all see / **With our ...**

So here is to Broad May & to her broad horn
May God send our master a good crop of corn
And a good crop of corn that may we all see / **With the ...**

And here is to Fillpail & to her left ear
Pray God send our master a happy New Year
And a happy New Year as e'er he did see / **With our ...**

And here is to Colly & to her long tail
Pray God send our master he never may fail
A bowl of strong beer, I pray you draw near
And our jolly wassail it's then you shall hear ...

Come butler, come fill us a bowl of the best
Then we hope that your soul in heaven may rest
But if you do draw us a bowl of the small
Then down shall go butler, bowl & all ...

Then here's to the maid in the lily white smock
Who tripped to the door & slipped back the lock
Who tripped to the door & pulled back the pin
For to let these jolly wassailers in ...

— trad. (English)

aka: "Wassail, Wassail." Coll by Ralph Vaughan Williams, rec in 1908 fr singer at an inn in Herefordshire. Cherry & Dobbin are horses. Broadmay, Fillpail & Collie are cows. On Xmas Revels *(Revels), Sylvia Woods* 3 Harps for Xmas *& Linda Russell* Sing We All Merrily. *In* The Joys of Xmas, FS N Am Sings, The Oxford B of Carols & Xmas Carols fr Many Countries. OS12

Green Grow the Rashes O

There's naught but care on ev'ry han'
In ev'ry hour that passes-o
What signifies that life o' man
An' 'twer not for the lasses-o

C - / Dm - / F C / Dm Am

Green grow the rashes-o (2x)
The sweetest hours that e'er I spend
Are spent among the lasses-o

The war'ly race may riches chase
An' riches still may fly them-o
An' tho' at last they catch them fast
Their hearts can ne'er enjoy them-o

But gie me a cannie hour at e'en
My arms about my dearie-o
An' war'ly cares an' war'ly men
May a' gae tapsalteerie-o!

— w: Robert Burns — m: trad. (Scottish)

War'ly=worldy, cannie=quiet, tapsalteerie=topsy-turvy. On Ewan MacColl S of Robt Burns *(FW8758) &* Scottish Drinking S *(Riverside) & Betty Sanders* S of Robt Burns *(Riverside). In* SO! *9:4 &* Reprints #8, FSEncyV1 & SFS of Eng Ire Scot & Wales. OS13

Hava Nagila

Hava nagila **(3x)** ve-nisma-cha **(repeat)**
Hava na-ranana **(3x)** ve-nisma-cha **(repeat)**

(in Am) E - Am E / / E Dm - E / /

Uru, uru achim
Ur'achim be-lev sa-me-ach **(4x)**
Ur'achim, ur'achim, be-lev sa-me-ach

Am - / - - G - / E EAm

— trad. (Hebrew)

A joyful energetic dance. The "ch" is pronounced similar to a "ch" in German or the Scottish "loch." Eng. transl: Let us rejoice & be happy / Awaken brothers & sisters with a happy heart. On Israel's Gr H & Guy Carawan Sing with. In SO! *9:1,* S for Eyal, Club Date FakeB, Hootenanny SB, 1001 Jumbo S, Gr Legal FakeB & FSEncy V1. OS14

Hevenu Shalom Alechem

Hevenu, shalom alechem **(3x)**
Hevenu, shalom, shalom, shalom alechem

Dm - / - Gm / A Dm / A ADm

— trad. (Hebrew)

A song of greeting or farewell. Often sung at weddings & other celebrations. Shalom alechem = Peace be with you. On My Israel Celebrates, Lion of Judah & Welcome to Israel. *In* Israel in S, Fav Hebrew S, S for Eyal, S of Praise V3, Harv of Jewish S & S Children Sing. OS15

Hey, Look Me Over

F9

Hey, look me over, lend me an ear
Fresh out of clover, mortgaged up to here
But don't pass the plate, folks, don't pass the cup
I figure whenever you're down & out the only way is up
And I'll be up like a rosebud, high on the vine
Don't thumb your nose, bud, take a tip from mine
I'm a little bit short of the elbow room but let me get me some
And look out (**2nd time:** Hear me shout), world, here I come!

G B7 / E Am / D GE / A D

/ " / " / Cmaj7F9 GE / AmD G

(bridge) Nobody in the world was ever without a prayer
How can you win the world if nobody knows you're there
Kid, when you need the crowd the tickets are hard to sell
Still you can lead the crowd if you can get up & yell

G - / F - / E - / Dsus4 D

— w: Carolyn Leigh — m: Cy Coleman

 – Fr their musical Wildcat. *In* Best Loved S of Am Stage, S for the Rotary Club & Best of Broadway. *Sheet music available from Hal Leonard Pub.* OS16

I Feel Pretty

I feel pretty, o so pretty
I feel pretty & witty & bright
And I pity any girl who isn't me tonight

(in 3/4) D - / - EmA / Bm EmA D -

I feel charming, o so charming
It's alarming how charming I feel
And so pretty that I hardly can believe I'm real

(bridge) See the pretty girl in that mirror there
Who can that attractive girl be
Such a pretty face, such a pretty dress, such a pretty smile
Such a pretty me

G - / - D / F#mC#7 F#m / Dm A7 -

C#7

I feel stunning & entrancing
Feel like running & dancing for joy
For I'm loved by a pretty wonderful boy!
— w: Stephen Sondheim m: Leonard Bernstein

 Fr their musical West Side Story. OS17

I've Got Sixpence

I've got sixpence, jolly jolly sixpence
I've got sixpence to last me all my life
I've tuppence to spend & tuppence to lend
And tuppence to send home to my wife – poor wife!

D - - A / D G DA D / D - G - / A - DA D

No cares have I to grieve me,
No pretty little maiden to deceive me
I'm as happy as a lark, believe me
As we go rolling, rolling home
Rolling home, rolling home
By the light of the silvery moo-oo-oon
Happy is the day when <u>we line up for our pay</u>*
As we go rolling, rolling home

[when the sailors get their pay; the soldiers/campers/counselors go away.]

A - D - / E7 - A7 - / D - G - / A - D -
/ " / A - D GA / " / " /

I've got fourpence, jolly jolly fourpence
I've got fourpence to last me all my life
I've tuppence to spend & tuppence to lend
And no pence to send home to my wife – poor wife!

I've got tuppence ...
I've tuppence to spend & no pence to lend
And no pence to send home to my wife – poor wife!

I've got no pence ...

— **trad. (Australian)**

A late 19th c. military song. In S Am Sings & S for the Rotary Club. OS18

Jubilee

Jubilee, wasn't it a jubilee? (2x)
Well, they were singing out together, they were shouting revelries
Jubilee, Lord, wasn't it a jubilee?

C G C G / C Am G - / Am F CG AmF / 1st /

They were dancing by the river, they were dancing by the sea
They were bouncing all the babies, up & down upon their knees
They were laughing out happy, they were crying out free
Jubilee, Lord, wasn't it a jubilee?

C G C - / G - C - / " / C G C (G)

They were banging on the banjos, they were picking on guitars
They were blowing out the bass notes on the crockery jars
They were sliding on the washboards, banging spoons upon their knees ...

They were coming from the valleys, they were coming from the towns
Well, they came to see the paddle wheel & the showboat clowns
They were coming from the farmlands, they were coming from the seas ...

Now, isn't it a picture, all these times gone by
Well, he used to tell me stories with a twinkle in his eye
And I wished I could have been there as I sat upon his knee
Jubilee, Granddad, I'll bet it was a jubilee

— **Bill Staines**

© Mineral River Music (BMI). Used by permission. — In his If I Were a Word *& on his* Whistle & the Jay, *Sally Rogers* The Unclaimed Pint *& Reid Miller* Jubilee. OS19

Keep on the Sunny Side

There's a dark & a troubled side of life
There's a bright, there's a sunny side, too
Tho' we meet with the darkness & strife
The sunny side we also may view

D G D - / - - A - / - - D - / A - D -

Keep on the sunny side, always on the sunny side
Keep on the sunny side of life
It will help us ev'ry day, it will brighten all the way
If we'll keep on the sunny side of life

D - G - / D - A - / D - G - / D A D -

The storm & its fury broke today
Crushing hopes that we cherish so dear
Clouds & storms will, in time, pass away
The sun again will shine bright & clear

Let us greet with the song of hope each day
Tho the moment be cloudy or fair
Let us trust in our Saviour always
Who keepeth everyone in His care

— **A.P. Carter & Gary Garett**

© 1928 by Peer International Corp. Copyright renewed. All rights reserved. Used by permission of CPP Belwin Inc. — On Carter Fam Mid the Green Fields of VA, The Orig, The Famous, & Their Last Recording. *Also on Smith Sisters* Bluebird, JE Mainer V1, *Lorre Wyatt* Roots & Branches, *New Lost City Ramblers* 20th Anniv Conc & S of the Depression. *In* SO! *17:3,* Readers Dig Fam SB of Faith & Joy. OS20

The Lads o' the Fair

Come bonny lass, lie near me & let the brandy cheer ye
For the road from Fife to Falkirk's
Lang & cold & wet & weary
My trade it is the weavin' at the bonnie toon o'Leven
And I'll drink the health o' the farmers' dames
Wha'll buy my cloth the morn

(in D) A - D GD / 1. D - / 2. D A :|| DA D

For ye can see them a', the lads o' the fair
Lads o' the Forth & the Carron water
Workin' lads & lads wi' gear
Lads wha' sell ye the provost's daughter
Soldiers back frae the German wars
Pedlars up frae the border
And lassies wi' an eye for mair than the kye
At the Trystin' Fair at Falkirk

D - / - GD :|| D GD / D A / GD ABm / D AD

O Geordie, lead the pony for the path is steep & stony
And we're three long weeks from the isle of Skye
And beasts are thin & bony
We'll take the last o' the siller & we'll buy oursels a gill or two
And we'll drink tae the lads wha'll buy our kye
In Falkirk town the morn

O stand here & I'll show ye there's the town below ye
But ye'd best bide here in the barn the nicht
For the night watch dinna know ye
My brother, he's a ploughman & I'm for the feein' now, man
And we'll drink tae the price o' the harvest corn / **In ...**

The work o' the weaver's over, likewise the day o' the drover
And the ploughboy sits on a tractor
Now too high to see the clover
The workin's no sae steady, but the lads are a' still ready
To drink the health o' the workin' man / **In Falkirk ...**

— **Brian McNeill**

© Kinmor Music. Used by permission. — The Falkirk Tryst began in the 18th c. as a cattle fair but gradually changed into a purely social event. Brian hails from Falkirk (in Scotland). In the Battlefield Band's Forward With Scotland's Past, *& on their* Home Is Where ..., *& Gaughan & Irvine* Parallel Lines. OS21

Landlord Fill the Flowing Bowl

Landlord fill the flowing bowl, until it doth run over **(2x)**
For tonight we'll merry, merry be **(3x)** tomorrow we'll be sober
G - D7 G / / G C D7 G - C D7 G

Here's to the man drinks water pure & goes to bed quite sober **(2x)**
Falls as the leaves do fall **(3x)** he'll be dead before October

Here's to the man who drinks good ale & goes to bed right mellow **(2x)**
Lives as he ought to live **(3x)** & dies a jolly good fellow

Here's to the maid who steals a kiss & runs & tells her mother
She's a foolish, foolish thing **(3x)** for she'll not get another

Here's to the maid who steals a kiss & stays to steal another
She's a boon to all mankind **(3x)** for she'll soon be a mother

— trad. (English)

In SO! *2:6 &* Reprints #10, SFest, FS Abecedary, Hootenanny SB, Golden Ency of FS, S For Pickin & Singin *&* FSEncy V1. OS22

Little Brown Jug

My wife & I live all alone
In a little brown hut we call our own
She loves gin & I love rum
Tell you what, don't we have fun

Ha, ha, ha, you & me
Little brown jug don't I love thee? (repeat)
G C / D7 G :|| 4x

'Tis you that makes my friends my foes
'Tis you that makes me wear old clothes
But here you are so near my nose
So tip her up & down she goes

Me & the wife & the little brown dog
Crossed the creek on a hollow log
The wife & the dog fell in kerplunk
But I held on to the little brown jug

If I had a cow that gave such milk
I'd dress her in the finest silk
Feed her on the choicest hay
And milk her forty times a day

When I die, don't bury me at all
Just pickle my bones in alcohol
Put a bottle o'booze at my head & feet
And then I know that I will keep

The rose is red, my nose is too
The violet's blue & so are you
And I guess, before I stop
I'd better take another drop!

— trad. (US)

In SFest, S for Pickin & Singin, Read 'Em & Weep, Club Date FakeB, Gr Legal FakeB, Treas of Am M, Life of the Party, Best Loved S of Am People, 1001 Jumbo S *&* FSEncyV2. OS23

Make Me a Pallet

Ddim

I know that I'd be satisfied
If I could hop that train & ride
If I make Atlanta with no place to go
Make me a pallet on your floor
G - D - / /D F♯ G Ddim/D A D

Make me a pallet on your floor
Make it right down by the door
Make it long, make it low, so my good gal won't ever know
Make ...
D A D - / / " / " /

Give everybody my regard
I'm goin' if I have to ride the rod
And if I make Atlanta with no place to go / **Make me ...**

I'm tired & I can't work no more **(2x)**
Well I'm tired, lonesome, weary & I can't work no more
Pretty baby now, **make ...**

— Joe Parrish

 — On Doc Watson Memories, *Country Gentlemen* Yesterday & Today V3, *Odetta &* the Blues & H.A.R.P. (Appleseed Recs). *In* The Blues Bag. OS24

Movin' Day

Landlord said this mornin' to me
"Give me your key, this place ain't free
I can't get no rent out of you
Pack up your clothes & skidoo you!"
Well I been waitin' til my Bill come home
He's my honey from the honeycomb
He'll have money cuz he told me so, this mornin'
C - / G7 C :|| F - / C - / D - G -

Because it's movin' day, movin' day
Rip up that carpet up off the floor
Pick up your overcoat & get out the door
Because it's movin' day, pack up your bags & get away
If you spent every cent, you can live out in a tent
Because it's movin', it's movin' day!
C - F - / G - / C - / - - F D7 / F - / G GC

Well Bill come in all covered with snow
I said "Hello, give me some dough
Here's the landlord waitin' for rent"
And Bill he says "I ain't got a cent"
Well we'll be leavin' just as quick as we can
You can try & catch me Mr. Landlord Man
I'll be headin' back to Dixieland, this mornin'

— Harry Von Tilzer & Sterling

On Charlie Poole V2, *Jim Kweskin* Jump for Joy, *Delaware Water Gap* String Band Music, *Critton Hollow Stringband* Poor Boy, *Cranberry Lake* Old Time Music *& rec by Holy Modal Rounders. In* SO! *36:4.* OS25

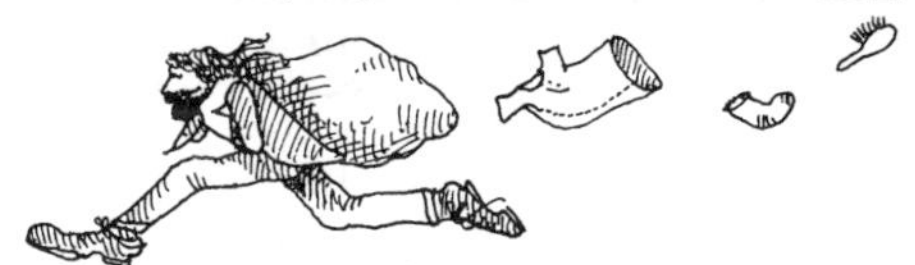

My Favorite Things

Raindrops on roses & whiskers on kittens
Bright copper kettles & warm woolen mittens
Brown paper packages tied up with strings
These are a few of my favorite things (in 3/4)
Em --- / Cmaj7 --- / Am D G C / G C Am B7

Cream colored ponies & crisp apple strudels
Door bells & sleigh bells & schnitzel with noodles
Wild geese that fly with the moon on their wings / **These ...**

Girls in white dresses with blue satin sashes
Snowflakes that stay on my nose & eyelashes
Silver white winters that melt into springs / **These ...**
E - - - / A - - - / " / " /

(tag) When the dog bites, when the bee stings
When I'm feeling sad
I simply remember my favorite things
And then I don't feel so bad
Em - Am B7 / Em C - / - - A - / G C Am D G - - -

— w: Oscar Hammerstein II — m: Richard Rodgers

 – Fr their musical Sound of Music. OS26

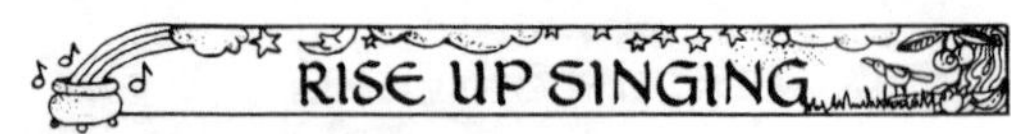

New River Train

I'm riding on that new river train (2x)
It's the same old train that brought me here
Is gonna take me back again

D - / - A / D G / A7 D

Darlin', you can't love one **(2x)**
You can't love but one & have any fun
Darlin', you can't love one

Darlin', you can't love but two **(2x)**
You can't love but two & still be true ...
Three / ...& still have me
Four / ...& love me any more
Five / ...& get your honey from my bee hive
Six / ...& do any tricks
Seven / ...& expect to get to heaven
Eight / ...& get thru the Pearly Gates
Nine / ...& still be mine

10. Darlin', you can't love Bert **(2x)**
 You can't love Bert if you've lost your shirt ...
11. Jane / You can't love Jane if you're insane ...
12. Darlin', you can't love them all **(2x)**
 The skinny & the fat, the short & the tall / Darlin' ...

— trad. (US – last 3 v. Raffi)

On Raffi More Singable S *& in his* Singable SB. *Doc Watson* Old Timey Conc, *Pete Seeger* Am Fav Bal V3, *Mark Graham* Natural Selections, *Nancy Raven* Hop Skip & Sing *& Strange Creek Singers. In* FSEncyV2, *Fred Waring* SB & Am Fav Bal. OS27

O Hanukah

O Hanukah, o Hanukah, come light the menora
Let's have a party we'll all dance the hora
Gather round the table we'll give you a treat
Shiny tops to play with & pancakes to eat
And while we are playing / The candles are burning low
One for each night they shed a sweet light
To remind us of days long ago **(repeat last 2 lines)**

Dm - A Dm / / F - C F / 1st /
Dm - - - / F Gm F A ||: Dm Gm (2x) / Dm A Dm - :||

Y'me hachanuka chanukat mikdashenu
Gil uv'simcha m'malim et libenu
Laila vayom s'vivonenu yisov
Sufganiyot nochal bam larov
Hairu hadliku nerot Chanuka rabim
Al hanisim v'al hanifla-ot
Asher chol'lu hamakabim

— trad. (Hanukah song)

aka: "Y'me Hachanuka." In J Eisenstein Gateway to Jewish S, FiresB of FS, Treas of Jewish FS, Fav Xmas Carols, V Fav of the V Young & V Pasternak Holidays in S. OS28

Old Rosin the Beau

I live for the good of my nation
And my sons are all growing low
But I hope the next generation
Will resemble Old Rosin, the Beau
 Resemble Old Rosin, the Beau **(2x)**
 I hope that the next generation
 Will resemble Old Rosin, the Beau

(in 3/4) C - / - Am / C CF / CG C
 C F / C Am / " / " /

I've traveled this country over
And now to the next I will go
For I know that good quarters await me
To welcome Old Rosin, the Beau / To welcome ...

In the gay round of pleasures I've traveled
Nor will I behind leave a foe
And when my companions are jovial
They will drink to old Rosin, the Beau ...

But my life is now drawn to a closing
As all will at last be so
So we'll take a full bumper at parting
To the name of Old Rosin, the Beau ...

When I'm dead & laid out on the counter
The people all making a show
Just sprinkle plain whiskey & water
On the corpse of old Rosin, the Beau ...

Then pick me out six trusty fellows
And let them stand all in a row
And dig a big hole in the meadow
And in it toss Rosin, the Beau ...

Then bring out two little brown jugs
Place one at my head & my toe
And do not forget to scratch on them
The name of Old Rosin, the Beau ...

— trad. (Irish)

aka: "Rosin the Bow." As all string players know, before you play you must rosin the bow. In Clancy Bros SB. OS29

(to same tune:) The Old Settler Song

I've wandered all over this country
Prospecting & digging for gold
I've tunneled, hydraulicked, & cradled
And I have been frequently sold ... **(same pattern as above)**

For one who got rich by mining
I saw there were hundreds grew poor
I made up my mind to try farming
The only pursuit that is sure ...

I rolled up my grub in my blanket
I left all my tools on the ground
I started one morning to shank it
For the paradise called Puget Sound ...

Arriving dead broke in midwinter
I found it enveloped in fog
And covered all over with timber
As thick as the hair on a dog ...

I staked me a claim in the forest
And set myself out to hard toil
For two years I chopped & I beavered
But I never got down to the soil ...

I tried to get out of the country
But poverty forced me to stay
Until I became an Old Settler
Now nothing could drive me away ...

No longer the slave of ambition
I laugh at the world & its sham
And think of my happy condition
Surrounded by acres of clams ...

— w: Judge Francis B. Henry — m: "Old Rosin the Beau"

 – aka: "Acres of Clams." Charlie King has written new anti-nuclear words to this same tune: see "Acres of Clams" in ECOLOGY. In Hootenanny SB, Best Loved S of the Am People, S of Work & Protest, S for Pickin & Singin, People's SB & 1004 FS.

The Ramblin' Rover

O there's sober men in plenty & drunkards barely 20
There are men of over 90 that have never yet kissed a girl
But gie me a ramblin' rover & frae Orkney down to Dover
We will roam the country over & together we'll face the world

DA D DG D / G D A G / 1st / G D A D

O there's many that feign enjoyment for merciless employment
Their ambition was this deployment since the minute they left the school
They save & scrape & ponder while the rest go out & squander
See the world & rove & wander & they're happier as a rule

I've roamed thru all the nations, ta'en delight in all creation
And I've tried a wee sensation where the company did prove kind
And when parting was no pleasure, I've drunk another measure
To the good friends that we treasure for they always are in our minds

If you're bent with arthritis, your bowels have got colitis
You have gallopin' bollockitis & you're thinkin' it's time you died
You've been a man of action, tho you're lyin' there in traction
You may gain some satisfaction thinkin' "Jesus at least I tried!"

— Andy M. Stewart

 On Andy Stewart *&* Silly Wizard Live in Am. OS30

Ring Around the Rosy Rag

I had a friend, a friend I could trust
He went into the park & got busted
Doing the ring around a rosy rag
Went in the park late at night
And he put a lot of people over 80 up tight
He was doing the ring around a rosy rag **(capo up or play in E)**

C E7 / F - / C D G - / 1st 2 / C DG C -

Ring around, ring around rose
Touch your nose & blow your toes &
Mind – doing the ring around a rosy rag (repeat)

We ought to send Officer Joe Strange
To some Australian mountain range
So we all can do the ring around the rosy rag
Would you like to put Philadelphia up tight one night?
One mass ring around the rosy in the middle of the night
Yes, we all should do the ring around a rosy rag

— Arlo Guthrie

 — When King was murdered in 1968, many cities exploded in riots. Philadelphia's then police chief, Frank Rizzo, responded by defining any assemblage of 3 or more people as "a riot." This particular "riot" occured in Rittenhouse Sq. On his Alice's Restaurant. OS31

Salty Dog

Let me be your salty dog or I won't be your man at all
Honey, let me be your salty dog
Salty dog (2x) let me be your salty dog / Honey ...

D B7 E E7 / A7 - D (A7) :||

Standin' on the corner with a hat in my hand
Wishin' for a woman what ain't got no man / **Honey ...**
Standin' on the corner with the low down blues
Gosh darn mud all over my shoes / **Honey ...**

God made a woman & he made her mighty funny
When you kiss her round the mouth it's as sweet as any honey ...
Worst day I ever had in my life
When my best friend caught me kissin' his wife ...

Hello Sara, I know you
One old slipper & a rundown shoe ...
Two old maids a-sittin' in the sand
Each one wishin' the other was a man ...

Man in the wildwood, sittin' on a log
Fingerin' a trigger at a hound & a hog ...
Pulled that trigger & the gun let go
Shot went wild to Mexico ...

— trad. (U.S.)

On Blue Sky Boys. *In* SO! *8:4,* Hootenanny SB *&* 1001 Jumbo FS. OS32

Somerset Wassail

Wassail & wassail, all over the town
The cup it is white & the ale it is brown
The cup it is made of the good ashen tree
And so is the malt of the best barley

D - - - / / G D G - / DG D A D

For it's your wassail & it's our wassail
And it's joy be to you & a jolly wassail

D A D G / DG D A D

O master & missus, are you all within?
Pray open the door & let us come in
O master & missus a-sitting by the fire
Pray think upon poor trav'lers, a-trav'ling in the mire

O where is the maid with the silver-headed pin
To open the door & let us come in?
O master & missus, it is our desire
A good loaf & cheese, & a toast by the fire

There was an old man, & he had an old cow
And how for to keep her he didn't know how
He built up a barn for to keep his cow warm
And a drop or two of cider will do us no harm
(this cho:) No harm boys harm **(2x)**
And a drop or two of cider ...

The girt dog of Langport he burnt his long tail
And this is the night we go singing wassail
O master & missus, now we must be gone
God bless all in this house til we do come again

— trad. (English) Coll by Cecil Sharp

Fr the Drayton wassailers in Somerset Co. On Roberts & Barrand Nowell Sing We Clear. *In* SO! *37:3 & in* The Oxford B of Carols, FS fr Somerset. OS33

There Is a Tavern in the Town

There is a tavern in the town, in the town
And there my true love sits him down, sits him down
And drinks his wine 'mid laughter free
And never, never thinks of me

C - - - / - - G G7 / C C7 F - / G7 - C -

Fare thee well, for I must leave thee, do not let this parting grieve thee
For remember that the best of friends must part, must part
Adieu, adieu, kind friends, adieu, yes adieu
I can no longer stay with you, stay with you
I'll hang my harp on a weeping willow tree
And may the world go well with thee

G7 - C - / G7 - CF C / → **last 4 lines of chorus are as verse**

He left me for a damsel dark, damsel dark
Each Friday night they used to spark, used to spark
And now my love once true to me
Takes that dark damsel on his knee

O dig my grave both wide & deep, wide & deep
Put tombstones at my head & feet, my head & feet
And on my breast carve a turtle dove
To signify I died of love

— trad. (English, a version of "The Butcher's Boy")

On Mitch Miller Sing Along w/Mitch. *In* SFest, FiresB of Love S, Golden Ency of FS, Readers Dig Fam SB, FSEncyV1, Am Treas of Gold Oldies. OS34

GOOD TIMES

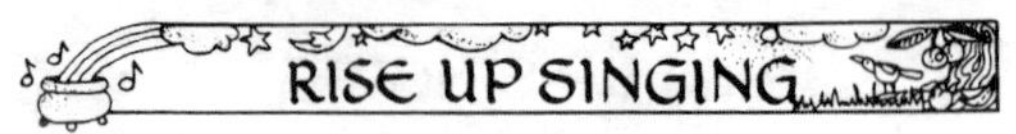

Tonight

Tonight, tonight, won't be just any night
Tonight there will be no morning star
Tonight, tonight, I'll see my love tonight
And for us stars will stop where they are

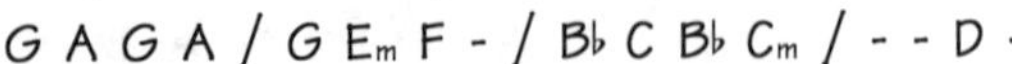

Today the minutes seem like hours, the hours go so slowly
And still the sky is light
O moon, grow bright & make this endless day
Endless night, tonight

Eb - Cm - / Bbm - A - / G A G Em / Bm Am7 G -

— w: Stephen Sondheim — m: Leonard Bernstein

© 1957 by Leonard Bernstein & Stephen Sondheim. International copyright secured. All rights reserved. Used by permission. — Fr their musical West Side Story. *This song represents the balcony scene fr Romeo & Juliet, w Maria (Juliet) here on a fire escape. On Mario del Monaco* World's Gr Love S. *In* Readers Dig Pop S that Will Live, S Am Sings *& Broadway SBs.* OS35

The Twelve Days of Christmas

On the first day of Christmas my true love gave to me
A partridge in a pear tree

D - - - A - D - / D G D A D - - -

On the 2nd day of Christmas my true love gave to me
2 turtle doves and a / partridge in a pear tree

D - - - A - D - / A - - - / D G D A D - - -

On the 3rd day ... to me / 3 French hens / 2 turtle doves & a ...

D - - - A - D - / A - - / A - - - / D G D A D - - -

On the 4th ... 4 calling birds / 3 French hens / 2 turtle doves & a ...

/ " / A - - / / A - - - / D G D A D - - -

... 5 golden rings

/ " / D - E - Â - - - / D - - / G - - / A - - - / D G D A D - - -

On the ... 6 geese a-laying ...

/ " / ||: A - - :|| * D - E - A - - - / D - - / G - - / A - - - / DGDA D - - -

... 7 swans a-swimming
... 8 maids a-milking
... 9 ladies dancing
... 10 lords a-leaping
... 11 pipers piping
... 12 drummers drumming

(for verses 6-12 insert as many of * chord line as needed until you get to "5 golden rings")

— trad. (English)

On Sylvia Woods 3 Harps for Xmas *& on* Xmas Revels. *In* FiresB of FS, SFest, S for Pickin & Singin, Treas of FS, Fred Waring SB, FSEncyV1 & S Along w World's Fav FS. OS36

Vive L'Amour

Let every good person here join in the song
Vive la compagnie!
Success to each other & pass it along
Vive la compagnie!
Vive la, vive la, vive l'amour **(2x)**
Vive l'amour, vive l'amour *[le roi]* / **Vive la compagnie!**

A - / AE A :||: A D / E A :||

A friend on your left & a friend on your right / **Viva ...**
In love & good fellowship let us unite ...

Now wider & wider our circle expands ...
We sing to our comrades in far away lands ...

(Parody) Vive La Cookery Maid

There once was a maiden to cooking school went
Vive la cookery maid!
*On dishes delicious her mind was intent / **Vive ...***
Her cap & her apron were both very neat
And she really looked most distractingly sweet
*But the things she concocted a goat couldn't eat / **Vive ...***

She tried to make doughnuts, but they wouldn't cook thru ...
She tried to make soup & they used it for glue ...
They used her plum pudding to poison the rats
Her griddle-cakes would have been good for door-mats
With her biscuits her brother disabled four cats ...

One day she made something, a pie so she said ...
'Twas tough as sole-leather & heavy as lead ...
She laid it aside & retired to her bed
A burglar came in & upon it he fed
When they woke in the morning the burglar was dead ...

— trad.

Sam Hinton learned the parody in 1935 fr Dr. Walter Penn Taylor. aka: "Vive la Compaigne." In SFest, Fred Waring SB, FiresB of Fun & Games, Pocketful of S & 1004 FS. OS37

Wassail Song

Here we come a-wassailing among the leaves so green
Here we come a-wandering so fair to be seen

D - - - / G D Em A //

Love & joy come to you & to you your wassail too
And God bless you & send you a happy New Year
And God send you a happy New Year

DG D (2x) / D GA D G / DBm GA D -

Our wassail cup is made of the rosemary tree
And so is your beer of the best barley / **Love & joy ...**

We are not daily beggars that beg from door to door
But we are neighbors' children that you have seen before

Call up the butler of this house, put on his golden ring
Let him bring us up a glass of beer, & better we shall sing

We have got a little purse of stretching leather skin
We want a little of your money, to line it well within

Bring us out a table & spread it with a cloth
Bring us out mouldy cheese & some of your Christmas loaf

God bless the master of this house, likewise the mistress too
And all the little children that round the table go

Good master & good mistress, while you're sitting by the fire
Pray think of us poor children who are wandering in the mire

— trad. (English)

aka: "Here We Come ..." On Wright & Reiman, *Nancy Raven* S for the Holiday *& on* Christmas Revels. *In* FiresB of FS & Christmas Carols fr Many Countries. OS38

There are lots of kinds of "good times", of course, besides partying, jugband music, "wenching" & liquid refreshment (the chief subjects touched on in this chapter). In fact, you could say that the whole book is on good times since it's about singing with your friends. Check out the following chapters for other kinds of play for all ages: CREATIVITY, GOLDEN OLDIES, LOVE, MOUTAIN VOICES, OUTDOORS and SEA. (Come to think of it, SEA deals mainly with the same subjects just listed above!)

Other songs of like subject include: "Blow the Candles Out," "John Barleycorn" (BALLAD) "Downtown," "Hot Time in the Old Town," "Moscow Nights" (CITY) "Applepickers Reel," "Buffalo Gals" (FARM) "All the Good People" (FRIEND) "Eddystone Light," "I Wish They'd Do It Now," "Martin Said to His Man" (FUN) "Cook with Honey," "Food Glorious Food," "You Ain't Goin Nowhere" (HOME) "I'm Gonna Be Silly" (MEN) "The Man that Waters the Workers Beer" (RICH) "Birthday Cake," "Foggy Foggy Dew," "Get Up & Go," "Those Were the Days," "Today" (TIME) & "Wild Rover" (TRAV).

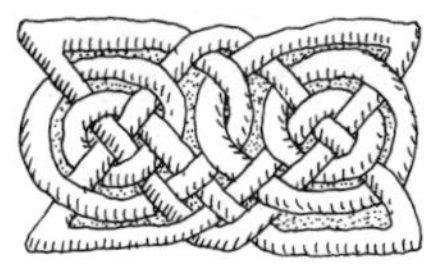

GOSPEL

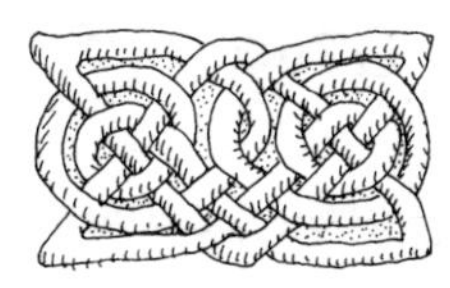

The songs in this chapter spring from the evangelical revival movements which have periodically swept the USA. They are basically composed (as opposed to "traditional") hymns, though the authorship of the older material is often obscure or controversial. Gospel music is equally strong in both Black and White churches. Uncredited songs are of unknown or widely disputed authorship.

Amazing Grace

Amazing grace! How sweet the sound
That saved a wretch *[soul]* like me
I once was lost & now am found
Was blind but now I see

(in 3/4) D - G D/- - A -/D D_7 G D/B_m A G D

'Twas grace that taught my heart to fear
And grace my fears relieved
How precious did that grace appear
The hour I first believed

The Lord has promised good to me
His word my hope secures
He will my shield & portion be
As long as life endures

Thru many dangers, toils & snares
I have already come
'Tis grace that brought me safe thus far
And grace will lead me home

When we've been there 10,000 years
Bright shining as the sun
We've no less days to sing God's praise
Than when we first begun

Allelujah **(3x)** Praise God! **(repeat)**

Amazing grace has set me free
To touch, to taste, to feel
The wonders of accepting Love
Have made me whole & real

— w: John Newton (1725-1807) — m: trad (in *Virginia Harmony*)

v.5 is by John P Rees. The last v. is by New York YM Quakers. Newton was the captain of a slaveship who experienced a religious conversion en route to America and decided to give up slaving. On J Collins Whales & Nightengales *& her* Best of, *Pete Seeger & Arlo Guthrie* Precious Friend, Ritchie Family *(FA2316), Willie Nelson* The Sound In Your Mind, *Stanley Bros* Uncloudy Day, *Bernice Reagon* FS: the South, *& J Ritchie & Doc Watson* At Folk City. *In Joan Baez* SB *& on her* Fr Every Stage. *In* S of the Spirit, 1001 Jumbo & FSEncy V2. OG02

Angel Band

The latest sun is sinking fast, my race is nearly run
My strongest trials now are past, my triumph is begun
O come Angel Band, come & around me stand
O bear me away on your snowy wings to my immortal home (2x) **(in 3/4)**

G C GD G / // D G D G / C G GD G / /

I know I'm near the holy ranks of friends & kindred dear
I've brushed the dew on Jordan's banks, the crossing must be near

I've almost gained my Heavenly home, my spirit loudly sings
The Holy ones, behold they come, I hear the noise of wings

O bear my longing heart to Him who bled & died for me
Whose blood now cleanses from all sin & gives me victory

— J. Hascall & William Bradbury, mid 19th c.

On Flatt & Scruggs S of Glory, *Redpath & Neustadt* Angels Hovering Round, *Stanley Bros* V1, *Carter Fam* Their Last Recording, *Emmylou Harris* Angel Band & Beach Mtn N Carolina V2. *In* SO! *21:3,* Bluegrass SB, FSEncy V2, Am FS for Christmas & Encore 101 Gospel Fav. OG03

Angels Hovering Round

1. There are angels hovering 'round **(2x)**
   There are angels, angels / Hovering 'round

D - - - / - - A - / D DA D G / D A D -

2. To carry the tidings home **(2x)** / To carry, carry the ...
3. To the New Jerusalem **(2x)** / To the New, the New ...
4. Let all who heareth come **(2x)** / Let all who, all who ...

— Philip P. Bliss, mid 19th c.

In Bliss' Gospel S *& on Readpath & Neustadt* Angels Hovering ... *&* SharonMountain Harmony *(Folk-Legacy FSI-86).* OG04

Blessed Assurance

Blessed assurance, Jesus is mine
O what a foretaste of glory divine
Heir of salvation, purchase of God
Born of His Spirit, washed in His blood

CCF C / A_mGD G / CCF C /FFG C

This is my story, this is my song
Praising my Savior all the day long (repeat)

/ " / D G / " / " / **(in 3/4)**

Perfect submission, all is at rest
I, in my Savior, am happy & blest
Watching & waiting, looking above
Filled with His goodness, lost in His love

— w: Fanny Crosby — m: Mrs Joseph F Knapp

On Ives Am Hymns. *In* 1001 Jumbo S & hymnals. OG05

Dwelling in Beulah Land

Far away the noise of strife upon my ear is falling
Then I know the sins of earth beset on ev'ry hand
Doubt & fear & things of earth in vain to me are calling
None of these shall move me from Beulah Land

A - - - / D A B_7 E / 1st / D AD AE A

I am living on the mountain underneath a cloudless sky (praise God!)
I am drinking at the fountain that never shall run dry
(O yes!) **I am feasting on the manna from a bountiful supply**
For I am dwelling in Beulah Land

A - - E / - A B_7 E / A A_7 D A / AD AE A -

Far below the storm of doubt upon the world is beating
Sons of men in battle long the enemy withstand
Safe am I within the castle of God's word retreating
Nothing there can reach me – 'tis Beulah Land

Let the stormy breezes blow, their cry cannot alarm me
I am safely sheltered here, protected by God's hand
Here the sun is always shining, here there's naught can harm me
I am safe forever in Beulah Land

Viewing here the works of God, I sink in contemplation
Hearing now His blessed voice, I see the way He planned
Dwelling in the Spirit, here I learn of full salvation
Gladly will I tarry in Beulah Land

— C. Austin Miles, 1911

Rec by Helen Schneyer (Folk Legacy). OG06

GOSPEL

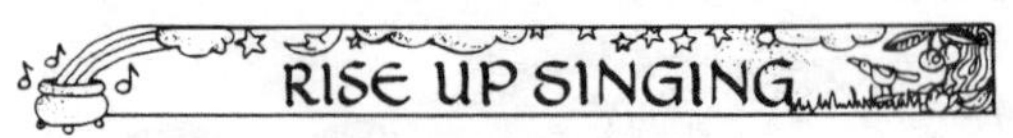

Farther Along

Tempted & tried, we're oft made to wonder
Why it should be thus all the day long
While there are others living about us
Never molested, tho' in the wrong

(in 3/4) DDG D / DDE A / 1st / DDA D

Farther along we'll know all about it
Farther along we'll understand why
Cheer up my brother *[people]*, **live in the sunshine**
We'll understand it all by & by

When death has come & taken our loved ones
Leaving our homes so lonely & drear
Then do we wonder why others prosper
Living as sinners year after year

Often I wonder why I must journey
Over a road so rugged & steep
While there are others living in comfort
While with the lost I labour & weep

"Faithful til death" saith our loving Master
Only a while to labor & wait
All of our toils will soon be forgotten
When we sweep thru the beautiful gate

— W.B.Stevens & R. Baxter

 – Others credit W.P.Jay. Woody Guthrie used this tune for his I've Got to Know *(see PEACE). In* SO! *6:4 & 44:4 &* Reprints *#1,* Bells of Rhymney, Hootenanny SB & Hymns of Glor Praise. *On* Hedy West V2, *Rondstadt Parton & Harris* Trio, *Miss. John Hurt* Worried Blues, *Cindy Mangsen* Longtime Trav & Stanley Bros V1 *(County738).* OG07

Give Me Oil in My Lamp

Give me oil in my lamp, keep me burning, burning, burning
Give me oil in my lamp, **I pray**
Give me oil in my lamp, keep me burning, burning, burning
Keep me burning **til the break of day**

C - F - / C - G - / C - F - / C G C -

Sing Hosanna! (3x) to the King of Kings *[break of day]*
(repeat)

/ " / G - CF C / " / G - C -

Give me truth as my guide, keep me seeking ...
Give me joy in my soul, keep me shining ...
Give me love in my life, keep me sharing ...
Give me umption in my gumption, help me function ...
(and for applepickers:)
Give me strength in my arms, keep me picking ...
... keep me picking til the end of the day

In Quaker SB & Singspiration #6. OG08

Gospel Changes

Prodigal Son, he'd been away awhile
He was working his way back home now over many a ragged mile
When he finally crossed the river & his father saw him near
There was a joyful sound for all the world to hear **(TD ↑ 5)**

G D Em - / C DG - / C - G Em / G D G -

I listened to what the Good Book said & it made good sense to me
Talkin' 'bout reapin' what you're sowin', people trying to be free
Now we've got new names & faces this time around
Gospel changes, Lord, still goin' down

G Bm C Em / G Bm C D / Em C B7 C / G D G -

Jesus, he did not doubt his gifts
Tho' he knew that he had not long to live
He took care of the business of teachin' us how to fly
Then he bowed his head & laid down to die

Jerusalem, I see you standing high
But if you lose your salvation there'll be no tears left to cry
Now some men worship a Golden Calf, while others are bought & sold
And if we live like that, brother we pay the toll

— Jack Williams

 Rec by John Denver and in John Denver SB. OG09

Gospel Ship

I have good news to bring & that is why I sing
All my joy with you I will share
I'm gonna take a trip on that old gospel ship
And go sailin' thru the air

C - - - / - - G - / C - - - / C G C -

I'm gonna take a trip on that old gospel ship
I'm goin' far beyond the sky
I'm gonna shout & sing, until the bells do ring
When I go sailing thru the sky

If you are ashamed of me, you ought not to be
And you'd better have a care
If too much fault you find, you'll sure be left behind
When I'm sailing thru the air

I can hardly wait, I know I won't be late
I'll spend all my time in prayer
And when my ship comes in I'll leave this world of sin
And go sailing thru the air

On Joan Baez In Concert *(VSD 2122) &* Country Music Album *(VSD 105/6) & rec by Dry Branch Fire Squad (Rounder).* OG10

I'll Fly Away

Some bright morning when this life is o'er, **I'll fly away**
To a home on God's celestial shore, **I'll fly away**
I'll fly away, O Lordy, I'll fly away (in the morning)
When I die, Hallelujah, by & by, I'll fly away

D - G D / - - DA D :||

When the shadows of this life have grown, **I'll ...**
Like a bird that prison bars has flown, **I'll ...**

Just a few more weary days & then ...
To a land where joys will never end ...

— Albert E. Brumley

 — Southern White gospel. On The Dillards Wheat Straw Suite, *Happy Traum* Am Stranger *& Bryan Bowers* By Heart. *In* SO! *36:1 &* Hymns of Glor Praise. OG11

I've Got That Joy

1. I've got that joy, joy, joy, joy **down in my heart**
Down in my heart, o Lordy, down in my heart
I've got that joy ... / **Down in my heart to stay**

A - - - / E - A - :||

2. I've got that peace that passeth understanding **down in ...**
3. I've got that wonderful love of my blessed redeemer ...
4. *I've got that opposition to conscription* ***down in ...***

In SO! *7:2 &* Reprints *#9 as "Down in My Heart."* OG12

If You Don't Love Your Neighbor

There are many people who will say they are Christians
And who live like Christians on the 7th day
But from Monday morning til the coming Sunday
They will fight their neighbor all along the way

D - - - / - - E A / D - - - / - - A D

O you don't love God if you don't love your neighbor
If you gossip about him, if you don't have mercy
If he gets into trouble & you don't try to help him
If you don't love your neighbor, then you don't love God

D - - - / A - D - / - - - - / - - A D

In the Holy Bible in the Book of Matthew
Read the 18th chapter from the 21st verse
Jesus plainly tells us that you must have mercy
There's a special warning in the 35th verse

There's a God in heaven & you've but to love him
If you want salvation & a Home on High
If you say that you love him when you hate your neighbour
Then you don't have religion, you just told a lie
On Hotmud Family Yrs in the Making. OG13

In the Garden

I come to the garden alone
While the dew is still on the roses
And the voice I hear falling on my ear
The Son of God discloses

(in 3/4) G - - - / C - G - / D - G - / A - D -

And He walks with me & He talks with me
And He tells me I am His own
And the joy we share as we tarry there
None other has ever known

G - D - / C - G - / - B7 Em C / G D G -

He speaks & the sound of His voice
Is so sweet the birds hush their singing
And the melody that He gave to me
Within my heart is ringing

I'd stay in the garden with Him
Tho' the night around me be falling
But He bids me go, thru the voice of woe
His voice to me is calling

— **C. Austin Miles**

The author was inspired to write this song after reading his favorite Bible chapter, John 20. In S of the Spirit, Treas of Hymns, Hymns of Glor Praise. *Rec by Bill Harrell & Virginians (Leather) & Tennessee Ernie Ford (Capitol).* OG14

Jesus Won't You Come By Here

Jesus won't you come by here **(2x)**
Jesus won't you come by here?
Now is a needed time **(2x) / Jesus won't you come by here?**

D - G GD / D - A - / D - G GD / D A DG D

Listen! can't you hear me call? **(2x) / Jesus ...**
Now is a needed time **(2x) / Jesus ...**

I'm down on my knees a-prayin' ...
Now is a needed time ...

And Daniel was in the lion's den, Daniel in the ...
He said Lord have a mercy on me, Lord have ...

He said Lord! you said you'd answer prayer ...
He said Lord! you said ...

Well now the Lord he sent an angel down ...
And the angel locked the lion's jaw ...
On Redpath & Neustadt Angels Hovering Round. *On Raffi* Rise & Shine *(as "Daniel") & in his* 2nd SB. *In* CFO Songs. OG15

Just a Closer Walk with Thee

Just a closer walk with Thee
Grant it Jesus is my plea
Daily walking close to Thee
Let it be, dear Lord, let it be

A - E7 - / - - A - / - A7 D - / A E7 A -

Thru the world of toil & snare
If I fall, dear Lord, who cares
Who with me my burden shares?
None but Thee, dear Lord, none but Thee

When my troubled life is o'er
Time for me will be no more
Then guide me gently, safely o'er
To Thy shore, dear Lord, to Thy shore
Became popular in Calif in the 1930s. Some sources credit Kenneth Morris. In SO! *9:4 &* Reprints *#5,* FS Abecedary, S for Pickin & Singing, Hymns of Glor Praise, Hootenanny SB & Am Treas of Golden Oldies. *On D Van Ronk* Sings the Blues, *T Rush* Mind Ramblin *& rec by Red Foley.* OG16

The Land Where We'll Never Grow Old

I have heard of a land on a far away strand
It's the beautiful home of the soul
Built by Jesus on high where we never will die
It's a land where we'll never grow old **(in 3/4)**

C - - - / F C G - / C - - - / F CCG C -

Never grow old (2x) / 'Tis the land where we'll never ...
Never grow old (2x) / In the land where we'll never grow old

C - F C / - - G - / C - F C / - G C -

When our work here is done & our life's crown is won
And our troubles & trials are o'er
All our sorrows will end & our voices will blend
With the loved ones who've gone on before

In that beautiful home where we'll never more roam
We shall be in that sweet by & by
Happy praise to the King thru eternity sing
'Tis a land where we never shall die

— **James C. Moore**

On Redpath & Neustadt Angels Hovering Round, *JJ Mainer* V 18. OG17

Leaning on the Everlasting Arms

Leaning (2x) / Safe & secure from all alarms
Leaning (2x) / Leaning on the everlasting arms

G - C - / G - - D / 1st / G - GD G

What a fellowship, what a joy divine / **Leaning ...**
What a blessedness, what a peace is mine / **Leaning ...**

What have I to dread, what have I to fear? ...
I have blessed peace with my Lord so near ...

— **w: Elisha A. Hoffman** — **m: Anthony J. Showalter**

On Stanley Bros V1, *Golden Ring 5 Days Singing, V1 (FolkLegacy). In* Hymns of Glor Praise & 1001 Jumbo S. OG18

Let the Lower Lights Be Burning

Brightly beams our Father's mercy
From His lighthouse evermore
But to us He gives the keeping
Of the lights along the shore

Let the lower lights be burning
Send a gleam across the wave
Some poor fainting, struggling seaman
You may rescue, you may save

D G / E A / D G / DAA D // G D / rest of chorus as verse

Dark the night of sin has settled (TD ↑ 5)
Loud the angry billows roar
Eager eyes are watching, longing
For the lights along the shore

Trim your feeble lamp, my brother!
Some poor seaman, tempest-tossed
Trying now to make the harbor
In the darkness may be lost

— Philip Bliss (1838-76)

The inspiration for this hymn was religious revivalist Dwight L. Moody's sermon about a shipwreck which happened because the lower lights on the shore were out altho the top light of the lighthouse was burning. Moody's moral was "The Master will take care of the great light; let us keep the lower lights burning." On Redpath & Neustadt Anywhere Is Home *(Philo). In* Treas of Hymns & Hymns of Glor Praise. OG19

Life Is Like a Mountain Railroad

Life is like a mountain RR with an engineer that's brave
We must make the run successful from the cradle to the grave
Watch the curves, the fills, the tunnels – never falter, never quail
Keep your hand upon the throttle & your eye upon the rail

D - G D / - - E A / D - G D / - - DDA D

Blessed Savior, thou wilt guide us til we reach the blissful shore
Where the angels wait to join us in thy praise forever more

G D - A / D G DDA D **(in 3/4)**

You will roll up grades of trial you will cross the bridge of strife
See that Christ is your conductor on this lightning train of life
Always mindful of obstruction, do your duty, never fail
Keep your hand ...

You will often find obstructions, look for storms of wind & rain
On a fill or curve or trestle, they will almost ditch your train
Put your trust alone in Jesus, never falter, never fail ...

As you roll across the trestle, spanning Jordan's swelling tide
You behold the union depot into which your train will glide
There you'll meet the Superintendant: God the Father, God the Son
With the hearty, joyous plaudit "Weary pilgrim, welcome home!"

— m: M. E. Abbey — w: Charles Tillman

aka: "Life's Railway to Heaven." On Bill Monroe I Saw the Light, *Marcus* Life's Railway to Heaven *(Folkways), Ives* S of Expanding Am *& Redpath & Neustadt* Anywhere Is Home *(Fretless 154). In* Bluegrass SB *&* 1001 Jumbo S. OG20

The Lighthouse

Let it shine on *[me]* **(2x)**
Let the *[your]* **light from the lighthouse shine on me (repeat)**

D - G - / D - - A / D - G - / D - DA D

My Lord he done just what he said / **Let your light ...**
He healed the sick & he raised the dead / **Let your light ...**

D - G D / - - - A / D - G D / - - DA D

I know I got religion & I ain't ashamed ...
Angels in heaven gonna write my name ...

Paul & Silas bound in jail ...
Ain't nobody gonna go their bail ...

On Redpath & Neustadt Angels Hovering Round. *Version with different verse pattern in* CFO Songs. OG21

Man in the Middle

Three men on a mountain, up on Calvary
And the man in the middle was Jesus, He died for you & me

Em - - - / A Em B7 Em // Em D - Em / 2nd / as chorus

Well the man on the left was a sinner, tied to a cross he bled
He could have been forgiven but he mocked the Lord instead
"You say you are the son of God, they nailed you to a tree
Come down, come down & save us, if God your father be"

Now the man on the right was a sinner too, but sorry for his sins
He begged the Lord's forgiveness & Jesus said to him
"Fear not, fear not this earthly death, before this day is o'er
You'll be with me in paradise, on heaven's golden shore!"

— Tom "Harley" Campbell

© 1980 Thomas E. Campbell. Used by permission. — On Michael McCreesh & Campbell Host of the Air, *Skyline* Stranded In the Moonlight. *Rec by Hot Rize (Flying Fish). In SO! 31:2.* OG22

Precious Lord, Take My Hand

Precious Lord, take my hand, lead me on, let me stand
I am tired, I am weak, I am worn
Thru the storm, thru the night, lead me on to the light
Take my hand, precious Lord, lead me home

(in 3/4) D D7 G - / D - A7 - / 1st / D A7 D -

When my way goes drear, precious Lord, linger near
When my life is almost gone
Hear my cry, hear my call, hold my hand, lest I fall / **Take ...**

When the darkness appears & the night draws near
And the day is past & gone
At the river I stand, guide my feet, hold my hand / **Take ...**

— Thomas A. Dorsey

© 1938 by Hill & Range Songs, Inc. Copyright renewed, assigned to Unichappell Music, Inc. (Rightsong Music, Publisher) International copyright secured. On Redpath & Neustadt Anywhere Is Home *(FR 154).* OG23

Precious Memories

Precious memories, unseen angels, sent from somewhere to my soul
How they linger ever near me & the sacred scenes unfold
Precious memories how they linger, how they ever flood my soul
In the stillness of the midnight, precious sacred scenes unfold

E AE E B7 / E AE EB7 E // - - A E / 2nd /

Precious father, loving mother, fly across the lonely years
And old home scenes of my childhood in fond memory appear

In the stillness of the midnight, echoes from the past I hear
Oldtime singing, gladness bringing, from that lovely land somewhere

As I travel on life's pathway knowing not what the years may hold
As I ponder, hope grows fonder, precious memories flood my soul

— Lonnie Combs & J. B. Wright

© 1966 by Stamps-Baxter Music (BMI). All rights reserved. Used by permission of the Benson Company Inc, Nashville TN — On Redpath & Neustadt Angels Hovering Round *& Dylan* Knocked Out. *In* 1001 Jumbo S. OG24

Put Your Hand in the Hand

Put your hand in the hand of the man who stilled the water
Put your hand in the hand of the man who calmed the sea
Take a look at yourself & you can look at others differently
By puttin' your hand in the hand of the man from Gallilee

D - A - / - - D - / - D7 G E / DBm EA DG D

Every time I look into the Holy Book I wanna tremble
When I read about the part where a carpenter cleared the temple
For the buyers & the sellers were no different fellas than what I profess to be
And it causes me pain to know we're not the people we should be

Momma taught me how to pray before I reached the age of seven
And when I'm down on my knees that's when I'm close to heaven
Daddy lived his life, eight kids & a wife, you do what you must do
But he showed me enough of what it takes to get you thru

— **Gene MacLellan**

© 1970 Beechwood Music of Canada. All rights for the US & Canada controlled by Beechwood Music Corp, 6920 Sunset Blvd, Hollywood CA 90028. All rights reserved. Used by permission. — Recs by Ocean (Black gospel rock gp), Donny Hathaway & Anne Murray. In Ency of Country M & Gr Legal FakeB. *On Joan Baez Blessed Are ... (VSD 6570/1).* OG25

The Royal Telephone

Central's never "busy," always on the line
You may call to Heaven almost anytime
'Tis a royal service free to one & all:
When you get in trouble give this royal line a call

A - D A / E - - A / - - D - / - A E A

Telephone to glory, O what joy divine
You can feel the current a-moving on the line
Built by God the Father for His loved & own
You can talk to Jesus thru this royal telephone

A - E - / - - A - / - - - D / - A E A

There will be no charges, telephone is free
It was built for service, just for you & me
There will be no waiting on this royal line
Telephone to glory always answers just in time

Fail to get an answer? Satan's crossed the wire
By some strong delusion or some base desire
Take away obstructions – God is on the throne
And you'll get your answer thru the royal telephone

Carnal combinations cannot get control
Of this line to glory anchored in the soul
Storm & trial cannot disconnect the line
Held in constant keeping by the Father's hand divine

— **F.M. Lehman**

Lehman was a Pittsburgh radio evangelist who wrote this song in the mid 1920s. On Jean Ritchie High Hills & Mtns. OG26

S-A-V-E-D

Some folks jump up & down all night & d-a-n-c-e
While others go to church to show their brand new h-a-t
And on their face they put great gobs of p-a-i-n-t
And then they'll have the brass to say they're s-a-v-e-d

G - C - / D - - G :||

It's g-l-o-r-y to know I'm s-a-v-e-d
I'm h-a-p-p-y because I'm f-r-double-e
I once was b-o-u-n-d in the chains of s-i-n
But it's v-i-c-t-o-r-y to know I've Christ within

I've seen some girls in our town who are so n-i-c-e
They do their hair in the latest style that's b-o-b-e-d
They go to parties every night, drink w-i-n-e
And then they'll have the nerve to say they're ...

I've seen some boys lean back & puff their s-m-o-k-e
While others chew & spit out all their j-u-i-c-e
They play their cards & shoot their guns & drink their p-o-p ...

I know a man, I think his name is B-r-o-w-n
He prays for prohibition & then he votes for gin
He helps to put the poison in his neighbor's c-u-p
And then he'll have the brass to say he's s-a-v-e-d

Sunday school song from 1920s. aka: "It's G-l-o-r-y to Know ..." On Weavers Trav On, *Delaware Water Gap* String Band Music, *Blue Sky Boys* Sunny Side of Life (orig *ver) & Robin & Linda Williams* 9 Til Midnight. *In SO! 38:4 &* S for Pickin & Singin. OG27

Shall We Gather at the River

Shall we gather at the river
Where bright angel feet have trod
With its crystal tide forever
Flowing by the throne of God?

C - - - / G7 - - - / C - - - / G - CF C

Yes, we'll gather at the river
The beautiful, the beautiful river
Gather with the saints at the river
That flows by the throne of God

F - C - / G7 - C - / F - C - / " /

On the bosom of the river
Where the Saviour King we own
We shall meet & sorrow never
'Neath the glory of the throne

Ere we reach the shining river
Lay we every burden down
Grace our spirits will deliver
And provide a robe & crown

Soon we'll reach the shining river
Soon our pilgrimage will cease
Soon our happy hearts will quiver
With the melody of peace

— **Robert Lowry, 1864**

aka: "Beautiful River." A Methodist revivalist hymn. In SO! 37:4, FiresB of FS, S Am S, Treas of Hymns. *Rec by Lost & Found (Rebel).* OG28

Somebody Touched Me

While I was praying, **somebody touched me (3x)**
Must have been the hand of the Lord

Glory, glory, glory, somebody touched me (3x)
Must have been ...

G - - - / C - - G / - - - - / G D GC G :||

While I was singing ...
While I was preaching ...

On Stanley Bros V4 & *The Dillards* Back Porch Bluegrass & Back Porch Majority. OG29

Stand By Me

When the storms of life are raging, **stand by me (stand by me) (2x)**
When my world is tossing me like a ship upon the sea
Thou who rulest wind & water, **stand by me (stand ...)**

D DG DG D / - - A - / G D F#m G / 1st /

In the midst of tribulations, **stand by me (stand ...) (2x)**
When the hosts of hell assail & my strength begins to fail
Thou who never lost a battle, **stand by me (stand ...)**

In the midst of faults & failures ... **(2x)**
When I do the best I can & my friends misunderstand
Thou who knowest all about me ...

In the midst of persecution ... **(2x)**
When my foes in battle array undertake to stop my way
Thou who saved Paul & Silas ...

When I'm growing old & feeble ... **(2x)**
When my life becomes a burden & I'm nearing chilly Jordan
O thou Lily of the Valley, **stand by me (stand by me)**

— **Charles A. Tindley**

Tindley is one of the most influential gospel writers of all time. His hymns are standards in all Black churches. His song "I'll Overcome Someday" was adapted by Zilphia Horton & others into the civil rights anthem "We Shall Overcome" (see FREE). In SO! 30:3 (see article in this issue on Tindley by Bernice Johnson Reagon) & Lift Every Voice & Sing. OG30

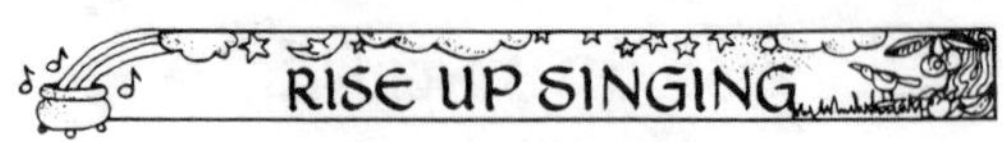

Sweet Hour of Prayer

Sweet hour of prayer, sweet hour of prayer
That calls me from a world of care
And bids me at my Father's throne
Make all my wants & wishes known
In seasons of distress & grief
My soul has often found relief
And oft escaped the tempter's snare
By thy return **sweet hour of prayer**

(in 3/4) C F / C G / C F / C GC
CF C / CF CG / " / " /

Sweet ... / The joys I feel, the bliss I share,
Of those whose anxious spirits burn
With strong desires for thy return!
With such I hasten to the place
Where God my Savior shows His face
And gladly take my station there
And wait for thee, **sweet hour of prayer!**

Sweet ... / Thy wings shall my petition bear
To Him whose truth & faithfulness
Engage the waiting soul to bless:
And since He bids me seek His face
Believe His Word & trust His grace
I'll cast on Him my every care
And wait for thee, **sweet hour of prayer**

Sweet ... / May I thy consolation share
'Til, from Mount Pisgah's lofty height
I view my home and take my flight:
This robe of flesh I'll drop and rise
To sieze the everlasting prize
And shout, while passing thru the air
"Farewell, farewell, **sweet hour of prayer!**"

— w: William W. Walford (1845) — m: William B. Bradbury (1861)
Rec by Tennessee Ernie Ford (Capitol). OG31

This Train

This train is bound for glory, **this train (repeat)**
This train is bound for glory, don't ride nothin' but the righteous and the holy
This train is bound for glory, **this train**

I: Am D Am - / - - E - / Am A Dm - / 1st /

This train don't carry no gamblers, **this train (repeat)**
This train don't carry no gamblers, no hot town women, no midnight ramblers
This train don't carry no gamblers, **this train**

This train is built for speed now / fastest train you ever did see
This train don't carry no liars / no hypocrites & no high flyers
This train don't pay no transportation / no Jim Crow no discrimination

II: D A D - / - - A - / D D7 G D / 1st /

1st chord line fits with rendition on Peter, Paul & Mary. *2nd version of melody is found in* SO! *10:1, in* Reprints #3, How Can We Keep fr Singing, Tribute to Woody, pt 1 *& W Guthrie* We Ain't Down Yet. *Also in Lomax* FS of NA, FS Abecedary, Eye Winker, FSEncyV2. *& on rec by Sonny Terry.* OG32

This World Is Not My Home

This world is not my home, I'm just a-passing thru
My treasures are laid up somewhere beyond the blue
The angels beckon me from heaven's open door
And I can't feel at home in this world anymore

D - G D / - - E A / 1st / D DG DA D

O Lord, you know I have no friend like you
If heaven's not my home then Lord what will I do
The angels beckon me from heaven's open door / And I ...

They're all expecting me & that's one thing I know
My Savior pardoned me & now I onward go
I know He'll take me thru tho' I am weak & poor / **And I ...**

I have a loving mother up in gloryland
I don't expect to stop until I shake her hand
She's waiting now for me in heaven's open door ...

Over in Canaan's land there'll be no dying there
Saints shouting victory, glory everywhere
Their songs of sweetest praise drift back from heaven's shore

— arr by Albert E. Brumley
Arr © Albert E. Brumley & Sons, All rights reserved. Used by permission. — White Pentecostal hymn. Guthrie used the tune for his I Ain't Got No Home *(see RICH). On Redpath & Neustadt* Angles Hovering Round *& J Loudermilk* Just Passin Thru V2. *In* Awakening Glory. OG33

Turn Your Radio On

Come & listen in to a radio station where the mighty hosts of Heaven sing
Turn your radio on, turn your radio on
If you want to hear the songs of Zion coming from the land of endless spring
Get in touch with God, turn your radio on

D - G D / - - AE A / 1st / D DA D -

Turn your radio on & listen to the music in the air
Turn your radio on, Heaven's glory share
Turn the lights down low & listen to the Master's radio
Get in touch with God, turn your radio on

Brother, listen in to a gloryland chorus
Listen to the glad hosannas roll / **Turn ...**
Get a little taste of joy awaiting
Get a little Heaven in your soul / **Get in touch ...**

Listen to the songs of the fathers & mothers
And the many friends gone on before / **Turn ...**
Some eternal morning we shall meet them
Over on the hallelujah shore / **Get in touch ...**

— Albert E. Brumley
© 1938 by Stamps-Baxter Music (BMI). Renewed 1966. All rights reserved. Used by permission of The Benson Co., Inc. Nashville TN. — On J Hartford Aero Plain *& Blue Sky Boys* Sunny Side of Life. *In* Guiding Star. OG34

We Need a Whole Lot More of Jesus

You can read it in the morning paper
You can hear it on the radio
How crime is sweeping the nation
This old world's about to go
We need a brand new case of salvation
To keep the love of God in our soul
We need a whole lot more of Jesus
And a lot less rock 'n' roll!

A - / D - / - A / B7 E // 1st 3 / E A

We need more old time camp meetings
And a lot more prayers of faith
Prayers that'll move the mountain
Save our souls from the burnin' wave ...

We need more old-fashioned preachers
Pouring out their hearts in prayer
When you're in their presence
You know that the Lord is there ...

— Wayne Raney
© 1958 Fort Knox Music Inc, Trio Music Co, Inc. & Oleta Publishing Co. Copyright renewed. All rights administered by Hudson Bay Music Inc. All rights reserved. Used by permission. On his Sings 18 of Their Most Requested Favs. OG35

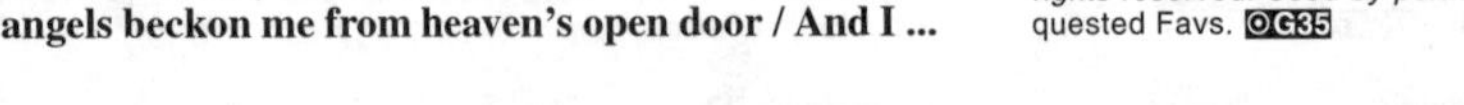

We'll Understand it Better By & By

We are tossed & driven on the restless sea of time
Somber skies & howling tempest oft succeeds a bright sunshine
In that land of perfect day, when the mists have rolled away
We will understand it better by & by

D - G D / - E A - / 1st / D A D -

By & by, when the morning comes
All the saints of God are gathered home
We'll tell the story how we've overcome
For we'll understand it better by & by (by & by)

We are often destitute of the things that life demands
Want of shelter & of food, thirsty hills & barren lands
We are trusting in the Lord & according to His word / **We ...**

Trials dark on every hand & we cannot understand
All the ways that God would lead us to that blessed Promised Land
But He guides us with His eye & we'll follow til we die
For **we'll ...**

Temptations, hidden snares, often take us unaware
And our hearts are made to bleed for a thoughtless word or deed
And we wonder why the test when we try to do our best
But **we'll ...**

— Charles A. Tindley
In SO! *30:3 &* Lift Every Voice & Sing *& on Sweet Homey In the Rock* Feel Something Drawing Me On *(FF 375).* OG36

What a Friend We Have in Jesus

What a friend we have in Jesus, all our sins & griefs to bear
What a privilege to carry everything to God in prayer
O what peace we often forfeit, o what needless pain we bear
All because we do not carry everything to God in prayer

D G D A / D G DA D / A D GD A / 2nd /

Have we trials & temptations, is there trouble anywhere?
We should never be discouraged, **take it to the Lord in prayer**
Can we find a friend so faithful who will all our sorrows share?
Jesus knows our ev'ry weakness, **take it ...**

Are we weak & heavy laden, cumbered with a load of care?
Precious Saviour still our refuge, **take ...**
Do thy friends despise, forsake thee? **Take ...**
In His arms He'll take & shield thee, thou wilt find a solace there

— w: Joseph Scriven **— m: Charles C. Converse**
aka: "Take It to ..." In S of the Spirit, 1001 Jumbo S, 50 Yrs of Country M, Treas of Hymns, Hymns of Glor Praise. *Rec by Tennessee Ernie. On Doc Watson* Down South *(SH-3742) & Sweet Honey In the Rock* We All ... Every One of Us *(FF 317).* OG37

When the Roll Is Called up Yonder

When the trumpet of the Lord shall sound & time shall be no more
And the morning breaks eternal bright & fair
When the saved of earth shall gather over on the other shore
And the roll is called up yonder, I'll be there

D - G D / - E A - / D D7 G D / - A D -

When the roll is called up yonder **(3x)**
When the roll is called up yonder, I'll be there

D - - - / A - - - / D D7 G - / D A D -

On that bright & cloudless morning when the dead in Christ shall rise
And the glory of His resurrection share
When His chosen ones shall gather to their home beyond the skies / **And ...**

Let us labor for the Master from the dawn til setting sun
Let us talk of all His wondrous love & care
Then when all of life is over & our work on earth is done ...

— James M. Black
On Willie Nelson Troublemaker *& in* Hymns of Glor Praise. OG38

Where Could I Go

Living below in this old sinful world
Hardly a comfort can afford
Striving alone to face temptations sore
Where could I go but to the Lord?

D - G D / - - A - / D D7 G D / DG DA D -

Where could I go, O where could I go
Seeking a refuge for my soul?
Needing a friend to save me in the end / Where ...?

Neighbors are kind, I love them ev'ryone
We get along in sweet accord
But when my soul needs manna from above / **Where ...?**

Life here is grand with friends I love so dear
Comfort I get from God's own word
Yet when I face the chilling hand of death ...

— J.B. Coats
 — On Stanley Bros V4 *& Emmylou Harris* Angel Band. *In* Golden Key. OG39

Will the Circle Be Unbroken

I was standing by my window on a cold & cloudy day
When I saw the hearse come rolling for to carry my mother away

D - G D / - - DA7 D

Will the circle be unbroken by & by, Lord, by & by?
There's a better home a-waiting in the sky, Lord, in the sky

Lord, I told that undertaker "Undertaker, please drive slow
For this body you're a-hauling, Lord, I hate to see her go"

I followed close behind her, tried to hold up & be brave
But I could not hide my sorrow when they laid her in the grave

Went back home, Lord, my home was lonesome, 'cause my mother, she was gone
All my brothers, sisters cryin', what a home, so sad and lone

One by one the seats were emptied, one by one, they went away
Now that family, they are parted. Will they meet again someday?

— Charles H. Gabriel (adapted)

Will the circle be unbroken, by & by Lord by & by
There's a better way to live now, we can have it if we try

I was singing with my sisters, I was singing with my friends
And we all can sing together, 'cause the circle never ends

I was born down in the valley where the sun refused to shine
But I'm climbing up to the highland, gonna make that mountain mine!

— new version by Cathy Winter, Betsy Rose & Marcia Taylor
New words © 1988 Authors. Used by permission. — Orig: "Can the Circle ..." Earliest recs by Metropolitan Quartet, Silver Leaf Quartet (of Norfolk VA) & Carter Fam. On Simmons & Gavin By Babel's Stream, *Country Gentlemen* Sing & Play *(FA2410), Dorsey Dixon* Babies in the Mill *(Testament), Baez* Country M Alb *& her* 1st 10 Yrs, *W Nelson* Troublemaker, *Doc Watson* Old Timey Conc, *Carter Fam* The Famous, *Pentangle* Reflection, *Blue Sky Boys* Presenting Strange Creek Singers *& Pete Seeger & A Guthrie* Prec Friend. *Also rec by Jack Elliott. In* SO! *16:3 &* Reprints *#11.* OG40

Most evangelically-oriented Christian bookstores carry a wide variety of gospel collections. Philo has issued 2 wonderful albums of gospel music by Jean Redpath, Lisa Neustadt & the Angel Band entitled Angels Hovering Round & Anywhere Is Home. An excellent source for the 2 Tindley hymns here & other Black gospel is Lift Every Voice & Sing (Church Hymnal Corp., New York, NY.)

Gospel songs elsewhere in this book include: "Love Will Guide Thee" [a rewrite of "I Will Guide Thee"], "What a Day of Victory" (HOPE) "Kumbaya / Come by Here" (LULL) T.A.Dorsey's "Peace in the Valley" (PEACE) & "Peace Like a River" (SACR).

For earlier traditional (pre-Emancipation) Black hymns, see SPIRITUALS. Early American White hymns (eg. "Babylon is Falling," "Bringing in the Sheaves," "I Will Arise") are in FAITH

Angel from Montgomery

I am an old woman named after my mother
My old man is another child that's grown old
If dreams were lightning, thunder were desire
This old house would have burnt down a long time ago

D G D G / D G A D :||

Make me an angel that flies from Montgom'ry
Make me a poster of an old rodeo
Just give me one thing that I can hold on to
To believe in this living is just a hard way to go

D C G D / / / D G A D

When I was a young girl, well I had me a cowboy
He weren't much to look at just a free rambling man
But that was a long time & no matter how I try
The years just flow by like a broken down dam

There's flies in the kitchen I can hear 'em there buzzing
And I ain't done nothing since I woke up today
How the hell can a person go to work in the morning
And come home in the ev'ning & have nothing to say

— w: John Prine

 — On his John Prine, *John Denver* Farewell Andromeda, Memorial Conc for Steve Goodman *& on Bonnie Raitt* Streetlights. OB37

Banks of the Ohio

I asked my love to go with me
To take a walk a little way
And as we walked & as we talked
About our golden wedding day

D - A7 - / - - D - / - D7 G - / D A7 D -

Then only say that you'll be mine
In no other arms entwine
Down beside where the waters flow
Down by the banks of the Ohio

I asked your mother for you, dear
And she said you were too young
Only say that you'll be mine
Happiness in my home you'll find

I held a knife against her breast
And gently in my arms she pressed
Crying "Willie, O Willie, don't murder me
For I'm unprepared for eternity"

I took her by her lily white hand
Led her down by where the waters stand
I picked her up & I pitched her in
Watched her as she floated down

I started back home twixt 12 & 1
Crying "My God, what have I done?
I've murdered the only woman I love
Because she would not be my bride"

— w: trad. (U.S.)

On Baez Country M Alb, *Stanley Bros* Legenday, *Monroe Bros* Feast Here, *Calif Slim* On the Mall *(SlimRec), Doc Watson* On Stage, *Grandpa Jones* Farm Alb *& New Lost City Ramblers* V2 & 20 Yrs. *In* SO! *7:4 &* Reprints *#1,* Hootenanny SB, S for Pickin & Singin *&* 1001 Jumbo S. OB38

Candy Man Blues

Candy Man, Candy Man **(3x)**
I wish I was in New Orleans, sittin' on a candy stand

D - - - / A7 - D - / - - - - / G D A7 D

Candy Man, Candy Man (3x)
I'd give anything in this God almighty world to get my Candy Man home

Little red light, little green light **(3x)**
Stop on the red, go on the green, gettin' my Candy Man home

Run get the pitcher, get the baby some beer **(6x)**
I wish I was in New Orleans, sittin' on a candy stand

Candy Man, salty dog **(3x)**
If you won't be my salty dog, I won't be your Candy Man

— w: trad (US)

On Van Ronk Just Dave, Your Basic *&* S for Aging Children. *On* Gr FSingers of the '60s, *Jack Elliott* Ramblin ..., *Patrick Sky* 2 Steps Forward, *Michael Cooney* Still Cooney, *John Renbourn* w/Stefan Grossman Live, *Grateful Dead* Am Beauty & Dead Set. *Mississippi John Hurt sings a rather different (& "racier") "Candy Man Blues." In* SO! *14:5 &* Reprints *#9.* OB39

Deep River Blues

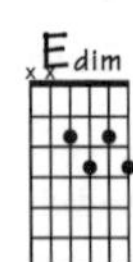

Let it rain let it pour
Let it rain a whole lot more
Cuz I've got them deep river blues
Let the rain drive right on
Let the wind sweep along / Cuz ...

E Edim E A7 / E - B7 - / 1st / E B7 E -

My gal Sal's a good ol' pal
Walks just like a water fowl / **Cuz ...**
Ain't no one to cry for me
And the fish all go out on a spree / **Cuz ...**

Give me back my old boat
I'm gonna sail her if she'll float ...
Goin' back to Mussel Shoals
Times are better back there I'm told ...

— w: arr & adap by A.D. "Doc" Watson

 — On Doc Watson On Stage *& Delmore Bros* I Got That Big River Blue *(orig rec). In* FSEncy V2. OB40

Eleanor Rigby

(intro) Ah, look at all the lonely people! **(2x)**

F - - - Am - - - / /

Eleanor Rigby picks up the rice in the church
Where a wedding has been – lives in a dream
Waits at the window wearing the face that she keeps
In a jar by the door – who is it for?

Am - - - / - F - - Am :||

All the lonely people, where do they all come from
All the lonely people, where do they all belong

Am7 - Am6 - F - Am - / /

Father McKenzie writing the words of a sermon
That no one will hear – no one comes near
Look at him working, darning his socks in the night
When there's nobody there – what does he care?

Eleanor Rigby died in the church & was buried
Along with her name – nobody came
Father McKenzie wiping the dirt from his hands
As he walks from the grave – no one was saved

— w: John Lennon & Paul McCartney

 — On Beatles 1962-66 & Revolver, *Tim Ware Group* Shelter fr the Norm *& Richie Havens* Mixed Bag. *In* Club Date FakeB. OB41

Every Night When the Sun Goes In

Ev'ry night when the sun goes in **(3x)**
I hang down my head & mournful cry

C AmG C - / Em Gm C C7 / F G Am - / C CG C -

True love don't weep, true love don't mourn **(3x)**
I'm going away on the morning train *[to Marble town]*

I wish to the Lord that train would come **(3x)**
To take me back to where I come from

I wish to the Lord my babe was born
A-sitting upon his papa's knee
And me, poor girl, was dead & gone
And the green grass growing over me

— w: trad. (So Appalachian)

In Cecil Sharp Eng FS of the So Appalachs, SO! *2:11 &* Reprints *#2, Lomax* Am Bals & FS, S for Pickin & Singin, Treas of Am FS, FSEncyV1, S Am Sings & FiresB of FS. *On* Fast Folk V2, *Weavers* SB, *Ian & Sylvia* 4 Strong Winds *& a rec by Harry Belafonte.* OB42

Frankie and Johnnie

Frankie & Johnnie were lovers, o Lordie how they could love
They swore to be true to each other, just as true as the stars above
He was her man, but he done her wrong

C - - C7 / F - - C // G - C -

Frankie & Johnnie went walking, John in his brand new suit
"Then o good Lord" says **F.** "don't my **J.** look real cute!" / **He ...**

F. she was a good woman & **J.** was a good man
And every dollar that she made went right into **J.**'s hand ...

F. went down to the corner just for a bucket of beer
She said to the fat bartender "Has my lovin'est man been here?" ...

"I don't want to cause you no trouble & I don't want to tell
 you no lie
But I saw your man an hour ago with a gal named Alice Bly
And if he's your man, he's a-doin' you wrong"

F. looked over the transom & found to her great surprise
That there on the bed sat **J.**, a-lovin' up Alice Bly ...

F. drew back her kimono, she took out her little 44
Root-a-toot-toot three times she shot, right thru that hardwood floor
She shot her man cuz he was doin' her wrong

"Roll me over easy, roll me over slow
Roll me on the side, cuz the bullet hurt me so
I was her man, but I done her wrong"

The judge said to the jury "It's as plain as plain can be
This woman shot her lover, it's murder in the second degree
He was her man, tho' he done her wrong"

This story has no moral, this story has no end
This story only goes to show that there ain't no good in men
They'll do you wrong just as sure as you're born

— w: trad (U.S.)

On Doc & Merle Watson Then & Now *& Josh White* The Legendary. *On (& in) Pete Seeger* Am Fav Bals V1 *(FA2320). In* Liberated Woman's SB, Treas of FS, Read 'em & Weep. OB43

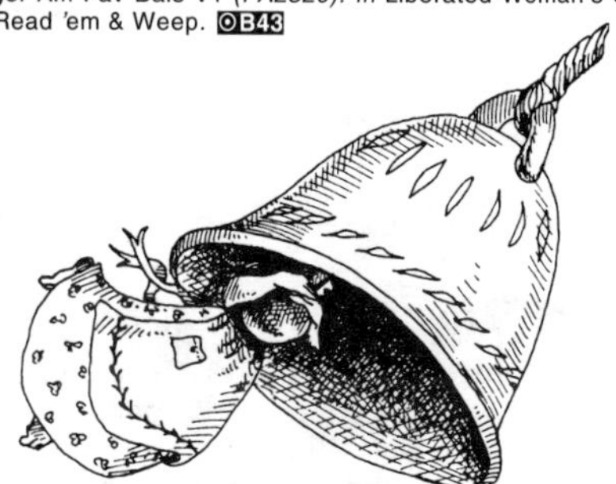

Hang on the Bell, Nellie

The scene is in a jailhouse, if the curfew rings tonight
The guy in number 13 cell will go out like a light
She knew her dad was innocent & so our little Nell
Tied her tender torso to the clapper of the bell

D - A D / - - - A / D - G - / A - - D

Hang on the bell Nellie, hang on the bell
Your poor father's locked in the old prison cell
As you swing to the left & you swing to the right
Remember the curfew must never ring tonight

D - G D / - - G A / " / " /

It all began when Nellie said "O, No!" to handsome Jack
She struggled as he tried to kiss her down by the RR track
Daddy came a-runnin' as the train sped down the line
Jack stepped back upon the track & paid the price of crime

They arrested dear old daddy & they took him before the law
The coppers said that handsome Jack warn't handsome any more
Nell, she came & pleaded but the jury did not care
They did not have a sofa so they sent him to the chair

They tugged upon the bell-rope but there was no ting-a-ling
They could not get the job done, no the curfew would not ring
Upstairs, poor Nell was swinging as below they tugged & heaved
Til suddenly a voice cried "Stop! the geezer's been reprieved'

This is the bedtime story that the warden loves to tell
The convicts listen to the tale of plucky little Nell
And how she saved her dad that night when the curfew
 would not ring
And tears stream down their faces as in harmony they sing:

— w: Tommie Connor, Clive Erard & Ross Parker

 — Fr the singing of Joe Hickerson. On his FS & Bals. *Rec by Chad Mitchell Trio (Kapp).* OB44

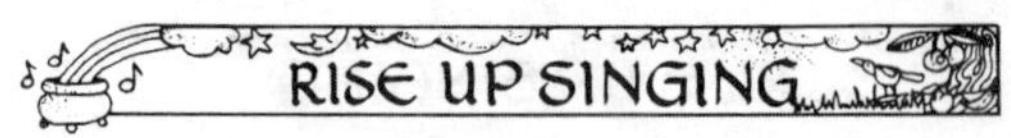

Hard Ain't it Hard

It's hard & it's hard, ain't it hard
To love one that never did love you
It's hard & it's hard, ain't it hard, great God!
To love one that never will be true

D G / D A / D G / DA D

There is a house in this old town
That's where my true love lays around
Takes other women right down on his knee
Tells them a tale that he won't tell me

First time I seen my true love
He was walkin' by my door
The last time I saw his falsehearted smile
He was dead on his coolin' board

Don't go to drinkin' & to gamblin'
Don't go there your sorrows to drown
This hard-liquor place is a low-down disgrace
The meanest damn place in this town

— w: arr & adap Woodie Guthrie

 — *In his* S by *& on his* Sings FS V2 *&* Gr S. *In* Golden Ency of FS, FSEncyV1, 1001 Jumbo S, *A Lomax* FS of NAm *&* S Am Sings. *On Cisco Houston* S of Woody Guthrie *(VSD-2131).* OB45

Hard Times Come Again No More

Let us pause in life's pleasures & count its many tears
While we all sup sorrow with the poor
There's a song that will linger forever in our ears
O, Hard Times, come again no more

D - A DG / D DA D - :||

'Tis the song, the sigh of the weary
Hard Times, Hard Times, come again no more
Many days you have lingered around my cabin door
O, Hard Times, come again no more

D - G D / - - DE A /

There's a pale drooping maiden who toils her life away
With a worn heart whose better days are o'er
Tho' her voice would be merry, 'tis sighing all the day / O ...

'Tis a sigh that is wafted across the troubled wave
'Tis a wail that is heard upon the shore
'Tis a dirge that is murmured around the lowly grave ...

While we seek mirth & beauty & music bright & gay
There are frail forms fainting at the door
Tho' their voices are silent, their pleading looks still say ...

— w: Stephen C. Foster

On Red Clay Ramblers Hard Times *& Cindy Mangsen* Long Time Trav. *In* SO! *35:4,* S That Changed the World *&* Treas of Stephen Foster. OB46

Heart Like a Wheel

Some say a heart is just like a wheel
When you bend it, you can't mend it
And my love for you is like a sinking ship
And my Heart is on that ship out in mid-ocean

D - A - / F♯m - Bm - / Em - A Em / Bm Em A D

They say that death is a tragedy
It comes once, then it's over
But my only wish is for that deep dark abyss
'Cause what's the use of living with no true lover

(bridge) It's only love & it's only love
That can wreck a human being & turn it inside out

D - Em A / Bm Em A D

When harm is done no love can be won
I know this happens frequently
What I can't understand, o please God hold my hand
Why this should have happened to me?

— w: Anna McGarrigle

 — On her rec with Kate McGarrigle & on Linda Ronstadt Heart Like a Wheel. OB47

House of the Rising Sun

There is a house in New Orleans, they call the Rising Sun
It's been the ruin of many a poor girl & me, o Lord, I'm one

(in 3/4)
I: Dm - A Dm / - C F A / Dm Dm7 Dm6 B♭ / Dm A Dm -

If I had listened what Mama said, I'd a been at home today
Being so young & foolish, poor boy, let a rambler lead me astray

Go tell my baby sister, never do like I have done
To shun that house in New Orleans, they call the Rising Sun

My mother she's a tailor, she sewed those new blue jeans
My sweetheart, he's a gambler Lord, drinks down in New Orleans

The only thing a gambler needs is a suitcase & a trunk
The only time he's satisfied is when he's on a drunk

One foot is on the platform & the other one on the train
I'm going back to New Orleans to wear that ball & chain

Going back to New Orleans, my race is almost run
Going back to spend the rest of my life beneath that Rising Sun

(in 3/4) II: Am C D F / Am C E - / 1st / Am E Am (E)

— w: coll, adap & arr with new words & new music by John A. Lomax, Alan Lomax & Georgia Turner

 — aka: Rising Sun Blues. On Jack Elliott, *Joan Baez* Bal B, *Doc Watson* & Son, *Van Ronk* Just Dave, *Jane Voss* Alb of S *& Weavers* Greatest Hits *(VSD 15/16). On (& in) Pete Seeger* Am Fav Bals *V2, also rec. by The Animals (see alt. chords). In* SO! *7:1* & Reprints #2, FSEncy V2, Golden Ency of S, Hootenanny SB, *A Lomax* FS of NAm & The Blues Bag. OB48

I Never Will Marry

One day as I rambled,_down by the seashore _
The wind it did whistle_and the waters did roar _
I spied a fair damsel make a pitiful cry
It sounded so lonesome in the waters nearby

(in D, 3/4) A D G - / D A DG D :||

I never will marry, I'll be no man's wife
I expect to live single all the days of my life
The shells in the ocean will be my deathbed
The fish in deep water swim over my head

My love's gone & left me, he's the one I adore
He's gone where I never shall see him any more
She plunged her dear body in the water so deep
She closed her pretty blue eyes in the waters to sleep

— w: new words & music by Mrs. Texas Gladden

 — The chorus is derived fr a British broadside ballad known in the US as "Down by the Sea Shore." Fred Hellerman wrote a new set of verses which was recorded by Joan Baez & the Weavers. On Kossoy Sisters Bowling Green, *Pete Seeger* Hoot at Carnegie Hall & Frontier Bals V2, *Weavers* Trav On & Songbag, *Bill Harrell & The Virgs* Bals & Bluegrass *& on* Blue Sky Boys. *In* SO! *10:2* & Reprints #2, FS Abecedary, Golden Ency of FS, Bells of Rhymney, Am Fav Bals, *A Lomax* FS of NAm & Baez SB. OB49

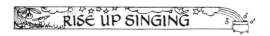

I Shall Be Released

_They say ev'rything can be replaced _
_Yet ev'ry distance is not near _
_So I remember ev'ry face _
_Of ev'ry man who put me here _

(capo up or in E) C - Dm - / Em FG C (F) :||

I see my light come shining / From the west unto the east
Any day now (2x) / I shall be released

They say ev'ry man [one] needs protection
They say ev'ry man must fall
Yet I swear I see my reflection
Some place so high above this wall

Standing next to me in this lonely crowd
Is a man who swears he's not to blame
All day long I hear him shout so loud
Crying out that he was framed

— w: Bob Dylan

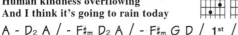

© 1967, 1976 Dwarf Music. All rights reserved. International copyright secured. Reprinted by permission. — On his At Budokan, Gr H V2 *& in his* Biograpghy. *On Joan Baez* Any Day Now, Fr Every Stage, Carry It On, *Peter Paul & Mary* Late Again, *The Band* Music fr Big Pink & Anthology V1, *Happy Traum* Bright Morning Stars, *Joe Cocker* With a Little Help From My Friends *(A&M SP 4182), Nina Simone* Greatest Hits *(RCA LSP-4374) & Rick Nelson* In Conc. *Rec by Bette Midler. In SO! 37:4.* OB50

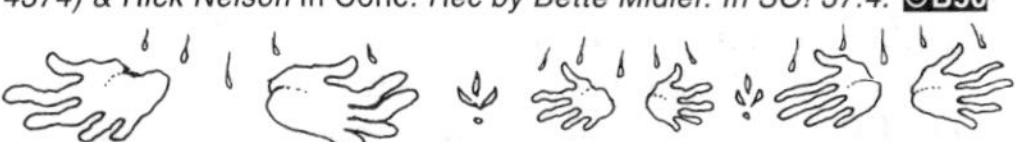

I Think It's Going to Rain Today

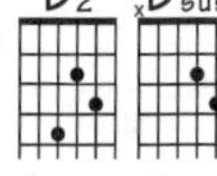

Broken windows & empty hallways
Pale dead moon in a sky streaked with grey
Human kindness overflowing
And I think it's going to rain today

A - D2 A / - F#m D2 A / - F#m G D / 1st /

Scarecrows dressed in the latest styles
With frozen smiles to keep love away / **Human kindness ...**

(bridge) Lonely, lonely
Tin can at my feet, think I'll kick it down the street
That's the way to treat a friend

Am7 Dm7 (2x) / C - Am - / F Dm7 Dsus D

Bright before me the signs implore me
"Help the needy & show them the way" / **Human ...**

— w: Randy Newman

© 1966 January Music Corp. All rights administered by Unichappe Music Inc. All rights reserved. Used by permnission. — On his Sail Away, *Ian Campbell Folk Gp* The Circle Game *& Dave Van Ronk. In* Judy Collins SB *& on her* In My Life. OB51

I'm So Lonesome I Could Cry

Hear that lonesome whipporwill, he sounds too blue to fly
The midnight train is moaning low,
I'm so lonesome I could cry

(in 3/4) C C ↓ C7 / F C CG C

Have you ever heard a robin grieve when leaves begin to die?
That means he's lost the will to live, I'm ...

Did you ever see a night so long, when time goes driftin' by?
The moon just went behind some clouds to hide its face & cry

The silence of a falling star lights up the purple sky
As I wonder where you are tonight, I'm ...

— w: Hank Williams

© 1949 by Acuff-Rose-Opryland Music, Inc. Copyright renewed, Assigned to Acuff-Rose-Opryland Music, Inc. & Aberbach Enterprises, Ltd. (Rightsong Music, Admin.) for the U.S.A. only. All rights outside the U.S.A. controlled by Acuff- Rose-Opryland Music, Inc. International copyright secured. All rights reserved. Printed in USA. Unauthorized copying, arranging, adapting, recording or public performance is an infringement of copyright. Infringers are liable under the law. — On Hank Williams, *Cathy Fink* Doggone My Time, *& Bashful Bro Oswald Dobro Dreamland. In* Country FakeB & Best FakeB Ever. OB52

Long Black Veil

Ten years ago on a cold dark night
Someone was killed 'neath the town hall light
The people who saw, they all agreed
That the slayer who ran looked a lot like me

D - - - / A - G D :||

The judge said "Son, what is your alibi?
If you were somewheres else, then you won't have to die"
I spoke not a word, tho' it meant my life
For I'd been in the arms of my best friend's wife

She walks these hills in a long black veil
Visits my grave when the night winds wail
Nobody knows, nobody sees
Nobody knows, but me

G D G D - / / D - G D / G A D -

The scaffold is high, eternity near
She stands in the crowd, she sheds not a tear
But sometimes at night when the cold winds moan
In a long black veil she cries o'er my bones

— w: Marijohn Wilkin & Danny Dill

© 1959 (renewed) Cedarwood Publishing Co. Inc. Nashville TN. International copyright secured. Made in USA. All rights reserved. Used by permission. — In SO! 15:2 & Reprints *#9 &* Ult Country FakeB. *In* Joan Baez SB *& on her* One Day At A Time & Country M Alb. *On Bill Monroe* Kentucky Mandolin, *Country Gentlemen* On the Rd *(FA2411), H Dickens & A Gerrard* Bluegrass, *The Band* Music From Big Pink *(Capitol SKAO 2955) & Eddie Alrock* Talk of the Town. OB53

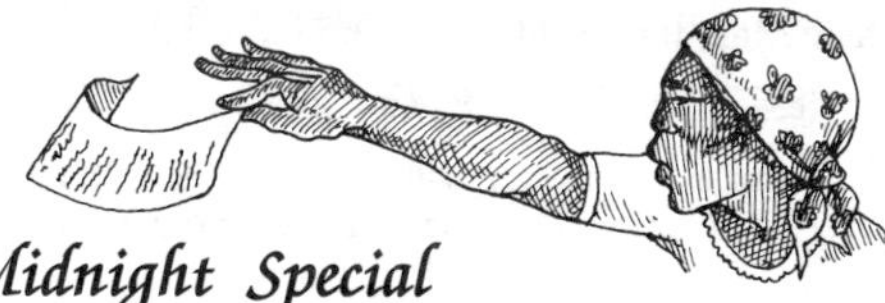

Midnight Special

Yonder come Miss-a Rosie, how in the world do you know?
Well, I knows her by the apron & the dress she wore
Umbrella on her shoulder, piece of paper in her hand
Well she's gonna tell the Governor "Please turn a-loose my man"

(in D) G - - - D - - - / A - - - D - :||

Let the midnight special shine its light on me
Let the midnight special shine its everlovin' light on me

G - - - D - - - / A - - - - D -

When you wake up in the mornin', when the ding-dong ring
Go marchin' to the table, meet the same old thing
Knife & fork are on the table, nothin' in my pan
Ever say anything about it, have trouble with the man

If you ever go to Houston, boy, you better walk right
Well, you better not squabble & you better not fight
Cuz the sheriff will arrest you & he'll take you down
And the judge will sentence you, you're penitentiary bound

I'm goin' away to leave you, cuz my time ain't long
The Man is gonna call me & I'll be gone
Be done all my weepin, whoppin, holl'in' & cryin'
Be done all my studyin' about my great long time

— w: Huddie Ledbetter

Coll & adap by John A. Lomax & Alan Lomax. TRO © 1936 (Renewed 1964) Folkways Music Publishers, Inc., NY, NY. International copyright secured. Made in USA. All rights reserved incl. public performance for profit. Used by permission. — The "midnight special" refers to an imaginary train which prisoners associated with their longings for freedom. As they lay in their cells at night they hoped the train's headlight would fall on them & they would be freed. On Pete Seeger Sings Leadbelly *& (on & in) his* Am Fav Bals V2. *On Ronnie Gilbert* The Spirit Is Free, *Weavers* SB, *Odetta* At the Horn, *Burl Ives* S of Expanding Am, *Merle Travis* Travis Pickin, *Sonny Terry & Brownie McGhee* Midnight Special *(Fantasy F-24721) & Blue Sky Boys* Presenting. *On Credence Clearwater Revival* In Conc, Credence Gold & Chronicle V2. *In* Peoples SB, FiresB of Am S, SFest, Golden Ency of FS, FS Abecedary, S Am Sings, FM Gr H, FSEncy V2 & 1001 Jumbo S. OB54

HARD TIMES & BLUES

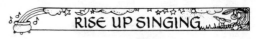

Motherless Child

Sometimes I feel like a motherless child **(3x)**
A long way from home (2x)

Em Em7 Em6 (or A7) Em / A Am Em -
Em Em7 Em6 C / Am B7 - Em / - B7 Em -

Sometimes I feel like I have no friend **(3x) / A long ...**
Sometimes I feel like I never been born ...
Sometimes I feel like I'm almost dead ...
Sometimes I feel like a feather in the air ...

But I know the lord's gonna help me along **(3x)**
Help me find my way back home **(2x)**

— w: trad. (Black Spiritual)
aka: "Sometimes I Feel ..." On (& in) Pete Seeger Am Fav Bals V3 *(FA2322). In* Peter Paul & Mary SB *& on their* S Will Rise. *On Dave Van Ronk* Van Ronk, *Odetta* The Essential & At Carnegie Hall, *Morgana King* Best of, The Essential *Paul Robeson (VSD 57/58) & Geoff Muldaur* Sleepy Man. *In* FSEncyV2 & FS Abecedary. OB55

Nowhere Man

He's a real Nowhere Man sitting in his Nowhere Land
Making all his nowhere plans for nobody
Doesn't have a point of view, knows not where he's going to
Isn't he a bit like you & me?

C G F C / F Fm C - :||

(bridge)
Nowhere Man, please listen, you don't know what you're missing
Nowhere Man, the world is at your command

Em F Em F / Em F - G

He's as blind as he can be, just sees what he wants to see
Nowhere Man can you see me at all? / **Doesn't have ...**

(bridge #2)
Nowhere Man, don't worry, take your time, don't hurry
Leave it all til somebody else lends you a hand

— w: John Lennon & Paul McCartney
 On Beatles Yesterday & Today & 1962-66. OB56

O Babe, it Ain't No Lie

One old woman, Lord, in this town
Keeps a-telling lies on me
Wish to my soul that she would die, Lord
She's telling lies on me

C - F - / C G C - :||

O, babe, it ain't no lie (3x)
This life I'm livin' is very hard

C DG C - / E7 - F - / - - C - / - CG C -

Been all around this whole round world
Lord, & I just got back today
Work all the week, honey, & I give it all to you
Honey baby, what more can I do?

— w: Elizabeth Cotten
 — On her FS & Instrumentals *(Folkways3526)* & Live *(Arhoolie1089). On Grateful Dead* For the Faithful. *In* SO! *9:4* & Reprints *#6* & FSEncyV2. OB57

Saint James Infimary

It was down in old Joe's barroom
On the corner by the square
The drinks were served as usual
And the usual crowd was there

Am E7 Am - / Am Dm Am E7 /
Am E7 Am F / Am E7 Am (E7)

Now on my left stood big Joe McKennedy
And his eyes were bloodshot red
And he looked at the gang around him
And these were the very words he said
"I went down to the St. James Infirmary
I saw my baby there
She was stretched out on a long white table
So cold, so pale & fair
17 coal-black horses
Hitched to a rubber-tired hack
7 girls goin' to the graveyard
And only 6 of 'em comin' back
Let her go, let her go, God bless her
Wherever she may be
She can ramble this wide world over
And never find another man like me
Now when I die please bury me
In my hightop Stetson hat
Just put a 20 dollar gold piece on my watch chain
So the Lord will know I died standing pat
I want six crap shooters for my pall bearers
And a chorus girl to sing me a song
Put a jazz band on my hearse wagon
Just to raise hell as we roll along
And now that you have heard my story
I'll take another shot of booze
If anyone should happen to ask you
Well, I've got the gambler's blues"

— w: trad. (US)
aka: "The Gambler's Blues." Apparently derived fr Br. street ballad "The Unfortunate Rake." On Dave Van Ronk Your Basic, *Spider John Koerner* Nobody Knows the Trouble, *Cab Calloway* Hi De Ho Man *(Columbia CG 32593) & Josh White* Sing a Rainbow. *In* SFest, FS Abecedary, The Blues Bag, S for Pickin & Singin, Treas of FS, 1001 Jumbo S, Golden Era of Nost M V4, FSEncy V2 & Sing Along w/ World's Fav FS. OB58

San Francisco Bay Blues

I got the blues when my baby left me by the San Francisco Bay
Ocean liner gone so far away
I didn't mean to treat her so bad, she was the best gal I ever had
Said goodbye, made me cry, gonna lay down my head & die

G C G G7 / C - G - / C - G E / A - D -

Well I ain't got a nickel & I ain't got a lousy dime
If she don't come back, I think I'm gonna lose my mind
But if she ever comes back to stay, it's gonna be another brand new day
Walkin' with my baby down beside the San Francisco Bay

/ " / C - B7 - / " / A D G -

Sittin' down lookin' thru my back door, wondrin' which way to go
Gal that I'm so crazy about, don't want me no more
Guess I'll take me a freight train cause I'm feelin' blue
Ride all the way to the end of the line thinkin' only of you

GC G (2x) / C - - G / C - G E / A - D -

Meanwhile in another city I'm just about to go insane
Thought I heard my baby the way she used to call my name
If she ever comes back to stay ...

/ " / C - - B7 / " / A D G -

— w: Jesse Fuller
 — On his Workin on the RR *(Topic), Ritchie Havens* Mixed Bag, *Weavers* Reunion 1963, *Tom Rush* Mind Rambling, *Patr Sky* Thru a Window & Ramblin' Jack Elliott *(Prestige). In* SO! *13:5* & Reprints *#7*, How Can We Keep fr Singing & FM Gr H. OB59

Send in the Clowns

Isn't it rich? Aren't we a pair?
Me here at last on the ground, you in mid air
Send in the clowns _ **(in C, 3/4 – freely)**

C - - F C - - / Cmaj7 - - - Fmaj7 - - - / G - - F **(2x)**

Isn't it bliss? Don't you approve?
One who keeps tearing around, one who can't move
Where are the clowns? Send in the clowns

C - - F C - - /Cmaj7 - - - Fmaj7 - - - /G - - F C - - Bm

(bridge) Just when I'd stopped opening doors
Finally knowing the one that I wanted was yours
Making my entrance again with my usual flair
Sure of my lines – no one is there

Em - - Bm **(2x)** / Em - - Am - - E

Am7 - - E - - Dm / Em - - Dm Gsus - - F

Don't you love farce? My fault, I fear
I thought that you'd want what I want – Sorry, my dear
But where are the clowns? Quick, send in the clowns
Don't bother they're here

C - - F C - - /Cmaj7 - - - Fmaj7 - - - /G - - F **(2x)**/C - - -

Isn't it rich, isn't it queer
Losing my timing this late in my career?
And where are the clowns? There ought to be clowns
Well, maybe next year

— w: Stephen Sondheim

 — Fr his musical A Little Night Music. *On Judy Collins* 1st 15 Yrs & Judith, *& Madeleine MacNeil* Soon Its Gonna Rain. *In* Gr S of 70's, Gr Legal FakeB *& Broadway SBs.* OB60

Stagolee

Stagolee was a bad man, everybody knows
Spent $100 just to buy him a suit of clothes
He was a bad man, that mean old Stagolee

E - - E7 / A7 - - E / B7 - - E

Stagolee shot Billy de Lyons, what do you think about that
Shot him down in cold blood because he stole his Stetson hat
He was a ...

Billy de Lyons said "Stagolee, please don't take my life
I've got two little babies & a darlin' loving wife / You're **a ...**"

"What do I care about your two little babies, your darling loving wife?
You done stole my Stetson hat & I'm bound to take your life"

The judge said "Stagolee, what you doin' here?
You done shot Mr. Billy de Lyons, you goin' to die in the electric chair"

12 o'clock they killed him, head reached up high
Last thing that poor boy said "My 6-shooter never lied"

— trad.

"Learned fr Woody Guthrie in 1940. I think he got it fr a phonograph record. Stagolee was supposed to have been an actual person around the turn of the century" – PS. Recs by Jesse Fuller & Dave Bromberg. In Am Fav Bals & S for Pickin & Singin. *On Doc Watson* Ballads From Deep Gap *(VSD-6576), Tom Rush* Blues, Songs, Ballads *(Prestige 7374) & Pete Seeger* Am Fav Bal V2 *(Folkways 2321).* OB61

Stealin', Stealin'

Now put your arms around me like a circle 'round the sun
You know I love you, Mama, when my easy ride is done
If you don't believe I love you, look what a fool I've been
If you don't believe I'm sinkin', look what a hole I'm in
Stealin', stealin', pretty mama don't you tell on me
I'm stealin' back to my same old used to be

C - - - /F - - - //C - - - / /C C7 F - /CA DG C -

The woman I'm a-lovin', she's my size & my height
She's a married woman so you know she treats me right

— w: Will Shade

 — Rec by Memphis Jug Band ca. 1930. On The Country Blues *(RBF RF1), Dave Van Ronk* Have To Have Fun *(Mercury), Jim Kweskin* America, *David Bromberg* Reckless Abandon *& Pete & Arlo* Together *(2R5 2214). In* SO! *14:4 &* Reprints *#10,* FSEncy V2 *&* How Can We Keep Fr S. OB62

Take this Hammer

Take this hammer (huh!) carry it to the captain (huh!) (3x)
You tell him I'm gone (huh!) tell him I'm gone (huh!)

D - A - / - - D - / - D7 G - / D A7 D -

If he asks you (huh!) was I running ... **(3x)**
You tell him I was flyin' ... tell him I was flyin' ...

If he asks you / was I laughing **(3x)**
You tell him I was crying / tell him I was crying

Don't want no / cornbread & m'lasses **(3x)**
They hurt my pride / they hurt my pride

— w: trad. (US)

On Leadbelly This Hammer *(Folkways), Pete Seeger* Sings Leadbelly, *Sparky Rucker* Heroes & Hard Times *(SIF1032), S Terry & B McGhee* Midnight Special *(Fantasy 24721), Martin, Bogan & Armstrong* That Old Gang of Mine *(FF 056) & Odetta* At the Horn & The Essential *(Vang). In* SO! *36:2,* Peoples SB, FiresB of Am S, SFest, Am FS for Children, Carry It On, FSEncy V2, S of Work & Protest *&* 1001 Jumbo S. OB63

Tom Dooley

Hang down your head, Tom Dooley, hang down your head & cry
Hang down your head, Tom Dooley, poor boy you're bound to die

G - - D7 / - - D7C G

I met her on the mountain & there I took her life
I met her on the mountain & stabbed her with my knife

Hand me down my banjo, I'll pick it on my knee
This time tomorrow it'll be no use to me

This time tomorrow, reckon where I'll be?
If it hadn'-a been for Grayson, I'd-a been in Tennessee

This time tomorrow, reckon where I'll be?
In some lonesome valley, a-hangin' on a white oak tree

— w: coll, adap & arr by Frank Warner, John A. Lomax, & Alan Lomax

 Fr the singing of Frank Profitt (FSA1). One of the most sensational murder cases of the mid 19th c. Thomas C. Dula was hanged in Wilkes Co. NC on 5/1/1868 for the murder of Laura Foster but the exact circumstances were & still are a matter of debate. The State Supreme Court concluded that Dula was courting both Foster & an Ann Melton. He contacted VD (which he believed to have gotten fr Laura) & passed it on to Ann. The latter was widely believed to have been an accomplice in his purported revenge against Laura. On Doc Watson, *Kingston Trio* Best of, V1 & 25 Yrs *& New Lost City Ramblers* V2 *(FA2397). In* SO! *11:5,* Best S of the Lomax Coll, *Lomax* FS of NA, SFest, FM Gr H *&* S Along w World's Fav FS. OB64

The Tracks of My Tears

People say I'm the life of the party
'Cause I tell a joke or two
Altho' I might be a-laughing loud & hearty
Deep inside I'm blue

C F - G / C F - C :||

So take a good look at my face
You'll see my smile looks out of place
If you look closer, it's easy to trace
The tracks of my tears — I need you, need you

C F - G / / / C F - C / F C F C

Since you left me if you see me with another girl
Seeming like I'm having fun
Altho' she may be cute, she's just a substitute
'Cause you're the permanent one

(bridge) Hey yeah yeah
Outside – I'm masquerading / Inside – my hope is fading
Just a clown – since you put me down
My smile is my makeup I wear since my breakup with you, baby

(C - F C) F C / C - F C / / / C - - - G -

— w: William ("Smokey") Robinson, Warren Moore & Marv Tarplin

 — On Motown Story V3, *Linda Ronstadt's* Greatest Hits *(Asylum 6E-106) & Smokey Robinson* Smokin. *In* The Top 100 Motown H. OB65

Trouble in Mind

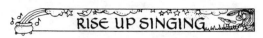

Trouble in mind, I'm blue, but I won't be blue always
For the sun will shine in my back door someday

E B7 E A7 / E B7 E (B7)

Trouble in mind, that's true, I have almost lost my mind
Life ain't worth livin', feel like I could die

I'm gonna lay my head on some lonesome RR iron
Let the 2:19 train ease my troubled mind

Trouble in mind, I am blue, my poor heart is beatin' slow
Never had such trouble in my life before

I'm going down by the river, gonna take me a rocking chair
And if the blues don't leave me, I'll rock on away from here

Well, trouble, o trouble, trouble on my worried mind
When you see me laughin', I'm laughin' just to keep from crying

— w: Richard M. Jones

© 1937 MCA Music Publishing, a division of MCA, Inc. 445 Park Ave, NY, NY 10022. Copyright renewed. International Copyright Secured. Made in USA. All rights reserved. Used by permission. On Josh White The Legendary, *Geoff Muldaur* Sleepy Man *& Whitstein Bros* Trouble Ain't Nothin. *In* SO! 6:2, B of the Blues & Readers Dig Fest of Pop S. *Rec by Nina Simone, Cisco Houston & Lightnin' Hopkins.* B66

Waterfall

Sometimes it takes a rainy day just to let you know
Everything's gonna be all right, all right

Bm - Em FG **(2x)** / C - G - A - - - D G D -

I've been dreaming in the sun, won't you wake me up someone
I need a little peace of mind
Wake me from this dream that I have dreamed so many times
I need a little peace of mind

D C G D / C Em D - :||

When you open up your life to the living
All things come spilling in on you
And you're flowing like a river, the Changer & the Changed
You got to spill some over **(3x)** over all!

Bb C D - / Em A D - / Em A D Bm /
BbC D **(3x)** A -

Filling up & spilling over it's an endless waterfall
Filling up & spilling over, over all (repeat)

Em A D Bm / Em A D - :||

(bridge) Like the rain falling on the ground
Like the rain falling all around

Em G D - / C G D -

— w: Cris Williamson

© 1975 Bird Ankles Music. Used by permission. On her Changer & the Changed *& in her* SB. B67

Wayfaring Stranger

I'm just a poor wayfaring stranger
A-traveling through this world of woe
But there's no sickness, no toil nor danger
In that bright world to which I go

Am E Am - / Dm - E - / Am E Am F / Dm Em Am -

I'm going there to see my father
I'm going there no more to roam
I'm just a-going over Jordan
I'm just a-going over home

F G C -/F G Am E/Am E AmG F/ " /

I know dark clouds will gather 'round me
I know my way is rough & steep
But beauteous fields lie just beyond me
Where souls redeemed their vigil keep

I'm going there to meet my mother
She said she'd meet me when I come
I'm only going over Jordan
I'm only going over home

I want to wear a crown of glory
When I get home to that bright land
I want to shout Salvation's story
In concert with that blood-washed band
I'm going there to meet my Saviour
To sing His praises for evermore
I'm only going over Jordan
I'm only going over home

— w: "White Spiritual"

In SO! 22:5 & 44:4, FSEncyV2, Joyful Singing, FiresB of FS, S of the Spirit & Treas of FS. *On Limelighters* Alive V2 *& Les Murdock* Wayfaring Stranger. *On Baez* David's Alb *& in her* Contemp Bal B. *In* Burl Ives SB *& on his* S of the Revolution. *On Pete Seeger* Frontier Bals V2 *(FA2176).* B68

We Can Work it Out

Try to see it my way: Do I have to
Keep on talking til I can't go on?
While you see it your way – run the risk of
Knowing that our love may soon be gone
We can work it out, we can work it out

G - - / D F G / - - - / D F G // C G C D

Think of what you're saying: You can get it
Wrong & still you think that it's all right
Think of what I'm saying: We can work it
Out & get it straight or say goodnight / **We ...**

(bridge) Life is very short & there's no
Time for fussing & / Fighting my friend
I have always thought that it's a
Crime – so I will / Ask you once again

Em - - - C - B7 / - Em ↓ - - :||

Try to see it my way – only time will
Tell if I am right or I am wrong
While you see it your way – There's a chance that
We might fall apart before too long ...

— w: John Lennon & Paul McCartney

© 1965 Northern Songs Ltd. All rights administered by Blackwood Music Inc. under license fr ATV Music (Maclen). All rights reserved. International copyright secured. Used by permission. On Beatles Yesterday & Today & 1962- 66 *& The Dillards* Decade Waltz. B69

Worried Man

It takes a worried man to sing a worried song **(3x)**
I'm worried now but I won't be worried long

G - - - / C - - G / - - - - / D - - G

I went across the river & I lay down to sleep **(3x)**
When I woke up, had shackles on my feet

The shackles on my feet had 21 links of chain **(3x)**
And on each link the initials of my name

I asked that judge "Tell me what's gonna be my fine?"
"21 years on the Rocky Mountain line!"

The train came to the station, 21 coaches long
The one I love is on that train & gone

I looked down the track as far as I could see
A little bitty hand was waving after me

If anyone should ask you who made up this song
Tell 'em 'twas I & I sing it all day long

— w: trad. (US)

On Weavers Trav On, *Kingston Trio* Sing a Song, Best of & 25 Yrs, *Carter Fam* The Famous *(Harmony/Col) &* Carter Family *(RCA), New Lost City Ramblers* 20 Yr Conc *(FF), Doc Watson* Elementary *(UA), Michael Cooney* Cheese Stands Alone, *W Guthrie* Lib. of Congress *& Mike Seeger* Old Time Country M. *In* Bells of Rhymney, Peoples SB, SFest, Golden Ency of S, & FSEncyV2. B70

Yesterday

Yesterday, all my troubles seemed so far away
Now it looks as though they're here to stay
O I believe in yesterday

C - Bm7 E Am - / F G C - / Am D F C

Suddenly, I'm not half the man I used to be
There's a shadow hanging over me
O yesterday came suddenly

(bridge) Why she had to go I don't know, she wouldn't say
I said something wrong, now I long for yesterday

Bm E AmG FAm G - C - / /

Yesterday, love was such an easy game to play
Now I need a place to hide away
O I believe in yesterday

— w: John Lennon & Paul McCartney

 — On Beatles Yesterday & Today, Help *(Brit. version),* Love Songs & 1962-66, *Roger Williams* Golden H & *Andy Williams* Shadow of Your Smile. *In Readers Dig* Festival of Pop S & Club Date Fake B. OB71

There are a many songs about difficult times in: BALLADS, MOUNTAIN VOICES, SEA, SPIRITUALS, TRAVEL and WORK.

Elsewhere in the book are: "Stewball" (AMER) "Bourgeois Blues" (CITY) "Before They Close the Minstrel Show" (CREATIVITY) "Lonesome Valley" (FAITH) "Deportee," "So Long," "Time's a Gettin' Hard" (FARM) "Fire & Rain," "My Rambling Boy," "Pack Up Your Sorrows" (FRIEND) "Bill Bailey," "Keep the Home Fires Burning" (GOLDEN) "Farther Along," "Will the Circle" (GOSPEL) "Nobody Knows You" (RICH) "Absalom," "Babylon," "When Jesus Wept" (SACRED) "Old Devil Time" (UNITY) "Custom Made Woman Blues" (WOMEN).

Prison Songs: *FREEDOM and STRUGGLE each have a number of songs about prisons & executions. Elsewhere, see: "Brennan on the Moor," "Geordie" (BALLAD) "Mr. Bojangles" (CREATIVITY) "How Can I Keep from Singing" (FAITH) "Down in the Valley" (LOVE) "Capt. Kidd" (SEA) "Thirsty Boots" (TRAVEL) "One Man's Hands" (UNITY) & "Joe Hill" (WORK).*

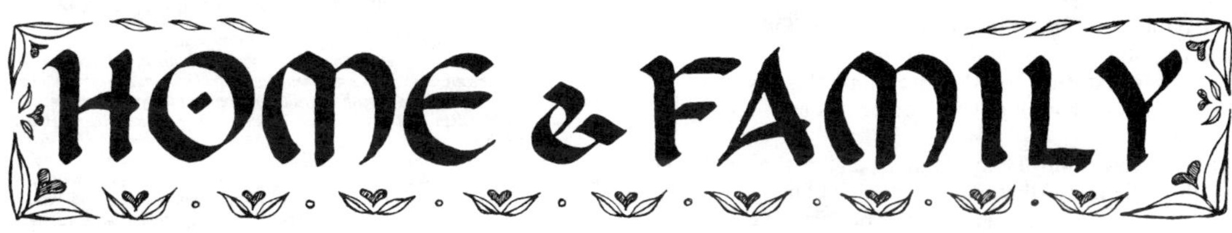

All I Really Need

All I really need is a song in my heart
Food in my belly & love in my family
All I really need is a song in my heart
And love in my family

D - - - / Em - A D / - - - - / Em A D -

And I need the rain to fall
And I need the sun to shine
To give life to the seeds we sow, to give the food we need to grow
All I really need is a song in my heart / & love in my family

Em A D - / / Em - F#m GA / D - - - / Em A D -

And I need some clean water for drinking
And I need some clean air for breathing
So that I can grow up strong & take my place where I belong ...

— w: Raffi

 — Words taken fr the UN Declaration of Rights of the Child: written for the International Year of the Child. On his Singable S for the V Young, Baby Beluga *& in his* Beluga B & 2nd SB. *Also on Susan Stark* Rainbow People. *In* SO! *37:2.* OH01

The Baby Tree

There's an island way out in the seas
Where the babies they all grow on trees
It's jolly good fun to swing in the sun
But you have to look out if you sneeze, you sneeze
But you have to look out if you sneeze

G - Em - / /C - G - /D - G Em /D - G -

You have to look out if you sneeze
For swingin' up there in the breeze
If you happen to cough you might very well fall off
Lord, you tumble, flop down on your knees, your ... / You ...

And when the stormy winds wail
And the breezes blow high in the gale
There's the funniest hoppin' & floppin' & droppin'
And fat little babies just hail, they hail / And fat ...

And the babies lie there in a pile
And the grown-ups come after awhile
And they always pass by the babies that cry
And they take only babies that smile, that smile
Take triplets or twins if they smile

— w: w: anon. — m: Rosalie Sorrels

 — Sorrels learned this orig fr her mother who found it in a book of children's poetry fr the early 1800s – she later got the words fr Olive Burt (author of Am Murder Bals & Their Stories*). In* SO! *20:3.* OH02

Babysitter Song

If it's fun for you then it's fun for me
If it's good enough for you then it's good enough for me
I want to go out with the whole family
And I don't want to stay home alone

D A / - D / - G / A D

I don't want to stay with a babysitter (3x)
No I don't want to stay home alone

A D / / D G / A D

I want to go out, I want to have fun
I want to go out with everyone
And I won't come home til the whole night is done
And I don't want to stay home alone

I don't know where you're going but it must be great
Or you wouldn't be worried when you think you're late
I just can't wait till I get grown
And I won't have to stay home alone

Maybe tomorrow I'll go downtown
Momma & Daddy they can stay back home
I'll get them a babysitter for to keep 'em company
And they can stay home like me

— w: Si Kahn

 On his Good Times & Bad Times *& John McCutcheon* Howjadoo. OH03

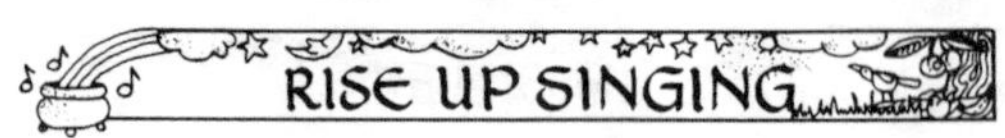

Back Home Again

There's a storm across the valley, clouds are rolling in
The afternoon is heavy on your shoulders
There's a truck out on the 4-lane a mile or more away
The whinin' of his wheels just makes it colder

C - F - / G - C - :||

He's an hour away from ridin' on your prayers up in the sky
And ten days on the road are barely gone
There's a fire softly burning, supper's on the stove
But it's the light in your eyes that makes him warm

Hey, it's good to be back home again – yes it is
Sometimes, this old farm feels like a long-lost friend
Hey, it's good to be back home again

F G C - / F G C F / G - C -

There's all the news to tell him, how'd you spend your time
And what's the latest thing the neighbors say?
And your mother called last Friday, "Sunshine" made her cry
And you felt the baby move just yesterday

And o the time that I can lay this tired old body down
And feel your fingers feather soft upon me
The kisses that I live for, the love that lights my way
The happiness that livin' with you brings me

It's the sweetest thing I know of just spending time with you
It's the little things that make a house a home
Like a fire softly burning & supper on the stove
And the light in your eyes that makes me warm

— John Denver

 — On his Back Home Again & Gr H V2. OH04

Be Kind to Your Parents

Be kind to your parents, tho' they don't deserve it
Remember they're grown-ups, a difficult stage of life
They're apt to be nervous & overexcited
Confused from their daily storm & strife

(capo up) D - A7 - / - - - D / 1st / A7 - D -

Just keep in mind, tho' it sounds odd, I know
Most parents once were children long ago (Incredible!)
So treat them with patience, & sweet understanding
In spite of the foolish things they do
Some day you may wake up & find you're a parent too

G - D - / A E A EmA / D - A7 -

A7 - D - / G - Gm A7 D -

— Harold Rome

 — Fr his musical Fanny. *On* Camp songs *(Folkways), Linda Arnold* Make Believe, *M Cooney* Pure Unsweetened *(Alliance) & Pete Seeger* Children's Concert at Town Hall & Young vs Old. OH05

Bisan

(intro) _Kanat lana min zazan_
Bayyaraton jamila wa dai 'aton dhalila
Yanamu fi afya iha nisan dai 'atuna
Kanas muha Bisan

Dm - - - / - A - Dm / - - A7 - / - - Dm -

Khuthuni ila Bisan, ila dia 'atish shita iyyah
Hunaka yashi 'ul hanan, 'alal hafafiren ramadiyyah

Dm - - - (2x) / C - - - Am - - -

Khuthuni ilath thuhairat, ila ghafwaten 'inda babi
Hunaka maddat 'ailah, u'aniqu samtati turabi

(bridge) Athkuru ya Bisan, ya mal 'abat tufula
Afya ukil khajula, wa kullu shai en kan
Babon wa shubbakan, baituna fi Bisan

DmA Dm (2x) / Dm A - Dm / Gm - - - C - Dm -

Khuthuni, khuthuni ma 'al hasasin ilath thilalil lati tabki
Rufufon minal 'aidin, 'ala haninen laha tahki
Khuthuni ila Bisan

as verse, adding: Dm - C - Dm -

— author unknown

Bisan is the name of an old Palestinian town, now within the borders of Israel & renamed Beit Shalan. This song, made famous by the Lebanese singer Fairouz, expresses the longing of the Palestinian (& any) people for a home & a homeland. Published by M. Chahine & Sons, Beirut, Lebanon. On Fairouz' albums, Bright Morning Star Live in the USA, *& in* Broadside *#159 (S for Peace & Justice in the Middle E). Trans of Arabic: "A long time ago we owned a beautiful orchard. A shady village in which April surrendered to sleep. The name of our village was Bisan/Take me to Bisan, to my winter village. There where tenderness thrives up to the grey edges/Take me to those long afternoons, to those peaceful naps against my door where I can hug the silence of the earth/I remember Bisan, a playground of innocence, humble dwellings, pastoral shadows, everything we called home: our home, Bisan/Take me, take me w the songbirds to those same shadows that now weep. Rows & rows of the Returning [fr the Diaspora] to a tenderness now reduced to words. Take me to Bisan."* OH06

Circle of the Sun

1. Babies are born **in a circle of the sun**
   Circle of the sun on their birthing day **(repeat)**
   Clouds to the north, clouds to the south
   Wind & rain to the east & the west
   But babies are born **in a circle of the sun**
   Circle of the sun on their birthing day

C - - - / CF C G C :||

C - - - / F C F G / C G C - / CF C G C

2. Children take their first step **in a circle of the sun**
   Circle ... on their walking day **(repeat) / Clouds ...**
3. Children speak their first word ... / ... their talking day
4. I hope to be married in a circle ... / ... my wedding day
5. And I hope to die ... / ... my dying day
   And spread my ashes ... / ... my dying day
   Clouds to the north ... /... the west
   But spread my ashes ... / ... on my dying day

— Sally Rogers

 — On her In the Circle of the Sun *(Thrushwood), in her* SB. *Also in* SO! *30:2,* New Folk Favs & Bright Morning Stars *(WAS).* OH07

Cook with Honey

Muffin warm & basket brown, smiling faces all around
Our dinner table, close together hand in hand _

D A7 D A7 :|| **as needed**

I always_cook with honey to sweeten up the night _
We always_cook with honey, tell me how's your appetite
For some sweet love? _

D A7 D A7 - / D A7 D A7 / D (A7)

Finding favor with your neighbor, well it can be so fine
It's easier than pie to be kind
We've been searching for so long, now our house is turned
Into a home

Well our door is always open & there's surely room for more
Cooking where there's good love is never any chore
So come & get to know us, there'll be a place set just for you
Sweet wine before dinner that is surely bound to soothe

— Valerie Carter

Don't You Push Me Down

Don't you push me, push me, push me
Don't you push me down (repeat)

C - - F / G7 - - C :||

You can play with me, you can hold my hand
We can skip together down to the pretzel man
You can wear my mommy's shoes, wear my daddy's hat
You can even laugh at me, **but don't you push me down – No!**

C F C F / G7 - - C / 1st / G7 - - - - C

You can play with me, we can build a house
You can take my ball & bounce it up & down
You can take my skates & ride them all around
You can even get mad at me, but don't ...

You can play with me, we can play all day
And you can use my dishes if you'll put them away
You can feed me apples & oranges & plums
And you can even wash my face, **but ...**

— Woody Guthrie

Family

Who's your Mama's Mama? **She's my** Grandma!
Who's your Daddy's Mama? **She's my** Grandma **too**
Grandma, Grandma, **I love you**
Who's your Mama's Daddy? **He's my** Grandpa
Who's your Daddy's Daddy? **He's my** Grandpa **too**
Grandpa, Grandpa, **I love you**

C - FC GC / C - FG C / F C G C :||

Lucky to be in the family
I belong to you & you belong to me

F C G C / /

Who's your Mama's sister? **She's my** auntie
Who's your Daddy's sister? **She's my** auntie **too**
Auntie, auntie **I love you**
Who's your Mama's brother? **He's my** uncle ...

Who's your Mama's sister's children? They're my cousins
Who's your Daddy's sister's children? They're my cousins too
Cousins, cousins, **I love you**
Who's your Mama's brother's children? Still more cousins
Who's your Daddy's brother's children? Still more cousins too ...

Who is my true family? Everybody
Everyone & everywhere & every color too
Family, family, I love you / **Lucky to be ...**

— Carol Johnson

Food Glorious Food

Food, glorious food! Hot sausage & mustard
While we're in the mood, cold jelly & custard
Peas, pudding & saveloys, what next is the question
Rich gentlemen have it, boys, in-dye-gestion!
Food, glorious food! We're anxious to try it
3 banquets a day, our favourite diet
Just picture a great big steak, fried, roasted or stewed
O food, wonderful food, marvelous food, glorious food!

G Dm C D / / G Am AmD AD / Bm Em A7 D7
/ " / / G Am Em A7 / GEm A7 AmD G

Food, glorious food! Don't care what it looks like
Burned, underdone, crude, don't care what the cook's like
Just thinking of growing fat, our senses are reeling
One moment of knowing that full-up feeling!
Food, glorious food! What wouldn't we give for
That extra bit more, that's all that we live for
Why should we be fated to do nothing but brood
O food, magical food, wonderful food, marvelous food
Fabulous food, beautiful food, glorious food!

2nd verse ends: GEm A7 **(2x)** / Am D G -

— Lionel Bart

For Baby (For Bobbie)

I'll walk in the rain by your side
I'll cling to the warmth of your tiny hand
I'll do anything to help you understand
I'll love you more than anybody can
    And the wind will whisper your name to me
    Little birds will sing along in time
    The leaves will bow down when you walk by
    And morning bells will chime

D G D - / G A D - / G A D Bm / D A D -
G A D - / // G A F#m Em (or D G) / " /

I'll be there when you're feeling down
To kiss the tears if you cry
I'll share with you all the happiness I've found
A reflection of the love in your eyes
    And I'll sing you the songs of the rainbow
    Whisper all the joy that is mine / **The leaves ...**

— John Denver

HOME & FAMILY

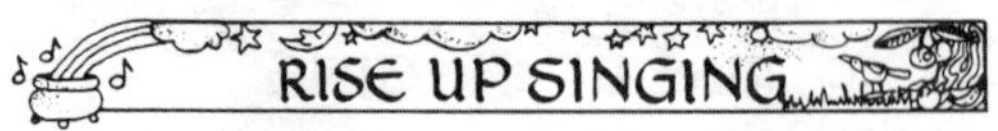

Free to Be You and Me

There's a land that I see where the children are free
And I say it ain't far to this land from where we are
Take my hand, come with me, where the children are free
Come with me, take my hand & we'll live

(in D) G - D - / A - G D / G - D - / A - G -

In a land where the river runs free
In a land thru the green country
In a land to a shining sea
And you & me are free to be you & me

DG DG / / DG D / F#m G D(G DG DG D)

I see a land bright & clear & the time's comin near
When we'll live in this land, you & me hand in hand
Take my hand, come along, lend your voice to my song
Come along, take my hand, sing a song

(2nd cho) For a land **where the river runs free**
For a land **thru the green country**
For a land where the horses run free
And you & me are ... me

Every boy in this land grows to be his own man
In this land every girl grows to be her own woman
Take my hand, come with me where the children are free
Come with me, take my hand & we'll run

(last cho) To a land **where the river runs free**
To a land **thru the green country**
To a land to a shining sea
To a land where the horses run free
To a land where the children are free / **And you & me ...**

— w: Bruce Hart — m: Lawrence Stephen

 — On Marlo Thomas & Friends Free to Be... OH13

Hearth and Fire

Hearth & Fire be ours tonight & all the dark outside
Fair the night & kind on you, wherever you may bide
And I'd be the sun upon your head, the wind about your face
My love upon the path you tread & upon your wanderings, peace

CF GC DmF G / F GC [1.] Dm G :|| [2.] DmG C

Song & wine be ours tonight & all the cold outside
Peace & warmth be yours tonight, wherever you may bide

Hearth & fire be ours tonight & the wind in the birches bare
O that the wind we hear tonight would find you well & fair

— Gordon Bok

 — Gordon's "comfort song for the 1980's." He writes: "It needs verses ... for different seasons & circumstances. If you come up with any, I hope you'll send them." On Bok Muir & Trickett A Water over Stone. *In his* Time & the Flying Snow & Bright Morning Stars *(WAS).* OH14

I Won't Grow Up

I won't grow up * (echo) I don't want to go to school *
Just to learn to be a parrot * & recite a silly rule *
If growing up means it would be beneath my dignity to climb a tree
I'll never grow up, never grow up, never grow up
Not me! not I! not me! not me!

D - Em - / A - D - / G F# Bm B7
E7 Em A / AD AD AD AD

I won't grow up * I don't want to wear a tie * (etc.)
And a serious expression, in the middle of July
And if it means I must prepare to shoulder burdens with a worried air
I'll never grow up, never grow up, never grow up
So there! not I! not me! so there!

(bridge) Never gonna be a man, I won't!
Like to see somebody try & make me
Anyone who wants to try & make me
Turn into a man, catch me if you can

G GD / / Em - / A -

I won't grow up, not a penny will I pinch
I will never grow a mustache, or a fraction of an inch
'Cause growing up is awfuller than all the awful things that ever were
I'll never grow up, never grow up, never grow up
No sir! not I! not me! no sir!

— w: Carolyn Leigh — m: Mark Charlap

 — Fr their musical Peter Pan. OH15

I'm Gonna Tell on You

I'm gonna tell, I'm gonna tell
I'm gonna holler & I'm gonna yell
And I'll get you in trouble for ev'rything you do
I'm gonna tell on you

(in 3/4) C - F C / - - D7 G / C - F C / - G C -

Well, I'm gonna tell where you hid the broom
So you wouldn't have to sweep up the room
Then Mamma will sweep the room up with you
And I'm gonna tell on you

I'm gonna tell that you busted that plate
And I'll tell about all them bananas you ate
I'll tell on you one time, I'll tell on you two / **And ...**

I'm gonna tell that you kicked me & you bit me
I'm gonna tell that you punched me & you hit me
But I won't tell Mama what I did to you / **And ...**

— Rosalie Sorrels

 — On her album, Michael Cooney Pure & Unsweetened, *Cathy Fink & Duck Donald* I'm Gonna Tell *& Faith Petric* Sing a S, Sing Along *(GentleWinds). In SO! 20:3 &* How Can We Keep from Singing. OH16

Isn't She Lovely

Isn't she lovely, isn't she wonderful
Isn't she precious, less than one minute old
I never thought thru love we'd be
making one as lovely as she
But isn't she lovely made from love

Bm7 E9 A11 D / / Gmaj7 F# Bm7 E9 / A11 - D -

Isn't she pretty, truly angel's best
Boy, I'm so happy, we have been heaven blessed
I can't believe what God has done, thru us
he's given life to one / **But isn't she...**

Isn't she lovely, life & love are the same
Life is Aisha, the meaning of her name
Londie, it could have not been done
without you who conceived the one
That's so very **lovely made from love**

Bm7 E9 A11 Gmaj7

— Stevie Wonder

 On his S in the Key of Life *& in his* Gr H & Top 100 Motown H. OH17

Joseph Dearest

Joseph lieber, Joseph mein
Hilf mir wiegen mein Kinderlein
Gott der wird dein Lohner sein
Im Himmelreich, der Jungfrau Sohn Maria
Eya, eya / Jesum Christ hat uns geborn Maria

(in 3/4) C -/ /Dm G /C DmG FC C//CAm CAm/ **4th**

Gerne, liebe Muhme mein
Helf ich dir wiegen dein Kinderlein
Dass Gott musse mein Lohner sein
Im Himmelreich, der Jungfrau Sohn Maria ...

Joseph dearest, Joseph mine
Help me rock this child of mine
Here mid sheep & friendly kine
We watch our babe in slumber softly dreaming
Slumber, slumber
See the babe in slumber softly dreaming

Gladly, dearest Mary mine
I will rock this child of thine
While God's stars above us shine
Here love's pure light upon us all is streaming ...

— trad. (German), Eng. Leah Felton

Appears in manuscript around 1500 fr Leipzig University for a mystery play acted around a crib in church. Also in Walther Gesangbuch *(1544),* Piae Cantiones, Mainzer Cantual *(1605),* The English Hymnal, Oxford B of carols, Friends Hymnal, Xmas Carols fr Many Countries *(G.Schirmer).* OH18

Kilkelly, Ireland

Kilkelly, Ireland, 18 & 60
My dear & loving son, John
Your good friend the schoolmaster, Pat McNamara's
So good as to write these words down
    Your brothers have all gone to find work in England
    The house is so empty & sad
    The crop of potatoes is sorely infected
    A third to half of them bad
And your sister Bridget & Patrick O'Donnell
Are going to get married in June
Your mother says not to work on the railroad
And be sure to come on home soon

(in 3/4)

Em G / D Em :||: G D / C D / Em G / D Em :||

Kilkelly, Ireland, 18 & 70
Dear & loving son, John
Hello to your missus & to your four children
May they grow healthy & strong
    Michael has got in a wee bit of trouble
    I guess that he never will learn
    Because of the the dampness there's no turf to speak of
    And now there's nothing to burn
And Bridget is happy you named a child for her
You know she's got six of her own
You say you found work but you don't say what kind
Oh when will you be coming home?

Kilkelly, Ireland, 18 & 80
Dear Michael & John, my sons
I'm sorry to give you the very sad news
That your dear old mother passed on
    We buried her down at the church in Kilkelly
    Your brothers & Bridget were there
    You don't have to worry she died very quickly
    Remember her in your prayers
And it's so good to hear that Michael's returning
With money he's sure to buy land
For the crop has been poor & the people are selling
At any price that they can

Kilkelly, Ireland, 18 & 90
My dear & loving son, John
I guess that I must be close on to 80
It's 30 years since you're gone
    Because of all the money you've sent me
    I'm still living out on my own
    Michael has built himself a fine house
    And Bridget's daughters are grown
Thank you for sending your family picture
They're lovely young women & men
You say that you might even come for a visit
What joy to see you again

Kilkelly, Ireland, 18 & 92
My dear brother John
I'm sorry that I didn't write sooner
To tell you that Father passed on
    He was living with Bridget, she says he was cheerful
    And healthy right down to the end
    You should have seen him playing with the grandchildren
    Of Pat McNamara, your friend
And we buried him alongside of Mother
Down at the Kilkelly churchyard
He was a strong & feisty old man
Considering his life was so hard
    And it's funny the way he kept talking about you
    He called for you at the end
    Oh, why don't you think about coming to visit
    We'd love to see you again

— Peter & Steve Jones

 — On Peter &Steve Jones (Clouds). On Moloney, O'Connell & Keane Kilkelly, The Coop 2-7 *& Laura Burns & Roger Rosen* Light This Night. *In* SO! *30:3.* OH19

Little Brand New Baby

Hey, little brand new baby
Your momma & your daddy think you're mighty nice
Hey, little brand new baby
I hope you have a mighty nice life

C FC / C G / C FC / CG C

Your daddy's lookin' mighty proud
Handin out cigars all around the town
Grinnin' like a 'possum & I think he's gonna crow
And I hope you have a mighty nice life

C F / C G / C F / CG C

Your mamma waited quite awhile
Carried you around for half a million miles
But you know it was worth it when you look at her smile / **And ...**

It all lies ahead of you & from this day
It won't be easy as you travel your way
But here's to your birth & I just want to say that / **I ...**

— Tom Paxton

 — For Andrew Arthur Okun, born Sept 29, 1962. On (& in) his Ramblin Boy *& Shaw Bros* The Best of. *In* Bells of Rhymney. OH20

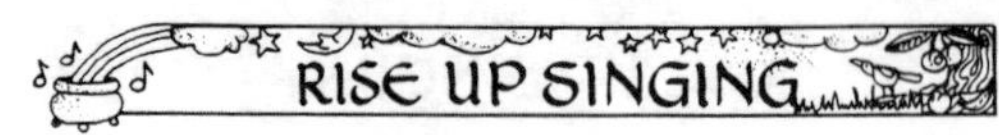

My Body

My body's nobody's body but mine
You run your own body, let me run mine

G - - D / - - - G **(Do twice for verse)**

My heart was made to be filled up with love
Not to be ordered or broken or shoved
My hands were made to hold other hands
Not to hold guns in faraway lands

My genes were made to pass on human traits
Not to be fried with your atomic waste
My womb was made to make kids when I please
Not to obey man-made laws & decrees

Our body's one body, one voice is heard
We each sing for freedom when we sing these words:

My nose was made to sniff & to sneeze
To smell what I want & to pick when I please
My lungs were made to hold air when I breathe
I am in charge of just how much I need!

My legs were made to dance me around
To walk & to run & to jump up & down
And my mouth was made to blow up a balloon
I can eat, kiss & spit, I can whistle a tune!

No one knows my body better than me
It tells me "Let's eat!" It tells me "Go pee!"
Don't hit me or kick me, don't push or shove
Don't hug me too hard when you show me your love

Sometimes it's hard to say "No!" & be strong
When the "No!" feeling comes, then I know something's wrong!
'Cause my body's mine from my head to my toe
Please leave it alone when you hear me say "No!"

Secrets are fun when they're filled with surprise
But not when they hurt us with tricks, threats & lies
My body's mine, to be used as I choose
Not to be threatened, or forced or abused!

— Peter Alsop (new v. Green Thumb Theatre, Vancouver, BC)
© 1985 Moose School Music (BMI). Used by permission. — On his Draw the Line & Wha' D'ya Wanna Do? *(FF298) & Tickle Tune Typhoon* All of Us Will Shine. *In* Here's to the Women & SO! *30:1.* OH21

My Little Girl

My little girl, teach me to laugh again
Run in the wind & tumble in the grass again
When you're so alive & running by my side
Then you teach me to laugh, little girl

A Bm / E A / - D / AE A

My little girl, teach me to cry again
To feel my pain & to stop & wonder why again
When you bow your head from something I have said
Then you teach me to cry, little girl

My little girl, teach me to love again
Put your arms around me & teach me how to hug again
When you know I'm sad & you touch me with your hand
Then you teach me to love, little girl

My little girl, teach me to live again
Let me be near you, & teach me how to give again
Life is fresh & new in everything you do
When you teach me to live, little girl

— Mary Dart
© 1975 Mary Dart. Used by permission. In S About People. OH22

No No No

(**spoken:** *Hey Dad? Can I have a puppy?)*
No no no, no no no, no no no, *no!* (3x) / Nooo! Nooo! Nooo!

(in 3/4) C - - G / - - - C / - - - F / - G C -

I never had one when I was your size
You really don't want one who barks & cries
Who wets on the carpet & chews up my shoes
And they carry diseases – they probably do
You're just a kid & I forbid you to have a puppy
Just do as I say: I've explained it to you

C - F - / C - G - / C - F - / C - G - - -
C - F - C - G - / - - - C

(There's nothing to do – can my friend come here to play?)
No no no ...!
When you have a friend here there's always such noise
You laugh & you play & you scatter your toys
And this house belongs to us grownups you see?
So go play with your crayons or watch the TV
You're just a kid & I forbid you to have any friends here
Just do as I say: I'm bigger than you

(Well I'm bored – can I smoke a cigarette?) **No, No, No ...!**
Just because I smoke doesn't mean you
Can huff & puff smoke rings like mature adults do
Smoking is bad for your lungs & your growth
I'm older, I know what is best for us both!
You're just a kid & I forbid you to smoke cigarettes
(Or anything else for that matter)
Just do as I say: don't do as I do!

(I'm getting angry – I feel like cussing!) **No, No, No ...!**
Damn it all NO! Because children who swear
Grow up to be stupid asses – so there!
"Tinkle" & "Kaa-kaa" are kid words to say
Stick with "pee-pee" & "poo-poo" & you'll be OK
You're just a kid & I forbid you to use grownup cuss words
Just do as I say: dirty words are taboo!

(You never let me do anything! I'm gonna have a tantrum!)
No, No, No ...!
That's an idea that's completely absurd
Children should only be seen & not heard
Just because I yell & shout & sometimes
Kick the cat, kick the chair & spank your behind
Doesn't mean that you have that luxury too
You have to go thru some frustrations, you see?
Especially if you want to grow up like me!
(Hey! Come back here! I'm speaking to you! Don't you slam that door! Wait until your mother gets home! Unlock this door! You're only a child! Only grown-ups get to have locked doors! Open! Open! Open! Waaaaaahhhh!)

— Peter Alsop
© 1980 Moose School Music (BMI). Used by permission. — On his Silly S & Modern Lullabies. OH23

The Old Folks at Home

Way down upon the Swannee River, far, far away
There's where my heart is turning ever, there's where the old folks stay
All up & down the whole creation, sadly I roam
Still longing for the old plantation & for the old folks at home
All the world is sad & dreary, everywhere I roam
O brothers, how my heart grows weary far from the old folks at home

C F C G7 / C F CG C :‖ G C F CG / 2nd

All 'round the little farm I wandered when I was young
Then many happy days I squandered, many the songs I sung
When I was playing with my brother, happy was I
O take me to my kind old mother, there let me live & die

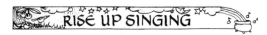

One little hut among the bushes, one that I love
Still sadly to my mem'ry rushes, no matter where I rove
When will I see the bees a-humming, all round the comb?
When will I hear the banjo strumming, down in my good old home?

— Stephen Foster

On (& in) Pete Seeger Am Fav Bal V3 *(FA2322). In* FiresB of FS & 100 S of Nostalgia. OH24

The Piney Wood Hills

I'm a rambler & rover & a wand'rer it seems
I've travelled all over chasing after my dreams
But a dream should come true & a heart should be filled
And a life should be lived on the Piney Wood Hills

G - Em - / / C - Am D / G D GC G

I'll return to the woodlands, I'll return to the snow
I'll return to the hills & the valleys below
I'll return as a poor man or a king if God wills
But I'm on my way home to the Piney Wood Hills

(bridge) I was raised on a song there
I've done right, I've done wrong there
And it's true I belong there
And it's true it's my home

C - / G - / A - / D - **(in 3/4, TD ↑ 5)**

From ocean to ocean I've rambled & roamed
And now I'll return to my Piney Wood home
Maybe someday I'll find someone who will
Love as I love my Piney Wood Hills

— Buffy Sainte Marie

 On her Many a Mile, Native Amer, I'm Gonna Be a Country Girl, Native No Amer Child & Best of. OH25

Short'nin' Bread

Three little children lyin' in bed
Two was sick & the other 'most dead
Sent for the doctor, the doctor said:
Feed those children on shortnin' bread

C - - - / - - G7 C :||

Mammy's little baby loves shortnin', shortnin'
Mammy's little baby loves shortnin' bread (repeat)

Put on the skillet, put on the lid
Mammy goin' to bake a little shortnin' bread
That ain't all she's goin' to do
Mammy goin' to make a little coffee too

The little child sick in bed
When he hear tell o' shortnin' bread
Popped up well, he dance an' sing
He almost cut the pigeon wing

I slip to the kitchen, slip up the lid
Filled my pocket full o' shortnin' bread
Stole the skillet, stole the lid
Stole the gal makin' shortnin' bread

They caught me with the skillet, they caught me with the lid
They caught me with the gal makin' shortnin' bread
Paid six dollars for the skillet, paid six dollars for the lid
Spent six months in jail, eatin' shortnin' bread

— trad. (Southern Black US)

On New Lost City Ramblers With Cousin Emmy *(FTS 31015) & JE Mainer* V3. *In* Golden Ency of FS, *Lomax* FS of NAm, Fred Waring SB, S Along w/World's Fav FS & FSEncyV2. OH26

Sons of (Fils de)

Sons of the sea, sons of the saint
Who is the child with no complaint
Sons of the great, sons unknown
All were children like your own
The same sweet smiles, the same sad tears
The cries at night, the nightmare fears
Sons of the great, sons unknown
All were children like your own **(in 3/4)**

D - - - / - - Em A / Em - A Em / A - D - / " / - - Em - / G F♯ Em B♭ / Em A Dsus D

Sons of tycoons, sons from the farms
All of the children ran from your arms
Thru fields of gold, thru fields of ruin
All of the children vanished too soon
In towering waves, in walls of flesh
Amid dying birds trembling with death / Sons of tycoons...

Sons of your sons, sons passing by
Children were lost in lullaby
Sons of true love, sons of regret
All of your sons you can never forget
Some built roads, some wrote the poems
Some went to war, some never came home / Sons of your sons...

— w: Eric Blau & Mort Shuman — m: Girard Jouannest

 — On Judy Collins Whales and Nightengales *& her* Colors. OH27

Sweet Potatoes

1. Soon as we all cook sweet potatoes **(3x)**
Soon as we all cook sweet potatoes, eat 'em right straight up!

(in E) B7 E B7 E :||

(counter melody): Roo **(4x)**, hoo roo, sing ho de dinkum!
Roo **(4x)** hoo roo, hoo roo!

2. Soon as supper's et, mammy hollers ... get along to bed
3. Soon we touch our heads to the pillow ... go to sleep right smart
4. Soon's the rooster crow in the mornin' ... got to wash our face
5. Soon's the school bus stops on the highway ... got to go to school

— Eng lyrics: H.W.Loomis, addl v. Pete Seeger
— m: trad (descant Hector Spaulding)

 — In SO! 13:3, Bells of Rhymney, FiresB Of Fun & Games & Twice 55 Brown B Of Community S. *On Pete Seeger* S & Playtime *(Folkways).* OH28

Sweet Sunny South

Take me back to the place where I first saw the light
To my sweet sunny south take me home
Where the wild birds sing me to sleep every night
O why was I tempted to roam?

D - - A / D - G - / D G D A - / D A D -

The path to our cabin they say has grown green
And the stones are quite mossy around
And I know that the faces & forms that I love
Now lie in the cold mossy ground

Take me back to the place where the orange trees grow
To my place in the evergreen shade
Where the flowers on the rivers green margins do grow
And share their wet scent with the glade

— trad. (US) coll by Cecil Sharp

In his Eng FS fr the So Appalach, *1932. On Baez* One Day at a Time & Country M Alb, *Mike Seeger* 2nd Annual Farewell Reunion *(Mercury), Smith Sisters* Mockingbird, *Carlie Poole* Old Time S & *New Lost City Ramblers* V4. *In* 1001 Jumbo S. OH29

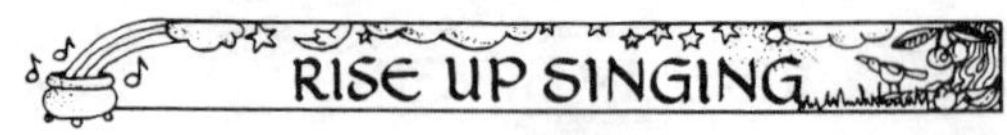

Teach Your Children

You who are on the road
Must have a code that you can live by
And so, become yourself
Because the past is just a goodbye

C F / C G :||

Teach your children well
Their father's hell did slowly go by
And, feed them on your dreams
The one they pick's the one you'll know by
And don't ever ask them why – if they tell you,
You'll just cry so, just look at them and sigh _
And know they love you _

C F / C G :|| C F / C Am FG / C -

And you, of tender years
Can't know the fears that your elders grew by
And so, please help them with your youth
They seek the truth before they can die

Teach your parents well
Their children's hell did slowly go by ...

— Graham Nash

 — *On* Crosby Stills & Nash Deja Vu, Gr H & 4-Way Street. *On Country Gentlemen* 25th Anniv *(Rebel).* OH30

What'll I Do with this Baby-o

What'll I do with this baby-o? (3x)
If he don't go to sleepy-o

D - A D :|| (4x)

Wrap him up in calico **(3x)**
Send him to his mammy-o

D - G D / D - A D :||

Wrap him up in a tablecloth **(3x)**
Throw him up in the fodderloft

Tell your daddy when he gets home **(3x)**
And I'll give old Blue your chicken bone

Pull his toes, tickle his chin **(3x)**
Roll him up in the countypin *[=counterpane]*

Dance him north, dance him south **(3x)**
Pour a little moonshine in his mouth

Everytime the baby cries, stick my finger in the baby's eye
That's what I'll do with the baby-o **(2x)**

— new & addl words & music by Jean Ritchie

 – In her Celeb of Life *& on her* At Folk City *(w/Doc Watson – Folkways). On Mike & Peggy Seeger (& in Ruth C Seeger)* Am FS for Children *(Rounder). In* SO! *9:4 & Reprints #5 (as "Prettiest ..."), Sharp* Eng FS of S App V2, All Our Lives, FSEncyV1 & Eye Winker. OH31

Where Is Love

Where is love? Does it fall from skies above?
Is it underneath the willow tree that I've been dreaming of?

GAm7 (3x) GG7 / C F Eb Am7D

Where is she who I close my eyes to see?
Will I ever know the sweet "hello" that's meant for only me?

Who can say where she may hide? Must I travel far & wide
Til I am beside the someone who I can mean something to?
Where, where is love?

GAm7 GG7 CD G / Am7D G F E /
Am7Em AmD G -

— Lionel Bart

 — Fr his musical & film Oliver! OH32

Why Oh Why

Why, o why, o why, o why? Why, o why, o why?
Because (4x) – Goodbye! (3x)

(in 3/4, TD ↑ 3) A - D A / D A E A

Why can't a dish break a hammer? **Why, o why, o why?**
Because a hammer's a hard head – **Goodbye! (3x)**

Why can't a bird eat an elephant? **Why...**
Because an elephant's got a pretty hard skin – **Goodbye ...**

Why can't a mouse eat a street car
Because a mouse's stomach ain't big enuf to hold no street car

Why does a horn make music
Because the horn-blower blows it

Why does a cow drink water
Because a cow gets thirsty just like you or me or anybody else

Why don't you fly up toward the moon
Because then I'll never be able to get back home again,
and see everybody again, might not get back home
never again, aaaaah...!

Why don't you answer my questions
Because I don't know the answers

— Woody Guthrie

 — (The 2nd lines of v3 & 6 should be sung holding the note following "Because" until the last 3 notes.) On his Gr S *& in his* SB. *On Odetta* Sings FS & Tribute to Woody Guthrie, pt 2. *In* SO! *10:3 & Reprints #12.* OH33

Wouldn't It Be Loverly

All I want is a room somewhere
Far away from the cold night air
With one enormous chair
O wouldn't it be loverly!

D G / D EA / D GEm / DBm EmA :||

Lots of choc'late for me to eat
Lots of coal makin' lots of heat
Warm face, warm hands, warm feet / **O ... loverly!**

/ " / " / " / DA D -

(bridge) O, so loverly sittin abso-bloomin-lutely still
I would never budge til spring crept over me winder sill

Em - A7 - / Bm F#m E7 A7

Someone's head restin' on my knee
Warm & tender as he can be
Who takes good care of me, o
Wouldn't it be
Loverly **(2x)** / Loverly **(2x)** / Loverly

D G/D EA/D GEm/DBm EmA/D EmA/D G/D -

— w: Alan Jay Lerner — m: Frederick Loewe

 — Fr their musical My Fair Lady. OH34

You Ain't Goin' Nowhere

Clouds so swift, rain won't lift
Gate won't close, railings froze
Get your mind off wintertime
You ain't goin' nowhere

G Am / C G :||

Whoo-ee! Ride me high
Tomorrow's the day my bride's gonna come
O, o, are we gonna fly
Down in the easy chair

I don't care how many letters they sent
Morning came & morning went
Pick up your money & pack up your tent / **You ...**

Buy me a flute & a gun that shoots
Tailgates & substitutes
Strap yourself to the tree with roots / **You ...**

Genghis Khan, he could not keep
All his kings supplied with sheep
We'll climb that hill no matter how steep
When we get up to it

— **Bob Dylan**

 — On his & The Band, Basement Tapes & Gr H *On Joan Baez* Any Day Now & 1st 10 Yrs. OH35

This chapter includes songs about children. For songs enjoyed by children, see PLAY and LULLABIES. For songs about emotional support & affection, see FRIENDSHIP. For songs about missing home, see TRAVEL. See also TIME & CHANGES.

Look for: "What Did You Learn in School Today" (AMER) "My Hometown" (CITY) "Mandolin Man," "My Old Man" (CREATIVITY) "My Father," "O Had I a Golden Thread," "Rhymes & Reason" (DREAMS) "Mammas Don't Let Your Babies," "My Sweet Wyoming Home," "Home on the Range" (FARM) "Chat with Your Mom," "Father's Whiskers," "I'm My Own Grandpa," "Squalor" (FUN) "Make Me a Pallet" (GOOD) "We Can Work It Out" (HARD) "All the Weary Mothers" (HOPE) "Hard Love," "Lovely Agnes" (LOVE) "Jenny's Gone," "Mountain Song," "Take Me Home" (MTN) "Deep Blue Sea," "May There Always Be Sunshine," "Mothers Daughters Wives" (PEACE) "Prodigal Son," "This Glorious Food" (SACRED) "Come Fare Away," "Rolling Home," "Ways of Man" (SEA) "Your Daughters & Your Sons" (STRUG) "Everything Possible" (UNITY) "Housewife's Lament" (WOMEN).

HOPE

All the Weary Mothers

All the weary mothers of the earth will finally rest
We will take their babies in our arms & do our best
When the sun is low upon the field
To love & music they will yield
And the weary mothers of the earth will rest

CF CG C↓ / CF C D G

C Em / Am F - / 1st /

And the farmer on his tractor & beside his plow
Will stand there in confusion as we wet his brow
With the tears of all the businessmen
Who see what they have done to him
And the weary farmers of the earth shall rest

And the aching workers of the world again shall sing
These words in mighty choruses to all will bring
"We shall no longer be the poor
For no one owns us any more"
And the workers of the world again shall sing

And when the soldiers burn their uniforms in every land
And the foxholes at the borders will be left unmanned
General, when you come for the review
The troops will have forgotten you
And the men & women of the earth shall rest

— **Joan Baez**

 On her Come fr the Shadows & Gracias a la Vida *(in Spanish).* OO02

Blackbird

Blackbird singing in the dead of night
Take these broken wings & learn to fly
All your life
You were only waiting for this moment to arise

DEm7 D - / Em7 F#7 Bm -

DE7 Em Gm / D E7 EmA D

Blackbird singing in the dead of night
Take these sunken eyes & learn to see
All your life
You were only waiting for this moment to be free

(bridge) Blackbird fly, blackbird fly
Into the light of the dark black night

C G F G C G F E7 / A7 D -

— **John Lennon & Paul McCartney**

 — In their Gr S of ... *& on Beatles* White Alb. *On Mary McCaslin* Old Friends *(Philo 1046)* & Blue Ridge Epitaph *(Piccadilly 3537). In* Club Date FakeB. OO03

Blowin' in the Wind

How many roads must a man walk down
Before you call him a man?
Yes & how many seas must a white dove sail
Before she sleeps in the sand?
Yes & how many times must the cannonballs fly
Before they're forever banned?
The answer, my friend, is blowin' in the wind
The answer is blowin' in the wind

C F C - / C F C G / C F C Am / C F G -
/ " / " // F G C Am / F G C -

How many times must a man look up
Before he can see the sky?
Yes & how many ears must one man have
Before he can hear people cry?
Yes & how many deaths will it take til he knows
That too many people have died?

How many years can a mountain exist
Before it's washed to the sea?
Yes & how many years can some people exist
Before they're allowed to be free?
Yes & how many times can a man turn his head
Pretending he just doesn't see?

— **Bob Dylan**

© 1962 Warner Bros. Inc. Renewed 1990 Special Rider Music. — In his SB & Biography *& on his* Freewheelin, Gr H V2 & At Budokan. *In* Peter, Paul & Mary SB *& their* Best of .... *On their* In the Wind & In Conc. *On Flatt & Scrugs* Changin Times *(CS9596), Baez* Fr Every Stage, *Patrick Sky* Thru a Window *& Kingston Trio* Best of, V2 *& on* Gr FSingers of the '60s. *In* SO! *12:4 & 44:4,* Gr S of the '60s, *Readers Dig* Fam SB. O004

Can't Kill the Spirit

Nobody can push back an ocean
It's gonna rise back up in waves
And nobody can stop a wind from blowin'
Can stop a mind from growin'
Somebody may stop my song from being sung
But the song will live on & on

A9 A7 / D2 Fmaj7 :|| (3x)

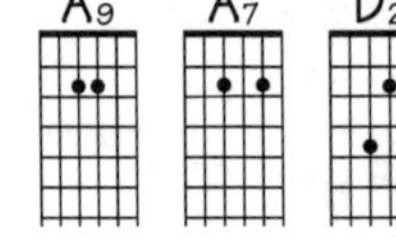

You can't kill the spirit
It's *[she's]* **like a mountain**
Old & strong
It *[she]* **lives on & on (repeat)**

A9 / A7 / D2 / Fmaj7 :||

Fmaj7

Nobody can stop a woman from feelin'
That she has to rise up like the sun
Somebody may change the words we're saying
But the truth will live on & on

— **Naomi Littlebear Morena**

© 1976 Naomi Littlebear Morena. Used by permission. — On her & the Izquierda Ensemble *& in her* Hermanas SB *(both available fr author c/o Quiet Thunder, 11046 Silver Run, Morena Valley CA 92388).* O005

Come and Go with Me

Come & go with me to that land **(3x)**
where I'm bound (repeat)

D - / G D / - - / A - / 1st 2 / D DA / DG D

There'll be freedom in that land **(3x)** where I'm bound...
There'll be justice in that land...
There'll be singin' in that land...
There'll be lovin' in that land...
There'll be no hunger in that land...

— **trad. (Black Spiritual)**

In SO! *6:2,* Sing Together Children, How Can We Keep From S. & FSEncyV2. *In* Peter Paul & Mary SB *& on their* A S Will Rise. *On* Odetta *& her* Bals & Blues *& Bernice Reagon* River of Life *(FF).* O006

The Faith of Man

One day a babe was born along the highway
A tiny, helpless thing upon the sand
And an Okie with a dream out on the byway
Took the babe & held it proudly in his hands

And the woman smiled a gentle smile of knowing
And whispered something softly in its ear
Perhaps a little prayer to help the growing
Perhaps a word of comfort thru the fear

D - G - / A - D - :|| (4x)

You can trust the moon to move the mighty oceans
You can trust the sun to shine upon the land
You take the little that you know & you do the best you can
And you see the rest with the quiet faith of man

G A D - / GD EmD A - / G A D G / Em A D -

A tractor makes its way along a fence line
The seeds are dropped precisely in the row
And if the rain is kind & the wind don't take the topsoil
Before too long the crops will start to show

Now the farmer sees the fields around him ripen
And whispers something low beneath his breath
Perhaps a little prayer to help the growing
Perhaps a word of thanks for all the rest

There's a storm tossed ship tonight out on the water
There's a soul that sails alone out on the blue
There's a dreamer with her eyes upon the heavens
They're all looking for a way to make it thru

— **Bill Staines**

© 1986 Mineral River Music (BMI). — On his Sandstone Cathedrals *& in* Movin' It Down the Line *&* SO! *33:3. On Priscilla Herdman* Darkness into Light. O007

Give Yourself to Love

Kind friends all gathered 'round, there's something I would say
That what brings us together here has blessed us all today
Love has made a circle that holds us all inside
Where strangers are as family & loneliness can't hide, you must

C Am F C / - Am F G /
C G F C / - Am FG F -

Give yourself to love, if love is what you're after
Open up your hearts to the tears & laughter
And give yourself to love, give yourself to love

C Am FG C / - Am G - / C Am FG C -

I've walked these mountains in the rain, I've learned to love the wind
I've been up before the sunrise to watch the day begin
I always knew I'd find you tho' I never did know how
But like sunshine on a cloudy day, you stand before me now, so

Love is born in fire, it's planted like a seed
Love can't give you everything but it gives you what you need
Love comes when you are ready, love comes when you're afraid
It will be your greatest teacher, the best friend you have made, so..

— **Kate Wolf**

© 1982 Another Sundown Publishing. In SO! *34:4 & 44:4 & on her* Give Yourself... *In* Worship in Song: A Hymnal for Friends. O008

Gracias a La Vida

Gracias a la vida_que me ha dado tanto _
Me dio dos luceros_que cuando los abro _
Perfecto distingo_lo negro del blanco _
Y en el alto cielo su fondo estrellado _
Y en las multitudes el hombre que yo_amo _ **(in Am)**

Dm E Am C / G - C - / Gm - F - / E - Am - / /

Gracias a la vida que me ha dado tanto
Me ha dado el oído que en todo su ancho
Graba noche y días grillos y canarios
Martillos, turbinas, ladridos, chubascos
Y la voz tan tierna de mi bienamado

Gracias... / Me ha dado el sonido y el abacedario
Con ,l las palabras que pienso y declaro
Madre, amigo, hermano, y luz alumbrando
La ruta del alma del que estoy amando

Gracias... / Me ha dado la marcha de mis pies cansados
Con ellos anduve ciudades y charcos
Playas y desiertos, montañas y llanos
Y la casa tuya, tu calle y tu patio

Gracias... / Me dió el corazon que agita su marco
Cuando miro el fruto del cerebro humano
Cuando miro el bueno tan lejos del malo
Cuando miro el fondo de tus ojos claros

Gracias... / Mi ha dado la risa y mi ha dado el llanto
Así yo distingo dicha de quebranto
Los dos materiales que forman me canto
Y el canto de ustedes que es el mismo canto
Y el canto de todos que es mi propio canto
I: in 6/8 II: in 4/4 on TD (same chords for both)

— Violeta Para

© 1970 by Editorial Musical Korn S.A.I.C. All rights for the USA administered by Rightsong Music, Inc. All rights reserved. Used by permission. – In SO! *22:5. On H Near & R Gilbert* Lifeline, *Marcia Taylor* Tinden *(Rainbow Snake007) & Baez* Gracias a la Vida *&* Best of. *Trans of Sp: "Thank you to the life that has given me song, that gave me 2 eyes which, when I open them, perfectly distinguish the black fr the white, the sparkling stars in the deep sky & among the multitudes the man I love."* OO09

The Great Storm Is Over

The thunder & lightning gave voice to the night
The little lame child cried aloud in her fright
Hush, little baby, a story I'll tell
Of a love that has vanquished the powers of hell

D - G D/GA D G D/- - G A/GA Bm G A

Alleluia, the Great Storm is over
Lift up your wings & fly (repeat)

D - A Bm / D G A - :|| **(in D)**

Sweetness in the air & justice on the wind
Laughter in the house where the mourners have been
The deaf shall have music, the blind have new eyes
The standards of death taken down by surprise

Release for the captives, an end to the wars
New streams in the desert, new hope for the poor
The little lame children will dance as they sing
And play with the bears & the lions in spring

Hush little baby, let go of your fear
The Lord loves His own & your mother is here
The child fell asleep as the lantern did burn
The mother sang on til her bridegroom's return

— Bob Franke

© 1982 Telephone Pole Music Publishing Co. (BMI). Used by permission. – In SO! *35:4. On his* One Eve. in Chicago *(GDSR 1766). Also on* The Coop *(July 1982) &* Live at the Bottom Line. *In Worship in Song: A Hymnal for Friends.* OO10

If We Only Have Love

If we only have love,_then tomorrow will dawn _
And the days of our years_will rise on that morn _
If we only have love_to embrace without fears _
We will kiss with our eyes,_we will sleep without tears _

C Am C Am / Dm G Dm G / 1st / Dm G - C

If we only have love with our arms open wide
Then the young & the old will stand at our side
If we only have love, love that's falling like rain
Then the parched desert earth will grow green again

E Am E Am / Dm G - C / 1st / Dm E Dm E

If we only have love for the hymn that we shout
For the song that we sing, then we'll have a way out

Am E Am7 D7 / Dm G - C

If we only have love we can reach those in pain
We can heal our own wounds, we can use our own names
If we only have love, we can melt all the guns
And pass on the world to our daughters & sons

If we only have love, then Jerusalem stands
And then death has no shadow, there are no foreign lands
If we only have love we will never bow down
We'll be tall as the pines, neither heroes nor clowns

Then with nothing at all but the little we are
We'll have conquered all time, all space, the sun & the stars

Am E Am E / F G - - C(Am C Am Fm G C -)

— orig Fr lyrics & m: Jacques Brel Eng: Mort Shuman & Eric Blau

© 1956 Lorraine Music Co.© 1968 Unichappell Music, Inc. (Rightsong Music, Publisher) International copyright secured. All rights reserved. Printed in USA. Unauthorized copying, arranging, adapting, recording or public performance is an infringement of copyright. Fr Jacques Brel is Alive & Well. OO11

Imagine

Imagine there's no heaven, it's easy if you try
No hell below us, above us only sky
Imagine all the people living for today

G C G C - / / CEm AmC D -

Imagine there's no countries, it isn't hard to do
Nothin' to kill or die for & no religions too
Imagine all the people living life in peace

You may say I'm a dreamer, but I'm not the only one
I hope someday you'll join us & the whole world will live as one

CD GB7 **(2x)** / CD GB7 CD G

Imagine no possessions, I wonder if you can
No need for greed nor hunger nor folk with empty hands
Imagine all the people sharing all the world / **You...**

— John Lennon

© 1971 Lenono Music. All rights controlled & administered by Blackwood Music, Inc. All rights reserved. Used by permission. — On his Imagine *& Joan Baez* Come for the Shadows *& her* Best of. OO12

It Could Be a Wonderful World

If each little kid could have fresh milk each day
If each working man had enough time to play
If each homeless soul had a good place to stay
It could be a wonderful world (2x)

(in 3/4) C G / - C / C7 F / G C / /

If we could consider each other
A neighbor, a friend, or a brother
It could be a wonderful, wonderful world
It could be a wonderful world (2x)

/ " / F C / " / " / /

If there were no poor & the rich were content
If strangers were welcome wherever they went
If each of us knew what true brotherhood meant / **It ...**

— w: Hy Zaret — m: Lou Singer

© 1947 Argosy Music Corp., NY. Copyright renewed. Used by permission. — On Faith Petric Sing a S, Sing Along *(GentleWind) & Susan Stark* Rainbow People. *In* S of Work & Protest *&* Children's S for a Friendly Planet. OO13

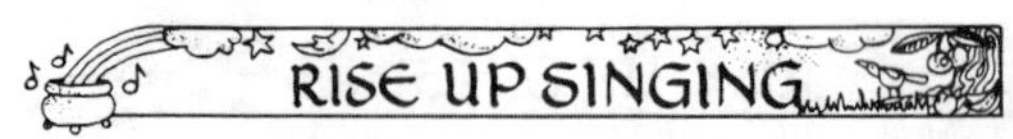

It's a Long Road to Freedom

It's a long road to freedom, a-winding steep & high
But when you walk in love with the wind on your wing
& cover the earth with the songs you sing
The miles fly by

D G D A / D G D Em / DG D

I walked one morning by the sea
And all the waves reached out to me
I took their tears, then let them be

D G D - / - A D DG / A AG D

I walked one morning at the dawn
When bits of night still lingered on
I sought my star, but it was gone

I walked one morning with a friend
And prayed the day would never end
The years have flown, so why pretend

I walked one morning with my King
[My heart one morning took to wing]
And all my winters turned to spring
Yet every moment held its sting

— Sr. Miriam Therese Winter

© 1966 Medical Mission Sisters, Phila., PA. Used by permission. On (& in) Medical Mission Sisters Joy is Like the Rain. O014

Julian of Norwich

Loud are the bells of Norwich & the people come & go
Here by the tower of Julian I tell them what I know
Ring out bells of Norwich & let the winter come & go
All shall be well again, I know

D - - - / // G D A - / D GA D -

Love, like the yellow daffodil is coming thru the snow
Love, like the yellow daffodil is Lord of all I know

Ring for the yellow daffodil, the flower in the snow
Ring for the yellow daffodil & tell them what I know

(as chorus)
All shall be well, I'm telling you: **let the winter come & go**
All shall be well again, I know

— Sydney Carter

© 1981, 1982 by Stainer & Bell, Ltd. Used by permission of Galaxy Music Corp. NY, NY, sole US agent. — Julian is widely considered one of the greatest mystics of medieval times. She had a room in Norwich Cathedral which had one opening facing outward (for the people who streamed to her for solace & advice) & a 2nd opening inward facing the sanctuary. On Lovely in the Dances: S of Sydney Carter *(Osmosys Recs) & in* S of Sydney Carter in the Present Tense Bk 1 *&* Worship in S. *On Bok Muir & Trickett* All Shall Be Well Again *&* Minneapolis Conc. O015

Let it Be

When I find myself in times of trouble, Mother Mary comes to me
Speaking words of wisdom: **let it be**
And in my hour of darkness, she is standing right in front of me
Speaking words of wisdom, **let it be**
Let it be (4x) / Speaking words of wisdom, let it be

(TD ↑ 7)
C G Am F / C G F C :|| Am G F C / - G F C

And when the broken hearted people living in the world agree
There will be an answer, **let ...**
For tho' they may be parted, there is still a chance that they will see / There ...

And when the night is cloudy there is still a light that shines on me
Shines until tomorrow, **let ...**
I wake up to the sound of music, Mother Mary comes to me
Speaking words of wisdom ...
(last cho:) Let it be (4x) / Whisper words of wisdom...

— John Lennon & Paul McCartney

© 1970 Northern Songs Ltd. All rights administered by Blackwood Music Inc. under license from ATV Music (Maclen). All rights reserved. International copyright secured. Used by permission. – On Beatles Let It Be *&* '67-'70, *Baez* Blessed Are, *Denver* Poems Prayers & Promises, *Mary McCaslin* Way Out West *(Philo), Aretha Franklin* Gr H *& rec by the Everly Bros. In* S of the Spirit, *Readers Dig* Fam SB of Faith & Joy *&* Quaker SB. O016

Light Is Returning

Light is returning, even tho' this is the darkest hour
No one can hold back the dawn

Dm - DmAm Dm / - DmAm Dm(Am Dm)

Let's keep it burning, let's keep the light of hope alive
Make safe our journey thru the storm

One planet is turning, circle on her path around the sun
Earth Mother is calling her children home

— Charlie Murphy

© 1984 Charlie Murphy (BMI). Used by permission. On his Canticles of Light. O017

Lo How a Rose

Lo how a Rose e'er blooming from tender stem hath sprung
Of Jesse's lineage coming as men of old have sung
It came a floweret bright amid the cold of winter
When half spent was the night

C - FC G Am F C Dm G C - :||
G Am G - C FC G Am / F C Dm G C -

Isaiah 'twas foretold it the Rose I have in mind
With Mary we behold it the Virgin Mother kind
To show God's love a right she bore to men a Savior
When half spent was the night

— w: German anon. 15th c, Eng Theodore Baker (1851-1934)
— m: German, 16th c. arr Michael Praetorius (1571-1621)

aka: "Es Ist Eim Ros." On Lindsay Haisley Armadillo 82, *Pete Seeger* Trad Xmas Carols *(FAS32311), Sylvia Woods* 3 Harps for Xmas *& Reilly & Maloney* Xmas Alb. *In* Oxford B of Carols *& in many hymnals.* O018

Love Grows One by One

Love grows one by one
Two by two & four by four
Love grows 'round like a circle
And comes back knocking at your front door

C - F C / F C D G / 1st / F C G C

Note by note we make a song
Voice by voice we sing it
Choir by choir we fill up the world
With the music that we bring it

G - - C / / Em - Am - / D - G -

So let me take your hand, my friend
We'll each take the hand of another
One by one we'll reach for all
Our sisters & our brothers

— Carol Johnson

© 1981 Carol Johnson, Noeldner Music (BMI) PO Box 6351 Grand Rapids MI 49506. All rights reserved. Used by permission. — On her Might As Well Make It Love. *In* Children's S for a Friendly Planet. O019

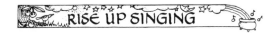

Love Is Come Again

Now the green blade riseth from the buried grain
Wheat that in the dark earth many days has lain
Love lives again that with the dead has been
Love is come again like wheat that springeth green

DmG Dm GA Dm / / Dm A Dm A / 1st /

In the grave they laid him, love whom men had slain
Thinking that never he would wake again
Laid in earth like grain that sleeps unseen / **Love...**

Forth he came at Easter, like the risen grain
He that for three days in the grave had lain
Quick from the dead my risen Lord is seen...

When our hearts are wintry, grieving or in pain
Thy touch can call us back to life again
Fields of our hearts that dead & bare have been...

— w: J.M.C. Crum (1872-1958) — m: trad. (Fr. carol "Noël Nouvelet")
aka: "Now the Green Blade Riseth." Fr Oxford B of Carols. *Reprinted by permission of Oxford University Press.* O020

Love Will Guide Us

If you cannot sing like angels
If you cannot speak before thousands
You can give from deep within you
You can change the world with your love **(in 3/4)**

E - A E - - / - - - B7 - / 1st / E - B7 E (A E)

Love will guide us, peace has tried us
Hope inside us will lead the way
On the road from greed to giving
Love will guide us thru the dark night

You are like no other being
What you can give no other can give
To the future of our precious children
To the future of the world where we live

Hear the song of peace within you
Heed the song of peace in your heart
Spring's new beginning shall lead to the harvest
Love will guide us on our way

— w: Sally Rogers — m: trad. "I Will Guide Thee"

A New Day

I can see a new day, a new day soon to be
When the storm clouds are all past
And the sun shines on a world that is free

(TD ↑ 2) C G - C / - F / CG C

I can see a new world, a new world coming fast
When all men are brothers *[we're all one people]*
And hatred forgotten at last

I can see a new man *[folk]*, a new man standing tall
With his *[our]* head*[s]* high & his *[our]* heart*[s]* proud
And afraid of nothing at all

— Les Rice

Ripple

If my words did sing with the voice of sunshine
And my tunes were played on the harp unstrung
Would you hear my voice come thru the music
Would you hold it close as if it was your own?

G - C - / - - - G / - - C - / G D C G

It's a hand-me-down, the thoughts are broken
Perhaps it's better left unsaid
And I don't know, don't really care
Let there be songs to fill the air

Ripple in still water
Where there is no pebble tossed, nor wind to blow

Am - D - / G C A D

Reach out your hand if your cup be empty
If your cup is full, may it be again
Let it be known there is a fountain
That was not made by the hand of man

There is a road, no simple highway
Between the dawn & dark of night
And where you go, no one may follow
That path is for your steps alone

You who choose to lead must follow
But if you fall, you fall alone
If you should stand, then who's to guide you?
If I knew the way, I would take you home

— w: Robert Hunter m: Jerry Garcia

The Rose

Some say love, it is a river that drowns the tender reed
Some say love, it is a razor that leaves your soul to bleed
Some say love, it is a hunger, an endless aching need
I say love, it is a flower & you its only seed

D - A - G GA D - / F#m - Bm - Em - A - / 1st /

It's the heart afraid of breaking that never learns to dance
It's the dream afraid of waking that never takes the chance
It's one who won't be taken, who cannot seem to give
And the soul afraid of dying that never learns to live

When the night has been too lonely & the road has been too long
And you think that love is only for the lucky & the strong
Just remember in the winter far beneath the bitter snows
Lies the seed that with the sun's love in the spring becomes the rose

— Amanda McBroom

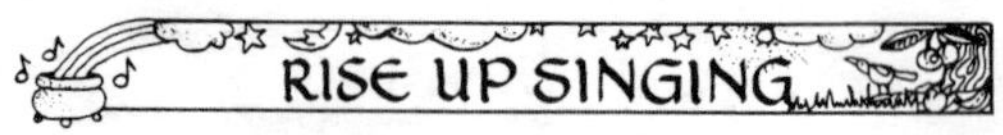

Somewhere

There's a place for us, somewhere a place for us
Peace & quiet & open air, wait for us somewhere

A - D G Em A D G / A - F#m Bm G C A -

There's a time for us, someday a time for us
Time together with time to spare, time to learn, time to care

A - D G Em A D G / A - F#m Bm G C Am F

(bridge) Someday, somewhere, we'll find a new way of living
We'll find a way of forgiving, somewhere

Bb - G - Dm - Em - / Bb Gm F - E - - -

There's a place for us, a time & place for us
Hold my hand & we're half-way there, hold my hand & I'll take you there
Somehow, someday, somewhere

as 2nd verse adding on: Bb - Gm - D - - -

— **w: Stephen Sondheim** — **m: Leonard Bernstein**

 – Fr their musical West Side Story. *On Andy Williams* Shadow of Your Smile. *In* S Am Sings & Broadway Sbs. O025

Thanksgiving Eve

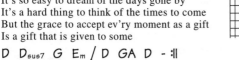

Dsus7

It's so easy to dream of the days gone by
It's a hard thing to think of the times to come
But the grace to accept ev'ry moment as a gift
Is a gift that is given to some

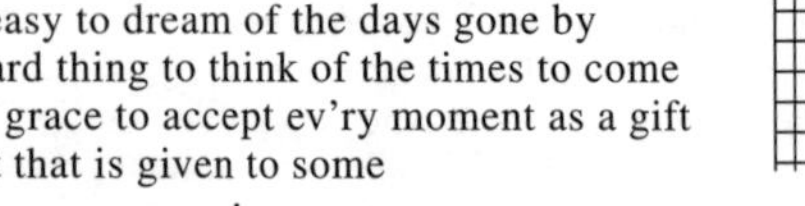

D Dsus7 G Em / D GA D - :||

What can you do with your days but work & hope
Let your dreams bind your work to your play
What can you do with each moment of your life
But love til you've loved it away / Love til you've...

A - C A / Bm G A - / 1st above / D GA D - / /

There are sorrows enough for the whole world's end
There are no guarantees but the grave
And the life that I live & the time I have spent
Are a treasure too precious to save

As it was so it is, as it is shall it be
And it shall be while lips that kiss have breath
Many waters indeed only nurture Love's seed
And its flower overshadows the power of death

— **Bob Franke**

 — On his One Evening in Chicago, *Claudia Schmidt* New Goodbyes Old Helloes, *Sally Rogers* In the Circle of the Sun, *Guy Carawan* The Land Knows You're There *& on* Garnet Rogers. *In* SO! *38:3 &* New Folk Favs. O026

That Cause Can Neither Be Lost Nor Stayed

That cause can neither be lost nor stayed
Which takes the course of what God has made
And is not trusting in walls & towers
But slowly growing from seeds to flowers

(in 3/4) C Am G C / Am Dm G C
Am Em F C / Am Ab CCG GCC

Each noble service that man has *[we have]* wrought
Was first conceived as a fruitful thought
Each worthy cause with a future glorious
By quietly growing becomes victorious

There by itself like a tree it shows
That high it reaches, as deep as it grows
And when the storms are its branches shaking
It deeper root in the soil is taking

Be then no more by a storm dismayed
For by it the full-grown seeds are laid
And tho' the tree by its might it shatters
What then if thousands of seeds it scatters!

— **orig Danish: Kristian Ostergaard Eng: J.C. Aaberg**
— **m: J. Nellemann (adap fr Danish folktune)**

Used by permission of Grandview College. — In Joyful Singing & S of All Time *(WAS) &* Friends Hymnal. O027

Turn Back O Man

Turn back, o man, foreswear thy foolish ways
Old now is earth & none may count her days
Yet thou her child whose head is crowned with flame
Still will not hear thine inner God proclaim
Turn back, o man, foreswear thy foolish ways

C FC DmG C / - FC Dm G / GAm (2x) DmC E
CG (2x) CD G / CG EAm DmC GC

Earth might be fair & all folk glad & wise
Age after age men's tragic empire rise
Built while they dream & in that dreaming weep
Would we but wake from out our haunted sleep / Earth might...

Earth shall be fair & all her people one
Nor til that hour shall God's whole hope be done
Now, even now, once more from earth to sky
Peals forth in joy that old undaunted cry: / "Earth shall..."

— **w: Clifford Bax (1886-1962)**
— **m: Genevan Psalter, 1551 ("Old 124th")**

Reprinted by permission of A.D.Peters & Co. Ltd. — In Joyful Singing *(WAS) & many hymnals. These words were put to a new tune in* Godspell. O028

Turning Toward the Morning

When the deer is bedded down & the bear is gone to ground
And the Northern goose has wandered off to warmer bay & sound
It's so easy in the cold to feel the darkness of the year
And the heart is growing lonely for the morning

C - F - / C - F G - / C - F - / C G F C

O my Joanie don't you know that the stars are swinging slow
And the seas are rolling easy as they did so long ago?
If I had a thing to give you, I would tell you one more time
That the world is always turning toward the morning

G - C - / " / " / " /

Now October's growing thin & November's coming home
You'll be thinking of the season & the sad things that you've seen
And you hear that old wind walking, hear him singing high and thin:
You could swear he's out there singing of your sorrows

When the darkness falls around you & the North Wind comes to blow
And you hear him call your name out as he walks the brittle snow
That old wind don't mean you trouble, he don't care or even know
He's just walking down the darkness toward the morning

It's a pity we don't know what the little flowers know
They can't face the cold November, they can't take the wind and snow
They put their glories all behind them, bow their heads & let it go
But you know they'll be there shining in the morning

Now my Joanie don't you know that the days are rolling slow
And the winter's walking easy as he did so long ago?
And if the wind should come & ask you "Why's my Joanie weeping so?"
Won't you tell him that you're weeping for the morning?

— **Gordon Bok**

 Publ. by Folk Legacy Records. In SO! *36:4 & his* Time & The Flying Snow, New Folk Favs & Bright Morning Stars *(WAS). On* Turning... *(w/Muir & Trickett).* O029

Weave Me the Sunshine

Weave, weave, weave me the sunshine
Out of the falling rain
Weave me the hope of a new tomorrow
And fill my cup again

(in C) F G C Am / / / D - G -

Well, I've seen the steel & the concrete crumble
Shine on me again
The proud & the mighty, all have stumbled
Shine on me again

Am - Em - / F G C Am / Am - D - / G - G7 -

They say that the tree of loving / **Shine on me again**
Grows on the banks of the river of suffering / **Shine...**

If only I can heal your sorrow...
I'll help you to find a new tomorrow...

Only you can climb the mountain...
If you want to drink at the golden fountain...

— Peter Yarrow

What a Day of Victory

When there's a roof & there's a bed
And the hungry have been fed
What a day of victory that will be
When men & women take their place
One multi-colored human race
What a day of victory that will be!

D - / G D / D - A - / 1st 2 / D A D -

What a day of victory victory / Vic-tory!
What a day of victory that will be
When hosannas glad we sing
Bells of peace & freedom ring
What a day of victory that will be!

When non-violence brings forth reason
And no jail or shouts of treason / **What a day...be**
When capital punishment is done
When world-wide amnesty has been won / **What...be!**

To bear a child each woman's choice
In her own "destiny" a voice...
Respected equally at last
Whatever color, creed or cast...

No nukes or neutron bombs that day
No way to peace, peace is the way...
Arms in museums where they belong
And it's love will make us strong...

— w: Marion Wade — m: trad. (hymn)

What the World Needs Now

What the world needs now is love, sweet love
It's the only thing that there's just too little of
What the world needs now is love, sweet love
No, not just for some, but for everyone **(in 3/4)**

Em7 Am7 **(2x)** / Dm7 F Em G / 1st / Dm7 - G G7

Lord we don't need another mountain
There are mountains & hillsides enough to climb
There are oceans & rivers enough to cross
Enough to last, til the end of time

Am7 - - - / Gm7 C Fmaj7 Dm7
/ Gm7 C Fmaj7 / Am7 D7 Dm7 G

Lord, we don't need another meadow
There are cornfields & wheat fields enough to grow
There are sunbeams & moonbeams enough to shine
O listen Lord, if you want to know

— w: Hal David — m: Burt Bacharach

Woyaya

We are going, heaven knows where we are going
We'll know we're there

(in 3/4) C - F Em Dm - / C - - -

We will get there, heaven knows how we will get there
We know we will

(bridge) It will be hard we know, & the
Road will be muddy & rough but we'll / Get there... **(into 2d v.)**

Am G F - / - - C G

(Interlude / tag)
Woyaya (woyaya), woyaya (woyaya) **(repeat ad lib)**

Dm7 - C - :|| **(ad lib)**

— Teddy Ose, Sol Amarfia, Loughty Lasisi Amao, Mac Tontoh, W. Richardson, R.M. Bailey & R. Bedau

*As you may have noticed this book is **full** of "hopeful songs" (both in the personal & the broader social sense). This obviously reflects the bias of those of us who put the book together (altho' we have managed to fit in some songs which let you sing about hard times as well...) The following index may be especially useful for the organizers of retreats, gatherings or workshops. (For some of the longer or harder songs, try just using choruses.) Chapters with too many songs to list individually include: FAITH, FREEDOM, FRIENDSHIP, GOSPEL, MEN, SACRED ROUNDS & CHANTS, SPIRITUALS, UNITY, and WOMEN. For couples retreats, see also GOLDEN OLDIES and LOVE.*

In addition, see: "Fashioned in the Clay" (CREAT) "Follow the Gleam," "O Had I a Golden Thread," "Over the Rainbow" (DREAM) "God Bless the Grass" (ECO) "Garden Song" (FARM) "Multiple Relationship Blues," "Squalor" (FUN) "Hey Look Me Over," "New River Train," "Vive l'Amour" (GOOD) "Motherless Child" (HARD) "All I Really Need," "Free to Be You & Me," "My Body" (HOME) "Angels Watchin over Me," "Kumbaya," "Lullabye [Like a Ship...]" (LULL) "Bless My Soul," "Mountain Song" (MTN) "Here Comes the Sun," "Morning Has Broken" (OUT) "Let There Be Peace," "May There Always Be Sunshine," "Study War No More" (PEACE) "If I Only Had a Brain," "You Can't Make a Turtle" (PLAY) "Banks of Marble" (RICH) "Black Socks," "Make New Friends," "More We Get Together," "Why Shouldn't My Goose" (ROUNDS) "Dona Dona," "If I Had a Hammer," "Look to the People," "Love's Gonna Carry Us," "Never Turning Back," "Singing for our Lives" (STRUG) "Circle," "I Like the Age I Am," "River, Turn Around," "Turn Turn Turn" (TIME) "One More Step," "Sailing Down My Golden River," "Thirsty Boots" (TRAV) "Mill Was Made of Marble," "Our Life is More Than Our Work," & "We Shall Not Be Moved" (WORK).

À la Claire Fontaine

A la claire fontaine, m'en allant promener
J'ai trouvé, l'eau si belle, que je m'y suis baigné,
Lui ya* longtemps que je t'aime, jamais je ne t'oublierai

D Em7 **(2x)** / DA BmD D EA / D GD D AD

J'ai trouvé, l'eau si belle, que je m'y suis baigné,
Sous les feuilles d'un chêne, je me suis fait sécher
(for each v. repeat 2nd line of last v. + new line)

Sous... / Sur la plus haute branche le rossignol chantait
Sur... / Chante, rossignol, chante, toi qui as le coeur gai, **(etc.)**
Tu as le coeur à rire, moi je l'ai-t-à pleurer
J'ai perdu ma maîtresse sans l'avoir mérité,
Pour un bouquet de roses que je lui refusai
Je voudrais que la rose fût encore au rosier
Et moi et ma maîtresse dans les mêm's amitiés

— trad. (Québeqois)

**lui ya=il y a (in French Canadian dialect.) Trans. of refrain: "Long have I loved you, I will never forget you." The fountain waters, oak leaves & nightengale are images of the singer's sadness at the loss of his lady. Sometimes called the "unofficial anthem of French Canada," it is said to have been brought to Canada from France as early as 1604 by Champlain's men. The words were known with a different tune in France. In Fowke & Johnston* Chansons de Québec/FS of Quebec. *On* Authentic M & F Dances of the World, *Lilianne Labbé, & Don Hinkley* Un Canadien Errant *(Philo PH 41069) & Shep Ginandes* Sings FS. *In* SO! *7:2,* FS & Footnotes, FSEncy V1 *& Trapp Fam* Enjoy Your Recorder. OL02

Abelard and Heloise

Abelard & Heloise were lovers in history
I don't know their story, I only remember their names

Dm A / B♭ A Dm **(Omit final Dm on verses 3 + 4)**

The Duke & the Duchess of Windsor were married
It made all the papers, he gave up his kingdom for love

Even if I built a marriage museum
Walked thru the turnstile, explored all the galleries

Even if I had a book by a poet
The one where he tells me the meaning of life

Still in the darkness it's all so elusive
I feel so frightened my hand reaches out for my wife

— Tom Gala

 — On Sally Rogers & Howard Bursen Satisfied Customers *(Thrushwood).* OL03

Annie Laurie

Maxwelton's braes are bonnie, where early fa's the dew
And it's there that Annie Laurie gave me her promise true
Gave me her promise true, which ne'er forgot will be
And for bonnie Annie Laurie I'd lay me doon an' dee

A D A E / A D AE A
AE A **(2x)** / AD A AE A

Her brow is like the snawdrift, her neck is like the swan
Her face it is the fairest, that e'er the sun shone on
That e'er the sun shone on, an' dark blue is her e'e / **And for...**

Like a dew on the gowan lying, is the fa' o' her fairy feet
An' like winds in summer sighing, her voice is low an' sweet
Her voice is low an' sweet, an' she's the world to me...

— William Douglas & Lady John Scott

On Jean Redpath A Fine S for Singing. *In* FiresB of Love S, FSEncyV1, Penguin SB, New Fellowship SB, Legendary Bals of Eng & Scot, S of Scot, Log Cabin S & Bals, 1001 Jumbo S, 100 S Of Nost, Fred Waring SB, S for the Rotary Club *&* Sing Along w/World's Fav Am FS. OL04

Annie's Song

You fill up my senses like a night in the forest
Like the mountains in springtime, like a walk in the rain
Like a storm in the desert, like a sleepy blue ocean
You fill up my senses, come fill me again **(in G & in 3/4)**

C D Em C G↓ - - / C↓ - - D↑ - -
/ " / C↓ - D G - - -

Come let me love you, let me give my love to you
Let me drown in your laughter, let me die in your arms
Let me lay down beside you, let me always be with you
Come let me love you, come love me again

— John Denver

 On his Back Home Again, An Evening With *&* Gr H V2. *In* Gr S of the '70s. OL05

The Bramble and the Rose

We have been so close together
Each a candle, each a flame
All the dangers were outside us
And we knew them all by name

A - E - / D D (or E) A - :||

See how the bramble & the rose / Intertwine
Love grows like the bramble & the rose
Often cruel, often kind *[Round each other we will twine]*

A E D A / D A E7 - / 1st / A F♯mE A -

Now I've hurt you & it hurts me
Just to see what we can do
To ourselves & to each other
Without really meaning to

So put your arms around me
And we'll sing a true love song
And we'll learn to sing together
Just to last a whole life long *[Sing & laugh the whole night long]*

(II cho.) A E D A / D E E7 - / 1st / D E A -

— Barbara Keith

 On Mary McCaslin The Bramble & the Rose *(Philo), Reilly & Maloney* Good Company *& Trapezoid* Cool of the Day. *Version I in SO! 38:4.* OL06

Bridget O'Malley

O, Bridget O'Malley you left me heart shaken
With a hopeless desolation, I'll have you to know
It's the wonders of admiration, your quiet face has taken
And your beauty will haunt me, wherever I go

C Em F Am / F Em Am F / - Em C F / - Em F C

The white moon above the pale seas, **(in 3/4)**
the pale stars above the thorn tree
Are cold beside my darling, but no purer than she
I gaze upon the cold moon, til the stars drown in the warm sea
And the bright eyes of my darling are never on me

My Sunday is weary, my Sunday it is gray now
My heart is a cold thing, my heart is a stone
All joy is dead in me, my life has gone away now
Another has taken my love for his own

The day is approaching when we were to be married
And it's rather I would die than live only to grieve
O meet me my darling ere the sun sets on the barley
And I'll meet you there on the road to Drumslieve

Is a Bhrígíd Óg ní Mháille, 's tú d'fhág mo croidhe cráidhte
'S gur fhág tú arraing an bhais trí chéart-lar mo chléib
Ta' na mílte feari ngradh led' éadan cíuin náireach
'S go dtug tú barr breaghtha o Thír Urradh maá's fíor

— trad. (Irish gaelic "Brígíd Óg Ní Mháille")

On Silly Wizard So Many Partings. *In* SO! *37:4.* OL07

Catch the Wind

In the chilly hours & minutes of uncertainty I long to be
In the warm hold of your loving mind
To feel you all around me & to take your hand along the sand
Ah but I may as well try & catch the wind

(in 6/8) C F C F / C FG C G / 1st / C FG CF C

When sundown pales the sky, I want to bide awhile behind your smile
And every where I'd look your eyes I'd find
For me to love you now would be the sweetest thing, 'twould make me sing / **Ah...**

(bridge) Didi, didi...

F Em F D G -

When rain has hung the leaves with tears I want you near to quell my fears
To help me to leave all my blues behind
Standing near your soul is where I want to be, I long to be...

— Donovan Leitch

 — On his Like It Is, Real, Gr H, Best of & Pye History of Pop. *Also on* Cher. *In* FM Gr H. OL08

Circle 'Round the Sun

O I love my baby & she's bound to love me some **(2x)**
Well she throws her arms around me just like a circle 'round the sun

A Em A Em G D A Em / / A Em G Em A Em A Em

I lay down last night, just to try to take my rest **(2x)**
But my thoughts they just kept wanderin' like them wild geese in the west

Now I know that sunrise, it's gonna shine in my backyard someday **(2x)**
And that wind's just bound to rise up, gonna blow, blow all my blues away

— James Taylor

 On his James Taylor *(Apple SKAO 3352).* OL09

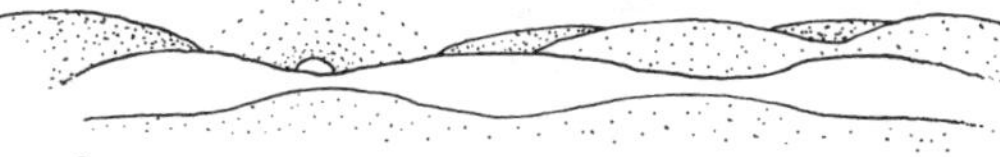

Colours

1. Yellow is the colour of my true love's hair
   In the morning when we rise (2x)
   That's the time (2x) I love the best

D - G D / G - D - / / A - G - D - - -

2. Blue is the colour of the sky...
3. Green is the colour of the sparkling corn...
4. Mellow is the feeling that I get / When I see her, mm hm...

5. Freedom is a word I rarely use
   Without thinkin mm hm **(2x)**
   Of the times **(2x)** when I've been loved

— Donovan Leitch

 On his Like It Is, Fairytale, Gr H, Pye History of Pop & Best of *& Joan Baez* Farewell Angelina *& in her* SB. *In* SO! *16:1 &* Reprints *#10.* OL10

Comin' Thro' the Rye

Gin a body meet a body, comin' thru the rye
Gin a body kiss a body, need a body cry
Ilka lassie has her laddie – nane, they say, hae I
Yet a' the lads they smile at me, when comin' thru the rye

D A DA D / / D A D G / DA **(3x)** D

Gin a body meet a body, comin' frae the toon
Gin a body greet a body, need a body froon
Among the train there is a swain I dearly love mysel'
But what's his name or what's his hame, I donna care to tell

— Robert Burns

In FiresB of Love S, Gr Legal Fake B, FSEncyV1. OL11

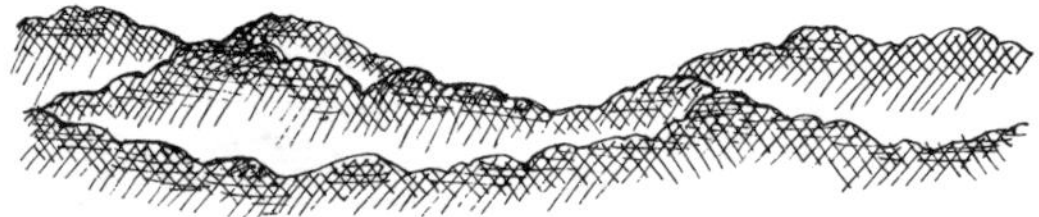

Danny Boy

O Danny Boy, the pipes, the pipes are calling
From glen to glen & down the mountain side
The summer's gone & all the roses falling
'Tis you, 'tis you must go & I must bide

But come ye back when summer's in the meadow
Or when the valley's hushed & white with snow
'Tis I'll be there in sunshine or in shadow
O Danny Boy, o Danny Boy, I love you so

C - F - / C - Dm G / C - F - / C G C -

C F C - / Am FC G - / C F C Am / C DmG C -

And when ye come and all the flowers are dying
If I am dead, as dead I well may be
You'll come & find the place where I am lying
And kneel & say an Ave there for me

And I shall hear, tho' soft you tread above me
And all my dreams will warmer, sweeter be
If you will bend and tell me that you love me
Then I shall sleep in peace, until you come to me

— w: Fred E. Weatherly

— m: trad. (Irish Londonderry Air)

Written in the 19th c. Weatherly was English. On Belafonte, Baez Diamonds & Rust, *J Cash* Orange Blossom Spec, *Bing Crosby* When Irish Eyes Are Smiling, *Limelighters* Alive, The Essential *Paul Robeson (Vanguard VSD 57/58) & adopted by Danny Thomas as his "theme song." In* S That Changed the World, FSEncyV1, S Am Sings & Best FakeB Ever. OL12

Do You Love an Apple

Do you love an apple, do you love a pear
Do you love a laddie with curly brown hair?
O still I love him, I can't deny him
I'll be with him wherever he goes **(in 3/4, capo up)**

G Am7 **(2x)** / G Am7 G D / G - C - / G - D G

Before I got married, I wore a black shawl
But now that I'm married, I wear buggerall

He stood at the corner, a fag in his mouth
Two hands in his pockets, he whistled me out

He works at the pier for nine bob a week
Come Saturday night he comes rolling home drunk

Before I got married I'd sport & I'd play
But now the cradle it gets in me way

— trad. (Irish)

On Best of Green Linnet, *Trapezoid* Now & Then. *On* Bothy Band *& their* 1975. *In* SO! *38:1.* OL13

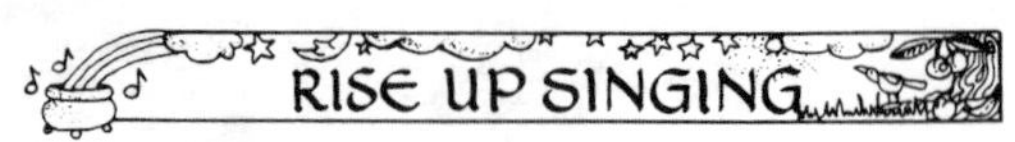

Dodi Li

Dodi li va-ani lo, ha-roeh bashoshanim (2x)

DmGm BbAm DmGm AmDm / /

Mi zot ola min hamidbar, mi zot olah
M'kuteret mor, mor ulevona, mor ulevona

Dm - - Gm / /

Libavtini achoti kalah, libavtini kala **(2x)**

Dm C FG A / /

U-ri tza-fon, u-vo-i teyman **(2x)**

Dm C F A / /

— w: Song of Songs — m: trad. (Israeli)

A beautiful Israeli couple dance. Trans: "My beloved is mine & I am his, he pastures his flock among the lilies/Who is that going up from the desert burning myrrh & frankincense?/ You have ravished my heart, my sister, my bride/ Awake, north wind & come, o south wind." In SO! *10:1. On* Israeli F Dances *(T646), Bikel* S of Israel *(Elektra), & Pasternak* Israel in S. OL14

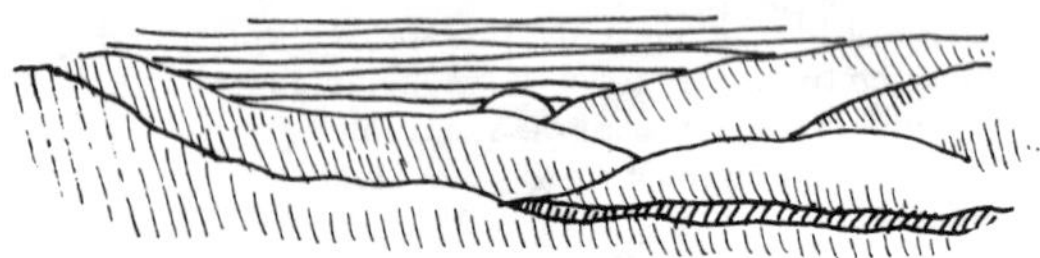

Down by the Sally Gardens

It was down by the Sally Gardens my love & I did meet
She passed the Sally Gardens with little snow white feet
She bid me take love easy, as the leaves grow on the tree
But I, being young & foolish, with her did not agree

CG FC FG C / / AmF GC FG C / 1st /

In a field by the river my love & I did stand
And on my leaning shoulder she laid her snow-white hand
She bid me take life easy, as the grass grows on the weirs
But I was young & foolish, & now am full of tears

— w: W.B. Yeats — m: unknown

In this poem (pub in his Crossways, *1889) Yeats attempted to reconstruct an old song from 3 lines he remembered an old peasant woman singing in the village of Ballisodare, Co. Sligo in the west of Ireland. In* SO! *11:5 &* Reprints *#8,* FSEncyV1 *&* FiresB of Love S. *On* Richard Dyer-Bennet, *Cambridge Singers* Lark in the Clear Air, *Clannad* In Conc, *Alfred Deller* Western Wind *(Vang) & Mary O'Hara* S for Ireland *(Shanachie).* OL15

Down in the Valley

Down in the valley, the valley so low
Hang your head over, hear the wind blow
Hear the wind blow, dear, hear the wind blow
Hang your head over, hear the wind blow

(in 3/4) D - - A7 / - - - D :||

Roses love sunshine, violets love dew
Angels in heaven, know I love you
Know I love you, dear...

If you don't love me, love whom you please
Throw your arms 'round me, give my heart ease...

Build me a castle 40 feet high
So I can see him as he rides by...

Write me a letter, send it by mail
Send it in care of Birmingham jail...

Writing this letter containing three lines
Answer my question "Will you be mine?"...

— trad. (So. Appalachian)

Reworking of an older song fr Br Isles. On Robin & Linda Williams Down in the Valley, *Kim Wallach* 2 Doz Children's S *& Frank Proffett* Sings FS *(FA2360). On (& in) Pete Seeger* Am Fav Bals V1 *(FA2320). On Ives* Bals & FS V2, S of Expanding Am *& in his* SB. *In* FiresB of FS, *Lomax* FS of NAm, Treas of FS, Fred Waring SB & Best Loved S of Am People. OL16

Every Day

Every day it's a-getting closer
Going faster than a roller coaster
Love like yours will surely come my way

D - G A / / D - G A D G D (A)

Every day it's a-getting faster
Everyone said Go ahead & ask her
Love like yours will surely come my way

(bridge) Every day seems a little longer
Every way love's a little stronger
Come what may, do you ever long for
True love from me

G - - - / C - - - / F - - - / Bb - A -

— Norman Petty & Charles Hardin

 On Buddy Holly Legend *& J Denver* Aerie. OL17

The First Time Ever I Saw Your Face

The first time ever I saw your face
I thought the sun rose in your eyes
And the moon & stars were the gifts you gave
To the dark & the empty skies, my love
To the dark & the empty skies

I: D A D - / - F#m G - / D Em D - / C - G D / C A D -

The first time ever I kissed your mouth **(TD ↑ 2)**
I felt the earth move in my hand
Like the trembling heart of a captive bird
That was there at my command, my love / That was there...

The first time ever I lay with you
And felt your heart beat close to mine
I thought our joy would fill the earth
And last til the end of time, my love...

II: Em A D - / Bm - F#m G / D A D - / C - D - / /

— Ewan MacColl

 — *I: on his & Peggy Seeger* New Britton Gazette 2 & Freeborn Man. *II: on Roberta Flack* 1st Take & Best of, *Peter Paul & Mary* See What Tomorrow Brings *& on* Hootenanny *(Prestige). In* SO! *12:3 &* Reprints *#6,* Hootenanny SB, Gr S of the '70s, Club Date FakeB, 100 of the Gr Easy Listening H, Best of the '70s *&* FM Gr H. OL18

Forty-Five Years

Where the earth shows its bones of wind-broken stone
And the sea & the sky are one
I'm caught out of time, my blood sings with wine
And I'm running naked in the sun
There's God in the trees, I'm weak in the knees
And the sky is a painful blue
I'd like to look around, but Honey, all I see is you

C - / G - / Dm F / G - / C - / G - / Dm FG C -

And I just want to hold you closer than
I've ever held any one before
You say you've been twice a wife & you're thru with life
Ah but Honey, what the hell's it for?
After 23 years you'd think I could find
A way to let you know somehow
That I want to see your smiling face 45 years from now

F - / CF C / F C / Dm G / 1st 2 / Dm G C -

The summer city light will soften the night
'Til you'd think that the air is clear
And I'm sitting with friends where 45 cents
Will buy another glass of beer
He's got something to say, but I'm so far away
That I don't know who I'm talking to
'Cause you just walked in the door & Honey, all I see is you

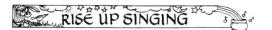

So alone in the lights on stage every night
I've been reaching out to find a friend
Who knows all the words, sings so she's heard
And knows how all the stories end
Maybe after the show she'll ask me to go
Home with her for a drink or two
Now her smile lights her eyes, but Honey, all I see is you

— Stan Rogers

 — Written for Diane in Cole Harbor, N.S. Stan requested that upon his death, his ashes be scattered in Cole Harbor in memory of the moment that created the song. On his Fogarty's Cove *& in his* S fr Fogarty's Cove. *On Priscilla Herdman* Forgotten Dreams *& in* SO! *29:3.* OL19

Hard Love

I remember growing up like it was only yesterday
Mom & Daddy tried their best to guide me on my way
But the hard times & the liquor drove the easy love away
And the only love I knew about was hard love

(in C – capo up) C - F -/Dm Em F C/ 1st /Dm Em F -

It was hard love, every hour of the day
When Christmas to my birthday was a million years away
And the fear that came between them drove the tears into my play
There was love in daddy's house, but it was hard love

And I recall the gentle courtesy you gave me as I tried
To dissemble in politeness all the love I felt inside
And for every song of laughter was another song that cried
This ain't no easy weekend, this is hard love

It was hard love, every step of the way
Hard to be so close to you, so hard to turn away
And when all the stars & sentimental songs dissolved to day
There was nothing left to sing about but hard love

So I loved you for your courage, & your gentle sense of shame
And I loved you for your laughter & your language & your name
And I knew it was impossible, but I loved you just the same
Tho' the only love I gave to you was hard love

It was hard love, it was hard on you, I know
When the only love I gave to you was love I couldn't show
You forgave the heart that loved you as your lover turned to go
Leaving nothing but the memory of hard love

So I'm standing in this phone booth with a dollar & a dime
Wondering what to say to you to ease your troubled mind
For the Lord's cross might redeem us, but our own just wastes our time
And to tell the two apart is always hard, love

So I'll tell you that I love you even thought I'm far away
And I'll tell you how you change me as I live from day to day
How you help me to accept myself & I won't forget to say
Love is never wasted, even when it's hard love

Yes, it's hard love, but it's love all the same
Not the stuff of fantasy, but more than just a game
And the only kind of miracle that's worthy of the name
For the love that heals our lives is mostly hard love

— Bob Franke

 — On his One Evening in Chicago, *Tony Rice* Me & My Guitar *& Claudia Schmidt* New Goodbyes & Old Hellos. *In* SO! *30:3.* OL20

Heat Wave

Whenever I'm with him, something inside
Starts to burnin' & I'm filled with desire
Could it be a devil in me
Or is this the way love's supposed to be?

Dm - Em - Am - - - / / Dm - Em - / F - G -

It's like a heat wave / Burnin' in my heart
I can't keep from cryin' / It's tearin' me apart

CF CF CF C / / / CF CF C **(tacit)**

Whenever he calls my name soft, low, sweet & plain
I feel, yeah yeah, well I feel that burnin' flame
Has high blood pressure got a hold on me
Or is this the way love's supposed to be?

Sometimes I stare into space, tears all over my face
I can't explain it, don't understand it, I ain't never felt like this before
Now that funny feelin' has me amazed
I don't know what to do, my head's in a haze

Yeah yeah, yeah yeah, whoa ho
Yeah yeah, yeah yeah, yeah, oh
Don't pass up this chance
This time it's a true romance

— Eddie Holland, Lamont Dozier & Brian Holland

 — aka: "Love Is Like a..." On Motown Story V1. *In* The Top 100 Motown H. *Rec by The Supremes, Martha Reeves & Vandellas (Motown) & Linda Ronstadt* Greatest Hits *(Asylum 6E-106).* OL21

Hey, That's No Way to Say Goodbye

I loved you in the morning, our kisses deep & warm
Your head upon the pillow like a sleepy golden storm
Many have *[loved]* before us, I know that we are not new
In city & in forest they smile like me & you
Now it's come to distances & both of us must try
Your eyes are soft with sorrow
Hey, that's no way to say Goodbye

C - - -/Am - - - /F - - - / 1st 2 /F -/G - - - C G -

I'm not looking for another as I wander in my time
Walk me to the corner, our steps will always rhyme
You know my love goes with you as your love stays with me
It's just the way it changes like the shoreline & the sea
Let's not talk of love or change or things we can't untie...

— Leonard Cohen

 — On his S of *&* Best of *& Judy Collins* Wildflowers *(Elektra EKS-74012).* OL22

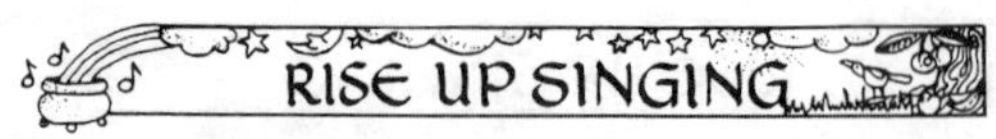

I Just Called to Say I Love You

No New Years Day to celebrate
No chocolate covered candy hearts to give away
No first of spring, no song to sing
In fact here's just another ordinary day

Am maj7

(capo up) G - - - / - - Am Am maj7 /
Am Am maj7 **(2x)** / Am D G -

No April rain, no flowers' bloom
No wedding Saturday within the month of June
But what it is is something true
Made up of these three words that I must say to you

I just called to say I love you
I just called to say how much I care
I just called to say I love you
And I mean it from the bottom of my heart

Am D G - / Am D Em - / / 1st /

No summer's high, no warm July
No harvest moon to light one tender August night
No autumn breeze, no falling leaves
Not even time for birds to fly to southern skies

No Libra sun, no Halloween
No giving thanks to all the Christmas joy you bring
But what it is, tho' old so new
To fill your heart like no three words could ever do

— Stevie Wonder

 In his Gr H & 100 Top Motown H. OL23

I Still Miss Someone

At my door the leaves are falling, a cold wild wind has come
Sweethearts walk by together, and I still miss someone

C F G - F G C - :||

I go out on a party and look for a little fun
But I find a darkened corner 'cause I still miss someone

(bridge) Tho' I never got over those blue eyes
I see them everywhere
I miss those arms that held me
When all the love was there

F G C - :|| **(4x)**

I wonder if she's sorry for leaving what we'd begun
There's someone for me somewhere and I still miss someone

— Johnny Cash & Roy Cash, Jr.

 — aka: "Blue Eyes." On J Cash Johnny *& in his* At Folsom Prison, *Baez* One Day At A Time *&* Country M Alb *& on* Linda Ronstadt *(Capital).* OL24

If Ever I Would Leave You

If ever I would leave you, it would not be in summer
Seeing you in summer, I never would go
Your hair streaked with sunlight, your lips red as flame
Your face with a lustre that puts gold to shame

(in G - capo up) Am7 D G Gmaj7 / Am D G G7
C D Bm G / C Am - D **(2nd v:** C Am G -**)**

But if I'd ever leave you, it couldn't be in autumn
How I'd leave in autumn, I never would know
I've seen how you sparkle when fall nips the air
I know you in autumn & I must be there

(bridge) And could I leave you running merrily thru the snow?
Or on a winter's evening when you catch the fire's glow?

B7 F♯ B7 - / E♭ E F♯m D7

If ever I would leave you, how could it be in springtime
Knowing how in spring I'm bewitched by you so?
O no, not in springtime! Summer, winter or fall!
No never could I leave you, at all

— w: Alan Jay Lerner — m: Fredrick Loewe

 Fr their musical Camelot. *On Robert Goulet* Gr H. *In Readers Dig* Fest of Pop S *& Broadway SBs.* OL25

If You Love Me

If you love me, if you love, love, love me
Plant a rose for me
And if you think you'll love me for a long, long time
Plant an apple tree

CG C / F C / / G C

The sun will shine, the wind will blow
The rain will fall & the tree will grow
And whether you comes or whether you goes
I'll have an apple & I'll have a rose

F - / C - / G - / CG C

Lovely to bite & nice to my nose
And every juicy nibble will be
A sweet reminder of the time you loved me
And planted a rose for me, & an apple tree

F - / CG C / Fm CG / CA♭ G - C

— Malvina Reynolds

 On her Held Over *& in her* SB. *On Jane Voss & Hoyle Osborne* Side By Side *(GentleWinds) & Rosalie Sorrels* Miscellaneous Abstract *(Green Linnet SIF 1042). In* SO! *38:3,* Bright Morning Stars, Sing the Good Earth & Here's to the Women. OL26

Juanita

Soft o'er the fountain, ling'ring falls the southern moon
Far o'er the mountain, breaks the day too soon
In thy dark eyes' splendor, where the warm light loves to dwell
Weary looks, yet tender, speak their fond farewell

> Nita, Juanita, ask thy soul if we should part
> Nita, Juanita, lean thou on my heart

(in 3/4) C G - C / / C F G C / / 1st / /

When in thy dreaming, moons like these shall shine again
And daylight beaming, prove thy dreams are vain
Wilt thou not relenting, for thine absent lover sigh
In thy heart consenting to a prayer gone by

> Nita, Juanita, let me linger by thy side
> Nita, Juanita, be my own fair bride

— trad.

On Faith Petric As We Were *& Pete Seeger* Bitter & the Sweet. *In* Sfest. OL27

The Last Thing on My Mind

It's a lesson too late for the learning
Made of sand, made of sand
In the wink of an eye my soul is turning
In your hand, in your hand

A D A AD / A E A - :||

Are you going away with no word of farewell?
Will there be not a trace left behind?
Well I could have loved you better, didn't mean to be unkind
You know that was the last thing on my mind

E - D A / D A E - / A D A - / E - A -

As we walk, all my thoughts are a-tumblin' / Round & round...
Underneath our feet the subway's rumblin' / Underground...

You've got reasons a plenty for goin' / This I know...
For the weeds have been steadily growing / Please don't go...

As I lie in my bed in the morning / Without you...
Each song in my breast dies a-borning / Without you...

— **Tom Paxton**

© 1964, 1969 United Artist Music Co. Inc. Rights assigned to SBK Catalogue Partnership. All rights controlled & administered by SBK U Catalog Inc. Used by permission of CPP Belwin Inc. On (& in) his Rambling Boy, *on* Even a Grey Day *(FF) & in his* Anthology. *On P,P&M* See What Tomorrow Brings, *Baez* Carry It On, *Doc Watson* Southbound *(Vang) &* Elementary *(UA) & Jose Feliciano* Feliciano. *On Judy Collins* Recollections, Conc *& in her* SB. *In* SO! *15:1 &* Reprints *#10.* OL28

Let It Be Me

I *[God]* bless the day I found you, I want to stay around you
And so I beg you, let it be me

(capo up) C G Am Em / F C FG C

Don't take this heaven from one, if you must cling to someone
Now & forever, let it be me

(bridge) Each time we meet love, I find complete love
Without your sweet love, what would life be?

F C F C / F C F E **(or:** D G**)**

So never leave me lonely, tell me you love me only
And that you'll always, let it be me

— **Eng: Mann Curtis** — **m: Gilbert Bécaud**

© 1955, 1957, 1960 France Music Co., NY. Sole selling agent MCA Music Publishing, All rights reserved. Used by permission. — Orig French: "Je t'appertiens" (w: Pierre Delanoe) was rec by Bécaud. Made popular here by Vicki Carr. On Everly Bros Pure Harmony *(WBR),* Orig Classics *(Arista),* 24 Orig Classics, *Mary McCaslin* Way Out West *(Philo) & Lettermen* Best of V2. *In Readers Dig* Treas of Bestloved S. OL29

Lovely Agnes

**O Agnes won't you go with me, we'll be married in style
And we'll cross Lake Michigan so blue & so wild
We'll cross over Lake Michigan til we come to the shore
And orchards will blossom for our babies as they're born**

(in 3/4)

AAD A - D/- A - E/A - - D/- A AAE A

O yes, I will go with you, leave Wisconsin behind
Tho' my parents think little of my life on a farm
O to leave the gay city life, to be "buried on a farm"
But I'll watch the orchards bloom in spring, spend the winters warm in your arms

Three children he gave her, Curtis, Addie & Dee
And their fourth child, little Gussie, came ten years after these
And she raised them with loving hand & with firmness of mind
And she raised them thru troubled times, Agnes strong-willed and kind

Now 3 score years have gone & passed like the fruit on the trees
And her children have children with babies on their knees
And they all join in the summertime on the Crystal Lake Shore
To greet lovely Agnes, now 12 years & 4 score

— **Sally Rogers**

©1980 by Sally Rogers. Pub by Thrushwood Press (BMI). Used by permission. — Written as a 92nd birthday present for her grandmother Agnes Challoner Rogers (whose parents said that she would be wasting her graduate work by moving to a rural Michigan). On her The Unclaimed Pint *(Wheatland) &* Closing the Distance *(FF – w/Claudia Schmidt) & in her* SB. *In* SO! *29:2.* OL30

Mairi's Wedding

**Step we gaily on we go, heel for heel & toe for toe
Arm in arm & on we go, all for Mairi's wedding**

E - A E / - - A B7

Over hill ways up & down, myrtle green & bracken brown
Past the sheeling thru the town, all for the sake of Mairi

Plenty herring, plenty meal, plenty peat to fill her creal
Plenty bonny bairns as weel, that's the toast for Mairi

Cheeks are bright as rowans are, brighter far than any star
Fairest of them all by far is my darling Mairi

— **trad. (Scottish)**

aka: "Marie's Wedding," "Lewis Bridal Song." In the Clancy Bros SB *& on their* The Boys Won't Leave the Girls Alone. *In Maggi Pierce* S fr Try Works *& Norman Buchan* 101 Scottish S. *On Geo & Gerry Armstrong* Anglo-Am FS. OL31

My Girl

I've got sunshine on a cloudy day
When it's cold outside, I've got the month of May
**I guess you say, what can make me feel this way?
My girl, talking 'bout, my girl**

G C G C / //G Am CD **(2x)** / G - C D

I've got so much honey, the bees envy me
I've got a sweeter song than the birds in the tree / **I...**

I don't need no money, fortune or fame
I've got all the riches, baby, one man can claim...

(tag) _I've got sunshine on a cloudy day with my girl,
I've even got the month of May with
My girl,_talkin' 'bout, talkin' 'bout talkin' 'bout my girl,
Woo, my girl, that's all I can talk about is my girl

G - Am D / / /

— **William (Smokey) Robinson & R. White (Bobby Rogers)**

© 1965 Jobete Music Inc. International copyright secured. Made in USA. All rights reserved. Used by permission of CPP Belwin Inc. — Rec by Smokey Robinson, Motown Story V2, 25 #1 H *(Motown) & in* The Top 100 Motown H. *On Mamas & Papas* 16 of Their Gr H, Gr H *& Best of. On Temptations* Anthology *(Motown),* All the Million Sellers *&* Gr H. OL32

O, No, John

On yonder hill there stands a creature
Who she is I do not know
I'll go & court her for her beauty
She must answer yes or no
O no John, no John, no John, no!

D A D A/ /D - Em A/D G A -//D G D A D - - -

My father was a Spanish captain
Went to sea a month ago
First he kissed me, then he left me
Bid me always answer no / **O no John...**

O, madam, in your face is beauty
On your lips red roses glow
Will you take me for your lover?
Madam, answer yes or no: **O...**

O madam, I will give you jewels
I will make you rich & free
I will give you silken dresses
Madam, will you marry me?...

O madam since you are so cruel
And that you do scorn me so
If I may not be your lover
Madam, will you let me go?...

Then I will stay with you forever
If you will not be unkind
Madam, I have vowed to love you
Would you have me change my mind?...

O hark, I hear the church bells ringing
Will you come & be my wife?
Or dear madam, have you settled
To live single all your life? / **O no John...**

— **trad. (Eng)**

In SFest, FS Abecedary *&* FS of Eng Ire Scot & Wales. *On* The Essential Paul Robeson *(VSD 57/58).* OL33

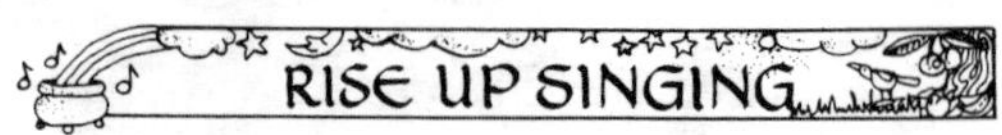

Plaisir d'Amour

Plaisir d'amour ne dure qu'un moment
Chagrin d'amour dure toute la vie

(in 3/4) D A D - G D A - / Bm A D G D A D -

The joys of love are but a moment long
The pain of love endures the whole life long

Your eyes kissed mine, I saw the love in them shine
You brought me heaven right then when your eyes kissed mine

My love loves me & all the wonders I see
A rainbow shines in my window, my love loves me

And now he's gone, like a dream that fades into dawn
But the words stay locked in my heartstrings My love loves me

— Jean Paul Martini il Tedesco 17th c. (Eng w: anon.)

18th c. (?) popular song. On Baez V2, Love S *& in her* SB. *Also in* FiresB of Love S, FSEncy V1, 1001 Jumbo S & S Am Sings. OL34

Red Is the Rose

Come over the hills my bonny Irish lass
Come over the hills to your darling
You choose the road, love, & I'll make a vow
That I'll be your true love forever

C Em Dm F/C Em F Em /F Em Dm F/C Em G C

Red is the rose that in yonder garden grows
Fair is the lily of the valley
Clear is the water that flows from the Boyne
But my love is fairer than any

It's down in Killarney's green woods that we strayed
When the moon & the stars they were shining
For the moon shone its rays on her locks of golden hair
And she said she'd be my love forever

It's not for the parting with my sister Kate
It's not for the grief of my mother
It's all for the loss of my bonny Irish lass
That my heart is breaking forever

— adap. & arr. by Tommy Makem

© Tin Whistle Music, 2 Longmeadow Rd, Dover NH 03820. All rights reserved. Used by permission. *— Learned from his mother Sarah Makem in Co. Armagh. The tune is nearly the same as "Loch Lomond" (which dates to late 1800s), but Tommy says these lyrics are very old & one cannot be certain which version is older. Joe Heaney sings a slightly different version. On Tommy Makem & Liam Clancy* 2 for the Early Dew *(Blackbird BLB1007). On Schooner Fare* Closer to the Wind. OL35

Roseville Fair

O the night was clear & the stars were shining
And the moon came up, so quiet in the sky
And the people gathered 'round & the band was a-tuning
I can hear them now playing Comin' thru the Rye

D - - G D - - - / A - - - D - - - :||

You were dressed in blue & you looked so lovely
Just a gentle flower of a small town girl
You took my hand & we stepped to the music
And with a single smile you became my world

And we danced all night to the fiddle & the banjo
Their drifting tunes seemed to fill the air
So long ago, but I still remember
When we fell in love at the Roseville Fair

G↓ - A D - A - / G - - A D - - - :||

Now we courted well & we courted dearly
And we'd rock for hours in the front porch chair
Then a year went by from the time that I met you
And I made you mine at the Roseville Fair

(to tune of chorus) So here's a song for all the lovers
And here's a tune that they can share
May they dance all night to the fiddle & the banjo
The way we did at the Roseville Fair

— Bill Staines

© Mineral River Music (BMI) Used by permission. *— In his* If I Were A Word *& on his* The Whistle of the Jay. *Also on Nancy Griffith* Once in a Very Blue Moon *(Philo), Debby McClatchy* Lady Luck *(SIF1017), Wendy Grosman* Roseville Fair *& Jim Ringer* Endangered Species. *In* SO! *36:2.* OL36

Since You Asked

What I'll give you since you've asked, is all my time together
Take the rugged, sunny days, the warm & rocky weather
Take the roads that I have walked along
Looking for tomorrow's time, peace of mind

Bm4

Em Bm4 G A / / C A / C A B G -

As my life spills into yours, changing with the hours
Filling up the world with time, turning time to flowers
I can show you all the songs
That I never sang to one man before

/ " / " / " / C A Bm G

(bridge) We have seen a million stones lying by the water
You have climbed the hills with me to the mountain shelter
Taken off the days, one by one
Setting them to breathe in the sun

G - A - / / C - - / C - Fmaj7 -

(as vs. 1) Take the lilies & the lace from the days of childhood
All the willow winding paths leading up & outward
This is what I give
This is what I ask you for, nothing more

— Judy Collins

© 1967 Rocky Mountain National Park Music Co. Inc. (ASCAP) Admin. by Good Flavor Songs, Inc., 515 Madison Ave., 28th Flr., NY, NY 10022. All rights reserved. Used by permission. *— In her* SB *&on her* Wildflowers, Recollections, 1st 15 Yrs & Colors. *On Smith Sisters* Mockingbird. OL37

Some Enchanted Evening

Some enchanted evening, you may see a stranger
You may see a stranger, across a crowded room
And somehow you know, you know even then
That somewhere you'll see her again & again

Eaug

C - G - / C Eaug Fmaj7Dm DmAmaj7

Dm DmE AmC FEm/Dm7 - Cmaj7 - **(v. 2 & 3** Dm G C -**)**

Some enchanted evening, someone may be laughing
You may hear her laughing, across a crowded room
And night after night, as strange as it seems
The sound of her laughter will sing in your dreams

(bridge) Who can explain it? Who can tell you why?
Fools give you reasons, wise men never try

GC DmC / GC DmD G

Some enchanted evening, when you find your true love
When you feel her call you, across a crowded room
Then fly to her side, & make her your own
Or all thru your life you may dream all alone

(tag) Once you have found her, never let her go **(2x)**

GC DmC / GC Dm7 - C -

— w: Oscar Hammerstein II — m: Richard Rodgers

© 1949 Richard Rodgers & Oscar Hammerstein II. Copyright renewed. Williamson Music Co., All rights administered by Chappell & Co., Inc. International copyright secured. All rights reserved. *— Fr their musical* South Pacific. *On Mantovani* Gr H & Some Enchanted Evening. *In* Pop S That Will Live *& Broadway Sbs.* OL38

Someone to Love Me

I wish I had someone to love me
Someone to call me his own
Someone to sleep with me nightly
I'm weary of sleeping alone

(in 3/4) G - C G / C G D - / G - C G / C D G -

Meet me tonight in the moonlight
Meet me tonight all alone
I have a sad story to tell you
That I'll tell by the light of the moon

Tonight is our last night together
Nearest & dearest must part
The love that has bound us together
Is shredded & torn apart

I wish I had ships on the ocean
Bind them with silver & gold
Follow the ship that he sails in
A lad of 19 years old

I wish I had wings of a swallow
Fly out over the sea
Fly to the arms of my true love
And bring him home safely to me

— **trad.**

aka: "I Wish I Had Someone to Love Me." On Caryl P Weiss With Her Head Tucked *& Sally Rogers* Circle of the Sun *& in her* SB. *In* SO! *36:1.* OL39

Spanish Is the Loving Tongue

Spanish is the loving tongue, bright as music, soft as spray
'Twas a girl I learned it from living down Sonora way
I don't look much like a lover, yet I say her love words over
Often when I'm all alone, **mi amor, mi corazón**

(capo up) G C G AmD / G C G DG
EmD CG G AmD / " /

Nights when she knew where I'd ride, she would listen for my spurs
Throw those big doors open wide, raise them laughin' eyes of hers
How my heart would near stop beating when I'd hear her tender greeting
Whispered soft for me alone: ***mi...***

Starlight on the patio, old señora nodding near
Me & Juana are talking low, so the madre would not hear
How those hours would go a flying & too soon I'd hear her sighing
While the moonlight brightly shone, ***mi...***

But one time I had to fly for a foolish gamblin' fight
And we said a swift goodbye, in that black unlucky night
When I loosed her arms from clingin', with her words the hoofs kept ringin'
As I galloped north alone: ***"Adios mi corazón"***

Never seen her since that night, I can't cross the Line you know
She was Mex and I was white *[I'm still wanted for that fight]*, like as not it's better so
Still I often kind of miss her since that last sad night I kissed her
Left her heart & lost my own: ***"Adios mi corazón"***

— **w: Charles Badger Clark Jr.** — **m: unknown**

aka: "A Border Affair" originally published by Clark as a poem in his Sun & Saddle Leather *in 1915. Early recording by Richard Dyer Bennett & on Judy Collins* Bread & Roses, *B Staines* Just Play One More Tune *(Folk Legacy), Liam Clancy* The Dutchman & Farewell to Tarwaithe, *Pete Seeger* Rainbow Quest *& Ian & Sylvia* 4 Strong Winds. *In SO! 38:2 & 44:4.* OL40

Tell Me Why

Tell me why the stars do shine?
Tell me why the ivy twine?
Tell me why the skies are blue?
And I will tell you just why I love you

(in 3/4) G - C G / - - A D / G - C B7 / E A D G

Because God made the stars to shine
Because God made the ivy twine
Because God made the skies so blue
Because God made you is why I love you

— **trad. (US)**

In Fred Waring SB *&* S for the Rotary Club. OL41

Until It's Time For You to Go

You're not a dream, you're not an angel, you're a man
I'm not a queen, I'm a woman, take my hand
We'll make a space in the lives that we planned
And here we'll stay until it's time for you to go

(capo up, in 3/4)
G (G, F♯, F) E / Am (A, G♯, G) D / 1st / Am D G -

Yes we're different, worlds apart, we're not the same
We laughed & played at the start like in a game
You could have stayed outside my heart, but in you came
And here we'll stay until it's time for you to go

(bridge) Don't ask why (of me), don't ask how (of me)
Don't ask forever (of me), love me, love me now

A♭ F G - **(2x)** / B7 - Em - A - D -

This love of mine had no beginning it has no end
I was an oak now I'm a willow, now I can bend
And tho' I'll never in my life see you again
Still I'll stay until it's time for you to go

— **Buffy Sainte-Marie**

 — On her Many A Mile *&* Best of, *Roberta Flack* Chap 2, *Doc & Merle Watson* Guitar Alb *(FF), & on* Cher. *In* Best of Pop S. OL42

Valley of Strathmore

By the clear & the winding streams
In the Valley of Strathmore
Where my love & I have been
Where we'll wander nevermore

(in C, in 3/4) C F C - / F - G - :||

But if Time was a thing Man could buy
All the money that I have in store
I'd give for one day by her side
In the Valley of Strathmore

Am G F - / - - G - / C F C - / F - G -

From the glen of the golden & green
I left for a land far away
Where sadness has never been seen
Aye & joy only costs a day's pay

In Strathmore there's a long working day
For a man wi' his hands on the ploo
But it's work I'd be happy tae dae
If at night I were lyin wi' you

As I take a long draught from my glass
O I'm drinking alone here again
And I try no' tae think o' my lass
For the old days will ne'er come again

— **Andy M. Stewart**

 On Silly Wizard So Many Partings, Best of *&* Live in Am. OL43

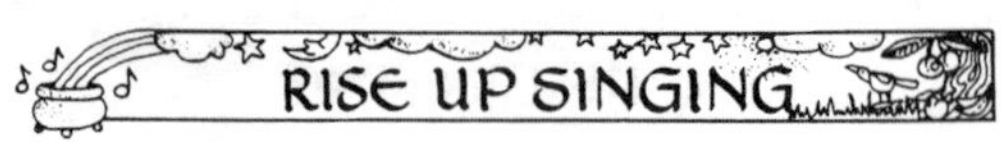

Wedding Song

(intro) He is now to be among you at the calling of your hearts
Rest assured this troubadour is acting on His part

C - G - / F - - C

The union of your spirits here has caused Him to remain
For whenever two or more of you are gathered in His name
There is love, there is love

C G F C / Am C G - // F --- C - (D - F - C -)

A man shall leave his mother & a woman leave her home
They shall travel on to where the two shall be as one
As it was in the beginning, is now & till the end
Woman draws her life from man & gives it back again
And **there is love, there is love**

(bridge) Then what's to be the reason for becoming man & wife
Is it love that brings you here or love that brings you life

F Dm G C / /

And if loving is the answer then who's the giving for?
Do you believe in something that you've never seen before?
Well, there's **love, there is love**

The marriage of your spirits here has caused Him to remain
For whenever two or more of you are gathered in His name
There is love, there is love

 aka: "There Is Love." On Paul Stookey Paul And *(WB).* OL44

Will You Love Me Tomorrow?

Tonight you're mine completely
You give your love so sweetly
Tonight the light of love is in your eyes
But will you love me tomorrow?

C - Dm G / C - F G / Em E Am C / F G C -

Is this a lasting treasure
Or just a moment's pleasure?
Can I believe the magic of your sighs?
Will you still love me tomorrow?

(bridge) Tonight with words unspoken
You say that I'm the only one
But will my heart be broken
When the night meets the morning sun?

F - Em - / F G C - / F - Em - / Am D Dm G

I'd like to know that your love
Is love I can be sure of
So tell me now & I won't ask again
Will you still love me tomorrow?

— Gerry Goffin & Carole King

 — On Carole King Tapestry, *Shirelles* Anthology *(RNDA1101), Linda Ronstadt* Retrospectives & A Diff Drum, *Roberta Flack* Best of & Cher. OL45

You Can Close Your Eyes

The sun is slowly sinking down
But the moon is rising
And this old world must still be spinning 'round
And I still love you

D GD A - / GD AG G - / 1st / GD AD (2x)

So close your eyes
You can close your eyes, it's all right
I don't know no love songs
And I can't sing the blues anymore
But I can sing this song
And you can sing this song when I'm gone

GD A / Em G Bm - / G A / C G Bm -
GA G / GA GA Bm -

I know there's gonna be another day
We gonna have a good time
Nobody's gonna take this time away
You can stay as long as you like

— James Taylor

 — On his Mud Slide Slim. *On Linda Ronstadt* Heart Like a Wheel *& Richie Havens* End of the Beginning. OL46

You Can't Hurry Love

(intro) I need love, love, to ease my mind
I need to find, find someone to call mine, but

C - F C / Em Am F G

(First Chorus)
Mama said "You can't hurry love, no you just have to wait"
She said "Love don't come easy, it's a game of give & take
You can't hurry love, no you just have to wait
You gotta trust, give it time, no matter how long it takes"

C - F C / Em Am F G :||

But how many heartaches must I stand
Before I find a love to let me live again
Right now the only thing that keeps me hanging on
When I feel my strength, yeah it's almost gone, I remember

Em - - - / Am - - - / F - - - / G - F -

(Second Chorus)
Mama said "You...wait" / She said "Love...take"
How long must I wait, how much more can I take
Before loneliness will cause my heart, heart to break?

No, I can't bear to live my life alone
I grow impatient for a love to call my own
But when I feel that I, I can't go on
These precious words keep me hanging on, I remember
(to first chorus)

(As intro) No love, love don't come easy
But I keep on waiting, anticipating
For that soft voice to talk to me at night
For some tender arms to hold me tight
I keep on waiting, I keep on waiting
But it ain't easy, it ain't easy when / **(to first chorus)**

C - F C / Em Am F G :|| (3x)

— E. Holland, L. Dozier, Brian Holland

 — On Temptations 25 #1 H, *Supremes* 25th Anniver *& Diana Ross* All the Gr H. *In* The Top 100 Motown H. OL47

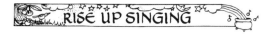

You've Really Got a Hold

I don't like you, but I love you
Seems that I'm always thinkin of you
Oh you treat me badly, I love you madly

C - - - / Am - - - / C - F - G

You've really got a hold on (me) (4x)
(2nd & 3rd cho add:) Baby, I love you & all I want you to do
Is just hold me (4x)

G C - - Am - - - / - - - F - / C - G -

I don't want you, but I need you
Don't want to kiss you, but I need to
Oh you do me wrong now, my love is strong now

I want to leave you, don't want to stay here
Don't want to spend another day here
Oh I want to split now, I can't quit now

— William (Smokey) Robinson

© 1962 by Jobete Music Co. International copyright secured. Made in USA. All rights reserved. Used by permission of CPP Belwin Inc. *— On Smoky Robinson & the Miracles* Smokin *& Laura Nyro* Gonna Take a Miracle. OL48

There are a number of love songs in the following chapters: BALLADS, DREAMS & FANTASIES, GOLDEN OLDIES, GOOD TIMES, HARD TIMES & BLUES, and MOUTAIN VOICES. For songs about love in the broader sense (eg. love for humanity) see HOPE. Also see FRIENDSHIP.

Addl love songs include: "Chelsea Morning," "Up on the Roof" (CITY) "Brand New Tennessee Waltz," "To Sing for You," "Waltz Across Texas" (CREAT) "Ca' the Ewes," "Desperado," "Red River Valley," "Someday Soon" (FARM) "Hippopotamus Song," "Multiple Relationship Blues" (FUN), "Careless Love" (MTN), "Loch Lomond," "Wild Mountain Thyme" (OUT) "Go to Joan Glover," "Joan Come Kiss Me Now," "Rose Rose" (ROUNDS) "Come Fare Away" (SEA) "In My Life," "Kisses Sweeter than Wine," "When I'm 64," "Tomorrow is a Long Time" (TIME) "& One More Step," "Coming Home to You," "You Were on my Mind" (TRAV).

LULLABIES

Abide with Me

Abide with me, fast falls the eventide
The darkness deepens, Lord, with me abide
When other helpers fail & comforts flee
Help of the helpless, o abide with me

CG Am C FG C / - FC DmD G
CG Am FA Dm / G CF CG C

Swift to its close ebbs out life's little day
Earth's joys grow dim, its glories pass away
Change & decay in all around I see
O Thou who changest not, abide with me

I need thy presence every passing hour
What but thy grace can foil the tempter's pow'r?
Who like thyself my guide & stay can be?
Thru cloud & sunshine, o abide with me

I fear no foe, with thee at hand to bless
Ills have no weight & tears no bitterness
Where is death's sting, where grave thy victory?
I triumph still if thou abide with me

Hold thou thy cross before my closing eyes
Shine thru the gloom & point me to the skies
Heav'n's morning breaks & earth's vain shadows flee
In life, in death o Lord abide with me

— w: Henry Lyte, 1820 — m: W.H. Monk, 1861

In Fred Waring SB, *Readers Dig* Fam SB, Gr Legal FakeB, Treas of Hymns, 1001 Jumbo S, S Am Sings *&* Hymns of Glor Praise. *Lyte was an English clergyman inspired by a visit to a dying friend who kept repeating the phrase "Abide with me."* OH36

All My Trials

Hush little baby, don't you cry
You know your mama was born to die
All my trials, Lord, soon be over **(* 1½ beats)**

D* C - / DF♯m F♯m G Em // D Bm Em - A - D -

The river of Jordan is muddy & cold
Well it chills the body but not the soul

I've got a little book with pages three
And every page spells liberty

If living were a thing that money could buy
You know the rich would live & the poor would die

There grows a tree in Paradise
And the pilgrims call it the tree of life

(bridge) Too late, my brothers!
Too late, but never mind

D - / F♯m - G -

— trad. (Spiritual)

1st printed in a book of songs for the Bahamas. In SO! 7:3 *&* Reprints #2, Hootenanny SB, FS Abecedary, Hootenany Tonight, FSEncyV2, 1001 Jumbo S & The Legal FakeB. *On* Cynthia Gooding *(Elektra) &* Bellafonte at Carnegie Hall. *On* Peter Paul & Mary, *their* In the Wind *& in their* Best of PPM SB. *In Joan Baez* SB *& on her* Ballad B. OH37

All the Pretty Little Horses

Hush-you-bye don't you cry, go to sleep-y little baby
When you wake you shall have all the pretty little horses
Blacks & bays, dapples & grays, coach & 6-a little horses

AmC GDm EmE Am / / C Am EmE Am

Way down yonder in the meadow, there's a poor l'il lambie
The birds & the butterflies peckin' out *[flutter round]* his eyes
The poor l'il thing cried "Mammy"

— coll, adapted & arr by John A. Lomax & Alan Lomax

TRO © 1934 & renewed 1962 Ludlow Music, Inc, NY, NY. Internat'l copyright secured. Made in USA. All rights reserved incl public performance for profit. Used by permission. *— The "lambie" which this slave sings about (as she rocks her master's child to sleep) is her own child – who has no one to sing her to sleep. In* Peter, Paul & Mary SB *& on their* In The Wind. *On* Lullaby Magic, *Bill Staines & Cynthia Price* Effective 101, *Pamela Ballingham* Earthmother Lullabies V1 *& Alfred Deller* Western Wind *(SRV73005). On Odetta* The Essential, At the Horn & At Carnegie Hall. *In* Am FS For Children, FiresB of Childrens S, Hootenanny SB, S That Made Am, FS & Footnotes, Treas of FS, FSEncyV1, FS N Am Sings *&* The Legal FakeB. OH38

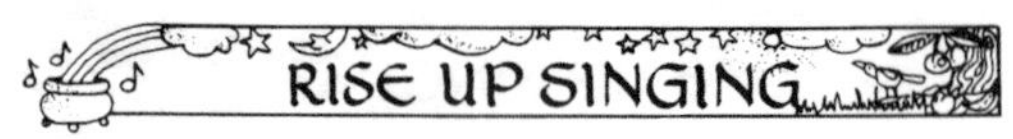

All Through the Night

Sleep my child & peace attend thee, **all thru the night**
Guardian angels God will send thee, **all...**
Soft the drowsy hours are creeping, hill & dale in slumber sleeping
I my longing vigil *[Love alone his watch is]* keeping, **all...**

DG EA GA D / / G - Em A / 1st

While the moon her watch is keeping...
While the weary world is sleeping...
O'er thy spirit gently stealing, visions of the light revealing
Breathes a pure & holy feeling...

— Eng w: Sir Harold Boulton — m: trad (Welsh Ar Hyd y Nos)

© J.B.Cramer & Co. Ltd., 23 Garrick St., London WC2E 9AX. Used by permission. On Peter Paul & Mary Peter Paul & Mommy, *Kevin Roth* Lullabies *(CMS), Paul Robeson* Essential, *Leo Kotke* Ice Water *& Mormon Tab Choir* Gr H. *In SO!* 37:2, Joyful Singing, Pocketful of S, FiresB of Am S, FSEncy V1, FiresB of Childrens S, Lulls & Night S, Lulls fr around the World, 1001 Jumbo, S for the Rotary Club, S We Sang *&* Fred Waring SB. OH39

Angels Watchin' Over Me

All night, all day, angels watchin' over me, my Lord
All night, all day, angels watchin' over me

D - G GD / D - DA D

Day is dyin' in the west – **Angels watchin' over me, my Lord**
Sleep my child & take your rest – **Angels watchin' over me**

Now I lay me down to sleep – **Angels...my Lord**
Pray the Lord my soul to keep – **Angels...me**

If I die before I wake...
Pray the Lord my soul to take...

Children, sleep, the moon is high...
You are safe & love is nigh...

— trad. (Black Spiritual) OH40

At the Gate of Heaven

At the gate of Heav'n little shoes they are selling
For the little barefooted angels there dwelling
Slumber, my baby (3x), a rru, a rru

D DG A7 - / / D G D A7 D DG DA D

God will bless the children so peacefully sleeping
God will help the mothers whose love they are keeping

A la puerta del cielo venden zapatos
Para los angelitos queandan descalzos
Duérmete, niño (3x) a rru, a rru

— Eng. w: Augustus D. Zanzig
— m: Spanish-American Folk Melody

© 1940 Birch Tree Group, Ltd. All rights reserved. Used by permission. In Sing Together *&* S of Many Nations *(WAS) &* Singing America. *In* SO! *36:4 as "La Puerta."* OH41

Aunt Rhody

Go tell Aunt Rhody (3x) the old grey goose is dead

D - A D **(2x)**

1. The one that she's been savin' **(3x)** to make a featherbed
2. The goslins are weepin' **(3x)** because their mammy's dead
3. The gander is mournin' **(3x)** because his wife is dead
4. She died in the millpond **(3x)** from standin' on her head
5. *She died of the small pox* **(3x)** *least that's what the doctor said*

— trad. (US)

This tune has been traced to a 1752 opera by Rousseau & perhaps predates that. On Weavers SBag, Gr H *& in their* SB. *On Jean Ritchie* The Most Dulcimer *(Green Linnet) &* Best of *(Prestige), Nancy Raven* People & Animals *& Bernice Reagon* FS:The South. *On (& in) Pete Seeger* Am Fav Bals V2 *(FA2321). In* Burl Ives SB *& on his* Bals & FS V1. *In* FSEncy V1, FS Abecedary, FiresB of Childrens S, Fred Waring SB, 1001 Jumbo S & FS N Am Sings. OH42

Bheir Me O

Bheir me o, horo van-oh
Bheir me o, horo van-ee
Bheir me o, o hooro ho
Sad am I without thee

(in 3/4) C - / - G7 / - - / - C

Thou'rt the music of my heart
Harp of joy, a cruit mo chruidh
Moon of guidance by night
Strength & light thou'rt to me

In the morning when I go
To the white & shining sea
In the calling of the seal
Thy soft calling to me

When I'm lonely, my white *(gentle)* heart
Dark the night & wild the sea
By love's light my foot finds
The old pathway to thee

— trad. (Scots Gaelic lullaby, v.2 Gordon Bok)

aka: "Eriskay Love Lilt." On Bok's Sea Djiril's Hymn *& in his* Time & the Flying Snow. *In* Sing thru the Seasons, 99 S For Children, Sing Together S to Children, Pocketful of S, Bright Morning Stars, Music in the Air *&* Voices of Am. OH43

Brahms' Lullaby

Lullaby & good night, with roses bedight
With lilies o'er spread is baby's wee bed
Lay thee down now & rest, may thy slumbers be blest **(2x)**

(in 3/4) C - - - / G - - C / F C G C / /

Lullaby & goodnight, thy mother's delight
Bright angels beside my darling abide
They will guard thee at rest, thou shalt wake on my breast **(2x)**

Guten Abend, gut' nacht! Mit Rosen bedacht
Mit naglein bestecht schlupf unter die Deck
Morgen fruh, wenn Gott will, wirst du wieder gewecht **(2x)**

Guten Abend, gut'Nacht! Von Englein bewacht
Die zeigen im Traum, dir Christkindlein's baum
Schlaf' nun selig und suss, schau' im Traum's Paradies **(2x)**

— Johannes Brahms (Eng. anon.)

On Kim Wallach Even More Children S *& Kevin Roth* Lullabies *(CMS). In* Lullabies & Night S, SFest, FiresB of Childrens S *&* Pocketful of S. OH44

Bye 'm Bye

Stars shining number, number one
Number 2, number 3, good Lord!
Bye m' bye, bye m' bye, good Lord / Bye m' bye

C - - - / - - Am G / C - Am G / C - - -

Stars shining number, number 4 / # 5, # 6, good Lord / Bye...

— trad.

In Ruth Crawford Seeger Am FS for Christmas, *Carl Sandburg* Am SBag, Bright Morning Stars *(WAS) &* FiresB of Childrens S. OH45

Day Is Done

Tell me why you're crying, my son
I know you're frightened like everyone
Is it the thunder in the distance you fear
Will it help if I stay very near? / I am here

G C / D G / - C / Em - Am D / G - - -

And if you take my hand, my son
All will be well when the day is done (repeat)
Day is done (when the day is done) (4x)

C G / D G :||: D - / G - :||

You ask me why I'm sighing, my son
You shall inherit what your elders have done
In a world filled with sorrow & woe
If you ask me why this is so, I really don't know

Tell me why you're smiling, my son
Is there a secret you can tell everyone?
Do you know more than those who are wise
Can you see what we all must disguise thru your loving eyes?

— Peter Yarrow

© 1969 Pepamar Music Corp. All rights reserved. Used by permission. — In Peter Paul & Mary SB, *on their* 10 Yrs & Peter Paul & Mommy. *In* The Legal FakeB. ©H46

Day Is Dying in the West

Day is dying in the west / Heav'n is touching earth with rest
Wait & worship while the night
Sets her evening lamps alight / Thru all the sky

G C G - / / D G D G / C G A D / A - D - **(in 3/4)**

Holy, holy, holy / Lord God of Hosts!
Heav'n & earth are full of thee
Heav'n & earth are praising thee / O Lord most high!

G - - - / - D G - / C - G - / D - G GGC / G D G -

Lord of life, beneath the dome / Of the universe, thy home
Gather us who seek thy face
To the fold of thy embrace / For thou art nigh

— w: Mary A. Lathbury, 1877 — m: Wm. F. Sherwin, 1877

By permission of the Chautauqua Institution. In FiresB of FS & hymnals. ©H47

Douglas Mountain

Cedars are growin' on Douglas Mountain
Cedars are growin' so high
Cedars are growin' on Douglas Mountain
Joinin' the earth to the sky **(2x)**

C - G C / D_{m7} G C - / D_{m7} G C EA_m
D_{m7} G_7 C - / G_7 - C -

Snows are a-fallin' on Douglas Mountain
Snows are a-fallin' so deep
Snows are a-fallin' on Douglas Mountain
Puttin' the bears to sleep **(2x)**

Trimmin' the wicks on Douglas Mountain
Shinin' my chimney so bright / Trimmin'...
So God can bring the night **(2x)**

Sun's goin' down on Douglas Mountain
Nights are so long & so cold / Sun's...
And I am feelin' old **(2x)**

— w: Arnold Sundgaard — m: Alec Wilder

TRO © 1965 & 1988 Hampshire House Publishing Corp. & Ludlow Music, Inc, NY, NY. International copyright secured. Made in USA. All rights reserved incl. public performance for profit. Used by permission. — On Raffi More Singable S *& in his* Singable SB *& on Priscilla Herdman* Stardreamer. *In* SO! *38:3 &* V Fav of the V Young *(WAS).* ©H48

Erev Ba

Shuv haeder noher, bimvu-ot hak'far
Ve-oleh ha-avak, mishviley afar
Vehar-cheyk od tzemed inbelim
Milavey et meshech hatz-lalim
Erev ba, erev ba

C D_m G C / - D_m G E
F GC / D_m G / CF D_mG C -

Shuv haruach locheysh, ben gidrot genim
Uv'tzameret hebrosh, Kver namotyoim
Vehar-cheyk, al ketef hagva-ot
Od noshkot karnayim achronot
Erev ba, erev ba

Shuv havared holem, halomot balat
U'forchim tochavim, bamerom 'at at
Veharcheyk ba'emek ha' afel
Melaveh hatanet bo halel
Layil rad, layil rad

— trad. (Israel)

On Welcome to Israel *(T605),* The Best of Israeli FDances *(T645),* Israel's Gr H *(T604) & Bikel* Harv of Israeli FS. *In* Gr S of Israel, The Isr Guitar B & Cassette *(T605),* Fav Hasidic & Isr Melodies for the Young Pianist. *Trans: "Again the flock is flowing towards the outskirts of the city, billows rise from the dusty paths & far away a couple of bees still greet the coming of the shadows. Evening comes/ Again the wind whispers between the fences of the gardens & in the tops of the firs doves are already resting. And far away the last rays still kiss the shoulders of the hills/ Once again the rose dreams secretly. Stars blossom above in the heavens slowly, slowly. In the dusky valley the coyote goes out to greet the coming of the night. Night has descended."* ©H49

God Bless the Moon (I See the Moon)

I see the moon & the moon sees me
God bless the moon & God bless me
There's grace in the cabin & grace in the hall
And the grace of God is over us all

ED E ED E / / E - A - / B_7 - ED E

I see the moon & the moon sees me
The moon sees the somebody I want to see
God bless the moon & God bless me
And God bless the somebody I want to see

— new words & music by Jean Ritchie

© 1969 Geordie Music Publishing Co. Box 361, Fort Washington NY 11050. On Jean Ritchie At Home. ©H50

Goodnight, Irene

Irene goodnight, Irene goodnight
Goodnight Irene (2x) I'll see you in my dreams

(in 3/4) E B_7 - E / EE_7 A B_7 E

Sometimes I live in the country, sometimes I live in town
Sometimes I have a great notion to jump into the river & drown

Quit ramblin' & quit gamblin', quit stayin' out late at night
Stay home with your wife & family, sit down by the fireside bright

I asked your mother for you, she told me you was too young
I wished to God I'd never seen your face, I's sorry you ever was born

I love Irene, God knows I do, I'll love her til the seas run dry
And if Irene turns her back on me, I'd take morphine & die

You cause me to weep, you cause me to mourn, you cause me to leave my home
But the very last words I heard her say was Please sing me one more song"

Foxes sleep in the forest, lions sleep in their dens
Goats sleep on the mountainside & pigs sleep in pens

Whales sleep in the ocean, zebras sleep on land
Hippos sleep by the riverside & camels sleep on sand

Coyote sleeps in the canyon, a birdie sleeps in a tree
And when it's time for me to rest my bed's the place for me

— Huddie Ledbetter & John A. Lomax (new v. Raffi & Debi Pike)

TRO © 1936 (renewed 1964) & 1950 (renewed 1978) Ludlow Music, Inc, NY, NY. International copyright secured. Made in USA. All rights reserved incl. public performance for profit. Used by permission. — On Weavers Together Again, Reunion 1963 *&* Gr H, *H Near & R Gilbert* Lifeline, *Patrick Sky* Thru a Window *& Ry Cooder* Chicken Skin Music. *On (& in) Pete Seeger* Am Fav Bals V3 *&* Sings Leadbelly. *In* Those Were The Days These Are The S, Best S fr the Lomax Coll, 110 S of Nostalgia, Treas of FS, *Raffi* Singable SB, Gr Legal FakeB, Life of the Party, Gold Era of Nost M V3 *& Lomax* FS of NAm. ©H51

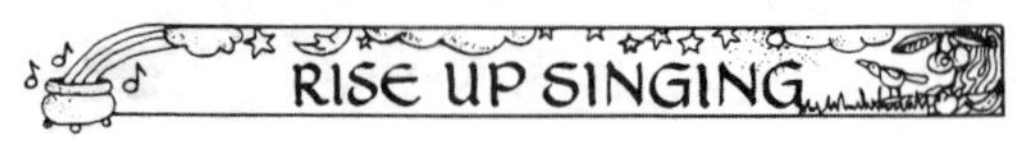

Hobo's Lullaby

Go to sleep you weary hobo
Let the towns drift slowly by
Can't you hear those steel rails hummin'?
That's the hobo's lullaby

D G / A D :||

Don't you worry 'bout tomorrow
Let tomorrow come & go
Tonight you're in a nice warm boxcar
Safe from all that wind & snow

I know your clothes are torn & tattered
And your hair is turning gray
Rest your head in weary slumber *[Lift your head & smile at trouble]*
You'll find peace & rest someday

I know the police give you trouble
They cause trouble everywhere
When you die you'll go to heaven
There'll be no policemen there

— Goebel Reeves

© 1961, 1962 Fall River Music Inc. All rights reserved. Used by permission. — On Woody Guthrie Hard Trav, Tribute to Woody Guthrie V2, *Arlo Guthrie* Hobo's Lullaby, *Jack Elliott* Hootenany *& Utah Phillips* All Used Up *(Philo1050). On Pete Seeger* World of, & Rainbow Race. *In SO! 38:2.* OH52

Hush Li'l Baby (The Mockingbird Song)

Hush li'l baby, don't say a word
Mamma's gonna buy you a mockin'bird

D A / - D

If that mockin'bird don't sing
Mamma's gonna buy you a diamond ring

If that diamond ring turn brass
Mamma's gonna buy you a lookin' glass

If that lookin' glass gets broke
Mamma's gonna buy you a billygoat

If that billygoat won't pull
Mamma's gonna buy you a cart & bull

If that cart & bull turn over
Mamma's gonna buy you a dog named Rover

If that dog named Rover won't bark
Mamma's gonna buy you a horse & cart

If that horse & cart fall down
You'll be the sweetest baby in town

— coll., adap. & arr. by John A. Lomax & Alan Lomax

© 1941 & renewed 1969 Ludlow Music, Inc, NY, NY. International copyright secured. Made in USA. All rights reserved Used by permission. In SO! 3:8, *Baez* SB, Lulls & Night S, Am FS for Children, FiresB Childrens S. *In* Weavers SB *& on* At Carnegie Hall. *On* Peter Paul & Mommy, *Kevin Roth* Lullabies, *Marcy Marxer* Jump Children, *Horseflies* Human Fly *& Joan Baez* In Concert *(VSD 2123).* OH53

Isle au Haut Lullabye

If I could give you three things, I would give you these
Song & laughter & a wooden home in the shining seas
When you see old Isle au Haut rising in the dawn
You will play in yellow fields in the morning sun

D Em A D :|| **(4x)**

Sleep where the wind is warm & the moon is high
Give sadness to the stars, sorrow to the sky

Do you hear what the sails are saying in the wind's dark song
Give sadness to the wind, blown alee & gone

Sleep now: the moon is high & the wind blows cold
For you are sad & young, & the sea is old

— Gordon Bok

© 1964 Timberhead Inc. Pub by Folk Legacy Records, Sharon CT. Used by permission. On Bok Muir & Trickett Turning toward the Morning. In Golden Link SB. OH54

John O' Dreams

_When midnight sings, good people homeward tread
_Seek now your blankets & your feather bed
_Home is the rover,_his journey over
_Yield up the nighttime to old John O'Dreams **(2x)**

G - CG / / G D - Em / G - CG / /

Across the hill the sun has gone astray
Tomorrow's cares are many dreams away
The stars are flying, your candles dying
Yield up the darkness to old John O'Dreams **(2x)**

Both man & master in the night are one
All things are equal when the day is done
The prince & ploughman, the slave & freeman

All find their comfort with old John O'Dreams **(2x)**
Now as you sleep the dreams come winging clear
The hawks of morning cannot harm you here
Sleep is your river, float on forever
And for your boatman choose old John O'Dreams **(2x)**

— w: Bill Caddick — m: adap fr Tchaikovsky Symphony #6

© 1967 Bill Caddick, Rough Music, 24 Parkdale, Tettenhall Rd., Wolverhampton WV1 4TE England. Used by permission. — On Bok Muir & Trickett Fashioned in Clay, *Garnet Rogers* The Outside Track *(Valerie1112), Clancy Bros* Live!, *Planxty* High Kings of Tara *(Tara), Jean Redpath* A Fine S for Singing *&* Mick Maloney. OH55

Kentucky Babe

Skeeters are a hummin' on the honeysuckle vine
Sleep, Kentucky Babe!
Sandman is a comin' to this little babe of mine / Sleep...
Silv'ry moon is shinin' in the heavens up above
Bob-o-link is pinin' for his little lady love
You are mighty lucky, Babe of old Kentucky
Close your eyes in sleep

Daug

(TD ↑ 5)

G Em **(2x)** / G - D - / Am D **(2x)** / A7 - D -
G Bm Em D / G Bm C D / D E♭ **(2x)** / D A D Daug

Fly away / Fly away Kentucky Babe, fly away to rest
Fly away
Lay your kinky wooly head on your mammy's breast
Um – um / Close your eyes in sleep

G - - - / G Em **(2x)** / Am - D - / Am D **(2x)**
E♭ - G - **(2x)** / G D G D G - - -

Daddy's in the canebrake with his little dog & gun / **Sleep...**
Possum for your breakfast when your sleepin' time is done...
Bogie man'll catch you sure unless you close your eyes
Waitin' just outside the door to take you by surprise
Best be keepin' shady, little colored lady / **Close your eyes...**

— w: Richard Henry Buck — m: Adam Geibel

In Fav S of the 90's, 100 S of Nost, Fred Waring SB, Gr Legal Fake B, 120 Am S, 1001 Jumbo S, Am Treas of Gold Oldies Sing Along World's Fav FS. OH56

Kumbaya

Kumbaya, my lord, kumbaya (2x)
O Lord, kumbaya **(in 3/4)**

C-F C-- / Em-F G-- / C-F **(2x)** / AmG C--

Someone's sleeping, Lord, kumbaya (3x) / O Lord...

Singing, dreaming, crying, laughing, etc.

Come by here, my lord, come by here **(3x)**
O Lord, come by here

— Traditional

Library of Congress Folk Archive has transcriptions of this song from the field in early 20th c. In SO! 8:1, Hootenanny SB, S of the Spirit, Sing Together, FS Abecedary, V Fav of the V Young, Children's S for a Friendly Planet, Quaker SB, S Am Sings & FS Ency V2. *In Joan Baez* SB *& on her* In Conc. *On Raffi* Baby Beluga *& in his* 2nd SB. *On Weavers* Trav On. OH57

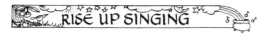

Liverpool Lullaby

O you are a mucky kid,
Dirty as a dustbin lid
When he finds out the things you did
You'll get a belt from your dad
O you have your father's nose
So crimson in the dark it glows
If you're not asleep when the boozers close
You'll get a belt from your dad

Dm - A Dm / - - - A / Dm - A Dm / - A Dm -
‖: Gm - Dm - / A - Dm - :‖

You look so scruffy lying there
Strawberry jam tufts in your hair
And in the world you haven't a care
And I have got so many
It's quite a struggle every day
Living on your father's pay
The bugger drinks it all away
And leaves me without any

Altho' we have no silver spoon
Better days are coming soon
Now Nellie's working at the loom
And she gets paid on Fridays
Perhaps one day we'll have a bash
When little ones provide the cash
We'll get a house in Knotting Ash
And buy your dad a brewery

O you are a mucky kid...belt from your dad **(as 1st v.)**
O you have your father's face
You're growing up a real hard case
But there's no one else can take your place:
Go fast asleep for Mammy

— Stan Kelly

 — In Judy Collins SB *& on her* In My Life. *On Ian Campbell Folk Gp* Rights of Man *& Caryl P Weiss* With Her Head. OH58

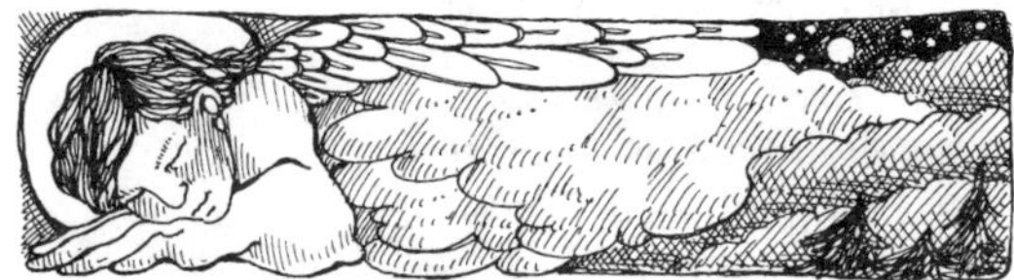

Lord Blow the Moon Out

Bed is too small for my tiredness
Give me a hilltop with trees
Tuck a cloud up under my chin
Lord blow the moon out please! **(in 3/4)**

Am - E Am / - F E - / Am - E Am / - F Am -

Rock me to sleep in a cradle of dreams
Sing me a lullaby of leaves / **Tuck...**

In 1004 FS, SFest & P Berrien Berends Whole Child/Whole Parent. OH59

Lullabye *(Like a Ship)*

Like a ship in the harbour, like a mother & child
Like a light in the darkness I'll hold you awhile

(in 3/4) A - E - / DE E A -

We'll rock on the water, I'll cradle you deep
And hold you while angels sing you to sleep

— Cris Williamson

 — On her Live Dream *& in her* SB. *On Susan Stark* Rainbow People. *In* Worship in Song: A Hymnal for Friends. OH60

Matthew, Mark, Luke and John

Matthew, Mark, Luke & John
Bless the bed that I lay on
Four corners to my bed
Four angels there be spread
One to watch & one to pray
Two to guide my soul away

G GD G - / F C G GD / G GD G
FC G / C GD G / F C G (GD)

God is the branch & I'm the flower
Pray God send that blessed hour
Now I lay me down to sleep
Pray the Lord my soul to keep
And in the morning when I awake
The Lord's path I'll surely take

— trad. (US)

Words with a new melody in Eliz Posten Children's SB. OH61

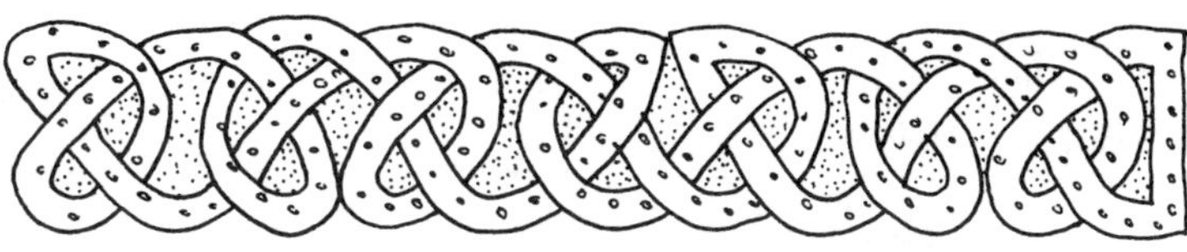

Morningtown Ride

Train whistle blowing, makes a sleepy noise
Underneath their blankets go all the girls & boys
Heading from the station, out along the bay
All bound for Morningtown, many miles away

G - C G / C G Am D / 1st / C G D G

Sarah's at the engine, Tony rings the bell
John swings the lantern to show that all is well
Rocking, rolling, riding, out along the Bay
All bound for Morningtown, many miles away

Maybe it is raining where our train will ride
But all the little travelers are snug & warm inside
Somewhere there is sunshine, somewhere there is day
Somewhere there is Morningtown, many miles away

— Malvina Reynolds

 — In her SB & Little Boxes *on her* Artichokes, Malvina Reynolds & Magical S. *On Raffi* Baby Beluga *& in his* 2nd SB. OH62

Now the Day Is Over

Now the day is over, night is drawing nigh
Shadows of the evening steal across the sky

GD G EmB7 EmEm7 / A7 D(D, C♯, B, B♭) D7 G

Jesus *[Spirit]*, give the weary calm & sweet repose
With thy tend'rest blessing may our eyelids close

Grant to little children visions bright of Thee
Guard the sailors tossing on the deep blue sea

Comfort every sufferer watching late in pain
Those who plan some evil, from their sin restrain

Thru the long night watches may thine angels spread
Their white wings above me watching 'round my bed

When the morning wakens then may I arise
Pure & fresh & sinless in thy holy eyes

— w: Sabine Baring-Gould — m: Joseph Barnaby

Written in the 1860's. In S of the Spirit, Fred Waring SB *& hymnals.* OH63

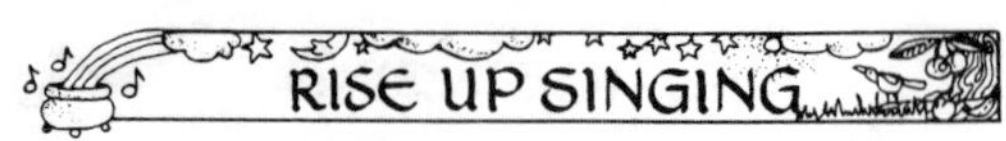

One Grain of Sand

1. One grain of sand
One grain of sand in all the world
One grain of sand
One little boy, one little girl

(very freely) Dm G / Dm F / Dm G / Am Dm

2. **One...** / One little star up in the sky
One... / One little you, one little I

3. ...One drop of water in the sea
...One little you, one little me

4. ...One leaf of grass on a windy plain
...We come & go again & again, again, etc.

5. I love you so **(4x)**
More than you will ever, ever, ever, ever, ever know

6. **One...**/ ...One little snowflake lost in the swirling storm
One.../ ...I'll hold you alone & keep you warm

7. ...One grain of sand on an endless shore
...One little life, who'd ask for more

8. One grain of sand **(6x)**

9. ...One little star up in the blue
...One little me, one little you

— Pete Seeger

 On his Dangerous S & Abiyoyo *& in his* Bells of Rhymney. *On Odetta & WHATFG (S of Pete Seeger V.1) & in his WHATFG.* OH64

Riddle Song

I gave my love a cherry that has no stone
I gave my love a chicken that has no bone
I gave my love a story that has no end
I gave my love a baby with no cryin'

D G - D / A D - A / / G - - D

How can there be a cherry that has no stone?
How can there be a chicken that has no bone?
How can there be a story that has no end?
How can there be a baby with no cryin'?

A cherry when it's bloomin' it has no stone
A chicken when it's pippin' it has no bone
A story of I love you it has no end
A baby when it's sleepin', it's no cryin'

— trad.

Riddle portion is part of Child Ballad #46 "Capt. Wedderburn's Courtship" On Pete Seeger World of, Am Fav Bal V2 *(FA2321) & (with E McColl)* Cold Snap. *On Doc Watson* Southbound, *Jean Ritchie* None But One *& Grandpa Jones* Farm Alb. *On Ives* S of the Colonies, Wayfaring Stranger *& in his* SB. *In* AmFavBals, SFest, FS Abecedary, S for Pickin & Singin, FSEncy V1, Treas of FS, *&* FiresB of FS. OH65

Skye Boat Song

Speed bonnie boat, like a bird on the wing
"Onward" the sailors cry!
Carry the lad that's born to be king
Over the sea to Skye

(in 3/4) C - G - / C F C G / 1st / C F C -

Loud the winds howl, loud the waves roar
Thunderclouds rend the air
Baffled our foes stand on the shore
Follow they will not dare

Am - Dm - / Am F Am - / 1st / Am F Am G

Tho' the waves leap, soft shall ye sleep
Ocean's a royal bed
Rocked in the deep, Flora will keep
Watch by your weary head

Many's the lad fought on that day
Well the claymore could wield
When the night came, silently lay
Dead on Culloden's field

Burned are our homes, exile & death
Scatter the loyal men
Yet e'er the sword cool in the sheath
Charlie will come again

— m: trad & Annie McLeod — w: Sir Harold Boulder 1884

After an unsuccessful Scottish uprising against the English in the 18th c., the Bonnie Prince Charlie, then still a child & the Stuart claimant to the Scottish throne, was sneaked across to the Isle of Skye, west of Scotland, to safety. On Kevin Roth Lullabies & Living & Breathing Wind *(FTS31080). In* FiresB of FS, SFest & Sing Along w/World's Fav FS. OH66

Stone Harbor Lullaby

The wind blows steady across the bay
Clay fish ring like bells
Papa sails the yellow boat
So swiftly thru the swells **(2x)**

C G C F / - C F C / F - C G / C - F - / - G C -

Now we'll slowly rock my little babe
Close your sleepy eyes
Listen to the lapping waves
Feel mama's heart close by **(2x)**

And when you're grown you will have a boat
A baby of your own
You will sing a lullaby
And know the love of home **(2x)**

— Judith Fox

 OH67

Summertime

Summertime & the livin' is easy
Fish are jumpin' & the cotton is high
O your pappy's rich & your mammy's good lookin'
So hush little baby, don't you cry

Em A **(3x)** Em Em7 / Am - - - B7 C7 B7 -
/ " / G Em Am C Em (A Em A)

One of these mornings you're gonna rise up singin'
Then you'll spread your wings & you'll take to the sky
Until that mornin' there ain't nothin' can harm you
With mammy & pappy standin' by

— w: Dubose Heyward — m: George Gershwin

 Fr their musical Porgy and Bess. On Carolyn Hester, Trad M of the Future, Sam Cooke The Legendary (RCA), Doc Watson Elementary, Madeleine MacNeil Soon Its Gonna Rain & No Strings Attached. In Readers Dig Treas of Bestloved S & Broadway SBs. OH68

Sweet and Low

Sweet & low, sweet & low, wind of the western sea
Low, low, breathe & blow, wind of the western sea
Over the rolling waters go, come from the dying moon & blow
Blow him again to me
While my little one, while my pretty one sleeps **(in 3/4)**

G C G C G D A D / G C G C D Em A D
D - G D **(2x)** / Em - C Cm / G D G D G - - -

Sleep & rest, sleep & rest, father will come to thee soon
Rest, rest on mother's breast, father will come to thee soon
Father will come to his babe in the nest, silver sails all out of the west
Under the silver moon
Sleep my little one, sleep my pretty one, sleep

— Alfred Tennyson & Joseph Barnaby

In SFest, Fred Waring SB & S Along w/World's Fav FS. *On Pat Carfra* Sleepy Heads. OH69

Sweet Baby James

There is a young cowboy, he lives on the range
His horse & his cattle are his only companions
He works in the saddle & he sleeps in the canyons
Waiting for summer his pastures to change **(in 3/4)**

C G F Em / Am F C Em / / F C Dm G - - -

As the moon rises he sits by his fire
Thinkin' about women & glasses of beer
And closing his eyes as the doggies retire
Sings out a song which is soft but it's clear
As if maybe someone could hear:

F - G C / Am F C G / 1st / Am F C - / D - G -

Goodnight, you moonlight ladies
Rockabye Sweet Baby James
Deep greens & blues are the colors I choose
Won't you let me go down in my dreams
And rockabye Sweet Baby James

C F G C / Am F C - / / Dm D G - / F G C -

The first of December was covered with snow
And so was the turnpike from Stockbridge to Boston
The Berkshires seemed dreamlike on account of that frosting
Ten miles behind me & 10,000 more to go

There's a song that they sing when they take to the hwy
A song that they sing when they take to the sea
A song that they sing of their home in the sky
Maybe you can believe it if it helps you to sleep
But singing works just fine for me

— James Taylor

 — On his Sweet Baby James & Gr H. *In* Gr S of '70s. OH70

Wynken, Blynken and Nod

Wynken, Blynken & Nod one night sailed off in a wooden shoe
Sailed on a river of crystal light into a sea of dew
"Where are you going & what do you wish?" the old moon asked the three
"We have come to fish for the herring fish that live in the beautiful sea
Nets of silver & gold have we" said **Wynken, Blynken & Nod**

Em A **(2x)** / D Bm Em A :|| Em A Em - A -

The old moon laughed & sang a song as they rocked on the wooden shoe
And the wind that sped them all night long ruffled the waves of dew
The little stars were the herring fish that lived in the beautiful sea
"Now cast your nets wherever you wish, never afeared are we!"
So cried the stars to **the fishermen three, Wynken...**

All night long their nets they threw to the stars in the twinkling foam
Then down from the skies came the wooden shoe, bringing the fishermen home
'Twas all so pretty a sail it seemed as if it could not be
And some folks thought 'twas a dream they dreamed of sailing that beautiful sea
But I shall name **the fishermen three...**

Wynken & Blynken are two little eyes & Nod a little head
And the wooden shoe that sailed the skies is a wee one's trundle bed
So shut your eyes while Mother sings of wonderful sights that be
And you shall see the beautiful things as you rock in the misty sea
Where the old shoe rocked **the fishermen three...**

— w: Eugene Field **— m: various settings**

For the melody which fits these chords, refer to our Teaching Tapes. Also on (with various melodies): Buffy Saint-Marie Sweet America, *Carly Simon* In Harmony, *Jonathan Edwards* Little Hands, Sesame Street Beat, *&* Lullaby Magic V1 *(Discovery Music).* OH71

Yea Ho, Little Fish

Come all ye bold fishermen, listen to me
I'll sing you a song of the fish in the sea
Yea ho, little fish, don't cry, don't cry
Yea ho, little fish, you be whale by & by

(in 3/4) C - F G / C - G C // F C G C / /

You go to fish school & can learn from a book
How not to get caught on the fisherman's hook / **Yea ho...**

Watch out, little fish, we're out after you
But you can escape away deep in the blue...

You just swim around the fisherman's bait
And you won't end up on the fisherman's plate...

— trad. (Australian)

On Ed Trickett Tellin Takes Me Home. OH72

Other lullabies & night songs in the book include: "Walk Shepherdess Walk" (DREAM) "Blackbird," "Somewhere" (HOPE) "Whiffenpoof Song" (GOLD) "Rock Me Roll Me, Rock Me to Sleep" (MEN) "Deep Blue Sea" (new words / PEACE) "Tallis Canon," "Tender Shepherd," "Vesper Hymn" (SACR) & "Dillan Bay" (SEA). [Songs about morning are mainly in OUTDOORS.]

The Boxer

I am just a poor boy tho' my story's seldom told
I have squandered my resistance
For a pocketful of mumbles, such are promises
All lies in jest, still a man hears what he wants to hear
And disregards the rest
Ooh la la la...

G - - Em / D - / - - G - / Em D C / - G / D - G -

When I left my home & my family I was no more than a boy
In the company of strangers
In the quiet of a railway station running scared
Laying low seeking out the poorer quarters
Where the ragged people go
Looking for the places only they would know

(bridge) Lie la lie...

Em - D - **(2x)** G -

Asking only workman's wages I come looking for a job
But I get no offers
Just a come-on from the whores on Second Avenue
I do declare there were times when I was so lonesome
I took some comfort there / Ooh la la...

Then I'm laying out my winter clothes & wishing I was gone
Going home
Where the New York City winters aren't bleeding me
Leading me – going home

G - - Em / D - / - - G - / Em - D - (- - G -)

In the clearing stands a boxer & a fighter by his trade
And he carries the reminders
Of every glove that laid him down or cut him til he cried out
In his anger & his shame, I am leaving, I am leaving
But the fighter still remains / Ooh la la...**(to bridge)**

G - - Em / D - / - - G - / - Em D C / - G / D - G -

— Paul Simon

© 1968 Paul Simon. All rights reserved. Used by permission. – In his S *of* Paul Simon *& on* Bridge Over Troubled Waters *& Gr H (both w/Art Garfunkel). On Dylan* Self Portrait. **Y01**

Changing as I Go

There was a time when I was as uptight as could be
I'd pretend I had no feelings wrapped up inside of me
No love or joy or pain, only anger would I show
But I began a-changing & I'm changing as I go

D - - - / G D E A / D - - - / G D DA D

As I go (I laugh & cry), as I go (I'm feelin' so fine)
My life it is a-changing as I go (Hallelujah)
Oh I want to shout & sing, for I've finally taken wing
And my life it is a-changing as I go

A - D - / - - A - / D - G D / - A D -

My life began to change & I began to lose my fear
When I expressed emotions to those I felt were dear
I began to see in life a sunshine & a glow
And I began a-changing as I go

My foggy, frozen self began to warm & clear
When I discarded dominance & threw away the fear
Of softness & of gentleness & letting feelings flow
And now I am a-changing as I go

So let me say to you who think you're masculine
Be wary & be cautious of the traps it puts you in
Suppression of your feelings, always putting on a show
When you can be a-changing as you go

(last cho)
As we go (we laugh & cry), as we go (we're feelin' so fine)
Our lives they are a-changing as we go, etc.

— w: Bruce Kokopeli
— m: trad. (hymn "The Old Account Was Settled Long Ago")

© 1988 Bruce Kokopeli. Used by permission. This was the theme song of the Cowardly Lion singing group in Seattle. **Y02**

For a Change

When I was 17 I could feel the rules
Don't get too close to anyone, keep your distance & be cool
Confused & quiv'ring like a newborn colt but we pushed it deep inside
All putting on a show while Lord, you know we were all so terrified **(capo up)**

G D C G / - D C D / C G C D / C - A D

For a change: when we're afraid, let's not hide it
For a change, when we hurt, reach out our hand
Each one of us can be the solution
If we love & work together for a change

G - C - / - - A D / G - C - / G D G -

After school came the nine to five, trying to stay afloat
Do your job & you'll move on up if you don't rock the boat
But the layoffs could come anytime so don't let friendship get in the way
If you help someone out they just might be the one tomorrow to take your place

It was in the fall of '70, my lottery number was low
Right in the middle of an undeclared war & I didn't want to go
But my country expected me to fight & so did the enemy
But it goes on & on if we don't stop & say let's live this differently

(bridge)
And I believe that we all feel it & it's the fear that makes it tough
But when we put our heart into our lives we'll be strong enough

Em - D7 - / C - D7 -

— Geof Morgan

© 1984 by Geof Morgan (BMI). Used by permission. — On his At the Edge *(FF). In* SO! *31:3.* **Y03**

The Frozen Logger

As I sat down one evening 'twas in a small cafe
A 40 year-old waitress to me these words did say:

(in 3/4) D A - D / DD7 G A D

"I see you are a logger & not just a common bum
For no one but a logger stirs his coffee with his thumb

My lover was a logger, there's none like him today
If you poured whiskey on it, he'd eat a bale of hay

He never shaved the whiskers from off of his horny hide
He'd drive them thru with a hammer & bite them off inside

My logger came to see me, 'twas on a winter's day
He held me in a fond embrace that broke three vertebrae

He kissed me when we parted, so hard he broke my jaw
I couldn't speak to tell him he forgot his mackinaw

I saw my logger lover go sauntering thru the snow
A-goin' gaily homeward at forty-eight below

The weather tried to freeze him, it tried its level best
At a hundred degrees below zero, he buttoned up his vest

It froze clear down to China, it froze to the stars above
At a thousand degrees below zero, it froze my logger love

They tried in vain to thaw him, & if you believe it, sir
They made him into axe blades to cut the Douglas fir

And so I lost my logger, & to this cafe I've come
And it's here I wait for someone who stirs his coffee with his thumb"

— James Stevens

TRO © 1951 renewed 1979 Folkways Music Publishers Inc., NY, NY. International copyright secured. Made in USA. All rights reserved incl pub performance for profit. Used by permission. — aka: "Logger Lover." In J Lomax FS of NAm, S for Pickin & Singin & SFest. *On Weavers* On Tour & Reunion at Carnegie Hall, pt 2, *Odetta* The Essential *(Vang) & Clancy Bros* Live! *(Vang).* ©Y04

A Gentle Song

Out here on this backroad just a few clouds in the sky
The hills seem so much drier than before
This mornin' is for backroads, walkin' here & thinkin'
How some things don't feel right anymore

D - G A / G A Bm - / G A D G / D G A -

Like the only way I know you is to stay so far apart
I guess I just don't know too much of you
'Cause we've never shared the times that hurt, the tenderness and tears
That's not the sort of thing men do

So here's a gentle song for you, my brother
A gentle song for you, my friend
And as we learn to sing, you're gonna hear our voices ring
In a gentle song for you, my brother

D G D - / / D F# Bm A / D G D -

Up the road a hawk is flying, everything's so still
Makes me want someone to share this day
Like a sister who has taught me much or a brother I know well
Where hugs & tears are all there is to say

Now the sun has gone behind the clouds I can feel the wind
Walking out here always brings me home
But now it's time to find some friends who feel the same as me
It makes no sense to walk this road alone

— Tom Hunter

© 1977 Tom Hunter. All rights reserved. Used by permission. He writes: "Somehow brotherhood has become one of those nice empty words with no guts. Paying attention to each other, to the anger, the gentleness, the visions, the real stuff & then doing smth about it puts the power back in brotherhood – maybe that's what we've learned from sisterhood." On his Coming Home. ©Y05

Goodbye, John Wayne

A shy, winning smile, not good with words
At home with the sky or a stampeding herd
Bigger than life that one could tame
Goodbye, John Wayne **(in 3/4)**

G ↓ - - / C ↓ - D / G G7 Em Eb - / C D G -

I watched the man you projected on screen
I tried to live up to the image I'd seen
A soul of warm stone, you never complained / Goodbye...

You saved the day, you won every fight
Your record was clean, you always were right
But not even you could live up to your name / Goodbye...

C D C G / Em - A D / " / " /

We all knew you'd make it, even when you looked so tired
And the way you handled love, I once admired
But it only brought me confusion & pain...

Yes, you had strength & that I can use
But you never tried to let anyone thru
I can't live behind walls with my feelings in chains...

— Geof Morgan

© 1980 Geof Morgan. Used by permission. On his At the Edge *(FF350) & in his* SB. ©Y06

Government on Horseback

The President stepped off the silver screen
He said "People put your lives here in my hands
We can turn our country's honor white again
Let the sulfur smoke of progress fill our land"

G C Bm C G / C - GC G / 1st / G D GC G

'Cause we've got government on horseback again
Back to the days when Congressmen were men
We can make it on our own, running on testosterone
It's government on horseback again

G - C - / - - G D / G - C - / G D G -

Help me give your land a golden goose
Turn our native corporations loose
High voltage lines will go the extra mile
Now it's power to the people, nuclear style

Blow out the lamp beside the golden door
We don't need cheap foreign labor any more
Without our unions & the E.R.A.
We will all have twice the jobs at half the pay

(tag) Back again, back again
We've got government on horseback again
It's back to home for mommies, bomb the hell out of the commies
It's government on horseback again

C - G - / - - D - / G - C - / G D G -

— Si Kahn

© 1984 Joe Hill Music (ASCAP). All rights reserved. Used by permission. — On his & John McCutcheon's Signs of the Times *(Rounder) & on* Swords Into Plowshares. *In SO! 32:4 (along w/feature article on Si Kahn). A takeoff on the song "Franklin D. Roosevelt's Back Again" (see Reprints #4).* ©Y07

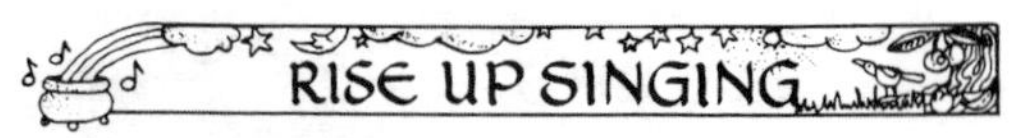

Hard Lovin' Loser

He's the kind of guy puts on a motorcycle jacket and he
weighs about a hundred & five
He's the kind of surfer got a hodaddy haircut
and you wonder how he'll ever survive
He's the kind of frogman using 20 lbs. of counterweights
and sinking in the sea like a stone
He's the kind of soldier got no sense of direction
and they sent him in the jungle alone
But when the frost's on the pumpkin & the little girls are jumpin'
He's a hard lovin' son-of-a-gun
He's got 'em waiting downstairs just to sample his affairs
And they call him a spoonful of fun

D - - - / / / // G - / D7 - / A7 G7 / D -

He's the kind of person going riding on a skateboard
and his mind's ragin' out of control
He's the kind of person goes to drive a Maserati
puts the key inside the wrong little hole
He's the kind of ski-bum tearing wild down the mountain
hits a patch where there ain't any snow
He's the kind of cowboy got a hot trigger finger
shoots his boot 'cause he's drawing kind of slow
But when he comes in for bowling, he's an expert at rolling
Sets the pins up & lays them right down
He's got them taking off their heels & they like the way he feels
And they call him a carnival clown

Well, he's got a parachute & screaming like Geronimo
and makes a little hole in the ground
He's the kind of logger when the man hollers "Timber!"
has to stop & look around for the sound
He's the kind of artist rents a groovy little attic
discovers that he can't grow a beard
He's a human cannonball, comes in for a landing
and he wonders where the net disappeared
But when he takes off his shoes, it won't come as news
That they're lining up in threes & in twos
He's got them pounding on the door, got them begging for
some more
And they call him whatever they choose

— **Richard Fariña**

© 1966 Warner Bros. Inc. All rights reserved. Used by permission. On his & Mimi's Best of *(Vang). In* Judy Collins SB *& on her* In My Life. **Y08**

He Ain't Heavy, He's My Brother

The road is long with many a winding turn
That leads us to who knows where, who knows where
But I'm strong, strong enough to carry him
He ain't heavy, he's my brother (capo up)

G D C Am / Em F Am D / G D Em E♭ / G Am G -

So on we go, his welfare is my concern
No burden is he to bear, we'll get there
For I know he would not encumber me / He ain't...

(bridge) If I'm laden at all, I'm laden with sadness
That everyone's heart isn't filled with the gladness
Of love for one another

Em D Em D / Bm Dm Bm Em / C A7 Am D

It's a long, long road from which there is no return
While we're on our way to there, why not share?
And the load doesn't weigh me down at all / He...

— **w: Bob Russell m: Bobby Scott**

© 1969 Harrison Music Corp/Jenny Music. International copyright secured. Used by permission. — The refrain orig spoken by a boy carrying his brother in Boy's Town. On Cher Gypsy Tramps *& Al Green* Soul Survivor. *In* Gr Legal FakeB, 1001 Jumbo S *&* Club Date FakeB. *Rec. by the Hollies & Neil Diamond* Rainbow *(MCA-2103).* **Y09**

Homophobia

Back when I was very young, I was a curious boy
One day my daddy caught me alone, he said "Son, you know
that ain't no toy
You keep playing with yourself, you'll never learn the
social rules
My son's gonna be a football hero, not one of those sissy
fools"

D - A7 D / / / /

**Now it's that homophobia! in the locker room when I
took gym
Homophobia! Lord, it keeps me from touchin' my friends**

G D A D / /

I can't remember who told me exactly, or when I first heard
But I could tell by the tone in the voice, the meaning of the
words
The women teachers who lived alone, everybody knew were
weird
And one day my taking a ballet class was something my
mother always feared

Well first I learned it was evil, then I got "liberated"
and learned it was sick
Now I see things differently but that early training just
won't quit
Sometimes it feels just like a wall or a river in me that froze
But tho' I can't really touch it, it keeps me from getting
too close

Well, out in Southern California, anything you do is fine
To be strange is to be normal, but you've still got to walk
a straight line
Holding hands with my friend Duncan, I may be risking a knife
"Hey, man, I was only kidding, here's a picture of my
kids and my wife"

— **Geof Morgan**

© 1980 Geof Morgan. (Last verse added 1981.) Used by permission. — In his SB *& on his* It Comes with the Plumbing *(Nexus). Also on* Walls to Roses *(Folkways) – an alb of men's liberation songs by a variety of artists.* **Y10**

I'm Gonna Be Silly

**I'm gonna be silly, take it all willy-nilly
I'm gonna be a fool, throw away the rules
gonna laugh when I don't know
I'm gonna be silly, maybe go dancing on a lily
I'm gonna be laughing with both hands clapping
when it comes my time to go**

(in D, capo up) G - D - / A - - D :||

I'm tired of planning my whole life away
Be quiet in class, keep off the grass & I can retire someday
That's a bunch of baloney, I'm retiring right now
I'm gonna be a clown, laugh much too loud
& roll in the grass with the cows (yecch!)

It's time for recess, time to go out & play
Gonna see the sunrise, send an eskimo pies
forget about making it rhyme (who cares!)
I swallowed that time clock & punched myself out
I'm gonna push on "Pull" doors, wear chartreuse underdrawers
give the sad face to somebody else, 'cause:

— **Geof Morgan**

© 1982 Transformation Music. Used by permission. On his Finally Letting It Go *(FF) & in his* SB. **Y11**

It Comes with the Plumbing

Well, you know that I'm not the strong silent type
With a muscle-beach body & Wheatena in my mind
And even tho' Rambo ain't who I want to be
I pass a mirror & I flex, instinctively

D A / - D / - G / DA D

Well, it comes with the plumbing (2x)
'Cause I'm a US certified male, still under warranty
It comes with the plumbing (2x)
It's so hard to change when you're raised to be a male machine

G - D - / A - D - :||

You know, it's just biology, the way my head turns around
When I'm walking up the street & see some woman walkin' down
It happens so fast looks like my neck might break
It's amazing what this body can take

You tell me I need to show more concern
My intellectual games only make you feel burned
You say what I'm feeling, I always conceal
But could you explain exactly what you mean by "feel?!"

Now I get so weary watching men compete
At everything we do, at home or on the street
Best job, best car, always gotta be on top
But now I'm the best "liberated" man at the shop (oops!)

— **Geof Morgan**

It's Only a Wee Wee

As soon as you're born grown-ups check where you pee
And then they decide just how you're gonna be
Girls pink & quiet, boys noisy & blue
Seems like a dumb way to choose what you'll do

G C / D G :||

It's only a wee-wee so what's the big deal?
It's only a wee-wee so what's all the fuss?
It's only a wee-wee & everyone's got one
There's better things to discuss!

Now girls must use make-up, girls' names & girls' clothes
And boys must use sneakers but not panty hose
The grown-ups will teach you the rules to their dance
And if you get confused they'll say "Look in your pants!"

If I live to be nine I won't understand
Why grown-ups are tot'ly obsessed with their glands
If I touch myself "Don't you do that!" I'm told
And they treat me like I might explode!

Grown-ups watch closely each move that we make
Boys must not cry & girls must make cake
It's all very formal & I think it smells:
Let's be abnormal & act like ourselves!

— **Peter Alsop**

John Wayne Image

I don't want your John Wayne Image
I don't want to dominate
I'll just be a human being
I'm taking back my life again

A - / D A / / E A

I don't want your corporations
I don't want to rape the land
Let me live without destroying
I'm taking back my life again

I don't want your business office
I don't want your suit & tie
I don't want to be valued

By my work until I die
Time has come for a changing image
All we want's the chance to give
Men & women who want a difference
Support for alternatives

I don't want male competition
I don't want to beat you down
Let me take your hand & love you
And we'll turn this world around

— **w: Bruce Kokopchi, Peter Kokopeli & Scott Glascock**
— **m: trad. "East Virginia"**

Let the Woman in You Come Through

(intro) You're holding in 'cause you're a
Man who never cries
I'm not as tough as you, my friend
But since you ask for my advice:

Dmaj7 D6

(in D capo up) Dmaj7 - / D6 - / D B7 / Em7 - A -

Let the woman in you come thru
She's trying to let you know she's there
She colors everything you do
And the man in you gets scared.

Dmaj7 - / D B7 / G - / A D

You like to dance, I've seen you dance
When you thought no one was there
I've heard sorrow in your voice
While you laugh like you don't care
It's hard to hide your gentle side
It's a lonely way to be
Take it from a friend who knows
An old, old friend like me

Dmaj7 - / D B7 / G - / Em7 A :||

You'll fight to prove that you're a man
You'll fight to prove you're right
You work hard & you play hard
And you stay up late at night
Working hard's a way to hide
From the dumb things some folks say
But holding tenderness inside
Is only throwing it away

So you tell me that I'm crazy
And I know you don't like kids
Especially little sissies
Yeah, I know you never did
But I've seen you with the tough ones
The ones the others all condemn
And you know that they're the frightened ones
And you know 'cause you're like them

(last cho) Let the woman in you come thru
Be a different kind of brave
She'll show you love's the difference
Between a free man & a slave

— **Peter Alsop**

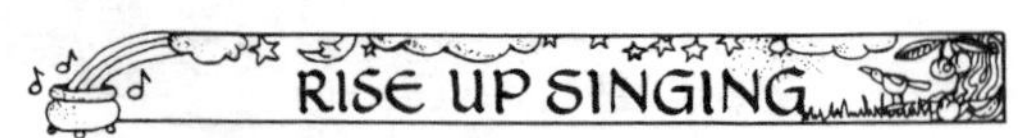

Rock Me, Roll Me

The hardest things to think about are things you feel the most
And thinking of you now, that's what I feel
Like storms that drag the ocean floor & lift it towards the coast
You bring my childhood back so close & real

C Dm G C / - F G - :||

Rock me, roll me, Daddy won't you hold me?
Keep me in your arms the whole night thru
Across the dreams of 30 years, they're sleeping side by side
The child in me, the newborn child that's you

F G C F / - C G - / F G C F / Dm G C -

It isn't just the making love, that's made you what you are
And brought the milk that keeps you growing strong
It's knowing that what you become depends on how I live
That makes me stare at you so hard & long

If all my past & future life was rolled up in a ball
Would you take it in your arms & hold it tight?
If the frightened child I used to be was standing by the door
Would you share your sleep with him tonight?

— Si Kahn

 OY16

Rock Me to Sleep

All I can hear are the crickets
And the whistle from some lonely freight
I've been working so hard to make everything right
But for now it'll just have to wait

(in 3/4) C - F - / C - G - / C - F - / - - G -

'Cause tonight I'd like you to rock me to sleep
I'd like you to sing me a song
I'm tired of trying to figure things out
And I'm tired of being so strong

C - FCG C / F - C - / / F FCG C -

I've never been too good at asking
I'm more apt to do it alone
And it's strange how a lot of us think something's wrong
If we can't do it all on our own

It's funny how times when you're hurting
Make what's so familiar seem strange
So when you need help, it's hardest to ask
And it always takes so long to change

— Tom Hunter

 OY17

Stouthearted Men

(intro) You who have dreams if you act they will come true!
To turn your dreams to a fact, it's up to you!
If you have the soul & the spirit, never fear it, you'll see it thru
Hearts can inspire other hearts with their fire
For the strong obey when a strong man shows them the way!

Am E7 F E7 / Am Em EmB7 E
DmE Am DmE F / C Em F C / F Am E -

Give me some men who are stouthearted men
Who will fight for the right they adore
Start me with 10 who are stouthearted men
And I'll soon give you 10,000 more, Oh!
Shoulder to shoulder & bolder & bolder
They grow as they go to the fore!
Then, there's nothing in the world can halt or mar a plan
When stouthearted men can stand together man to man!

A - / - E / BmE BmE / BmE AE
A - / AF# Bm / G A E A / G AF# BmE A

— w: Oscar Hammerstein II — m: Sigmund Romberg

 OY18

What to Do

I'm still dizzy from my first cigarette
I'd tell you of my first drunk but mostly I forget
Father, can you tell me the false from true
Mother, can you tell me what to do

C G / Am G // C G / AmD G

I just bought a razor & I'm learning to shave
I don't want a burial in an early grave / **Father...**

I was never good at sports, always sickly & frail
Could I take five years in the Lewisburg jail?...

I first kissed Betsy just the other day
I'm not sure I'm ready to go & run away

What should I do in answer to the call?
I don't want to kill, no, I don't want to kill
I just don't want to kill at all

C G / Am - / - G

— Steve & Peter Jones

 OY19

With a Little Bit of Luck

The Lord above gave man an arm of iron
So he could do his job & never shirk
The Lord above gave man an arm of iron **but**
With a little bit of luck, with a little bit of luck
Someone else'll do the blinkin' work
With a little bit (3x) of luck you'll never work

(capo up) G D G - / / C - - B7
C CD D G/C D G -/D - G - - D G -

The Lord above made man to help his neighbor
No matter where, on land or sea & foam
The Lord above made man to help his neighbor but
With...luck / When he comes around you won't be home
With...bit (3x) of luck you won't be home

(bridge) O you may walk the straight & narrow
But with a little bit of luck you'll run amok

C - G - / A - D -

The gentle sex was made for man to marry
To tend his needs & see his food is cooked
The gentle sex was made for man to marry but
With ...luck **(2x)** / You can have it all & not get hooked
With a little bit **(3x)** of luck you won't get hooked
With a little bit **(3x)** of blooming luck!

— w: Alan Jay Lerner — m: Frederick Loewe

 OY20

The Woman She Hold Up

The woman she work outside of the house
Just the same for the man
The man he don't say she cannot work
Like some other husband
    When she come home from work she cook the meal
    He always help clean the dish
    And after she wash all the baby's clothes
    He give all the children a kiss
She say husband, dear, you a good husband
You always give help when I ask
But since you are the Liberated Man
From now on all the housework is your task, & he say:

The woman she hold up half the sky
Maybe even more
The man he hold up the other half
But sometimes his arms get sore

C F / G C :|| **(8x)**

Now the Liberated man, he is very couth
When he go out on a date
He let the woman pay for her own way
And he never hold open the gate
    He talk all night of the book he read
    By the feminist woman writer
    And after the concert by Holly Near
    Back to his bedroom he invite her
When she say "No", he say "I don't understand
I thought you were Liberated too?"
She say "Yes, I am – but you seem to forget
The woman Liberated from you!"

So woman beware of the sensitive man
You know the wolf wear the wool of the sheep
Sometimes the best intention & the kindest of words
Just remind you that talk, it come cheap
    Watch out for the man who say he not perfect
    The way he know the perfect man do
    Whenever he's wrong you will have to pay twice
    When he tell all of his faults to you
Tell him you know of a good therapist
Who can help him if anyone can
And last of all don't even trust the one
Who write the song about the Liberated Man

— Willie Sordill

© 1985 Willie Sordill. Pub by Folkstream Music (BMI). Used by permission. On Swords into Ploughshares. **OY21**

For other songs about men, see espec. the following chapters: FRIENDSHIP, UNITY, and WORK. There is a also special index of songs about personal change at the end of HOPE. See also: "Joseph Dearest" (HOME) "Mary Ellen Carter" (SEA) & "Ballad of Erica Levine" (WOMEN).

MOUNTAIN VOICES

The songs in this section are nearly all songs which spring from the life and experience of people in the Southern Appalachians. Many are about coal mining (both from the miners' viewpoint & the viewpoint of people whose land is stripmined) but others are lovesongs, playsongs, hymns, etc. rooted in Appalachia. Songs are traditional Appalachian unless otherwise noted.

Ballad of Springhill

In the town of Springhill, Nova Scotia
Down in the dark of the Cumberland Mine
There's blood on the coal and the miners lie
In the roads that never saw sun nor sky **(2x)**

(TD ↑ 5) Am G Am G / Am C D Em
F D G Em / Am G Am G / Am G AmG E

In the town of Springhill, you don't sleep easy
Often the earth will tremble and roll
When the earth gets restless, miners die
Bone & blood is the price of coal **(2x – each last line)**

In the town of Springhill, Nova Scotia
Late in the year of '58
Day still comes & the sun still shines
But it's dark as the grave in the Cumberland Mine

Down at the coal face, miners working
Rattle of the belt & the cutter's blade
Rumble of rock & the walls close round
The living & the dead men two miles down

Twelve men lay two miles from the pit shaft
Twelve men lay in the dark & sang
Long hot days in a miner's tomb
It was three feet high & a hundred long

Three days passed & the lamps gave out
And Caleb Rushton he up & says
"There's no more water or light or bread
So we'll live on songs & hope instead"

Listen for the shouts of the bareface miners
Listen thru the rubble for a rescue team
Six hundred feet of coal & slag
Hope imprisoned in a three foot seam

Eight long days & some were rescued
Leaving the dead to lie alone
Thru all their lives they dug their graves
Two miles of earth for a marking stone

— Peggy Seeger

© 1961 Stormking Music Inc. All rights reserved. Used by permission. — aka: "Springhill Mine Disaster." On their Freeborn Man (Rounder). In SO! 9:4, Reprints #4 & Hootenanny SB. On Gr FSingers of the '60s (Vanguard), Bikel FSinger's Choice, Peter Paul & Mary A S Will Rise & rec by Martin Carthy. **OM41**

Bless My Soul (Sweet Wind)

I can hear the sweet winds blowin' thru the valleys & the hills
I can hear the sweet winds blowin' as I go, as I go
I can hear the sweet winds blowin' thru the valleys & the hills
Well I'm goin' home to Jesus *[West Virginia, or Carolina...]*
bless my soul, bless my soul

C ↓ F C / / C F G / 1st / /

I can see the morning breakin'...
I can hear (see, feel) the people stirrin'...

— Bill Staines

© 1974 Folk Legacy Records. Used by permission. — aka: "I Can Feel The Sweet Wind." In his If I Were A Word, Voices fr the Mountains, Sing The Good Earth, Bright Morning Stars *&* V Fav of the V Young. *On Rick Kirby & Michael Kline* They Can't Put It Back. M42

Bright Morning Stars

1. Bright morning stars are rising **(3x)**
Day is a-breakin' in my soul

(in E ↑ 2) D - - - / A - - - / D - - - / A - G D

2. O where are our dear fathers?...
3. They are down in the valley praying...
4. O where are our dear mothers?...
5. They have gone to heaven shoutin'...

6. *...brothers?*
7. *...in the fields a-ploughin' [sowin' seeds of gladness]*
8. *...sisters?* 9. *...by the streams a-dancin'*

— trad. arr. by Tony & Irene Saletan

© 1970 Tony & Irene Saletan. Hillgreen Music (BMI). Used by permission. — On their album (FSI-37) & Penny Whistlers, *Bright Morning Star* Arisin, *Sharon Mtn Harm* Pennywhistlers & A Cool Day & Crooked Corn *(Nonesuch), Judy Collins* Running for My Life, *Happy Traum* Bright... *County Down* Living in the Country, *Kevin Roth* Living & Breathing Wind *(FTS31080) & Emmy Lou Harris* Angel Band. *In* SO! *18:5 &* Reprints *#12,* FS N Am Sings, How Can We Keep fr Singing & Voices fr the Mountains. M43

Careless Love

Love, o love, o careless love! **(3x)**
O look what love has done to me!

E B_7 E - / - - B_7 - / E E_7 A A_m / E B_7 E -

Once I wore my apron low
You'd follow me thru wind & snow

Now my apron strings won't tie
You pass my cabin door right by

You pass my door, you pass my gate
But you won't get by my "38"

What o what will Mother say
When I come home the family way?

She'll tear her hair, she'll bide her tongue
For she did the same when she was young

What o what will Father say?
He ain't my real pa anyway!

On Dave Van Ronk Sings Bals & Blues *(FS3818) &* Black Mtn Blues, *Hudson River Revival alb & Mike Seeger* 2nd Anniv Reunion. *On (& in) Pete Seeger* Am Fav Bals V2 *(FA2321). In* Burl Ives SB *& on his* S of the Revolution. *In* SFest, Hootenanny SB, FSEncyV1, *Lomax* FS of NAm, FS Abecedary, FiresB of FS, *Sandburg* Am SBag, Treas of FS & Here's to the Women. M44

Cindy

You ought to see my Cindy, she lives away down South
She's so sweet the honey bees swarm around her mouth
Git along home, Cindy, Cindy, git along home I say
Git along home, Cindy, Cindy, I'll marry you some day

D - - A / D G DA D // G - D - / G - A D

The first I seen my Cindy, she was standing in the door
Her shoes & stockings in her hand, her feet all over the floor

She took me to her parlor, she cooled me with her fan
She said I was the prettiest thing in the shape of mortal man

She kissed me & she hugged me, she called me sugar plum
She throwed her arms around me, I thought my time had come

Cindy got religion, she had it once before
But when she heard my old banjo, she 'uz the first one on the floor

When Cindy got religion, she shouted all around
She got so full of glory, she shook her stockings down
[or: knocked the preacher down]

I wish I had a needle as fine as I could sew
I'd sew the girls to my coattail & down the road I'd go

I wish I was an apple a-hangin' on a tree
And every time my Cindy passed, she'd take a bite o' me

Cindy in the springtime, Cindy in the fall
If I can't have my own Cindy, I'll have no girl at all

On Pete Seeger Goofing-off Suite *(FA2045), Frank Proffitt* Sings FS *(FA2360), New Lost City Ramblers* V4 *& Mike Seeger* 2nd Anniv Reunion. *In* SFest, Am Fav Bals, *Lomax* FS of NAm, FS Abecedary, Treas of FS, Treas of Am S, FSEncy V1, Best Loved S of the Am People, FS Am Sings & Peoples SB. M45

Coal Mining Woman

I used to come home every night – what would I see?
A pile of talking beer cans where my husband used to be
The only time he got off his butt was when he got on my back
If marriages are made in heaven, you can just take this one back

CF C F C / F C - G / 1st / F C G C

I told him I was tired but he never heard a word I said
The only words he seemed to hear were "food" & "beer" & "bed"
I was waiting on tables for tips each day, waiting on him each night
If I'd a had the money I'd have been long gone out of sight

Now I'm one mile down & 50 ft. high
Drawing good wages & drawing the line
'Cause you can't ride the train if you can't buy the ticket
I'm a coal mining woman just claiming what's mine

F - - C / F - D G / C G C F / - C G C

I'm a safety inspector now, working down in the hole
Making a living & living alone
Some of these men they say I don't earn my pay
We'd sure as hell be equal if the roof caved in today

So come all you women who live in these hills
You can't own your life if you can't pay the bills
If you can't get your husband to treat you just right
Better shut down the portals & walk out on strike!

— Si Kahn

© Joe Hill Music (ASCAP). All rights reserved. Used by permission. M46

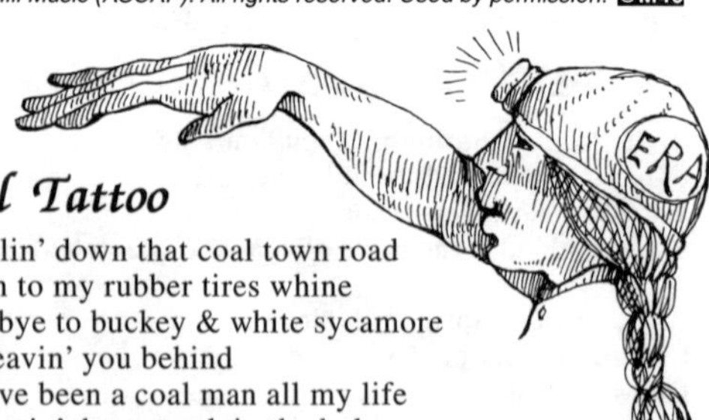

Coal Tattoo

Travelin' down that coal town road
Listen to my rubber tires whine
Goodbye to buckey & white sycamore
I'm leavin' you behind
I've been a coal man all my life
Layin' down track in the hole
Got a back like an ironwood bent by the wind
Blood veins blue as the coal **(2x)**

E_m - C E_m / C D E_m - :|| G - D G / G D C G
G - C G / C D C - / E_m D E_m -

Somebody said that's a strange tattoo
You have on the side of your head
I said that's the blue print left by the coal
Just a little more & I'd be dead
But I love the rumble & I love the dark
I love the cool of the slate
But it's on down the new road lookin' for a job
This travelin' & lookin' I hate **(2x)**

I've stood for the union, walked in the line
Fought against the company
Stood for the U.M.W. of A.
Now who's gonna stand for me?
I got no house & I got no pay
Just got a worried soul
And this blue tattoo on the side of my head
Left by the number nine coal **(2x)**

Some day when I die & go
To heaven, the land of my dreams
I won't have to worry on losin' my job
To bad times 'n' big machines
I ain't gonna pay my money away
And lose my hospital plans
I'm gonna pick coal while the blue heavens roll
And sing with the angel bands **(2x)**

— Billy Edd Wheeler

© 1964 Quartet Music Inc. & Bexhill Music. All rights on behalf of Quartet Music administered by WB Music Corp. Used by permission. — aka: "Coal Town Road." On his Wild Mtn Flowers *(FF85), Rich Kirby & Michael Kline* They Can't Put It Back, *Pete Kennedy* Rhythm Ranch, *Jim Croce* Junk Food Junkie, Candie & Guy Carawan *& rec by the Kingston Trio. In* Judy Collins SB *& on her* Conc. *In* Voices fr the Mtns. OM47

The Coming of the Road

O now that our mountain is growing
With people hungry for wealth
How come it's you that's a-going
And I'm left alone by myself?
We used to hunt the cool caverns
Deep in our forest of green
Then came the road & the tavern
And you found a new love it seems

G D Em - / C D G - / - D Em A / C - D - :||

Once I had you & the wildwoods
Now it's just dusty roads
And I can't help from blamin' your going
On the coming, the coming of the roads

G A D - / C D G - / G D F E* / C - D - G - - -

Look how they've cut all to pieces (*or G D C A)
Our ancient poplar & oak
And the hillsides are stained with the greases
That burned up the heavens with smoke
You used to curse the bold crewmen
Who stripped our land of its ore
Now you've changed & you've gone over to them
And you've learned to love what you hated before

Once I thanked God for my treasure
Now like rust it corrodes
And I can't help from blaming your goin'
On the coming, the coming of the roads

— Billy Edd Wheeler

© 1964 Quartet Music, Inc. & Bexhill Music. All rights on behalf of Quartet Music administered by WB Music Corp. Used by permission. — On his Wild Mtn Flowers *(FF85), Prisc Herdman* Darkness into Light *(FF) & rec by Johnny Darrell & Anita Carter. In* Judy Collins *& on her* 5th Alb. *In* Survival SB & Voices fr the Mtns. OM48

MOUNTAIN VOICES

Copper Kettle

Get you a copper kettle, get you a copper coil
Fill it with new-mixed corn mash & never more you'll toil
You just lay there by the juniper while the fires burn bright
You just watch them jugs a-fillin' in the pale moonlight

(in 3/4) CG C CG7 C / E Am D G //

Am E Am E / Am Dm AmE Am (G)

Fill your fire with hickory, hickory, ash & oak
Don't use no green or rotten wood or they'll git you by the smoke

My daddy he made whiskey, my grandad he did, too
We ain't paid no whiskey tax since 1792

I'd rather have corn whiskey, than anything I know
I'd rather be here on moonshine hill than down in the town below

God bless you, copper kettle, may you never stop
Just let us hear that whiskey goin' "Drop, drop, drop"

— Albert F. Beddoe

TRO © 1953 (renewed 1981), 1961, & 1964 Melody Trails Inc., NY, NY. International copyright secured. All rights reserved. Used by permission. — In SO! 14:6, Joan Baez SB & FS Abeceday. *On Dylan* Self Portrait. OM49

Cripple Creek

I got a gal at the head of the creek
Go up to see her 'bout the middle of the week
Kiss her on the mouth, just as sweet as any wine
Wraps herself around me like a sweet pertater vine

D - G D / - - A7 D :||

Goin' up Cripple Creek, goin' on a run
Goin' up Cripple Creek to have a little fun
Goin' up Cripple Creek, goin' in a whirl
Goin' up Cripple Creek to see my girl

D - - - / - - A7 D :||

Girls on the Cripple Creek 'bout half grown
Jump on a boy like a dog on a bone
Roll my britches up to my knees
I'll wade old Cripple Creek when I please

Cripple Creek's wide & Cripple Creek's deep
I'll wade old Cripple Creek afore I sleep
Roads are rocky & the hillside's muddy
And I'm so drunk that I can't stand steady

Kids up on Cripple Creek they so free
Jump on your lap like a squirrel up a tree
We hold on tight when things feel bad
Laugh when you're happy & cry when you're sad

One time it rained 'bout a week or more
I never saw such mud before
We ran 'round naked like little greased pigs
Stood on our heads & danced a jig

When grandma died at a hundred & two
We danced & we sang like she asked us to
Folks drove in from miles around
To help lay grandma in the ground

Loving __________**(friend's name)** *is so easy*
Cuz I love her **(him)** *& she* **(he)** *loves me*
If I had all the gold on earth
It still wouldn't touch what a good friend's worth

— new v. Peter Blood

New words © 1988 Sing Out Corp. — On Best of Buffy Sainte-Marie, *Pete Seeger* The Essential & Darling Corey, *Doc Watson & Jean Ritchie* At Folk City, *The Dillards* Homecoming, *Leo Kottke* Mudlark & 1971-1976, *Guy Carawan* S with, *J.E. Mainer* V14 & V20, *Michael Cooney* Still Cooney *(Front Hall), Stanley Bros* On Radio *(Country) & Don MacLean* Solo. *In* 1001 Jumbo SB, *Lomax* FS of NAm & FSEncyV2. OM50

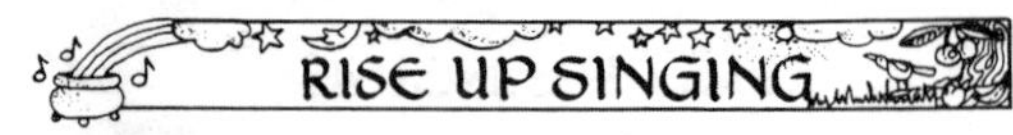

Dark as a Dungeon

Come all you young fellas so fair & so fine
And seek not your fortune way down in the mine
It will form as a habit & seep in your soul
Til the stream of your blood is as black as the coal

(in 3/4) A - D E / A - D A :||

Well it's dark as a dungeon & damp as the dew
Where the dangers are double & the pleasures are few
Where the rain never falls & the sun never shines
Well it's dark as a dungeon way down in the mines

E - A - / E - D A / - - D E / A - D A

It's many a man I have known in my day
Who lived but to labor his whole life away
Like a fiend with his dope or a drunkard his wine
A man must have lust for the lure of the mine
The morning, the evening, the middle of day
They're the same to the miner who labors away
And the one who's not careful will never survive
One fall of the slate & you're buried alive
I hope when I die & the ages shall roll
My body will blacken & turn into coal
Then I'll look from the door of my heavenly home
And pity the miner that's diggin' my bones

— **Merle Travis**

© 1947 American Music Inc. Copyright renewed, assigned to Unichappell Music Inc. (Rightsong Music, Publisher) International copyright secured. All rights reserved. Printed in USA. On his FS of the Hills *(orig rec) &* Back Home. *On Weavers* Together Again, *Patr Sky* Thru a Window, *Jim Kweskin* America *& Grandpa Jones* With Ramona. *In* SO! *3:8 & 44:4 Lomax* FS of NAm *&* S of Work & Protest. OM51

Darlin' Corey

Wake up, wake up, darlin' Corey!
What makes you sleep so sound?
The revenue officers are comin
Gonna tear your still-house down

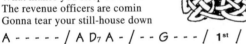

A - - - - - / A D7 A - / - - G - - - / 1st /

Go 'way, go 'way, darlin' Corey
Quit hangin' 'round my bed
Pretty women run me distracted
Corn likker's killin' me dead
[Corn liquor ruin my body / Pretty women gone to my head]

The first time I saw darlin' Corey
She was standin' by the door
Her shoes & stockin's in her hands
And her feet all over the floor

The next time I saw darlin' Corey
She was standin' by the banks of the sea
She had a pistol strapped around her body
And a banjo on her knee

The last time I saw darlin' Corey
She had a wine glass in her hand
She was drinkin' that sweet pizen likker
With a low-down gamblin' man

Dig a hole, dig a hole in the meadow
Dig a hole in the cold, cold ground
Go & dig me a hole in the meadow
Just to lay darlin' Corey down

Don't you hear them bluebirds a-singin'?
Don't you hear that mournful sound
They're preachin' Corey's funeral
In the lonesome graveyard ground

In SO! 7:3, 44:4 & Reprints #2, FSEncyV2, Hootenanny SB, Lib'd Woman's SB, Treas of Am S & S for Pickin & Singin. On Weavers Together Again, At Carnegie Hall & Gr H. On Doc Watson & the Boys (UA), The New Lost City Ramblers 20 Yr Conc (FF), Pete Seeger Darling Corey (FS2003) & Gr H, & Ives Wayfaring Stranger. OM52

Draglines

Draglines at my heart, they're tearing us apart
And the mountainside where we were born –
must I weep &
Mourn for the land, it took ten million years to form?
Now all my eyes can see are just the bleeding scars across
The mountainside, across the mountainside

C F C F / C F G G7 :|| C F C -
(last chorus) C F C F C -

Coalport, PA, just a little town
Tucked too far away for anyone to know
But the folks born & raised for six generations
Working day by day, trying to keep themselves a home

C F G G7 / / / C F C (G)

Our neighbors down the road, they farmed twelve acres
Worked a heavy load, poor as dirt tho' they tried
Til the coal company came thru, said "We'll mine your land
Take the burden off of you & we'll see that you get by"

First they tore down their house where their grandma
And all the kids were born, they just brushed it all aside
Then came the big machines, ripped up the trees
And muddied all the streams while the family stood & cried

(last cho) **Draglines at my heart, they're tearing us apart**
And the mountainside where we were born – o take
warning that
The storm clouds will come & block out the sun that's
Shining on the folks who seek their fortunes off the families
Who have died, trying to survive **across the mountainside**

— **Deborah Silverstein**

© 1977 Author/Happy Valley Music (BMI). Used by permission. — On They'll Never Keep Us Down *(Rounder 4012),* Swords into Plowshares *(FolkTrad), Peggy Seeger* Fr Where I Stand, *New Harm Sisterhood Band* And Ain't I a Woman *(Ladyslipper) & Guy Carawan* S of Struggle & Celeb *(FF).* OM53

Green Rollin' Hills

O the green rolling hills of West Virginia
Are the nearest thing to heaven that I know
Tho' the times are sad & drear & I cannot linger here
They will keep me & never let me go

D A D D7 / G - A - / D - G - / D A D -

My daddy said don't ever be a miner
For a miner's grave is all you'll ever own
Well it's hard times everywhere, I can't find a dime to spare
These are the worst times I've ever known

So I'll move away into some crowded city
In some northern factory town you'll find me there
Tho' I leave the past behind, I will never change my mind
These troubled times are more than I can bear

Well I traveled to a crowded northern city
So far away & lonesome from my home
There were no jobs anywhere & I could not linger there
So I started out once more to search & roam

While traveling all around the open country
Finding people in the same sad shape as me
This one lonely thought came clear, we've nothing left to fear
We must fight & win the battle to be free

But someday I'll go back to West Virginia
To the green rolling hills I love so well
Yes, someday I'll go home & I know I'll right the wrongs
And these troubled times will follow me no more

— **Bruce Phillips (v3,4 S. Worcester, v5 H. Dickens/A. Gerrard)**

© 1971 by On Strike Music. All rights administered by Music Management, PO Box 174, Pleasantville NY 10570. Used by permission. — In Voices fr the Mtns. *On Dickens & Gerrard* Hazel & Alice. OM54

Jenny's Gone Away

Jenny's gone away, Jenny's gone to Ohio*
Jenny's gone away
*[*later v. use: Cleveland town, Detroit town, Baltimore, etc.]*

D Em A DG / DA D

Jenny's wearing strings & rags, **Jenny's gone away (repeat)**

D DEm D Em / A DG DA D

Jenny was a pretty gal don't you know, **Jenny's...**
Worked until her hair turned gray, **Jenny's...**

Jenny's hill got stripped away...
Strip mine operators had their way...

Starvation was her baby's fate...
Caseworker said she was a burden to the state...

The army took Jenny's brother today...
He'll come home in a pine box & stay, but...

Jenny's man died in the Farmington mine...
Company insurance didn't treat her so kind, &...

Jenny didn't want to go away...
The company took her place to stay, &...

— **w: Rich Kirby & Michael Kline**
— **m: Charlie Tart & Phillip Kennedy**

Words © 1971 Kirby & Kline. Music 1960 Tart & Kennedy. Used by permission. — On Kirby & Kline They Can't Put It Back *(June Appal). In* Voices fr the Mtns. *Orig words ("Ginnie's Gone to Ohio") in* How Can We Keep fr Singing. OM55

Jesus, Jesus, Rest Your Head

Jesus, Jesus, rest your head, you has got a manger bed
All the evil folk on earth sleep on feathers at their birth
Jesus, Jesus, rest your head, you has got a manger bed

C F C - (2x) / F C Dm C F C Dm G
C F C - C F G C

Have you heard about our Jesus?
Have you heard about his fate?
How his mammy went to that stable
On that Christmas Eve so late?
Winds were blowing, cows were lowing
Stars were glowing, glowing, glowing

Am7 - Dm Am / F Dm E Am :||
F Dm C Dm / Am Dm Am G

To that manger came then wise men
Bringing things from hin & yon
For the mother & the father
And the blessed little Son
Milkmaids left their fields & flocks
And sat beside the ass & ox

John Jacob Niles published an arrangement adap fr the singing of 3 people in Hardin Co. KY. Sheet music & colls are avail fr G.Schirmer/Music Sales. Also in S of the Spirit. OM56

John Henry

John Henry was a little baby
Sittin' on his papa's knee
He picked up a hammer & a little piece of steel
Said "Hammer's gonna be the death of me, **Lord, Lord!**
Hammer's gonna be the death of me"

(TD ↑ 3) A - / - E / A D7 / / AE A

The captain said to John Henry
"Gonna bring that steam drill 'round
Gonna bring that steam drill out on the job
Gonna whop that steel on down **Lord, Lord** / Whop..."

John Henry told his captain
"A man ain't nothin' but a man
But before I let your steam drill beat me down
I'd die with a hammer in my hand..."

John Henry said to his shaker
"Shaker, why don't you sing?
I'm throwin' 30 lbs. from my hips on down
Just listen to that cold steel ring..."

John Henry said to his shaker
"Shaker, you'd better pray
'Cause if I miss that little piece of steel
Tomorrow be your buryin' day!'"

The shaker said to John Henry
"I think this mountain's cavin' in!"
John Henry said to his shaker, "Man
That ain't nothin' but my hammer suckin' wind!"

The man that invented the steam drill
Thought he was mighty fine
But John Henry made 15 ft.
The steam drill only made nine...

John Henry hammered in the mountain
His hammer was striking fire
But he worked so hard, he broke his poor heart
He laid down his hammer & he died...

John Henry had a little woman
Her name was Polly Ann
John Henry took sick & went to his bed
Polly Ann drove steel like a man...

John Henry had a little baby
You could hold him in the palm of your hand
The last words I heard that poor boy say
My daddy was a steel-driving man...

They took John Henry to the graveyard
And they buried him in the sand
And every locomotive comes a-roaring by
Says "There lies a steel-driving man..."

Well every Monday morning
When the bluebirds begin to sing
You can hear John Henry a mile or more
You can hear John Henry's hammer ring...

This story can apparently be traced to a real event which took place in the Swannanoa Tunnel in West Virginia in the 1870's. In SO! 21:6 & 34:1 (guitar instrum), Am Fav Bals, Treas of FS, Lomax FS of NAm, FS Abecedary, Peoples SB, FSEncyV2, Bluegrass SB & Am FS for Children. On Gr FSingers of the 60's, Big Bill Broonzy Mem Alb, Hudson River Revival alb, Bill Monroe Sings Country S, Sparky Rucker Heroes & Hard Times (SIF1032), Odetta The Essential & At Carnegie Hall, Stanley Bros Shadows of the Past, McCutcheon Howjadoo, Dave Van Ronk Sings Bals & Blues, Black Mtn Blues & Gamblin Blues, Limelighters Alive V1, Pete Seeger John Henry, 3 Saints, 4 Sinners & Carry It On, Happy Traum Relax Your Mind, New Lost City Ramblers V5", Cooney The Cheese Stands Alone", Woody Guthrie Sings FS, Joe Hickerson Drive Dull Care V1. OM57

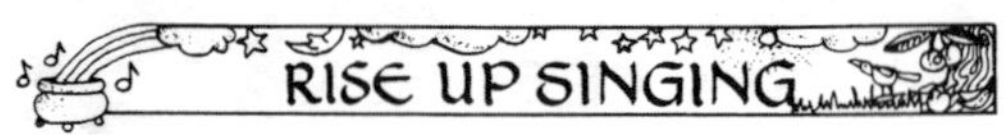

The L&N Don't Stop Here Anymore

O when I was a curlyheaded baby
My daddy set me down upon his knee
Said Son, you go to school & learn your letters
Don't be no dusty miner like me"

(TD ↑ 3) Am Em Am - / / / Em - Am -

For I was born & raised at the mouth of Hazard Holler
Coal cars roarin' & a rumblin' past my door
Now they're standin' rusty, row all empty
And the L&N don't stop here anymore

G - Am - / / Am G Am - / Em - Am -

I used to think my daddy was a black man
With scrip enough to buy the company store
But now he goes downtown with empty pockets
And his face as white as February snow

Last night I dreamed I went down to the office
To get my payday like I done before
Them old cudsy vines* had covered up the doorway
And there was trees & grass, well a-growin' thru the floor

I never thought I'd live to love the coal dust
Never thought I'd pray to hear the tipple roar
But, Lord, how I wish that grass could change to money
Them greenbacks fill my pockets once more

— Than Hall (Jean Ritchie)

*© 1963, 1971 Geordie Music Publishing Inc. Used by permission. — *Kudzu vines were imported fr Japan as a ground cover for spoilbanks fr new hwys & strip mines but have grown out of control & taken over many wooded areas in the South. On* her High Hills & Mtns, Time for Singing *& in her* Celebration of Life. *On Devilish Merry* The Ghost of His Former Self, *Magpie* Working My Life Away, *Lorre Wyatt* Roots & Branches, *Bluestein Fam* Trav Blues *& Kevin Roth* Sings & Plays *(FA2367). In* SO! *36:1 & 44:4.* ⊙M58

Man of Constant Sorrow

I am a man of constant sorrow
I've seen trouble all my days
I bid farewell to old Kentucky
The place where I was born & raised

I: (in C) G C / Am Dm :||

For six long years I've been in trouble
No pleasure here on earth I found
For in this world I'm bound to ramble
I have no friends to help me now

It's fare you well, my own true lover
I never expect to see you again
For I'm bound to ride that northern railroad
Perhaps I'll die upon this train

You may bury me in some deep valley
For many years where I may lay
Then you may learn to love another
While I am sleeping in my grave

Maybe your friends think I'm just a stranger
My face you never will see no more
But there is one promise that is given
I'll meet you on God's golden shore

II: (in G but a cappella) D C / Am G :||

(New verses:) *I Am a Girl of Constant Sorrow*

My mother, how I hated to leave her
Mother dear, she now is dead
But I had to go & leave her
So my children could have bread

For breakfast, we had bulldog gravy
For supper, we had beans & bread
The miners don't have any dinner
And a tick of straw they call a bed

Well, our clothes are always ragged
And our feet are always bare
And I know if there's a Heaven
That we all are going there

Well, we call this Hell on earth, friends
I must tell you all goodbye
O I know you all are hungry
O my darling friends, don't cry

— new v. Sara Ogan Gunning

II: In SO! *14:1 &* Reprints *#7,* FS Abecedary, Bluegrass SB, Here's to the Women & FSEncyV2. *On Sandy Patton* Frank Proffitt Mem Alb *(FSA36), J Collins* Girl of Const Sorrow, *Ralph Stanley* Plays Requests *&* Live In Japan, *Country Gentlemen* Yesterday & Today V2, *The Dillards* Roots & Branches, *Mike Seeger* Oldtime Country M *& Peggy Seeger* A Song for You & Me. *I: In* Peter Paul & Mary SBook *& on their* Best of . *In* Joan Baez SB *& on her* V Early. ⊙M59

A Mole in the Ground

I wish I was a mole in the ground
Yes, I wish I was a mole in the ground
If I was a mole in the ground, I'd root that mountain down
And I wish I was a mole in the ground

C G C - / F - C - / - - F C / - G C -

Well, Kimpy wants a nine dollar shawl
Yes, Kimpy wants a nine dollar shawl
When I come over the hill with a forty dollar bill
'Tis, baby where you been so long?

I've been in the pen so long / Yes I've...
I've been in the pen with the rough & rowdy men
'Tis baby, where you been so long?

O I don't like a railroad man / No I...
A railroad man will kill you when he can
And drink up your blood like wine

O I wish I was a lizard in the spring / Yes I...
If I's a lizard in the spring I'd hear my darling sing
And I wish I was...

O Kimpy, let your hair roll down /Kimpy...
Let your hair roll down & your bangs curl round
O Kimpy, let ...

— Bascom Lamar Lunsford

aka: "I Wish I Was..." Rec by author. Also on M Cooney Singer of Old S, *J McCutcheon* How Can I Keep fr Singing, *Larry Hanks* Tying a Knot *(Long Sleeve104), Doc & Merle Watson* Red Rocking Chair *(FF), Fast Folk* V 2-7, *Patrick Sky* 2 Steps Forward *& Pine River Boys* Our Back. *In Lunsford & Stringfield* 30 & 1 FS fr the So Mtns, SO! *22:4,* FS N Am Sings & Bright Morning Stars. ⊙M60

Mountain Dew

There's an old hollow tree just a little way from me
Where you lay down a dollar or two
You go round the bend & you come back again
With **that good old mountain dew**

G - / C G / - - / GD G

They call it that good old mountain dew (mountain dew)
And them that refuse it are few (quite a few!)
If you hush up your mug, then I'll give you a jug
Of that good old mountain dew!

My uncle Bill has a still on the hill
Where he runs off a gallon or two
The buzzards in the sky get so drunk they can't fly
From sniffing **that...**

My Aunty June had a brand new perfume
It had such a sweet smelling phew (P. U.!)
Imagine her surprise when she had it analyzed
It was nothing but...

The preacher come by with a tear in his eye
[with his head h'isted high]
He said that his wife had the flu
He said that I ort to give him a quart of...

My brother Nort, he is sawed off & short
He measures about four foot two (four – two!)
But he feels like a giant when you give him a pint of...

Mr. Roosevelt told me just how he felt
The day that the dry law went thru:
If your likker's too red, it will swell up your head
Better stick to...

— Scott Weisman & Bascomb L. Lunsford

© 1945 Tannen Music, Inc. and Tree Publishing Co., Inc. Copyright renewed. All rights reserved. Used by permission. *— In* SO! *13:5 &* Reprints *#7,* FSEncyV2, FS Abecedary, Bluegrass SB, S for Pickin & Singin *&* SFest. *On Lulubelle & Scotty* Have I Told You Lately *(OldHomestead), Lee Allen* I'm Leaving You Darling, *Ralph Stanley* Live in Japan *(Rebel2202), Doc Watson* Old Timey Conc *(Vang), Clancy Bros* Hearty & Hellish *& Grandpa Jones* Farm Alb, Sings for Hee Haw & The Legend. OM61

Mountain Song

I have dreamed on this mountain
Since first I was my mother's daughter
And you can't just take my dreams
Away – not with me watching
You may drive a big machine
But I was born a great big woman
And you can't just take my dreams
Away – without me fighting

(better a cappella) Am - / G Am / - DmEm / Am - :||

(bridge) This old mountain raised my many daughters
Some died young, some are still living
If you come here for to take our mountain
Well, we ain't come here to give it

Am - / Dm Am :||

I have dreamed on this mountain
Since first I was my mother's daughter
And you can't just take my dreams
Away – not with me watching
No, you can't just take my dreams
Away – without me fighting
No, you can't just take my dreams away

as 1st v. once thru → Dm FEm / Am - / - DmEm Am -

— Holly Near

©1978 Hereford Music (ASCAP) Used by permission. *— On her* Imagine My Surprise, *Meg Christian* Face the Music *& rec by Reel World String Band. In* SO! 38:4 & Singing for Our Lives. OM62

My Home's Across the Blue Ridge Mountains

1. My home's across the Blue Ridge *[Smoky]* Mountains **(3x)**
And I never expect to see you any more, more, more **(2x)**

D - / A D / - - / A D / /

2. I'm leavin' on a Monday mornin'...
3. Rock my baby, give her candy...
4. Where's the weaving that *[finger-ring]* I gave you?...
5. How can I keep myself from crying?...

— Thomas C. Ashley

© 1938 Southern Music Publishing Co. Inc. Copyright renewed. All rights reserved. Used by permission of CPP Belwin Inc. *— In* SO! *11:1 &* Reprints *#6,* Hootenanny SB & FSEncy V2. *On Joan Baez* David's Alb *&* Country M Alb, *Doc Watson* Old Timey Conc *(Vang), Sparky Rucker* A Home in Tennessee *(GW1004), Happy Traum* Bright Morning Stars *& Tracy & Eloise Schwarz* Fam Band. *In* Bright Morning Stars. OM63

Old Dan Tucker

Now old Dan Tucker's a fine old man
Washed his face in a fryin' pan
Combed his head with a wagon wheel
And died with a toothache in his heel

Get out the way, old Dan Tucker
You're too late to get your supper
(repeat above, or:) Supper's over & dinner's a-cookin'
And old Dan Tucker's just standin' there lookin'

G - / - DG :|| **cho:** G C / D G :||

Now old Dan Tucker is come to town
Riding a billy goat, leading a hound
Hound dog bark & the billy goat jump
Landed Dan Tucker on top of the stump

Now old Dan Tucker he got drunk
Fell in the fire & kicked up a chunk
Red hot coal got in his shoe
And oh my lord, how the ashes flew

Now old Dan Tucker is come to town
Swinging the ladies round & round
First to the right & then to the left
Then to the girl that he loves best

— Dan Emmet

This was the big hit song of 1844 & is another example of a minstrel tune that got taken back into folk tradition & further changed. On (& in) Pete Seeger Am Fav Bals V1 *(FA2320). In* Burl Ives SB *& on his* Bals & FS V1 *&* S of North & South. *On JE Mainer* V19 *& Tracy & Eloise Schwarz* Fam Band. *In* Trea of Am S, FSEncy V1 & FS N Am Sings. OM64

Old Joe Clark

Old Joe Clark's a fine old man, tell you the reason why
He keeps good likker 'round his house, good old Rock & Rye
Fare ye well, Old Joe Clark, fare ye well, I say
Fare ye well, Old Joe Clark, I'm a-goin' away

E - - D / E - ED E :||

Old..., the preacher's son, preached all over the plain
The only text he ever knew was High, low, jack & the game

Old... had a mule, his name was Morgan Brown
And every tooth in that mule's head was 16" around

Old... had a yellow cat, she would neither sing nor pray
She stuck her head in the buttermilk jar & washed her sins away

Old... had a house, 15 stories high
And every story in that house was filled with chicken pie

I went down to Old Joe's house, he invited me to supper
I stumped my toe on the table leg & stuck my nose in the butter

Now I wouldn't marry a widder, tell you the reason why
She'd have so many children, they'd make those biscuits fly

I wouldn't marry that old maid, tell you the reason why
She blows her nose in the corn-bread & calls it pumpkin pie

16 horses in my team, the leaders they are blind
And every time the sun goes down, there's a pretty girl on my mind

18 miles of mountain road & 15 miles of sand
If I ever travel this road again, I'll be a married man

In SO! *10:4, 34:2 (banjo instrum) &* Reprints *#4,* FSEncyV1, SFest, Hootenanny SB & FS Abecedary. *On Mike & Peggy (& in Ruth) Seeger* Am FS for Children *(Rounder). On Pete Seeger* Frontier Bals V2 *(FA2176),* Darling Corey & Bitter & the Sweet. *On Michael Cooney* Pure Unsweetened, *John Hartford* Morning Bugle, *New Lost City Ramblers* V5 & 20th Anniv Conc, *Guthrie* Lib. of Congress, *Robbie Clemment* Magic Place, *The Dillards* Homecoming *& Merle Travis & Grandpa Jones* Farm & Home. OM65

Paradise

When I was a child, my family would travel
Down to western Kentucky where my parents were born
And there's a backwoods old town that's often remembered
So many times that my memories are worn

(in 3/4) D - G D / - - A D :||

And Daddy won't you take me back to Muhlenberg County
Down by the Green River where Paradise lay?
Well I'm sorry my son, but you're too late in asking
Mr. Peabody's coal train has hauled it away

Well sometimes we'd travel right down the Green River
To the abandoned old prison down by Adrien Hill
Where the air smelled like snakes & we'd shoot with our pistols
But empty pop bottles was all we would kill

Then the coal company came with the world's largest shovel
And they tortured the timber & stripped all the land
Well, they dug for their coal til the land was forsaken
Then they wrote it all down as the progress of man

When I die, let my ashes float down the Green River
Let my soul roll on up to the Rochester Dam
I'll be halfway to heaven with Paradise waiting
Just five miles away from wherever I am

— John Prine

© 1971 Walden Music, Inc. & Sour Grapes Music. Used by permission. All rights reserved. — Paradise was an actual town in E. Kentucky before the area was completely demolished by the Peabody Coal Co.'s stripping operations. On his 1st alb & German Afternoons, *John Denver* Rocky Mtn High, *Jim Ringer* Waitin for the Hard Times *& rec by Country Gentlemen (Vang). In SO! 22:3,* Voices fr the Mtns & Bluegrass SB. OM66

Pretty Saro

Down in some lone valley in some lonesome place
Where the wild birds do whistle & their notes do increase
Farewell pretty Saro, I'll bid you adieu
And I'll dream of pretty Saro wherever I go

(TD ↑ 2) D Em D A / / / /

Your parents don't like me so I understand
They want a freeholder & I have no land
I cannot maintain you on silver & gold
Nor buy all the fine things that a big house can hold

If I were a merchant & could write a fine hand
I'd write my love a letter so that she'd understand
But I'll travel down the river where the waters o'erflow
And I'll dream of pretty Saro wherever I go

— arr & adap Jean Ritchie

© 1940, 1964 Geordie Music Publishing Co. Used by permission. — On her The Most Dulcimer *(GR714), Judy Collins* First 15 Yrs & Maid of Const Sorrow, *Kim Wallach* Coldest Winter, *Pete Seeger* God Bless the Grass, *Joel Mabus* Faeries & Fools *(FF296), Doc Watson* Home Again *& Watson Fam* Tradition. *On Mike & Peggy (& in Ruth) Seeger* Am FS for Children *(Rounder). In SO! 10:4 &* Reprints *#5,* Bells of Rhymney, Joyful Singing, *Sharp* English FS of So. App & FS N Am Sings. OM67

Roll in My Sweet Baby's Arms

Ain't going to work on the railroad
Ain't going to work on the farm
Lay around the shack til the mail train comes back
Then I'll roll in my sweet baby's arms

G - / - D7 / G C / D7 G

Roll in my sweet baby's arms (2x)
Lay around the shack til the mail train comes back
Then I'll roll in my sweet baby's arms

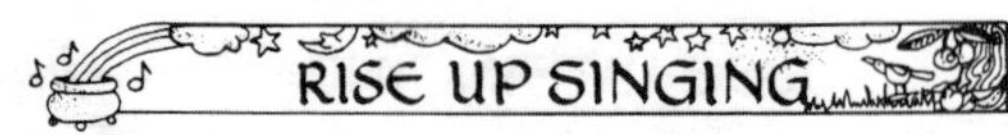

Can't see what's the matter with my own true love
She done quit writing to me
She must think I don't love her like I used to
Ain't that a foolish idea?

Sometimes there's change in the ocean
Sometimes there's change in the sea
Sometimes there's change in my own true love
But there's never no change in me

Mama's a ginger cake baker
Sister can weave & can spin
Dad's got an interest in that old cotton mill
Just watch that old money roll in

They tell me that your parents do not like me
They have drove me away from your door
If I had all my time to do over
I would never go there any more

Now where was you last Friday night
While I was locked up in jail?
Walking the streets with another man
Wouldn't even go my bail

In SO! 13:3 & Reprints #7 & FSEncyV2. *Rec by Buster Carter & Preston Young (1927), The Monroe Bros, and Flatt & Scruggs. Also on* Gr FSingers of the 60's, *Stanley Bros* On Radio *(Country 780), Doc & Merle Watson* Bals fr Deep Gap, *Jack Elliott* Ramblin, *Dillard & Clark* Thru the Morning *& New Lost City Ramblers* V3 *(FA2398).* OM68

Shady Grove

Cheeks as red as the bloomin' rose, eyes of the deepest brown
You are the darlin' of my heart, stay til the sun goes down

Em D EmD Em / /

Shady Grove, my little love, Shady Grove, my dear
Shady Grove, my little love, I'm goin' to leave you here

Went to see my Shady Grove, she was standin' in the door
Shoes & stockin's in her hand, little bare feet on the floor

Wish I had a big, fine horse, corn to feed him on
Pretty little girl stay at home, feed him when I'm gone

Shady Grove, my little love, Shady Grove, I say
Shady Grove, my little love, don't wait til Judgment Day!

In SO! 12:1 & Reprints #5, Hootenanny SB, 1001 Jumbo S, *Lomax* FS of NAm, Celeb of Life *&* FSEncyV2. *On Bryan Bowers* By Heart, *Jean Ritchie* Best of *(Prestige) &* Marchin Across the Grass, *Doc Watson* Memories *(UA), JEMainer* V13 *& Bob Carlin* Fiddle Tunes for Banjo *(Rounder).* OM69

Sixteen Tons

Now some people say a man's made out of mud
But a poor man's made out of muscle & blood
Muscle & blood, skin & bone
[They say] A mind that's weak & a back that's strong

Em ↓ C B7 / /Em - Am - /Em - - B7 /

You load 16 tons & what do you get?
Another day older & deeper in debt
St. Peter, don't you call me cause I can't go
I owe my soul to the company store

/ " / / " /Em - B7 Em (↓ C - B7 **etc.**)

I was born one morning when the sun didn't shine
I picked up my shovel & I walked to the mine
I loaded 16 tons of number one coal
And the straw boss hollered Well bless my soul!

I was born one morning in the drizzling rain
Fighting & trouble is my middle name
I was raised in the bottoms by a momma hound
I'm mean as a dog but I'm gentle as a lamb

If you see me coming, you better step aside
A lot of men didn't & a lot of men died
I got a fist of iron & a fist of steel
If the right one doesn't get you then the left one will

— Merle Travis

 — The refrain line was a favorite expression of Merle's miner father. 8 yrs after Merle released the song on his Back Home *album it became a Tennessee Ernie Ford hit. Also on Weavers* At Carnegie Hall & Gr H. *In* SO! *3:3,* S of Work & Protest, Carry It On, *Lomax* FS of NAm & Ult Country FakeB. **OM70**

Take Me Home, Country Roads

Almost heaven, West Virginia
Blue Ridge Mountains, Shenandoah River
Life is old there, older than the trees
Younger than the mountains, growing like a breeze

G - Em - / D - C G :||

Country roads, take me home
To the place I belong
West Virginia, Mountain Mama
Take me home, country roads

G - D - / Em - C - / G - D - / C - G -

All my memories, gather round her
Miner's lady, stranger to blue water
Dark & dusty, painted on the sky
Misty taste of moonshine, teardrop in my eyes

(bridge) I hear her voice, in the morning hours she calls me
Radio reminds me of my home far away
Drivin' down the road, I get a feelin' that I should have
Been home yesterday, yesterday

Em D G - / C G D - / Em F C G / D - D7 -

— Bill Danoff, Taffy Nivert & John Denver

 — In John Denver SB *& on his* Poems Prayers & Promises, Gr H *& An Eve with. On Carter Fam* Trav Minstrel Band *(CBS). In Readers Dig* Fest of Popular S, Gr S of the '70s *&* Best of the '70s. **OM71**

Voices from the Mountains

You'd better listen to the voices from the mountains
Tryin' to tell you what you just might need to know
'Cause the empire's days are numbered, if you're countin'
And the people just get stronger, blow by blow

(in E) E - / - B7 / A E / A B7

You'd better listen when they talk about strip minin'
It's gonna turn the rollin' hills to acid clay
If you're preachin' all about that silver linin'
You'll be talkin' til the hills are stripped away

You'd better listen to the cries of the dyin' miners
Better feel the pain of the children & the wives
We gotta stand & fight together for survival
And that's bound to mean a change in all our lives

In explosions or from black lung they'll be dyin'
And the operator's guilty of this crime
But the killin' won't be stopped by all your cryin'
We gotta fight for what we need, let's seize the time!

— Rutthy Taubb (formerly Ruthie Gorton)

 — On Peggy Seeger Fr Where I Stand *(FW8563), Guy Carawan* The Land Knows You're There. *In* SO! *24:2,* Friction in the System, Voices fr the Mtns & Out Loud. **OM72**

A goldmine of songs, pictures & lifestories of Appalachian people can be found in Guy & Candie Carawan's Voices from the Mountains *(University of Illinois Press, 1982). Another excellent source is Jean Ritchie's* Celebration of Life *(Geordie Music Publishing, PO Box 361, Fort Washington 11050).*

For other Appalachian songs in this book see: "Cherry Tree Carol" (BALLAD) "Brightest & Best," "Babylon is Falling," "I Will Arise," "Wondrous Love" (FAITH) "New River Train," "Salty Dog" (GOOD) "Aunt Rhody" (LULL) "O Susannah," "She'll Be Comin Round the Mtn" (PLAY) "Shenandoah" (SEA) "Gone Gonna Rise Again" (TIME) "Taft Hartley," & "Which Side Are You On?" (WORK). Also see the GOSPEL chapter and Artists Index listings for: Elizabeth Cotton, New Lost City Ramblers, John Jacob Niles, Jean Ritchie, Doc Watson, and Hedy West.

For non-Appalachian songs about mountains, hiking, etc. see OUTDOORS.

OUTDOORS

All Things Bright and Beautiful

All things bright & beautiful, all creatures great & small
All things wise & wonderful, the Lord God made them all

I: D - - D7 G D A - / D - - Bm D A D -

Each little flower that opens, each little bird that sings
God made their glowing colors, God made their tiny wings

God made the deer & rabbits, the squirrels brown & gray
The fishes in the river, the butterflies so gay

And all the dogs & horses, the friendly cows & sheep
God giveth us his flowers & animals to keep

II: (cho) CF C GD G / CF CAm CG C
(vs:) GD G **(2x)** / Am DG GD GG7

— w: Cecil Frances Alexander, 1848
— m: W.R. Waghorne, 1906

In many hymnals. **OE27**

The Ash Grove

The ash grove how graceful, how plainly 'tis speaking
The harp thru it playing has language for me
Whenever the light thru its branches is breaking
A host of kind faces is gazing on me
The friends of my childhood again are before me
Each step wakes a memory as freely I roam
With soft whispers laden its leaves rustle o'er me
The ash grove, the ash grove alone is my home

(in 3/4) D - Em A/D G A D :|| 1st /Bm - E7 A /1st 2 /

My laughter is over, my step loses lightness
Old countryside measures steal soft on my ear
I only remember the past & its brightness
The dear ones I mourn for again gather here
From out of the shadows their loving looks greet me
And wistfully searching the leafy green dome
I find other faces fond bending to greet me
The ash grove, the ash grove alone is my home

(version II) Down yonder green valley where streamlets meander
When twilight is fading I pensively roam
Or at the bright noontide in solitude wander
Amid the dark shades of the lonely ash grove
'Twas there while the blackbird was cheerfully singing
I first met that dear one, the joy of my heart
Around as for gladness the bluebells were ringing
Ah! then little thought I how soon we should part

D - Em A / D G A D :|| 1st / Bm - E7 A / 1st 2

Still glows the bright sunshine over valley & mountain
Still warbles the blackbird its note from the tree
Still trembles the moonbeam on streamlet & fountain
But what are the beauties of nature to me?
With sorrow, deep sorrow, my heart is laden
All day I go mourning in search of my love
Ye echoes! Oh tell me, where is the sweet loved one
He *[she]* sleeps 'neath the green turf down by the ash grove

— trad.

In Omnibus of Fun, Sing Together, Gambit B of Children's S *&* FS of Eng, Ire, Scot & Wales. OE28

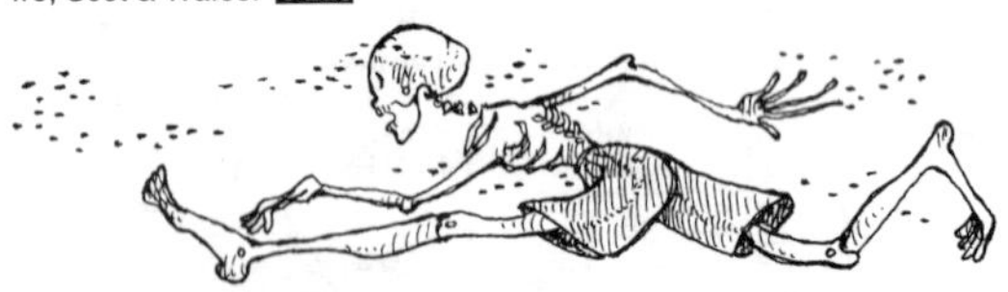

Black Fly Song

'Twas early in the Spring, when I decide to go
To work up in the woods in North Ontario
And the unemployment office said they'd send me thru
To the Little Abitibi with the survey crew

(capo up) C Am / F Em :||

But the black flies, the little black flies
Always the black fly no matter where you go!
I'll die with the black fly a-picking my bones
In North Ontar-i-o-i-o, in North Ontar-i-o

Am - / C - / Dm - - / - Em E7 Am

Now the man Black Toby was the captain of the crew
And he said "I'm gonna tell you boys what we're gonna do
They want to build a power dam & we must find a way
For to make the Little Ab flow around the other way"

So we surveyed to the east & surveyed to the west
And we couldn't make our minds up how to do it best
Little Ab, Little Ab, what shall I do?
For I'm all but goin crazy on the survey crew

It was black fly, black fly everywhere
A-crawlin' in your whiskers, a-crawlin' in your hair
A-swimmin' in the soup & a-swimmin' in the tea
O the devil take the black fly & let me be

Black Toby fell to swearin' cuz the work was gettin' slow
And the state of our morale was a-gettin' pretty low
And the flies swarmed heavy, it was hard to catch a breath
As you staggered up & down the trail talkin' to yourself

Now the bull cook's name was Blind River Joe
If it hadn't been for him we'd've never pulled thru
For he bound up our bruises & he kidded us for fun
And he lathered us with bacon grease & balsam gum

At last the job was over, Black Toby said "We're thru
With the Little Abitibi & the survey crew"
'Twas a wonderful experience & this I know
I'll never go again to North Ontario!

— Wade Hemsworth

 — In SO! 8:2 & Reprints #3 & Bells of Rhymney. *On* Jackie Washington, *Bill Staines* Just Play 1 More Tune *& Guy Carawan* S with. OE29

Captain Kidd (Hymn)

Thru all the world below God is seen all around
Search hills & valleys thru, there He's found
The growing of the corn, the lily & the thorn
The pleasant & forlorn, all declare God is there
In the meadows drest in green there He's seen

Dm Am Dm Am / Dm Am Dm - / Dm Am CDm Am
/ " / DmBb Am Dm - **(better a cappella)**

See springs of water rise, fountains flow, rivers run
The mist that veils the sky hides the sun
Then down the rain doth pour, the ocean it doth roar
And beat upon the shore, all to praise in their lays
That God who ne'er declines His designs

The sun with all his rays, speaks of God as he flies
The comet in her blaze: God she cries
The shining of the stars, the moon when she appears
His sacred name declares, see them shine all divine
The shades in silence prove: God's above

Then let my station be here on earth, as I see
The cont'nents, lights & seas all agree
Thru all the world is made, the forest & the glade
Nor let me be afraid, tho' I dwell on the hill
Since nature's works declare: God is there

— w: trad. (early US) m: Captain Kidd

aka: "Thru All the World Below." 1st sung in Maryland in the early 19th c. Pub in William More Columbian Harmony *(1825), an early book in the "Sacred Harp" tradition of shapenote hymnsinging. Also in SO! 38:4, Geo Jackson* Spir FS of Early Am *(1937) & Alan Lomax* FS of N Am. *For other tune sources see SEA.* OE30

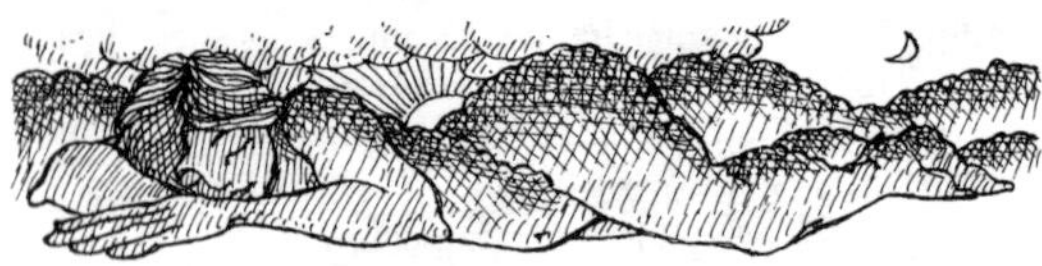

Crawdad

You get a line & I'll get a pole, **honey**
You get a line & I'll get a pole, **babe**
You get a line & I'll... & we'll go down to the crawdad hole
Honey, sugar baby, mine

D - / - A7 / DD7 G7 / DA7 D

Get up old man, you slept too late, **honey**
Get up...late, **babe**
Get up...late, crawdad man done passed your gate / **Honey...**

Yonder come a man with a sack on his back...
  packin' all the crawdads he can pack...
The man fall down & he bust his sack...
  hey, look at them crawdads back in back...
What you gonna do when the lake goes dry...
  sit on the bank & watch the crawdads die...
What you gonna do when the crawdads die...
  sit on the bank until I cry...
Crawdat sittin' on the river bank...
  pickin' his teeth with a two by four plank...
Look at that crawdad crawlin' round...
  He's the mayor of Crawdad Town...
I heard the duck say to the drake...
  there ain't no crawdads in this lake...

— trad. (US)

In SO! *4:1 &* Reprints *#4,* Am Fav Bals, Golden Ency of FS, S for Pickin & Singin, 1001 Jumbo S, FS Ency V2, FS Abecedary, S Fest, Am Treas of Gold Oldies & S Am Sings. *On Pete Seeger* & Big Bill Broonzy *(FS3864), Calif Slim* On the Mall *(SlimRecs), Doc Watson* Old Time Conc *(Vang), Sparky Rucker* A Home in Tenn., *Purly Gates & David Levine* Singin On A Star *(GentleWinds), Nancy Raven* People & Animals *& rec by Alan Arkin.* OE31

De Colores

De colores, de colores se visten los campos en la primavera
De colores, de colores son los pajaritos que vienen de afuera
De colores, de colores es el arco iris que vemos lucir
Y por eso los grandes amores de muchos colores me gustan a mí (2x)

(in 3/4) C - - - G7 - / - - - - C -
C - - - F / F C G C / /

Canta el gallo, canta el gallo con el quiri **(4x)** qui-i
La gallina, la gallina con el cara **(5x)**
Los polluelos, los polluelos con el pío **(4x)** pi
Y por eso los grandes ... (2x)

— trad. (Mexican)

This old spanish song is a favorite of the United Farmworkers. Sp trans: The fields dress up in colors in the spring. In colors the little birds come from far off. In... the rainbow lights the sky. And that's why those big many- colored loves are what I like / The rooster sings with his cockadoodle do, the hen with her cluck cluck, the baby chicks with their cheep cheep. Then they all start at once. And that's... On Baez Gracias a la Vida, *Sarah Pirtle* 2 Hands Hold the Earth *& on (& in) Seeger et al* Carry It On. *In Raffi* 2nd SB *& on his* One Light, One Sun. *In* SO! *25:3 & 44:4 &* Sing the Good Earth *(WAS).* OE32

Edelweiss

Edelweiss, Edelweiss
Every morning you greet me
Small & white, clean & bright
You look happy to meet me
Blossoms of snow may you bloom & grow
Bloom & grow forever
Edelweiss, Edelweiss
Bless my homeland forever (in 3/4)

G D G C / G Em C D / G D G C / G D G -
D - G - / C A D D7 / G G7 C Cm / " /

— w: Oscar Hammerstein II — m: Richard Rodgers

 Fr their musical Sound of Music. *In Broadway SBs.* OE33

Everybody's Talking

Everybody's talking at me, I don't hear a word they're saying
Only the echoes of my mind
People stop & staring, I can't see their faces
Only the shadows of their eyes

C - C7 - / G7 - C - :||

(bridge)
I'm going where the sun keeps shining thru the pouring rain
Going where the weather suits my clothes
Banking off of the northeast wind, sailing on a summer breeze
Skipping over the ocean like a stone

Dm G C C7 / F G C - :||

Everybody's talking at me, I can't hear a word they're saying
Only the echoes of my mind
I won't let you leave my love behind **(2x)**

C - C7 - / G7 - C - / / /

— Fred Neil

 — On his Everybody's Talkin *(Capital) &* Other Side of This Life, *Lena Horne* The Essential, *&* Midnight Cowboy *soundtrack. In* Club Date Fake B, Gr Legal Fake B, Best of the '70s, 100 of the Grtst Easy Listening H *&* 50 Yrs of Country. OE34

Finjan

Haru-ach noshevet k'rira
Nosifa kesam lamdura
Vechach bizro-ot argaman
B'esh ya-aleh ke korban
Ha-esh me-havhevet, shira melavlevet
Sovev lo, sovev ha-finjan

Am Dm / E Am :|| AmE Am / /

Lalala...

FC Dm AmE Am / / AmE Am

The wind is so cool in the night
The logs on the fire are bright
And sparks all a-dancing arise
A-shining like stars in the skies
The singing is hearty & soon thru the party
Around & around goes finjan

— Hebrew: Chaim Hefer Eng: Teddi Schwartz & Arthur Kevess
— m: Moshe Wilensky

aka: "Hafinjan." Hebrew ACUM, Israel. Eng © 1988 Teddi Schwartz. All rights reserved. Used by permission. — "Finjan is an Arabic name for an old type of coffee pot, held by its long handle over an open flame. After a hard day's work, the pioneers in Israel would often build a fire, sing & relax & pass around Finjan." On Havanagila Festival – El Al *(Tara). In* SO! *39:2,* Israel in S, Fav Hebrew S *&* Harv of Jewish S. OE35

Flower Carol

Spring has now unwrapped the flowers, day is fast reviving
Life in all her growing powers toward the light is striving
Gone the iron touch of cold, winter time & frost time
Seedlings working thru the mold now make up for lost time

D - GA D/ /DA BmD GA D/DA BmA DA G D

Herb & plant that winter long slumbered at their leisure
Now bestirring green & strong, find in growth their pleasure
All the world with beauty fills, gold the green enhancing
Flowers make glee among the hills & set meadows dancing

Thru each wonder of fair days God himself expresses
Beauty follows all his ways as the world he blesses
So as he renews the earth, artist without rival
In his grace of glad new birth, we must seek revival

Earth puts on her dress of glee, flowers and grasses hide her
We go forth in charity – brothers all beside her
For, as man this glory sees in the awakening season
Reason learns the heart's decrees and hearts are led by reason

Praise the Maker, all ye saints; He with glory girt you
He who skies and meadows paints fashioned all your virtue
Praise him, seers, heroes, kings, heralds of perfection
Brothers, praise him, for he brings all to resurrection!

— Eng trans: *Oxford Book of Carols*
— m: trad. (same as "Good King Wenceslas")

JM Neale used the tune to this very old Latin carol ("Tempus Adest Floridum") which appears in the 1582 manuscript Piae Cantiones *for his 19th c. composition "Good King Wenceslas." aka: "Spring Has Now..." On John Roberts & Tony Barrand* Nowell Sing We Clear V3. *In* Oxford B of Carols, Friends Hymnal *&* Joyful Singing. OE36

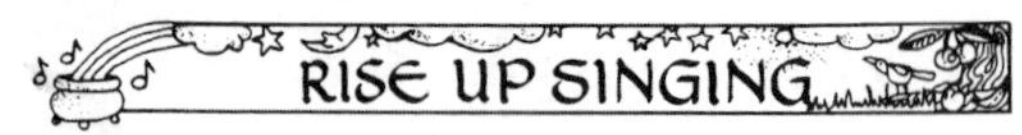

For the Beauty of the Earth

For the beauty of the earth
For the glory of the skies
For the love which from our birth
Over & around us lies
Lord of all, to thee we raise
This our hymn of grateful praise

D - G D / G - A D :|| D - A Bm / G D A D

For the wonder of each hour
Of the day & of the night
Hill & vale & tree & flower
Sun & moon & stars of light

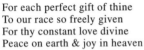

For the joy of human love
Brother, sister, parent, child
Friends on earth & friends above
For all gentle thoughts & mild

For each perfect gift of thine
To our race so freely given
For thy constant love divine
Peace on earth & joy in heaven

— w: F.S. Pierpont, 1864 — m: Conrad Kocher, 1838

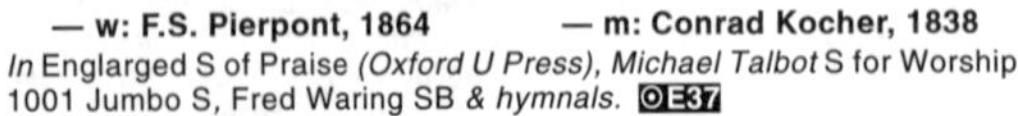

In Englarged S of Praise *(Oxford U Press), Michael Talbot* S for Worship, 1001 Jumbo S, Fred Waring SB *& hymnals.* OE37

The Happy Wanderer

I love to go a-wandering along the mountain track
And as I go I love to sing, my knapsack on my back
Valderi, valdera, valderi, valdera-hahaha hahahaha
Valderi, valdera, my knapsack on my back
(substitute last phrase of each verse)

A - - E/- A DE A/E A E A/E A DE A

I love to wander by the stream that dances in the sun
So joyously it calls to me Come join my happy song
Valderi... / ...valdera Come join my happy song

I wave my hat to all I meet & they wave back to me
And blackbirds call so loud & sweet from every greenwood tree

High overhead the skylark wing, they never rest at home
But just like me they love to sing as o'er the world we roam

O may I go a-wandering until the day I die
And may I always laugh & sing beneath God's clear blue sky

— Eng. w: Antonia Ridge m: Friedrich W. Moller

 — Orig. German. On Susan Stark Rainbow People. *In* Good Fellowship S & V Favs of the V Young *(both WAS)*, Fred Waring SB, 1001 Jumbo S & Golden Era of Nost M. OE38

Here Comes the Sun

Little darlin,' it's been a long cold lonely winter
Little darlin,' it feels like years since you've been here

D - Gmaj7 A7 / /

Here comes the sun (2x) & I say / It's all right

D - Gmaj7 E7 / D (GD GD A7)

Little... the smiles returning to their faces
...it feels like years since it's been here

...I feel the ice is slowly melting
...it feels like years since it's been clear

(Tag:) Sun, sun, sun, here it comes

FC G D - :|| **(repeat ad lib)**

— George Harrison

 Sheet music is available fr Warner Bros. Music. On Beatles Abbey Road & '67-'70, Richie Havens Alarm Clock & Bennet Hammond Walking on Air. In Club Date FakeB. OE39

Joy Is like the Rain

I saw raindrops on my window, joy is like the rain
Laughter runs across my pain, slips away & comes again
Joy is like the rain

DEm AD Em GA D - / G D A D / Em GA D -

I saw clouds upon a mountain, joy is like a cloud
Sometimes silver, sometimes gray, always sun not far away
Joy is like a cloud

I saw Christ in wind & thunder, joy is tried by storm
Christ asleep within my boat, whipped by wind yet still afloat
Joy is tried by storm

I saw raindrops on the river, joy is like the rain
Bit by bit the river grows til all at once it overflows
Joy is like the rain

— Sr. Miriam Therese Winter

 — On (& in) their Joy Is Like the Rain *(AVS101). In* S of the Spirit. OE40

Loch Lomond

By yon bonnie banks & by yon bonnie braes
Where the sun shines bright on Loch Lomond
Where me & my true love were ever wont to be
On the bonnie, bonnie banks of Loch Lomond

C Am F G / /F Am Dm FG / C Am DmG C

O you'll take the high road & I'll take the low road
And I'll be in Scotland before you
But me & my true love will never meet again
On the bonnie, bonnie banks of Loch Lomond

I mind where we parted in yon shady glen
On the steep, steep side of Ben Lomond
Where in deep purple hues the Highland hills we viewed
And the moon coming out in the gloaming

The wee birdies sing & the wild flowers spring
And in sunshine the waters are sleeping
But the broken heart will ken no second spring again
And the world does not know how we're greeting

— trad. (Scottish late 1800s)

Tune is the same as "Red is the Rose" (see LOVE). In FiresB of FS & 1004 FS, Grtst Legal Fake B, FS Ency V1, S That Changed the World, 1001 Jumbo S & Oxford Scot SB *(as "The Bonny Banks").* OE41

Lord, I Got Some Singing to Do

The Lord made all the world in just 6 days
And in the 7th day we sing His praise
For land so green & sky so blue
Lord, Lord, I've got some singing to do

Am - Dm E / / Am G C Dm / Am - E Am

Lord, Lord I've got some singin' to do (3x)
Don't take me, Lord, too soon

Am - D E / Am - Dm Am / 1st / Am E Am -

I'll sing about the moon, the queen of night
Who touches all the world with her silver light
And guides my way the whole night thru / **Lord...**

I'll sing about the sun, my friend the sun
Who says Get up, get up, the day's begun
And warms my way the whole day thru / **Lord...**

I'll sing about the rain, the gentle rain
That falls upon the mountains & the plain
And weeps for me the dark days thru...

I'll sing about the wind who brings to me
The songs of those I love, where they may be
For, Lord, I know they're singin' too...

— Robert Schmertz

 In SO! 8:1 & Reprints *#8. On Folksmiths* We've Got Some Singing to Do *(FA2407).* OE42

Morning Has Broken

Morning has broken like the first morning
Blackbird has spoken like the first bird
Praise for the singing, praise for the morning
Praise for the springing fresh from the Word

(in 3/4) C - Dm G F C / - Em Am D G -

C F - C Am D / G C F G C (F C)

Sweet the rain's new fall sunlit from heaven
Like the first dew fall on the first grass
Praise for the sweetness of the wet garden
Sprung in completeness where His feet pass

Mine is the sunlight, mine is the morning
Born of the one light Eden saw play
Praise with elation, praise every morning
God's re-creation of the new day

— w: Eleanor Farjeon **— m: trad. (Scottish Gaelic)**

 — On Cat Stevens Teaser & the Firecat *&* Gr H *& on Judy Collins* Trust Your Heart. *In* S of the Spirit, Pilgrim Hymnal, Sing the Good Earth *&* 1001 Jumbo S. OE43

O What a Beautiful Morning

There's a bright golden haze on the meadow **(2x)**
The corn is as high as an elephant's eye
An' it looks like it's climbin' clear up to the sky

C G C G / C G Am F / C G C F / C Dm Em G

(in 3/4)

O what a beautiful morning
O what a beautiful day
I've got a beautiful feelin'
Everything's goin' my way

C - F - / C - G - / C - F - / C G C -

All the cattle are standin' like statues **(2x)**
They don't turn their heads as they see me ride by
But a little brown mav'rick is winkin' her eye

All the sounds of the earth are like music **(2x)**
The breeze is so busy it don't miss a tree
And an ole weepin' willer is laughin' at me!

(tag:) Everything's goin' my way / O what a beautiful day

C G C G / C G C -

— w: Oscar Hammerstein II **— m: Richard Rodgers**

 — Fr their musical Oklahoma. *In* Bert Hill SB, Sing the Good Earth *& Broadway SBs.* OE44

Pleasant and Delightful

It was pleasant & delightful on one midsummer's morn
When the green fields & the meadows they were buried in corn
And the blackbirds & thrushes sang on ev'ry green tree
And the larks they sang melodious at the dawning of the day
And the larks they sang melodious **(3x)** at the dawning...

(in 3/4) G - GGD G / - D A D / G - - D

G C GGD G // C D G D / G C GGD G

A sailor & his true love were out walking one day
Said the sailor to his true love "I am bound far away
I am bound for the East Indies, where the loud cannons roar
And I'm going to leave me Nancy, she's the girl that I adore
And I'm going to leave my Nancy **(3x)**, she's the girl..."

Said the sailor to his true love "Well I must be on my way
For our topsails they are hoisted & our anchors are weighed
Our big ship, she lies a-waiting for the next flowing tide
And if ever I return again, I will make you my bride" / & if...

Then a ring from offen her finger she instantly drew
Saying "Take this, dearest William, & me heart will go too"
And as he stood embracing her, tears from her eyes fell
Saying May I go along with you? O no, my love, farewell!"...

— trad. (English)

Aka: "Life on the Rolling Sea." Fr the singing of Lou Killen In SO! *19:4 & 44:4 &* How Can We Keep fr Singing. *On Sam Larner* Now is the Time for Fishing *(FG3507) & on* Blow Ye Winds in the Morning *(Revels).* OE45

(Parody) Cosmic and Freaky

It was cosmic & freaky one midsummer's day
The vibes from the meadow just blew me away
And the blackbirds & thrushes they were into their own thing
And the larks got off on music, man like all they did was sing
And the larks got off on music **(3x)**, man like all...sing

As a freak & his old lady were a-trippin' thru the heather
Said the freak to his lady "Man, my head's not together
So I'm trucking out to Frisco where the alpha waves run free
And the highs you reach on skateboards have transcended LSD..."

Well, a painting of his Earth Shoes she instantly drew
Saying "This is where I'm at, man, I'm still tuned in with you"
As they dug each other's headspace, tears from her eyes he could see
She said "Can't I come?" & he said "No, man, don't lay that trip on me"...

He said, "Listen man, we're getting heavy, I'm not into what's going down
The taxi meter's running & I'm turned off this town
But you'll still be my old lady if you're ever near San Francisco
'Cause after all, man, you're a Pisces – & I'm a Scorpio..."

— new w: Grit Laskin

 On his Unmasked.

Road to the Isles

A far croonin' is a-pullin' me away
As take I wi' my cromack to the road
The far Coolins are a-puttin' love on me
As step I with the sunlight for my load

D - G - / - E A - / D - G - / D A D -

Sure by Tummel & Loch Rannoch & Lochaber I will go
By heather tracks wi' heaven in their wiles
If it's thinkin' in your inner heart braggart's in my step
You've never smelled the tangle of the Isles
(Last cho:) The far Coolins are a-puttin' love on me
As step I wi' my cromack to the Isles

It's by Shiel water the track is to the west
By Aillort & by Morar to the sea
The cool cresses I am thinkin' of for pluck
And bracken for a wink on Mother's knee

The blue islands are a-pullin' me away
Their laughter puts the leap upon the lame
The blue islands from the Skerries to the Lewis
Wi' heather honey taste upon each name

— w: Kenneth MacLeod

— m: Patricia Kennedy-Fraser & Marjorie Kennedy-Fraser

Fr Marjorie Kennedy Fraser, Songs of the Hebrides. *— Cromack=crook-handled walking stick, Coolins=mtns on the Isle of Skye, west of Scotland.* OE46

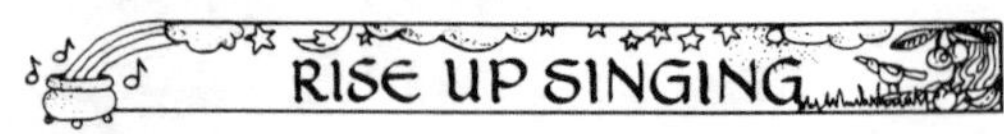

(Americanized Version:) *The Border Trail*

It's the far Northland that's a-calling me away
As take I with my packsack to the road
It's the call on me of the forest in the North
As step I with the sunlight for my load

D - G - / - E A - / D - G - / D A D -

By Lake Duncan & Clear water to Bearskin I will go
Where you see the loon & hear its plaintive wail
If you're thinking in your inner heart there's swagger in my step
You've never been along the Border trail
(Last cho only – softly) **It's the far Northland that's a-calling me away**
As take I with my packsack to the road

It's the flash of paddle blades a-gleaming in the sun
A canoe softly skimming by the shore
It's the tang of pine & bracken coming on the breeze
That calls me to the water ways once more

(winter v.) It's the hiss & glide of skis on newly fallen snow
It's the sparkle of the sun on snow & hoar
It's the snap & tingle of cold air upon the face
That calls me to the snowcapped peaks once more

(as cho) To Mt Washington, Mt Mansfield & to Cannon I will go
Where the thrills of skiing make an endless tale
If you're thinking in your inner heart there's braggart in my talk
You've never skied along the snowbound trail

W: Carol Preston M: "Road to the Isles." In 1956 Girlscout Pocket Handbook *© Boosey and Hawkes a.k.a. "The Far Northland."*

Rocky Mountain High

He was born in the summer of his 27th year
Comin' home to a place he'd never been before
He left yesterday behind him, you might say he was born again
You might say he found a key to every door

(in C) C - F G / C - F - / C Am F G / 2nd /

When he first came to the mountains, his life was far away
On a road & hangin' by a song
But the string's already broken & he doesn't really care
It keeps changin' fast & it don't last for long

But the Colorado Rocky Mountain high
I've seen it rainin' fire in the sky
The shadows in the starlight are softer than a lullaby
Rocky Mountain high – in Colorado (2x)

F G C - / / F G C F - / C - F - / /

He climbed cathedral mountains, he saw silver clouds below
He saw everything as far as you can see
And they say that he got crazy once & tried to touch the sun
And he lost a friend but kept his memory

Now he walks in quiet solitude, the forests & the streams
Seeking grace in every step he takes
His sight has turned inside himself to try & understand
The serenity of a clear blue mountain lake

And that Colorado Rocky Mountain high / I've ...sky
You can talk to God & listen to the casual reply / **Rocky...**

Now his life is full of wonder, but his heart still knows some fear
Of the simple things he cannot comprehend
When they try to tear the mountains down to bring in a couple more
More people, more scars upon the land

(3rd cho:) And that Colorado... / ...sky
Friends around the campfire & everybody's high...
(Final cho:) And that...sky
I know he'd be a poorer man if he never saw an angel fly...

— John Denver & Mike Taylor

 — On his Rocky Mtn High, Gr H & Evening with. *In* Gr S of the '70s. OE47

Rolling Hills of the Borders

When I die, bury me low
Where I can hear the bonny Tweed flow
A sweeter place I never did know
The rolling hills of the borders

(in 3/4) D - G D / - - E7 A / Bm - G D / - - A D

I've traveled far & wandered wide
Seen the Hudson & the Clyde
Courted by Loch Lomond's side
But I dearly love the borders

Well do I have mind the day
With my lass I strolled by the Tay
But all its beauty fades away
Among the hills of the borders

There's a certain place of mind
Bonny lassies there you'll find
Men so sturdy, yet so kind
Among the hills of the borders

— Matt McGinn

© 1967 Janetta Music, Scotland. Used by permission. On his ...Again (Transatlantic). On The Golden Ring 5 Days Singing V1 (FSI41) & in SO! 21:2. OE48

(Parody) *The Rolling Mills of New Jersey*

When I die, bury me low
Where I can hear the petroleum flow
A sweeter sound I never did know
The Rolling Mills of New Jersey

In Hoboken, there will be
Trash as far as the eye can see
Enough for you, enough for me
The garbage cans of New Jersey

Down in Trenton there is a bar
Where the bums come from near & far
They come by truck, they come by car
The lousy bums of New Jersey

When first I started to roam
I traveled far away from Bayonne
Then I sat down & wrote this poem
I wrote an ode to New Jersey

— John Roberts & Tony Barrand

© 1983 John Roberts & Tony Barrand. Used by permission. On their Live at Holsteins! *(FHR31).*

Sakura (Cherry Trees)

Sakura! sakura! / Yayo-i no sora wa
Miwatasu kaghiri, / Kasumi ka? kumo ka?
Ni-o-i zo izuru / Iza ya! Iza ya! / Mini yuka-n

Am Em (2x) / Am - - F / Am F Am E / Am Dm (2x)
Am F Am E / Am Dm (2x) / Am F Dm E

Cherry trees (2x) / Bloom so bright in April breeze
Like a mist or floating cloud / Fragrance fills the air around
Shadows flit along the ground / Come, o come! (2x)
Come, see cherry trees!

— trad. (Japanese) Eng: Katherine F. Rohrbough

English © 1956 World Around Songs, Inc. Used by permission. On Pete Seeger Goofing Off Suite & Darlin Corey. *In* Bright Morning Stars *(WAS).* OE49

Seneca Canoe Song (Kayowajineh)

Kayowajineh, yo ho hey yo ho
Kayowajineh. Kayowajineh-eh
Kayowajineh yo ho hey
Kayowajineh Kayowajineh-eh **(sing a capella)**

D - - - / - A - D / A Bm D - / - A - D

— trad. (Native American)

This song was taught to Ray Fadden by Jesse Cornplanter, a Seneca. "It's important not to change it. Keep that unusual extra beat (yo ho) in the middle of the first line. Sing it high, with a good lungful of air to push it out." – PS. On Pete Seeger Circles & Seasons *& in his* Carry It On. OE50

Soon It's Gonna Rain

(intro) Hear how the wind begins to whisper
See how the leaves go streaming by
Smell how the velvet rain is falling
Out where the fields are warm & dry
Now is the time to run inside & stay
Now is the time to find a hideaway, where we can stay

G D Em D / / / / Em B7 Em F Em - - -
Em B7 Em F Em - - Cdim G7 - - -

Soon it's gonna rain, I can see it
Soon... I can tell / Soon... what're we gonna do?

Cmaj7 Am7 **(2x)** / Cmaj7 Am7 Em A
Fmaj7 D7 Dm7 G Cmaj7 Am7 **(2x)**

Soon... I can feel it
...I can tell / ...what'll we do with you?

(bridge) We'll find four limbs of a tree we'll
Make four walls & a door we'll
Bind it over with leaves &
Run inside & stay

Dm7 - F G / Cmaj7 Am7 Em Am / 1st / Am D Dm G

Then we'll let it rain all around us
Then we'll let it rain, rain pell mell
And we won't complain if it never stops at all
We'll laugh & sing within our own four walls

Cmaj7 Am7 **(2x)** / Cmaj7 Am7 Em A
Fmaj7 D7 Dm7 - A7 - - - /Dm Em F G C - - -

— w: Tom Jones — m: Harvey Schmidt

 — Fr their musical The Fantasticks. *On Madeleine MacNeil* Soon Its Gonna Rain *& Tony Bennett* Many Moods of. OE51

Sound of Music

(intro) My day in the hills has come to an end I know
A star has come out to tell me it's time to go
But deep in the dark green shadows are voices that urge me to stay
So I pause and I want and I listen
For one more sound, for one more lovely thing that the hills might say

C - G - / C - Db - / G C G C / Cm Bb / 3rd /

The hills are alive with the sound of music
With songs they have sung for a thousand years
The hills fill my heart with the sound of music
My heart wants to sing every song it hears

C - B7 - / C - F G / C - B7 - / CF G C -

My heart wants to beat like the wings of the birds that rise
From the lakes to the trees
My heart wants to sigh like a chime that flies
From a church on a breeze

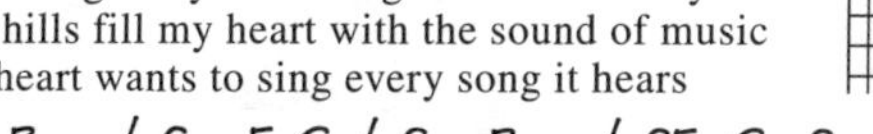

FDdim C / / /D G

To laugh like a brook when it trips & falls
Over stones on its way
To sing thru the night
Like a lark who is learning to pray

FDdim C / / Am Em / AmD G

(as v. 1) I go to the hills when my heart is lonely
I know I will hear what I've heard before
My heart will be blessed with the sound of music
And I'll sing once more

C - B7 - / C - F Fm / C Em F - / Dm G C -

— w: Oscar Hammerstein II — m: Richard Rodgers

 — Fr their musical Sound of Music. *In Broadway SBs.* OE52

Spirit of God

Spirit of God in the clear running water
Blowing to greatness the trees on the hill
Spirit of God in the finger of morning

(in 3/4) C - F C / - - D G / C F Em FCC

Fill the earth, bring it to birth
And blow where you will
Blow, blow, blow til I be
But breath of the Spirit blowing in me

F C F C / Dm G C - / F Em Dm C / F C G C

Down in the meadow the willows are moaning
Sheep in the pastureland cannot lie still
Spirit of God, creation is groaning / **Fill...**

I saw the scar of a year that lay dying
Heard the lament of a lone whippoorwill
Spirit of God, see that cloud crying...

Spirit of God, ev'ryone's heart is lonely
Watching & waiting & hungry until
Spirit of God, we long that you only / Fulfill **the earth...**

— Sr. Miriam Therese Winter

 On (& in) their Joy Is Like the Rain *(AVS101) & in* Worship in Song: A Hymnal for Friends. OE53

Swimming Song

This summer I went swimming
This summer I might have drowned
But I held my breath & I kicked my feet
And I moved my arms around / I moved my arms around

C - / G Am / - F / G Am / G C

This summer I swam in the ocean
And in a swimming pool
I got salt in my wound, cleaned my eyes
I'm a self-destructive fool / A self...

This summer I did the backstroke
And you know that that's not all
I did the breaststroke & the butterfly
And the old Australian crawl / The old...

This summer I swam in a public place
And a reservoir to boot
At the latter I was informal
At the former I wore my suit / I wore my swimming suit

This summer I did swan dives
And jackknifes for you all
And once when you weren't looking
I did a cannonball / I did...

— Loudon Wainwright III

 On his Attempted Mustache, Scruggs Revue Anniv Special, New Riders of the Purple Sage New Riders, Mary McCaslin Sunny Calif (Philo) & on Kate & Anna McGarrigle. OE54

They Call the Wind Maria

Way out here they've got a name for rain & wind & fire
The rain is Tess, the fire's Joe & they call the wind Maria *
Maria blows the stars around & sends the clouds a-flying
Maria makes the mountains sound like folks up there were dying
Maria, Maria / They call the wind Maria

C Am (2x) / C Em FG C / C Am C -
F Em FG C // F - Em - / F G C -

Before I heard Maria's name & heard her wail & whining
I had a gal & she had me & the sun was always shining
But then one day I left that gal, I left her far behind me
And now I'm lost, so goddam lost, not even God can find me...

Out here they've got a name for rain, for wind & fire only
But when you're lost & all alone, there ain't no word but lonely
I feel just like the restless wind, without a star to guide me
Maria blow my love to me, I need my love beside me...

— w: Alan Jay Lerner — m: Frederick Loewe

** Maria is pronounced "Mah-rye-uh."* *— Fr their musical* Paint Your Wagon. *On Country Gentlemen* Yesterday & Today V3 *(Rebel SLP 1535) & Kingston Trio* 25 Yrs. *In Broadway SBs.* OE55

Urge for Going

When I woke up today & found the frost perched on the town
It hovered in a frozen sky & gobbled summer down
When the sun turns traitor cold
And shivering trees are standing in a naked row
I get the urge for going & I never seem to go

D C - D / - - C D / G F / G F A - / 1st

And I get the urge for going when the meadow grass is turning brown
Summertime is falling down, winter's closing in

CG D CG D / CG D DC D

And I had a girl in the summertime with summer colored skin
And not another man in town my darling's heart could win
But when the leaves fell trembling down
And bully winds did rub their faces in the snow
She got the urge for going & I had to let her go
And she got **the urge... when the meadow grass was...**

The warriors of winter give a cold triumphant shout
All that stays is dying, all that lives is getting out
See the geese in chevron flight
Flapping & a-racing on before the snow
They've got the urge for going, they've got the wings to fly
And they get **the urge for going...**

So I'll ply the fire with kindling, pull the blankets to my chin
I'll lock the vagrant winter out & bolt my wandering in
I'd like to call back summertime
And have her stay for just another month or so
She's got the urge for going & I guess she'll have to go
And she gets **the urge for going...is turning brown**
All her empires are **falling down & winter's closing in**
And I get **the urge for going...** / Summertime is **falling...**

— Joni Mitchell

 In SO! 18:4. On Dave Van Ronk *(Polydor) & Tom Rush* The Circle Game. OE56

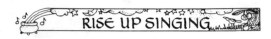

Wild Mountain Thyme

O the summertime is coming & the trees are sweetly blooming
And the wild mountain thyme grows around the purple heather

DG D G D / GD Bm Em G

Will you go, lassie go & we'll all go together
To pluck wild mountain thyme all around the blooming heather
Will you go lassie go?

/ " / " / DG D -

I will build my love a bower by yon crystal flowing fountain
And on it I will pile all the flowers of the mountain

If my true love will not go, I can surely find another
Where the wild mountain thyme grows around the purple heather

I will build my love a shelter on yon high mountain green
And my love shall be the fairest that the summer sun has seen

— trad. (Scottish)

In SO! 13:2 & Reprints #6, 1004 FS, How Can We Keep fr Singing? *&* Judy Collins SB *& on her* Maid of Const Sorrow. *On Joan Baez* Farewell Angelina & Love S Alb, *Judy Small* Reunion *& Madeleine MacNeil* Soon It's Gonna Rain. OE57

You Fill the Day

You fill the day with your glory & your power
You fill the night with your quiet & your deep love

(in C capo up) C Em F CG / /

Run with your head up in the wind (2x) the wind
Your head held high, your soul an open door
And breathe the wind that makes you free (2x)

C G C CG / EmAm DmG / CF G / F G

Stand with your face up in the sun (2x) the sun
Your head held high, your soul an open door
And feel the warmth that makes you free (2x)

Lie with your face up in the rain (2x)... / **Your...door**
And drink the rain that makes you free (2x)

Walk hand in hand with one you love (2x)... / **Your...**
And hold the hand that makes you free (2x)

— Joe Wise

 On his Hand in Hand. OE58

There are a number of other songs about nature, weather, the seasons, hiking, etc. in the following chapters: ECOLOGY, FARM & PRAIRIE, LOVE, LULLABIES, MOUNTAIN VOICES and ROUNDS.

Other songs on this subject include: "On Ikley Moor Bah t'At" (FUN) "By the Light of the Silvery Moon," "Shine On Harvest Moon," "Trail of the Lonesome Pine" (GOLD) "Blackbird," "Turning toward the Morning" (HOPE) & "Foggy Foggy Dew" (TIME).

Andorra

I want to go to Andorra, Andorra, Andorra
I want to go to Andorra, it's a place that I adore
They spent $4 & 90¢ on armaments & their defense
Did you ever hear of such confidence? Andorra, hip hurrah!

G - D G / - - A D / C G B7 Em / C G CD G

In the mountains of the Pyrenees there's an independent state
Its population 5000 souls & I think they're simply great
One hundred seventy square miles big & it's awf'lly dear to me
Spends less than $5 on armaments & this I've got to see

G - D - / - - G - / - - C - / G Em AD G

It's governed by a council, all gentle souls & wise
They've only $5 for armaments & the rest for cakes & pies
They didn't invest in a tommy-gun or a plane to sweep the sky
But they bought some blanks for their cap pistols to shoot on their 4th of July

They live by the arts of farm & field & by making shoes & hats
And they haven't got room in their tiny land for a horde of diplomats
They haven't got room in their tiny land for armies to march about
And if anyone comes with a war budget, they throw the rascals out

I wandered down by the Pentagon, this newspaper clipping in hand
I hollered I want to see everyone in MacNamara's band
I said "Look what they did in Andorra, they put us all to shame
The least is first, the biggest is last, let's get there just the same"

The general said "My dear boy [girl] you just don't understand
We need those things to feel secure in our great & wealthy land"
I said "If security's what you need I'll get a couch for you
A head-shrinker is cheaper & quicker & a damn sight safer too!"

— Malvina Reynolds **(last 2 v. Pete Seeger)**

 — In her Little Boxes. *In* SO! 12:3 & S that Changed the World. *On Pete Seeger* The Bitter & the Sweet. OP26

Bashana Haba'ah

Bashana haba'ah neyshev al hamirpeset
Venispor tziporim nodedot
Yeladim bahufsha yesahaku tofeset
Beyn habayit l'veyn hasadot

Em C D G / Am B7 Em - / - C D7 G / Am B7 Em E7

Od tir'eh, od tir'eh, kama tov yih'ye
Bashana bashana haba'ah (repeat)

Am D7 G Em / Am B7 Em E7 / 1st / Am B7 Em -

Soon the day will arrive when we will be together
And no longer will we live in fear
And the children will smile without wond'ring whether
On that day dark new clouds will appear
Wait & see, wait & see, what a world there will be
If we share, if we care – you & me (repeat)

Some have dreamed, some have died, to make a bright tomorrow
And their vision remains in our heart
Now the torch must be passed with hope & not with sorrow
And a promise to make a new start / **Wait & see...**

— Hebrew: Ehud Manor **— Music: Nurit Hirsch**

 — This is a peace song written after the 6 Day War. In Israeli Guitar B, Israel in S & Harv of Jewish S *(all pub by Tara).* OP27

Carry It On

There's a man by my side walkin'
There's a voice inside me talkin'
There's a word needs a-sayin'
Carry it on, carry it on (2x)

D - / A D / - - / A D / /

They will tell their lyin' stories
Send their dogs to bite our bodies
They will lock us in their prisons / **Carry...**

All their lies be soon forgotten
All their dogs are gonna lie there rottin'
All their prison walls will crumble...

If you can't go on any longer
Take the hand of your sister & brother
Every victory's gonna bring another!...

For the dream never-ending
You can hear the voices blending
Loud & clear, their echoes sending:...

Thru the air the song is winging
Down the years, hope keeps springing
No more tears! We're still singing:...

— Gil Turner **(new v. Marion Wade)**

 — In Sing For Freedom. *In (& on) Pete Seeger* Carry It On. *In* Judy Collins SB *& on her* #5 & 15 Yrs. *On Baez* One Day at a Time, Carry It On, 1st 10 Yrs & Country M Alb. *On* Broadside Singers. OP28

Children of Darkness

Now is the time for your loving, dear
And the time for your company
Now when the light of reason fails
And fires burn on the sea
Now in this age of confusion
I have need for your company

(in 3/4, capo up) D GD / DC D / - - / C A / **1st 2**

It's once I was free to go roaming in
The wind of a springtime mind
It's once the clouds I sailed upon
Were sweet as lilac wine
So why are the breezes of summer, dear
Enlaced with a grim design?

And where was the will of my father when
We raised our swords on high?
And where was my mother's wailing when
Our flags were justified?
And where will we take our pleasures when
Our bodies have been denied?

For I am a wild & a lonely child
And the child of an angry man
Now with the high wars raging, I
Would offer you my hand
For we are the children of darkness and
The prey of a proud, proud land

— Richard Fariña

 On his & Mimi's Reflections in a Crystal Wind *&* Best of. *On Baez* Contemp Bal B. OP29

PEACE

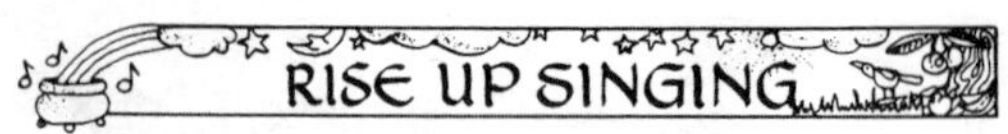

The Cruel War

The cruel war is raging & Johnny has to fight
I want to be with him from morning til night
I want to be with him, **it grieves my heart so**
O let me go with you: **No, my love, no**

G Em Am Bm / Em C D7 (or GC) G :||

I'll go to your captain, get down upon my knees
10,000 gold guineas I'd give for your release
10,000 gold guineas, **it grieves my heart so**
Won't you let me go with you? O no, my love no

Tomorrow is Sunday & Monday is the day
Your captain calls for you & you must obey
Your captain calls for you, **it... / Won't you...**

Your waist is too slender, your fingers are too small
Your cheeks are too rosy to face the cannonball
Your cheeks are too rosy, **it grieves...**

Johnny, o Johnny, I think you are unkind
I love you far better than all other mankind
I love you far better than tongue can express
Won't you let me go with you? O, yes, my love, yes

I'll pull back my hair, men's clothes I'll put on
I'll pass for your comrade as we march along
I'll pass for your comrade & none will ever guess
Won't you let me go with you? Yes, my love, yes

— trad.

Based on Lib. of Congress field recording of Charles Ingenthron in Walnut Shade, MO, made by Vance Randolph. In SO! *14:2,* Reprints *#8,* FSEncyV1, The Legal FakeB *&* Lib'd Woman's SB. *On Peggy Seeger* FS *&* Bals *& Cher* V2. *On* Peter Paul & Mary, *their* Best of *& in their* SB. OP30

Deep Blue Sea

1. Deep blue sea, baby, deep blue sea **(3x)**
Now there's peace in all the lands & o'er the deep blue sea

DGD- G-D-/DGD- G-A- / 1st /D---G DAD-

2. Sleep my child, you are safe & sound **(3x)** for / **Now...**
3. Just yesterday war clouds hung so low **(3x)** but...
4. Love of life finally turned the tide **(3x)** and...

— w: John Bell **— m: trad. ("Deep Blue Sea")**

Words © 1982 John Bell. Used by permission. "When my daughter was 6 1/2, she said as we were driving to school one day 'Daddy, they won't have a war before I'm 21, will they?' Before I could respond, she added 'Or at least they don't shoot little girls before they're 7, do they?' Not long after this I was singing her to sleep & found myself taking an old tune to form a song of reassurance that we adults can sing to the children of the world" — JB. On Peace Gathering S. *For tune sources see SEAS.* OP31

Draft Dodger Rag

I'm just a typical American boy
From a typical American town
I believe in God & Senator Dodd
And in keeping old Castro down
'N when it came my time to serve
I knew "Better dead than red"
But when I got to my old draft board, Buddy
This is what I said:

G - / A - / D7 - / - G :||

"Sarge, I'm only 18, I got a ruptured spleen
And I always carry a purse
I got eyes like a bat & my feet are flat
And my asthma's gettin' worse
O think of my career, my sweetheart dear
My poor old invalid aunt
Besides I ain't no fool, I'm a-goin' to school
And I'm workin' in a defense plant

I got a dislocated disc & a racked-up back
I'm allergic to flowers & bugs
And when the bombshell hits, I get epileptic fits
And I'm addicted to a thousand drugs
I got the weakness woes & I can't touch my toes
I can hardly reach my knees
And if the enemy came close to me
I'd probably start to sneeze

I hate Chou En-Lai & I hope he dies
But one thing you gotta see
That someone's gotta go over there
And that someone isn't me
So I wish you well Sarge, give 'em hell
Yeah, kill a thousand or so
And if you ever get a war without blood & gore
Well, I'll be the first to go!"

— Phil Ochs

© 1964 by Appleseed Music, Inc. All rights reserved. Used by permission. — On his I Ain't Marchin' Anymore *(Elektra) &* Chords of Fame *(A&M) & Pete Seeger* Dangerous S. *In* SO! *15:1 &* Reprints *#9.* OP32

Hymn for Nations

Brother, sing your country's anthem
Shout your land's undying fame
Light the wondrous tale of nations
With your people's golden name
Tell your father's noble story
Raise on high your country's sign
Join, then, in the final glory
Brother, lift your flag with mine!

C - - G / / / C - G C
G C G C / G E AmD G / C - - G / C - G C

Hail the sun of peace, new rising
Hold the war clouds closer furled
Blend our banners, O my brother
In the rainbow of the world!
Red as blood, & blue as heaven
Wise as age, & proud as youth
Melt our colors, wonder woven
In the great white light of Truth!

Build the road of peace before us
Build it wide & deep & long
Speed the slow & check the eager
Help the weak & curb the strong
None shall push aside another
None shall let another fall
March beside me, O my brother
All for one, & one for all!

— w: Josephine Daskam Bacon (3rd v. Don West)
— m: Ludwig van Beethoven (9th Symphony, 1824)

© 1934 UN Assoc of Gr Britain & Ireland. All rights reserved. — In SO! *6:1 &* Reprints *#1 &* Friends Hymnal. OP33

I Ain't Marchin Anymore

I marched to the battle of New Orleans
At the end of the early British war
A young land was a-growin', the young blood started flowin'
But I ain't marchin' anymore
I killed my share of Indians in a thousand different fights
I was there at the Little Big Horn
I saw many men a-lyin', I saw many more a-dyin' / **But...**

D - A - / / D Em C Bm / G - A - :||

'Cause it's always the old who lead us off to war
Always the young to fall
Take a look at what we've won with a sabre & a gun
Tell me, was it worth it all?

G - D - / G D Em - / 1st / G - A -

And I stole California from the Mexican land
I fought in the bloody Civil War
I even killed my brothers & so many others / **But...**
And I marched to the battle of the German Trench
In the war that was bound to end all war
I must have killed a million men & now they want me back again...

And I flew the final mission over Japanese skies
Set off that mighty mushroom roar
When I saw those cities burnin', I knew that I was learnin' that...
Now the congressmen are screamin' as they close the missle plant
United Fruit screams at the Cuban shore
Call it peace or call it treason, call it love or call it reason...

— Phil Ochs

© 1964 Appleseed Music Inc. All rights reserved. Used by permission. — On his I Ain't Marchin'... *&* Chords of Fame. *In SO! 16:1 & 44:4 &* S that Changed the World. *On Bright Morning Star* Live in the US. OP34

I Come and Stand

I come & stand at every door
But none can hear my silent tread
I knock & yet remain unseen
For I am dead, for I am dead

(in 3/4) D C - D / / G D C D / Em - C D

I'm only seven altho' I died
In Hiroshima long ago
I'm seven now as I was then:
When children die, they do not grow

My hair was scorched by swirling flame
My eyes grew dim, my eyes grew blind
Death came & turned my bones to dust
And that was scattered by the wind

I need no fruit, I need no rice
I need no sweets or even bread
I ask for nothing for myself
For I am dead, for I am dead

All that I ask is that for peace
You fight today, you fight today
So that the children of this world
May live & grow & laugh & play!

— w: Nazim Hikmet (Eng: Jeanette Turner)
— m: James Walter ("Great Silkie") **— arr. Pete Seeger**

w: *© 1966 Stormking Music Inc.* ***m:*** *© 1966 Folk Legacy Records. All rights reserved. Used by permission. — Hikmet was a great people's poet who was a prisoner of conscience for a number of yrs in his native Turkey. aka: "Dead Little Girl of Hiroshima." In SO! 11:5, Reprints #5, WHATFG, Anne Hills rec on WHATFG (S of Pete Seeger VI). On Pete Seeger* I Can See a New Day, *Susan Stark* Child of the Nuclear Age, *Byrds* 5th Dimention, *Sally Rogers* Generations *& rec by Joan Baez. For tune sources see BALLADS.* OP35

I Didn't Raise My Boy to Be a Soldier

Ten million soldiers to the war have gone
Who may never return again
Ten million mothers' hearts must break
For the ones who died in vain
Head bowed down in sorrow, thru the lonely years
I heard a mother murmur thru her tears

C - - Am / D G C G / C - Em -
- B7 Em - / F G C G / D - G G7

I didn't raise my boy to be a soldier
I brought him up to be my pride & joy
Who dares to place a musket on his shoulder
To shoot some other mother's darling boy?
Let nations arbitrate their future troubles
It's time to lay the sword & gun away
There'd be no wars today, if mothers all would say:
"I didn't raise my boy to be a soldier!"

C A D - / G - C G / Am - G - / D - G -
/ " / G - E7 - / A - D - / C Am G C

What victory can cheer a mother's heart
When she looks at her blighted home
What victory can bring her back
All she cares to call her own
Let each mother answer in the years to be
Remember that my boy belongs to me

— w: Alfred Bryan **— m: Al Piantadosi**

© 1914 (renewed 1942) by Leo Feist Inc. All rights of Leo Feist Inc. assigned to SBK Catalogue Partnership. All rights administered by SBK Feist Catalog. International copyright secured. Made in USA. All rights reserved. Used by permission of CPP Belwin Inc. — On Guy Carawan The Land Knows You're There *(FF391). In* Golden Era of Nost M V1. OP36

I Feel Like I'm Fixin' to Die Rag

Come on all of you big strong men
Uncle Sam needs your help again
He's got himself in a terrible jam
Way down yonder in Vietnam
So put down your books & pick up a gun
We're gonna have a whole lot of fun!

(in G) D - / G - :|| E A / D G

And it's 1, 2, 3, what are we fighting for?
Don't ask me, I don't give a damn – next stop is Vietnam
And its 5, 6, 7, open up the pearly gates
There ain't no time to wonder why – whoopie, we're all gonna die!

A7 D7 G - / D - G - / 1st / E A D G

Come on, generals, let's move fast
Your big chance has come at last
Now you can go out & get those Reds
The only good Commie is one that's dead
You know that peace can only be won
When we've blown 'em all to kingdom come!

Come on, Wall Street, don't be slow
Why, man, this is war Au-go-go
There's plenty good money to be made
Supplying the army with tools of the trade
Just hope & pray if they drop the Bomb
They drop it on the Viet Cong!

Come on, mothers, throughout the land
Pack your boys off to Vietnam
Come on, fathers, don't hesitate
Send your sons off before it's too late
You can be the first one on your block
To have your boy come home in a box

— Joe McDonald

© 1965 Joe McDonald. © 1977 Alkatraz Corner Music (BMI). Used by permission. — rec by Country Joe & the Fish. In SO! 16:3 & Reprints #11. Also on Gr FSingers of the '60s. OP37

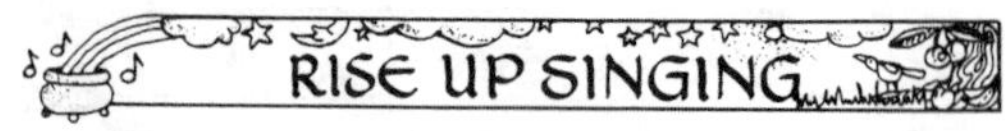

I've Got to Know

I've got to know, yes, I've got to know, friend
Hungry lips ask me wherever I go
Comrades & friends all a-falling around me
I've got to know, yes, I've got to know!

D - G D / - - E A / D - G D / - - A D

Why do your war boats ride on my waters?
Why do your death bombs fall from my skies?
Tell me, why do you burn my farm & my town down?
I've got to know, friend, I've got to know!

What makes your boats haul death to my people?
Nitro blockbusters, big cannons & guns?
Why doesn't your ship bring food & some clothing?
I've sure got to know, folks, I've sure got to know!

Why can't my two hands get a good pay job?
I can still plow & plant, I can still sow!
Why did your lawbook chase me off my good land?
I'd sure like to know, friend, I've just got to know!

What good work did you do, I'd like to ask you
To give you my money right out of my hands?
I built your big house here to hide from my people
Why do you crave to hide so, I'd love to know!

You keep me in jail & you lock me in prison
Your hospital's jammed & your crazyhouse full
What make your cop kill my trade union worker?
You have to talk plain, 'cause I sure have to know!

Why can't I get work & cash a big pay-check?
Why can't I buy things in your place & your store?
Why close my plant down & starve all my buddies?
I'm asking you sir, 'cause I've sure got to know!

— w: Woody Guthrie **— m: trad ("Farther Along")**

TRO © 1963 Ludlow Music, Inc, NY, NY. Made in USA. All rights reserved incl. public performance for profit. Used by permission. International copyright secured. — In his SB, SO! *1:6,* Reprints #1 *&* Bells of Rhymney. *On Sweet Honey in the Rock* Feel Smth Drawing Me. *For tune sources see GOSPEL.* OP38

Johnny, I Hardly Knew You

With your guns & drums & drums & guns, **huroo, huroo (2x)**
With your guns & drums & drums & guns, the enemy nearly slew you
O my darling dear you looked so queer
& Johnny, I hardly knew you

Em - D - / Em - G B7 /
Em D C B7 / EmA CD EmC Em

Where are your eyes that were so mild...**(3x)**
that looked upon the world & smiled
O why did you run from me & the child **& Johnny...**

Where are your legs that used to run...**(3x)**
when first you went to carry a gun
I fear your dancing days are done **&...**

You haven't an arm you haven't a leg...**(3x)**
you're an eyeless, boneless, chickenless egg
You'll have to be put with a bowl to beg **&...**

They're rolling out the guns again...**(3x)**
but they'll never take our sons again
No they'll never take our sons again
yes, Johnny I'm swearing to you

— trad. (Irish)

Ironically the tune from this great antiwar song was used for "When Johnny Comes Marchin Home," a song which glorifies soldiering. On Clancy Bros & Tommy Makem *(TLP1042) & their* Hearty & Hellish *(Shanachie). In* Irish SB, *Bikel* FS & Footnotes, FS Abecedary, FSEncyV2 *&* FiresB of FS. OP39

Last Night I Had the Strangest Dream

Last night I had the strangest dream I'd ever dreamed before
I dreamed the world had all agreed to put an end to war
I dreamed I saw a mighty room, filled with women & men
And the paper they were signing said they'd never fight again

C - F C / G EmAm DmG C / F C G C / /

And when the paper was all signed & a million copies made
They all joined hands & bowed their heads & grateful prayers were prayed
And the people in the streets below were dancing round & round
While swords & guns & uniforms were scattered on the ground

— Ed McCurdy

TRO © 1950 (renewed 1978), 1951 (renewed 1979) & 1955 (renewed 1983) Almanac Music Inc., NY, NY. International copyright secured. Made in USA. All rights reserved incl pub performance for profit. Used by permission. — aka: "Strangest Dream." In Weavers SB *& on their* Gr H. *In Pete Seeger* Am Fav Bals *& on his* World of & Love S for Friends & Foes *(FA2453). In* Joan Baez SB *& on her* V Early. *On Simon & Garfunkel* Wed AM, *Limelighters* Alive v2, *Guy Carawan* S with *(FG3544) & Susan Stark* Child of the Nucl Age. *In* SO! *2:1 & 44:4 &* Lift Every Voice, Childrens S for a Friendly Planet *&* Worship in Song: A Hymnal for Friends. OP40

Let There Be Peace on Earth

Let there be peace on earth & let it begin with me
Let there be peace on earth, the peace that was meant to be
With God as our Father, brothers all are we
[With God our Creator, children all are we]
Let me *[us]* **walk with my brother** *[each other]* **in perfect harmony**

CAm DmG C DmG / C B7 EmB7 G7
Am Em F C / AmD G AmD G

Caug

Let peace begin with me, let this be the moment now
With ev'ry step I take, let this be my solemn vow
To take each moment & live each moment in peace eternally
Let there be peace on earth & let it begin with me

1st 2 above / C Caug F D / CE FC FG C

— Sy Miller & Jill Jackson

© 1955 by Jan-Lee Music. Copyright renewed 1983. Used by permission. On Internatl Childrens Choir S for a Peaceful World *(UNICEF). In* S of the Spirit, Best of Popular S *&* Children's S for a Friendly Planet. OP41

May There Always Be Sunshine

May there always be sunshine
May there always be blue sky
May there always be mama
May there always be me

D - / - Em / - A / - D

Poost vsegda boodyet solntse
Poost vsegda boodyet nyeba
Poost vsegda boodyet mama
Poost vsegda boodoo ya

— w: orig. Russian Lev Oshanin, Eng. Thomas Botting
— m: Arkadi Ostrovsky

© 1964 by MCA Music Canada, a division of MCA Canada Ltd, Willowdale, Ontario. Sole selling agent MCA Music Publishing, a division of MCA, Inc., New York NY 10019. — Written by a Russian schoolchild. On Swords Into Plowshares, Peace Gathering S, *Pete Seeger* Strangers & Cousins *&* Pete & Arlo Together, *Sarah Pirtle* 2 Hands Hold the Earth *(GentleWinds), Michael Cooney* Pure Unsweetened *(Alliance) & Susan Stark* Rainbow People *(as Poost Fsegdah). In* Children's S for a Friendly Planet. OP42

Mrs. McGrath

"O Mrs. McGrath" the sergeant said
"Would you like to make a soldier out of your son Ted?
With a scarlet coat & a big cocked hat
Now Mrs. McGrath, wouldn't you like that?"

Wid yer too-ri-aa, fol-the-diddle-aa
Too-ri-oori-oori-aa (repeat) (pron. "ri" as "rye")

G - - D/ /G C G D/G D G D|: G Em G -/Em D G - :||

So Mrs. McGrath lived on the seashore
For the space of seven long years or more
Til she saw a big ship sailing into the bay
"Hullaloo, buballoo & I think it is he!"

"O Captain dear, where have ye been?
Have you been sailing on the Mediterreen?
Or have you any tidings of my son Ted?
Is the poor boy living or is he dead?"

Then up comes Ted without any legs
And in their place two wooden pegs
She kissed him a dozen times or two
Saying "Holy Moses, 'tisn't you"

"O then were ye drunk or were ye blind
That ye left yer two fine legs behind?
Or was it walking up the sea
Wore yer two fine legs from the knees away?"

"O I wasn't drunk & I wasn't blind
But I left my two fine legs behind
For a cannonball on the fifth of May
Took my two fine legs from the knees away"

"O then, Teddy me boy" the widow cried
"Yer two fine legs were yer mama's pride
Them stumps of a tree wouldn't do at all
Why didn't ye run from the big cannon ball?

All foreign wars I do proclaim
Between Don John & the King of Spain
And by herrin's! I'll make them rue the time
That they swept the legs from a child of mine

O then, if I had ye back again
I'd never let ye go to fight the King of Spain
For I'd rather my Ted as he used to be
Than the King of France & his whole Navee!"

— trad. (Irish)

On Pete Seeger Sing Out with Pete, Wimoweh *&* I Can See a New Day. *In* SO! *6:4 &* Reprints #1, Hootenanny SB, *Bikel* FS & Footnotes, FSEncyV2, FS of Eng Ireland Scotland & Wales *&* S That Changed the World. OP43

Mothers, Daughters, Wives

The first time it was fathers, the last time it was sons
And in between your husbands marched away with guns & drums
And you never thought to question, you just went on with your lives
'Cause all they'd taught you who to be was mothers, daughters, wives

G - - D / G - C D / G - C G / Am - C D

You can only just remember, the tears your mothers shed
As they sat & read their papers thru the lists & lists of dead
And the gold frames held the photographs that mothers kissed each night
And the doorframes held the shocked & silent strangers from the fight

It was 21 years later with children of your own
The trumpet sounded once again & the soldier boys were gone
And you drove their trucks & made their guns & tended to their wounds
And at night you kissed their photographs & prayed for safe returns

And after it was over, you had to learn again
To be just wives & mothers when you'd done the work of men
So you worked to help the needy & you never trod on toes
And the photos on the pianos struck a happy family pose

Then your daughters grew to women & your little boys to men
And you prayed that you were dreaming when the call-up came again
But you proudly smiled & held your tears as they bravely waved goodbye
And the photos on the mantlepieces always made you cry

And now you're getting older & in time the photos fade
And in widowhood you sit back & reflect on the parade
Of the passing of your memories as your daughters change their lives
Seeing more to our existence than just mothers, daughters, wives

— Judy Small

 — On Judy Small, *Prisc Herdman* Seasons of Change, *Ronnie Gilbert* The Spirit Is Free *(Redwood) & Margaret Christl* Looking Towards Home. *In* SO! *30:1 & 44:4 &* Here's to the Women. OP44

No Man's Land

Well how do you do Private William McBride
Do you mind if I sit here down by your graveside
And rest for awhile in the warm summer sun?
I've been walking all day & I'm nearly done

And I see by your gravestone you were only 19
When you joined the glorious fallen in 1916
Well I hope you died quick & I hope you died clean
Or Willie McBride was it slow & obscene?

G - C Am / D - G D / 1st / D - C G
G - Am - / " / G - Am - / " /

Did they beat the drum slowly, did they play the fife lowly?
Did the rifles fire o'er you as they lowered you down?
Did the bugles sound the last post in chorus?
Did the pipes play the "Flowers o' the Forest"?

D - C G / / Am - D - / G C D G

And did you leave a wife or a sweetheart behind
In some loyal heart is your memory enshrined
And tho' you died back in 1916
To that faithful heart are you forever 19?

Or are you a stranger without even a name
Forever enclosed behind some glass pane
In an old photograph torn & tattered & stained
And fading to yellow in a brown leather frame?

But the sun shining now on these green fields of France
The warm wind blows gently & the red poppies dance
The trenches have all vanished under the plow
No gas, no barbed wire, no guns firing now

But here in this graveyard it's still no man's land
The countless white crosses in mute witness stand
To man's blind indifference to his fellow man
And a whole generation who were butchered & damned

And I can't help but wonder now, Willie McBride
Do all those who lie here know why they died?
Did you really believe them when they told you the cause?
Did you really believe that this war would end wars?
The suffering the sorrow the glory the shame
The killing, the dying, it was all done in vain
For Willie McBride it all happened again
And again & again & again & again

— Eric Bogle

 — On his Scraps of Paper & Live in Person , *June Tabor* Ashes & Diamonds *(Topic), Bok Muir & Trickett* Ways of Man *(FolkLeg), Prisc Herdman* Forgotten Dreams *& on* S for Peace. *In* SO! *28:4.* OP45

No More Genocide

Why do we call them the enemy
This struggling nation that's won independence across the sea?
Why do we want these people to die?
Why do we say North and South, o why, o why, o why?

C - Dm - / Em - Dm - / C - Dm - / Em - Dm C

Well that's just a lie! one of the many & we've had plenty
I don't want more of the same
No more genocide in my name!

Am - F G / Am - F G / F G Am -

Why are our history books so full of lies
When no word is spoken of why the Indian dies & dies?
Or that the Chicanos love the California land
Do our books all say it was discovered by one White man?

Why are the weapons of the war so young?
Why are there only rich ones around when it's done?
Why are so many of our soldiers black or brown?
Do we think it's because they're good at cutting other people down?

Why do we support a colony
When Puerto Rican people are crying out to be free?
We sterilize the women & rob the copper mines
Do we think that people will always be so blind?

Nazi forces grow again, ignorance gives them a place
The Klan is teaching children to hate the human race
Where once there was a playground, now an MX missile plant
Do they think it's fun to see just how much we can stand?

— **Holly Near**

© 1972 Hereford Music (ASCAP). Used by permission. — On her Hang in There, Lifeline *(w/Ronnie Gilbert) & in her* Words & M. *Also on* Out of the Darkness – S for Survival *(Fire on the Mtn4001 c/o Kaleidoscope Rec, PO Box O, El Cerrito CA 94530).* OP46

Oseh Shalom

Oseh shalom bimromov, hu ya-aseh shalom aleynu
V'al kol yisrael, v'imru, imru am,n
Ya-ase shalom ya-ase shalom, al,nu v'al kol yisrael **(2x)**
Ya-ase shalom ya-ase shalom, shalom al,nu v'al kol yisrael **(2x)**

Dm - Gm Dm / C Dm A ADm // D7Gm CF DmA A
D7Gm CF DmA ADm / Dm Am Dm EAm / /

— **trad. (Hebrew)**

This is a Jewish prayer for peace that is recited at the end of the Amidah, the silent prayer recited in all three daily prayer services. Translation: "May the One who creates peace in the heavens, make peace for us and all over Israel. Amen." On Israel's Gr H *(Tara T604). In* Harv of Jewish Wedding M, Israeli Band B, Israeli Guitar B & Cass., Hebrew S & Israel in S. OP47

Peace In the Valley

I am tired & so weary, but I must toil on
Til the Lord comes to call me away
Where the morning's so bright & the Lamb is the Light
And the night, night is as fair as the day

D - G - / D Bm E7 A / D - G - / D EA D -

There'll be peace in the valley for me someday
There'll be peace in the valley for me, O Lord I pray
There'll be no sadness, no sorrow, no trouble I'll see
There'll be peace in the valley for me **(in 3/4)**

G - D - / - E A - / D D7 G E7 / D EA D -

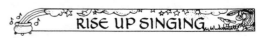

Well the bear will be gentle & the wolf will be tame
And the lion will lay down by the lamb
And the beasts from the wild will be led by a child
I'll be changed, changed from this creature that I am

— **Rev. Thomas A Dorsey**

© 1933 by Thomas A. Dorsey. Copyright renewed, assigned to Unichappell Music Inc. (Rightsong Music, Publisher). International copyright secured. Printed in USA. Unauthorized copying, arranging, adapting, recording or public performance is an infringement of copyright. Infringers are liable under the law. — aka: "There'll Be... In 1939" "while Hitler was rumbling his war chariots" Dorsey was riding on a train in Southern Indiana thru a serene valley past farm animals, a brook, trees. "It made me wonder what's the matter with humanity? Why couldn't man live in peace like those animals down there?" In Treas of Best Loved S. *Rec by Red Foley, Elvis Presley & Lost & Found.* OP48

Peace Is

Feel the cool breeze blowing thru the smoke & the heat
Hear the gentle voices & the marching feet
Singing call back the fire, draw the missiles down
And we'll call this earth our home

D - G D / F#m - G A / Bm A G F#m / Em - A -

Peace is the bread we break / Love is the river rolling
Life is a chance we take / When we make this earth our home
Gonna make this earth our home

G D G D / G D G A / 1st / Em - A - / G A D -

We have known the atom, the power & pain
We've seen people fall beneath the killing rain
If the mind still reasons & the soul remains
It shall never be again

Peace grows from a tiny seed
As the acorn grows into the tallest tree
Many years ago I heard a soldier say
"When people want peace, better get out of the way!"

— **Fred Small**

© 1983 Pine Barrens Music (BMI). Used by permission. On his The Heart of the Appaloosa *& in his* Breaking from the Line. *In* SO! *36:1 &* Peace Gathering S. OP49

A Song of Peace (Finlandia)

_This is my song, O God of all the nations
_A song of peace, for lands afar & mine
_This is my home, the country where my heart is
_Here are my hopes, my dreams, my holy shrine
_But other hearts in other lands are beating
_With hopes & dreams as true & high as mine

C G GF GC / C G GF C
|: C Am AmC GDm / DmG C [1. FDm E :| [2. ending CG C

My country's skies are bluer than the ocean
And sunlight beams on clover leaf & pine
But other lands have sunlight too, and clover
And skies are everywhere as blue as mine
O hear my song, thou God of all the nations
A song of peace for their land & for mine

— **w: Lloyd Stone — m: Jean Sibelius ("Finlandia")**

© 1934 Lorenz Pub. Co., renewal secured 1964. Used by permission. — In Pocketful of S *(WAS),* Friends Hymnal & Children's S for a Friendly Planet. OP50

Study War No More

1. Gonna lay down my sword & shield **down by the riverside**
Down by the riverside, down by the riverside
Gonna lay down my sword & shield **down by the riverside**
And study war no more

I ain't a-gonna study war no more (6x)

(TD ↑ 9) E - - - / B7 - E - :||: A - / E - / B7 - E - :||

2. Gonna put on that long white robe...
3. Gonna put on that starry crown...
4. Gonna walk with the Prince of Peace...

5. Gonna shake hands around the world...
6. Gonna lay down those atom bombs...

Gonna lay down my income tax / I ain't a-gonna pay for war no more
Gonna lay down my GE stock / & live off war no more
Gonna lay down my Honeywell job / & work for war no more
Gonna...those Congressional hawks / & vote for war no more

— trad. (Black Spiritual – new v. anon.)

Aka: "Down By The Riverside." On Pete Seeger At Carnegie Hall *(FA2412),* Sing Out w/Pete *&* Wimoweh, *on Weavers* Reunion 1963, *Sally Rogers* Peace by Peace *(KidsRecs) & Sweet Honey In the Rock* We All Every One of Us *(FF 317). In* S of Work & Protest, FS Abecedary, *Bikel* FS & Footnotes, S of the Spirit, SFest, Children's S for a Friendly Planet, Quaker SB *&* S That Changed the World. **©P51**

There Were Roses

My song for you this evening, it's not to make you sad
Nor for adding to the sorrows of this troubled northern land
But lately I've been thinking & it just won't leave my mind
I'll tell you of two friends one time, who were both good friends of mine
Allan Bell from Banagh, he lived just across the fields
A great man for the music & the dancing & the reels
O'Malley came from South Armagh to court young Alice fair
And we'd often meet on the Ryan Road & the laughter filled the air

(in D) D - GA D/Bm A G -/ 1st /Bm A G D :||

There were roses, roses / There were roses
And the tears of the people ran together

G D G D / G D - / Bm A G -

Tho' Allan he was Protestant & Sean was Catholic born
It never made a difference for the friendship it was strong
And sometimes in the evening when we heard the sound of drums
We said It won't divide us, we always will be one
For the ground our fathers plowed in the soil it is the same
And the places where we say our prayers have just got different names
We talked about the friends who died & we hoped there'd be no more
It's little then we realized the tragedy in store

It was on a Sunday morning when the awful news came round
Another killing has been done just outside Newry Town
We knew that Allan danced up there, we knew he'd liked the band
When we heard that he was dead, we just could not understand
We gathered at the graveside on that cold & rainy day
And the minister he closed his eyes & prayed for no revenge
And all of us who knew him from along the Ryan Road
We bowed our heads & said a prayer for the resting of his soul

Now fear it filled the countryside, there was fear in every home
When a car of death came prowling 'round the lonely Ryan Road
A Catholic would be killed tonight to even up the score
"O Christ! it's young O'Malley that they've taken from the door"
Allan was my friend he cried, he begged them with his fear
But centuries of hatred have ears that cannot hear
An eye for an eye was all that filled their minds
And another eye for another eye, til everyone is blind

(1st 4 lines/1st v.:) So my song for you... ...friends of mine
I don't know where the moral is, or where this song should end
But I wondered just how many wars are fought between good friends
And those who give the orders are not the ones to die
It's Bell & O'Malley & the likes of you and I

— Tommy Sands

© 1985 Elm Grove Music. Used by permission. — On his Singing of the Times *(SpringRecs) &* There Were Roses, *Mick Maloney et al* There Were Roses *(Green Linnet). In* SO! *31:3.* **©P52**

Two Brothers

Two brothers on their way, two brothers on their way
Two brothers on their way, one wore blue & one wore gray
One wore blue & one wore gray as they marched along their way
The fife & drum began to play **all on a beautiful morning**

Am G Am G / Am G Am GAm

AmG AmD CD AmB7 / C Bm CD Em

One was gentle, one was kind **(2x)**
One came home, one stayed behind, a cannonball don't pay no mind
A cannonball don't pay no mind, if you're gentle or if you're kind
It don't think of the folks behind **all...**

Two girls waiting by the railroad track **(2x)**
Two girls waiting by the railroad track, one wore blue and one wore black
One wore blue & one wore black waiting by the railroad track
For their darlings to come back **all...**

— Irving Gordon

© 1951, renewed 1979, Welbeck Music Corp. All rights for the USA & Canada controlled & administered by April Music Inc. under license from ATV Music (Welbeck). Used by permission. — Rec by the Kingston Trio. On Weavers On Tour *and in their* SB. **©P53**

Universal Soldier

He's 5 feet 2 & he's 6 feet 4
He fights with missiles & with spears
He's all of 31 & he's only 17
He's been a soldier for a thousand years

(in C) F G C Am / F G C - / F G Em Am / F - Dm G

He's a Catholic, a Hindu, an atheist, a Jain
A Buddhist & a Baptist & a Jew
And he knows he shouldn't kill & he knows he always will
Kill you for me, my friend, & me for you

And he's fighting for Canada, he's fighting for France
He's fighting for the U.S.A.
And he's fighting for the Russians, he's fighting for Japan
And he thinks we'll put an end to war that way

And he's fighting for democracy, he's fighting for the Reds
He says it's for the peace of all
He's the one who must decide who's to live & who's to die
And he never sees the writing on the wall

But without him how would Hitler have condemned him at Dachau?
Without him Caesar would have stood alone
He's the one who gives his body as the weapon of the war
And without him all this killing can't go on

He's the universal soldier & he really is to blame
His orders come from far away no more
They come from him & you & me & people can't you see
This is not the way we put an end to war

(new words) *The Universal Citizen*

They are business women, union workers, teachers, even priests
They say "A strong defense will save men's lives"
They have to give their money because it is the law
Yet without this money killing can't go on

They are universal citizens, they really are to blame
Their money goes to carry on the war
It comes from them & you & me, it isn't hard to see
This is not the way we put an end to war

— Buffy Sainte-Marie (new v. anon.)

© 1963 Caleb Music. All rights reserved. Used by permission. — On her It's My Way & Best of. *On Donovan* Fairytale, Like It Is, Best of *&* Pye History of Pop. *In* SO! *15:1 & 44:4 &* Reprints *#9 &* Here's to the Women. **©P54**

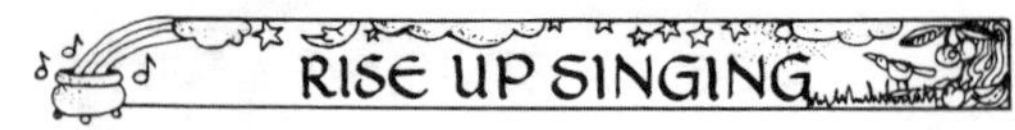

What If the Russians Don't Come?

My town has a plan for its civil defense
We'll all take Route 70 when it gets tense
My wife sewed directions in my underclothes
So I'll know where to run when the big whistle blows
We had a rehearsal last Saturday night
And all things considered, our town did all right
Except on the ramp when that truck tried to pass
And it took us three hours to clean up the glass

C G / - C / - F / D G :||

What if the Russians don't come?
What if they like where they're from?
What if they're not in the mood to invade?
What if they're tired or drunk or afraid?
What would we do if their gen'rals just said "This is dumb"
What if the Russians don't come?

(in 3:4) G CC_7 / F CC_7 / / / F C G / - C

I've learned about Russians since I was a tyke
And here's what I know about what they are like
They don't believe in God & they never have fun
They're brain-washed & dull & they all weigh a ton
And in the Olympics whenever we meet
Their women are men & their judges all cheat
But maybe you shouldn't rely just on me
'Cause I've not seen a Russian except on TV

What if the Russians have lives?
What if they're husbands & wives?
If they come home late from work on the bus
And have to fix dinner for children that fuss
They might be too tired to come put us under their thumb...

The president says we're behind in the race
And we need his new missile just to keep pace
If we don't stay up with them lap after lap
The Russians will come blow us right off the map
Well I may be dumb, but sometimes I forget
What I've got against all these folks I ain't met
I can't figure out why they want World War III
Could it be they're wonderin' the same about me?

What if the Russians are scared?
What if they're all unprepared?
Maybe that Ivan's as tired as I am
Tired of worrying about Uncle Sam?
Why don't we stop before one of us does something dumb?...

— Phil Hoose

© 1983 Phillip M. Hoose, Precious Pie Music, Inc (BMI). Used by permission. For lead sheet/cassette write Precious Pie, 8 Arlington St, Portland ME 04101. On Charlie King Feelings of Fire. *In* SO! *30:4.* OP55

Where Have All the Flowers Gone?

1. **Where have all the flowers gone? – long time passing**
Where have all the flowers gone? – **long time ago**
Where... gone? – girls have picked them every one
When will they ever learn? When will they ever learn?

C A_m F G / / / F C F G C -

2. **Where have all the** young girls gone?... **(3x)** – they've taken husbands every one / **When will they...**
3. **Where...the** young men gone? – gone for soldiers every one
4. **Where...the** soldiers gone? – gone to graveyards every one
5. **Where...the** graveyards gone? – gone to flowers every one

— Pete Seeger (with addl v. by Joe Hickerson)

© 1961 by Fall River Music Inc. All rights reserved. Used by permission. — Inspired by 3 lines of an old Ukrainian folksong in Mikhail Sholokhov's And Quiet Flows the Don. *On his* World of, WHATFG & Gr H *& in his* Bells of Rhymney. *In* SO! *11:5 &* Reprints #4, Hootenanny SB *& Readers Dig* Fest of Pop S. *In* Baez SB *& on her* V Early, Peter Paul & Mary, *Flatt & Scruggs* Changin Times, *& Kingston Trio* Best of, 25 Yrs & College Conc. *Rec by Marlene Dietrich.* OP56

The Willing Conscript

O Sergeant, I'm a draftee & I've just arrived in camp
And I've come to wear the uniform & join the martial tramp
And I want to do my duty but one thing I do implore
You must give me lessons, Sgt., for **I've never killed before**

C CF CG C / / F C FC G / C CF CG C

To do my job obediently is my only desire
To learn my weapon thoroughly & how to aim & fire
To learn to kill the enemy & then to slaughter more
I'll need instruction, Sgt., for **I've...**

O there are rumors in the camp about our enemy
They say that when you see him he looks just like you & me
But you deny it, Sgt., & you are a man of war
So you must give me lessons, for **I've...**

Now there are several lessons that I haven't mastered yet
I haven't got the hang of how to use the bayonet
If he doesn't die at once, am I to stick him with it more?
O I hope you will be patient, for **I've...**

The hand grenade is something that I just don't understand
You've got to throw it quickly or you're apt to lose a hand
Does it blow a man to pieces with its wicked, muffled roar?
O I've got so much to learn because **I've...**

O I want to thank you, Sgt., for the help you've been to me
For you've taught me how to slaughter & to hate the enemy
And I know that I'll be ready when they march me off to war
And I know that it won't matter that **I've...**

— Tom Paxton

© 1963 by Cherry Lane Music Publishing Co. Inc. All rights reserved. Used by permission. — On his Ain't That News *& in his* Rambling Boy. *On Pete Seeger* Little Boxes & Other Broadsides *(FV 9020) & in* SO! *35:4 &* S That Changed the World. OP57

With God on Our Side

O my name it means nothin',_my age it means less _
The country I come from_it's called the Midwest _
I's taught & brought up there_the laws to abide _
And that the land I live in_has God on its side _

(G) CB_m B_mD G GC / G GC G GC
G GC G - / CB_m B_mD G - **(capo up)**

O the history books tell it, they tell it so well
The cavalries charged, the Indians fell
The cavalries charged, the Indians died
O the country was young with God on its side

The Spanish-American War had its day
And the Civil War too was soon laid away
And the names of the heroes I's made to memorize
With guns in their hands & God on their side

O the first World War, well it came & it went
The reason for fighting I never did get
But I learned to accept it, accept it with pride
For you don't count the dead with God on your side

When the second World War came to an end
We forgave the Germans & then we were friends
Tho' they murdered six million, in the ovens they fried
The Germans now too have God on their side

I've learned to hate Russians all thru my whole life
If another war comes, it's them we must fight
To hate them & fear them, to run & to hide
And accept it all bravely with God on our side

But now we got weapons of the chemical dust
If fire them we're forced to, then fire them we must
One push of the button & a shot the world wide
And you never ask questions with God on your side

In many a dark hour I been thinkin' 'bout this
That Jesus Christ was betrayed by a kiss
But I can't think for you, you have to decide
Whether Judas Iscariot had God on his side

So now as I'm leavin' I'm weary as hell
The confusion I'm feelin' ain't no tongue can tell
The words fill my head & fall to the floor
If God's on our side, He'll stop the next war

— **Bob Dylan**

© 1963 Warner Bros. Inc. Renewed 1991 Special Rider Music. Used by permission. — On his Times They Are A-Changin *& in his* SB. *On Joan Baez* In Conc #2 & 1st 10 Yrs *& Jack Elliott* Bull Durham. *In* SO! *13:5 & Reprints #7.* ©P58

There are a number of peace songs in the chapters ECOLOGY, HOPE, SACRED ROUNDS & CHANTS, and STRUGGLE. Other songs on this theme include: "Tenting Tonight," "Your Flag Decal" (AMER) "Eli Eli," "Old Hundredth" [new v. by Pete Seeger] (FAITH) "Wild West Is Where..." (FUN) "All I Really Need" (HOME) "What to Do" (MEN) "We Hate to See Them Go" (RICH) "There Are Three Brothers," "One Submarine" (ROUND) & "Turn Turn Turn" (TIME).

Some others songs on war & soldiers include: "Battle of New Orleans," "Spoon River" (AMER), "Arthur McBride" (BALLAD) "One Morning in May" (GOOD) "Barrett's Privateers," & "The Grey Funnel Line" (SEA).

Authorship for many children's songs is especially difficult to trace because of how quickly such songs move into a mouth-to-mouth folk process. Songs in this section are of unknown authorship unless otherwise noted. We apologize if we have failed to credit the author of any of these songs, or any others in the book.

Aikendrum

There was a man lived in the moon **(3x)**
There was a man lived in the moon **& his name was Aikendrum**

D G D A7 / D G DA7 D

And he played upon a ladle (3x)
He played upon a ladle & his name was Aikendrum

And his hair was made of spaghetti...
And his eyes were made of meatballs...
And his nose was made of cheese...
And his mouth was made of pizza...

This was originally a Scottish FS, much altered in the folk process. In SO! *17:3 &* Reprints *12,* FiresB of Children's S & Oxford Scottish SB. *In Raffi* Singable SB *& on his* Singable S for the V Young. *On Robbie Clement* Magic Place, *Kim Wallach* 2 Doz Childrens S *& Roxanne & Dan Keding In* Came That Rooster. ©K23

Alouette

Alouette, gentille Alouette / Alouette, je te plumerai

Je te plumerai <u>la tête</u> **(2x)**
Et <u>la tête</u> **(2x) / Alouette (2x) / O**

C - G C / // C G - GC ||: G7 - :|| **(as needed)**

Alouette... / ...plumerai / Je te plumerai le bec **(2x)**
Et le bec *[le nez]* **(2x) / Et** la tête **(2x) / Alouette...**

le cou / le dos / les ailes / la queue / les jambes /
les pattes *[les pieds]*

— **trad. (Québecquois)**

"Alouette" means skylark. Trans. of French: "Gentle Alloutte, I will pluck you! I'll pluck your head, beak (nose), neck back wings, tail, knees feet." On Ted Heath & Korean Orphan Choir We Sing Because We're Happy. In Joyful Singing (WAS), FiresB of FS, Golden Ency of FS, Goodtimes SB, The Ditty Bag, S for Pickin & Singin, Gr Legal FakeB, S Am Sings & Sing Along w World's Fav FS. ©K24

Arrabella Miller

Little Arrabella Miller found a woolly caterpillar
First it crawled upon her mother, then upon her baby brother
All said "Arrabella Miller, take away that caterpillar!"

D - G D G D A D / D G D A **(2x)** / 1st /

To the tune of "Twinkle Twinkle Little Star." ©K25

Baby Beluga

Baby beluga in the deep blue sea
Swim so wild & you swim so free
Heaven above & the sea below
And a little white whale on the go

D - / - A7 / - - / - D

Baby beluga / Baby beluga
Is the water warm, is your mama home
With you so happy?

G - / D - / E - / A7 -

Way down yonder where the dolphins play
Where you dive & splash all day
Waves roll in & the waves roll out
See the water squirtin' out of your spout

Baby beluga / O baby beluga
Sing your little song, sing for all your friends
We like to hear you

When it's dark, you're home & fed
Curl up snug in your water bed
Moon is shining & the stars are out
Good night, little whale, good night

Baby beluga / O baby beluga
With tomorrow's sun another day's begun
You'll soon be waking

Baby beluga in the deep blue sea
Swim so wild & you swim so free
Heaven above & the sea below
And a little white whale on the go
(as last line) You're just a little white whale on the go

— **Raffi & D. Pike**

© 1980 by Homeland Publishing, a division of Troubadour Records Ltd. All rights reserved. Used by permission. — On Raffi Baby Beluga *& in his* 2nd SB, Baby Beluga B & SO! *35:4.* ©K26

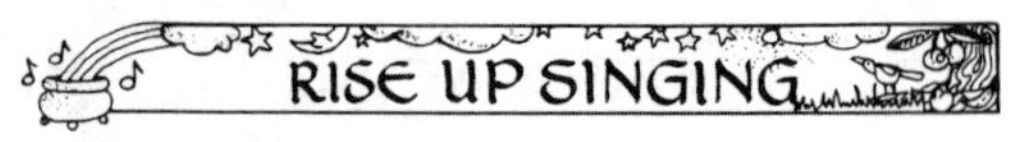

Beans in My Ears

My Mommy said not to put **beans in** my **ears**
Beans in my **ears, beans in** my **ears**
My Mommy said not to put **beans in** my **ears**
Beans in my **ears!**

D - A / - D :||

Now why would I want to put **beans in** my **ears?...**
You can't hear your teacher with **beans in** your **ears...**
O maybe it's fun to have **beans in** our **ears...**
Hey, Charlie, let's go & put **beans in** our **ears...**
WHAT'S THAT YOU SAY? **(2nd child:)** Let's put **beans...**
YOU'LL HAVE TO SPEAK UP! I'VE GOT **BEANS...**
Hey, Mommy, I've gone & put **beans in** my **ears...**
That's nice son, just don't put those **beans in** your **ears...**
I think that all grown-ups have **beans in** their **ears...**

— Len H. Chandler, Jr.

 — Chandler states that he has the distinction of being the only songwriter in history to have his song publicly banned by the NY Board of Health. In SO! 15:2 & Reprints #10 & Club Date FakeB. *On Pete Seeger* Dangerous S. OK27

Biscuits in the Oven

Biscuits in the oven, gonna watch 'em rise (3x)
Right before my very eyes

C - G7 - / /C C7 F D7 / G7 - C -

When they get ready gonna jump & shout **(3x)**
Roll my eyes & bug them out (hey hey!)

Gonna clap my hands & stomp my feet **(3x)**
Right before the very next beat

Gonna look both ways when I cross the street **(2 pauses) (3x)**
Gonna take my time when the light turns green

— Bill Russell

 — In Raffi Baby Beluga B *&* 2nd SB *& on his* Baby Beluga. OK28

Boom Boom

A horse & a flea & the 3 blind mice
Sat on a curbstone shooting dice
The horse he slipped & fell on the flea
"Whoops!" said the flea "there's* a horse on me!"

G Bm C D / /G Am Bm C / D - - -

Boom, boom, ain't it great to be crazy? (2x)
Giddy & foolish the whole day thru
Boom, boom, ain't it great to be crazy?

G Em Am D / /C Bm Am G / - - D G

Way down South where bananas grow
A flea stepped on an elephant's toe
The elephant cried with tears in his eyes
"Why don't you pick on someone your size?"

Eli, Eli, he sells socks
5¢ a pair & a dollar a box
The longer you wear 'em the shorter they get
You put 'em in the water & they don't get wet

**orig "that's a horse" (old slang for "that's a joke on me.") On Raffi* The Corner Grocery Store *& in his* Singable SB *& in* FiresB of Children's S. OK29

Brush Your Teeth

When you wake up in the morning & it's quarter to one
And you want to have a little fun
You brush your teeth **(brushing sounds) (2x)**

When wake up in the morning & it's quarter to 2
And you want to find something to do / **You...**
3: ...And your mind starts humming twiddle de dee...
4: ...And you think you hear a knock on your door...
5: ...And those birds just start to come alive...

— trad. adap & arr by Raffi & Louise Dain Cullen

 — On Cathy Fink Grandma Slid Down the Mountain *& Raffi* Singable S for V Young *& in his* Singable SB. OK30

Buckingham Palace

They're changing guard at Buckingham Palace
Christopher Robin went down with Alice
Alice is marrying one of the guard
"A soldier's life is terrible hard" **(pause) says Alice**

G GD G - / /C G / D7 G - GD G -

They're... / ...Alice / We saw a guard in a sentry box
"One of the sergeants looks after their socks" – **says...**

...We looked for the King but he never came
"Well, God take care of him, all the same..."

...They've great big parties inside the grounds
"I wouldn't be King for a hundred pounds..."

...A face looked out, but it wasn't the King's
"He's much too busy a-signing things..."

..."Do you think the King knows all about me?"
"Sure to, dear, but it's time for tea" – **says Alice**

— w: A.A.Milne — m: H. Fraser-Simson

 In A.A.Milne The Pooh SB, The King's Breakfast *&* 14 S fr When We Were Very Young. OK31

Don't Put Your Finger Up Your Nose

Don't put your finger up your nose
'Cause your nose knows that's not the place it goes
You can sniffle, you can sneeze, but I'm asking you please
Don't put your finger up your nose

G - / C - / D - / - G

Don't stick your finger in your ear
'Cause then your ear will find it hard to hear
You can thump & you can tug it, but please don't plug it
Don't stick your finger in your ear

Don't put your finger in your eye
That's not a thing you ought to try
You can blink it, you can wink it, but I don't think it
Would be good to put your finger in your eye

Don't stick your finger down your throat
'Cause that'd just make you start to choke
Then up will come your dinner & you'll start to look much thinner
Don't stick your finger down your throat

— Barry Louis Polisar

 — On his Naughty S for Boys & Girls. *In his* Noises fr under the Rug *& SO! 31:4.* OK32

Down By the Bay

1. **Down by the bay where the watermelons grow**
   Back to my home I dare not go
   For if I do my mother will say
   Did you ever see a goose kissing a moose? **down by the bay!**

G D7 / - G / C G / - D7G

2. **Down...**/ Did you ever see a whale with a polka-dot tail?...
3. Did you ever see a fly wearing a tie?
4. Did you ever see a bear combing his hair?
5. Did you ever see llamas eating their pajamas?
6. Did you ever have a time when you couldn't make a rhyme?
7. This doggone song's gone on too long

On Raffi Singable S for the V Young *& in his* Singable SB. OK33

Five Little Ducks

5 little ducks went out one day
Over the hills & far away
Mother duck said "Quack, quack, quack, quack"
But only 4 little ducks came back

C - F C / - F G7 - / C - F C / - Dm G7 C

4 little ducks went out one day / Over... / Mother...
But only 3 little ducks came back, **(etc.)**

One little duck went out one day...
But none of the 5 little ducks came back

Sad mother duck went out one day / Over...
Mother duck said QUACK! QUACK! QUACK! QUACK!
And all of the 5 little ducks came back

On Raffi Rise & Shine *& in his* 2nd SB. *On Rachel Buchman* Hello Everybody! *In* Eye Winker. OK34

The Foolish Frog

Way down south in the yankety-yank,
 a bullfrog jumped from bank to bank
Just because he'd nothing better for to do
He stubbed his toe & fell in the water,
 you could hear him holler for a mile & a quarter
Just because he'd nothing better for to do

E - A - / B7 - E B7 / E - A - / B7 - E -

There's lots of folks just like that foolish frog of mine
Get themselves in trouble trying to pass the time
Lot's of folks just like that foolish frog of mine
Because they've nothing better for to do

"May Irwin's Frog Song" (1890s), made popular by Mae Murray. Aka: "Yankety Yank." In SO! *5:4,* Reprints *#4 & Pete's* Bells of Rhymney. *On his* Birds, Beasts, Bugs, 3 Saints, 4 Sinners *&* John Henry. OK35

The Fox

The fox went out on a chilly night
Prayed for the moon to give him light
For he'd many a mile to go that night
Before he reached the town-o / Town-o **(2x)**
He'd many a mile to go that night
Before he reached the town-o

D - / - A / D G / DA D / A D / G D / A D

He ran til he came to a great big bin
The ducks & the geese were put therein
Said "A couple of you will grease my chin
Before I leave this town-o..."

He grabbed the grey goose by the neck
Slung the little one over his back
He didn't mind their quack-quack-quack
And the legs all dangling down-o...

Old mother Pitter-patter jumped out of bed
Out of the window she cocked her head
Crying "John, John, the grey goose is gone
And the fox is on the town-o!..."

John, he went to the top of the hill
Blew his horn both loud & shrill
The fox, he said "I better flee with my kill
He'll soon be on my trail-o..."

He ran til he came to his cozy den
There were the little ones: 8, 9, 10
They said "Daddy, Daddy, you better go back again
'Cause it must be a mighty fine town-o..."

Then the fox & his wife without any strife
Cut up the goose with fork & knife
They never had such a supper in their life
And the little ones chewed on the bones-o...

— (adap by) Burl Ives

© 1945 by MCA Music Publishing, a div. of MCA Inc. NY, NY 10019. Copyright renewed. Used by permission. — (This song goes back at least to 15th c. – © is for arrangement.) On his Bals & FS *& in his* SB, *on (& in) Pete Seeger* Am Fav Bal V2, *on Odetta* At the Horn & The Essential, *Bellafonte* Mark Twain, *Faith Petric* Sing a S Sing Along, *Nancy Raven* People & Animals *& rec by the Kingston Trio. In* SFest, FS Abecedary, Sing the Good Earth, FSEncy V1, FS N Am Sings *&* FS of Old New England. OK36

Froggie Went a-Courtin'

Froggie went a-courtin' & he did ride, **a-huh, a-huh**
Froggie went a-courtin' & he did ride
Sword & pistol by his side, **a-huh, a-huh**

D - - - / - GD / D A7 D -

Well, he rode down to Miss Mouse's door... **(2x)**
Where he had often been before, **a-huh, a-huh**

He took Miss Mousie on his knee
Said "Miss Mousie will you marry me?"

"I'll have to ask my Uncle Rat
See what he will say to that"

"Without my Uncle Rat's consent
I would not marry the President"

Well, Uncle Rat laughed & shook his fat sides
To think his niece would be a bride

Well, Uncle Rat rode off to town
To buy his niece a wedding gown

"Where will the wedding supper be?"
"Way down yonder in a hollow tree"

"What will the wedding supper be?"
"A fried mosquito & a roasted flea" *[2 green beans & a black-eyed pea]*

First to come in were two little ants
Fixing around to have a dance

Next to come in was a bumble bee
Bouncing a fiddle on his knee

Next to come in was a fat sassy lad
Thinks himself as big as his dad

Thinks himself a man indeed
Because he chews the tobacco weed

And next to come in was a big tomcat
He swallowed the frog & the mouse & the rat

Next to come in was a big old snake
He chased the party into the lake

On Mike & Peggy (& in Ruth) Seeger Am FS for Children (Rounder). On (& in) Pete Seeger Am Fav Bals V4 (FA2323) & on his Am FS for Children. On The Dildine Fam, Doc Watson Home Again (Vang), Sparky Rucker A Home in Tennessee, John McCutcheon How Can I Keep fr Singing, B Hinkley & J Larson Out in Our Meadow & Spider John Koerner Nobody Knows the Trouble I've Been (RHR 12). In SFest, Treas of FS, FSEncyV1, Sing to Children (WAS) & Burl Ives SB. OK37

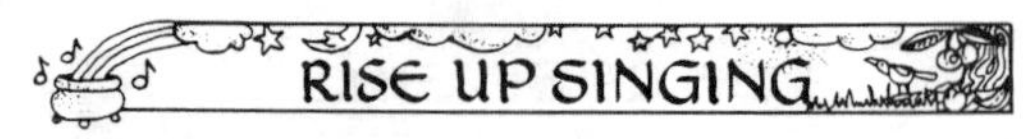

Going to the Zoo

Daddy's taking us to the zoo tomorrow
Zoo tomorrow, zoo tomorrow
Daddy's taking us to the zoo tomorrow
We can stay all day

D - / A D :||

We're going to the zoo zoo zoo
How about you you you?
You can come too too too
We're going to the zoo zoo zoo

G - / D - / A - / DG G

See the elephant with the long trunk swingin'
Great big ears & long trunk swingin'
Sniffin' up peanuts with the long trunk swingin' / **We...**

See all the monkeys scritch scritch scratchin'
Jumpin' all around & scritch scritch scratchin'
Hangin' by their long tails scritch...

Big black bear all huff huff a-puffin'
Coat's too heavy, he's huff huff...
Don't get too near the huff... / Or you won't stay all day

Seals in the pool all honk honk honkin'
Catchin' fish & honk honk...
Little seals **(high pitched voices)** honk... / **We can...**

(slower & slower) We stayed all day & I'm gettin' sleepy
Sitting' in the car gettin' sleep sleep sleepy
Home already & I'm sleep sleep sleepy / We have stayed...
We've *been* **to the zoo...** / So have... / You came...

But! **(faster)** Mommy's taking us to the zoo tomorrow...

— Tom Paxton

 — In his Ramblin' Boy *& on* Marvellous Toy. *In* SO! *14:4. On Raffi* Singable S for the V Young *& in his* Singable SB. *On* Peter, Paul & Mommy *&* Going to the Zoo. OK38

The Green Grass Grew All Around

O there was once a tree, a pretty little tree
The prettiest little tree **that you ever did see**
O the tree was in a hole & the hole in the ground

And the green grass grew all around, all around
The green grass grew all around

G - - - / D - G - ||: G :|| **(as needed)** GD GC / GD G

Now on this tree there was a limb
The prettiest little *limb* that you ever did see
The limb on the tree & the tree in a hole & the hole in the ground

And the green grass grew...

Now on this limb there was a branch...
On this branch there was a bough...
On this bough there was a twig...
On this twig there was a leaf...
On this leaf there was a nest...
In this nest there was a bird...
On this bird there was a feather...
On this feather there was a flea...

An older version of this song is called "The Rattling Bog." On The Dildine Family, *Nick Seeger* A S or 2 for You *(GentleWinds), Clancy Bros* At Home *(Everest) & Pete Seeger et al* Carry It On. *In* Tom Glaser Treas, Joyful & FiresB of Fun & Games. OK39

Green, Green Rocky Road

When I go by Baltimore, ain't no carpet on the floor
Come along & follow me, must go down to Galilee, singin'

Green, green rocky road, promenade in green
Tell me who ya love, tell me who ya love

E - - AE / //E AE EA E / - AE E -

See that crow up in the sky, he don't walk well he just fly
He don't walk & he don't run, keep on flappin' to the sun

Hooka, tooka, soda cracker, does your mama chew tobacker?
If your mama chew tobacker, hooka, tooka, soda cracker

If you see me comin' fast, sweep the yard & cut the grass
Girls who kiss are bound to fall, boys who kiss will soon tell all

— Len Chandler & Robert Kaufman

 — "Green, Green Rocky Road" was collected by Harold Courlander from the children of Lilly's Chapel School in York, AL, & appears in his Negro S fr Alabama. *Len Chandler & Bob Kaufman reworked it, added some new v. & Len scored it in* A Rootin' Tootin' Hootenanny *(FM310). In* SO! *14:4 &* FS Am Sings. *On Joanna Cazden* Gr Illusion, *Dave Van Ronk* In the Trad. *(Prestige) &* S for Aging Children *(Cadet), Fred Neil* Everybody's Talkin, *County Down* Living in the Country, *Harvey Reid* Nothin' but Guitar, *Guy Carawan* Green Rocky Road *& Kevin Roth* High on a Mtn *(FolkTrad).* OK40

Gum Song

Chomp chomp, nibble nibble, yum yum yum
I love to chew on my chewing gum
My chewing gum's so good & sweet
It makes me happy from my head to my feet

D A / - D / - G / D AD

I love to pull my gum out far
And pluck on it like a big guitar
I wind it around my thumb with care
'Cause nobody likes it if it gets in my hair

Blowing a bubble's mighty tough
You've got to stick your tongue out enough
Now I'm ready, just look at me
And I'll blow you a bubble as big as a tree

Sometimes when I'm chewing gum
I make it flat with the top of my tongue
I make it flat, then I take it out
And it makes a map of the top of my mouth

My gum makes pops & cracks & clicks
Against my teeth & against my lips
When I'm all alone, no one else around
I love to hear that chewing gum sound

— Mary Dart

 In her S About People. OK41

Here's to Cheshire, Here's to Cheese

O there was a little frog who lived in a well
Ding dang dong go the wedding bells
And a pretty little mouse lived under a mill
Ding dang dong go the wedding bells

Here's to cheshire, here's to cheese
Here's to the pears & the apple trees
And here's to the lovely strawberries
Ding dang dong go the wedding bells

D - G A / D A D - :|| D - D_{maj7} - / G - D A / **1st 2**

Well, Froggy went a-courtin' & he did ride / **Ding...**
Now Miss Mouse you must decide / **Ding...**

I'll have to ask my uncle Rat
And see what he does say to that

Well, uncle Rat says I'm much afraid
If you don't marry Froggy you'll die an old maid

Well the knot was tied secure & fast
She's off her uncle's hands at last

Well open the oysters, spill the champagne
Never will there be such a feast again

But as they were going it hot & strong
The good gray cat comes prowlin' along

She sprang thru the window right out of the yard
She didn't bring no invitation card

Uncle Rat like a hero stood
Puss wet her whiskers in his blood

Miss Mousie made a dive for a crack
Puss made a pounce & broke her back

Where was the valiant frog the while
He just about broke the four minute mile

Well this is the end of him & her
There won't be no tadpoles covered in fur

— new words & new music adaptation by Leslie Haworth

 — On Hootenany (Prestige), John McCutcheon Howjadoo *(Rounder) & Tom Smith* Chip Off the New Block *(GentleWinds).* OK42

Hoppity

Christopher Robin goes hoppity **(4x)** hop
Whenever I tell him politely to stop it
he says he can't possibly stop
If he stopped hopping he couldn't go anywhere,
poor little Christopher couldn't go anywhere
That's why he always goes hoppity **(4x)** hop
Hoppity **(6x)** hop!

C G C F C G C - / /
C G C - Dm Am G - / 1st / /

— w: A.A. Milne — m: Harold Fraser-Smith

 In A.A.Milne The Pooh SB, 14 S fr When We Were Very Young & The King's Breakfast. OK43

A Horse Named Bill

I had a horse his name was Bill
And when he ran he couldn't stand still
He ran away one day
And also I ran with him

(TD ↑ 3) A - / D DE / A - / E7 A

He ran so hard he couldn't stop
He ran into a barber shop
He fell exhausted
With his teeth in the barber's left shoulder

Now my horse Bill found a grocery store
He ate some food & then he ate some more
He ate & he ate / & also I ate with him

Now my horse Bill he ate some more
He stayed all night in that grocery store / He ate...

Now my horse Bill saw a circus tent
He lifted up the flap & under he went
He saw & he saw / & I also saw with him

Now my horse Bill got into a race
The very next thing he was up in space / He saw...

Now my horse Bill he was no fool
One day he went to the school / He saw [learned]...

Now if you'd like to sing this song
Just open your mouth & sing along
Sing high, sing low, sing squeaky, sing together

(other trad. verses) *Sarah the Whale*

In Frisco Bay there lives a whale
And she eats pork chops by the pail
By the hatbox, by the pillbox
By the hogshead & schooner

Her name is Sarah *[Lena]* & she's a peach
But don't leave food within her reach
Or babies or nursemaids *[airedales]*
Or chocolate ice cream sodas

She loves to laugh & when she smiles
You can see her teeth for miles & miles
And her spareribs & her adenoids
And things too fierce to mention

She knows no games so when she plays
She rolls her eyes for days & days
She vibrates & yodels
And breaks the Ten Commandments

I went up in a balloon so big
The people on earth they looked like a pig
Like flieses, like fleases
Like mouses & like alligators

The balloon turned us with the bottom side higher
It fell on the wife of a country squire
She made a noise like a dog-hound
Like a steamboat and like dynamite

O what can you do in a case like that?
O what can you do but sit on your hat
Or your toothbrush or your grandmother
Or anything else that's helpless! *[helpful*]*

— w: trad. (new v. Gene Bluestein) — m: Dixie

**Ada at age 3 insisted that these things are helpful so some of us sing it that way. New v.* *— On Bluestein Fam* A Horse Named Bill *(Greenhay c/o FF). In SO! 12:2 & Reprints #6,* FSEncyV2, *Sandburg* Am SBag, *Lomax* FS of NAm & FiresB of Children's S. OK44

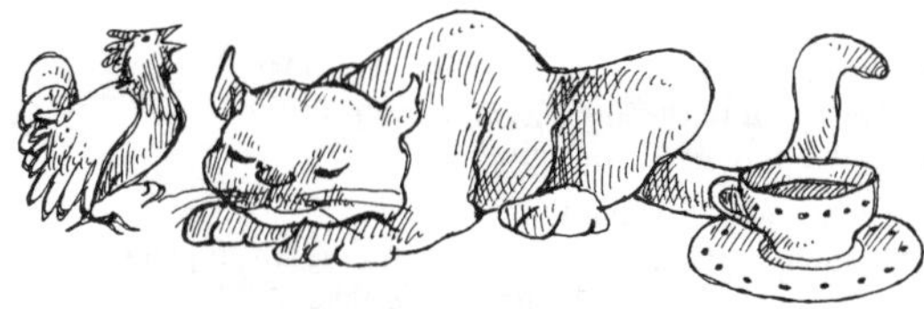

I Had a Rooster

I had a *rooster* & the *rooster* pleased me
I fed my *rooster* on a green berry tree
The little rooster went "cock-a-doodle doo, dee
Doodle-dee (3x) doo"

C - / - G7 / C F / CF GC

I had a cat & the cat pleased me
I fed my cat on a green berry tree
The little cat went "meow, meow" (repeat line fr each v.)
The little rooster went...

/ " / " ||: C - :|| as needed C F / CF GC

pig: The little pig went "oink, oink, oink"...
cow: The little cow went "moo, moo"...
baby: The little baby went "waah, waah"... etc.

On The Dildine Fam *(GentleWinds), Gary Lapow* Your Brightest Light, *Rachel Buchman* Hello Everybody *& Kim Wallach* 2 Doz Children's S. *In SO! 6:3 & Reprints #2,* FiresB of Children's S *&* Eye Winker. OK45

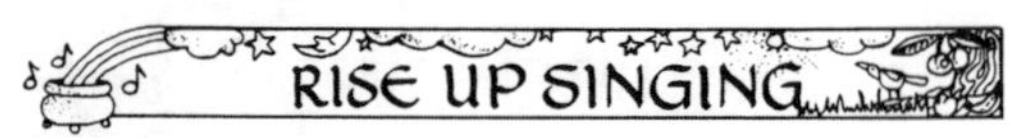

I Know an Old Lady

I know an old lady who swallowed a fly
And I don't know why she swallowed the fly
Perhaps she'll die

G - / A D / DG G

I know an old lady who swallowed a spider
That wiggled & jiggled & tickled inside her
She swallowed the spider to catch the fly
And I don't know why...

/ " / " / G - / A D / DG G

...bird / How absurd to swallow a bird!
She swallowed the bird to catch the spider
That wiggled & jiggled...

/ " / " ||: G - :|| **as needed** A D / G - / A D / DG G

...cat / Imagine that - to swallow a cat!
She swallowed the cat to catch the bird
She swallowed the bird to catch the spider, that...

...dog / What a hog, to swallow a dog!...

...goat / She opened her throat & in walked that goat...

...cow / I don't know how she swallowed a cow...

I know an old lady who swallowed a horse
(spoken) She's dead, of course!

— w: Rose Bonne **— m: Alan Mills**

© 1952, 1954 Peer International (Can.) Ltd. Copyright renewed. All rights reserved. Used by permission of CPP Belwin Inc. — In SO! 5:1, Bells of Rhymney, Fires B of Children's S *&* Treas of Am S. *On Ives* FS Dramatic & Humorous, *Warner & Davis* Old Time S for Kids, *Kevin Roth* Unbearable Bears *& Kim Wallach* 2 Doz Children's S. OK46

I Wanna be a Dog

O I wanna be a dog! **h, h, h, h (make 4 "dog pants")**
Wanna wag my tail **h, h, h, h**
Chase cars & knock over garbage cans
Bite the lady who brings the mail

A - / D - / E - / - A

O I wanna be a dog **h,...** / I wanna drool on the floor...
Get pats on the head, chase cats, get fed
Chew your shoes & bark at the door

O I wanna be a dog / I wanna dig big holes
I wanna sniff French poodles & basset hounds
And pee on telephone poles

O I wanna be a dog / I wanna big wet nose
I wanna run in the street, get mud on m'feet
And jump up onto your clothes!

(Bridge – without "pants")
O I wanna have dog breath / I wanna learn to growl
Scratch fleas & ticks & run after sticks
I want the moon to make me howl!

D - / A - / E - / - A

O I wanna be a dog / I wanna sleep on the ground
Bein' human these days is a-gettin' too cra-zy
I just wanna be a hound!

— Barry Louis Polisar (adap. Peter Alsop)

© 1979 by Barry Louis Polisar. Used by permission. — Orig last v: "I've got a college degree but all I want to be, is somebody else's pet." On his S for Well-behaved Children *& in* Noises fr under the Rug *(both Rainbow Morning M). In SO! 36:3. This adaptation on Peter Alsop* Wha' D'Ya Wanna Do?. OK47

I With I Were a Little Thugar Bun

I with I were a wittle thugar bun (thugar bun)
I with I were a wittle thugar bun
I'd thlippy & I'd thlidy down everyone's inthidie
I with I were a wittle thugar bun

D A / - D / G D / A D

I with I were a wittle cake of thope **(2x)**
I'd thlippy & I'd thlidy over everybody's hidie / ...thope

I with I were a monkey in the thoo
I'd thit upon a thelf & I'd thquat my wittle thelf

I with I were a wittle muthkitoe
I'd buthie & I'd bitie under everybody's nightie

I with I were a fithie in the thea
I'd thwim around tho cute without a bathing thuit

I with I were a wittle thafety pin
And evrything that'th buthted I'd hold until I ruthted

I with I were a wittle thlippewy woot
I'd thtick up in the twail & I'd flop you on your tail

I with I were a wittle bog of mud
I would oothe & I would goothe inthide everybody's thoothe

I with I were a wittle can of beer
I'd go down with a thllurp & come up with a burp

I with I were a wittle Englith Thpawow
I'd thit up on a thteeple & I'd thpit on all the people

I with I were a wittle kangawoo
I'd hippy & I'd hoppy inthide my mother's pockie

I with I were a thpoon of cathter oil
I'd lubricate the chathies of all the lads & lathies

I with I were a wittle thtripèd thkunk
I'd thit up in the treethes & perfume all the breethes

In SFest. Pronounce "th" as in the when it replaces a "z" sound. OK48

I'm a Little Teapot

I'm a little teapot short & stout
Here is my handle, here is my spout
When I get all steamed up hear me shout
Just tip me over & pour me out

C - F C / F C G C / - - F C / - F G C

I'm a little black seed, plant me in a row
Water me & feed me, watch me up & grow
From little seed to seedling, flower to fruit
I'm a happy little plant from tip to root

— Clarence Kelley & George Sanders

© 1939 Kelman Music Corp., renewed 1967 by Marilyn Sanders O'Bradovich. International copyright secured. All rights reserved. On Kim Wallach Even More Children's S *& in* Eye Winker. OK49

I'm in the Mood

I'm in the mood for singing. **Hey, how about you? (2x)**
I'm in the mood for singing, singing **along with you**
Hey, hey, what do you say? I'm in the mood for that today
Hey, hey, what do you say? I'm in the mood for that!

D - - A / - - - D / - - - G / - D A D / /

I'm in the mood for clapping...
I'm in the mood for whistling...
I'm in the mood for stomping...
I'm in the mood for singing...

— Raffi

© 1982 by Homeland Publishing, a division of Troubadour Records Ltd, All rights reserved. Used by permission. On his Rise & Shine *& in his* 2nd SB. OK50

I've Been to London

I've been to London, I've been to Dover
I've travelled this wide world all over
Over, over, three times over
Drink all the brandywine & turn the glasses over

D - - - / / D - G D / - - A D

Sailing east, sailing west
Sailing over the ocean
You better watch out when the waves begin to shout
Or you'll lose your friend in the ocean

D - - - / - - A - / D - - - / - - A D

A play party game. OK51

I've Been Working on the Railroad

I've been workin' on the railroad all the livelong day
I've been workin' on the railroad just to pass the time away
Can't you hear the whistle blowin'? Rise up so early in the morn
Can't you hear the captain shoutin' Dinah blow your horn!

D - G D / - - E A / - D G F#* / G D DA D

Dinah won't you blow **(3x)** your horn **(repeat)** **(* or use D)**

D G A D / /

Someone's in the kitchen with Dinah
Someone's in the kitchen I know
Someone's in the kitchen with Dinah
Strummin' on the old banjo

D - / - A / D G / DA D

A-playin' fee fi fiddle-y-i-o / Fee fi fiddle-y-i-o-o-o-o
Fee fi fiddle-y-i-o / Strummin' on the old banjo

First appeared in print in Carmina Princetonia *(1894). On Raffi* More Singable S *& in his* Singable SB. *On Pete Seeger* S & Playtime, *Sparky Rucker* Heroes & Hard Times *(SIF1032) &* A Home in Tennessee *(GW). In* SFest, S for Pickin & Singin & FiresB of FS. OK52

If I Only Had a Brain

(the scarecrow:)
I could while away the hours, conferrin' with the flowers
Consultin' with the rain
And my head, I'd be scratchin' while my thoughts were busy hatchin' / If I only had a brain
I'd unravel every riddle for any individdle
In trouble or in pain
With the thoughts I'd be thinkin', I could be another Lincoln
If I only had a brain

D - G - / D - - - / G - A - / DG D - - :||

(bridge) O I could tell you why
The ocean's near the shore
I could think of things I never thunk before
And then I'd sit & think some more

G - F#m - / Em A D - / Em A Bm - / E7 - A7 -

I would not be just a nuffin, my head all full of stuffin'
My heart all full of pain
And perhaps I'd deserve you & be even worthy erv you
If I only had a brain

(the tinwoodsman:)
When a man's an empty kettle he should be on his mettle
And yet I'm torn apart
Just because I'm presumin' that I could be kinda human
If I only had a heart
I'd be tender I'd be gentle & awful sentimental
Regarding love & art
I'd be friends with the sparrows & the boy that shoots the arrows
If I only had a heart

Picture me a balcony
Above a voice sings low
Wherefore art thou, Romeo?
I hear a beat – how sweet!

Just to register emotion, Jealousy, Devotion
And really feel the part
I would stay young & chipper & I'd lock it with a zipper
If I only had a heart

(the cowardly lion:)
Life is sad believe me missy, when you're born to be a sissy
Without the vim & verve
But I could change my habits, never more be scared of rabbits
If I only had the nerve
I'm afraid there's no denyin' I'm just a dandelion
A fate I don't deserve
But I could show my prowess, be a lion, not a mowess
If I only had the nerve

O I'd be in my stride
A king down to the core
O I'd roar the way I never roared before
And then I'd rrwoof & roar some more

I would show the dinosaurus, who's king around the forres'
A king they better serve
Why with my regal beezer I could be another Caesar
If I only had the nerve

— w: E. Y. Harburg **— m: Harold Arlen**

 Fr their musical The Wizard of Oz. *On* Claudia Schmidt. OK53

If You're Happy and You Know It

1. **If you're happy & you know it,** clap your hands **(2x)**
If you're happy & you know it, let everybody show it
If you're happy & you know it, clap your hands

G D / - G / C G / D G

2. stamp your feet 3. slap your knees 4. do a dance
5. shout Amen! 6. do all five **(etc.)**

Based on trad hymn "Watch Your Eyes" (which has the same tune). On Bob McGrath Sing Along w/Bob, *Marcy Marxer* Jump Children *(Rounder), Roxanne & Dan Keding* In Came That Rooster *& in* V Fav S of the V Young. OK54

In the Fashion

A lion has a tail & a very fine tail
And so has an elephant & so has a whale
And so has a crocodile & so has a quail
They've all got tails but me

D A D A / / G D G D / G A D -

If I had a sixpence I would buy one
I'd say to the shopman "Let me try one"
I'd say to the elephant "This is my one"
They'd all come round to see

Then I'd say to the lion "Why you've got a tail
And so has the elephant & so has the whale
And look! There's a crocodile: he's got a tail
You've all got tails like me!"

— w: A.A. Milne **— m: Harold Fraser-Smith**

 In A.A.Milne 14 S fr When We Were Very Young, The King's Breakfast & The Pooh SB. OK55

Itsy Bitsy Spider

The itsy bitsy spider climbed up the water spout
Down came the rain & washed the spider out
Out came the sun & dried away the rain
And the itsy bitsy spider climbed up the spout again

D - A D / / / /

On Mike & Peggy (& in Ruth) Seeger Am FS for Children *(Rounder), Bob McGrath* Sing Along w/Bob, *Sharon, Lois & Bram* Mainly Mother Goose *& Kim Wallach* Even More Children's S. *In* Singing Games, FiresB of FS & V Favs of the V Young. OK56

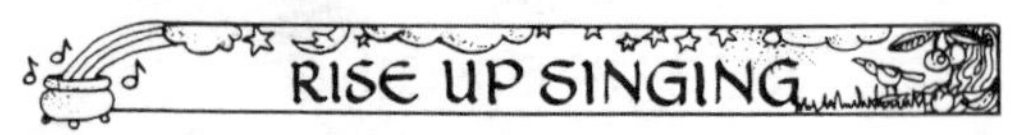

Jig Along Home

I went to the dance & the animals come
The jaybird danced with horseshoes on
The grasshopper danced til he fell on the floor
Jigalong, jigalong, jigalong home

Jig jiga jig jiga jigalong home (2x)
Jig along, jig along, jig along home
Jig jiga jig jiga jigalong home

E B7 / - E / E A / EB7 E :||

Fishing worm danced the fishing reel
Lobster danced on the peacock's tail
Baboon danced with the rising moon / **Jigalong...**

Mama rat took off her hat
Shook the house with the old tom cat
The alligator beat his tail on the drum / **Jigalong...**

The boards did rattle & the house did shake
The clouds did laugh & the world did quake
New moon rattled some silver spoons...

The nails flew loose & the floors broke down
Everybody danced around & around
The house come down & the crowd went home...

— **Woody Guthrie**

 — On Raffi Corner Grocery Store *& in his* Singable SB. OK57

Let's Do the Numbers Rumba

Let's do the numbers rumba (3x)
Numbers rumba all day long

Number One **(3x)** is straight but fun
Number One **(3x) all day long – O! / Let's...**

D EmA / A D / D Em / A D // D - - EmA / A - - D

Number 2 **(2x)**, 2 big feet on a kangaroo / Number 2 **(3x) all...**
Number 3 **(2x)**, 3 bananas on a banana tree...
Number 4 **(2x)**, we'll dance rumba all over the floor...

— **David Lee Walden**

 — On Raffi Rise & Shine *& in his* 2nd SB. OK58

Little House

Theirs is a little house, theirs is
In a pear tree full of pearses
Well they're birds you see, they live in a tree
Where they don't need ladders or stairses

D - A - / /G D G D / G - A D

They're happy & free from careses
They never have to run from bearses
And pears are free, they're birds you see
From the world or any other careses

Theirs is a little house, theirs is
With little bird beds & chairses
Did you ever hear of any house near
As nice a little house as theirs is?

— **w: Josef Berger** —**m: Nick Klonaris**

 — In SO! *9:4 &* Reprints #4. *On* Babysitters *(Vang), Lavender Jane* Loves Women, *Raffi* Everything Goes *& Faith Petric* Sing-a-S Sing Along *(GW).* OK59

The Little White Duck

There's a little white duck sitting in the water
A little white duck **doing what he oughter**
He took a bite of a lily pad
Flapped his wings & he said "I'm glad
I'm a little white duck sitting in the water
Quack! quack! quack!"

D - - A / - - - D / G - D - / E - A - / D - - A / - - D -

There's a little green frog swimming in the water
A little green frog **doing...oughter**
He jumped right off of the lily pad
That the little duck bit & he said "I'm glad
I'm a little green frog swimming... / Glug! Glug! Glug!"

There's a little black bug floating on the water / A...
He tickled the frog on the lily pad
That the little duck bit & he said "I'm glad
I'm a little black bug floating... /Bzz! Buzz! Bzz!"

There's a little red snake playing in the water / A...
He frightened the duck & the frog so bad
He ate the bug & he said "I'm glad
I'm a little red snake playing... / Hiss! Hiss! Hiss!"

Now there's nobody left sitting in the water / Nobody...
There's nothing left but the lily pad
The duck & the frog ran away – I'm sad
'Cause there's nobody left sitting... / Boo! Hoo! Hoo!

— **w: Bernard Zaritzky** — **m: Walt Barrows**

 — On Ives Sings 5 Early Tunes *& Raffi* Everything Goes. *In Tom Glazer* Treas of FS & Eye Winker. OK60

Mail Myself to You

I'm a-gonna wrap myself in paper
I'm gonna daub myself with glue
Stick some stamps on top of my head
I'm gonna mail myself to you

D A / / D G / D AD

I'm a-gonna tie me up in a red string
I'm gonna tie blue ribbons too
I'm a-gonna climb up in my mailbox
I'm gonna mail myself to you

When you see me in your mailbox
Cut the string & let me out
Wash the glue off my fingers
Stick some bubble-gum in my mouth

Take me out of my wrapping paper
Wash the stamps off my head
Pour me full of ice cream sodies
Tuck me in my nice warm bed

— **Woody Guthrie**

 — In his SB, SO! *13:1 &* V Favs of the V Young. *On* Tribute to Guthrie V2, *Pete Seeger* We Shall Overcome, *Guy Carawan* My Rhinoceros *& Faith Petric* Sing a S Sing Along *(both GW).* OK61

Marvelous Toy

When I was just a wee little lad full of health & joy
My father homeward came one night & gave to me a toy
A wonder to behold it was with many colors bright
And the moment I laid eyes on it it became my heart's delight

D A7 D A7 / G D E7 A7 / D A7 D G / G D A D A7

It went "Zip" when it moved & "Bop" when it stopped and "whirr" when it stood still
I never knew just what it was & I guess I never will

D A7 D G / G D A7 D

The first time that I picked it up I had a big surprise
For right on its bottom were two big buttons
that looked like big green eyes
I first pushed one & then the other & then I twisted its lid
And when I set it down again, here is what it did

It first marched left & then marched right
& then marched under a chair
And when I looked where it had gone it wasn't even there
I started to sob & my daddy laughed,
for he knew that I would find
When I turned around, my marvelous toy chugging from behind

Well the years have gone by too quickly it seems
& I have my own little boy
And yesterday I gave to him my marvelous little toy
His eyes nearly popped right out of his head
& he gave a squeal of glee
Neither one of us knows just what it is
but he loves it just like me
(final cho) It still goes **Zip when it moves...**

— Tom Paxton

© 1961 Cherry Lane Music Inc. All rights reserved. Used by permission. — On his Marv Toy. *Kevin Roth* Somebody Give Me Direction *&* Don't Wait for Me. *In* SO! *14:1 &* Reprints *#10.* OK62

Mr. Sun

O Mr. Sun, Sun, Mr. Golden Sun, please shine down on me
O Mr. Sun, Sun, Mr. Golden Sun, hiding behind a tree
These little children are asking you
to please come out so we can play with you
O Mr. Sun, Sun, Mr. Golden Sun, please shine down on me!

G A D G / - A - D / G D G D / G A D G

Adaptation of "Mr. Moon." On Raffi Singable S for the V Young *& in his* Singable SB. OK63

My Dreydel

I have a little dreydel, I made it out of clay
And when it's dry & ready, my dreydel I will play
O Dreydel (3x) I made it out of clay
Dreydel (3x) my dreydel I will play

D - - A / - - - D :||

I love to spin the dreydel, my top that plays a game
At Hanukah we play it when candles are aflame
O... my top that plays a game / ...when candles are aflame

My dreydel has four corners & a letter on each face
To remind us of the miracle that long ago took place
O... with a letter on each face / ...a miracle took place

The letters also tell us just who will lose or win
I have a pile of walnuts – I am ready, let's begin!
O... I wonder who will win? / ...I am ready, let's begin!

— m: S. E. Goldfarb; orig.
— w: Sam Grossman / addl v. Sam Hinton

Orig version fr The S We Sing *by Harry Coopersmith: United Synagogue of America. Reprinted by permission of The Board of Jewish Education of Greater NY. — On* Hanukkah S for Children, S for Hanukkah, *Jeff Klepper & Dan Freelander* Shalom Rav-kol B'Seder *& in* Hebrew Festival Melodies *(all Tara). On Raffi* Singable S for the Very Young *& in his* Singable SB. *In* More S We Sing, New Jewish SB *&* More S to Grow On. *On Nancy Raven* S for the Holiday. OK64

My Rhinoceros

1. My rhinoceros is silly, when we go for an auto ride
If he doesn't want to go with us, he runs to his room and hides
My rhinoceros (2x), he has such a beautiful smile
My rhinoceros (2x), but he smiles only once in a while

(in 3/4) CG C CG C / // F C G C / /

2. My rhinoceros loves donuts, he eats them night & morn
But he doesn't have any pockets so he carries them on his horn...
3. My rhinoceros gets dirty & Mama tells him to scrub
But there is no room for the water when he gets into the tub...
4. My rhinoceros gets thirsty when he goes to bed at night
He always asks for a drink of water after you turn out the light...
5. My rhinoceros gets tired & he has to take him a nap
But you have to tell him a story & let him sit on your lap...
6. My rhinoceros gets happy, he likes to dance all day
When he's dancing around his room it's best to keep out of his way...

— Edward Lipton

© 1970 by Edward Lipton. All rights reserved. Used by permission. — In his S for Singing *&* SO! *32:1. On* We're Going to the Zoo *& Guy Carawan* My Rhinoceros *(GW).* OK65

Octopus's Garden

I'd like to be under the sea
In an octopus' garden in the shade
He'd let us in, knows where we've been
In his octopus' garden in the shade
I'd ask my friends to come & see
An octopus' garden with me
I'd like to be under the sea
In an octopus' garden in the shade

C - Am - / F C G - / C - Am - / F G C -
F - - - / C - G - // " / " /

We would be warm below the storm
In our little hideaway beneath the wave
Resting our head on the sea bed
In an octopus' garden near a cave
We would sing & dance around
Because we know we can't be found / **I'd like...**

We would shout & swim about
The coral that lies beneath the waves
O what joy for every girl & boy
Knowing they're happy & they're safe
We would be happy you & me
No one there to tell us what to do
I'd like to be under the sea
In an octopus' garden with you **(3x)**

— Richard Starkey

© 1969 Startling Music Ltd. Used by permission. — On Beatles Abbey Rd *&* 1967-70. *On Raffi* One Light One Sun *& his* 2nd SB. OK66

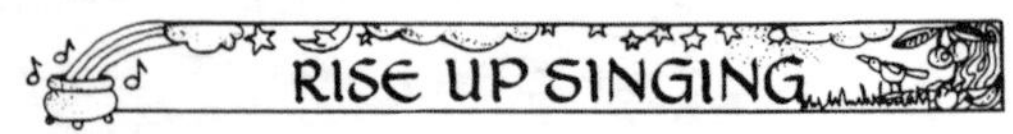

Oh Susanna

I come from Alabama with a banjo on my knee
I'm goin' to Lou'sianna my true love for to see
It rained all night the day I left, the weather it was dry
The sun so hot I froze to death, Susanna don't you cry

Oh Susanna, oh don't you cry for me
For I come from Alabama with a banjo on my knee

D - - A7 / D - DA D :|| G - D A / D - DA D

I had a dream the other night, when everything was still
I dreamed I saw Susanna a-coming down the hill
A buckwheat cake was in her mouth, a tear was in her eye
Says I "I'm comin' from the South: Susanna don't you cry"

— Stephen Foster

On Cathy Fink Grandma Slid Down *(Rounder) &* Grandma's Patchwork Quilt. *On Sparky Rucker* A Home in Tennessee *(GW). On (& in) Pete Seeger* Am Fav Bals V2. *In* FS Abecedary, FiresB of FS & Treas of Steph Foster. OK67

Old MacDonald

1. **Old MacDonald had a farm, E-I-E-I-O**
And on this farm he had some chicks, **E-I-E-I-O**
With a chick chick **here & a** chick chick **there**
Here a chick, **there a** chick, **everywhere a** chick chick
Old MacDonald had a farm, E-I-E-I-O

D GD DA D / ||: D - / - - :||* D GD DA D

2. ducks – quack quack *** as needed**
3. turkeys – gobble gobble
4. pigs – oink oink
5. a Ford – rattle rattle

(repeat 3rd & 4th lines of each v. previously sung)

*1. **Old MacDonald had a band E-I-E-I-O***
And in that band he had a** guitar **E-I-E-I-O
With a strum strum here & a... **(etc. as above)**
2. jug – whoof whoof **(blowing noise)** *3. banjo – plunk plunk*
4. drum – ratatat 5. tuba – oompah 6. some singers – la la

— new v. by Raffi & Ken Whiteley

© 1976 by Homeland Publishing, a div of Troubadour Records Ltd. All rights reserved. Used by permission. — On Raffi Singable S for the V Young *& in his* Singable SB. *Orig song on Kim Wallach* 2 Doz Childrens S *& in* SFest & Eye Winker. OK68

On Top of Spaghetti

On top of spaghetti all covered with cheese
I lost my poor meatball when somebody sneezed

(in 3/4, in C) F C / G7 C

It rolled off the table & onto the floor
And then my poor meatball rolled out of the door

It rolled in the garden & under a bush
And then my poor meatball was nothing but mush

The mush was as tasty as tasty could be
And early next summer it grew to a tree

The tree was all covered with beautiful moss
It grew great big meatballs & tomato sauce

So if you eat spaghetti all covered with cheese
Hold on to your meatball & don't ever sneeze

— w: Tom Glaser
— m: trad. (On Top of Old Smokey) — arr: Tom Glazer

© 1961 Songs Music Inc. Scarborough NY 10510. Lyrics reprinted herein by permission. All rights reserved. — In his Eye Winker Tom Tinker *& on Paul Strausman* Rainbows Stones & Dinosaur Bones *(GW) & Bob McGrath* Sing Along w/Bob. OK69

Over in the Meadow

Over in the meadow in a pond in the sun
Lived an old mother duck & her little duck one
"Quack" **said the mother,** "quack" **said the** one
And they quacked & were happy in their pond in the sun

D - Em A7 / D - A7 D / A7 - - - / D - A7 D

Over in the meadow in a stream so blue
Lived an old mother fish & her little fishes two
"Glub" **said the mother,** "Glub, glub" **(2x) said the** two
And they swam & were happy in the stream so blue

Over...in a nest in the tree / bird – birdies three / "tweet" **(3x)**
And they sang & were happy in their nest in the tree

Over...on a rock by the shore / frog – four / "croak" **(4x)**
And they croaked & were happy on the rock by the shore

Over...in a big bee hive / bee – five / "bzz" **(5x)**
And they buzzed & were happy in the big bee hive

Over...in the noonday sun
There was a pretty mother & her baby one
"Listen" said the mother "to the ducks & the bees
To the frogs & the fish & the birds in the trees"
"bzz" **(5x)** said the 5, "croak" **(4x)** said the 4
"tweet" **(3x)** said the 3, "glub" **(2x)** said the 2,
"quack" said the 1
And the little baby laughed just to hear such fun

— adap Lee Hays & Doris Kaplan

© 1968 by Sanga Music Inc. All rights reserved. Used by permission. — On Raffi Baby Beluga *& in his* Baby Beluga B & 2nd SB. OK70

Peanut Butter

Peanut, peanut butter! (& jelly & jelly) (2x)
First you take the grapes & you squish 'em, you squish 'em **(2x)**

Then you take the peanuts & you mash 'em, you mash 'em...
Next you take the bread & you spread it, you spread it...
Then you take the sandwich & you eat it, you eat it...

In SO!*32:2. On Cathy Fink* Granma Slid Down *(Rounder), Paul Strausman* Camels Cats & Rainbows *(GW) & Kim Wallach* 2 Doz Childrens S. OK71

Puff (the Magic Dragon)

Puff, the magic dragon, lived by the sea
And frolicked in the autumn mist in a land called Honalee
Little Jackie Paper loved that rascal Puff
And brought him strings & sealing wax & other fancy stuff

O-Puff... (cho = 1st 2 lines repeated twice)

G Bm C G / C G A D / 1st / C GEm AD GD

Together they would travel on a boat with billowed sail
Jackie kept a lookout perched on Puff's gigantic tail
Noble kings & princes would bow whene'er they came
Pirate ships would lower their flags when Puff roared out his name

A dragon lives forever, but not so little boys
Painted wings & giants' rings make way for other toys
One gray night it happened, Jackie Paper came no more
And Puff that mighty dragon, he ceased his fearless roar

His head was bent in sorrow, green scales fell like rain
Puff no longer went to play along the cherry lane
Without his lifelong friend, Puff could not be brave
So Puff that mighty dragon sadly slipped into his cave

— Peter Yarrow & Leonard Lipton

© 1963 Pepamar Music Corp. (ASCAP). Renewed 1991 Silver Dawn Music. All rights reserved. Used by permission. — On Peter Paul & Mary Moving, 10 Yrs, Best of & In Conc. *In* The Legal FakeB. OK72

Put Your Finger in the Air

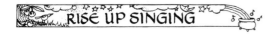

1. **Put your finger** in the air, in the air **(2x)**
   Put your finger in the air & leave it about a year
   Put your finger in the air, in the air

C - / - G7 / C FC / CG C

2. **Put your finger on your** head, **on your** head **(2x)**
   Put your finger on your head, tell me is it green or red?...
3. nose – & feel the cold wind blow...
4. shoe – & leave it a day or two...
5. chin – that's where the food slips in...
6. cheek – & leave it about a week...
7. **Put your finger on your** finger, on your finger **(2x)**
   Put your finger on your finger & your finger on your finger...
8. **Put your** fingers all together, all together **(2x)**
   Put your fingers all together both in dark & stormy weather...

— Woody Guthrie

TRO © 1954 (renewed 1982) Folkways Music Publishers Inc., NY, NY. International copyright secured. Made in USA. All rights reserved incl. public performance for profit. Used by permission. — In SO! *29:2 &* FiresB of Children's S. *On Pete Seeger* Children's Concert at Town Hall *(Columbia cassette 46185).* OK73

Riding in My Car

Brrrm brm brm... **(car noises to tune)**

C G7 / G7 C / C F / G7 C

Take me riding in the car car **(2x)**
Take you riding in the car car
I'll **take you riding in my car**

Click clack open up the door, girls
Click, clack open up the door, boys
Front door, back door, clickety clack
Take you riding in my car

Climb climb, rattle on the front seat
Spree I spraddle on the back seat
Turn my key, step on my starter / **Take...**

Engine it goes brrrm, brrrm **(2x)**
Front seat, back seat, boys & girls...

Trees & the houses walk along **(2x)**
Truck & a car & a garbage can...
Boom buh buh, buh buh buh buh, boom buh boom
Boom boom, buh buh buh buh, boom buh boom **(2x)**
Boom boom, buh buh buh buh, boom

Ships & the little boats chuck along **(2x)**
Brrrm buh buh, boom boom, boom buh boom / **Take...**

I'm a-gonna send you home again **(2x)**
Boom boom, buh buh boom, rolling home / **Take...**

I'm gonna let you blow the horn **(2x)**
A-oora, a-oorah, a-oogah, oogah / I'll **take...**

— Woody Guthrie

TRO © 1954 (renewed 1982) Folkways Music Publishers Inc. NY, NY. International copyright secured. Made in USA. All rights reserved incl pub performance for profit. Used by permission. — On his S to Grow On, Hard Trav, Gr S *& in his* SB. *On Peter Paul & Mary* In Conc, *Jack Elliot* Sings the S of Guthrie *& Pete Seeger* Children's Concert at Town Hall. *In Bikel* FS & Footnotes. OK74

Rise and Shine

The Lord said to Noah there's gonna be a floody, floody **(2x)**
The whole world is **(clap)** gonna be muddy, muddy
Children of the Lord – So:

C - F - /   / C - F C / - G C -

Rise & shine & give God the glory, glory (2x)
Rise & shine & (clap) give God the glory, glory
Children of the Lord!

The Lord said to Noah you better build an arky, arky **(2x)**
Build it out of **(clap)** birchy barky, barky / **Children...**

The animals came on board they came on by twosies, twosies
Elephants & **(clap)** kangaroosies, -oosies

It rained & rained for 40 nights & daisies, daisies
Almost drove those **(clap)** animals crazy, crazy

Noah he looked up & saw a dovey, dovey
Saw it up in **(clap)** heaven abovey, -bovey

The sun came out & dried up the landy, landy
Everything was fine & dandy, dandy

The animals came off, came off by threesies, threesies
They'd heard about those **(clap)** birds & beesies, beesies

This is the end of, the end of my story, story
Everything is **(clap)** hunky-dory, -dory

— trad. (Black Spiritual)

In FSEncyV1, Story of the Spirituals. OK75

Rubber Blubber Whale

My daddy bought me a **rubber blubber** whale **(2x)**
How I love my **R.B.**, **R.B.**, **R.B.**
How I love my **R.B.** whale, blubber whale
How I love my **R.B.** whale

C - - - / F - - C / F C F C / - - F - / C G C -

My sister wanted my **R.B.** whale **(2x)**
Yes I really love her, but she cannot have my **R.B.**
R.B., **R.B.** whale, blubber whale
R.B., **R.B.** whale

So my momma bought another **R.B.** whale **(2x)**
R.B., **R.B.**, **R.B.**, **R.B.**
R.B., **R.B.** whale, blubber whale
R.B., **R.B.** whale

I went swimming with my **R.B.** whale **(2x)**
Swimming with my **R.B.**, **R.B.**, **R.B.**
R.B., **R.B.** whale, blubber whale
R.B., **R.B.** whale

I took a bath with my **R.B.** whale **(2x)**
R.B., **R.B.**, **R.B.**, **R.B.**
R.B., **R.B.** whale, blubber whale
R.B., **R.B.** whale

And I rub-a-dubbed my **R.B.** whale **(2x)**
Rub-a-dubbed my **R.B.**, **R.B.**, **R.B.**
Rub-a-dubbed my **R.B.** whale, blubber whale
Rub-a-dubbed my **R.B.** whale

Everybody rub-a-dub your **R.B.** whale **(2x)**
Rub-a-dub your **R.B.**, **R.B.**, **R.B.**
Rub-a-dub your **R.B.** whale, blubber whale
Rub-a-dub your **R.B.** whale

— Si Kahn

© Joe Hill Music (ASCAP). All rights reserved. Used by permission. — On We're Going to the Zoo, *John McCutheon* Howjadoo *& Robin & Linda Williams* Down in the Valley *(GW).* OK76

Shake My Sillies Out

1. Gotta shake, shake, shake my sillies out
   Shake, shake, shake my sillies out **(2x)**
   And wiggle my waggles away

D G D - / A - D - :||

2. Gotta clap, clap, clap my crazies out
   Clap, clap, clap my crazies out **(2x)** / **And wiggle...**
3. Gotta jump, jump, jump my jiggles out... / **& wiggle...**
4. Gotta growl, growl, growl my grumpies out... / **& wiggle...**
5. **(slower)** Gotta yawn, yawn, yawn my sleepies out...

— Raffi

© 1977 by Homeland Publishing, a division of Troubadour Records Ltd. All rights reserved. Used by permission. — On his More Singable S *& in his* Singable SB. OK77

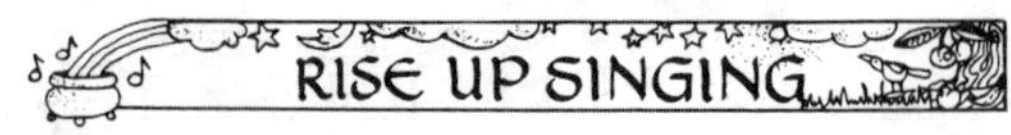

She'll Be Comin' 'Round the Mountain

She'll be comin' 'round the mountain **when she comes**
(toot toot!) **(2x)**
She'll be comin' 'round the mountain, she'll be...mountain
She'll be comin' 'round the mountain when she comes
(toot toot!)

D - - - / - - A - / D D7 G - / D A D -

She'll be ridin' six white horses **when she comes**
(whoa back!)...
She'll be wearin' pink pajamas when... (scratch scratch!)...
O we'll all go out to meet her... ("Hi, babe!")
O we'll kill the old red rooster... (hack hack!)
O we'll all have chicken & dumplin's... (yum yum!)
O she'll have to sleep with grandpa... (snore snore!)

A parody of the old camp meeting song "Old Ship of Zion" which goes back to the 1830s or earlier, adapted by mountaineers & then spread to RR work crews in the West. On Mike & Peggy Seeger (& in Ruth Seeger) Am FS for Children *(Rounder), Sharon Lois & Bram* One Elephant, Deux Elephants, *Pete Seeger* Am FS for Children, *John Denver* Rocky Mtn Holiday, *Nick Seeger* A S or 2 for You, *Reid Miller* Jubilee, *Sparky Rucker* A Home in Tennessee *(GW) & Jim Kweskin* Lives Again *(MR 52782). In* SO! *20:3,* FiresB of FS, *Lomax* FS of NAm, SFest, FSEncyV1, *&* FiresB of Fun & Games. OK78

Skip to My Lou

Lost my partner, what'll I do? **(3x)**
Skip to my lou my darling

D - / A7 - / D - / A7 D

Skip, skip, skip to my lou **(3x)**
Skip to my lou my darling

I'll get another one prettier than you **(3x) / Skip...**
Little red wagon painted blue...
Flies in the buttermilk, two by two...
Flies in the sugar bowl, shoo shoo shoo!...
Going to Texas, two by two...
Cat's in the cream jar, what'll I do?...

Young people in most 19th c. (& some 20th c.) midwestern rural communities were barred from dancing for relig reasons. Dancing was considered sinful but playing games wasn't. As a result play party games evolved such as this one, accompanied by clapping & singing but no instruments – some as intricate as a modern square dance. In Am Fav Bals *& on Mike & Peggy Seeger* Am Folk Songs For Children *(Rounder 80021, 2, 3), Pete Seeger* S & Playtime *& Bob McGrath* Sing Along w/Bob. OK79

Sodeo

Here we go Sodeo, Sodeo, Sodeo
Here we go Sodeo, all night long
Step back Sally, Sally, Sally
Step back Sally, all night long

C - - - / - - G C :||

I went to the plaza & what did I see?
A big fat man from Calgary
I bet you $5 I can catch that man **(2x)**

To the front, to the back, to the see-saw side **(2x)**

C - - - :||

I went to the doctor, the doctor said
Ooh, ah, I got a pain in my side
Ooh, ah, I got a pain in my stomach
Ooh, ah, I got a pain in my head

C - - - :|| **(4x)**

On Raffi More Singable S *& in his* Singable SB. OK80

Teddy Bears' Picnic

If you go down in the woods today
You're sure of a big surprise
If you go down in the woods today
You'd better go in disguise
For every bear that ever there was
Will gather there for certain because
Today's the day the Teddy bears have their picnic

Am E Am E / Am E Am - / C G C G / C G C -
Dm - G - / C - F C / F C F C G7 - C -

Every Teddy bear who's been good
Is sure of a treat today
There's lots of marvelous things to eat
And wonderful games to play
Beneath the trees where nobody sees
They'll hide & seek as long as they please
'Cause that's the way the Teddy bears have their picnic

If you go down to the woods today
You'd better not go alone
It's lovely down in the woods today
But safer to stay at home
For every bear that ever there was
Will gather there for certain because
Today's the day the Teddy bears have their picnic

(interlude) Picnic time for Teddy bears
The little Teddy bears are having a lovely time today
Watch them, catch them unawares
And see them picnic on their holiday
See them gaily gad about
They love to play & shout, they never have any care
At six o'clock their Mummies & Daddies will take
them home to bed
Because they're tired little Teddy bears

C - - - / - - Dm G7 / - - - - / - - C G7
C - - - / - C7 F - / - - C - / Dm G7 C -

— w: Jimmy Kennedy — m: John W. Bratton

 — On We're Going to the Zoo, *Dave Van Ronk* S for Aging Children *(CA50044), Rosenhonz* Tickles You *(RSRecs) & Kevin Roth* Unbearable Bears. *In* The Legal FakeB. OK81

Ten Little Frogs

<u>Ten</u> **green & speckled frogs, sat on a speckled log**
Eating some most delicious bugs (yum, yum!)
One jumped into the pool, where it was nice & cool
Then there were <u>nine</u> **green speckled frogs (glub glub)**

C F / C G / C F / CG C

<u>Nine</u> **green & speckled frogs, (etc.)**

— L.B.Scott & Virginia Pavelko

 Fr their Singing Fun. *aka: "5 Little Frogs." On Raffi* Singable S for the V Young *& in his* Singable SB. OK82

There's a Hole in the Bottom of the Sea

1. **There's a** <u>hole</u> **in the middle of the sea (2x)**
   There's a <u>hole</u>**, There's a** <u>hole</u>
   There's a <u>hole</u> **in the middle of the sea**

G - D - / - - G - / D - - - / - - G -

2. **There's a** log in the hole **in the middle of the sea (2x)**
   There's a log**, there's a** log
   There's a log in the hole **in the middle of the sea**

G - - D - / - - - G - / D - - - / - - - G -

3. **There's a** bump on the log in the hole **in the middle of the sea...**

G* D - / D* G - / D - - - / D* G -

(* repeat chord 4 - 8x as needed)

4. **There's a** frog on the bump on the log in the hole **in the middle of the sea...**
5. **There's a** fly on the frog on the bump on the log in the hole **in the middle of the sea...**
6. **There's a** wing on the fly on the frog on the bump on the log **in the hole in the middle of the sea...**
7. **There's a** flea on the wing on the fly on the frog on the bump on the log in the hole **in the middle of the sea...**

In SO! *26:2,* Eye Winker & FiresB of Fun & Games. *On Nick Seeger* A S or 2 for You *(GW).* OK83

This Old Man

This old man, he played one
He played knick-knack on my thumb
With a knick-knack paddy-wack give your dog a bone
This old man came rolling home

D - / G A / D - / A AD

This old man, he played 2 / He played...on my shoe...
3 – on my knee / 4 – door / 5 – hive / 6 – sticks
7 – up in heaven / 8 – on my pate / 9 – on my spine
10 – once again

This old man, he plays *one*
He plays *one on his old drum*
O yes, yes, yes, uh huh
He plays one on his old drum, ***uh huh***

D - / - D_7 / G - D - / A_7 G_7 D -

2 – on his kazoo / 3 – on his ukelele / 4 – on his guitar
5 – with his friend Clive

(tag) *This old man, he plays one. This old man, he plays 2 ...This old man he plays 5 – knick knack, paddy whack!*

— new words by Raffi, D. Pike, B. & B. Simpson

 On (& in) Raffi Baby Beluga & in his 2nd SB. — Orig version on Mike & Peggy (& in Ruth) Seeger Am FS for Children *(Rounder). On Kim Wallach* 2 Doz Childrens S *& Pete Seeger* Am FS for Children. *Also in* FSEncy V1, Eye Winker & V Favs for the V Young *(WAS).* OK84

Throw it Out the Window

Old Mother Hubbard went to the cupboard
To fetch her poor dog a bone
But when she got there the cupboard was bare
So she threw it **out the window**
The window (2x) / the second-story window
But when she got there the cupboard was bare
So she threw it **out the window**

D - / - A / - - / - D // - - / - A / - - / - D

Old King Cole was a merry old soul
And a merry old soul was he
He called for his pipe & he called for his bowl
And threw them **out the window**
The window, the second-story window
He called for his pipe & he called for his bowl
And threw them **out the window**

Little Bo Peep has lost her sheep
And doesn't know where to find them
But leave them alone, when they come home
She'll throw them **out the window...**

O where, o where has my little dog gone?
O where, o where can he be?
With his ears cut short & his tail cut long
I'll throw him **out the window...**

Yankee Doodle went to town
A-riding on a pony
He stuck a feather in his cap
And threw **it out the window...**

A-tisket a-tasket
A green & yellow basket
I wrote a letter to my love
And threw it out the **window... (etc.)**

(Can substitute 1st 3 lines of many nursury rhymes & other songs for addl v.) On Trout Fishing in America. In FiresB of Fun & Games & V Favs of the V Young. OK85

We're Off to See the Wizard

(intro) Follow the yellow brick road **(2x)**
Follow **(5x)** the yellow brick road
Follow the rainbow over the stream, follow the fellow who follows a dream
Follow **(5x)** the yellow brick road

CG C (2x) / C FG D G / F C FG C / 2nd /

We're off to see the Wizard, the wonderful Wizard of Oz
We hear he is a Whiz of a Wiz if ever a Wiz there was
If ever o ever a Wiz there was, the Wizard of Oz is one becoz
Becoz **(5x)** / Becoz of the wonderful things he does **(whistle)**
We're off to see the Wizard, the wonderful Wizard of Oz!

CG C D_mG C / F GF D_7 G / F C D_mG C
C E_mF G - / GD_7 G (2x) / CG C D_mG C

— E.Y.Harburg & Harold Arlen

 — Fr their musical The Wizard of Oz. *In* Those Wonderful Yrs. OK86

Wheels on the Bus

The wheels on the bus go round & round
Round & round, round & round
The wheels on the bus go round & round
All around the town

D - / A D :||

The wipers on the bus go swish swish swish...
The driver on the bus goes "Move on back!"...
The people on the bus go up & down...
The horn on the bus goes beep beep beep...
The baby on the bus goes "Wah wah wah!"...
The parents on the bus go Sh sh sh...

In Raffi 2nd SB *& on his* Rise & Shine, *Kim Wallach* 2 Doz Childrens S *& Bob McGrath* Sing Along w/Bob. *Also in* V Fav of the V Young. OK87

When I First Came to this Land

1. **When I first came to this land I was not a wealthy man**
So I got myself a farm & I did what I could
And I called my farm: "muscle in my arm"
But the land was sweet & good & I did what I could

C FC FC GC / C FC G C

||: FC GC :|| * **(* as needed)** C FC G C

2. **When...man / So I got myself a** shack **& I...**
And I called my shack "break my back"
And I called my farm "muscle in my arm" / **But the land...**
3. cow – no milk now 4. horse – dead of course
5. duck – out of luck
6. dog – what a hog! 7. pig – dance a jig
8. wife – run for your life [joy of my life]
9. son – my work's done [child – free & wild]

— Oscar Brand

 On his Best of. *In* SO! *7:3 &* Reprints #2. *On Roxanne & Dan Keding* In Came That Rooster, *Kim Wallach* 2 Doz Childrens S, *& MF Rhoads & J Pearse* Together. *On (& in) Pete Seeger* Am Fav Bals V3. *In SO! 7:3,* Singing Holidays & FSEncyV2. OK88

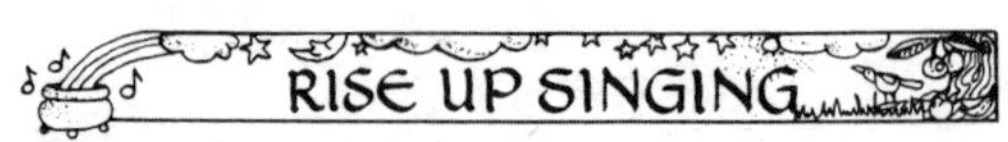

Who Built the Ark

Who built the ark? – Noah, Noah!
Who built the ark? – Brother Noah built the ark

D - G - / D - A D

Now didn't old Noah build the ark?
He built it out of hickory bark
He built it long, both wide & tall
Plenty of room for the large & small

||: D - - - / - - A D :||

Now in came the animals 2 by 2
Hippopotamus & kangaroo
Now in came the animals 3 by 3
Two big cats & a bumblebee

Now in came the animals 4 by 4
2 thru the window & 2 thru the door
Now in came the animals 5 by 5
5 little sparrows doin' the jive

Now in came the animals 6 by 6
The elephant laughed at the monkey's tricks
Now in came the animals 7 by 7
4 from home & the rest from heaven

Now in came the animals 8 by 8
Some were on time & the others were late
Now in came the animals 9 by 9
Some were shoutin' & some were cryin'

Now in came the animals 10 by 10
5 black roosters & 5 black hens
Now Noah says "Go & shut that door
The rain's started dropping & we can't take more"

This song is a reworking of a Black Spiritual. On Mike & Peggy Seeger Am Folk Songs for Children, *Bluestein Fam* Horse Named Bill, *Raffi* More Singable S *& in his* Singable SB. K89

Yellow Submarine

In the town where I was born lived a man who sailed the sea
And he told us of his life in the land of submarines

(in D) A D Em A / /

So we sailed up to the sun til we found the sea of green
And we lived beneath the waves in our yellow submarine

We all lived in a yellow submarine
A yellow submarine, a yellow submarine (repeat)

A - / - D / - A / - D

And our friends are all aboard, many more of them live next door
And the band begins to play: **(make band noises together)**

As we live the life of ease, everyone of us has all we need
Sky of blue & sea of green in your yellow submarine

— John Lennon & Paul McCartney

 — On Beatles Yellow Submarine & 1962-66. *In* Club Date FakeB. K90

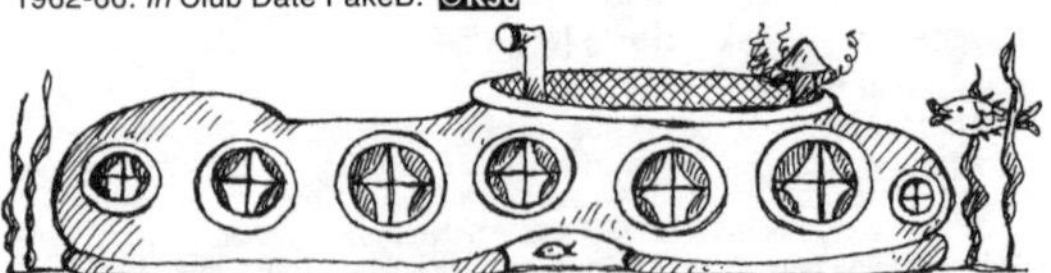

You Can't Make a Turtle Come Out

You can't make a turtle come out **(2x)**
You can coax him or call him or shake him or shout, but
You can't make a turtle come out, come out
You can't make a turtle come out

(in 3/4) C G C G / C G C C7 / F D7 Em A Dm G CCG C / F G C -

If he wants to stay in his shell **(2x)**
You can knock on the door but you can't ring the bell &...

Be kind to your four-footed friends **(2x)**
A poke makes a turtle retreat at both ends &...

So you'll have to patiently wait **(2x)**
And when he gets ready he'll open the gate, but...

And when you forget that he's there **(2x)**
He'll be walking around with his head in the air, but...

— Malvina Reynolds

 — On her Artichokes & Funny Bugs *& in her* Cheerful Tunes for Lutes & Spooks, Little Boxes *&* SB. *Also on Ginni Clemens* Long Time Friends, *Jay Ungar & Lyn Hardy* A Place To Be *& Cathy Fink et al* Grandma's Patchwork Quilt. *In* SO! *27:6.* K91

*There are many excellent records & tapes of children's music which have been brought out in the last several years. The editor's favorite is the Canadian singer Raffi. His albums are distributed in the US by A&M Records, and in Canada by Troubadour Records (6043 Yonge St., Willowdale, Ont. M2M-3W3. He has published 2 books (*The Singable Songbook & The 2nd Raffi Songbook*) which include music to all the songs on his first 6 albums. These are distributed in Canada by Chappell Music (85 Scarsdale Rd, Unit 101, Don Mills, Ontario M3B 2R2.)*

Mike & Peggy Seeger have issued a three volume collection on Rounder with all the songs in their mother Ruth Crawford Seeger's collection Amer FS for Children. *Malvina Reynolds, Pete Seeger, Peter Paul & Mary, Peter Alsop, Woody Guthrie & many other folksingers all have produced special children's albums. Carol Johnson is one of many lesser-known artists focusing specifically on writing songs for children. Her albums can be obtained from: Noeldner Music, PO Box 6351, Grand Rapids MI 49506.*

The PLAY chapter includes basically songs which are favorites of children. Songs about children are mainly in HOME & FAMILY. Slightly more adult playful/humorous songs are found in FUNNY SONGS. LULLABIES have their own chapter.

Here is a list of animal songs in this book: "Stewball," "Tennessee Stud" (AMER) "Little Brown Dog" (DREAM) "Waydy Bug" (ECO) "Cat Came Back," "Eddystone Light," "Hippopotamus Song," "Rooster Song," "Waltzing with Bears" (FUN) "All the Pretty Little Horses," "Aunt Rhody," "Goodnight Irene" (new v. Raffi), "Mockingbird Song" (LULL) "Mole in the Ground" (MTN) "Kookabura," "Ride-a-cock Horse," "Why Shouldn't My Goose" (ROUNDS) & "A Place in Choir" ["All God's Critters"], "Under One Sky" (UNITY).

Other children's songs include: "Cockles & Mussels," "I Live in a City" (CITY) "Do Re Mi," "Sarasponda," "Sur le Pont" (CREAT) "Down on the Farm" (ECO) "The Garden Song" ["Inch by Inch"] "Oats Peas Beans," "Pick a Bale o' Cotton" (FARM) "Go Down Moses," "Michael Row" (FREE) "I've Got Sixpence" (GOOD) "May There Always Be Sunshine," "Study War No More" (PEACE) "I Had a Little Overcoat" (RICH) "Down at the Station," "Scotland's Burning" (ROUNDS) "Casey Jones," "Daddy What's a Train" (TRAV) "I'm a Little Cookie," "In the Very Middle," "Magic Penny" (UNITY) "The Witch Song" (WOMEN) & "The Bread Song" (WORK).

Banks of Marble

I've traveled round this country
From shore to shining shore
It really makes me wonder
The things I heard & saw

C G C - / F - C - / G - C - /   /

I saw the weary farmer
Plowing sod & loam
I heard the auction hammer
Just a-knocking down their home

But the banks are made of marble
With a guard at every door
And the vaults are stuffed with silver
That the farmer *[seaman, etc.]* **sweated for**

C - - - / G - C - / - - FC C / G - C -

I saw the seamen standing
Idly by the shore
I heard the bosses saying
"Got no work for you no more"

I've seen the weary miners
Scrubbing coal dust from their backs
And I heard their children crying
"Got no coal to heat the shack"

I've seen my brothers working *[My brothers & my sisters]*
Thru out this mighty land *[Are at work throughout this land]*
I pray we'll get together
And together make a stand

(last cho) Then we'll own those **banks of marble**
With no **guard at any door**
And we'll share those vaults of silver
That the workers **sweated for!**

— Les Rice

© 1950 (renewed) by Stormking Music, Inc. All rights reserved. Used by permission. *In* SO! *1:1 & 44:4* & Reprints #8, Bells of Rhymney, Hootenanny SB & Carry It On. *On Pete Seeger* Banks of Marble, *Weavers* Trav On & Reunion 1963. OC26

Big Rock Candy Mountain

(intro) One evening as the sun went down
And the jungle* fires were burning
Down the track came a hobo hiking
He said "Boys, I'm not turning
I'm heading for a land that's far away
Beside that crystal fountain
I'll see you all this coming fall
In the Big Rock Candy Mountain"

DA DA/DA D/   /   /GD GD/G A/ 1st 2 /

In the... / It's a land that's fair & bright
The handouts grow on bushes
And you sleep out ev'ry night
The boxcars are all empty
And the sun shines every day
I'm bound to go where there ain't no snow
Where the sleet don't fall & the winds don't blow / In...

D -/G D/   /Em A/ 1st 2 /GD GD/   /A D

O the buzzing of the bees in the cigarette trees
By the soda water fountain
Near the lemonade springs where the bluebird sings
On the Big Rock Candy Mountain

D - / G D / A D /   /

In... / You never change your socks
Little streams of alky-hol
Come trickling down the rocks
O the shacks all have to tip their hats
And the RR bulls are blind
There's a lake of stew & gingerale too
And you can paddle all around it in a big canoe / **In...**

In... / The cops have wooden legs
The bulldogs all have rubber teeth
And the hens lay soft-boiled eggs
The box-cars all are empty
And the sun shines every day
I'm bound to go where there ain't no snow
Where the sleet don't fall & the winds don't blow / **In...**

In... / The jails are made of tin
You can slip right out again
As soon as they put you in
There ain't no short-handled shovels
No axes, saws nor picks
I'm bound to stay where you sleep all day
Where they hung the jerk that invented work / **In...**

— Harry McClintock

**A hobo jungle was a patch of ground usually nr the RR tracks, where tramps, hobos & migrants would camp overnight, waiting for the right freight train to take them out. aka: "Rock Candy Mtn." McClintock also wrote "Hallelujah, I'm A Bum."* *In* SO! *30:2*, FSEncyV2, FS Abecedary, S That Changed the World, 120 Am S, *Lomax* FS of NAm, & S Am Sings. *On (& in) Pete Seeger* Am Fav Bals V1 *On Ives* S of Expanding Am & Bals & FS V3. OC27

Brother, Can You Spare a Dime?

(intro:) They used to tell me I was building a dream
And so I followed the mob
When there was earth to plough or guns to bear
I was always there, right on the job
They used to tell ... dream / With peace & glory ahead
Why should I be standing in line / Just waiting for bread

Am Dm6/Am DmG/C B7/Dm6 E/1st /Am G/C E/Am E

Once I built a RR, I made it run / I made it run against time
Once I built a RR, now it's done
Brother, can you spare a dime?

Am EG / Dm Am /   / E - Am (E)

Once I built a tower, up to the sun / Bricks & mortar & lime
Once I built a tower, now it's done / **Brother...**

(bridge) Once in khaki suits, gee we looked swell
Full of that Yankee-Doodly-dum
Half a million boots went slogging through Hell
And I was the kid with the drum

Am - / - E :||

Say, don't you remember, you called me "Al"
It was "Al" all the time
Say don't you remember, I was your pal / **Buddy...**

— w: E. Y. Harburg   **— m: Joe Gorney**

© 1932 (renewed) Warner Bros. Inc. All rights reserved. Used by permission. *In* SO! *30:1*, 100 Best S of the '20s & '30s, *Readers Dig* Fest of Popular S, & S That Changed the World. *On Judy Collins* Judith, *Peter Paul & Mary* See What Tomorrow, *Tom Jones* Wales, *Weavers* Gr H & *Prisc Herdman* Forgotten Dreams *(FF)*. OC28

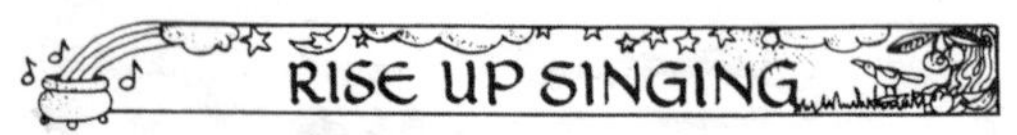

The Commonwealth of Toil

In the gloom of mighty cities, mid the roar of whirling wheels
We are toiling on like chattel slaves of old
And our masters hope to keep us ever thus beneath their heels
And to coin our very life blood into gold

C F / C G / C F / CG C

But we have a glowing dream of how fair the world will seem
When each man can live his life *[we all can live our lives]* **secure & free**
When the earth is owned by labor & there's joy & peace for all
In the Commonwealth of Toil that is to be

G C / C G / C F / CG C

They would keep us cowed & beaten, cringing meekly at their feet
They would stand between each worker & his bread
Shall we yield our lives up to them for the bitter crust we eat?
Shall we only hope for heaven when we're dead?

They have laid our lives out for us to the utter end of time
Shall we stagger on beneath their heavy load?
Shall we let them live forever in their gilded halls of crime
With our children doomed to toil beneath their goad?

When our cause is all triumphant & we claim our Mother Earth
And the nightmare of the present fades away
We shall live with love & laughter, we who now are little worth
And we'll not regret the price we have to pay

— w: Ralph Chaplin m: trad ("Nellie Bly")

One of the great songwriters of the Industrial Workers of the World. In SO! *15: 2 &* Reprints *#8*, S of Work & Protest *& The* IWW SB. OC29

Do Re Mi (Guthrie)

Lots of folks back East, they say, leavin' home ev'ry day
Beatin' the hot old dusty way to the California line
'Cross the desert sands they roll getting out of that old dust bowl
They think they're going to a sugar bowl, but here is what they find:
Now the police at the port of entry say
You're number 14,000 for today

G - C - / D - G - / 1st / D - G - - / D - - - / /

O if you ain't got the do re mi, folks
If you ain't got the do re mi
Why you better go back to beautiful Texas
Oklahoma, Kansas, Georgia, Tennessee
California is a garden of Eden
A paradise to live in or see
But believe it or not, you won't find it so hot
If you ain't got the do re mi

G - - - / - - D - / - - - - / - - G -
/ " / G - C - / G DG C G / - CD G -

If you want to buy your home or farm that can't do nobody harm / Or take your vacation by the mountain or sea
Don't swap your old cow for a car, you'd better stay right where you are
You'd better take this little tip from me
'Cause I look thru the want ads every day
But the headlines in the papers always say:

— Woody Guthrie

 – On his Bound for Glory *(Folkways)*, Gr S *(Vang)*, Lib. of Cong *(Elektra)*, Dust Bowl Bals *(Folkways)*, 1940-46 *(WB) &* Legendary Performer. *On* Tom Rush *(Elektra)*, Ry Cooder, Tribute to Woody Guthrie pt 1, *Pete Seeger & Arlo Guthrie* Prec Friend *& Bluestein Fam* Let the Dove Come In. *In* SO! *12:4 &* Reprints *#6.* OC30

Going Down the Road

I'm blowin' down this old dusty road
Yes, I'm blowin' down this old dusty road
I'm blowin' down this old dusty road, **Lord God**
And I ain't a-gonna be treated this way

D - / G D / / A D

I'm going where the water tastes like wine **(3x) / And...**
I'm going where them dust storms never blow...
They say I'm a dust-bowl refugee...
I'm looking for a job at honest pay...
My children need three square meals a day...
Your $2 shoe hurts my feet...
Takes a $10 shoe to fit my feet...
I'm goin' down this old dusty road...

— Woody Guthrie & Lee Hays

 – In Woody Guthrie SB *& on his* This Land, Legendary Performer, Gr S, Lib. of Cong, Bonneville Dam, Dust Bowl Bals, We Ain't Down Yet *&* Sings FS V2. *In* S of Work & Protest *&* People's SB, FS Abecedary, S That Changed the World, Treas of Am S, S Am Sings *&* FSEncyV2. *On Eliz Cotton* FS & Instrums. OC31

Hallelujah, I'm a Bum

O why don't you work like other men do?
How the hell can I work when there's no work to do?
Hallelujah, I'm a bum – Hallelujah, bum again!
Hallelujah, give us a handout to revive us again

(in 3/4) D - - - / - - - A / D - - A / D G A D

I went to a house, I knocked on the door
The lady said "Scram, bum, you've been here before!"

Whenever I get all the money I earn
The boss will go broke & to work he must turn

O I love my boss, he's a good friend of mine
That's why I am starving out on the bread line

O why don't you save all the money you earn?
If I didn't eat, I'd have money to burn

— w: Harry McClintock
— m: John J. Husband ("Revive Us Again")

On Utah Phillips We Have Fed You All *(Philo)*, All Used Up *(Philo) &* Sings the S of the IWW. *On Earl Robinson* Strange Unusual Eve. *In* S of Work & Protest, FiresB of FS, SFest, Carry It On, S for Pickin & Singin, S That Changed the World, Treas of Am S *&* FSEncyV1. OC32

How Can a Poor Man Stand Such Times & Live?

There once was a time when everything was cheap _
But now prices nearly puts a man to sleep _
When we pay our grocery bill
we just a-feel like makin' our will
Tell me how can a poor man stand such times & live?

D A D - / - - A - / D - G D // D A D -

I remember when drygoods were cheap as dirt
We could take two bits & buy a dandy shirt
Now we pay three bucks or more,
maybe get a shirt that another man wore / **Tell me...**

Well I used to trade with a man by the name of Gray
Flour was 50¢ for a 24 lb. bag
Now it's a dollar & a half beside
just like a-skinnin' off a flea for the hide...

O the schools we have today ain't worth a cent
But they see to it that every child is sent
If we don't send every day we have a heavy fine to pay...

Prohibition's good if 'tis conducted right
There's no sense in shooting a man til he shows flight
Officers kill without a cause,
then complain about funny laws...

Most all preachers preach for gold & not for souls
That's what keeps a poor man always in a hole
We can hardly get our breath,
taxed & schooled & preached to death...

O it's time for every man to be awake
We pay 50¢ a pound when we ask for steak
When we get our package home
a little wad of paper with gristle & bone...

Well the doctor comes around with a face all bright
And he says in a little while you'll be all right
All he gives is a humbug pill,
a dose of dope & a great big bill...

— Blind Alfred Reed

© 1930 Peer International Corp. Copyright renewed. All rights reserved. Used by permission of CPP Belwin Inc. – In SO! 20:2. On New Lost City Ramblers S of the Gr Depression *(FH5264) & in their* SB *& rec by Ry Cooder.* OC33

I Ain't Got No Home in This World

I ain't got no home, I'm just a rambling round
Just a wand'rin' worker, I go from town to town
The police make it hard wherever I may go
And I ain't got no home in this world anymore

D - G D / - - E A / 1st / D - DA D

My brothers & my sisters are stranded on this road
A hot, dusty road that a million feet have trod
Rich man took my home & drove me from my door / **And I...**

Was a-farmin' on the shares & always I was poor
My crops I laid into the banker's store
And my wife took down & died upon the cabin floor...

Now as I look around it's mighty plain to see
This wide wicked world is a funny place to be
The gambling man is rich & the working man is poor...

— new w & m adaptation Woody Guthrie

from trad. gospel ("This World Is Not My Home") TRO © 1961 & 1963 Ludlow Music, Inc, NY, NY. International copyright secured. Made in USA. All rights reserved incl. public performance for profit. Used by permission. – On his Legendary Performer, Gr S, Lib. of Congress & Dust Bowl Bals. *On* Tribute to Woody Guthrie, pt1 *& Magpie* Working My Life Away. *In SO! 6:2 & Reprints #2. For orig version see GOSPEL.* OC34

I Am Changing My Name to Chrysler

O the price of gold is rising out of sight
And the dollar is in sorry shape tonight
What a dollar used to get us now won't get a head of lettuce
No the economic forecast isn't bright
But amidst the clouds I spot a shining ray
I begin to glimpse a new & better way
I've devised a plan of action,
worked it down to the last fraction
And I'm going into action here today

GC G*/ C G / D GE / A D
/ " / C B7 / C GE / AD G (*cho: GD G)

I am changing my name to "Chrysler"
I am going down to Washington, D.C.
I will tell some power broker "What you did for Iacocca
Would be perfectly acceptable to me!"
I am changing my name to "Chrysler"
I am leaving for that great receiving line
When they hand a million grand out,
I'll be standing with my hand out
Yes sir, I'll get mine

When my creditors come screaming for their dough
I'll be proud to tell them all where they can go
They won't have to yell & holler,
they'll be paid to the last dollar
Where the endless streams of money seem to flow
I'll be glad to show them all what they must do
It's a matter of a simple form or two
It's not just remuneration, it's a lib'ral education
Makes you kind of glad that I'm in debt to you

Since the first amphibian crawled out of the slime
We've been struggling in an unrelenting climb
We were hardly up & walking before money started talking
And it said that failure is an awful crime
It's been that way a millennium or two
Now it seems there is a different point of view
If you're a corporate titanic & your failure is gigantic
Down in Congress there's a safety net for you

— Tom Paxton

© 1980 Accabonac Music. All rights reserved. Used by permission. – On his The Paxton Report *(FF), Pete Seeger & A Guthrie* Prec Friend & NSLT. *In SO! 29:2.* OC35

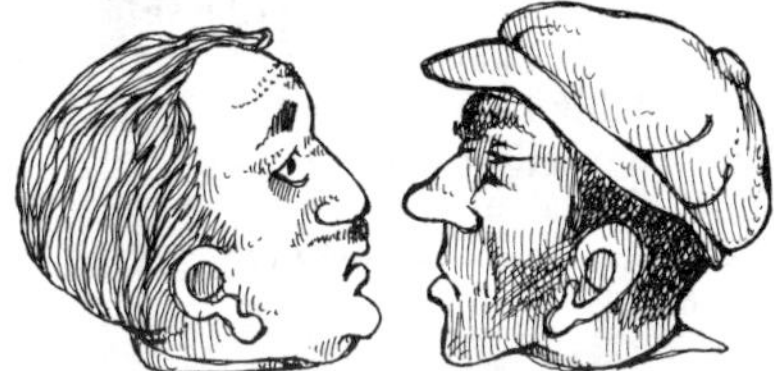

I Don't Want Your Millions Mister

I don't want your millions, Mister
I don't want your diamond ring
All I want is the right to live, Mister
Give me back my job again

C - / F C / / G C

I don't want your Rolls Royce, Mister
I don't want your pleasure yacht
All I want is food for my babies
Give to me my old job back

I know you have the land deed, Mister
The money is all in your name
But where's the work that you did, Mister
I'm demanding back my job again

We worked to build this country, Mister
While you enjoyed a life of ease
You've stolen all that we built, Mister
Now our children starve and freeze

Think me dumb if you wish, Mister
Call me green or blue or red
Just one thing I sure know, Mister
My hungry babies must be fed

Take the two old parties, Mister
No difference in them I can see
But with a Farmer-Labor Party
We could set the people free

You never earned those millions, Mister
They were produced by working hands
We're taking back our own wealth, Mister
Winning back our lives & lands

— w: Jim Garland (new v. Peter Blood)
— m: trad. "East Virginia"

© 1947 (renewed) by Stormking Music Inc. All rights reserved. Used by permission. – Garland was a miner & the brother of Aunt Molly Jackson, an impt songwriter/organizer for the miners' union. Unfortunately, Minnesota's Farmer-Labor Party is now "no different" from the other 2! In SO! 30:2, Carry It On, Children's S for a Friendly Planet, S That Changed the World, *Lomax* FS of NAm, S of Work & Protest, People's SB *& Weavers* SB. *On Pete Seeger* S of Struggle & Protest, Hard Hitting S *&* Can't You See This System. *On Tom Rush* Mind Rambling. OC36

RICH & POOR

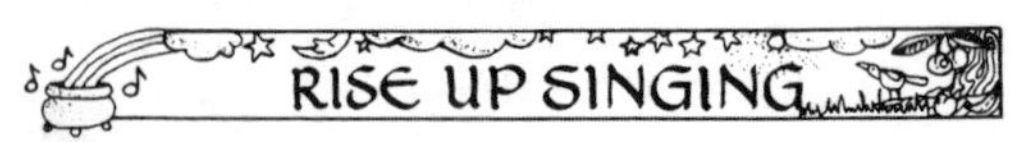

I Had a Little Overcoat

1. **I had a little overcoat, as old as can be**
   Tralala lalalala lalala
   What I'd ever do with it, I just couldn't see / Tralala...
   So I thought a little while
   And made myself a jacket in the very latest style
   Tralalala lalala (2x) / Made a jacket in the very latest style

C CG C - / G - C - :|| F - - - / - - C -
Am - Em G / C G CG C

2. **I had a little jacket, it was old as can be...**
   What... / So I thought a little while
   And made myself a vest in the very latest style
   Tralala...made a vest in the very latest style
3. **I had a little vest... / ...& made myself a tie**
4. tie / button
5. button / nothing
6. nothing / song

1. **Hob ikh mir a mantl fun fartsaytikn shtof / Tralala...**
   Hot dos nit in zikh kayn gantsenem shtokh / Tralala...
   Darum, hob ikh zikh batrakht
   Un fun dem mantl, a rekl gemakht
   Tralala... / Fun dem mantl, a rekl gemakht
2. **Hob ikh mir a rekl... fun dem rekl, a vestl gemakht**
3. vestl / shnipsl
4. shnipsl / knepl
5. knepl / gornitl
6. gornit / dos lidele

— trad (Yiddish), Eng words Teddi Schwartz & Arthur Kevess

Eng words ©1988 Teddi Schwartz. All rights reserved. Used by permission. *– "This is a song abt resilience in the face of adversity & satisfaction derived fr creative problem solving. eg. what if you have 2 children & one egg? Make an omelet! And when you are down to absolutely nothing? Well you can always make a song out of it." — TS. In her* Tumbalalaika & Other Jewish S. *On recs by Dave Sears, Lydia Davis. Paul Kaplan's "I Had an Old Coat" (SO! 32:3) is another song based on the Yiddish original.* OC37

If I Were a Rich Man

(spoken) What would have been so terrible
if I had a small fortune?
If I were a rich man, daidle, deedle, daidle
Digguh, digguh, deedle, daidle dum
All day long I'd biddy biddy bum
If I were a wealthy man!
Wouldn't have to work hard, daidle ... / ...dum
If I were a biddy, biddy rich
Digguh, digguh deedle daidle man **(TD ↑ 3)**

A - / AEm A / Dm Am / [1.] - E :|| [2.] AmE A

I'd build a big tall house with rooms by the dozen
Right in the middle of the town
A fine tin roof with real wooden floors below
There would be one long staircase just going up
And one even longer coming down
And one more leading nowhere, just for show

Dm G / C E / Dm E A - / Dm G / C A / Dm F E -

I'd fill my yard with chicks & turkeys & geese
And ducks for the town to see & hear
Squawking just as noisily as they can
And each loud quack & cluck & gobble & honk
Will land like a trumpet on the ear
As if to say: here lives a wealthy man (sigh) / **If I were...**

I see my wife, my Golde, looking like a rich man's
Wife with a proper double chin
Supervising meals to her heart's delight
I see her putting on airs & strutting like a peacock
Oh! What a happy mood she's in
Screaming at the servants day & night

(freely) The most important men in town will come to fawn
on me
They will ask me to advise them like Solomon the wise
"If you please, Reb Tevye, pardon me, Reb Tevye"
Posing problems that would cross a Rabbi's eyes – boi
Boi-boi-boi **(2x)** boi!

A - F - / Dm - B♭ - / Gm - - - / A - / - -

(as end of verse) And it won't make one bit of difference
If I answer right or wrong
When you're rich they think you really know

Dm G / C A / Dm F E -

If I were rich I'd have the time that I lack
To sit in the synagogue & pray
And maybe have a seat by the eastern wall
And I'd discuss the holy books with the learned men
Seven hours every day
This would be the sweetest thing of all (Sigh)

If I were... (1st 6 lines of chorus →) ... daidle, dum

(tag) Lord who made the lion & the lamb
You decreed I should be what I am
Would it spoil some vast eternal plan
If I were a wealthy man?

Dm Am / / / FE A

— w: Sheldon Harnick — m: Jerry Bock

© 1964 by Alley Music Corp & Trio Music Co, Inc. All rights administered by Hudson Bay Music Inc. All rights reserved. Used by permission. *– Fr the musical* Fiddler on the Roof. *In* Top 100 Movie Themes & Broadway SBs. OC38

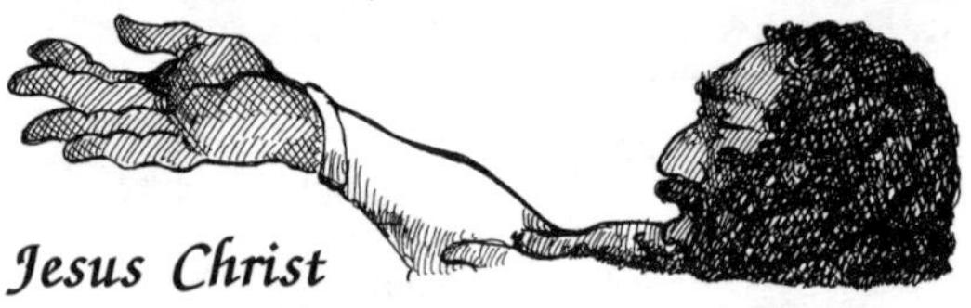

Jesus Christ

Jesus Christ was a man that traveled thru the land
Hard working man & brave
He said to the rich "Give your goods to the poor"
So they laid Jesus Christ in his grave

D GD / D A / DD7 GD / DA D

Jesus was a man, a carpenter by hand
His followers true & brave
But the cops & legislators called them dangerous agitators
So they laid Jesus Christ in his grave

G D / - A / D GD / DA D

He went to the preacher, he went to the sheriff
Told them all the same:
"Sell all your jewelry & give it to the poor"
So they laid Jesus Christ in his grave

When Jesus came to town the working folks around
Believed what he did say
The bankers & the preachers they nailed him on the cross
And they laid Jesus Christ in his grave

When the love of the poor shall one day turn to hate
When the patience of the workers gives way
"Would be better for you rich if you never had been born"
So they laid Jesus Christ in his grave

This song was written in New York City
Of rich men, preachers & slaves
Yes if Jesus preached today like he preached in Galilee
They would lay Jesus Christ in his grave

— w: Woody Guthrie — m: trad. ("Jesse James")

TRO ©1961 & 1963 Ludlow Music, Inc, NY, NY. International copyright secured. Made in USA. All rights reserved incl. public performance for profit. Used by permission. *– On his* Orig Recordings, Gr S, 1940-46 *(WB),* Bound for Glory *& in his* SB. *Also on* Tribute to W Guthrie pt2. *In* SO! *10:4,* Reprints #9 & Ewan MacColl SB. *Tune is in* Am Fav Bals, SFest & SO! Reprints #4. OC39

King of the Road

"Trailer for sale or rent – rooms to let: 50 cents
No phone, no pool, no pets" – I ain't got no cigarettes
Ah but, two hours of pushing broom buys an 8 by 12 four-bit room
I'm a man of means by no means, King of the road

A D E A / - D E - / A D E A // - D E A

Third boxcar, midnight train – destination: Bangor, Maine
Old worn out suit & shoes, I don't pay no union dues
I smoke old stogies I have found, short but not too big around
I'm a man...

(bridge) I know every engineer on every train
All of the children & all of their names
And every handout in every town
And ev'ry lock that ain't locked when no one's round

A D / E A / A D / E -

(on Teaching Disc modulate bridge up one half step to Bb)

— **Roger Miller**

© 1964 by Tree Publishing Co. Inc. 8 Music Square West, Nashville TN 37203. International copyright secured. Made in USA. All rights reserved. Used by permission. – In Gr S of the '60s. OC40

The Man That Waters the Workers' Beer

I'm the man, the very fat man who waters the workers' beer (2x)
And what do I care if it makes them ill, or if it makes them terribly queer?
I've a car & a yacht & an aeroplane & I waters the workers' beer

D - A D / - - AE A / G - D DA / D - A D

Now when I makes the workers' beer I puts in strych-i-nine
Some methylated spirits & a drop of paraffin
But since a brew so terribly strong might make them terribly queer
I reaches my hand for the water tap **& I waters the...beer**

Now a drop of beer is good for a man who's thirsty & tired & hot
And I sometimes has a drop for myself from a very special lot
But a fat & healthy working class is the thing that I most fear
So I reaches my hand for the water tap **& I waters...**

Now ladies fair beyond compare & be ye maid or wife
O sometimes lend a thought for one who leads a sorry life
The water rates are shockingly high & malt is shockingly dear
And there isn't the profit there used to be in wat'ring...

— **Paddy Ryan**

© Workers Music Assoc, UK. All rights reserved. Based on a trad. Irish song "The Son of a Gambolier". Orig published 1939 by Brit Workers Music Assoc. – On Roberts & Barrand Live at Holsteins! *& rec by Faith Petric (Bay). In* Labor Party SB *(1955),* S of Work & Protest & FSEncyV2. OC41

Nobody Knows You When You're Down & Out

Once I lived the life of a millionaire
Spent all my money & I didn't care
Taking my friends out for a mighty good time
Buying high priced liquor, champagne & wine

But then I began to fall so low
I didn't have a dollar, I had no place to go
Well if I ever get my hands on a dollar again
I'll hold on to it til the eagle grins

C E A - / Dm A DmA Dm /
F D7 CE A / [1.] D - Ab G :|| [2.] D - G C

Nobody knows you / When you're down & out
In my pocket not one penny
And when it comes to friends, I haven't any

But when I get back on my feet again
Everybody wants to be my long lost friend
It's mighty strange without a doubt
Nobody knows you when you're down & out

— **Jimmy Cox**

© 1923, 1924 by MCA Music Publishing, a division of MCA Inc. NY, NY 10019. Copyright renewed. All rights reserved. Used by permission. – In SO! *18:6 &* Weavers SB. *On Bessie Smith* Any Woman's Blues, *Rory Block* I'm in Love, *Odetta* & the Blues, *Josh White* The Legendary *& rec by Martin, Bogan & Armstrong.* OC42

The Preacher and the Slave (Pie in the Sky)

Long-haired preachers come out ev'ry night
Try to tell you what's wrong & what's right
But when asked How 'bout something to eat?"
They will answer in voices so sweet: **(in 3/4)**

G C G - / - - D - / G C G - / - D G -

You will eat, bye & bye
In that glorious land above the sky
Work & pray, live on hay
You'll get pie in the sky when you die (That's a lie!)

G - D - / - - G - / - - C - / G D G -

O the Starvation Army they play
And they sing & they clap & they pray
Til they get all your coin on the drum
Then they'll tell you when you're on the bum

If you fight hard for children & wife
Try to get something good in this life
You're a sinner & bad man, they tell
When you die you will sure go to Hell

Holy Rollers & Jumpers come out
And they holler, they jump & they shout
Give your money to Jesus" they say
He will cure all diseases today"

Workingmen of all countries, unite
Side by side we for freedom will fight
When the world & its wealth we have gained
To the grafter we will sing this refrain:

(last cho) You will eat bye & bye
When you've learned how to cook & to fry
Chop some wood, 'twill do you good
And you'll eat in the sweet bye & bye (that's no lie!)

— **w: Joe Hill** — **m: Gospel ("Sweet Bye & Bye")**

In SO! *26:4,* Carry It On, *Lomax* FS of NAm, S That Changed the World & Treas of Am S. *On Weavers* Trav On, *Joe Glaser* S of Joe Hill, *Earl Robinson* Strange Unusual Eve, *Utah Phillips* We Have Fed You All *(Philo),* All Used Up *(Philo),* Sings S of IWW *& in his* Starlight on the Rails. OC43

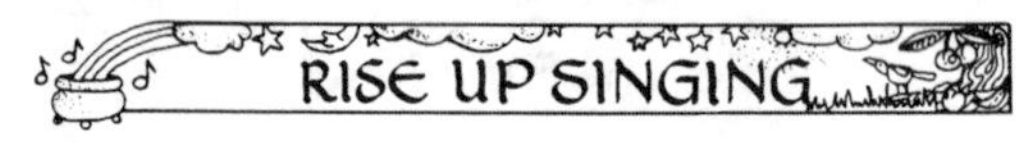

Rich Man and the Poor Man

There was a rich man & he lived in Jerusalem
Glory hallelujah, hi ro jerum
He wore a silk hat & his coat was very sprucium
Glory hallelujah, hi ro jerum

Hi ro jerum, hi ro jerum
Skinamalinka doolium, skinamalinka doolium
Glory hallelujah, hi ro jerum

D - / - AD :|| D G / D - / - AD

At his gate there stood a human wreckium / **Glory...**
He wore a bowler hat with the rim around his neckium / **Glory...**

The poor man asked for a piece of bread & cheesium
The rich man replied "I'll send for the policium"

Well the poor man died & his soul went to heavium
He danced with the angels til a quarter past elevium

The rich man died but he didn't fare so wellium
He couldn't go to heaven so he had to go to hellium

He called for a whiskey & a soda to consolium
But the Devil said "Come & shovel on the coalium!"

The moral of this story is riches are no jokium
So we'll all go to heaven cuz we all are stony-brokium!

— anon. (Brookside Labor College)

aka: "The Poor & the Rich." Derived fr the parable of Lazarus & the rich man. In a songbk pub at Brookside, one of the 1st schools for workers in the US (1921, Katonah, NY). In SO! *33:1,* Peoples SB, S of Work & Protest, S for Pickin & Singin & FSEncyV2. OC44

Rigs of the Time

No wonder that butter's a shilling a pound
See the rich farmers' daughters how they ride up and down
When you ask them the reason they cry "O, alas"
There's a war on in France and the cows have no grass

Am C Dm E / / Am Em Am Em / Am C DmDmE Am (in 3/4)

Singing Honesty's all out of fashion
These are the rigs of the time, time, my boys
These are the rigs of the time

Am G Am - / Am G FFGGC / Dm Em Am -

O 'tis of an old butcher, I must bring him in
He charge two shillings a pound & thinks it no sin
Slaps his thumb on the scale-weights & makes them go down
He swears it's good weight, yet it wants half a pound

Now next is the baker, I must bring him in
He charge fourpence a loaf & thinks it no sin
When he do bring it in, it's not bigger than your fist
And the top of the loaf is popped off with the ye'st

O next is the publican, I must bring him in
He charge fourpence a quart, he thinks it no sin
When he do bring it in, the measure is short
The top of the pot is popped off with the froth

Here's next to the tailor who skimps on our clothes
And next to the shoemaker who pinches our toes
We've nought in our bellies, our bodies are bare
No wonder we've reason to curse & to swear

And next there's the lawyer, you plainly will see
He'll plead for your case for a very large fee
All day he will talk proving all wrong is right
He'll make you believe that a black horse is white

And next there's the parson, he'll soon have your soul
If you stick to the Book you will keep off the dole
He'll give you his blessing & likewise his curse
Put his hand in your pocket & walk off with your purse

And next there's the doctor, I nearly forgot
I believe in my heart he's the worst of the lot
He'll tell you he'll cure you for half you possess
And when you are buried he'll take all the rest

Now the very best plan that I can find *[to bring this to an end]*
Is to pop them all up in a high gale of wynd *[wind]*
And when they get up, the cloud it will burst
And the biggest old rascal come tumbling down first

— trad. (English)

In SO! *29:3 & P Kennedy* FS of Britain & Ireland. *On Martin Carthy* Out of the Cut *(Topic), Michael Cooney* The Cheese Stands Alone & Still Cooney. OC45

Satisfied Mind

How many times have you heard someone say
If I had his money I'd do things my way
But little they know that it's so hard to find
A rich man or woman with a satisfied mind

(in D) A G D - / / GA A D - / 1st /

Once I had money, I had fortune & fame
Had all that I needed to make a start in life's game
Then suddenly it happened I lost every dime
But I'm richer by far with a satisfied mind

For money won't buy back your youth when you're old
Or a friend when you're lonely or a heart that's grown cold
The wealthiest person is a pauper at times
Compared to the man with a satisfied mind

When my life is ended & my time has run out
My friends & relations I'll leave them no doubt
But one thing's for certain when it comes my time
I'll leave this old world with a satisfied mind

— Red Hays & Jack Rhodes

 — On Joan Baez Farewell Angelina, Bright Morning Star Arisin, *Mary McCaslin* Epitaph, *Bryan Bowers* The View fr Home, *John McCutcheon* Gonna Rise Again *(Rounder), Dylan* Saved *& Ian & Sylvia* Play One More. OC46

Shake Sugaree

I have a little song, won't take long
Sing it right, once or twice
O Lord o me, didn't I shake Sugaree
Ev'rything I got is done in pawn (2x)

C - - - / F - - - // F - G C / C G C - / /

I pawned my watch, I pawned my chain
Pawned everything that was in my name / **O Lord...**

I pawned my buggy, house & cot
Pawned everything that was on my lot

I pawned my chair, I pawned my bed
Don't have nowhere to lay my head

I have a little secret I ain't gonna tell
I'm goin' to heaven in a ground pea shell

I pawned my house, I've pawned my home
Pawned everything that I own

I pawned my tobacco, I pawned my pipe
Pawned everything that was in my sight

I know something I ain't gonna tell
I'm goin' to heaven & I ain't goin' to –

I pawned my hat, I pawned my shoes
Pawned everything that I could use

I chew my tobacco, I spit my juice
I would raise cain, but it ain't no use

— Elizabeth Cotten

 — On her Shake Sugaree *(FTS31003) &* E Cotten V2 *(FG3537). Fred Neil* Everybody's Talkin *(SM294) & Art Thieme* That's the Ticket. *In* SO! *16:2 &* Reprints #11 *&* How Can We Keep fr Singing. OC47

The Soup Song

I'm spending my nights in the flop house
I'm spending my days on the street
I'm looking for work & I find none
I wish I had something to eat
Soup, soup, they gave me a bowl of soup (2x)

GC G / - D / GC G / CD G // G C D G / /

I spent 15 years in the factory **(in 3/4)**
I did everything I was told
They said I was faithful & loyal
Now why am I out in the cold

I saved 15 bucks with my banker
To buy me a car & a yacht
I went down to draw out my fortune
And this is the answer I got:

I went out to fight for my country
I went out to bleed & to die
I thought that my country would help me
But this was my country's reply:

When I die & I get up to heaven
St. Peter will let me right in
He can tell by the soup that they fed me
That I was unable to sin

— **w: Maurice Sugar** — **m: trad. (My Bonnie")**

"I wrote this song in the avalanche of sit-down strikes in 1937. During mealtime in the plant kitchens of the factories long lines of workers would stand, bowls in hand, singing the 'Soup Song' with great gusto" — MS. In SO! *23:3,* Hard-hitting S, Carry It On, FSEncyV1, Peoples SB *&* S of Work & Protest. OC48

There But for Fortune

Show me a prison, show me a jail
Show me a prisoner whose face is growin' pale
And I'll show you a young man with many reasons why
And there but for fortune go you or I

(capo up) C Fm C Fm/C Am D G/C Am F Dm

Em C Dm G **(last chorus add:)** C (Fm C -)

Show me an alley, show me a train
Show me a hobo who sleeps out in the rain / **And I'll...**

Show me the whiskey stains on the floor
Show me a drunken man as he stumbles out the door...

Show me a country where the bombs had to fall
Show me the ruins of the buildings once so tall
And I'll show you a young land...
And there but for fortune go you or I, you or I

— **Phil Ochs**

 — On his In Conc & Chords of Fame, *Baez* Gr H *&* 1st 10 Yrs *& on* Gr FSingers of the '60s. *In* SO! *15:2,* FM Gr H & Club Date FakeB. OC49

Tramp On the Street

Only a poor man was Lazarus that day
When he lay down by the rich man's gate
Well he begged for some crumbs from the rich man to eat
But they left him to die like a tramp on the street

I: D - G - / A - D - / 1st / D A D -

He was somebody's darling, he was some mother's son
Once he was fair & once he was young
Some mother rocked him, little darling to sleep / But **they**...

Jesus, who died on Calvary's tree
Gave his life blood for you & for me
They pierced thru his side, Lord, his hands & his feet
Then **they left him to die...**

He was Mary's own darling, he was God's chosen son
Once he was fair & once he was young
Mary she rocked him, little darling, to sleep
But he was only a tramp found dead on the street

If Jesus should come & knock on your door
Would you let him come in & pick from your store?
Would you turn him away with nothing to eat?
Would you leave **him to die like a...**?

When the battle is over & victory's won
Everyone mourns for the poor man's son
*Red, white & blue & victory's sweet / **But they left him...***

II: D DG D - / - - E A / 1st / D DA DG D

(both versions in 3/4)

— **Grady & Hazel Cole**

 – In SO! *14:6 &* Reprints *#9. On Baez* David's Alb, Country M Alb, Contemp Bal B, *Peter Paul & Mary* Late Again, *Jack Elliott* Bull Durham, Ramblin *& rec by Blue Sky Boys.* OC50

Waltzing Matilda

Once a jolly swagman camped by a billabong
Under the shade of a coolibah tree
And he sang as he watched & waited til his billy boiled
You'll come a waltzing Matilda with me!"

C G Am F / C - G - / C G Am F / C - G C

Waltzing Matilda **(2x)**
You'll come a waltzing Matilda with me!
And he sang as he watched... (3rd line of each v.)
You'll come a waltzing Matilda with me

C - F - / " / " / " /

Down came a jumbuck to drink at the billabong
Up jumped the swagman & grabbed him with glee
And he sang as he stowed that jumbuck in his tucker bag...

Up rode the squatter, mounted on his thoroughbred
Down came the troopers, one, two, three
"Where's that jolly jumbuck you've got in your tucker bag?"...

Up jumped the swagman, sprang into the billabong
"You'll never catch me alive!" said he
And his ghost may be heard as you pass by that billabong...

— **A. B. Banjo" Paterson**

 — Jumbuck=sheep. On Louis Killen Old S, Old Friends, *Josh White* In Memoriam *& Enoch Light* Far Away. *In* SFest, *R Dig* Fest of Pop S, S That Changed the World, FSEncy V1, S Am Sings, FiresB of FS, Joyful Singing *&* Pocketful of S *(both WAS).* OC51

RICH & POOR

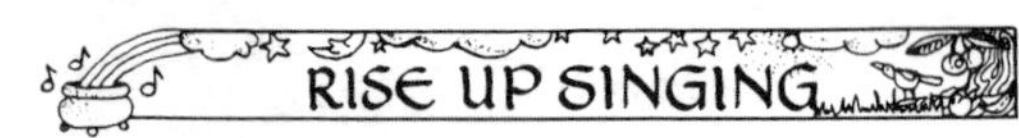

We Hate to See Them Go

(intro) Last night I had a lovely dream
I saw a big parade with ticker tape galore
And men were marching there the like I'd never seen before

D A D - / G - D - / E - - A

The bankers & the diplomats are going in the army
O happy day! I'd give my pay to see them on parade
Their paunches at attention & their stripéd pants at ease
They've gotten patriotic & they're going overseas
We'll have to do the best we can & bravely carry on
So we'll just keep the laddies here to manage
while they're gone

D Bm E A / / G - D - / E - AE A
G - D - / Bm E A D

O – we hate to see them go!
The gentlemen of distinction in the army

D - G D / A D A D

The bankers & the diplomats are going in the army
It seemed too bad to keep them from the wars they love to plan
We're all of us contented that they'll fight a dandy war
They don't need propaganda, they know what they're
fighting for
They'll march away with dignity & in the best of form
And we'll just keep the laddies here to keep the lassies warm

The bankers & the diplomats are going in the army
We're going to make things easy cause it's all so new
and strange
We'll give them silver shovels when they have to dig a hole
And they can sing in harmony when answering the roll
They'll eat their old K-rations from a hand-embroidered box
And when they die, we'll bring them home & bury them in
Fort Knox

— **Malvina Reynolds**

© 1959 Schroder Music Co. (ASCAP) Berkeley CA 94704. All rights reserved. Used by permission. *— aka: "Bankers & the Diplomats." On her album (Cassandra) & in her* Little Boxes. *In SO! 20:3. On Cooney* The Cheese Stands Alone, *Sally Rogers & Claudia Schmidt* Closing the Distance *& Bluestein Fam* Let the Dove Come In. OC52

World Turned Upside Down

(The Diggers' Song)

In 1649 to St. George's Hill
A ragged band they called the Diggers
came to show the people's will
They defied the landlords, they defied the laws
They were the dispossessed reclaiming what was theirs

C - G (or Dm) - / F - C G / 1st / F CG C -

"We come in peace" they said "to dig & sow
We come to work the lands in common
and to make the waste ground grow
This earth divided we will make whole
So it will be a common treasury for all

The sin of property we do disdain
No man has any right to buy & sell the earth for private gain
By theft & murder they took the land
Now everywhere the walls rise up at their command

They make the laws to chain us well
The clergy dazzle us with heaven or they damn us into hell
We will not worship the god they serve
The god of greed who feeds the rich while poor folk starve

We work, we eat together, we need no swords
We will not bow to the masters or pay rent to the lords
Still we are free, tho' we are poor
You Diggers all, stand up for glory, stand up now!"

From the men of property, the orders came
They sent the hired men & troopers
to wipe out the Diggers' claim
Tear down their cottages, destroy their corn
They were dispersed, but still the vision lingers on

"You poor take courage, you rich take care
This earth was made a common treasury for everyone to share
All things in common, all people one
We come in peace" – the order came to cut them down

— **Leon Rosselson**

© 1975 Leon Rosselson. c/o Fuse Records, 28 Park Chase, Wembley Park, Middlesex, England HA9 8EH. Used by permission. *— The Diggers were one of many radical movements (incl. the first Quakers) that sprang up during the time of Oliver Cromwell. They were one of the first groups anywhere to articulate a clearly socialist view of society. They actively resisted efforts of landowners to fence in and take over ownership of what were originally large tracts of land held in common by villages. On his* For the Good of the Nation *& his* That's Not the Way It's Got To Be *(w/Roy Bailey, FuseRecs). In SO! 24:4. On Dick Gaughan* A Handful of Earth *& Billy Bragg* Betw the Wars. OC53

Other songs about economic issues can be found in the chapters CITY, FARM & PRAIRIE, MOUNTAIN SONGS, TRAVELIN' and WORK. Songs elsewhere in the book include: "Mercedes Benz," "This Land" (AMER) "Hard Times Come Again No More" (HARD) "All I Really Need," "Food Glorious Food" (HOME) "Hobo's Lullaby," "Liverpool Lullaby" (LULL) "I've Got to Know" (PEACE) "Ego Sum Pauper," "Hey Ho Nobody Home," "O Joy Upon This Earth," "Poor Mr. Morgan," "There Are Three Brothers Named Dupont" (ROUNDS) & "I Got Shoes" (SPIRS).

Where an asterisk (*) appears above music, a second part or repeated parts may enter at this place. Authors of rounds are unknown unless otherwise noted.

A Ram Sam Sam

1. A ram sam sam **(2x)**
   Guli **(5x)** ram sam sam **(repeat)**
2. A rafi, a rafi
   Guli **(5x)** ram sam sam **(repeat)**

— trad. (Morocco) R02

Ah Poor Bird

Ah poor bird / take thy flight
Far above the sorrows / of this sad night!

— Public Domain R03

Apple Trees in Bloom

Sweet the evening air of May / soft my cheek caressing
Sweet the unseen lilac spray / with its scented blessing
White & ghostly / in the gloom
Shine the apple / trees in bloom / Apple trees in bloom!

— Betty Aswith R04

Black Socks

Black socks they / never get dirty, the
Longer you wear them the / stronger they get
Sometimes I / think I should launder them
Something keeps telling me / "Don't wash them yet, not
Yet, not yet"

— Public Domain R05

Canoe Round

My paddle's keen & bright / flashing like silver
Follow the wild goose flight / dip, dip & swing

Dip, dip & swing her back / flashing like silver
Follow the wild goose track / dip, dip & swing

— Margaret Embers McGee, 1918 R06

Chairs to Mend

1. Chairs to mend, old chairs to mend!
2. Mackerel, fresh mackerel!
3. Any old rags? Any old rags?

— Public Domain R07

Chickens Get into the Tomatoes

1. The chickens get into the tomatoes **(2x)**
2. Even the rabbits inhibit their habits when carrots are green **(2x)** – squash
3. **(on up beats)** _Squash_squash_squash_squash **(2x)**

This is a speaking round. For rhythm see Sing the Good Earth. R08

Come Follow

1. Come follow, follow, follow, follow, follow, follow me
2. Whither shall I follow, follow, follow
   Whither shall I follow, follow thee?
3. To the greenwood, to the greenwood
   To the greenwood, greenwood tree!

— Public Domain R09

ROUNDS

Down at the Station

1. Down at the station early in the morning
2. See the little puffabillies all in a row
3. See the station master pull the little handle
4. Puff puff, toot toot! off they go

— **Public Domain** OR10

Ego Sum Pauper

1. Ego sum pauper
2. Nihil habeo
3. Cor meum dabo

Translation of Latin: "I'm a poor man. I have nothing. I give my heart." OR11

French Cathedral Round

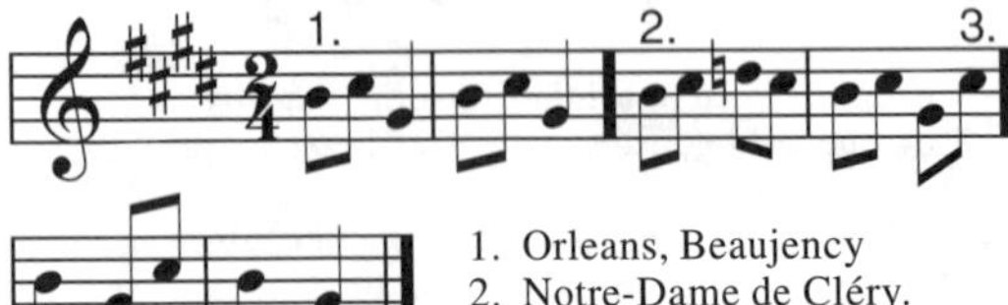

1. Orleans, Beaujency
2. Notre-Dame de Cléry.
3. Vendome, Vendome

These are the names of different towns in France which have famous bells. OR12

Gibberish

Can you dig that crazy / gibberish? _
Can you dig it_/ can you dig it? _ **(repeat)**
O look, there's a chicken / comin' down the road
O look, there's another one / sittin' on the fence
Ma-a!_/ Ma-a!_/ Get that son-of-a-gun / off my tractor

Another speaking round. On Tom Smith Chip Off The New Block *(GW). In* Sing the Good Earth. OR13

Go to Joan Glover

1. Go to Joan Glover and
2. tell her I love her and
3. By the light of the moon
4. I will come to her

— **Public Domain** OR14

Have You Seen the Ghost of John?

1. Have you seen the ghost of John?
2. Long white bones & the rest all gone
3. Oo! Oo!
4. Wouldn't it be chilly with no skin on?

— **Public Domain** OR15

Hey Ho, Nobody Home

1. Hey ho, nobody home.
2. No meat nor drink nor money have I none
3. Still I will be merry!

On Peter Paul & Mary Moving. OR16

I Love the Flowers

1. I love the flowers, I love the daffodils
2. I love the mountains, I love the rolling hills
3. I love the firelight when the light is low
4. Boom-ti-ada **(4x)**

D Bm Em A / / / /

— **Public Domain** OR17

I Sat Down with the Duchess to Tea

1. I sat down with the duchess to tea
2. It was just as I feared it would be.
3. The rumblings abdominal were simply phenomenal
4. And everyone thought it was me

(alt. words/Quaker version)

1. I sat down in the Meeting with thee
2. Prim & proper as a Quaker could be... **(as above)**

— **Public Domain** OR18

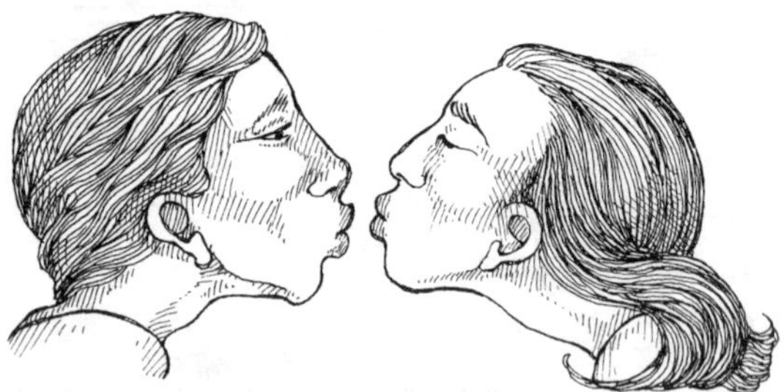

Joan, Come Kiss Me Now

1. Joan, come kiss me now
2. Once again for our love, gentle
3. Joan, come kiss me now

— **Public Domain** OR19

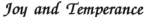

Joy and Temperance

1. Joy & temperance & repose!
2. Slam the door on the doctor's nose **(2x)**.
3. The Doctor's nose, the doctor's nose.
   Slam, slam the door on the doctor's nose!

— **Public Domain** OR20

Kookaburra

Kookaburra sits in the old gum tree
Merry merry king of the bush is he
Laugh kookaburra **(2x)** / Gay your life must be

Kookaburra ... / Eating all the gumdrops he can see
Stop kookaburra **(2x)** / Leave some there for me

Kookaburra ... / Counting all the monkeys he can see
Stop kookaburra **(2x)** / That's not a monkey, that's me!

— **Marion Sinclair**

Fr An Australian Camp Fire Song Book, pub by The Girl Guides Assoc of Australia. Used by permission. OR21

Lachend, Lachend

Lachend, lachend / lachend, lachend
Kommt der Sommer / übers Feld
Übers Feld kommt er / lachend, ha ha ha
Lachend übers / Feld

— **Cesar Bresgen**

Eng trans: "Laughing, laughing, summer comes over the field." OR22

Make New Friends

Make new friends & / keep the old
One is silver & the / other gold

— **Public Domain** OR23

Morning Comes Early

Morning comes early & / bright with dew
Under your window I'll / sing to you
Up then my comrades / up then my comrades
Let us be greeting the / morn so new

Why do you linger so / long in bed?
Open your windows & / show your head
Up then with singing / up then with singing
Over the meadow the / sun shines red

— **trad. (Slovakian folksong)** OR24

Music Alone Shall Live (Die Musici)

1. Himmel unde Erde mussen vergehn
2. Aber die Musici **(2x)**
3. Aber die Musici, bleiben bestehn

1. All things shall perish from under the sky
2. Music alone shall live **(2x)**
3. Music alone shall live, never to die

— **Public Domain** OR25

My Dame Had a Lame Tame Crane

1. My dame had a lame tame crane
2. My dame had a crane that was lame
3. Come mistress Jane to my dame's lame tame
4. Crane. Feed her & return again

— **Public Domain** OR26

O How Lovely Is the Evening

1. O how lovely is the evening **(2x)**
2. When the bells are sweetly ringing **(2x)**
3. Ding dong **(3x)**

1. O, wie wohl ist mir am Abend **(2x)**
2. Wenn zur Ruh die Glocke lautet **(2x)**
3. Bim, bam **(3x)**

— trad. (German) OR27

O Joy Upon This Earth

1. O Joy upon this earth to live & see the day.
2. When Rockefeller, Sr. shall up to me & say
3. Brother *[Comrade]*, can you spare a dime?

— Fred Holland & Charles Seeger

© 1934 Fred Holland & Charles Seeger. Used by permission. OR28

One Bottle of Pop

1. 1 bottle of pop, 2 bottles of pop, 3 bottles... 4... 5... 6... 7 bottles of pop, POP!
2. Don't chuck your muck in our dustbin **(3x)**
   [Amer. version: Don't throw your trash in my backyard]
   Don't chuck your muck in our dustbin, our dustbin's full
3. Fish & chips & vinegar, vinegar, vinegar
   Fish & chips & vinegar, pepper **(3x)** POP!

1. 1 submarine, 2 submarines, 3... 7 submarines – Stop!
2. Don't put your base in my backyard **(3x)**
Don't put your base in my backyard 'cause my backyard's green
3. World peace & harmony, harmony, harmony
World peace & harmony, harmony & love

— new version ("One Submarine") Bruce Kokopeli

© 1988 Bruce Kokopeli. Used by permission. It springs from the nonviolent movement to oppose deployment of Trident submarines in the Seattle area. On Paul Strausman Camels Cats & Rainbows. OR29

Poor Mr. Morgan

1. Poor Mr. Morgan cannot pay his income tax
2. Pity poor Morgan, he cannot pay
3. He's dead broke, he hasn't got a cent

— Elie Siegmeister

© 1988 Elie Siegmeister. Used by permission. OR30

Ride a Cock Horse

1. Ride-a-cock horse to Banbury Cross
2. To see a fine lady upon a white horse
3. Rings on her fingers & bells on her toes
4. She shall have music. 5. Wherever she goes

On Nancy Raven Wee Songs. OR31

Rose, Rose

1. Rose **(4x)** 2. Shall I ever see thee wed?
3. Aye marry, that thou wilt 4. If thou but stay

— Public Domain OR32

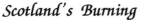

Scotland's Burning

Scotland's burning **(2x)** / Watch out **(2x)**
Fire, Fire! **(2x)** / Pour on water **(2x)**

— **Public Domain** OR33

Sumer Is Icumen In

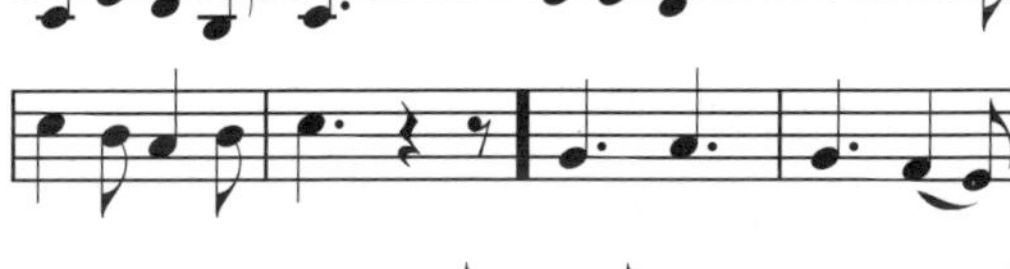

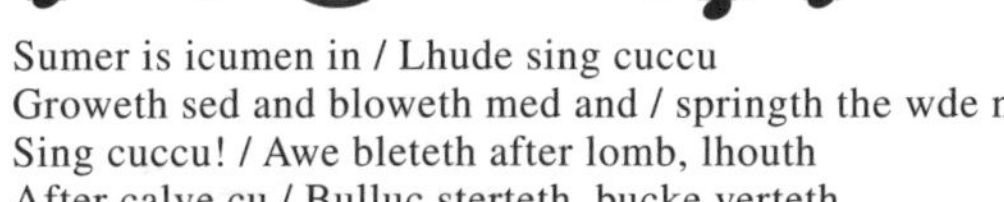

Sumer is icumen in / Lhude sing cuccu
Groweth sed and bloweth med and / springth the wde nu
Sing cuccu! / Awe bleteth after lomb, lhouth
After calve cu / Bulluc sterteth, bucke verteth
Murie sing cuccu! / Cuccu, cuccu
Wel singes thu cuccu. Ne / swik thu naver nu!

Summer is a-coming in / Loudly sing cuckoo
Seed now grows & mead now blows & / springs the wood anew
Sing cuckoo! / Ewe is bleating after lamb, cow
After calf lows too / Bullock starting, buck now browsing
Merry sing cuckoo! / Cuckoo, cuckoo
Well sing thou cuckoo. O / sing thou ever new!

Basses or Altos:

Sing, cuckoo, now, Sing cuckoo!

(can be sung throughout song)

There is valid evidence which indicates that this song is the oldest example of part-music in existence. The original 13th c. manuscript is in the British Museum. Middle English: nu=now, verteth prob.=turns, ne swik thu=cease thou. OR34

There Are Three Brothers

1. There are three brothers named Dupont, patriots are they
   They make their profits from munitions in an honest way
2. They love their country, right or wrong
   But when yen or lira come along, they
3. Always very cheerfully to any nation sell
   Shells that will all armor pierce & armor that will stop each shell

— **Elie Siegmeister**

 OR35

To Stop the Train

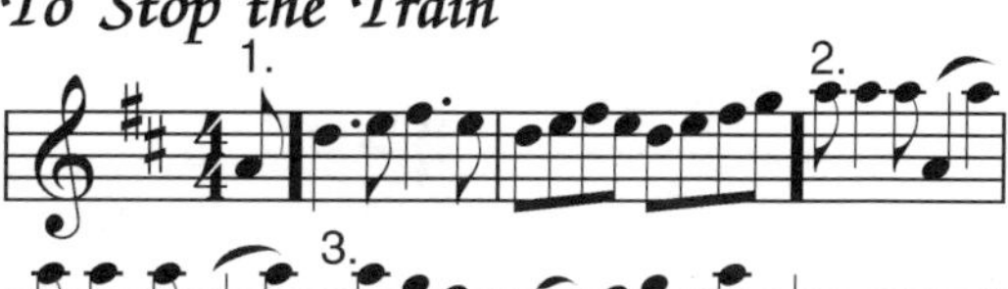

1. To stop the train in cases of emergency, just
2. Pull on the chain! Pull on the chain!
3. Penalty for improper use five pounds.

— **James Wild**

 — On Kim Wallach 2 Doz Children's S. OR36

White Sands and Gray Sands

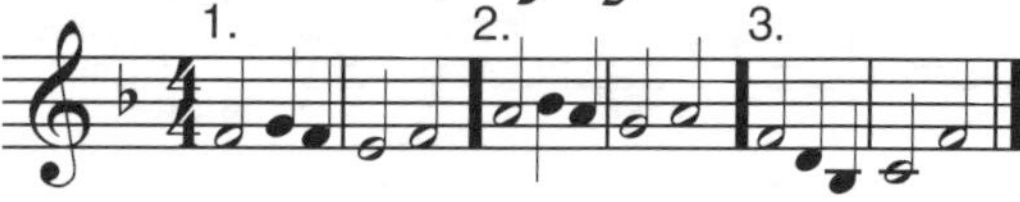

1. White sands & gray sands
2. Who'll buy my white sands?
3. Who'll buy my gray sands?

— **Public Domain** OR37

Why Shouldn't My Goose

1. Why shouldn't my goose 2. Sing as well as thy goose?
3. When I paid for my goose 4. Twice as much as thine!

— **Public Domain** OR38

Sacred Rounds & Chants

These are religious rounds and rounds "with a message" (eg. about peace). The chapter also includes a number of short or very repetitive songs which aren't rounds – but which can be sung quietly over and over in a group to help draw people together into a sense of the Divine Presence. Songs are traditional unless otherwise noted. New parts enter at asterisk (*) in rounds with many parts.

Absalom

1. O Absalom, my son, my son **(2x)**
2. Would to God I had died for thee, my son **(2x)**
3. O Absalom, my son, my son **(2x)**

Derived fr II Samuel 18:33. O035

Alleluia (Three Rounds)

(slash marks indicate new Alleluia)

1. Alleluia **(2x)**
2. Alleluia **(5x)**
3. Alleluia, Alleluia **(4x)**

— William Boice.

Boice was a contemporary of Mozart. When informed that Mozart had borrowed somewhat fr one of his melodies, Boice's response was that "Mozart takes ordinary things & turns them into pearls."

1 & 2. Alleluia, alleluia

1 & 2. Alleluia **(4x)** 3. Alleluia **(2x)**

— from W. A. Mozart (1756-91) O036

Babylon

1. By the waters, the waters of Babylon
2. We sat down & wept & wept for thee, Zion
3. We remember **(3x)** thee, Zion

Words fr Psalm 137, expressing the longing of the exiled Jewish people for their homeland. Music by William Billings, Boston, ca. 1780. On Don McLean Amer Pie. O037

Building Bridges

1. Building bridges between our divisions
2. I reach out to you, will you reach out to me?
3. With all of our voices & all of our visions
4. Friends, we could make such sweet harmony

Composed by the women of Greenham Common peace occupation in England in 1983. This transcription used by permission of Elizabeth Cave. O038

Circle Chant

Circle round for freedom, circle round for peace
For all of us imprisoned, circle for release
Circle for the planet, circle for each soul
For the children of our children: keep the Circle whole!

Am C F Dm / F - - C :||

— **Linda Hirschhorn**

© 1982 Linda Hirschhorn. Used by permission. On her Routes & Wings *(Oyster Albums c/o Redwood). In SO! 32:2.* O039

Dona Nobis Pacem

1. Do-na no-bis pa-cem, pacem. Do-na no-bis pa-cem
2. Dona no-bis pacem. Dona nobis pa-cem
3. Dona no-bis pacem. Dona nobis pa-cem

Eng trans: "Give us peace." O040

Haida Haida

1. Haida haida, haidada daida, haida, haida haida **(2x)**
2. Haida, haidada daida, haida, haida haida **(2x)**

This is a "nigun," a Jewish song without words used to create a special feeling, as during prayer. See also "Shabat Shalom." O041

Hava Nashira

1. 2. & 3. Hava nashira, shir' haleluia! **(3x)**

Trans of Hebrew: "Let us sing together, sing alleluia." O042

The Prodigal Son (melody is slightly different)

1. I shall arise & go unto my Father
2. And shall say unto him "Father, I have sinned against heaven & before thee
3. And am no more worthy to be callèd thy son"

But he came & raised me up & dried my tears with gladness
He had fresh bread & good things brought
& laid them out before me
And sang to God thanksgiving that his child had come home

2nd v. of "Prodigal Son" is by Peter Blood © 1978. Sing Out Corp. Used by permission. O043

Hineh Ma Tov

1. Hineh ma tov u'mana'yim, shevet achim gam yachad **(2x)**
2. Hineh ma tov, shevet achim gam yachad **(2x)**

Psalm 133. Trans. of Hebrew: "Behold how good & pleasant it is for brothers & sisters to live together in unity." O044

Hymn for Russian Earth

1. If the people lived their lives
2. As if it were a song for singing out of light
3. Provides the music for the stars
4. To be dancing circles in the night

— Yuri Zaritsky & Eugene Friesen

On Paul Winter Conc for the Earth. ⊙O45

I Am an Acorn

1. I am an acorn, the packet, the seed
2. God is within me, & God is the tree
3. I am unfolding the way I should be
4. & 5. Carved in the palm of His hand **(2x)**

[Sown in the soil of God's land **(2x)***]*

— Carol Johnson

 On her Might As Well Make It Love. ⊙O46

I Circle Around

I circle around (around, around) **(2x)**
The bound'ries of the earth (the bound'ries of the sky)
Wearing my long-wing feathers as I fly (wearing ...)

Em - - - / / C D Em - / / Em EmD Em - / /

— Arapaho (Native American)

aka: "Long Wing Feather." This haunting chant is in Friction in the System. *On Tickle Tune Typhoon* Circle Around. ⊙O47

Jubilate

Jubi- / late Deo / Jubilate Deo / Allelu- / ia!

— Michael Praetorius

Pron: "You-bee-lah-tay." Trans of Latin: "Be joyful unto God, Alleluia!" ⊙O48

Peace Is Flowing

Peace is flowing like a river
Flowing out of you & me
Flowing out into the desert
Setting all the captives free

E - - - / B7 - E - :||

(other v. substitute:) love, healing, etc.

On Patricia McKernon & Linda Worster River of Light, Peace Gathering S *(New Song Library).* ⊙O49

Peace Like a River

I've got peace like a river **(3x) in my soul (repeat)**

Am - - - - - E - / Am - - - - AmE Am -

I've got tears like the raindrops...
I've got joy like a fountain...
I've got *pain like an arrow / fear like an iceberg / strength like a mountain / love like the sunshine / de-termination!*

— Marvin V. Frey (new v. anon.)

 — Rec by Sharon Mtn Harmony (FolkLegcy) & on Peace Gathering S. *In* S of the Spirit. ⊙O50

Peace Round

1. O What a goodly thing 2. If the children of all men
3. Could dwell together 4. In peace

— Jean Ritchie

 On her At Home *& on Nan Hoffman* A Thousand Cranes. ⊙O51

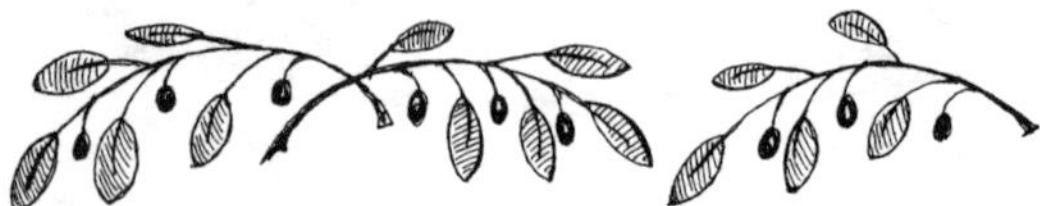

Peace Song

1. Peace **(4x)** 2. Wars have been & wars must cease
3. We must learn to live together 4. Peace **(3x)**

— w: anon. m: Rose, Rose (see ROUNDS)

By kindness of Broadside Magazine, *Children's Songs issue # 158.* ⊙O52

3 other rounds to same tune:

1. Love **(4x)** 2. People we are made for love
3. Love each other as thyself, for 4. God is love

1. Child **(4x)** 2. Will we ever see you grown?
3. We are working for your future 4. We love you so

1. Dear Friends **(2x)** 2. Let me tell you how I feel
3. You have given me such riches 4. I love you so

Ring in the New Year

1. Ring it in, ring in the new year **(2x)**
2. Bells are ringing, bells are ringing **(2x)**
3. Peace & love throughout the new year **(2x)**
4. Joy, joy, joy! **(2x)**

— Alix & Anne Herrmann

© 1971 Alix & Anne Herrmann. Used by permission. On Kim Wallach Even More Children's S. **0053**

Rise Up, O Flame

Rise up, o / flame / by thy light / glowing
Show to us / beauty / vision & / joy

— Public Domain **0054**

River of Light (Springs Forth a Well)

I've got a river of light flowing out of me
Makes the lame to walk & the blind to see
Opens prison doors, sets the captives free
I've got a river of light flowing out of me

G - - - / - - A7 D / 1st / G GD GAm7 G

Spring forth a well inside my soul
Spring forth a well & make me whole
Spring forth a well & let me see
That light that shines in me

River of Light is by L. Casebolt & Betty Carr Pulkingham. "Springs Forth a Well" is traditional. This arrangement is © 1978 Linda Worster & Patricia McKernon. Used by permission. On their River of Light. **0055**

Seek Ye First

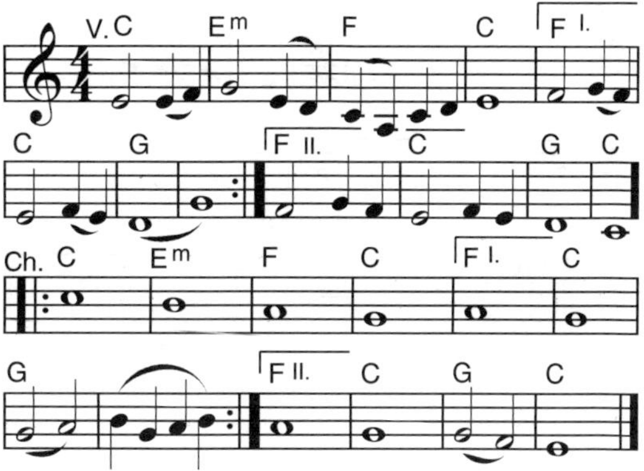

Seek ye first the Kingdom of God
And His *[its]* righteousness
And all these things shall be added unto you
Sing "Allelu, alleluia"

Alleluia, allelu-ia, alleluia. Sing "Allelu, alleluia"

Ask & it shall be given unto you
Seek & ye shall find
Knock & the door shall be opened unto you
Sing "Allelu, alleluia"

Man does *[We do]* not live by bread alone
But by every word
That proceeds from the mouth of the Lord
Sing "Allelu, alleluia"

— Karen Lafferty

Words derived from Matt 6:13, 7:7; Deut.8:3. © 1972 Maranatha! Music. All rights reserved. International copyright secured. Use by permission only. **0056**

Shabat Shalom

Bim bam, bim bim bim bam
Bim bim bim, bim bim bam **(repeat)**

Am - Dm Am / - Em Am - :||

Shabat shalom, shabat shalom / Shabat **(4x)** shalom **(repeat)**

Am Dm Am Dm / Am Dm Em Am :||

Shabat shabat, shabat shabat shalom **(2x)**

Am - G Am / /

Shabat shalom ... / Bim bam ...
A song greeting the Sabbath. **0057**

Shaker Life

1. Come life, Shaker life! Come life eternal!
   Shake, shake out of me all that is carnal **(repeat)**
2. I'll take nimble steps, I'll be a David
   I'll show Michael twice how he behavèd! **(repeat)**

Fr one of the early Shaker communities (early 19th c.?) — a spirited dance, acc. by shaking motions, ending abruptly. On Early Shaker Spirituals *(Rounder) & Molly Scott* Honor the Earth. *In Andrews* The Gift to be Simple. **0058**

Shalom Chaverim

Shalom chaverim / shalom chaverim / shalom / shalom
Le hit ra-ot / Le hit ra-ot / shalom / shalom

Glad tidings we bring / of peace on earth / goodwill / toward men
Of peace on earth / of peace on earth / goodwill / toward men

— Hebrew w: trad. Eng w & new m arrangement: Paul Campbell

 — Literal trans of Hebrew: "Farewell (or peace), friends, until we meet again." Rec by Weavers (Vang). O059

Spirit of the Living God

Spirit of the living God, fall afresh on me **(2x)**
Melt me, mold me, fill me, use me
Spirit of the living God, fall afresh on me

C - GC F C AmG C - / /
F - C - D - G G7 / 1st /

— Daniel Iverson

 In A Time for Singing *& Michael Talbot* S for Worship. O060

Tallis Canon

All praise to thee my God this night
For all the blessings of the light
Keep me, o keep me, King of Kings
Within thine own almighty wings
[Keep me, o keep me, Lord of Life
Within thy love & tender sight]

— Thomas Kenn (1695) & Thomas Tallis (1585) O061

Tender Shepherd

Tender shepherd, tender shepherd
Watches over all his sheep
One, say your prayers & two, close your eyes &
Three safe & happily fall asleep

C Dm7 C Dm7 / / / /

Tender shepherd, tender shepherd
You forgot to count your sheep
One in the meadow, two in the garden
Three in the nursery fast asleep

— w: Carolyn Leigh — m: Mark Charlap

 — Fr their musical Peter Pan. *On McCutcheon* Howjadoo *(Rounder).* O062

This Glorious Food (Vegetable Grace)

1. Thank you for this food, this food
   This glorious, glorious food
2. And the animals & the vegetables
   And the minerals who made it possible!

— Patricia McKernon

 aka: "Vegetable Grace." O063

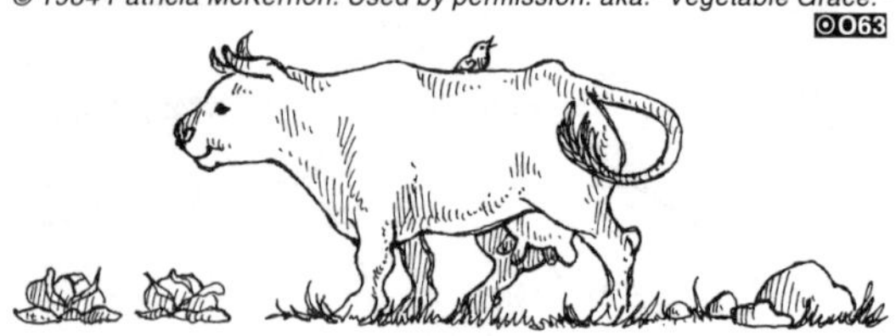

Ubi Cartias

Ubi caritas et amor
Ubi caritas, Deus ibi est

D A Bm - Em D E A / D A Bm - G A D -

— Jacques Berthier

From Music from Taizé, V1. *In* Worship in Song & Taize SBs. O064

Vesper Hymn

Hark! the vesper hymn is stealing o'er the waters soft & clear
Nearer yet & nearer pealing, soft it breaks upon the ear
Jubilate, jubilate, jubilate, amen

— w: Thomas Moore
—m: Russian Air adapted by Max V. Exner

There are several versions of this round. O065

Vine and Fig Tree (Lo Yisa Goy)

1. And every man *[one]* 'neath his *[their]* vine & fig tree
   Shall live in peace & unafraid **(repeat)**
2. And into plowshares beat their swords
   Nations shall learn war no more **(repeat)**
3. Love to your neighbor and
   Love to the Spirit of all life **(repeat)**

1. Lo yisa goy el goy cherev
   Lo yilmedu od milchama **(repeat)**
2. Lo yisa goy el goy cherev
   Lo yilmedu od milchama **(repeat)**

— Hebrew fr Hebrew Bible, Eng. Leah M. Jaffa & Fran Minkoff

Eng.
— On Bright Morning star Arisin. **OO66**

We Are the Flow

We are the flow, we are the ebb
We are the weavers, we are the web

Em - / EmC Em

— Shekinah Mountainwater

 On her S & Chants of the Goddess *(Moonspell tapes).* **OO67**

When Jesus Wept

1. When Jesus wept, the falling tear
2. In mercy flowed beyond all bound
3. When Jesus groaned, a trembling fear
4. Seized all the guilty world a-round

— William Billings (1746-1800) OO68

See also: "We Are All One Planet" (ECO) "Mi Y'Malel" (the first part of this song is a round), "Peace I Ask of Thee o River" (FAITH) "Can't Kill the Spirit" (HOPE) "Peace Is" (PEACE) & "Turning of the World" (UNITY).

Selections in this section are traditional North American or British Isles sea songs where not otherwise noted.

A-Rovin'

In Plymouth town there lived a maid
Bless you young women
In Plymouth town there lived a maid
O mind what I do say
In Plymouth town there lived a maid
And she was mistress of her trade
I'll go no more a-roving with you, fair maid
A-roving, a-roving / Since roving's been my ru-i-in
I'll go no more a-roving with you, fair maid

DA AD / A D / DA AD / AE A
‖: G D / A DA / DA DG DA D :‖

I took this fair maid for a walk / **Bless you...**
I took this fair maid for a walk / **O mind...**
I took... / And we had such a loving talk
I'll go no more a roving with you, fair maid...

O didn't I tell her stories too **(3x)**
Of the gold I found in Timbuktu / **I'll...**
Her eyes are like two stars so bright **(3x)**
Her face is fair, her step is light
Her cheeks are like the rosebuds red **(3x)**
There's wealth of hair upon her head
I put my arm around her waist **(3x)**
She said "Young man, you're in great haste"
I took this fair maid on my knee **(3x)**
She said "Young man, you're rather free!"

This was a favorite street tune in 17th c. England before becoming one of the oldest capstan shanties. In FiresB of FS, SFest, Treas of FS, S for Pickin & Singin, People's SB, FS for Fun, Penguin SB, Sea S & Shanties, *Cecil Sharp* FS V2, *Silverman* How to Play the Guitar, FS Abecedary, S Am Sings, Shanties for the 7 Seas *&* FSEncyV2. **OS40**

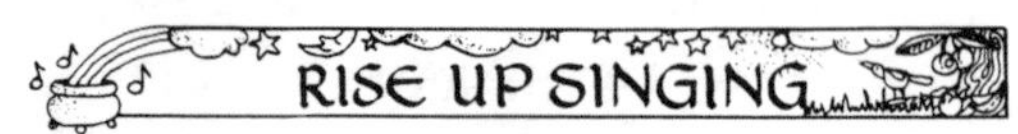

Barret's Privateers

O the year was 1778
How I wish I was in Sherbrooke now!
A letter of marque came from the king
To the scummiest vessel I'd ever seen

(in C) C - G C / - F C G / C G C - / - - - F

God damn them all! I was told
We'd cruise the seas for American gold
We'd fire no guns, shed no tears
Now I'm a broken man on the Halifax pier
The last of Barrett's privateers

G C - F / C F C F / G C G F / C F C F / - - G C

O Alcide Barrett, cried the town / **How I wish...**
For 20 brave men all fishermen who
Would make for him the Antelope's crew

The Antelope sloop was a sickening sight / **How...**
She'd a list to the port & her sails in rags
And the cook in the scuppers had the staggers & jags

On the King's birthday we put to sea / **How...**
We were 91 days to Montego Bay
Pumping like madmen all the way

On the 96th day we sailed again / **How...**
When a bloody great Yankee hove in sight
With our cracked fourpounders we made to fight

The Yankee lay low down with gold / **How...**
She was broad & fat & loose in her stays
But to catch her took the Antelope two whole days

Then at length we stood two cables away...
Our cracked fourpounders made an awful din
But with one fat ball the Yank stove us in

The Antelope shook & pitched on her side...
Barrett was smashed like a bowl of eggs
And the main trunk carried off both my legs

So here I lay in my 23rd year...
It's been six years since we sailed away
And I just made Halifax yesterday

— **Stan Rogers**

 — On his Fogarty's Cove, Betw the Breaks *& in his* S fr Fogarty's Cove. *On Alan Reid & Brian McNeil* Side Tracks. *In SO! 35:4.* OS41

Blow the Man Down

As I was a-walking down Paradise Street / **To me...**
To me way, aye, blow the man down
A pretty young damsel I chanced for to meet / **Give...**
Give me some time to blow the man down (in 3/4)

C - - - / - Am Dm G / Dm G Dm - / G - - C

She was round in the counter & bluff in the bow / **To me...**
So I took in all sail & cried "Way enough now!" / **Give...**

I hailed her in English, she answered me clear
"I'm from the Black Arrow, bound to the Shakespeare"

She says to me "Will you stand treat?"
"Delighted" says I "for a charmer so sweet"

So I tailed her my flipper & took her in tow
And yardarm to yardarm, away we did go

I bought her a two shilling dinner in town
And trinkets & laces & bonnet & gown

We walked & we talked & her name it was Gwen
I kissed her a couple & kissed her again

I says "Will you marry a seafaring man?"
She says "I'll ask Mother to see if I can."

Along comes a sailor, they call him Half Ton,
He says to her "Mother" she murmurs "My son!"

She says to him "Son, here is your new dadee"
But I says "I'm bound for the rolling sea"

"Blow" refers to a blow of the fist. On Roberts & Barrand Across the Western Ocean, *Pete Seeger* Frontier Bals V1 *(FA2175) & Burl Ives* S of the Sea *& in his* SB. *In* SFest, FiresB of FS, FS Abecedary, FSEncyV2, Treas of FS, S That Changed the World, *&* Shanties fr the 7 Seas. OS42

Blow Ye Winds of Morning

'Tis advertised in Boston, New York & Buffalo
500 brave Americans a-whaling for to go
Singing, blow ye winds in the morning, blow ye winds, high-O!
Clear away your running gear & blow, boys, blow!

D - - - / G D E A / D - - - / G D A D

They take you to New Bedford that famous whaling port
And hand you to some land-sharks to board & fit you out

They tell you of the clipper-ships a-going in & out
And say you'll take 500 sperm before you're 6 months out

It's now we're out to sea, my boys, the wind comes on to blow
One half the watch is sick on deck, the other half below

But as for the provisions, we don't get half enough
A little piece of stinking beef & a blamed small bag of duff

Next comes the running rigging which you're all supposed to know
"Lay aloft, you son-of-a-gun or overboard you go!"

The skipper's on the quarter-deck a-squinting at the sails
When up aloft the lookout sights a school of spouting whales

"Now clear away the boats, my boys & after him we'll travel
But if you get too near his fluke, he'll kick you to the devil!"

Now we have got him turned up, we tow him alongside
We over with our blubber-hooks & rob him of his hide

Next comes the stowing down, my boys, 'twill take both night & day
And you'll all have 50¢ apiece on the 190th day

When we get home, our ship made fast & we get thru our sailing
A winding glass around we'll pass & damn this blubber whaling!

In SO! *2:12 &* Reprints #3, Hootenanny SB, S of Work & Protest, FSEncyV2, S Am Sings, Shanties fr the 7 Seas & Clancy Bros SB. *In* Burl Ives SB *& on his* S of the Sea, *Tommy Makem* S of *& Kingston Trio* At Large. OS43

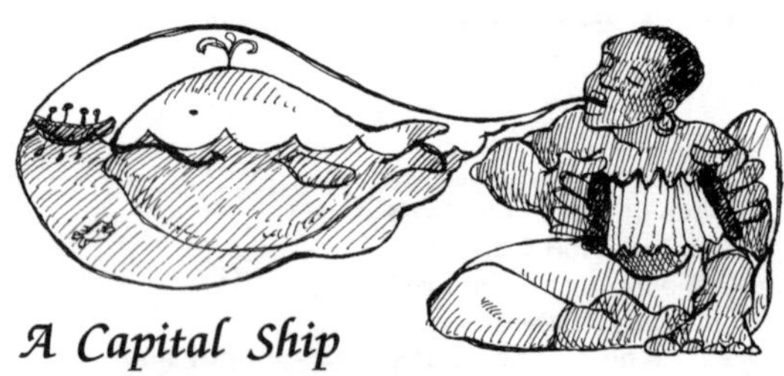

A Capital Ship

A capital ship for an ocean trip
Was the "Walloping Window Blind"
No wind that blew dismayed her crew
Or troubled the captain's mind
The man at the wheel was made to feel
Contempt for the wildest blow-ow-ow
Tho' it oft appeared when the gale had cleared
That he'd been in his bunk below

C - / G C / F G / D G / C - / G G / C - / G C

So, blow ye winds, heigh-ho
A-roving I will go
I'll stay no more on England's shore
So let the music play-ay-ay
I'm off for the morning train
To cross the raging main
I'm off to my love with a boxing glove
10,000 miles away

C - / F C / - - / G G / C - / F C / - - / G C

The bo'sun's mate was very sedate
Yet fond of amusement too
He played hop-scotch with the starboard watch
While the captain tickled the crew
The gunner we had was apparently mad
For he sat on the after ra-ai-ail
And fired salutes with the captain's boots
In the teeth of a booming gale

The captain sat on the commodore's hat
And dined in a royal way
Off pickles & figs & little roast pigs
And gunner bread each day
The cook was Dutch & behaved as such
For the diet he served the crew-ew-ew
Was a couple of tons of hot-cross buns
Served up with sugar & glue

Then we all fell ill as mariners will
On a diet that's rough & crude
And we shivered & shook as we dipped the cook
In a tub of his gluesome food
All nautical pride we cast aside
And we ran the vessel asho-o-ore
On the Gulliby Isles where the poopoo smiles
And the rubbily ubdugs roar

Composed of sand was that favored land
And trimmed with cinnamon straws
And pink & blue was the pleasing hue
Of the ticke-toe teaser's claws
We sat on the edge of a sandy ledge
And shot at the whistling bee-ee-ee
While the rugabug bats wore waterproof hats
As they dipped in the shining sea

On rugabug bark from dawn till dark
We dined till we all had grown
Uncommonly shrunk when a Chinese junk
Came up from the Torrible Zone
She was stubby & square, but we didn't much care
So we cheerily put to sea-ea-ea
And we left all the crew of the junk to chew
On the bark of the rugabug tree

— Charles Edward Carryl

In his Capital Ship *(Whittlesey 1963), Harry Devlin* Walloping Window Blind *(Van Nostrand 1968),* FiresB of Children's S, SFest & Joyful Singing. OS44

Captain Kidd

My name was Robert Kidd, **as I sailed, as I sailed**
My name was Robert Kidd, **as I sailed**
My name was Robert Kidd & God's laws I did forbid
And much wickedness I did, **as I sailed, as I sailed**
(II:) And much wickedness I did, as I sailed

I: E B7 E - B7 / E B7 E A B7 - / E - A B7 / A - B7 E

My father taught me well, **as I sailed, as I sailed**
My father...**as I sailed**
My father...to shun the gates of Hell
But yet I did rebel, **as I sailed, as I sailed** / But yet...

He put a Bible in my hand... & I sunk it in the sand
Before I left the strand, **as I...**

Then I murdered William Moore... & left him in his gore
Not many leagues from shore, **as...**

And being cruel still... my gunner I did kill
And his precious blood did spill, **as...**

And being nigh to death... I vowed with every breath
To walk in wisdom's way...

My repentance lasted not... my vows I soon forgot
Damnation was my lot...

To Execution Dock I must go, I must go, I must go / To...
To Execution Dock while thousands round me flock
To see me on the block, I must go, I must go / To see...

II: Dm Am Dm C / F Dm Am Dm - / Dm C Am C Dm Am
Dm Am Dm Am / " /

Altho looked on as a particularly vicious pirate, Kidd's reputation appears more due to balladmakers' fancy than historical fact. In fact a close look at Kidd's trial gives the impression he was framed for political reasons & his hanging a gross miscarriage of justice. In SO! *10:2 &* Reprints *#4 (chords I),* Treas of FS, *Lomax* FS of NAm *(chords II),* Read 'Em & Weep, Treas of Am FS *&* FSEncyV2. *On Dick Wilder* Badmen, Heroes & Pirate S *(Elektra).* OS45

Come Fare Away with Me (Marnie)

Bright is the morning & brisk is the weather
Steady the wind o'er the sweet-singing sea
Proudly the tall ship a-rides in the harbor
Come fare away with me **(in 3/4)**

G - C G / - - A D / G - C G / - D G -

Marnie, come fare away / Come fare away with me
There's an island of dreams / Over the rolling sea

Sails at the ready, she's bound for Newfoundland
Hasten, my darling, & do not delay!
Trees tall & green there & fish by the millions / **Come...**

Leave your belongings, for things do but bind us
Hemmed-in the life here, it won't do for me
Fretting & troubles, we'll leave them behind us
There is a land that's free

Lace on your stout shoes of good Highland leather
Bring your warm shawl & a cup for the tea
There'll be a new life, we'll build it together / **Come...**

— Jean Ritchie

 – Aka: "Marnie." In her Celeb of Life *& on her* At Home. *Also on Ed Trickett* The Telling Takes Me Home *(FolkLeg) & Art Thieme* On the Wilderness Rd. OS46

Deep Blue Sea

1. Deep blue sea, baby, deep blue sea **(3x)**
   It was Willy what got drownded in the deep blue sea

D G D - G - D - / D G D - G D A -
/ " / D - - - D G D A D -

2. Wrap him up in a silken shroud **(3x) / It was Willy...**
3. Dig his grave with a silver spade...
4. Lower him down with a golden chain...

In SO! *5:3 &* Reprints *#4,* Hootenanny SB, *&* FSEncy V2. *On Odetta* Bals & Blues *& Pete Seeger* Sing Out w Pete & W Voices Together *(FA2452) & in his* Am Fav Bal. *For new words to this song see PEACE.* OS47

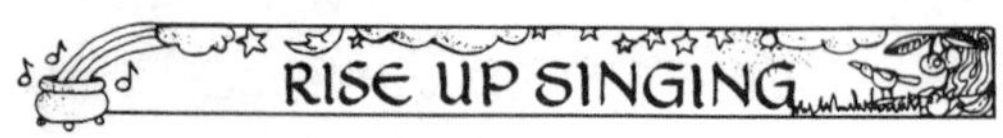

Dillan Bay

Dillan Bay, **laddie-o** / Dillan-dau, **laddie-ay**
Dillan Bay, **laddie-o** / All the boats are gone

A D / A DE / A D / AE A

Gone away, laddie-o / Gone awa', laddie-ay
Gone away, laddie-o / With their tops'ls high

Tops'ls high, laddie-o / Tops'ls low, laddie-ay
Tops'ls high, laddie-o / When the wind's away

Wind's away, laddie-o / Wind's awa', laddie-ay
Wind's away, laddie-o / Down in Dillan Bay

— Gordon Bok

 On his Seal Djiril's Hymn *& in his* Time & the Flying Snow. OS48

Drunken Sailor

What shall we do with the drunken sailor? **(3x)**
Early *[pron. "er-lie"]* **in the morning**
Hooray, up she rises (3x)
Early in the morning

Dm - / C - / Dm - / DmC Dm :||

Put him in the long boat til he's sober **(3x) / Early...**
Pull out the plug & wet him all over
Put him in the bilge & make him drink it
Put him in a leaky boat & make him bale her
Tie him to the scuppers with the hose pipe on him
Shave his belly with a rusty razor
Tie him to the topmast while she's yardarm under
Heave him by the leg in a runnin bowline
Keel haul him til he's sober
That's what we do with the drunken sailor!

Rec by Burl Ives & in his SB, *Schooner Fare* Day of the Clipper. *In* SFest, FiresB of FS, FS Abecedary, S for Pickin & Singin, Treas of FS, S Am Sings, FS N Am Sings, Shanties fr the 7 Seas *&* FSEncyV2. OS49

Farewell to Tarwathie

Farewell to Tarwathie, adieu Mormond Hill
And the dear land of Crimmond I bid ye farewell
I'm bound out for Greenland & ready to sail
In hopes to find riches in hunting the whale

(in 3/4) E - A E / / / /

Adieu to my comrades for a while we must part
And likewise the dear lass wha' fair won my heart
The cold ice of Greenland my love will not chill
And the longer our absence, more loving we'll feel

Our ship is well-rigged & she's ready to sail
Our crew they are anxious to follow the whale
Where the icebergs do float & the stormy winds blow
And the land & the ocean are covered with snow

O the cold coast of Greenland is barren & bare
No seed-time or harvest is ever known there
The birds here sing sweetly on mountain & dale
But there is na' a birdie to sing to the whale

There is no habitation for a man to live there
And the king of that country is the fierce Greenland bear
And there'll be no temptation to tarry long there
Wi' our ship bumper full we will homeward repair

On Judy Collins Whales & Nightingales, 1st 15 Yrs, Colors & Recollections. *On Liam Clancy* The Dutchman *&* Farewell to Tarwaithe, *Kevin Roth* Mtn Dulcimer, *Harvey Reid* Nothin But Guitar *& rec by Claudia Schmidt. In Peggy Seeger & Ewan MacColl* The Singing Island, *1960, Ewan MacColl* FS & Bals of Scotland *&* The Coffeehouse SB. OS50

Fiddler's Green

As I rode by the dockside one evening so rare
To view the still waters & take the salt air
I heard an old fisherman singing this song
Oh take me away boys, the time is not long

C F C Am / C F C G / F C G - / Am F C G **(in 3/4)**

Dress me up in me oilskins & jumper
No more on the docks I'll be seen
Just tell me old shipmates I'm takin a trip, mates
And I'll see you someday on Fiddler's Green

C G C - / F C G - / F - C - / G - - C

O Fiddler's Green is a place I've heard tell
Where fishermen go if they don't go to hell
Where the weather is fair & the dolphins do play
And the cold coast of Greenland is far, far away

Where the sky's always blue & there's never a gale
Where the fish jump on board with a swish of their tails
Where you lie at your leisure, there's no work to do
And the skipper's below makin' tea for the crew

When you get back to dock & your long trip is thru
There's pubs, there's clubs & there's lassies there too
The girls are all pretty & the beer is all free
And there's bottles of rum growin' on every tree

Well I don't want a harp nor a halo, not me
Just give me a breeze & a good rollin' sea
And I'd play me old squeezebox as we'd sail along
With the wind in the rigging to sing me this song

— John Connelly

 In SO! 20:4, Wind That Shakes the Barley *&* S That Changed the World. *On Liam Clancy* The Dutchman *&* Farewell to Tarwaithe, *Schooner Fare* Closer to the Wind, *Kevin Roth* Dulcimer Man, *Evelyn & Bob Beers* Seasons of Peace *& rec by Sara Grey.* OS51

Golden Vanity

There was a ship that sailed upon the Lowland sea
And the name of our ship was the Golden Vanity
And we feared she would be taken by the Spanish enemy
As we sailed upon **the lowland, lowland, low** *[land]*
We sailed upon **the lowland sea**

(capo up) G - D Em / Am A D -
/ 1st / Am D G Em / Am D G -

Then up spoke our cabin boy & boldly outspoke he
And he said to our captain "What will you give to me
If I swim alongside of the Spanish enemy
And sink her in the **lowland, lowland, low**
And sink her in **the lowland sea?"**

"O I will give you silver & I will give you gold
And my own fair young daughter, your bonny bride shall be
If you'll swim alongside of the Spanish enemy
And sink her in **the lowland, lowland, low...**"

Then the boy he made him ready & overboard sprang he
And he swam alongside of the Spanish enemy
And with his brace & auger in her side he bored holes 3
And sank her in **the lowland...**

Then quickly he swam back to the cheering of the crew
But the captain would not heed him, for his promise he did rue
And he scorned his poor entreatings when loudly he did sue
And left him in **the lowland...**

Then roundabout he turned & swam to the port side
And up unto his messmates full bitterly he cried
"O messmates, draw me up, for I'm drifting with the tide
And I'm sinking in **the lowland...**"

Then his messmates took him up, but on the deck he died
And they sewed him in his hammock that was so large & wide
And they low'red him overboard, but he drifted with the tide
And sank beneath **the lowland...**

— **Child Ballad #286**

In SO! *12:5 &* Reprints *#6 & #7,* Hootenanny SB, *A Lomax* FS of NAm, FiresB of FS, Shanties fr the 7 Seas, FSEncyV2, SFest, FS Abecedary *& Sharp* Eng FS of S Appalach. *On rec by Carter Fam,* Blow Ye Winds In the Morning *(RS1084), Pete Seeger* Am Bals, *Red Clay Ramblers* Stolen Love, *Bok Muir & Trickett* The Ways of Man, *Ives* FS Dramatic & Humorous, S of the Sea *& in his* SB. *On Caryl P Weiss* With Her Head Tucked, *Fast Folk* V2-2, *Dry Branch Fire Squad* Fannin the Flames *& Kim Wallach* Even More Children's S. OS52

Greenland Fisheries

'Twas in 18 hundred & 53
And of June the 13th day
That our gallant ship her anchor weighed
And for Greenland bore away, **brave boys**
And for Greenland bore away

D - - - / - - A - / D - G A / D G A - / D A D -

The lookout in the crosstrees stood
With a spyglass in his hand
There's a whale **(2x)**, there's a whalefish he cried
And she blows at every span, **brave boys...**

The captain stood on the quarter-deck
And a fine little man was he
"Overhaul! Overhaul! Let your davit-tackles fall
And launch your boats for sea..."

Now the boats were launched & the men aboard
And the whale was in full view
Resolvèd was each seaman bold
To steer where the whalefish blew...

We stuck that whale, the line paid out
But she gave a flourish with her tail
The boat capsized & four men were drowned
And we never caught that whale...

"To lose the whale," our captain said
"It grieves my heart full sore
But oh! to lose four gallant men
It grieves me ten times more...

The winter star doth now appear
So, boys, we'll anchor weigh
It's time to leave this cold country
And homeward bear away..."

O Greenland is a dreadful place
A land that's never green
Where there's ice & snow & the whalefish blow
And the daylight's seldom seen...

The Lomax version of the song has a somewhat more realistic version of the 3rd to the last verse: "Bad news (2x)" our captain he cried / For it grieved his heart full sore / But the losing of that hundred barrel whale / It grieved him 10 times more... Aka: "Greenland Whale Fishery." In SO! *1:10 &* Reprints *#1. In A & J Lomax* Our Singing Country, *A Lomax* FS of NAm *&* Best S fr the Lomax Coll. *In* SFest, Carry It On, Wind That Shakes the Barley, Dubliners SB, FS EncyV2 & S of Newfoundland Outports. *On* Gr FSingers of the 60s, *Michael Cooney* Singer of Old S *(FrontHall) & The Coop* V1-1. *On Weavers* SBag, Reunion at Carnegie Hall, Trav On *& in their* SB. OS53

The Grey Funnel Line

Don't mind the rain nor the rollin' sea
The weary night never worries me
But the hardest time in a sailor's day
Is to watch the sun as it dies away
It's one more day on the Grey Funnel Line

E - / - B7 / E A / EA EA // E EB7 E

The finest ship that sailed the sea
Is still a prison for the likes of me
But give me wings like Noah's dove
I'd fly up harbour to the girl I love / **It's...**

Every time I gaze behind the screws
Makes me long for old Peter's shoes
I'd walk down that silver lane
And take my love in my arms again

O Lord, if dreams were only real
I'd have my hands on that wooden wheel
And with all my heart I'd turn her round
And tell the boys that we're homeward bound

I'll pass the time like some machine
Until the blue water turns to green
Then I'll dance on down that walk ashore
And sail the Grey Funnel Line no more

— **Cyril Tawney**

 — The "Grey Funnel Line" is the British Navy. In SO! *20:1. On* Sara Grey *(FSI38), Maddy Prior & June Tabor* Silly Sisters *& Jean Redpath & Lisa Neustadt* Anywhere Is Home *(Philo).* OS54

Haul Away, Joe

When I was a little lad & so my mother told me
Way, haul away, we'll haul away, Joe
That if I did not kiss the girls, my lips would grow all mouldy
Way, haul away, we'll haul away, Joe

Am G - Em / Am G GEm Am :||

King Louis was the king of France before the revolution
But then he got his head cut off which spoiled his constitution

O once I had a German girl & she was fat & lazy
Then I got a Brooklyn gal, she damn near drove me crazy

So I got a Chinese girl & she was kind & tender
She left me for a Portuguee, so young & rich & slender

Way, haul away, I'll sing to you of Nancy
Way, haul away, she's just my cut & fancy

O once I was in Ireland, a-digging turf & praties
But now I'm in a Yankee ship, a-hauling on sheets & braces

The cook is in the galley, making duff so handy
And the captain's in his cabin drinkin' wine & brandy

Way, haul away, the good ship is a-bowling
Way, haul away, the sheet is now a-blowing

Way, haul away, we'll haul away together
Way, haul away, we'll haul for better weather

On Bikel FSinger's Choice, *Ives* S of the Sea *(& in his* SB*), Judy Small* One Voice in the Crowd *(Redwood) & Clancy Bros* Gr H. *In* SFest, Treas of FS, FS N Am Sings, Shanties fr the 7 Seas & FiresB of Fun & Games. OS55

Hieland Laddie

Was you ever in Quebec, **Bonnie Laddie, Hieland Laddie?**
Stowing timber on the deck, **my Bonnie Hieland Laddie**

Am DmAm Dm Em / Am DmAm DmEm Am

Hey, ho & away we go, Bonnie Laddie, Hieland Laddie
Hey, ho, away we go, my Bonnie Hieland Laddie

FC GC Dm Em / FC GC DmEm Am

Was you ever in Callao, **Bonnie Laddie...?**
Where the girls are never slow, **my Bonnie...**

Was you ever in Mobile Bay / Loading cotton by the day
Was you on the Brummalow / Where Yankee boys are all the go
Was you ever in Dundee / There some pretty ships you'll see
Was you ever in Merrimashee / Where you make fast to a tree
Was you ever in Aberdeen / Prettiest girls you've ever seen

Wm Doerflinger traces this song back to at least the 1840s. In Canada it evolved into a children's song "Donkey Riding." "Merrimashee"=Miramichi River in New Brunswick province. In SO! *10:3 &* Reprints *#5,* Shanties for the 7 Seas, FSEncyV2 & Bells of Rhymney. *On Ives* Down to the Sea in Ships *(Decca)), Alan Mills* More S to Grow On *(FC7009) & Relativity* Gathering Place *(Green Linnet).* Donkey Riding *is on Milt Okun* I Sing of Canada *(SLP71).* OS56

The Hills of Isle Au Haut

It's away & to the westward is the place a man should go
Where the fishing's always easy, they've got no ice or snow
But I'll haul down the sail where the bays come together
Bide away the days on the hills of Isle au Haut

(in D) A - GA D / //G D G D/ /

Now the Plymouth girls are fine, they put their hearts in your hand
And the Plymouth boys are able, first-class sailors, every man

Now, the trouble with old Martier, you don't try her in a trawler
For those Bay of Biscay swells, they roll your head from off your shoulder

The girls of Cascais, they are strong across the shoulder
They don't give a man advice, they don't want to cook his supper

Now, the winters drive you crazy & the fishing's hard & slow
You're a damn fool if you stay, but there's no better place to go

— **Gordon Bok**

© 1970 Timberhead, Inc. Used by permission. Pub by Folk Legacy Records. — On his A Tune for November *& in his* Time & Flying Snow. *On Happy Traum* Bright Morning Stars *& on County Down* Hills of.... *In* SO! *26:2 &* Golden Link SB. OS57

Jamaica Farewell

Down the way where the nights are gay
And the sun shines brightly on the mountain top
I took a trip on a sailing ship
And when I reached Jamaica I made a stop

C F / CG C :||

But I'm sad to say that I'm on my way
Won't be back for many a day
My heart is down, my head is turning around
Had to leave a little girl in Kingston town

C F / G C / C F / CG C

Sounds of laughter everywhere
And the dancers swinging to & fro
I must declare that my heart is there
Tho' I've been from Maine to Mexico

Down at the market you can hear
Ladies cry out while on their heads they bear
Ake rice, salt fish are nice
And the rum is fine anytime of year

— **Irving Burgie**

© 1955 Shari Music Publishing Corp. © renewal 1983 to Irving Burgie – assigned 1983 to Lord Burgess Music Publishing Co./Cherry Lane Music Publishing Company Inc. All rights reserved. Used by permission. – On Kingston Trio, *Kim Wallach* 2 Doz Children's S *& Martin Bogan & Armstrong* That Old Gang of Mine. *In* 1001 Jumbo S. *Rec by Harry Belafonte.* OS58

The John B. Sails

We sailed on the sloop John B., my grandfather & me
'Round Nassau town we did roam
Drinkin' all night, got into a fight
Well I feel so break up, I wanna go home

D - - - / - - A - / D - G - / D A D -

So hoist up the John B. sails, see how the mainsail sets
Send for the captain ashore, I wanna go home
O let me go home, please let me go home
I feel so break up, I wanna go home!

Well the first mate he got drunk, broke up the people's trunk
Constable had to come & take him away
Sheriff John Stone, please leave me alone
I feel so break up, I wanna go home

The cook he got the fits, ate up all of my grits
Then he went & ate up all of my corn
O let me go home, please let me go home
This is the worst trip I've ever been on

— **words & music adapted by Lee Hays**

TRO © 1951 (renewed 1979) Folkways Music Publishers Inc, NY, NY. International copyright secured. Made in USA. All rights reserved incl. public performance for profit. Used by permission. – aka: "Sloop John B.," "Wreck of the John B." Orig pub in Carl Sandburg Am Songbag, *1927. Rec by A Lomax fr the singing of Bahaman Blacks, Nassau, 1935. In his* FS of N Am. *On* Kingston Trio *(Capitol) & their* 25 Yrs, *Beach Boys* Pier Sounds, Sunshine Dream *&* Made in USA. *On Michael Cooney* Still Cooney *(FrontHall). In Weavers* SB *& on their* Gr H. *In* FS Abecedary, S for Pickin & Singin, FSEncyV2 *&* SFest. OS59

Lord Franklin

It was homeward bound one night on the deep
Swinging in my hammock I fell asleep
I dreamed a dream & I thought it true
Concerning Franklin & his gallant crew

D - G - / Em - A - / D - G D / - A G D

With 100 seamen he sailed away
To the frozen ocean in the month of May
To seek that passage around the pole
Where we poor seamen do sometimes go

Thru cruel hardships his men they strove
Their ship on mountains of ice was drove
Where the Eskimo in his skin canoe
Was the only one who ever came thru

In Baffin's Bay where the whalefish blow
The fate of Franklin no man may know
The fate of Franklin no tongue can tell
Lord Franklin along with his sailors do dwell

And now my burden it gives me pain
For my long-lost Franklin I'd cross the main
10,000 pounds would I freely give
To say on earth that my Franklin do live

aka: "Lady Franklin's Lament." On his 2nd attempt, Franklin set out with 2 ships loaded with luxuries instead of extra food. He was never heard of again. (Remains later indicated that all died of lead poisoning fr badly canned food.) Lady Franklin mounted 5 rescue operations herself fr a public fund drive after the Admiralty washed its hands of the affair. On K Burke & M O'Domnhail Promenade, *Martin Carthy* 2nd Alb *(Topic), Margaret Christl* Looking Towards Home, *Brecon Beacon* Feast or Famine *& Ewan MacColl & Al Lloyd* Off to Sea Once More V2. *In* Liverpool Lullabies *& Beryl Davis* FS fr Spin #2. *Dylan wrote new words to this tune in his song "Bob Dylan's Dream" on his* Times They Are a-Changin'. *In* SO! *35:2 & 44:4.* OS60

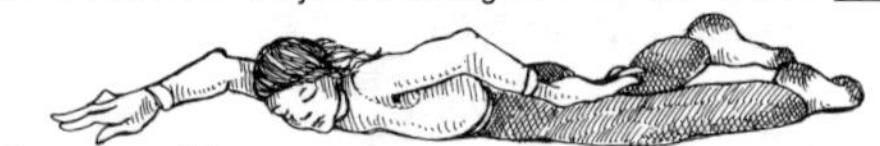

Mary Ellen Carter

She went down last October, in a pouring driving rain
The Skipper, he'd been drinking & the Mate, he felt no pain
Too close to Three Mile Rock & she was dealt her mortal blow
And the Mary Ellen Carter settled low
There was just us five aboard her when she finally was awash
We'd worked like hell to save her, all heedless of the cost
And the groan she gave as she went down, it caused us to proclaim
That the Mary Ellen Carter would rise again

G - CD G / Am - C D / G - C G
1. Am - D - :|| 2. Am D G -

Well, the owners wrote her off, not a nickel would they spend
"She gave 20 years of service, boys, then met her sorry end
But insurance paid the loss to us, so let her rest below"
Then they laughed at us & said we had to go
But we talked of her all winter, some days around the clock
For she's worth a quarter million, afloat & at the dock
And with every jar that hit the bar we swore we would remain
And make the Mary Ellen Carter rise again

Rise again, rise again
That her name not be lost to the knowledge of men
Those who loved her best & were with her to the end
Will make the Mary Ellen Carter rise again

Am D G - / C - G D / G - CD G / 1st /

All spring, now we've been with her on the barge lent by a friend
Three dives a day in a hard hat suit & twice I've had the bends
Thank God it's only 60 ft. & the currents here are slow
Or I'd never have the strength to go below
But we patched her rents, stopped her vents, dogged hatch and porthole down
Put cables to her, 'fore & aft & girded her around
Tomorrow, noon, we hit the air & then take up the strain
And watch the Mary Ellen Carter rise again

For we couldn't leave her there, you see, to crumble into scale
She'd saved our lives so many times, living through the gale
And the laughing drunken mates who left her to a sorry grave
They won't be laughing in another day
And you, to whom adversity has dealt the final blow
With smiling bastards lying to you everywhere you go
Turn to & put out all your strength of arm & heart & brain
And, like the Mary Ellen Carter, rise again

(last cho) Rise again, rise again
Tho' your heart it be broken & life about to end
No matter what you've lost, be it a home, a love, a friend
Like **the Mary Ellen Carter, rise again!**

— Stan Rogers

 — On his Betw the Breaks *& in his* S fr Fogarty's Cove *& on Schooner Fare* Alive. *In* SO! *29:3.* OS61

Northwest Passage

Ah for just one time I would take the Northwest Passage
To find the hand of Franklin reaching for the Beaufort Sea
Tracing one warm line through a land so wide & savage
And make a Northwest Passage to the sea

C G F Am / F C Dm F / 1st / F CG C -

Westward from the Davis Strait 'tis there 'twas said to lie
The sea route to the Orient for which so many died
Seeking gold & glory, leaving weathered broken bones
And a long forgotten lonely cairn of stones

F C - G / F C - F / F Am C F / - C Am -

Three centuries thereafter, I take passage overland
In the footsteps of brave Kelso, where his "sea of flowers" began
Watching cities rise before me, then behind me sink again
This tardiest explorer, driving hard across the plain

(4th line, 2nd v: F C G F)

And thru the night, behind the wheel, the mileage clicking West
I think upon Mackenzie, David Thompson & the rest
Who cracked the mountain ramparts & did show a path for me
To race the roaring Fraser to the sea

How then am I so different from the first men thru this way?
Like them I left a settled life, I threw it all away
To seek a Northwest Passage at the call of many men
To find there but the road back home again

— Stan Rogers

 – On his Northwest Passage *& in his* S fr Fogarty's Cove. *On Margaret Christl* Looking towards Home. OS62

Nova Scotia Farewell

The sun was sinkin' down in the west
The birds were singin' on every tree
All nature seemed to be at rest
But still there was no rest for me

G - - - / Em - - - / G D - - / Em C Bm Em

Farewell to Nova Scotia, the sea-bound coast
May your mountains dark & dreary be
For when I am far away on the briny ocean tossed
Will you ever heave a sigh & a wish for me?

I grieve to leave my native land
Grieve to leave my comrades all
And my aged loving parents who I always held so dear
And the bonnie, bonnie lass who I do adore

I have three brothers & they are at rest
Their arms are folded on their chests
But a poor weary sailor just like me
Must be tossed & driven on the dark blue sea

On Ian & Sylvia Northern Journey, *their* Gr H V2, *Tommy Makem* The Bard of Armagh *& Diane Oxner* Sings Trad FS fr Nova Scotia. *In Fowke* FS of Canada. OS63

Rio Grande

O say were you ever in Rio Grande / **O Rio**
It's there that the river flows down golden sand
And we're bound for the Rio Grande

(in 3/4) C - G C / - - G - / F C G C / - G C -

Then away, love, away / Way down Rio
So fare ye well my pretty young gal
For we're bound for the Rio Grande

C G C - / " / " / " /

And goodbye, fare you well, all you ladies of town / **O...**
We've left you enough for to buy a silk gown / **And we're...**

So it's pack your donkey & get under way
The girls we are leaving can take our half-pay

Now you Bowery ladies, we'd have you to know
We're bound to the Southward, o Lord let us go

We'll sell our cod for molassas & rum
And come home before Thanksgiving comes

Rio Grande refers to Rio Grande do Sul in Brazil. In SO! *1:7 &* Reprints #4, Hootenanny SB, SFest, FiresB of FS, S for Pickin & Singin, Trea of Am S, Shanties fr the 7 Seas & FSEncyV2. *On Ned Bachus* Raisin d'etre. OS64

Rollin' Down to Old Maui

It's a damn tough life full of toil & strife we whalermen undergo
And we don't give a damn when the gale is done how hard the winds did blow
'Cause we're homeward bound from the Arctic Ground with a good ship taut & free
And we won't give a damn when we drink our rum with the girls of Old Maui

Rolling down to Old Maui, me boys, rolling down to Old Maui
We're homeward bound from the Arctic Ground, rolling...

EmB7 **(3x)** Em / ||: G D Em B7 / 1st :||

Once more we sail with the northerly gale thru the ice & wind & rain
Them coconut fronds, them tropical lands we soon shall see again
Six hellish months we've passed away on the cold Kamchatka Sea
But now, we're bound from the Arctic Ground, **rolling...**

Once more we sail the northerly gale towards our island home
Our main mast sprung, our whaling done & we ain't got far to roam
Our stun's'l bones is carried away, what care we for that sound
A living gale is after us, thank God we're homeward bound

How soft the breeze thru the island trees, now the ice is far a-stern
Them native maids, them tropical glades is awaiting our return
Even now their big brown eyes look out hoping some fine day to see
Our baggy sails, running 'fore the gales, **rolling...**

Maui=pron. "Mau-WEE." On Stan Rogers Betw The Breaks *& in his* S fr Fogarty's Cove. *In Gale Huntington* S the Whalemen Sang, *Joanna Colcord* S of Am Sailormen *& Stan Hugill* S of the Sea. *On* Steady as She Goes: S & Chanties fr the Days of Commercial Sail *(Collector1928).* OS65

Rolling Home

Up aloft & in the rigging blows a wild & rushing gale
Like a monsoon in the springtime, filling out each well-known sail

G - - C / D G D G

Rolling home (3x) across the sea
Rolling home to old New England* rolling home, dear land, to thee!

And the waves we leave behind us seem to murmur as they rise
We have tarried here to bear you to the land you dearly prize

Full 10,000 miles behind us & a thousand miles before
Ancient ocean waves to waft us to the well-remembered shore

Newborn breezes swell to send us to our childhood's welcome skies
To the glow of friendly faces & the glance of loving eyes

— Charles Mackay

**or: to merrie England, or dear old Scotland, etc. Tune is same as "Kevin Barry" (see STRUG). In* Burl Ives SB *& his* Sea S, *Stan Hugill* Shanties & Sailors S & S of the Sea, *Frank Shay* Am Sea S & Chanteys, Pious Friends *& his* Iron Men, *Whall* Sea S & Shanties, *Doerflinger* Shantymen. *On Archie Fisher & Garnet Rogers Off the Map (Snow Go New Golden Ring 5* Days Singing V2 *(FolkLeg) & Caryl P Weiss* With Her Head Tucked. OS66

Run, Come, See Jerusalem

'Twas 19 hundred & 29
Run come see, run come see!
(**sung over the preceding:** I remember that day pretty well)
'Twas 19 hundred & 29
Run come see, Jerusalem

D -/- A7 / D G / DA7 D

Why then, there was a talk about a storm in our island
Run... (my God, what a beautiful morning!)
They were talkin' about a storm in our island / **Run...**

Well there were three sails leaving from the harbour
(with the women & children on board) There...
These sails was the Ethel & Myrtle & Pretoria
(my God, they were bound for Andros) The Ethel...
Right then, well the Ethel was bound for Stanniard Creek
(with the women & children on board) Yes the Ethel...
My God, well the Myrtle was bound for French Creek
(my God, what a beautiful morning!) Well the Myrtle...
O Lord, Pretoria was out on the ocean
(dashing from side to side from waves) Well Pretoria...
Great God, well the big sea built up in the northwest
(well the children run looking for their mothers) When...
My God & the first sea hit the Pretoria
(& the children come grabbing for their mommas) The...
My God & the sailor go downward for the bottom
(& the captain come grabbing for the tiller) The...
Now George Brown he was the captain
(he shouts "My children come pray") Now...
He said "Come now, witness your judgement"
(& the women all crying for the Daniel-God) "Come..."
There was 33 souls on the water
(swimming & praying to the good Lord) There were...

— Blake Alphonso Higgs ("Blind Blake")

 — In SO! 3:12 & Reprints #3 & FS Ency V2. *On Seeger & A Guthrie* Prec Friend, *Bok Muir & Trickett* Water Over Stone, *Jean Redpath & Lisa Neustadt* Anywhere Is Home *(Philo) & rec by the Weavers.* OS67

Safe in the Harbor

Have you stood by the ocean on a diamond-hard morning
And felt the horizon stir deep in your soul?
Watched the wake of a steamer as it cut thru blue water
And been gripped by a fever you just can't control?
O to throw off the shackles & fly with the seagulls
To where green waves tumble before a driving sea wind
Or to lie on the decking on a warm summer evening
Watch the red sun fall burning beneath the earth's rim

(in 3/4) C Em F C / C Dm C G / 1st / Em Dm G C / 1st / Em Dm C G / 1st / Em Dm CCG C

But to every sailor comes time to drop anchor
Haul in the sails & make the lines fast
You deep water dreamer, your journey is over
You're safe in the harbor at last (2x)

C Em F G / / C G F G / C G F - / /

Some men are sailors, but most are just dreamers
Held fast by the anchors they forge in their minds
Who in their hearts know they'll never sail over deep water
To search for a treasure they're afraid they won't find
So in sheltered harbours they cling to their anchors
Bank down their boilers & shut down their steam
And wait for the sailors to return with bright treasures
That will fan the dull embers & fire up their dreams

And some men are schemers who laugh at the dreamers
Take the gold from the sailors & turn it to dross
They're men in a prison, they're men without vision
Whose only horizon is profit & loss
So when storm clouds come sailing across your blue ocean
Hold fast to your dreaming for all that you're worth
For as long as there's dreamers, there will always be sailors
Bringing back their bright treasures from the corners of earth

— **Eric Bogle**

© Larrikin Music, PO Box 162, Paddington NSW 2021 Australia. All rights reserved. Used by permission. *This was written as a tribute to Stan Rogers. – On his* Where the Wind Blows *(Flying Fish) & Margaret Christl* Looking towards Home. OS68

A Sailor's Prayer

Tho' my sails be torn & tattered & the mast be turned about
Let the night wind chill me to my very soul
Tho' the spray might sting my eyes & the stars no light provide
Give me just another morning light to hold

D - - - / G A D - :||

And I will not lie me down this rain a-raging
I will not lie me down in such a storm
And if this night be unblessed I shall not take my rest
Til I reach another shore

A - D - / /D - G - / A - D -

Tho' the only water left is but salt to wound my thirst
I will drink the rain that falls so steady down
And tho' night's blindness be my gift & there be thieves upon my drift
I will praise this fog that shelters me along

And tho' my mates be drained & weary & believe their hopes are lost
There's no need for their bones on that blackened bottom
And tho' death waits just off the bow, they shall not answer to him now
He shall stand to face the morning without us

— **Rod McDonald**

© 1978, 1986 author. Blue Flute Music (ASCAP). Used by permission. *— In SO! 29:3. On his* No Commercial Traffic *(HR800), Jean Redpath & Lisa Neustadt* Anywhere Is Home *(Philo), Bok* All Shall Be Well Again *(FolkLeg), Jim Couza* Sailor's Prayer, *Hudson River Sloop Singers* Proud Old River *& Free Hot Lunch* Wa Ha Music *& rec by Mtn RR & Happy Traum (HomespunTapes).* OS69

Shenandoah

1. **O Shenandoah,** I long to see you
   Away, you rollin' river
   O Shenandoah, I long to see you
   Away, we're bound away
   'Cross the wide Missouri

C - F C / F G C - / F G Am -
C - - - / Am - G C

2. **O Shenandoah,** I love your daughter...
3. **O...** I'm bound to leave you...
   O... I'll not deceive you...
4. For seven years, I've been a rover...
5. But I'll return to be your lover...

Strange "inland" words for a sea song, but this is the way it goes & who would change it? On Odetta Sings FS, *Pete Seeger (& in)* Am Fav Bal V2 *(FA2321) & Spider John Koerner* Nobody Knows the Trouble. *In* Burl Ives SB *& on his* S of the Sea. *In* SO! *33:4 & 44:4,* SFest, FS Abecedary, *Readers Dig* Family SB, FSEncyV2, Shanties fr the 7 Seas, *&* FiresB of FS. OS70

Ship Titanic

O they built the ship Titanic for to sail the ocean blue
And they thought they had a ship that the water could ne'er go thru
It was on her maiden trip that the iceberg hit the ship
It was sad when that great ship went down

D - G D / - - E A / 1st / D A D -

O it was sad, it was sad
It was sad when that great ship went down
(to the bottom of the)
Husbands & wives, little children lost their lives
It was sad when that great ship went down

G - D - / - - A - / D D7 G D (or Ddim) / D A D -

O they sailed out from England & were almost to the shore
When the rich refused to associate with the poor
So they put them down below where they were the first to go...

The boat was full of sin & the sides about to burst
When the captain shouted "A-women & children first!"
O the captain tried to wire, but the lines were all on fire...

O they swung the lifeboats out o'er the deep & raging sea
When the band struck up with "Nearer My God to Thee"
Little children wept & cried as the waves swept o'er the sides...

aka: "The Titantic." The supposedly unsinkable R.M.S. Titanic was hit by an iceberg on her gala maiden voyage fr Southampton to NYC on 4/14/1912 with a loss of 1,513 lives. The most poignant of the many songs written about this event was the one Leadbelly recorded: on the story that the famed Black prizefighter Jack Johnson had been refused passage on the trip because the captain "wouldn't carry no coal" (!) In SO! *10:2 &* Reprints #2, SFest *&* FiresB of Fun & Games, FS Abecedary *&* FSEncyV2. *On* S of Camp *(FC7510), Leadbelly* Last Sessions, *Pete Seeger* Am Bals *(FA2319), Bob Gibson* There's A Meetin *& Eric Von Schmidt* Folk Blues. OS71

South Australia

In South Australia I was born
Heave away, o haul away!
In South Australia round Cape Horn
We're bound for South Australia

C - - - / - - G - / C - G C / /

Haul away you rolling kings
We'll heave away, haul away
Haul away, we're bound to sing
We're bound for South Australia

F - C - / - - G - / F - C - / - - G C

As I walked out one morning fair / **Heave away...**
'Twas there I met Miss Nancy Blair / **We're bound...**

There ain't but one thing grieves my mind
To leave Miss Nancy Blair behind

O when we whallop 'round Cape Horn
You'll wish to God you'd never been born

I wish I was in Australia's strand
With a glass of whisky in my hand

Port Adelaide's a grand old town
There's plenty of girls to go around

aka: "Australia." 1st coll (in Newcastle-upon-Tyne in England) & pub by Laura Smith in her M of the Waters *(late 19th c.) On A.L.Lloyd* Blow Boys Blow *(TLP1026), Clancy Bros* The Boys Won't Leave the Girls Alone *& in their* SB. *In* SO! *10:1 &* Reprints #9, SFest, How Can we Keep fr Singing, Shanties fr the 7 Seas *&* FSEncyV2. OS72

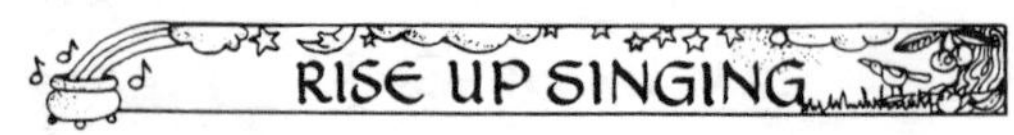

Turn Ye to Me

The stars are shining cheerily, cheerily
Horo, Mhairi-dhu: turn ye to me
The seabird is crying wearily, wearily / **Horo...**

(in C & 3/4) F - C - / Am C G C :||

Cold are the stormwinds that ruffle his breast
But warm are the downy plumes lining his nest
Cold blows the storm there, soft falls the snow there
Horo...

F - G C / G F C G / C F C Dm / Am C G C

The waves are driving wearily, wearily / **Horo...**
The seabird is crying drearily, drearily / **Horo...**

Hushed be thy moaning, lone bird of the sea
Thy home on the rock is a shelter to thee
Thy home is the angry wave, mine but the lonely grave...

— Christopher North (1785-1854)

Pron: long e's in cheerily, wearily, etc. as long a's (as in chair), ch in cheerily as a j. On Gordon Bok Seal Djiril's Hymn *(FolkLeg).* OS73

The Ways of Man

The ways of man are passing strange
He buys his freedom & he counts his change
Then he lets the wind his days arrange
And he calls the tide his master

(in D) D - A D / G A - Bm / G - D Bm / D - G -

O the days (2x) / O the fine long summer days
The fish come a-rolling in the bays
And he swore he'd never leave me

But the days grow short & the year gets old
And fish won't stay where the water's cold
So if you're going to fill the hold
You've got to go offshore to find them

So they go outside on the raging deep
And they pray the Lord their souls to keep
But the wave will roll them all to sleep
And the tide will be their keeper

O the tide **(2x)** / O you dark & you bitter tide
If I can't have him by my side
I guess I've got to leave him

Lord, I know that the day will come
When one less boat comes slogging home
I don't mind knowing that he'll be the one
But I can't spend my whole life waiting

O the tide **(2x)** / O the dark & the bitter tide
If I can't have him by my side
The water's welcome to him

I gave you one, I gave you two
The best that rotten old boat could do
And you'll have it all before you're thru
Well I've got no more to give you

— Gordon Bok

© 1977 Timberhead Inc. Used by permission. Pub by Folk Legacy Records, Sharon CT. On Bok Muir & Trickett The Ways of Man. *In SO! 36:4.* OS74

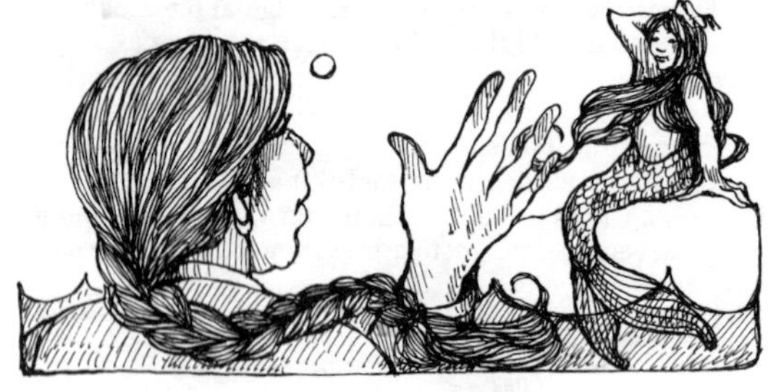

When I Was a Fair Maid

When I was a fair maid about 17
I 'listed in the navy for to serve the queen
I 'listed in the navy a sailor lad to stand
For to hear the cannons rattling & the music so grand
And the music so grand **(2x)**
For to hear the cannons rattling & the music so grand

G - C - / D - - - / G D G D / C G D G

D - G D / C G D G

Well the officer that 'listed me was a tall & handsome man
He said you'll make a sailor, so come along my man
My waist being tall & slender, my fingers long & thin
And the very soon they learned me I soon exceeded them
I soon exceeded them **(2x)** / And the very soon...

Well they sent me to bed & they sent me to bunk
To lie with a sailor I never was afraid
But taking off my blue coat sure it often makes me smile
For to think I was a sailor & a maiden all the while...

Well they sent me up to London for to guard the Tower
And I'm sure I might be there til my very dying hour
But a lady fell in love with me, I told her I was a maid
O she went unto the Captain & my secret she betrayed...

Well the Captain he came up to me & he asked if this was so
O I dare not **(3x)** say no
It's a pity we should lose you, such a sailor lad you made
It's a pity we should lose you, such a handsome young maid...

So it's fare thee well Captain you've been so kind to me
And likewise my shipmates I'm sorry to part with thee
But if ever the navy needs a lad, a sailor I'll remain
I'll put out my hat & feathers & I'll run the riggin' again...

On Sally Rogers The Unclaimed Pint *& Tríona níDhomhnaill* Tríona *(Gael-Linn). In SO! 36:1 & Sally Rogers SB.* OS75

There are many good collections of sea songs (Lomax, etc.). One very complete collection currently available is Songs from the Seven Seas ©1984 Routledge & Keegan-Paul $12.95.

Other maritime songs include "I've got sixpence" (GOOD), "I've Been to London" (PLAY), "Er-i-ee, Erie Canal" (TRAV).

The term "White Spirituals" has been used to refer to early American traditional (White) hymns. This chapter, however, follows the narrower, more popular understanding of the term "Spiritual" in being limited to Black Spirituals – that is, traditional religious songs which spring out of early Black American experience, primarily during the period of slavery.

Balm in Gilead

There is a balm in Gilead, to make the wounded whole
There is a balm in Gilead, to heal the sin-sick soul

D - - A / D - BmA D

Sometimes I feel discouraged & think my work's in vain
But then the Holy Spirit revives my soul again

D EmA D A / D EmA F♯m G

If you can preach like Peter, if you can pray like Paul
Go home & tell your neighbor: "Christ died to save us all"

In SO! *2:1 &* Reprints *#5*, Hootenanny SB, FSEncyV2, S of Praise v1 *&* A Time for Singing. *On* Songs of Praise alb 1 *(W/GC7608).* ⊙R40

Children, Go Where I Send Thee

Children, go where I send thee / How shall I send thee?
I'm gonna send thee 1 by 1 / 1 for the little bitty baby
Was born, born / Born in Bethlehem

D - / / / 𝄆 D - 𝄇 * D G / DA D

Children go... How...?
*** repeat 1-12x as needed**
I'm gonna send thee 2 by 2 / 2 for Paul & Silas
1 for the little bitty baby / **Was born...**

3 for the Hebrew Children
4 for the 4 who stood at the door
5 for the gospel preachers
6 for the 6 that never got fixed
7 for the 7 that never got to heaven
8 for the 8 who stood at the gate
9 for the 9 who looked so fine
10 for the 10 commandments
11 for the 11 who went up to Heaven
12 for the 12 Apostles

On Lib. of Cong. Negro Religious S *(AAFSL10 recorded 1942 in an Arkansas prison), Weavers* At Carnegie Hall, *Christmas Revels* Wassail Wassail, *Jonathan Edwards* Little Hands *& on* John Fahey *In* SO! *35:1 &* S of the Spirit. ⊙R41

Daniel

Didn't my Lord deliver Daniel (3x)?
Didn't my Lord deliver Daniel? Then why not every man

Em - / Am Em / - - / B7 Em

He delivered Daniel from the lion's den
Jonah from the belly of the whale
And the Hebrew children from the fiery furnace
Then why not every man *[one]*?

Am - / Em - / Am Em / B7 Em

The moon run down in a purple stream
The sun forbear to shine
And every star will disappear
King Jesus shall be mine

I set my foot on the Gospel ship
And the ship began for to sail
It landed me over on Canaan's shore
And I'll never come back no more

On Raffi Rise & Shine *& in his* 2nd SB. *In* Treas of FS, Story of the Spirituals, FS Am Sings & FSEncyV2. *On* The Essential *Paul Robeson.* ⊙R42

Deep River

Deep river, my home is over Jordan
Deep river, Lord I want to cross over into camp ground

C FG C Em / C7 F𝄐 DmG C

O don't you want to go to that gospel feast
That promised land where all is peace?
O don't you want to go to that promised land where all is peace

Am Em Am Em / / C Em F E7

I'll go up to Heaven & take my seat
And cast my crown at Jesus' feet
I'll go up to Heaven & cast my crown at Jesus' feet

When I get to Heaven I'll walk about
There's nobody there to turn me out
When I get to Heaven there's no one there to turn me out

In SO! *24:6, James Walden Johnson* B of Negro Spirituals, *1925,* Pocketful of S, Treas of Am S, 120 Am S, S Am Sings *&* Sing Along w World's Fav FS. *On Kim & Reggie Harris* Music & the Underground Railroad & The Essential *Paul Robeson.* ⊙R43

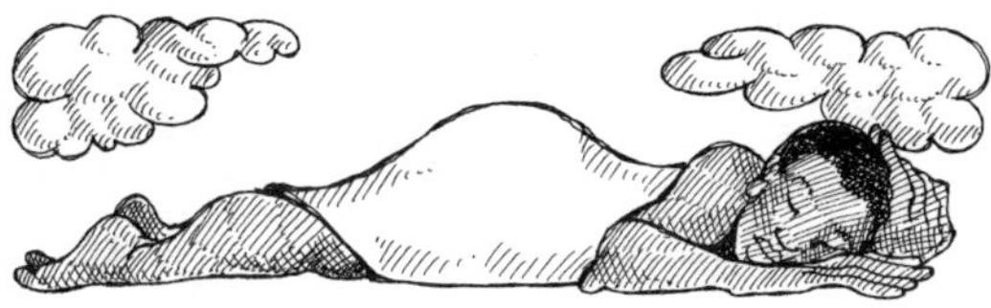

Do, Lord

Do Lord, o do Lord, o do you remember me? (3x)
Look away beyond the blue *[horizon]*

G - - - / C - - G / - - B7 Em / G D G -

1. I've got a home in glory land that outshines the sun...
2. I took Jesus as my saviour, you take him too...

cho: trad, v1: Rev. Everett George Washington, v2: Marvin Frey In S of the Spirit *&* 1001 Jumbo SB. ⊙R44

Don't You Weep After Me

When I'm dead & buried, **don't you weep after me (3x)**
O I don't want you to weep after me

D - - A / - - - D / - D7 G D / - A7 D -

On the good ship Zion, **don't you...**
King Peter is my captain... Sailing on the ocean...
Jordan is my river... When I do cross over...
O look-a Mary... When I'm on my journey...
She's a-lookin' over Jordan...
Bright angels are the sailors...

aka: "When I'm on My Journey". On Chad Mitchell Trio Mighty Day on Campus. *In* Bright Morning Stars *&* V Favs of the V Young. ⊙R45

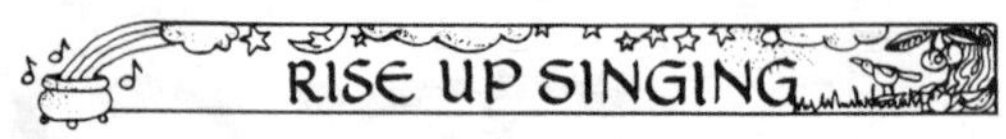

Every Time I Feel the Spirit

Ev'ry time I feel the spirit
Movin' in my heart I will pray (repeat)

(in C) F - C - / - AmG C - :||

Up on the mountain when my Lord spoke
Out of His mouth came fire & smoke
And all around me it looked so fine
I asked my Lord if all was mine

C - - - / - G C - :||

O I have sorrows & I have woe
And I have heartache here below
But while God leads me I'll never fear
For I am sheltered by His care

In Fenner Religious FS of the Negro *(1874)*, Pocketfull of S, Sing Together Children, S of the Spirit *&* 1004 FS. *On* The Essential *Paul Robeson (VSD 57/58)*. OR46

Ezekiel Saw the Wheel

Ezekiel saw the wheel, way up in the middle of the air
Ezekiel saw the wheel, way in the middle of the air
And the little wheel runs by faith & the big wheel runs by the grace of God
It's a wheel in a wheel, way in the middle of the air

D - - - / - - DA7 D :||

Some go to church for to sing & shout, **way in the middle...**
Before six months they are all turned out, **way...**

GD D DA7 D / /

Let me tell you, brother, what a hypocrite'll do...
He'll talk about me & he'll talk about you...

One of these days about 12 o'clock...
And this old world goin' to reel & rock...

On Bryan Bowers By Heart, *Sally Rogers & Claudia Schmidt* Closing the Distance *& Woody Guthrie* The Early Yrs. *In* SFest, Treas of FS, S That Changed the World, *Fenner* Religious FS of the Negro *(1874) &* S Am Sings. OR47

Free at Last

Free at last! Free at last!
I thank God almighty I'm free at last! (repeat)

D - - - / - - - G / D - - Bm / D - AD // D - - G / / as cho.

One of these mornings bright & fair
I thank God I'm free at last!
I'm gonna put on my wings & try the air
Thank God almighty I'm free at last

Old Satan's mad because we're glad...
He missed a crowd he thought he had...

On Kim & Reggie Harris Group M & the Underground Railroad. *In* 1004 FS, *Johnson* 2nd B of Negro Spirituals, *1926 &* FSEncyV2. OR48

Go Tell It On the Mountain

Go tell it on the mountain, over the hills & everywhere
Go tell it on the mountain that Jesus Christ was born

D - - - A - D GA / D - - DG D A D -

When I was a sinner, I prayed both night and day
I asked the Lord to help me & he showed me the way

D - - - A - D - / - - - - E - A A7

When I was a seeker, I sought both night and day
I asked my Lord to help me & he taught me to pray

The Lord made me a watchman upon the city wall
And if I am a Christian, I am the least of all

On Charlie Murphy Catch the Fire, *Christmas Revels* Wassail Wassail *(RC 1082) & Simon & Garfunkel* Wed. Morning 3AM. *In* SO! *2:6*, Weavers SB, Hootenanny SB, V Fav of the V Young, SFest, S for Pickin & Singin, Story of the Spirituals, *Fenner* Religious FS of the Negro *(1874)*, FSEncyV2. OR49

Good News

Good news, chariot's a-comin' (3x)
And I don't want it to leave me behind

G - / D G / - - / GD G

There's a long white robe in heaven, I know **(3x)**
And I don't want it to leave me behind

G - / - DG / G - / GD G

There's a better land in this world, I know...
There's a pair of wings in heaven, I know...
There's a starry crown in heaven, I know...
There's a golden harp in heaven, I know...

In FSEncy V2 *& Fenner* Religious FS of the Negro *(1874). Rec by Kingston Trio.* OR50

He's Got the Whole World

1. He's got the whole world **in his hands**
   He's got the big wide world **in...**
   He's got the whole world **in...**
   He's got the whole world in his hands

D - / A - / D - / A D

2. He's got you & me, brother... / sister / brother
   He's got the whole world in his hands
3. He's got the itty bitty baby...
4. He's got the sun & the moon / the wind & the rain / sun...
5. He's got everybody...

1st collected by Frank Warner fr Sue Thomas, in 1933. In Marion Kirby Collection of Negro Exultations *& Boatner* Spirituals Triumphant, *1927. On Raffi* Rise & Shine *(& in his* 2nd SB*), Tickle Tune Typhoon* All of Us Will Shine, *Odetta* The Essential *(Vanguard) &* At the Horn. *In* V Fav of the V Young, S of the Spirit, Eye Winker, Quaker SB, S Am Sings *&* Story of the Spirituals. OR51

He's My Rock, My Sword, My Shield

He's my rock, my sword, my shield – He's my wheel in the middle of the wheel
He's my lily of the valley, He's my bright & shining star
Makes no difference what you say, I'm gonna serve my Lord today
I'm gonna keep on serving Jesus *[the Spirit]* til I die

G - C G / - - A D / 1st / G GD G(C G)

— P.D. OR52

I Got Shoes

I got a shoe, you got a shoe
All God's children got shoes
When I get to heaven gonna put on my shoes
Gonna tromp all over God's heaven
Heaven (2x) / Everybody talkin' 'bout heaven ain't a-goin' there
Heaven (2x) / Gonna tromp all over God's heaven

G - - - / / G - C - / G C G -
D - G - / - - C - / G - D - / G D G -

I got a robe, **you got a** robe... **Gonna** shout...
I got a harp... **Gonna** play **all over God's heaven...**
I got wings... **Gonna** fly **all over...**
I got a song... **Gonna** sing **all over...**
I got a ski... Gonna shuss all over God's heaven...

aka: "Heaven, Heaven". *In* SFest, FS Abecedary, S That Changed the World *&* Sing Along w World's Fav FS. OR53

I Know the Lord

O I know the Lord, I know the Lord
I know the Lord's laid his hands on me (repeat)

D - / A D :||

Did ever you see the like before
I know the Lord's laid his hands on me
King Jesus preachin' to the poor?
I know the Lord's laid his hands on me

O wasn't that a happy day / **I know...**
When Jesus washed my sins away? / **I know...**

Some seek the Lord & don't seek him right...
They fool all day & trifle all night...

My Lord has done just what He said...
He's healed the sick & raised the dead...

In The 2nd B of Negro Spirituals, *Story of the Spirituals, A Time for Singing.* ⊙R54

I'm Gonna Do What the Spirit Says

I'm gonna do **what the Spirit says** do **(2x)**
And what the Spirit says do **I'm gonna** do**, Lord, Lord**
I'm gonna do **what the spirit says** do

Am - / - E / Am Dm / AmDm Am

I'm gonna move **when the Spirit says** move**...**
(**Substitute:** pray, fight, sing, dance)
I'm goin' to jail **when the Spirit says** jail...

aka: "Gonna Do" On Raffi More Singable S, *in his* Singable SB *as "You Gotta Sing." On* Peace Gather S *(NSL). In* SFF & ESF. ⊙R55

Jacob's Ladder

1. We are climbing Jacob's ladder **(3x)**
   Soldiers of the cross
   [Brothers, sisters, all! or *Children of the Lord!]*

C - - - / G - F C / - - F C / - G C -

2. Every round goes higher, higher
3. Sinners, do you love your Jesus?
4. If you love him, why not serve him?
5. Rise, shine, give God glory!
6. We are climbing higher, higher

New cho is by Pete Seeger. See also "Sara's Circle" in WOMEN & "We Are Building A Strong Union" in WORK. In Allen (et al) Slave S of the U.S. *(1867),* SO! *11:1* & Reprints *#7,* WHATFG, Pilgrim Hymnal, Friends Hymnal, S for Pickin & Singing, FS Abecedary, FSEncy V2, *Lomax* FS of NA, & SFest. *On Bernice Reagon* River of Life *(FF),* HARP & The Essential *Paul Robeson (VSD 57/58).* ⊙R56

Joshua (The Battle of Jericho)

Joshua fought the battle of Jericho
Jericho, Jericho
Joshua fought the battle of Jericho
And the walls came tumbling down

Dm - / A7 Dm :||

You may talk about the men of Gideon
You may brag about the men of Saul
But there's none like good old Joshua
At the battle of Jericho

Dm A7 / / Dm - / A7 Dm

Up to the walls of Jericho
They marched with spears in hand
Come blow them ram horns Joshua said
'Cause the battle is in our hands

Then the lamb ram sheep horns began to blow
The trumpets began to sound
Joshua commanded the children to shout
And the walls came tumbling down

Well I've heard God's voice on the mountaintop
In the desert & by the sea
Crying "Rise up against those city walls
And you too shall be free!"

— New verse by Peter Blood

© 1988 Sing Out Corp. All rights reserved. aka: "Battle of Jericho." On Odetta The Essential *(Vanguard),* Sings Bals & Blues & At Carnegie Hall, *Pete Seeger* Sampler *(FA2043),* The Essential *Paul Robeson (VSD (57/58) & Weavers* Sbag. *In* Am Fav Bals, People's SB, FS Abecedary, *Johnson* B of Negro Spirituals, *1924,* Treas of FS, S That Changed the World & FSEncyV2. ⊙R57

Let Us Break Bread

Let us break bread together on our knees **(2x)**
When I fall on my knees with my face to the rising sun
O Lord have mercy on me

CAm FG CF C / Em FD GD G

C C7 F Fm / CAm FG CF C

Let us drink wine...
Let us praise God...

As sung by Laura Duncan. aka: "Break Bread." In SO! *1:7* & Reprints *#1,* Pilgrim Hymnal, A Time for Singing & FSEncyV2. *On Baez* Recently. ⊙R58

Lord, I Want to Be a Christian

Lord, I want to be a Christian **in-a my heart, in-a my heart**
Lord, I want to be a Christian**, in-a my heart**
In-a my heart (in-a my...), **in-a my heart** (in...)
Lord I want to be a Christian **in-a my heart**

C - FC C / / CF F FC CAm / 1st /

Addl verses: more loving, more faithful, more holy, like Jesus

In Pilgrim Hymnal & Friends Hymnal. ⊙R59

Mary Had a Baby

1. Mary had a baby, **O Lord**
   Mary had a baby, **O my Lord!**
   Mary had a baby, **O Lord**
   The people keep a-coming & the train done gone

E - A E / - - A B7 / 1st / E - B7 E

2. What did she name him? 8. Star shined above him
3. She called him Jesus 9. Shepherds knelt before him
4. Where was he born? 10. Wise men bro't him presents
5. Born in a stable 11. Herod tried to find him
6. Where did they lay him? 12. So they fled away to Egypt
7. Laid him in a manger 13. Angel flew above them

In SO! *4:1* & Reprints *#3* & FSEncyV1. *On Mike & Peggy Seeger (& in Ruth Seeger)* Am FS for Children *(Rounder)* & *Pete Seeger* Trad Christmas Carols *(FAS32311).* ⊙R60

My Lord, What a Morning

My Lord what a mornin' (3x)
When the stars begin to fall

D - - - / - - A - / D - Bm G / D A D -

1. You'll hear the trumpet sound
   To wake the nations underground
   Lookin' to my God's right hand
   When the stars begin to fall

/ " / GD GD A - / D A Bm G / " /

2. You'll hear the sinner mourn / **To wake...**
3. You'll hear the Christians shout...

On Sandy Paton Frank Proffitt Memorial Album. *In* The B of Am Negro Spirituals, *Lomax* FS of NA, Friends Hymnal, *Fenner* Religious FS of the Negro *(1874),* S That Changed the World & FiresB of FS. *Rec by Kingston Trio & the Seekers.* ⊙R61

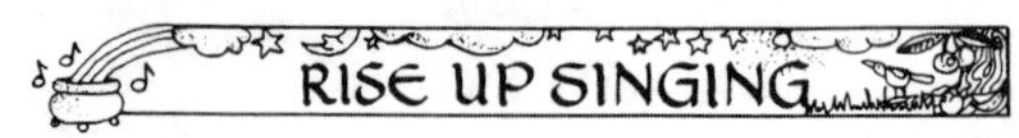

Nobody Knows the Trouble I've Seen

Nobody knows the trouble I've seen
Nobody knows but Jesus *[my sorrow]*
Nobody knows the trouble I've seen
Glory hallelujah!

D - - - / - - A - / D - - Bm / D A D -

Sometimes I'm up, sometimes I'm down / **O yes Lord!**
Sometimes I'm almost to the ground / **O yes Lord!**

D - - - / - - A - / D - - Bm / D A D -

Altho' you see me goin' 'long so / **O yes...**
I have my trials here below...

One day when I was walkin' 'long...
The element opened & Love came down...

What makes old Satan hate me so? ...
'Cause he got me once & let me go...

I never shall forget that day...
When Jesus wiped my sins away...

On Burl Ives S of North & South, *The Dillards* Wheat Straw Suite *& rec by Paul Robeson & by Marion Anderson. In* S That Changed the World, 120 Am S, Best Loved S of Am People, FSEncyV2, S Am Sings, Story of the Spirituals *&* FiresB of FS *& Allen et al* Slave S of the US *(1867)*. OR62

O, What a Beautiful City

O what a beautiful city (3x)
Twelve gates to the city, hallelujah!

D - - - / A - D A / 1st / D G D A D G D -

Three gates in the east, three gates in the west
There's three gates in the north & three gates in the south
There's twelve gates to the city, hallelujah!

D - - - / / D G D A D G D -

Who are those children there dressed in red? / **There's...**
Must be the children that Moses led / **There's...**

D - - - / D G D A D G D - :||

Who are those children there dressed in black?
Must be the hypocrites turning back

When I get to heaven gonna sing & shout
Ain't nobody there gonna keep *[kick]* me out

— new words & adaptation of words & music by Marion Hicks

aka: "Twelve Gates." *© 1958 (renewed) by Stormking Music Inc. All rights reserved. Used by permission. Marion Hicks was a cook in Brooklyn who taught this trad. song to the Seeger family. Earliest recording by Sonny Terry. In* SO! 8:1 & Reprints #2, Weavers SB & Joan Baez SB, FSEncyV2 *&* FiresB of Fun & Games. *On Pete Seeger* I Can See a New Day, Trad Xmas Carols *(FAS32311)*, World of *& in his* Am Fav Bals. *On Judy Collins* Golden Apples, *Dave Van Ronk* Sings Ballads & Blues, Black Mtn Blues *&* Gamblin Blues, *Tim O'Brien* Hard Year Blues *& Happy Traum* Bright Morning Stars. OR63

Old Time Religion

Give me that old time religion (3x)
And that's good enough for me

G - / D7 G / - C / GD7 G

It was good for the Hebrew children **(3x) & that's...**
It was good for Paul & Silas **(3x)**...

New humorous verses to this song can be found in FUNNY SONGS on p. 74. On Simon & Gavin By Babel's Stream *(Trad)*, *Ralph Stanley* I'll Wear a White Robe *(Rebel)*, *JJMainer* V18 *& W Guthrie* The Early Yrs. *In* S That Changed the World, Treas of Hymns, Hymns of Glor Praise *&* Sing Along w World's Fav FS. OR64

Over My Head

Over my head, there's trouble in the air (3x)
There must be a God somewhere

D DA D - / A - D - / - DF# Bm - / Em A D -

Substitute: weepin', singin', prayin', joy, freedom **etc.**

(last v.) Over my head there's victory in the air! **(3x)**
I know there's a God somewhere

In Sing For Freedom *&* Everybody Sing Freedom. OR65

Up Over My Head

Up over my head (echo) **I see freedom in the air** (echo) **(3x)**
And I really do believe, I said I really do believe there's a God somewhere

DG D (2x) / A - DG D / D D7 G Gm / DBm EA DG D

Up over my head, I hear praying in the air (3x)
And I really do believe...
(other v.) I hear music, I feel Jesus, etc.

— adapted by Betty Mae Fikes from a traditional spiritual

© 1968, 1989 Betty Mae Fikes. Used by permission. Introduced at the Sing For Freedom Conference in Atlanta, GA 1964. In Sing For Freedom *&* SO! *34:4 & on* I'm Gonna Let It Shine *(Round River Records)*. OR66

Pretty Little Baby

1. Virgin Mary had a little baby
   O, glory hallelujah
   O, pretty little baby
   Glory be to the newborn King!

Em - B7 Em / - C - D / G C D Em / G - B7 Em

2. Mary what you gonna name that pretty little baby?
3. Some call him one thing, think I'll name him Jesus
4. Some call him one thing, think I'll name him 'Manuel

aka: "Virgin Mary," "Mary What You Gonna Name..." In SO! *8:3 &* Reprints #2, FSEncy V2, Hootenanny SB, Joan Baez SB & Story of the Spirituals. *On* Carolyn Hester, Great FS of the '60s, *Peggy Seeger* Best of *& Guy Carawan* S with. OR67

Rise Up, Shepherd

There's a star in the East on Christmas morn
Rise up shepherd & follow
It will lead to the place where the Saviour's born
Rise up shepherd & follow

G - D - / - C D - / G - D Bm / D A G D

Leave your sheep & leave your lambs / Rise up...
Leave your ewes & leave your rams / Rise up...
Follow, follow / Rise up shepherd & follow
Follow the star of Bethlehem / Rise up...

D - G D / D C D - / D - G D / D A G D
D - - - / " / D - G Bm / " /

If you take good heed to the angel's words / **Rise...**
You'll forget your flocks you'll forget your herds...

In SO! *1:7 &* Reprints #1, Hootenanny SB, *Lomax* FS of NAm, S of the Spirit, FiresB of FS, FSEncy V1, FS N Am Sings *& Fenner* Religious FS of the Negro. *On Pete Seeger* Trad Xmas Carols *(FAS 32311) & Nancy Raven* S for the Holiday. OR68

Rock-a My Soul

Rock-a my soul in the bosom of Abraham (3x)
O rock-a my soul!

D - - - / A7 - - - / D - - - / A7 - D -

When I went down in the valley to pray / **O rock...**
My soul got happy & I stayed all day / **O...**

Am D Am D / Bm - F#m -
Asus7 A7 **(2x)** / Asus7 A7 D -

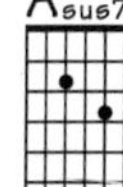

When I was a mourner just like you...
I mourned & mourned til I come thru...

(bridge: chords as chorus)
So high, can't get over it / So low, can't get under it
So wide, can't get 'round it / **O...**

"So high..." was orig part of another song. aka: "Oh, a-Rock-a My Soul." On Peter Paul & Mary In Conc *& Doyle Lawson & Quicksilver* Rock My Soul *(Sugar Hill SH-3717). In Allen et al* Slave S of the US *(1867)*, Legal FakeB, & S Am Sings. *Tune to verse is in* Fireside B of FS. OR69

Seek and You Shall Find

Seek & you shall find
Knock & the door will be opened
Ask & you shall be answered
When the love come tumblin' down

C - - - / F - - F (or C) / C - Am - / C G C -

O you look in the Bible & what do you see?
When the love come tumblin' down
That you shall know the truth & it will make you free
When the love come tumblin' down

F C F C / - G C - / F C F C / - G C -

You've got to love your neighbor, like the Lord has done
You've got to walk three miles if he asks for one

If you want to go to heaven where the Saints all go
You've got to try to make a heaven while you're here below

— Trad. adap & arr by Pete Seeger.
— New verses by Sam Hinton

Used by permission. Sam learned the chorus & part of 1st stanza in Crockett, Texas, around 1931. In SO! *32:4 &* Religious FS of the Negro. *On Pete Seeger* Where Have All the Flowers Gone *and in* Where Have All the Flowers Gone. OR70

Sinner Man

O sinner man, where you gonna run to? (3x)
All on that day!

Dm - / C - / Dm - / DmC Dm

Run to the rock, the rock was a-melting...
Run to the sea, the sea was a-boiling...
Run to the moon, the moon was a-bleeding...
Run to the Lord, Lord won't You hide me...
O sinner man, you oughta been a-praying...

In SO! *8:1,* Hootenanny SB, FSEncyV2, FS Abecedary, Eng FS of SAPP *&* S for Pickin & Singin. *In* Weavers SB *& on their* Reunion at Carnegie Hall, pt 2, Trav on *& Guy Carawan* S with *(FG3544).* OR71

Standing in the Need of Prayer

It's a-me (3x), o Lord
Standin' in the need of prayer (repeat)

D - - - / - A D - / - - - Bm / D A D -

1. Not my brother nor my sister **but it's me, o Lord**
Standin' in the need of prayer (repeat)
2. Not my preacher nor my teacher **but it's me...**
3. Not my mother nor my father
4. Not my neighbor nor a stranger

On Country Gentlemen Sing & Play *(FA2410). In* SFest, FSEncyV2, S of the Spirit *&* S Along w Worlds Fav FS. OR72

Steal Away

Steal away, steal away / Steal away to Jesus!
Steal away, steal away home / I ain't got long to stay here

D - - - / - - A D / - - G Â / D - A D

1. My Lord, He calls me / He calls me by the thunder
The trumpet sounds within-a my soul / I ain't...here

G - D - / - - - - / - - G A / D - A D

2. Green trees are bending / Poor sinner stands a-trembling
3. My Lord calls me / He calls me by the lightning

On Kim & Reggie Harris Group Music & the Undergd RR. *In* SFest, FiresB of FS, FS Abecedary, Joyful Singing, Friends Hymnal, S for Pickin & Singin, Story of the Spirs, *Fenner* Religious FS of the Negro *&* S That Changed the World. OR73

Swing Low, Sweet Chariot

Swing low, sweet chariot
Comin' for to carry me home (repeat)

D - G D / - - A - / D D7 G D / - A D -

I looked over Jordan & what did I see
Comin' for to carry me home
A band of angels comin' after me / **Comin'...**

I'm sometimes up & sometimes down
But still I know I'm heavenly *[freedom]* bound

If you get there before I do
Tell all my friends that I'm comin' too

If I get there before you do
I'll cut a hole & pull you thru

On (& in) Pete Seeger Am Fav Bals V3 *(FA2322) & Baez* Fr Every Stage. *On Raffi* Corner Groc Store *& in his* Singable SB. *On Stanley Brothers* Vol 4 *(County 754). In* SO! *20:3,* S of the Spirit, FS Abecedary, SFest, FiresB of FS, *Fenner* Relig S of the Negro *&* Story of the Spirs. OR74

Walk in Jerusalam

I want to be ready (3x)
To walk in Jerusalem just like John

(TD ↑ 2) C - - - / F - C - / C - F C / - - G C

John said the city was just four square
Walk in Jerusalem just like John
And he declared he'd meet me there / **Walk...**

C - F - / C - G C :||

O John, o John, what do you say?
That I'll be there in the coming day

When Peter was preaching at Pentecost
He was endowed with the Holy Ghost

In SO! *2:10 &* Reprints #4, Hootenanny SB, Joyful Singing *&* FSEncyV2. *On The Dillards* Mtn Rock, *Doc Watson* Old Timey Conc *(Vang), Bryan Bowers* The View fr Home *& Hot Mudd Fam* Til We Meet Again. OR75

Were You There?

Were you there when they crucified my Lord? **(2x)**
O sometimes it causes me to / Tremble, tremble, tremble
Were you there when they crucified my Lord?

C FG CF C / Em FC GD G
C - - C7 / F - G - / C FG CF C

Were you there when they nailed him to the tree?...
Were you there when they pierced him in the side?...
Were you there when the sun refused to shine?...
Were you there when they laid him in the tomb?...

On Burl Ives S of North & South. *In* Friends Hymnal, S of Worship *(M Talbot), Fenner* Relig FS of the Negro *&* Golden Ency of FS. OR76

When the Saints Go Marching In

(intro) *We are trav'ling in the footsteps*
Of those who've gone before
But we'll all be reunited [But if we stand & fight united]
On a new & sunlit shore [Then a new world is in store]

D G / D A / D G / DA D

O when the Saints go marching in **(2x)**
O Lord I want to be in that number
When the Saints go marching in

D -/- A7 / D G / DA D

And when the sun refuse *[begins]* to shine...
When the moon turns red with blood...
On that hallelujah day...
O when the trumpet sounds the *[a]* call...

(bridge: as intro) *Some say this world of trouble*
Is the only one we need
But I'm waiting for that morning
When the new world is revealed
O when the new world is revealed...

When the revelation *[revolution]* comes...
When the rich go out & work...
When the air is pure & clean...
When we all have food to eat...
When our leaders learn to cry... **(make up your own)**

Intro & bridge by The Weavers © 1951 & renewed 1979 Folkways Music Publishers, Inc., NY, NY. All rights reserved. Used by permission. New v. at end by Peter Blood © 1976 Sing Out Corp. All rights reserved. In SO! 2:6, SFest, S for Pickin & Singin & S That Changed the World. *On Ralph Stanley* Live at McClure VA *(Rebel). In* Weavers SB *& on their* At Carnegie Hall, Reunion 1963 *&* Gr H. OR77

The Woman at the Well

Jesus met the woman at the well **(3x)**
And He told her ev'rything she'd ever done

G - - - / C - G - / - - B7 Em / A7 D7 GC G

He said "Woman, woman, where is your husband? **(3x)**
I know ev'rything you've ever done"

She said "Jesus, Jesus, I ain't got no husband **(3x)**
And you don't know ev'rything I've ever done"

He said "Woman woman you've got five husbands **(3x)**
And the one you have now he's not your own"

She said "This man, this man, he must be prophet! **(3x)**
He done told me ev'rything I've ever done"

Based on John 4. On Dave Van Ronk Sunday Strut *(Philo) & Dave, Ian & Sylvia* 4 Strong Winds. *On Peter Paul & Mary* In Conc *& in their* SB. OR78

Many of these spirituals can be found in 2 excellent collections: Songs of Zion, 1981, Abingdon Press, Nashville, TN, & Lead Me, Guide Me, 1987, GIA Publications, Chicago, IL.

A great many of the songs in the FREEDOM section as well as union songs in WORK were originally derived from Black Spirituals. Black Spirituals elsewhere in the book include: "Preacher Went Down" (FUN) "Motherless Child" (HARD) "Come & Go with Me" (HOPE) "Angels Watchin' Over Me", "All My Trials" (LULL) "Study War No More" (PEACE) "Rise & Shine," "Who Built the Ark?" (PLAY). For "White Spirituals" see "Bringing in the Sheaves," "I Will Arise," "Lonesome Valley" (FAITH) & "Wayfaring Stranger" (HARD).

Asikatali

Asikatali, nomas'ya bozh, sizimiseli nkululeko **(2x)**
Unzima lomtwalo, ufuna madoda (2x)

(in 3/4) D A DDA D / // / /

Tina bantwan laseh Afrik', sizimisela nkululeko **(2x)**
Unzima lomtwalo...

We do not care if we go to prison, we'll keep on until our freedom's won **(2x)**
A heavy load, a heavy load! & it will take some strong souls (2x)

We are the children of Africa, we'll keep on until our freedom's won **(2x)**

— w: anon. (African National Congress)
— m: trad. (Zulu)

Written on picket lines in So Africa. Brought to the US in 1959 by Mary Louise Hooper. Popularized by Chipo Watakama. Rec by The Spinners (in UK), Bev Grant & the Human Condition & on This Land Is Mine: African Freedom S *(FW5588). In* SO! 26:3, S for Peace *(Oak, 1966),* Broadside Mag & Children's S for a Friendly Planet. OJ30

Bella Ciao

We are women **& we are** marching
Bella ciao (3x), ciao, ciao!
We are marching **for liberation,**
We want a revolution now!

Em -/ / Am Em / B7 Em

We are angry & we are fighting / **Bella...**
We are fighting for liberation / **We want a...**

Other verses:
We are workers/building, artists/weaving, poets/singing mothers/caring, children/growing, fathers/crying, soldiers/dying
lovers/dreaming, sisters/we're all together, people/marching

— these v: anon. (US) **— m: trad. (Italian folksong)**

This song was orig about women workers in the rice fields of Northern Italy. It has evolved thru many versions in different languages as partisan songs, liberation songs, etc. In SO! 20:3 *& on* NSLT. *2 of the earlier versions in Italian were part of a Italian stage production entitled "Bella Ciao" & an album is available for this show.* OJ31

Dona Dona

On a wagon bound for market
Lies a calf with a mournful eye
High above him, there's a swallow
Flying freely thru the sky

Am E Am E / Am Dm Am E
/ " / Am Dm AmE Am

How the winds are laughing
They laugh with all their might
Laugh & laugh the whole day thru
And half the summer's night (dona dona)
Dona dona dona dona, dona dona dona doe (2x)

G - C - / /G - C Am / E - Am -
E - Am - G - C E / - - Am - Dm E Am -

"Stop complaining!" says the farmer
"Who told you a calf to be?
Why don't you have wings to fly with
Like that swallow, proud & free?"

Calves are easily bound & slaughtered
Never knowing the reason why
But whoever treasures freedom
Like the swallow will learn to fly

Oyfin furl ligt a kelbl
Ligt gebundn mit a shtrik
Hoykh in himl flit a shvelbl
Freyt zikh dreyt zikh hin un tzurik

Lakht der vint in korn, lakht un lakht un lakht
Lakht er op a tog a gantzn, un a halbe nakht
Hey, dona, dona, dona... dona da

Shrayt dos kelbl, zogt der poyer
Verzhe heyst dikh zayn a kalb?
Volst gekent dokh zayn a foygl
Volst gekent dokh zayn a shvalb

Bidne kelber tut men bindn
Un men shlept zey un men shekht
Ver s'hot fligl, flit aroyftzu
Iz bay keynem nit kayn k'nekht

— **Yiddish: Aaron Zeitlin Eng: Arthur Kevess & Teddi Schwartz**
— **m: Sholem Secunda**

© 1940, 1956 by Mills Music Inc. Copyright renewed. All rights reserved. Used by permission of CPP Belwin Inc. *— Orig written in Yiddish for the show* Esterke *in 1940. The song was banned in South Korea at one point as "leftist" & "violence-producing". In Kevess & Schwartz* Tumbalalaika. *On* Joan Baez *(Vang) & in her* SB, *Donovan* Best of & Pye History of Pop *& on* Hava Nagila Festival-El Al *(Tara).* OJ32

Elizabeth Gurley Flynn

Elizabeth was a woman who couldn't be kept down
She was an organizer who roamed from town to town
Fighting with her sisters out on the picket lines
Building us a future, Elizabeth seized the time

D - G D / - - E7 A / D - G D / - - A D

Like Elizabeth Gurley Flynn, who never did give in –
Gonna
Build the revolution & you know we're gonna win (repeat)

G - D - / A - D - :||

Elizabeth was a woman, the bravest in her day
She fought for socialism & she would always say:
"We've got to get together, so we can all be free
We'll change the lives of women & win our liberty"

We've got to heed her message, for what she says is true
We'll join hands with our sisters in what we have to do
With working folk & young folk, red, white, black, yellow, brown
We'll build a people's movement & tear the system down!

— **Marge Cooper**

© 1971 by Margery Himel. All rights reserved. *In* All Our Lives. OJ33

Freiheit

Die Heimat ist weit / Doch wir sind bereit
Wir kämpfen und siegen für dich / Freiheit!

DG D / A D / G D / A D

Spanish heavens spread their brilliant starlight
High above our trenches in the plain
From the distance morning comes to greet us
Calling us to battle once again

DA D / / A D / AE A

We'll not yield a foot to Franco's fascists
Even tho' the bullets fall like sleet
With us stand those peerless men, our comrades
And for us there can be no defeat!

— **w: Karl Ernst** — **m: Paul Dessai**

© 1943 Edward B. Marks Co. Copyright renewed. All rights reserved. Used by permission. *On* 6 S for Democracy, S of the Spanish Civil War, V1 *(Folkways), & Pete Seeger* Sing Out w... & Wimoweh. *In* People's SB & FiresB of FS, S That Changed the World & FSEncyV1. OJ34

Sie fliehen vorbei, wie nächtliche Schatten
Kein Mensch kann sie wissen, kein Jäger erschiessen
Es bleibet dabei: **Die Gedanken sind frei (2x)**

(capo up, in 3/4) G - DG/ /D G D G/C G D G/ /

Ich denke was ich will und was mich beglücket
Doch alles in der Still, und wie es sich schicket
Mein Wünsch und Begehren kann niemand verwehren
Es bleibet dabei **Die...**

Und sperrt man mich ein im finsteren Kerker
Das alles sind rein vergebliche Werke
Denn meine Gedanken zerreissen die Schranken
Und Mauern entzwei...

Die Gedanken sind frei, my thoughts freely flower
Die Gedanken sind frei, my thoughts give me power
No scholar can map them, no hunter can trap them
No one can deny, die Gedanken sind frei **(2x)**

I think as I please & this gives me pleasure
My conscience decrees this right I must treasure
My thoughts will not cater to duke or dictator / No one...

And should tyrants take me & throw me in prison
My thoughts will burst free like blossoms in season
Foundations will crumble & structures will tumble
And free folk will cry "Die Gedanken sind frei!"

— **Eng words by Arthur Kevess**

© 1950 (renewed) by Appleseed Music Inc. All rights reserved. Used by permission. *In* SO! *1:6 &* Reprints #8, Hootenanny SB, Bells of Rhymney, S of Work & Protest, Quaker SB, S That Changed the World, A Time for Singing *&* S of the Spirit. *On Seeger* Dangerous S. OJ35

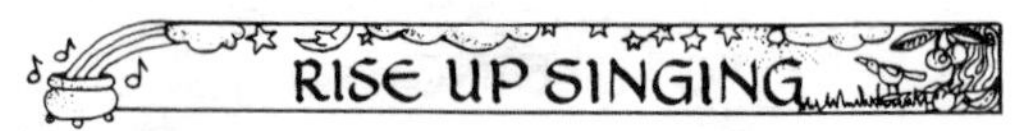

Hay Una Mujer

Michelle Peña Herrera, Nalvia Rosa Meña Alvarado
Cecilia Castro Salvadores, Ida Amelia Almarza

Am - - - - - - E / Am E Am E - Dm E Am

Hay una mujer desaparecida (2x) / En Chile (3x)
And the junta, and the junta knows
And the junta knows where she is
And the junta knows where they are hiding her, she's dying
Hay una mujer desaparecida (2x) / En Chile (3x)

Am - F E (2x)/Dm - E - Am/E- -Am/E- -/- - - Am/1st2

Clara Elena Cantero, Elisa del Carmen Escobar
Eliana Maria Espinosa, Rosa Elena Morales

— Holly Near

© 1978 Hereford Music (ASCAP). Used by permission. On her Imagine My Surprise *&* Lifeline *(w Ronnie Gilbert) & on Weavers* Together Again. *In* SO! *29:3,* New Folk Fav & Here's to the Women. OJ36

If I Had a Hammer

1. **If I had a** hammer, **I'd** hammer **in the morning**
I'd hammer **in the evening, all over this land**
I'd hammer **out danger, I'd** hammer **out a warning**
I'd hammer **out love between my brothers & my sisters all over this land**

C Em F G (2x) / C - D - G - - -
C - F G Am - F G / F C F C F C G - C - - -

2. If I had a bell, I'd ring it in the morning...
3. If I had a song, I'd sing it in the morning...
4. Well I got a hammer & I got a bell
And I got a song to sing all over this land
It's the hammer of justice, it's the bell of freedom
It's a song about **love between...**

— Lee Hays & Pete Seeger

© TRO 1958 (renewed 1986) & 1962 Ludlow Music, Inc., New York, N.Y. International copyright secured. Made in USA. All rights reserved incl. public performance for profit. Used by permission. aka: "The Hammer Song." On Weavers Travelin On, Gr H & Reunion 1963. *On Pete Seeger* World of, Love S fr Friends & Foes, Sing Out with Pete, Wimoweh, Prec Friend *(w Arlo Guthrie) &* S of Pete Seeger *V.1 & V.2. On* Peter Paul & Mary, *their* Best of *&* 10 Yrs *& Odetta* At Carnegie Hall. *In* Am Fav Bal, Carry It On, Children's S for a Friendly Planet, FM Gr H *&* WHATFG. OJ37

It Could Have Been Me

Students in Ohio & down at Jackson State
Shot down by a vicious fire one early day in May
Some people cried out angry "You should have shot more of them down"
But you can't bury youth my friend, youth grows the whole world round

(in C) F C F C / F C F G / C Am F Am / F - - C

It could have been me but instead it was you
So I'll keep doing the work you were doing as if I were two
I'll be a student of life, a singer of songs,
a farmer of food & a righter of wrongs
It could have been me but instead it was you
And it may be me dear sisters & brothers before we are thru
But if you can die* for freedom – freedom (3x)
If you can die for freedom, I can too
*(**other v. substitute:** sing, live, fight)

F - C - / F - G - / F - Em -
/ " / " / C Am - D / F - C -

The junta took the fingers from Victor Jara's hands
They said to the gentle poet "Play your guitar now if you can"
Well, Victor started singing til they shot his body down
You can kill a man but not a song when it's sung the whole world 'round

A woman in the jungle so many wars away
Studies late into the night, defends a village in the day
Altho' her life & struggle are miles away from me
She sings a song & I know the words & I'll sing them til she's free

One night in Oklahoma, Karen Silkwood died
Because she had some secrets big companies wanted to hide
Well they talk of nuclear safety, they talk of national pride
But we all know it's a death machine & that's why Karen died

Our sisters are in struggle, from Vietnam to Wounded Knee
From Mozambique to Puerto Rico & they look to you & me
To fight against the system that kills them off & takes their land
It's our fight too if we're gonna win, we've got to do it hand in hand

(last cho) It's gonna be me & it's gonna be you
So we'll keep doing the work we've been doing until we are thru
We'll be students of life, singers of song, farmers of food & fighters so strong
It's gonna be me & it's gonna be you
But it will be us dear sisters & brothers before we are thru
'Cause if you can fight for freedom, freedom **(3x)**
If you can fight for freedom, we can too!

— Holly Near

© 1974 Hereford Music (ASCAP). New verses 1983. Used by permission. On her Live, Holly Near *& in her* Words & Music. OJ38

Kevin Barry

Early on a Sunday morning, high up on a gallows tree
Kevin Barry gave his young life, for the cause of liberty
Only a lad of 18 summers, yet there's no one can deny
That he went to death that morning, nobly held his head up high

G - - D / - - - G :||

"Shoot me like an Irish soldier, do not hang me like a dog
For I fought for Ireland's freedom on that dark September morn
All around that little bakery where we fought them hand to hand
Shoot me like an Irish soldier, for I fought to free Ireland"

Just before he faced the hangman in his lonely prison cell
British soldiers tortured Barry, just because he would not tell
All the names of his companions, other things they wished to know
"Turn informer & we'll free you" – proudly Barry answered "No!"

Another martyr for old Ireland, another murder for the crown
Well they can kill the Irish, but they can't keep their spirits down!

— trad. (Irish)

In S of Work & Protest, People's SB, FS of Eng, Ire, Scot & Wales *& Clancey Bros* SB *& their* Rising of the Moon. *Tune "Rolling Home" (see SEA).* OJ39

Look to the People

We're gonna look to the people for courage
In the hard times comin' ahead
We're gonna sing & shout, we're gonna work it out
In the hard times comin' ahead
With people's courage **(3x)** / We can make it

C - F C / - - G - / C - F C / - G C -
C G F C - - - / / / G - - - C - - -

Addl verses: loving, laughing, power, music, chutzpah

— Ruth Pelham

© 1982 Ruth Pelham (ASCAP), PO Box 6024 Albany NY 12206. Used by permission. aka: People's Courage. On her Look to the People *(FF) &* Under One Sky *(GW), Guy Carawan* The Land Knows You're There *(FF),* Swords into Plowshares alb & Peace Gathering S *(NSL).* OJ40

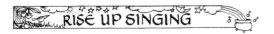

Love's Gonna Carry Us

It's been a long hard time, it's gonna be a long steep climb
But no one's gonna change our minds, 'bout what we gotta do
And when the road gets rough, everybody's saying "Just give it up"
All of our friends' sweet love, gonna carry us thru

DG D G - / DG D A - / 1st / DG DA D -

We don't have the money, but we got the will
We got voices talking the truth that can never be stilled
But they're gonna threaten, you know they have killed to get their way
But this movement we are building will not go away

G - D - / - Bm A - / G - GF#m Em / D A G -

Beware of the heroes, beware of the stars
'Cause a victory is hollow, if it ain't really ours
We're talking 'bout changes, not just changing the faces at the top
They say that freedom is a constant struggle & you can't ever stop

Now we're gonna argue, we don't always agree
But we can't let anger blind us to all we can be
'Cause we need the laughter & we need the tears to wash us clean
We need sisters & brothers beside us to follow the dream

— Fred Small

© 1981 Pine Barrens Music (BMI). Used by permission. On his Love's Gonna... *In his* Breaking fr the Line. *Also on Guy Carawan* The Land Knows You're There *(FF391) & Laura Burns & Roger Losen's* Light This Night. OJ41

MacPherson's Farewell

Fareweel ye dungeons dark & strong
Fareweel, fareweel to thee
MacPherson's time will no' be long
On yonder gallows tree

(in D) D Bm Em A/D - G A / 1st /D G A -

Sae rantin'ly, sae wantonly
Sae dauntin'ly, gaed he
He played a tune & he danced it 'roon
Beneath the gallows tree

D - A - / D - G - / 1st / Bm G A -

It was by a woman's treacherous hand
That I was condemned to dee
Below a ledge at a window she stood
And a blanket threw o'er me

The reprieve was comin' o'er the Bridge o'Banff
Tae set MacPherson free
But they pit the clock a quarter afore
And they hanged him tae the tree

The Laird o' Grant, that Highland sant
That first laid hands on me
He played the cause on Peter Broon
To let MacPherson dee

— trad. (Scottish)

MacPherson was sent to the gallows on 11/16/1700 & asked to play his fiddle one last time. He offered his fiddle to any member of the clan who would play this tune at his wake. When no one offered, he smashed his fiddle over the executioner's head & flung himself fr the ladder, ending his life. For a similar situation with a happier ending, see "Hang on the Bell, Nellie" in HARD TIMES. In SO! 10:3 & Reprints #5, Hootenanny SB, FSEncy V1 *& Bikel* FS & Footnotes. *On Raphael Boguslav* S from a Village Garret *(RLP12-638). On Clancy Bros* The Boys Won't Leave the Girls Alone, Gr H *& in their* Irish SB. OJ42

Never Turning Back

[We're] Gonna keep on walking forward
Keep on walking forward **(2x)**
Never turning back (2x)

C - / - G / C F / / CG C

Gonna keep on walking proudly **(3x) / Never...**
Gonna keep on singing loudly...
Gonna light this night together...

Gonna reach across our borders... **(Charlie King)**
Gonna keep on loving boldly... **(Judy Small)**
Gonna work for change together...
Gonna raise this house with strong hands... **(L.Burns/R.Rosen)**
Gonna show our children courage...
Gonna weave our lives with shining thread...

— Pat Humphries

© 1985 Hereford Music. Used by permission. In SO! *32:1. On Laura Burns & Roger Rosen* Light This Night *(FF) & Judy Small* One Voice in the Crowd *(Redwood).* OJ43

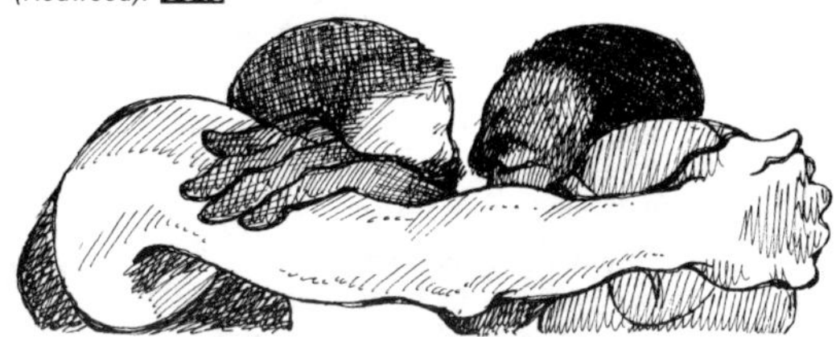

Once to Every Man and Nation

Once to every man *[soul]* & nation
Comes the moment to decide
In the strife of truth with falsehood
For the good or evil side
Some great cause, God's new Messiah
Offering each the bloom or blight
And the choice goes by forever
'Twixt that darkness & that light

Em B7Em B7 Em / GD GEm AmB7 Em :||
G D Em B7 / Em Am EmAm B7 / 1st 2

Then to side with truth is noble
When we share her wretched crust
'Ere her cause bring fame & profit
And 'tis prosperous to be just
Then it is the brave man chooses
While the coward stands aside
Til the multitude make virtue
Of the faith they had denied

By the light of burning martyrs
Jesus' bleeding feet we track
Toiling up new Calvaries ever
With the cross that turns not back
New occasions teach new duties
Time makes ancient good uncouth
They must upward still & onward
Who would keep abreast of truth

Tho' the cause of evil prosper
Yet 'tis truth alone is strong
Tho' her portion be the scaffold
And upon the throne be wrong
Yet that scaffold sways the future
And behind the dim unknown
Standeth God within the shadow
Keeping watch above His own

— w: James Russell Lowell, 1844 **— m: Welsh hymn**

In many hymnals. Lowell was a major abolitionist leader. OJ44

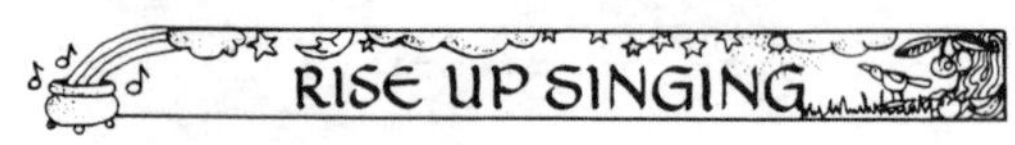

The Patriot Game

Come all you young rebels & list while I sing
For love of one's land is a terrible thing
It banishes fear with the speed of a flame
And makes us all part of the patriot game

(in 3/4) A D A E A - / E A - D A - / / **1st**

My name is O'Hanlon, I'm just gone 16
My home is in Monaghan & there I was weaned
I learned all my life cruel England to blame
And so I'm a part of the patriot game

It's barely a year since I wandered away
With the local battalions of the bold I.R.A.
I read of our heros & wanted the same
To play up my part in the patriot game

This Ireland of mine has for long been half-free
6 counties are under John Bull's monarchy
But still De Valera is *[most of our leaders are]* greatly to blame
For shirking his *[their]* part*[s]* in the patriot game

They told me how Connolly was shot in his chair
His wounds from the fighting all bleeding & bare
His fine body twisted all battered & lame
They soon made me part of the patriot game

And now as I lie with my body all holes
I think of those traitors who bargained & sold
I'm sorry my rifle has not done the same
For the traitors who sold out the patriot game

— Dominic Behan

© 1964 & 1965 Clifford Music Ltd, London, England. TRO — Essex Music, Inc. NY, controls all publication rights for the USA & Canada. International copyright secured. Made in USA. All rights reserved incl. public performance for profit. Used by permission. *IRA member Fergal O'Hanlon & the poet Sean South were shot during an attack on Dungannon Barracks in May 1957. Behan, a famous Irish playwright, wrote this song later that year. De Valera was the Prime Minister of the Irish Republic. Dylan used this tune for "With God on Our Side" (see PEACE) In* SO! *10:2, 44:4 &* Reprints *#3 &* FSEncyV1. *On Judy Collins* Whales & Nightingales, *Clancy Bros* In Person at Carnegie Hall *(Col),* Liam Clancy *(Vang) & Kingston Trio* Time to Think. **OJ45**

The Peatbog Soldiers (Moorsoldaten)

Wohin auch das Auge blicket / Moor und Heide nur ringsherum
Vogelsang uns nicht erquicket,
Eichen stehen kahl und krumm
Wir sind die Moorsoldaten,
Und ziehen mit dem Spaten ins Moor

Em C Em C / Am Em B7 Em / G - - C / **2nd**

(D) G - D B7 / Em - Am B7 Em - - -

Auf und nieder geh'n die Posten / Keiner, keiner kann hindurch
Flucht wird nur das Leben kosten!
Vierfach ist umzäunt die Burg / **Wir...**

Doch für uns gibt est kein Klagen / Ewig kann's nicht Winter sein
Einmal werden froh wir sagen / "Heimat, du bist wieder mein"
Dann zieh'n die Moorsoldaten / Nicht mehr **mit dem Spaten...**

Far & wide as the eye can wander,
Heath & bog are everywhere
Not a bird sings out to cheer us,
Oaks are standing, gaunt and bare
We are the peatbog soldiers,
Marching with our spades to the bog

Up & down the guards are pacing / No one, no one can go thru
Flight would mean a sure death facing,
Guns & barbed wire greet our view / **We...**

But for us there is no complaining / Winter will in time be past
One day we shall cry rejoicing
"Homeland dear, you're mine at last!"
Then will the peatbog soldiers / March no more with **spades...**

— w: Johann Esser & Wolfgang Langhaff — m: Rudi Goguel

© 1964 by Stormking Music Inc. All rights reserved. Used by permission. *In* SO! *16:4,* S of Work & Protest, S That Changed the World, FS Ency V1, Peoples SB, FiresB of FS & Bells of Rhymney. *On* S of the Spanish Civil War V1 *& Pete Seeger* Strangers & Cousins. **OJ46**

El Pueblo Unido

De pié cantar, que vamos a triumfar
Avanzan ya banderas de unidad
Y tu vendras marchando junto a mí
Y así verás tu canto y tu bandera
Florecer la luz de un rojo amanecer
Anunciara la vida que vendrá

Em G Am B7 / / Am D GB7 Em / Am B7 Em E7
Am D GB7 Em / Am B7 EmB7 Am

De pié *[Hay que]* cantar el pueblo va a triunfar
Será mejor la vida que vendrá
A conquistar vuestra felicidad
Y en un clamor mil voces de combate sealzaran
Dirán canción *[Mira que acción]* de libertad
Con desición la patria vencerá

Y ahora el pueblo que se alza en la lucha
Con voz de gigante gritando "¡Adelante!
(chant) El pueblo unido jamás será vencido"

Am - / Gdim - / Em - B7 - ||: Em G Am B7 :||

La patria está formando la unidad
Del norteal sur se mobilizará
Desdeel salar al vientre mineral
Al bosqueaustral unido en la lucha y el trabajo ideal
La patria cubrirán su paso ya anuncia el porvenir

De pié *[Hay que]* cantar, el pueblo va a triumfar
Millones ya imponen la verdad
De acero son, ardiente *[al vientre]* batallón
Sus manos van llevando la justicia y la razon
Mujer *[De un pie]* con fuego y con valor
Ya estás aquí junto al trabajador

— w: anon. — m: Sergio Ortega, ca. 1972

Prob the most important song of the Nueva Canción movement in Latin America. Rec by Quilapayun. Trans of cho: "And now the people are rising up in the struggle, with great voice crying 'Forward!' The people united can never be defeated." **OJ47**

The Rebel Girl

There are women of many descriptions
In this queer world as everyone knows
Some are living in beautiful mansions
And are wearing the finest of clothes
There are blueblooded queens & princesses
Who have charms made of diamonds & pearls
But the only & thoroughbred lady / Is the Rebel Girl

C F C - / F Fm C - / C F C - / D7 - G -
/ " / F - E7 - / A7 - Dm - / D7 G C -

That's the Rebel Girl, that's the Rebel Girl
To the working class she's a precious pearl
She brings courage, pride & joy / To the fighting Rebel Boy
We've had girls before, but we need some more
In the Industrial Workers of the World
For it's great to fight for freedom / With a Rebel Girl

C - F - / G - C - / - - G - / - - C -
/ " / G F E7 - / A7 - Dm F / D G C -

Yes, her hands may be hardened from labor
And her dress may not be very fine
But a heart in her bosom is beating
Warm & true to her class & her kind
And the grafters in terror are trembling
When her spite & defiance she'll hurl / For **the only...**

— Joe Hill

Written by Hill in jail, Feb 1915 & dedicated by him to the then youthful Wobbly leader Elizabeth Gurley Flynn. In IWW Songs, SO! *1:7 &* Reprints *#1,* FSEncyV1, Here's to the Women, & Lib'd Women's SB. *On Anne Romaine* Take A Stand *(FF).* OJ48

The Rising of the Moon

O then tell me Sean O'Farrell, tell me why you hurry so?
Hush me buchall, hush & listen & his cheeks were all aglow
I bear orders from the captain, get you ready quick & soon
For the pikes must be together **by the Rising of the Moon**
By the Rising of the Moon, by the Rising of the Moon
For the pikes must be together **by the Rising of the Moon**

C - G - / F C F C :|| 3x

O then tell me Sean O'Farrell where the gathering is to be?
In the old spot by the river, right well known to you & me
One more word, for signal token whistle up the marching tune
With your pike upon your shoulder **by the Rising...**

Out of many a mud wall cabin, eyes were watching thru the night
Many a manly heart was throbbing, for the coming morning light
Murmurs ran along the valley like the banshee's lonely croon
And a thousand pikes were flashing **by...**

There beside the singing river, that dark mass of men were seen
Far above their shining weapons hung their own beloved green
Death to every foe & traitor, forward strike the marching tune
And hurrah me boys for freedom, 'tis the Rising of the Moon
'Tis the Rising...

— trad. (Irish)

In SO! 3:11, Bikel FS & Footnotes, FSEncy V1, FS of Eng, Ire, Scot & Wales, Clancy Bros SB & on their Irish S of Rebellion & Hearty & Hellish. *Also on Peter Paul & Mary* See What Tomorrow Brings, *Limelighters* Alive V1 *& J Collins* Maid of Const Sorrow. OJ49

Roddy McCorley

O see the fleet-foot hosts of men, who speed with faces wan
From farmstead & from thresher's cot along the banks of Ban
They come with vengeance in their eyes, too late, too late are they
For **young Roddy M'Corley goes to die, on the Bridge of Toome today**

D - GA D / D GD GEm A / / 1st

Up the narrow street he stepped, smiling proud & young
About the hemp-rope on his neck, the golden ringlets clung
There's ne'er a tear in his blue eyes, both glad & bright are they / **As young...**

When he last stepp̀ed up that street his shining pike in hand
Behind him marched in grim array, a stalwart earnest band!
For Antrim Town! **(2x)** he led them to the fray / **As...**

There's never a one of all your dead more bravely fell in fray
Than he who marches to his fate on the Bridge of Toome today
True to the last **(2x)** he treads the upward way...

— Ethna Carberry

M'Corley was a local leader in Co. Antrim in the Rebellion of 1798. He was captured by the British & executed in Toomebridge. In SO! *11:2 &* Reprints *#4,* Hootenanny SB, *&* FSEncyV1. *On Kingston Trio* College Conc, *Clancy Bros &* Tommy Makem *(TLP1042) & in their* SB. OJ50

Singing for Our Lives

We are a gentle, angry people
And we are singing, singing for our lives (repeat)

D - G D / A - D A / D - G D / A - G D

1. a justice-seeking people
2. an anti-nuclear *[anti-racist, anti-sexist]* people
3. young & old together
4. gay & lesbian people *[gay & straight together]*
5. a land of many colors

— Holly Near

© 1979 Hereford Music (ASCAP). Used by permission. Written following the murder of San Francisco Mayor George Moscone & Supervisor Harvey Milk. aka: "Gentle Loving People." On her Lifeline *(w Ronnie Gilbert) & in her* Singing for Our Lives. *Also in Children's S for a Friendly Planet.* OJ51

Solidarity Forever

When the union's inspiration, thru the workers' blood shall run
There can be no power greater anywhere beneath the sun
Yet what force on Earth is weaker than the feeble strength of one
But the union makes us strong
Solidarity forever! (3x) / For the union makes us strong

G - - - / C - G - / - - - Em / C D G - :||

Is there aught we hold in common with the greedy parasite
Who would lash us into serfdom & would crush us with his might?
Is there anything left to us but to organize & fight? for...

It is we who plowed the prairies, built the cities where they trade
Dug the mines & built the workshops, endless miles of RR laid
Now we stand outcast & starving 'mid the wonders we have made, but...

It is we that wash the dishes, scrub the floors & chase the dirt
Feed the kids & send 'em off to school & then we go to work
Where we work for half wages for a boss that likes to flirt...

All the world that's owned by idle drones is ours & ours alone
We have laid the wide foundations, built it skyward stone by stone
It is ours not to slave in, but to master & to own, while...

They have taken untold millions that they never toiled to earn
But without our brain & muscle not a single wheel can turn
We can break their haughty power, gain our freedom when we learn that...

In our hands is placed a power greater than their hoarded gold
Greater than the might of armies magnified a thousand-fold
We can bring to birth a new world from the ashes of the old, for

Llevaremos en la sangre la grandeza sindical
No tendrá poder más grande_el laborismo mundial
Compañero, si_eres d,bil con tu fuerza individual
Con solidaridad *[Que viva nuestra unión]*
Solidaridad por siempre (3x) / Con la fuerza sindical

Más que_el oro_atesorado es el poder sindical
Es más fuerte que_una_armada y mejor que_un arsenal
Crearemos nueva vida en el campo laboral / **Con...**

En los campos de Delano luchan per su libertad
Todos los trabajadores quieren ya vivir en paz
Y por esos companeros nos tenemos que juntar / **Con...**

Vamos vamos campesinos los derechos a pelear
Con el corazón en alto y con fe en unidad
Las olas del mar la injusticia va a indunar / **Con...**

— w: Ralph Chaplin (feminist v., last 4 v. United Farm Workers, Faith Petric, Marcia Taylor & Sally Rogers)
— m: "Battle Hymn of the Republic"

In SO! *20:3,* FSEncyV1, S That Changed the World, Carry It On, *S of* Work & Protest *& Am Fav Bals. On Joe Glazer* Sings Labor S *& Pete Seeger* Talking Union *&* Carry It On, *Anne Romaine* Take A Stand *(FF), Utah Phillips* We Have Fed You All *(Philo), Earl Robinson* Strange Unusual Eve., *Almanac Singers* Talking Union *& Bobbie McGee* Bread & Raises. *Alt "jazzier" melody ("Rockin' Solidarity") in* WHATFG. OJ52

The Times They Are A-Changin'

Come gather round people wherever you roam
And admit that the waters around you have grown
And accept it that soon you'll be drenched to the bone
If your time to you is worth savin'
Then you better start swimmin' or you'll sink like a stone
For the times they are a-changin'

C Am F C / - Am F G / 1st / C Am G -

G - - - / C - G C **(capo up)**

Come writers & critics who prophesy with your pens
And keep your eyes wide, the chance won't come again
And don't speak too soon for the wheel's still in spin
And there's no tellin' who that it's namin'
For the loser now may be later to win / **For the...**

Come senators, congressmen, please heed the call
Don't stand in the doorways don't block up the hall
For those who get hurt will be those who have stalled
There's a battle outside & it's ragin'
It'll soon shake your windows & rattle your walls...

Come mothers & fathers thru out the land
And don't criticize what you don't understand
Your sons & your daughters are beyond your command
Your old road is rapidly agin'
Please get out of the new one if you can't lend a hand...

The line it is drawn the curse it is cast
The slow one now will later be fast
As the present now will later be past
The order is rapidly fadin'
And the first one now will later be last...

— **Bob Dylan**

© 1963 Warner Bros. Inc. Renewed 1991 Special Rider Music. All rights reserved. Used by permission. *On his* Biograph, Gr H V2, At Budokan, Times They Are... *& in his* SB. *On Peter, Paul & Mary* In Conc *& in their* Best Of. *On Simon & Garfunkel* Wed Morning 3 AM, *Pete Kennedy* Bound for Glory *(Rosewood) & Beach Boys* Party. OJ53

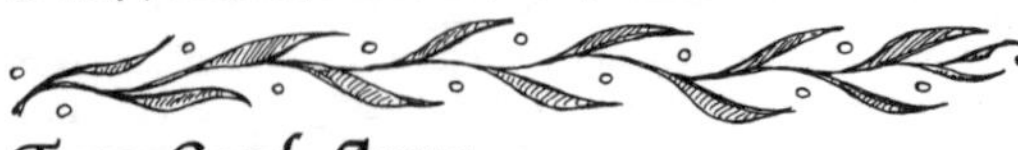

Two Good Arms

Who will remember the hands so white & fine
That touched the finest linen, that poured the finest wine
Who will remember the genteel words they spoke
To name the lives of two good men a nuisance or a joke

C - Dm - / G - F C :||

All who know these two good arms
Know I never had to rob or kill
I can live by my own two hands & live well
And all my life I have struggled
To rid the earth of all such crimes

/ " / " / F - C↓ Dm - / C↓ Dm - / G - C -

Who will remember Judge Webster Thayer
One hand on the gavel, the other resting on the chair
Who will remember the hateful words he said
Speaking to the living in the language of the dead

Who will remember the hand upon the switch, that
Took the lives of two good men in the service of the rich
Who will remember the one who gave the nod, or the
Chaplain standing near at hand to invoke the name of God

We will remember this good shoemaker
We will remember this poor fish peddler
We will remember all the strong arms & hands
That never once found justice in the hands that rule this land

(last cho) And all who knew these two good men
Knew they never had to rob or kill
Each had lived by his own two hands & *[they had]* lived well
And all their lives they had struggled
To rid the earth of all such crimes

And all our lives we must struggle
To rid the earth of all such crimes!

— **Charlie King**

© 1978 Charlie King/Pied Asp Music (BMI). Used by permission. *At the height of the "Red Scare" in 1920, two Italian immigrant union activists in Boston were framed on murder charges. Nicola Sacco & Bartolomeo Vanzetti were electrocuted in 1927 despite world-wide appeals on their behalf. On his* Somebody's Story *(RainbowSnake) &* 2 Good Arms, *Holly Near & Ronnie Gilbert* Lifeline *& Roy Bailey* Freedom Peacefully. *In SO! 31:2,* Carry It On *&* Broadside. OJ54

Victor Jara

Victor Jara of Chile lived like a shooting star
He fought for the people of Chile with his songs & his guitar
His hands were gentle, his hands were strong

D - G D / G D Em G / A7 AG D -

Victor Jara was a peasant, worked from a few years old
Sat upon his father's plow & watched the earth unfold

When the neighbors had a wedding, one of the children died
His mother sang all night for them with Victor by her side

He grew up to be a fighter against the people's wrongs
He listened to their grief & joy & turned them into songs

He sang about the copper miners & about those who worked the lands
He sang about the factory workers & they knew he was their man

He campaigned for Allende working night & day
He sang take hold your brothers' *[your brothers' & sisters']* hands, the future begins today

Then the generals seized Chile, they arrested Victor then
They caged him in a stadium with 5000 frightened men

Victor stood in the stadium, his voice was brave & strong
And he sang for his fellow prisoners til the guards cut short his song

They broke the bones in both his hands, they beat him on the head
They tore him with electric shocks & then they shot him dead

— **w: Adrian Mitchel m: Arlo Guthrie**

© 1977 by Adrian Mitchell & Arlo Guthrie. Rights administered by Arloco Music Inc. All rights reserved. Used by permission. *On Guthrie's* Amigo. *See Jara's song* Plegaria a un Labrador *in FARM for comments on Jara's work and his death. In* SO! *37:1.* OJ55

Viva la Quince Brigada

1. Viva la Quince Brigada, **rhumbala, rhumbala, rumbala (2x)**
Que se ha cubierta de gloria, ay **Manuela, ay Manuela (2x)**

Am - E - / / Am AmG GF FE E / /

2. Luchamos contra los Morros **rhumbala... (2x)**
Mercenarios y fascistas, **ay Manuela... (2x)**
3. Solo es nuestro deseo / Acabar con el fascismo, **ay...**
4. En el frente de Jarama / No tenemos ni aviones, ni tanques, ni cañones, **ay Manuela (1x only)**
5. Ya salimos de España / Para luchar en otros frentes...

— **as sung by the International Brigade – Spanish Civil War (1937-39)**

— **adapt by Bart Van Der Schelling**

© 1964 by Stormking Music Inc. All rights reserved. Used by permission. *On* S of the Spanish Civil War, V1 *(Folkways), Pete Seeger* I Can See A New Day, Circles & Seasons *&* The Essential. *In* Peoples SB, Bells of Rhymney *&* S That Changed the World. OJ56

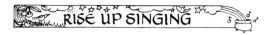

Wasn't That a Time?

Our fathers bled at Valley Forge, the snow was red with blood
Their faith was warm at Valley Forge, their faith was brotherhood

(in A) G - - - A - - - G A - / G - - - A D - E - A -

Wasn't that a time, wasn't that a time
A time to try the soul of man, wasn't that a terrible time!

A - - - - - / - - - G A - G A -

Brave men who died at Gettysburg now lie in soldier's graves
But there they stemmed the slavery tide & there the faith was saved

Informers took their Judas pay to tell their sorry tale
The gangs in Congress had their way & free souls went to jail

How many times we've gone to kill in freedom's holy name
And children died to save the pride of rulers without shame

Our faith cries out, we have no fear! We dare to reach our hand
To other neighbors far & near, to friends in every land
(last cho) Isn't this a time, isn't this a time!
A time to free the soul of man – isn't this a wonderful time!

— **Lee Hays & Walter Lowenfels**

 On Weavers Together Again, *Seeger* Wimoweh *& Peter Paul & Mary* A Song will Rise. *In SO! 36:1.* OJ57

What's That I Hear?

What's that I hear now ringin' in my ear?
I've heard that sound before
What's that I hear now ringin' in my ear?
I hear it more & more
It's the sound of freedom callin' / Ringin' up to the sky!
It's the sound of the old ways a-fallin'
You can hear it if you try! **(2x)**

(in G) C Em A D / G C D :||

G D / G F / G D / C Em D / /

What's that I see now shinin' in my eyes
I've seen that light before
What's that I see...eyes / I see it more & more
It's the light of freedom shinin' / Shinin' up to the sky
It's the light of the old ways a-fallin'
You can see it if you try **(2x)**

What's that I feel now beatin' in my heart?
I've felt that beat before
What's that I feel... / I feel it more & more
It's the rumble of freedom callin' / Climbin' up to the sky
It's the rumble of the old ways a-fallin'
You can feel it if you try **(2x)**

— **Phil Ochs**

 On his All the News That's Fit to Sing *& in* A Time For Singing. OJ58

When the Ship Comes In

O the time will come when the winds will stop
And the breeze will cease to be breathin'
Like the stillness in the wind 'fore the hurricane begins
The hour that the ship comes in
Then the sea will split & the ships will hit
And the shore line sands will be shaking
Then the tide will sound & the waves will pound
And the morning will be breaking

C Em F C / Am F C - / 1st / C G F C -

Em - F C / Em F C - / " / C F G F C -

O the fishes will laugh as they swim out of the path
And the seagulls they'll be a-smiling
And the rocks on the sand will proudly stand / **The hour...**
And the words that are used for to get the ship confused
Will not be understood as they're spoken
O the chains of the sea will have busted in the night
And be buried at the bottom of the ocean

A song will lift as the mainsail shifts
And the boat drifts on to the shore line
And the sun will respect every face up the deck / **The...**
Then the sands will roll out a carpet of gold
For your weary toes to be a-touchin'
And the ship wise men will remind you once again
That the whole wide world is watchin'

O the foes will rise with the sleep still in their eyes
And they'll jerk from their beds & think they're dreamin'
But they'll pinch themselves & squeal & they'll know that it's for real / **The hour...**
Then they'll raise their hands sayin' we'll meet all your demands
But we'll shout from the bow your days are numbered
And like Pharaoh's triumph they'll be drowned in the tide
And like Goliath they'll be conquered

— **Bob Dylan**

 On his Times They Are A-Changing *& in his* SB. *On Peter Paul & Mary* S Will Rise *& in their SB. On Arlo Guthrie* Hobo's Lullaby. OJ59

You Can Get It If You Really Want

You can get it if you really want (3x)
But you must try, try & try / Try & try
Til you succeed at last

C G F - / / / F - G - / / C G F - **(2x)**

Persecution you must bear
Win or lose you got to get your share
Got your mind set on a dream
You can get it tho' hard it may seem

C G F - / / Em - F - / G - - -

Rome was not built in a day
Opposition will come your way
But the harder the battle you see
It's the sweeter the victory

— **Jimmy Cliff**

 — On his The Harder They Come. OJ60

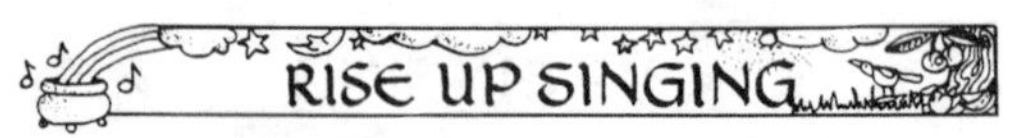

Your Daughters and Your Sons

They wouldn't hear your music & they pulled your paintings down
They wouldn't read your writing & they banned you from the town
But they couldn't stop your dreaming & a victory you have won
For **you sowed the seeds of** freedom **in your daughters & your sons**
In your daughters & your sons, in your...
You sowed the seeds of freedom **in your...**

G - D - / G GC C G / 1st / G C D G
D - G D / G C D G

Your weary smile it proudly hides the chain marks on your hands
When you bravely strived to realize the rights of every man
And tho' your body's bent & low, a victory you've won
For **you sowed the seeds of** justice **in your...**

I don't know your religion but one day I heard you pray
For a world where everyone can work & the children they can play
And altho' you never got your share of the fruits that you have won
You sowed the seeds of equality...

They taunted you in Belfast & they tortured you in Spain
And in that Warsaw ghetto they tied you up in chains
In Vietnam & Chile when they came with tanks & guns
It was there **you sowed the seeds of** peace...

And now your music's playing & the writing's on the wall
And all the dreams you painted can be seen by one & all
And now you've got them thinking & the future's just begun
For **you sowed the seeds of freedom...**

— Tommy Sands

© 1979 Elm Grove Music. Used by permission. On his Singing of the Times *& in* Sands Family SB. *Also on Dick Gaughan* S for Peace *& in* SO! *31:1.* OJ61

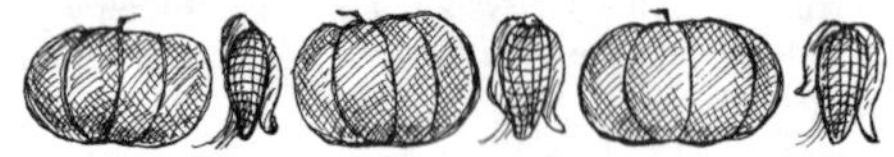

For other songs about social change, see ECOLOGY, FREEDOM, HOPE, MTN VOICES (on miners union & stripmining struggles), PEACE, WOMEN, and WORK (union songs). For songs about the struggles of migrant workers & of small farmers see FARM & PRAIRIE. For songs about personal struggles see HARD TIMES & BLUES (incl special index on prison songs).

Other social change songs include "Cutty Wren" (related to peasant uprisings – BALS) "How Can I Keep fr Singing" (FAITH) "Joshua", "Wade in the Wate"r & "When the Saints Go Marchin' In" ["When the Revolution Comes"] (SPIRS).

TIME & CHANGES

The Activity Room (Mrs. Abrams)

Would you like to play bridge & have a nice cup of tea in the morning Mrs. Abrams
We'll be starting out at ten, Mrs. Iltis & Flora Hazleton
What we need is a "fourth," Ida Yancy's not here she's at her sister's in New Jersey
So Mrs. Abrams will ya play, what d'ya say?

D - B7 - / Em A DF D :|| **(capo up)**

Well, I haven't played bridge since my husband died it's been a while Mrs. Riley
I hardly can remember the rules I'm really rusty & I know I'd feel like a fool
But since you ask, I could give it a go Mrs. Iltis has a book she'd lend it I know
So Mrs. Riley it's tea at ten, I'll see you then

Would you like to play pool in the tournament we could be partners Mr. Gaffney?
There's a game that starts at two Mr. Sheen & Ted Fine against me & you
Yes you're my pick, you bank 'em in every time we could each win a trophy
So Mr. Gaffney will you play, what d'ya say?

I like to catch a few winks, take a snooze at noon I get so tired Mr. Rosen
And there are times when I'm so stiff I can barely keep ahold of the darned cue stick
But since you ask it doesn't feel like rain, last night I slept great with those pink pills for the pain, so
Mr. Rosen I'll see you at two, we'll take 'em on, me & you

Would you like to play horn in the orchestra? you'd be terrific Mr. Lopez
We'll be tuning up at three, your friend Hal Hirsch'll play the timpani, we'll play
Some Gershwin & Brahms & some J.S. Bach, can you even believe we're gonna try a little pop & some rock?
So Mr. Lopez will you play, what d'ya say?

My lip is not in shape, my horn is worn & old it's at my brother's Mrs. Malcolm
My sight reading's very slow, it's been years I'd hold you back I know
But since you ask I could just stop by I could fill in for awhile, if you need me
So Mrs. Malcolm I'll see you at three, for some do, re - I'll even bring my brother with me, to the do, re -
And thanks for asking me to the do re mi, me, do re me

D - B7 - / Em A DF D / 1st / Em A (2x) / 2nd

— Ruth Pelham

© 1982 Ruth Pelham ASCAP. Used by permission. — aka: "Mrs Abrams." On her Look to the People *(Flying Fish 399), Reilly & Maloney* Backstage, *Holly Near & Ronnie Gilbert* Lifeline *(Redwood 404) & on* Swords Into Plowshares. *In* SO! *29:3.* OT02

Auld Lang Syne

Should auld acquaintance be forgot & never brought to mind?
Should auld acquaintance be forgot & days of auld lang syne
For auld lang syne, **my dear**, for auld lang syne
We'll tak' a cup o' kindness yet, for auld lang syne

|: D A D G / D A GA D :||

We twa ha'e ran aboot the braes & pu'd the gowans fine
We've wandered many a weary foot sin auld lang syne
Sin auld lang syne, **my dear**, ... / We've wandered...

We twa ha'e sported i' the burn frae mornin' sun til dine
But seas between us braid ha'e roared sin auld lang syne...

And here's a hand my trusty frien' & gie's a hand o' thine
We'll tak' a cup o' kindness yet for auld lang syne...

||: G D G C / G D - G :||

— w: Robert Burns — m: trad.

I: In FiresB of FS, FiresB of Fun & Games, Golden Ency, FS Ency V1 *&* Fred Waring SB. *On* David Grisman *(Rounder) & on* Tannahill Weavers *(GreenLinnet). II: In* SO! *31:1 & Jean Redpath* S of Robt Burns V2. OT03

Birthday Cake

"We're gonna let second grade out early today"
Which made little Mikey kinda blue
'Cause he just turned seven years old that day
And he thought he'd get a party at school
He walked to his house & **he's taken off his guard**
There's **chairs & tables all over the yard**
And his friends jumped up & they hollered real hard
"Happy Birthday to you!"

D - G D / - A D - :|| A - D - / / 1st 2

It makes me think of the good old days
Happy Birthday to you
You sure grew out of your baby ways / Happy...
7th (later v: 22nd, 92nd) **birthday we wish you many more**
Health & wealth & friends by the score
So cut the cake & let's eat some more / Happy...

Mike's 22 now & he's working for his Pop
And his head's full of business thru & thru
They were putting in a whole new system at the shop
And he forgot he had a birthday due
Got back home **& he's taken off his guard**
There were **chairs & tables all over the yard...**

Now it's old man Michael in a rocking chair
Admiring the view
He's still got all his teeth & he's still got all his hair
And today he's 92
He turns in his seat **& he's taken off his guard** / There's...

— Tina Liza Jones

© 1984 Swan & Quill Pub. Co. — aka: "Cut The Cake". In SO! *31:1 &* V Fav of the V Young. *On McCutcheon* Howjadoo *(Rounder).* OT04

Changes

Sit by my side, come as close as the air
Share in my memories of gray
Wander in my world, dream about the pictures
That I play of changes

F G C Am / F G Em / F Dm G C / F G C -

Green leaves of summer turn red in the fall
To brown & to yellow they fade
Then they have to die trapped within the circle time
Parade of changes

Scenes of my young years were warm in my mind
Visions of shadows that shine, til
One day I returned & found they were the victims
Of the vines of changes

The world spinning madly it drifts thru the dark
Swims thru a hollow of haze
A trip around the stars, a journey thru the universe
Ablaze with changes

Movements of magic will glow in the night
All fears of the forest are gone, but
When the morning breaks they're swept away by
golden drops of / Dawn of changes

Passions will part to a strange melody
As fires will sometimes burn cold
Like petals in the wind, we're puppets to the silver
Strings of soul of changes

Your tears will be trembling now we're somewhere else
One last cup of wine I will pour
I'll kiss you one more time & leave you on the rolling
River shore of changes

— Phil Ochs

© 1965 Barricade Music Inc. (ASCAP). All rights administered by Almo Music Corp. (ASCAP). International copyright secured. Used by permission of CPP Belwin Inc. — On his In Conc, The War Is Over *&* Chords Of Fame. *On Ian & Sylvia* Play One More *&* Best of. OT05

Circles

All my life's a circle, sunrise & sundown
Moon rolls thru the nighttime til daybreak comes around
All my life's a circle, still I wonder why
Seasons spinning 'round again, years keep rolling by

C - - Dm / - - G C / - - - F / - G - C

Seems like I've been here before, can't remember when
I get this funny feeling, we'll be together again
No straight lines make up my life, all my roads have bends
No clearcut beginnings, so far no dead ends

I've met you a thousand times, I guess you've done the same
Then we lose each other, it's like a children's game
But now I find you here again, the thought comes to my mind
Our love is like a circle, let's go round one more time

— Harry Chapin

© 1972 The Harry Chapin Foundation. Used by permission. — On his Sniper & Other Love S *(Elek) & Limelighters* Alive V1 *(GNP/Crescendo). On Pete Seeger & Arlo Guthrie* Prec Friend. *In* SO! *36:3.* OT06

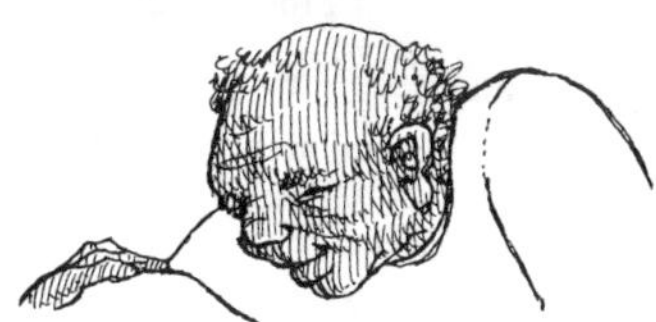

Circle Game

Yesterday a child came out to wonder
Caught a dragonfly inside a jar
Fearful when the sky was full of thunder
And tearful at the falling of a star

C F C - / - F G - / C F Em - / F G C -

And the seasons they go round & round
And the painted ponies go up & down
We're captive on a carousel of time
We can't return, we can only look
Behind from where we came
And go round & round & round in the circle game

C FC / / F - C - / F - / Em F / Em FG C -

Then the child moved ten times round the seasons
Skated over ten clear frozen streams
Words like "when you're older" must appease him
And promises of someday make his dreams

16 springs & 16 summers gone now
Cartwheels turn to carwheels through the town
And they tell him "Take your time it won't be long now
Til you drag your feet to slow the circles down"

Years spin by & now the child is 20
Tho' his dreams have lost some grandeur coming true
There'll be new dreams, maybe better dreams & plenty
Before the last revolving year is thru

— Joni Mitchell

© 1966 Siquomb Publishing Corp. All rights reserved. Used by permission. — On her Ladies of the Canyon, Miles Of Aisles *& in her* SB. V.1. *On Ian & Sylvia* Gr H & So Much For Dreaming, *Buffy Saint-Marie* Best of & Fire & Fleet & Candlelight, *Tom Rush* Circle Game *&* Classic Rush *& the Ian Campbell Folk Gp* Circle Game. OT07

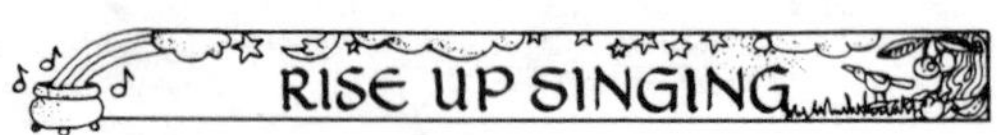

The Dutchman

The Dutchman's not the kind of man to keep his thumb
jammed in the dam / That holds his dreams in
But that's a secret only Margaret knows
When Amsterdam is golden in the morning Margaret brings
him breakfast / She believes him
_He thinks the tulips bloom beneath the snow
He's mad as he can be, but Margaret only sees that sometimes_
Sometimes she sees her unborn children in his eyes_

C - - - / Dm7 - - - / G - C - :|| F G C - / /

Let us go to the banks of the ocean
Where the walls rise above the Zuider Zee
Long ago I used to be a young man
And dear Margaret remembers that for me

F - C - / Dm7 G C - / F G C - / Dm7 G C -

The Dutchman still wears wooden shoes, his cap & coat
are patched with love / That Margaret sewed in
_Sometimes he thinks he's still in Rotterdam _
He watches tugboats down canals & calls out to them
when he thinks he / knows the captain
_Til Margaret comes to take him home again _
Thru unforgiving streets that trip him tho' she holds his
arm
Sometimes he thinks that he's alone & calls her name

The windmills whirl the winter in, she winds his muffler
tighter / They sit in the kitchen
Some tea with whiskey keeps away the dew
He sees her for a moment, calls her name, she makes
the bed up / Humming some old love song _
She learned it when the tune was very new
He hums a line or two, they hum together in the night
The Dutchman falls asleep & Margaret blows the candle out

— Michael Peter Smith

© 1971, 1978 Duchess Music Corp. Used by permission. All rights reserved. — On his Michael Smith, *Steve Goodman* Somebody Else's Troubles, Unfinished Business & the Essential, *Liam Clancy* The Dutchman & Farewell to Tarwaithe *(Plainsong), Shaw Bros* Best of, *George Turman* One Thing For Certain *& Josh White Jr.* Sing a Rainbow. OT08

The Foggy, Foggy Dew

When I was a bachelor, I lived all alone
I worked at the weaver's trade
And the only only thing I did that was wrong
was to woo a fair young maid
I wooed her in the wintertime, part of the summer too
And the only, only thing I did that was wrong
was **to keep her from the foggy, foggy dew**

D G A D / / A D A D / 1st /

One night she knelt close by my side when I was fast asleep
She threw her arms around my neck & then began to weep
She wept, she cried, she tore her hair
ah me, what could I do?
So all night long I held her in my arms just to...

Again I am a bachelor, I live with my son
we work at the weaver's trade
And every single time I look into his eyes
he reminds me of the fair young maid
He reminds me of the wintertime & of the summer too
And the many, many times that I held her in my arms just...

— trad.

In FiresB of FS, SFest, *Sharp* Eng FS of App V2, FS Abecedary, S for Pickin & Singing, FSEncy V1 *&* Treas of FS. *On Burl Ives* Bal & FS V3, S of the Colonies *& in his* SB, *Clancy Bros* Irish S of Rebellion, *Hedy West* Bals *(Topic), Odetta* My Eyes Have Seen *(Vang), Liam Clancy* The Dutchman & Farewell to Tarwaithe *(Plainsong) & Josh White* In Memoriam. OT09

Get Up and Go

How do I know my youth is all spent?
My get up & go has got up & went
But in spite of it all I'm able to grin
And think of the places my get up has been

(in 3/4) D A / E A / D A / E EA

Old age is golden, so I've heard said
But sometimes I wonder as I crawl into bed
With my ears in a drawer, my teeth in a cup
My eyes on a table until I wake up
As sleep dims my vision, I say to myself
"Is there anything else I should lay on the shelf?"
But tho' nations are warring & business is vexed
I'll still stick around to see what happens next

A E / - A / D A / [1.] B7 B7E :|| [2.] E EA

When I was young, my slippers were red
I could kick up my heels right over my head
When I was older, my slippers were blue
But still I could dance the whole night thru
Now I am older, my slippers are black
I huff to the store & I puff my way back
But never you laugh: I don't mind at all
I'd rather be huffing than not puff at all!

I get up each morning & dust off my wits
Open the paper & read the obits
If I'm not there, I know I'm not dead
So I eat a good breakfast & go back to bed

— w: trad. **— m: Pete Seeger**

TRO © 1964 Melody Trails, Inc. International copyright secured. All rights reserved. Used by permission. — On his Pete & Arlo Together, Young vs Old *& Weavers* Together Again. *In his* WHATFG, SO! *15:2 &* Reprints *#9 &* Bells of Rhymney. OT10

Gone, Gonna Rise Again

I remember the year that my grandaddy died
Gone, gonna rise again
They dug his grave on a mountainside / **Gone...**
I was too young to understand
The way he felt about the land
But I could read his history in his hands / **Gone...**

D C D - / C - G D - - - :||

D - - - / G - A - - - / **1st 2 above**

It's corn in the crib & apples in the bin / **Gone...**
Ham in the smokehouse & cotton in the gin / **Gone...**
Cows in the barn & hogs in the lot
You know he never had a lot
But he worked like the devil for the little he got...

These apple trees on the mountainside...
He planted the seeds just before he died...
I guess he knew that he'd never see
The red fruit hanging from the tree
But he planted those seeds for his children & me...

High on a ridge above the farm...
I think of my people that have gone on...
Like a tree that grows in the mountain ground
The storms of life have cut 'em down
But the new wood springs from the roots underground...

— Si Kahn

© Joe Hill Music (ASCAP). All rights reserved. Used by permission. — On his New wood *(JuneAppal), Lucha* Means Struggle *(tape) & J McCutheon* Gonna Rise Again *(Rounder). In his* SB, SO! *24:2,* Bright Morning Stars, Sing The Good Earth *& Guy Carawan* Voices Fr the Mtns. OT11

The Goodnight-Loving Trail

Too old to wrangle or ride on the swing
You beat the triangle & you curse everything
If dirt was a kingdom, then you'd be the king
On the Goodnight Trail, on the Loving Trail

C - G - / - - C - / - - F - - / C G C F -

Our Old Woman's lonesome tonight
Your French harp blows like the lone bawling calf
It's a wonder the wind don't tear off your skin
Get in there & blow out the light

C - G - / C G C F - / C Am G - / - - F C

With your snake oil & herbs & your liniments too
You can do anything that a doctor can do
Except find a cure for your own goddam stew / **On the...**

The cookfire's gone out & the coffee's all gone
The boys are all up & they're raising the dawn
You're still sitting there, lost in a song / **On...**

I know that some day I'll be just the same
Wearing an apron instead of a name
There's nothing can change it, there's no one to blame
(tune repeats) For the desert's a book writ in lizards & sage
It's easy to look like an old torn out page
Faded & cracked with the colors of age / **On the...**

— **Bruce Phillips**

 — On (& in) his Starlight on the Rails *& Ed Trickett* Tellin takes Me Home. OT12

Granderfather's Clock

My grandfather's clock was too large for the shelf
So it stood 90 years on the floor
It was taller by half than the old man himself
Tho' it weighed not a pennyweight more
It was bought on the morn of the day that he was born
And was always his treasure & pride
But it stopped short, never to go again
When the old man died

D A D G / D A D - :|| D - A - / D E A - / 1st 2

90 years without slumbering (tic toc, tic toc)
His life seconds numbering (tic toc, tic)
But it stopped short... / When the old man died

D GD D - / / D A D G / D A D -

In watching its pendulum swing to & fro
Many hours had he spent as a boy
And in childhood & manhood the clock seemed to know
And to share both his grief & his joy
For it struck 24 when he entered at the door
With a blooming & beautiful bride / **But it stopped...**

Now my grandfather said that of those he could hire
Not a servant so faithful he found
It wasted no time & it had but one desire
At the end of each week to be wound
And it stayed in its place, not a frown upon its face
And its hands never hung by its side / **But...**

It rang an alarm in the dead of the night
An alarm that for years had been dumb
And we knew that his spirit was pluming its flight
That his hour of departure had come
Still the clock kept the time, with a soft & muffled chime
As we silently stood by his side...

— **Henry Clay Work**

On E Trickett "Gently Down the Stream of Time", B Staines "Old Wood & Winter Wine" (MineralRiver), Bryan Bowers "Home Home On The Road" (FF), Purly Gates & David Levine "Singin On A Star" (GW), Reid Miller "Jubilee", Larry Hanks "Tying a Know" (LS104), Country Gentlemen "On The Rd" (Folkways2411) & Grandpa Jones "Old Time Collection". In S for the Rotary Club, Sing Along w World's Fav FS, FSEncyV1, Burl Ives SB, SFest & Best Loved S of Am People. OT13

Hello in There

We had an apartment in the city
Me & Loretta liked living there
It'd been years since the kids had grown
A life of their own, left us alone
John & Linda live in Omaha
And Joe is somewhere on the road
We lost Davy in the Korean War
And I still don't know what for, don't matter anymore

(in G) G Am D - / / Bm - C - / G - D - :||

Ya know that old trees just grow stronger
And old rivers grow wilder ev'ry day
Old people just grow lonesome
Waiting for someone to say "Hello in there, hello"

F - G - / / Bm - C - / G - D - G -

Me & Loretta we don't talk much more
She sits & stares thru the back door screen
And all the news just repeats itself
Like some forgotten dream, that we've both seen
Someday I'll go & call up Rudy
We worked together at the factory
But what could I say when he asks "What's new?"
"Nothing, what's with you?" "Nothing much to do"

So if you're walking down the street sometime
And spot some hollow ancient eyes
Please don't just pass 'em by & stare,
As if you didn't care. Say "Hello in there, hello"

(as cho) G Am D - / / Bm - C - / G - D - G -

— **John Prine**

 — On his John Prine, *J Baez* Diamonds & Rust *& Kevin Roth* The Other Side of the Mtn *(FTS31045).* OT14

I Like the Age I Am

I like the age I am
It's a wonderful life, no matter when
So if I'm a hundred or if I am 10
I like the age I am

(in 3/4) A D / E B7E / A AD / E A

Now some kids at 7 wish they were 11
And then want to be 13
When they finally arrive, then they wish they could drive
And can't wait until they're 18
Then they think 21 is when they'll have some fun
And "prime" is at least 25
And then 30 comes 'round & they start feeling down
'Cause they think they are ready to die

(in 4/4) A Bm / E A :||

D A / D E / D AF#m / **(in 3/4)** E A

Now some people lie & say they're 29
When really they're 40 or 50
And I just don't know why anybody would hide
All the years that have made 'em so nifty!
'Cause it's great being new & it's grand being old
And it's excellent in between
Different things to be learned at every turn
If you don't fall asleep at the wheel

Now if folks are so dumb that they like being young
But think being old is a shame
Well what's that to you? It's a lie, it's not true!
And there's no need to play that game
So when somebody says "How old are you?"
There's no need to stutter or lie
Just tell 'em flat out with a smile & a shout
"I'm ____ (fill in your age) years old today!"

— **Carol A. Johnson**

In My Life

There are places I remember
All my life, tho' some have changed
Some forever not for better
Some have gone & some remain
All these places have their moments
With lovers & friends I still can recall
Some are dead & some are living
In my life, I've loved them all

C ↓ Am C / F Fm C - :||

Am - F - / B♭ - C - / Am - D7 - / F Fm C -

But of all these friends & lovers
There is no one compares with you
And these memories lose their meaning
When I think of love as something new
I know I'll never lose affection
For people & things that went before
I know I'll often stop & think about them
In my life I love you more

— **John Lennon & Paul McCartney**

Kisses Sweeter Than Wine

When I was a young man & never been kissed
I got to thinkin' over what I had missed
I got me a girl, I kissed her & then
O lord, I kissed her again

F C Dm C / Am - Dm - :||

O / Kisses sweeter than wine (repeat)

F - Am / Dm C D9 - :||

D9

I asked her to marry & be my sweet wife
And we would be so happy the rest of our life
I begged & I pleaded like a natural man
And then, o Lord, she gave me her hand

I worked mighty hard & so did my wife
A-working hand in hand to make a good life
With corn in the fields & wheat in the bins
And then, o Lord, I was the father of twins

Our children they numbered just about four
And they all had sweethearts knocking at the door
They all got married & they didn't hesitate
I was, o Lord, the grandfather of eight

Now that I'm old & ready to go
I get to thinking what happened a long time ago
We had a lot of kids, trouble & pain
But, o Lord, I'd do it again

— **w: The Weavers** — **m: Huddie Ledbetter**

Lies

At last the kids are gone now for the day
She reaches for the coffee as the school bus pulls away
Another day to tend the house & plan
For Friday at the Legion when she's dancing with her man
Sure was a bitter winter, but Friday will be fine, and
Maybe last year's Easter dress will serve her one more time
She'd pass for 29 but for her eyes
But winter lines are telling wicked lies

G - D - / Em C G D :|| G - D -
Em - C - / G - D - / Am D G -

All lies / All those lines are telling wicked lies
Lies, all lies
Too many lines there in that face, too many to erase
Or to disguise they must be telling lies

AmG CD C - / G GAm D -
/ " / G - A - / C D G -

Is this the face that won for her the man
Whose amazed & clumsy fingers put that ring upon her hand?
No need to search that mirror for the years
The menace in their message shouts across the blur of tears
So this is Beauty's finish! Like Rodin's "Belle Heaulmiere"
The pretty maiden trapped inside the ranch wife's toil & care
Well, after seven kids, that's no surprise
But why cannot her mirror tell her lies?

Then she shakes off the bitter web she wove
And turns to set the mirror, gently, face down by the stove
She gathers up her apron in her hand
Pours a cup of coffee, drips Carnation from the can
And thinks ahead to Friday, 'cause Friday will be fine!
She'll look up in that weathered face that loves hers,
line for line / To see that maiden shining in his eyes
And laugh at how her mirror tells her lies

— Stan Rogers

© 1981 Fogarty's Cove Music Inc (Pro Canada). All rights reserved. Used by permission. — On his Northwest Passage *& in his* S fr Fogarty's Cove *& on Prisc Herdman* Seasons of Change *(FF).* OT18

Old Friends

Old friends, old friends
Sat on their park bench like bookends
A newspaper blown thru the grass falls on the
Round toes, on the high shoes / Of the old friends

F_{maj7} C_{maj7} - **(2x)**/ D_{m7} G C A_m - / D_{m7} - A_m G -
A_m - C_{maj7} - / F A_{m7} - -

Old friends / Winter companions, the old men
Lost in their overcoats, waiting for the sunset
The sounds of the city sifting thru trees settle like
Dust on the shoulders / Of the old friends

F_{maj7} C_{maj7} - / D_{m7} G F_{maj7} E_{m7} - / D_{m7} G C A_m -
D_{m7} G E_{m7} A_m - / G - F - / A_{m7} - - -

(bridge) Can you imagine us years from today
Sharing a park bench quietly?
How terribly strange to be 70

D_{m7} G C_{maj7} - / F F_m C - / D_{m7} G A_m - -

Old friends / Memory brushes the same years
Silently sharing the same fear

F_{maj7} C_{maj7} - / D_{m7} G F_{maj7} E_{m7} - / " /

— Paul Simon

© 1968 Paul Simon. All rights reserved. Used by permission. — In his S of. *On his & Garfunkel's* Bookends *&* Gr H *& on Richie Havens* On Stage. *In Complete Paul Simon.* OT19

One Day at a Time

I live one day at a time
I dream one dream at a time
Yesterday's dead & tomorrow is blind
And I live one day at a time

C F C - / - F G - / C F C F / C G C -

Tho' you're surprised to see me back at home
You don't know how I miss you when you're gone
Don't ask how long I plan to stay, it never crossed my mind
'Cause **I live...**

There's a swallow flyin' across a cloudy sky
Searchin' for a patch of sun, so am I
Don't ask how long I have to follow him, perhaps I won't
in time / But **I live...**

— Willie Nelson

© 1965 Tree Publishing Co., Inc., 8 Music Square West, Nashville, TN 37203. International copyright secured. Made in USA. All rights reserved. Used by permission. — On his Country Winners *(Pickwick), Baez* One Day At A Time *& John Wilcox* Stages of My Life. OT20

Passing Through

I saw Adam leave the garden with an apple in his hand
I said, "Now you're out, what are you gonna do?"
"Plant my crops & pray for rain, maybe raise a little Cain
I'm an orphan now & only passing thru"

D - G D / - - A - / 1st / D A D -

Passing thru, passing thru
Sometimes happy, sometimes blue, glad that I ran into you
Tell the people that you saw me passing thru

D - - - / - D_7 G - / D A D -

I saw Jesus on the cross on that hill called Calvary
"Do you hate mankind for what they done to you?"
He said, "Talk of love not hate, things to do it's gettin' late
I've so little time & I'm just passing thru"

Well, I shivered with George Washington one night at
Valley Forge
"Why do the soldiers freeze here like they do?"
He said "Men will suffer, fight, even die for what is right
Even tho' they know they're only passing thru"

I was at Franklin Roosevelt's side just a while before he died
He said "One world must come out of World War II
Yankee, Russian, white or tan, young & old in every land
We're all people & we're only passing thru"

*Gandhi spoke of freedom one night, I said "Man we've
gotta fight"
He said "Yes but love's the weapon we must use
For with killing no one wins, it's with love that peace begins
It takes courage when you're only passing thru"*

*I was talking with the crew of the ketch, The Golden Rule
"From these prison walls tell folks what we tell you
That if the bombs begin to fall, they will kill us one & all
We're in the same boat & we're only passing thru"*

— w: Dick Blakeslee (last 2 v. anon.) — m: trad. (gospel)

© Sing Out Corp. All rights reserved. On Pete Seeger Love S for Friends & Foes *(FA2453) & in his Am Fav Bals.* OT21

River

I was born in the path of the winter wind
And raised where the mountains are old
The springtime waters came dancing down
And I remember the tales they told

The whistling ways of my younger days
Too quickly have faded on by
But all of their memories linger on
Like the light in a fading sky

(in 3/4) D - G D / - - A - / D - G D / - A D - :||

River, take me along
In your sunshine, sing me your song
Ever moving & winding & free
You rolling old river, you changing old river
Let's you & me river run down to the sea!

D D_{maj7} G A/ /G - A D/G D G D/G A - G - D

I've been to the city & back again
I've been moved by some things that I've learned
Met a lot of good people & I called them friends
Felt the change when the seasons turned

I heard all the songs that the children sing
And listened to love's melodies
I've felt my own music within me rise
Like the wind in the autumn trees

Someday when the flowers are blooming still
Someday when the grass is still green
My rolling waters will round me bend
And flow into the open sea

So here's to the rainbow that followed me here
And here's to the friends that I know
And here's to the song that's within me now
I will sing it where'er I go

— Bill Staines

© Mineral River Music (BMI). Used by permission. — On his Bridges, The Whistle of the Jay *& in his* If I Were A Word. *On Madeleine MacNeil* Soon It's Goin to Rain *& on* Coffeehse Extempores. *In New Folk Favs.* OT22

September Song

When I was a young man courting the girls
I played me a waiting game
If a maid refused me with tossing curls

I let the old earth take a couple of whirls
While I plied her with tears in lieu of pearls
And as time came around she came my way
As time came around she came

(in C) G7 Am / / / Dm7 C / Fm Am / G Am / G C

O it's a long, long while from May to December
But the days grow short, when you reach September
When the autumn weather turns the leaves to flame
One hasn't got time for the waiting game
O the days dwindle down to a precious few
September, November
And these few precious days I'll spend with you
These precious days I'll spend with you

Cm Ab C - / D7 Fm C - :|| Fm - Cdim - / / 1st 2

When you meet with the young men early in spring
They court you in song & rhyme
They woo you with words & a clover ring

But if you examine the goods they bring
They have little to offer but the songs they sing
And a plentiful waste of time of day
A plentiful waste of time

— w: Maxwell Anderson — m: Kurt Weill

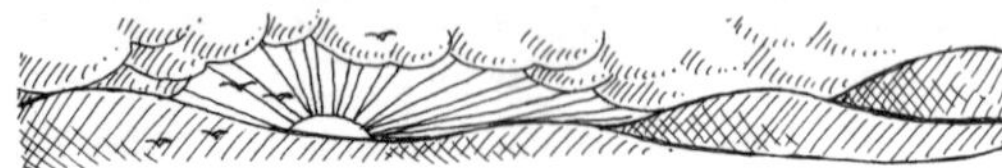

Sunrise, Sunset

Is this the little boy I carried?
Is this the little girl at play?
I don't remember growing older / When did they?
When did she grow to be a beauty?
When did he grow to be so tall?
Wasn't it yesterday when they were / small? **(in 3/4)**

Em B7 Em -/- B7 Em E7/Am E Am -/F# - B7 -
/ " / " /Am E Am F#/B7 - - -

Sunrise, sunset (2x) / Swiftly flow the days
Seedlings turn overnight to sunflowers
Blossoming even as we gaze
Sunrise, sunset (2x) / Swiftly fly the years
One season following another
Laden with happiness & tears

Em B7 **(2x)** / Em - - E7 / Am D G Em / Am B7 Em -
/ " / " /Am B7 Em A7/ " /

Now is the little boy a bridegroom
Now is the little girl a bride
Under the canopy I see them / Side by side
Place the gold ring around her finger
Share the sweet wine & break the glass
Soon the full circle will have come to / pass

— w: Sheldon Harnick — m: Jerry Bock

Sweeet Song from Yesterday

Hold back the days in which I'm living
So far from home, so far from free
Hold back the ways we've all been given
And let a sweet song from yesterday wash over me

A - E - / Bm E A - / A - D - / AD A E A

If we should meet like ships a-passin'
Some stormy night upon the blue
We may not speak, but for the asking
I'd let a sweet song from yesterday wash over you

When it seems your dreams ain't worth the dreamin'
When you can't find your way through
And when your schemes ain't worth the schemin'
Just let a sweet song from yesterday wash over you

— Bob Zentz

Those Were the Days

Once upon a time there was a tavern
Where we used to raise a glass or two
Remember how we laughed away the hours
And dreamed of all the great things we would do

Em - / E7 Am / - Em / F# B7

Those were the days my friend, we thought they'd never end
We'd sing & dance forever & a day
We'd live the life we choose, we'd fight & never lose
For we were young & sure to have our way
La, la, la...
Those were the days, o yes, those were the days

Em Am / D G / Am Em / B7 Em // - Am / B7 Em

Then the busy years went rushing by us
We lost our starry notions on the way
If by chance I'd see you in the tavern
We'd smile at one another & we'd say:

Just tonight I stood before the tavern
Nothing seemed the way it used to be
In the glass I saw a strange reflection
Was that lonely person really me?

Thru the door there came familiar laughter
I saw your face & heard you call my name
O my friends, we're older but no wiser
For in our hearts the dreams are still the same!

— Gene Raskin

Time Has Made a Change in Me

Time has made a change since my childhood days
Many of my friends have gone away
Some I never more in this life will see
Time has made a change in me

(in 3/4) D - G D / A7 - G D / - - G D / - A7 D -

Time has made a change in the old home place
Time has made a change in each smiling face
And I know my friends can plainly see / Time...

G - D - / - - E A / D - G D / - A7 D -

When I reach my home in the great somewhere
With my friends who wait to meet me over there
Free from pain & care I'll forever be / **Time...**

— anon. (US)

Rec by John McCutcheon, the Speer Fam & by Sharon Mtn Harmony (FLegcy). On Kim Wallach Short Sisters. OT27

Today

Today while the blossoms still cling to the vine
I'll taste your strawberries & drink your sweet wine
A million tomorrows will all pass away
Ere I forget all the joy that is mine today

(in 3/4) C Am F G / /C C7 F Fm
C Am Dm G - C (Am F G)

I'll be a dandy & I'll be a rover
You'll know who I am by the song that I sing
I'll feast at your table & sleep in your clover
Who cares what tomorrow shall bring

C Am F G / / /F G C (G)

I can't be contented with yesterday's glories
I can't live on promises winter to spring
For now is my moment, today is my story
I'll laugh & I'll cry & I'll sing

— Randy Sparks

 — On J Denver An Evening w... *& rec by the New Christy Minstrels. In* Life of the Party, Best of the '70s *&* 50 Yrs of Country M. OT28

Tomorrow Is a Long Time

If today was not an endless highway
If tonight was not a crooked trail
If tomorrow wasn't such a long time
Then lonesome would mean nothing to me at all

A D A - / /D E A - / /

Yes & only if my own true love was waitin'
And I could hear her heart a softly poundin'
Only if she was lyin' by me
And I in my bed once again

D E A - / / /D E - A - - -

I can't see my reflection in the water
Can't speak the sounds that show no pain
I can't hear the echo of my footsteps
Can't remember the sound of my own name

There's beauty in the silver singin' river
There's beauty in the sunrise in the sky
But none of these & nothin' else can touch the beauty
That I remember in my own true love's eyes

— Bob Dylan

 — Inspired by an ancient anon. poem: "O Western Wind, where wilt thou blow?/That the small rain down may rain/Christ, that my love were in my arms/And I in my bed again." On his Gr H V2 *& in his* SB. *On J Collins* 5th Alb & Recollections, *Sandy Denny* Who Knows Where the Time, *Kingston Trio* Once Upon a Time *& Ian & Sylvia* 4 Strong Winds. OT29

Try to Remember

Bbmaj7

Try to remember the kind of September
When life was slow & o so mellow
Try...September / When grass was green & grain was yellow
Try...September / When you were a tender & callow fellow
Try to remember & if you remember / Then follow...

(capo up, in 3/4) C Am Dm G/Cmaj7 Am7 Dm G :||
Em7 Am Dm G / Cmaj7 Fmaj7 Bbmaj7 G / 1st / /

Try to remember when life was so tender
That no one wept except the willow
Try...tender / That dreams were kept beside your pillow
Try...tender / That love was an ember about to billow
Try to remember & if you remember / Then follow

Deep in December, it's nice to remember
Altho' you know the snow will follow
Deep...remember / Without a hurt the heart is hollow
Deep... / The fire of September that made us mellow
Deep in December our hearts should remember / And follow

— w: Tom Jones m: Harvey Schmidt

 — Fr their musical The Fantasticks. *On Ray Conniff* World of H *& Andy Williams* Shadow of Your Smile. *In Readers Dig* Pop S that Will Live *& Broadway SBs.* OT30

Turn Around

Where are you going, my little one, little one
Where are you going, my baby, my own?
Turn around & you're two, turn around & you're four
Turn around & you're a young girl going out of my door
Turn around, turn around / (repeat 4th line:) Turn...door

C Em F G / / C C7 F Fm / C Dm G C
C - C7 - / F Em G C

Where are you going, my little one, little one
Little dirndls & petticoats, where have you gone?
Turn around & you're tiny, turn around & you're grown
Turn around & you're a young wife with babes of your own

— Malvina Reynolds, Alan Greene & Harry Belafonte

 — In Malvina Reynolds SB & Little Boxes. *In* SO! *10:1 &* Reprints *#5,* 1001 Jumbo S & FM Gr H. *On Pete Seeger* World of, *Sally Rogers* Love Will Guide Us *(FF), Neil Diamond* Primitive, *Kingston Trio* Time to Think *& Prisc Herdman* Darkness Into Light *(FF).* OT31

Turn, Turn, Turn

To everything – turn, turn, turn
There is a season – turn, turn, turn
And a time for ev'ry purpose under heaven

G - C G Am7 /G - C G Am7 - /D - - - G - - -

A time to be born, a time to die
A time to plant, a time to reap
A time to kill, a time to heal
A time to laugh, a time to weep

D - G - / / /C - D - G - - -

A time to build up, a time to break down
A time to dance, a time to mourn
A time to cast away stones
A time to gather stones together

A time of war, a time of peace
A time of love, a time of hate
A time you may embrace
A time to refrain from embracing

A time to gain, a time to lose
A time to rend, a time to sew
A time to love, a time to hate
A time of peace: I swear it's not too late!

— w: Book of Ecclesiastes — adap & m: Pete Seeger

 — On his Bitter & the Sweet, Gr H *&* World of. *On Judy Collins* 3rd Alb & Recollections *& rec by The Byrds. In his* WHATFG, SO! *14:4, 44:4 &* Reprints *#9,* Gr S of the '60s, Those Were the Days *&* S of the Spirit. *On* WHATFG *(S of Pete Seeger V.1 – rec by Bruce Cockburn).* OT32

When I'm Gone

There's no place in this world where I'll belong **when I'm gone**
And I won't know the right from the wrong **when I'm gone**
And you won't find me singin' on this song **when I'm gone**
So I guess I'll have to do it while I'm here

D - Bm - / Em - A - / D F#m Bm - / Em A D -

And I won't feel the flowing of the time **when...**
All the pleasures of love will not be mine **when...**
My pen won't pour out a lyric line **when... / So...**

And I won't breathe the brandy air...
And I can't even worry 'bout my cares...
Won't be asked to do my share...

And I won't be running from the rain...
And I can't even suffer from the pain...
There's nothing I can lose or I can gain...

Won't see the golden of the sun...
And the evenings & the mornings will be one...
Can't be singing louder than the guns...

All my days won't be dances of delight...
And the sands will be shifting from my sight...
Can't add my name into the fight...

And I won't be laughing at the lies...
And I can't question how or when or why...
Can't live proud enough to die...

— Phil Ochs

 — On his Chords of Fame *&* In Conc *& Magpie* If It Ain't Love *(Rounder). In SO! 25:1.* OT33

When I'm Sixty-Four

When I get older losing my hair many years from now
Will you still be sending me a valentine, birthday greetings, bottle of wine?
If I'd been out til quarter to three would you lock the door?
Will you still need me, will you still feed me, when I'm 64?

D - - A / - - - D / - - - G / GBb DB7 E7A D
(capo up)

_Ooh _ _ / You'll be older too
Ah, and if you say the word_ / I could stay with you

Bm BmG A Bm / - - F# - / Bm - Em - / G A D -

I could be handy mending a fuse when your lights have gone
You can knit a sweater by the fireside, Sunday mornings, go for a ride
Doing the garden, digging the weeds, who could ask for more?

Every summer we can rent a cottage in the Isle of Wight if it's not too dear / We shall scrimp & save
Grandchildren on your knee / Vera, Chuck & Dave

Send me a postcard, drop me a line stating point of view
Indicate precisely what you mean to say, yours sincerely wasting away
Give me an answer, fill in a form, mine forevermore...

— John Lennon & Paul McCartney

 — On the Beatles Sgt. Pepper's Lonely Hearts Club Band *& John Denver* Rhymes & Reasons. *In* Club Date FakeB. OT34

Life Stages: On birth see "Isn't She Lovely?" & "Little Brand New Baby" (HOME). HOME & FAMILY and FRIENDSHIP include many songs on childhood & parenting. Songs on courting & marriage are mainly in GOLDEN OLDIES or LOVE. Wedding songs include "Lovely Agnes," "Mairi's Wedding," "Wedding Song" (LOVE) & "Sunrise Sunset" (TIME). HOPE has some particularly good songs dealing with death (eg. "Love Will Guide Us," "Thanksgiving Eve," "Turning toward the Morning"). See also "Will the Cirlce Be Unbroken" (GOSP) "Eleanor Rigby" (HARD) "Danny Boy" (LOVE) "Bright Morning Stars" (MTN), "Gone Gonna Rise Again," & "When I'm Gone" (TIME). "Circle of the Sun" & "Kilkelly" (both in HOME) deal with all of these stages of life.

For other songs on the passage of time, life changes & growing older see: "Thyme" (BALS) "Dancing at Whitsun" (CREAT) "Bring Me a Rose" (FRIEND) "I Wish They'd Do It Now" (FUN) "Jubilee" (GOOD) "Farther Along," "Land Where We'll Never Grow Old," "Precious Memories" (GOSP) "Yesterday" (HARD) "Forty-five Yrs," "Spanish Is the Loving Tongue," "Until It's Time for You to Go" (LOVE) "Ash Grove," "Urge for Going" (OUT) "Times They Are a-Changing" (STRUG) "City of New Orleans" (TRAV) "Old Devil Time" (UNITY) "All Used Up," & "Too Old to Work" (WORK).

Bamboo

You take a stick of bamboo **(3x)** you throw it in the water
O, o, Hannah! (repeat)
River, she comes down (2x)

D C D C / D C D - :|| D C D - / /

You travel on the river **(3x)** you travel on the water/ **O...**

My home's across the river **(3x)** my home's across the water...

— Dave Van Ronk

 — On Peter Paul & Mary *& in their* SB. OY23

Un Canadien Errant

Un Canadien errant banni de ses foyers **(2x)**
Parcourait en pleurant des pays étrangers **(2x)**

(in 3/4) D - - A / /A - - D / G D A D

Un jour trist' et pensif assis au bord des flots **(2x)**
Au courant fugitif, il adressa ces mots: **(2x)**

"Si tu vois mon pays, mon pays malheureux **(2x)**
Va dire á mes amis que je me souviens d'eux" **(2x)**

— w: A. Gerin-LaJoie **— m: trad.**

Words are by a young student shortly after Canada's most serious revolution, the MacKenzie-Papineau Rebellion of 1837, during which several rebels were hanged & many others were exiled or fled to the US. Trans of French: "A Canad exile banished fr home to a foreign land / One sad morning, wandering by the banks of a rushing river, he spoke these words: / 'If you see my homeland that is so troubled, tell my friends I remember them.'" On Ian & Sylvia, their Gr H *&* Best of. *On Ned Bacchus* Raisin d'tre *& Lilianne Labbé & Don Hinkley* Un Canadien Errant. *In* Bells of Rhymney & FS of Canada. OY24

Carolina in My Mind

In my mind I'm gone to Carolina
Can't you see the sunshine
can't you just feel the moon shine?
And ain't it just like a friend of mine
to hit me from behind
Yes, I'm gone to Carolina in my mind

C F G - / F G **(2x)** / C Am F D / C FG C -

Karen she's a silver sun, you'd best
walk her way & watch it shine
Watch her watch the morning come
A silver tear appearin' now I'm cryin', ain't I? / **Gone...**

There ain't no doubt in no one's mind that
love's the finest thing around
Whisper somethin' soft & kind – and
Hey, babe the sky's on fire, I'm dyin', ain't I / **Gone...**

C Bb F G/Am F G -/F Am CD FG/C FG C - :||

Dark & silent late last night, think I
might have heard the highway call
Geese in flight & dogs that bite – and
Signs that might be omens says I'm goin', goin'... / **Goin'...**

(bridge) Now with a holy host of others standin' 'round me
Still I'm on the dark side of the moon
And it seems like it goes on like this forever
You must forgive me if I'm up and / **Gone to...**

F G Am - / Em Dm F G / Bb F C -

Bb Dm F G / C FG C -

— James Taylor

 — On his Sweet Baby James *&* Gr H *& John Denver* Take Me To Tomorrow. Y25

Casey Jones

Come all you rounders if you want to hear
The story of a brave engineer
Casey Jones was the rounder's name
On the "six-eight" wheeler, boys, he won his fame
The caller called Casey at half past four
He kissed his wife at the station door
He mounted to the cabin with the orders in his hand
And he took his farewell trip to that promis'd land

Casey Jones mounted to his cabin
Casey Jones with his orders in his hand
Casey Jones mounted to his cabin
And he took his...land **(last line of each v.)**

A - - - / - - B7 E / A - - - / - - E A :|| 3x

He looked at his water & his water was low
He looked at his watch & his watch was slow
He turned to his fireman & this is what he said
"Boy, we're going to reach Frisco, but we'll all be dead"
He turned to the fireman, said "Shovel on your coal
Stick your head out the window, see the drivers roll
I'm gonna drive her til she leaves the rail
For I'm eight hours late by that Western Mail"

Casey Jones – I'm gonna drive her / ...til she...rail
...I'm gonna... / For I'm eight hours late...Mail

When he pulled up that Reno hill
He whistled for the crossing with an awful shrill
The switchman knew by the engine's moan
That the man at the throttle was Casey Jones
When he was within six miles of the place
There No. 4 stared him straight in the face
He turned to his fireman, said "Jim, you'd better jump
For there're two locomotives that are going to bump"

...two locomotives / ...going to bump
...two locomotives / For there're two...bump

Casey said just before he died
"There're two more roads I would like to ride"
The fireman said "Which ones can they be?"
"O the Northern Pacific & the Santa Fe"
Mrs. Jones sat at her bed a-sighing
Just to hear the news that her Casey was dying
"Hush up children, & quit your cryin'
For you've got another poppa on the Salt Lake Line"

...got another poppa / ...on the Salt Lake Line
...got another poppa / For you've got...Line

— w: T. Lawrence Seibert — m: Eddie Newton

On Dave Van Ronk Somebody Else *(Philo), Pete Seeger* Dangerous S, *Earl Robinson* Strange Unusual Eve, *JE Mainer* V3 *& Grateful Dead* Workingman's Dead. *In* FiresB of FS, *A Lomax* FS of NAm, Best Loved Am FS, Gambit B of Children's S, *Glen Rounds* The Story Of A Brave Engineer, Read 'em & Weep. *See WORK for Joe Hill's parody of this song.* Y26

City of New Orleans

Ridin' on the City of New Orleans
Illinois Central, Monday mornin' rail
15 cars & 15 restless riders
Three conductors, 25 sacks of mail

C G C - / Am F C - / - G C - / Am G C -

All along the southbound odyssey
the train pulls out of Kankakee
Rolls along past houses, farms & fields
Passin' towns that have no name
freight yards full of old Black men
And the graveyards of rusted automobiles

Am - Em - / G - D - / Am - Em - / G - C -

Good mornin' America, how are you?
Don't you know me, I'm your native son?
I'm the train they call the City of New Orleans
I'll be gone 500 miles when the day is done

F G C - / Am F C CG

C G Am D / BbF G C -

Dealin' card games with the old men in the club car
Penny a point, ain't no one keepin' score
Pass the paper bag that holds the bottle
And feel the wheels grumblin' neath the floor

And the sons of Pullman porters & the sons of engineers
Ride their fathers' magic carpet made of steam
Mothers with their babes asleep, rockin' to the gentle beat
And the rhythm of the rails is all they dream

Night time on the City of New Orleans
Changin' cars in Memphis, Tennessee
Halfway home & we'll be there by mornin'
Thru the Mississippi darkness rollin' down to the sea

But all the towns & people seem to fade into a bad dream
And the steel rail still ain't heard the news
The conductor sings his song again
"The passengers will please refrain"
This train has got the disappearin' RR blues
(last cho) Goodnight, **America, how are you?...**

— Steve Goodman

 — On his alb (Buddah), A Guthrie Hobo's Lullaby, *J Collins* Judith *& J Denver* Aerie. *Also on* Best of the '70s *&* Country Gentlemen *(Vang). In SO! 21:3 & 44:4.* Y27

TRAVELING

Coming Home to You

My heart says stop, my heart says go
I see the road & I seem to know
I seem to know just what to do
I'm coming home to you

D - G D / - - - A / D - G D / - A D -

A thousand miles of doubt & pain
Shall I travel it again?
A thousand times I think of you
I hear such music in your name

D - C - / G - - - / D - C - / G - - A - - -

I climb the trees, wade the streams
I heal, yet still I yearn, it seems
My arms reach out as if to you
The lovely birch trees nod & gleam

The woods, they shelter & they snare
Bird wings rustle thru the air
They fly off like I flew from you
But soon return to nestle there

I climb as high as I can go
Upon these rocks, the woods below
At the top I'm free from you
Til I recall your face & know

I know that I can live alone
Out in this place & feel at home
I think I'd like to live with you
My love is yours altho' I've roamed

— **Claudia Schmidt**

© 1981 Flying Fish Music (BMI). Used by permission. On her Midwestern Heart *(FF).* OY28

Daddy, What's a Train?

"Daddy, what's a train? Is it something I can ride?
Does it carry lots of grown up folks & little kids inside?
Is it bigger than our house?" – well, how can I explain
When my little boy asks me, "Daddy, what's a train?"

D G / D EA / D G / D AD

I remember when I was a boy living by the track
Us kids'd gather up the coal in a great big gunny sack
And then we'd hear the warning sound as the train pulled into view
And the engineer would smile & wave as she went rolling thru

(spoken) She blew so loud & clear, that we covered up our ears
And counted cars as high as we could go
I can almost hear the steam & the big old drivers scream
With a sound my little boy will never know

G D / E A / D G / A D

I guess the times have changed & kids are different now
Some don't even seem to know that milk comes from a cow
My little boy can tell the names of all the baseball stars
But I remember how we memorized the names on RR cars

(spoken) The Wabash & T.P., Lackawana & I.C.
Nickel Plate & the good old Santa Fe
Names out of the past, and I know they're fading fast
Every time I hear my son look up & say:

Well we climbed into the car & drove down into town
Right up to the depot house but no one was around
We searched the yard together for something I could show
But I knew there hadn't been a train for a dozen years or so

(spoken) All the things I did when I was just a kid
How far away the memories appear
And it's plain enough to see, they still mean a lot to me
'Cause my ambition was to be an engineer

— **Bruce ("U. Utah") Phillips**

© 1976 On Strike Music. All rights administered by Music Management, P.O. Box 174, Pleasantville NY 10570. Used by permission. — On his Good Though! *(Philo) & in his* Starlight on the Rails. *In* SO! *28:6,* FS Abecedary, & Bluegrass SB. *On Monroe Bros* Feast Here Tonight, *G Carawan* Jubilee *(JuneAppal) & J Glazer* Union Train *(Collector). Also rec by Pete Seeger.* OY29

Dock of the Bay

Sittin' in the mornin' sun
I'll be sittin' when the evenin' comes
Watchin' the ships roll in
And I watch 'em roll away again

Sittin' on the dock of the bay
Watchin' the tide roll away
Sittin' on the dock of the bay / Wastin' time

D F♯ / G E :‖ D B / / D E / D B

I left my home in Georgia / Headed for the Frisco Bay
I have nothin' to live for
Look like nothin's gonna come my way

(interlude) Looks like nothin's gonna change
Everything still remains the same
I can't do what ten people tell me to do
So I guess I'll remain the same

DA G / / / C - A -

Sittin' here restin' my bones
Wish this loneliness would leave me alone
2,000 miles I roam / Just to make this dock my home

— **Otis Redding & Steve Cropper**

© 1968 & 1975 East/Memphis Music & Time Music Co, Inc. All rights for the USA & Canada administered by East/Memphis Music, 8025 Melrose Ave, L.A. CA 90046. International copyright secured. Made in USA. All rights reserved. Used by permission of CPP Belwin Inc. — Rec by Otis Redding & by Bob Gibson. Also on Huston Ives Cisco. *In* FS Abecedary & World's Best Loved S of the '60s. OY30

Done Laid Around

Done laid around, done stayed around this old town too long
Summer's almost gone, summer almost gone
Done laid around, done stayed around this...long
And I feel like I want to travel on

D - - - / - - G D / - - - - / Em A D -

The chilly wind will soon begin & I'll be on my way
Gone a lonesome day, gone a lonesome day
The chilly wind will soon begin...way / **& I feel like...**

There's a lonesome freight at 6:08, coming thru the town
I'll be homeward bound **(2x)** / There's a...

Done hung around & sung around this old town all year
Winter's almost here **(2x)** / Done hung...

— **Paul Clayton, Larry Ehrlich, David Lazar & Tom Six**

© 1958 (renewed) by Sanga Music Inc. All rights reserved. Used by permission. — In SO! *8:1 &* Reprints #3. OY31

Early Morning Rain

In the early mornin' rain with a dollar in my hand
With an achin' in my heart & my pockets full of sand
I'm a long way from home & I miss my loved one so
In the early mornin' rain with no place to go

(in D) A AG D - / Em - D - / Em EmG G D - / 1st /

Out on runway number nine, big "707" set to go
But I'm stuck here on the grass where the cold wind blows
Well the liquor tasted good & the women all were fast
There she goes, my friend, she's rollin' now at last

Hear the mighty engines roar, see the silver wings on high
She's away & westward bound, far above the clouds she'll fly
Where the mornin' rain don't fall & the sun always shines
She'll be flyin' o'er my home in about three hours time

Well this old airport's got me down, it's no earthly good to me
'Cause I'm stuck here on the ground, cold & drunk as I can be
You can't jump a jet plane like you can a freight train
So I best be on my way in the early mornin' rain

— Gordon Lightfoot

 — On his Gord's Gold & Best of. *On Judy Collins* 5th Alb, 10 Yrs & Recollections, *Ian & Sylvia* Early Morning & Best of, *Peter Paul & Mary* See What Tomorrow Brings & Best of, *Dylan* Self Portrait & *Tony Rice* Me & My Guitar. *In* SO! *19:2* & Gr Legal FakeB. **OY32**

The E-ri-ee

We were 40 miles from Albany, forget it I never shall
What a terrible storm we had that night on the E-ri-e Canal

G - GD G / GD GC GD G

O the E-ri-e was a-rising & the gin was getting low
And I scarcely think we'll get a drink
Til we get to Buffalo (2x)

G - GD G / GD GC / GD G / /

We were loaded down with barley, we were chuck up full of rye
And the captain, he looked down at me with his goddamn wicked eye

Our captain, he came up on deck with a spyglass in his hand
And the fog it was so 'tarnal thick that he couldn't spy land

Two days out from Syracuse, the vessel struck a shoal
And we like to all been foundered on a chunk o' Lackawanna coal

We hollered to the captain on the towpath treadin' dirt
He jumped on board & stopped the leak with his old flannel shirt

Our cook she was a grand old gal, she had a ragged dress
We hoisted her upon the pole as a signal of distress

The winds begin to whistle & the waves begin to roll
And we had to reef our royals on the raging Canal

When we got to Syracuse, the off-mule he was dead
The nigh mule got blind staggers & we cracked him on the head

O the girls are in the Police Gazette, the crew are all in jail
And I'm the only living sea cook's son that's left to tell the tale

— trad. (US)

On All Star Hootenanny, *Faith Petric* Sing A S Sing Along *& rec by Burl Ives. In* SFest, S for Pickin & Singin, Treas of FS, FSEncy V2 & FiresB of Fun & Games. **OY33**

The Erie Canal

I've got a mule & her name is Sal
15 miles on the Erie Canal!
She's a good old worker & a good old Pal / **15 miles...**
We've hauled some barges in our day
Filled with lumber coal & hay
And we know every inch of the way / From Albany to Buffalo

Am - Dm E / Am - E Am :|| C - - G
Am - - E / Am - Dm E / Am - E Am G

Low bridge, everybody down
Low bridge, for we're comin' to a town
And you'll always know your neighbor, you'll always know your pal
If you've ever navigated on the Erie Canal

C - - G / C - CG C / C G C G / C F CG C

You'd better get along on your way old Gal / **15...**
You can bet your life I'd never part with Sal / **15...**
Get up there, mule, here comes a lock
We'll make Rome 'fore 6 o'clock
And back we'll go to our home dock
Right back home to Buffalo

— trad. (US)

In SO! *2:2* & Reprints *#4*, Hootenanny SB, SFest, Read 'em & Weep, FSEncyV2 & FiresB of FS. *On J & A Lomax* Am Bals & FS. *On Pete Seeger (& in)* Am Fav Bals, Frontier Bals V1 *(FA2175)* & 50 Sail. *On Weavers* SBag, Gr H & Trav On. **OY34**

Five Hundred Miles

If you miss the train I'm on, you will know that I am gone
You can hear the whistle blow a hundred miles
A hundred miles **(4x)**
You can hear the whistle blow a hundred miles

(in D) I: A D Em G / Em A D - :||

Lord I'm 1, Lord I'm 2, Lord I'm 3, Lord I'm 4
Lord I'm 500 miles away from home
Away from home **(4x)** / Lord I'm... **(repeat 2nd line)**

Not a shirt on my back, not a penny to my name
Lord, I can't go back home this a-way / This a-way **(4x)**...

II: D Bm Em G / Em - A - / 1st / Em AG D -

— Hedy West

 — aka: "Railroader's Lament." In SO! *13:2* & Reprints *#6. On* Peter Paul & Mary, *their* In Conc & 10 Yrs (V. II). *On Country Gentlemen* 25th Anniv *(Rebel)*, *Kingston Trio* College Conc & Fast Folk 3-9. *In* FM Gr H. **OY35**

Four Strong Winds

4 strong winds that blow lonely, 7 seas that run high
All those things that don't change come what may
For our good times are all gone & I'm bound for movin' on
I'll look for you if I'm ever back this way

D Em A D / - Em A - / 1st / G Em A -

Guess I'll go out to Alberta, weather's good there in the fall
Got some friends that I can go to workin' for
Still I wish you'd change your mind if I asked you one more time
But we've been thru that a hundred times before

If I get there 'fore the snow flies & things are goin' good
You could meet me if I sent you down the fare
But by then it would be winter, not too much for you to do
And the winds sure do blow cold way out there

— Ian Tyson

 — On Ian & Sylvia Gr H, 4 Strong Winds & Best of. *On Judy Collins* Living, *Flatt & Scruggs* Changin Times *(CS9596)* & *Tony Rice* Me & My Guitar. *In* The Legal FakeB. **OY36**

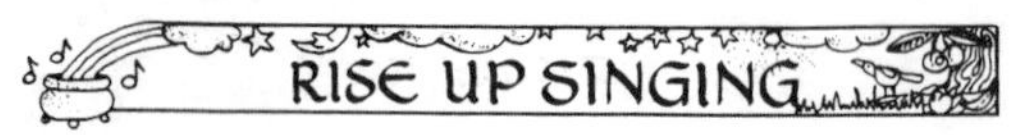

Freight Train

Freight train, freight train, run so fast (2x)
Please don't tell what train I'm on
So they won't know what route I'm gone

C G / - C / E F / CG C

When I'm dead & in my grave
No more good times here I crave
Place the stones at my head & feet
And tell them all that I'm gone to sleep

When I die, Lord, bury me deep
Way down on old Chestnut Street
So I can hear old "No. 9"
As she come rolling by

— Elizabeth Cotten

© Elizabeth Cotten Estate. All rights reserved. — Libba Cotten (as she was known to her friends) composed this song & taught it to the Seegers & other folk artists in the New York area. Some English folksingers learned the song from the latter, adapted it slightly & filed copyright forms for the song. Libba was unable to win the rights back to her song in a court battle on the song in the '50s. On her FS & Instrumentals, When I'm Gone *(FW3537) &* Live *(Arhoolie). On Peter Paul & Mary* In the Wind, *Jim & Jesse* Freight Train, *Baez* V Early, *Happy & Artie Traum* Hard Times, *Patrk Sky* Thru a Window, *New Lost City Ramblers* 20th Anniv Conc *(& in their* SB*), Eve Bluestein* Deep Shady Grove *& on* Bob Dylan. *In* SO! *14:4 &* Reprints *#9,* Bluegrass SB, V Fav of the V Young *&* FS Ency V1. OY37

Goodbye to the Thirty-Foot Trailer

The old ways are changing, ye canna deny
The day o' the traveller's over
There's nowhere to gang & there's nowhere to bide
So fareweel to the life o' the rover

A - - - / - - - E / A E A D / A - E_7 A

(in 3/4)

Goodbye to the tent & the old caravan
To the tinker, the gypsy, the traveling man
And goodbye to the 30 foot trailer

A - D E / / A - E_7 A

Fareweel to the cant & the traveling tongue
Fareweel to the Romany talking
The buying & selling, the old fortune-telling
The knock on the door & the hawking

You've got to move fast to keep up wi' the times
For these days a man canna daunder
There's a bye-law to say ye maun be on your way
And another to say you can't wander

Fareweel to the besoms of heather & broom
Fareweel to the creels & the basket
The folks o' today they would far sooner pay
For a thing that's been made oot o' plastic

The old ways are passing & soon they'll be gone
For progress is aye a big factor
It's sent to afflict us & when they evict us
They tow us away wi' a tractor

Fareweel to the pony, the cob & the mare
The reins & the harness are idle
You don't need the strap when you're breaking up scrap
So fareweel to the bit & the bridle

Fareweel to the fields where we've sweated & toiled
At pu'lin' & shawin' & liftin'
They'll soon hae machines & the travelling quaens
And their menfolk had better be shifting

— Ewan MacColl

© 1964 by Stormking Music Inc. All rights reserved. Used by permission. maun=must, besoms=brushes, brooms, cob=short stocky horse, shawin=showing turnips by removing the foliage & roots, quaens=women & girls. On his & Peggy Seeger Freeborn Man *(Rounder/Blackthorne) & Ian Campbell Folk Gp* Rights of Man. *In* SO! *17:2 &* Reprints *#12.* OY38

Hard Traveling

I been havin' some hard travelin', **I thought you knowed**
I been havin' some hard travelin', **way down the road**
I been doin' some hard travelin', hard ramblin', hard gamblin'
I been havin' *[hittin']* some hard travelin', Lord

D - - - / - - E A / D - G - / D A D -

I been ridin' them fast rattlers, **I thought...**
I been ridin' them flat wheelers, **way down...**
I been ridin' them dead enders, blind passengers, pickin' up cinders / **I been havin' some...**

I been hittin' some hard rock minin'...
I been leanin' on a pressure drill...
Hammer flyin' & air hose suckin', six foot of mud & I sure been a-muckin' & / **I been hittin' some...**

I been workin' that Pittsburgh steel...
I been pourin' that red hot slag...
I been blastin', I been firin', I been duckin' red hot iron...

I been hittin' some hard harvestin'...
North Dakota to Kansas City...
Cuttin' that wheat, stackin' that hay, tryin' to make 'bout a dollar a day...

I been layin' in a hard-rock jail...
I been layin' out 90 days...
Mean old judge, he says to me "90 days for vagrancy"...

I been hittin' that Lincoln Highway...
I been hittin' that "66"...
Heavy load & a worried mind, lookin' for somethin' that's hard to find...

— Woody Guthrie

TRO © 1959 (renewed 1987), 1963 & 1972 Ludlow Music, Inc, NY, NY. International copyright secured. Made in USA. All rights reserved incl. public performance for profit. Used by permission. — On his Hard Trav, Sings FS, Gr S, 1940-46 *& in his* SB. *On (& in) Pete Seeger* Am Fav Bal V2, *Jack Elliott* Talking Woody *&* Sings the S of Guthrie, *Limelighters* Alive V2 *& Kingston Trio* 25 Yrs. *In A Lomax* FS of NAm, S That Changed the World, 50 Yrs of Country M *&* People's SB. *On & in his* Roll on Coumbia. OY39

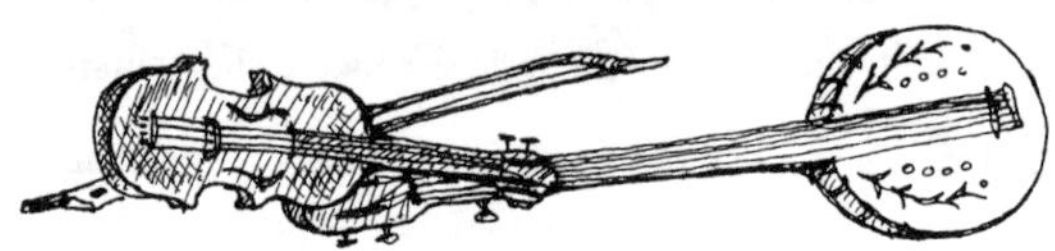

Here's to You Rounders

I never knew my grandad / he was always on the bum
Every September he'd grab him a southbound / & he'd ride
Then along about Christmas, me & my brother
Would get a few coins in the mail
We couldn't spend them, they were all he could send
From the Mexico City jail

C ↓ / FG C / 1st / F G / E_m CE_m / F G / 1st 2

Back in the '30s when the going got rough
Old grandad he hit the road
Mother was young then & only remembers / his name
Then granny got work in the old canning factory
And took in some wash on the side
She promised herself she'd never forgive him
A promise she kept til she died

So here's to you rounders & here's to you RR bums
I hope that you make it home soon
Here's to the women who married for love
And lived with the man in the moon

F C / G C / F C / GF C ↓

One time near the end, he rolled into town
He was riding the Greyhound line
I guess he got old & those boxcars were harder / to climb
He dropped his last dime in a call to my granny
But "No" was her only reply
She hung up the phone, she cussed him in German
But I saw the pain in her eyes

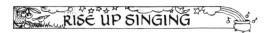

I never knew my grandad / he was always on the bum
The Salvation Army wrote us a note / when he died
Now me & my brother we carry the memory
Of a face we never did see
Like some foreign coin that lies cold in the pocket
Of a young boy's dirty blue jeans

— **Don Lange**

Home Again

Sometimes I wonder if I'm ever gonna make it home again
It's so far & out of sight
I really need someone to talk to & nobody else
Knows how to comfort me tonight
Snow is cold, rain is wet
Chills my soul right to the marrow
I won't be happy til I see you alone again
Til I'm home again & feelin' right

C Cmaj7 - FC / FAm DmF C C(G) :||
Am - C - / F C Dm DmG / 1st 2 /

— **Carole King**

Homeward Bound

I'm sittin' in a railway station, got a
ticket for my destina-/tion
On a tour of one night stands, my suitcase & guitar in hand
And every stop is neatly planned for a poet & a one-man band

G - Bm - / Dm - E - / Am - F - / G - D -

Homeward bound, I wish I / was – homeward bound_
Home – where my thought's escaping
home – where my music's playing
Home – where my love lies waiting silently for me

G - C - / /G Am7 G Am7 / G Am7 D G

Everyday's an endless stream of cigarettes & magazines
And each town looks the same to me, the movies & the factories
And every stranger's face I see reminds me that I long to be

Tonight I'll sing my songs again, I'll play the game & pretend
But all my words come back to me in shades of mediocrity
Like emptiness in harmony, I need someone to comfort me

— **Paul Simon**

I Can't Help But Wonder

It's a long & dusty road, it's a hot & a heavy load
And the folks I meet ain't always kind
Some are bad & some are good
some have done the best they could
Some have tried to ease my troublin' mind

C - FAm Dm / G - C - :||

And I can't help but wonder where I'm bound (2x)
And I can't help but wonder where I'm bound

Dm CG CEm Am / Dm CG C -

I have been around this land just a-doin' the best I can
Tryin' to find what I was meant to do
And the faces that I see are as worried as can be
And it looks like they are wonderin' too

I had a little gal one time, she had lips like sherry wine
And she loved me til my head went plumb insane
But I was too blind to see, she was driftin' away from me
And one day she left on the morning train

I've got a buddy from home but he started out to roam
And I hear he's out by Frisco Bay
And sometimes when I've had a few
his voice comes singin' thru
And I'm goin' out to see him some old day

If you see me passing by & you sit & wonder why
And you wish that you were a rambler, too
Nail your shoes to the kitchen floor
lace 'em up & bar the door
Thank your stars for the roof that's over you

— **Tom Paxton**

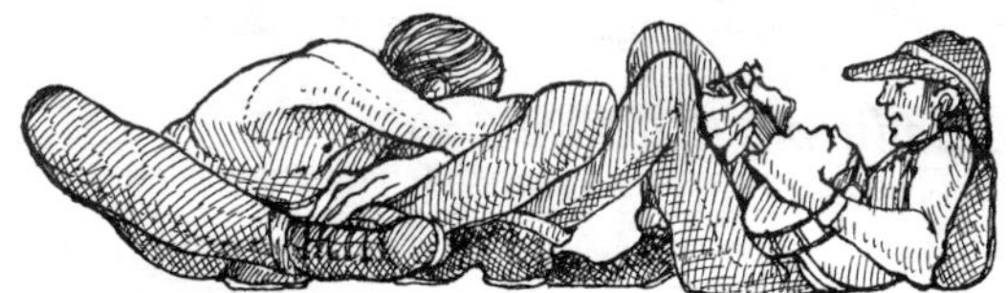

Lonesome Traveler

I am a lonely & a lonesome traveler **(3x)**
And I'm a-travelin' on

(capo up) Am - - - / Dm - Am - / 1st / Dm E Am -

I traveled cold & then I traveled hungry **(3x) / & I'm...**
I traveled with the rich man & traveled with the poor man...
Gonna keep on a-travelin' on the road to freedom...
One of these days I'm gonna stop all my travelin'...

— **Lee Hays**

The Motorcycle Song

I don't want a pickle, just want to ride on my motorsickle
And I don't want to tickle, I'd rather ride on my motorsickle
And I don't want to die, just want to ride on my motorcy-cle

G - - - G CG G - / /
CG Cmaj7G G - G C G -

Late last night the other day I thought I'd go up & see Ray
So I went up & I saw Ray, there was only one thing
Ray could say was:

G - - - - - - - / /

Late last week I was on my bike, run into a friend named Mike
I run into a friend named Mike, Mike no longer has a bike
he cries:

— **Arlo Guthrie**

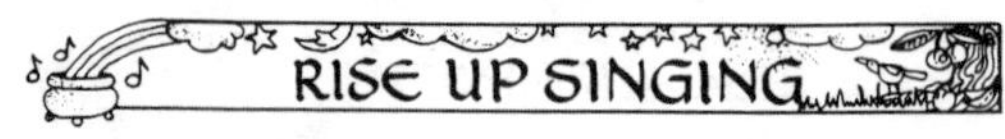

One More Step

One more step along the world I go **(2x)**
From the old things to the new
Keep me traveling along with you

D - A - / - - D - / - - G D / - A DG D

And it's from the old I travel to the new
Keep me traveling along with you

F#m G - D / - A DG D

'Round the corners of the earth I turn
More & more about the world I learn
All the new things that I see
You'll be looking at along with me

As I travel thru the bad & good
Keep me traveling the way I should
Where I see no way to go
You'll be telling me the way, I know

Give me courage when the world is rough
Keep me loving tho' the world is tough
Leap & sing in all I do / **Keep me traveling...you**

You are older than the world can be
You are younger than the life in me
Ever old & ever new / **Keep me...**

— Sydney Carter

 — In his Green Print for Song. OY46

Paddy on the Railway

In 18 hundred & 41
I put me corduroy breeches on
I put me corduroy breeches on
To work upon the railway

Filly-me-oori-oori-ay *[Patsy-ori-ori-ay]* **(3x)**
To work upon the railway **(last line of each v.)**

I: Em - / D - / Em - / EmD Em

In 18 hundred & 42
I left the Old World for the new
Bad cess to the luck that brought me thru
To work upon the railway

When Pat left Ireland to come here
And spend his latter days in cheer
His bosses they did drink strong beer
While Pat worked on the railway

It's "Pat, do this!" & "Pat, do that!"
Without a stocking or cravat
And nothing but an old straw hat
To work upon the railway

And when Pat lays him down to sleep
The wiry bugs around him creep
And the divil a bit can poor Pat sleep
While working upon the railway

In 18 hundred & 43
'Twas then I met sweet Biddy McGee
And an ilegant wife she's made for me
While working on the railway

In 18 hundred & 46
They pelted me with stones & sticks
And I was in wan hell of a fix
From working on the railway

In 18 hundred & 47
Sweet Biddy she died & went to Heaven
If she left one child, she left 11
To work upon the railway

In 18 hundred & 48
I learned to take me whisky straight
'Tis an elegant drink & can't be bate
For working on the railway

II: D - / A - / D - / A D :II

— trad. (US)

aka: "Patsy-ori-ori-ay." On Sam Hinton The Real McCoy *(Decca). In* S Fest & FiresB of FS. OY47

Rock Island Line

I say, the Rock Island Line is a mighty good road
I say, the Rock Island Line is the road to ride
O the Rock Island Line is a mighty good road
If you want to ride you got to ride it like you find it
Get your ticket at the station on the Rock Island Line

G - - - / - - A D / 1st / C7 - G - / D - - G - - -

Jesus died to save our sins
Glory be to God, gonna need him again

G - - - / D - - G

A-B-C, double X-Y-Z
Cat's in the cupboard but he can't see me

Little Evelina sitting in the shade
Figuring on the money I ain't made

I may be right & I may be wrong
I know you're gonna miss me when I'm gone

— new w & m arrangement by Huddie Ledbetter

— edited with new addl material by Alan Lomax

 — On Leadbelly's Rock Island Line. *On Weavers* At Carnegie Hall, Reunion at Carnegie Hall pt2 & Gr H. *On Jack Elliott* Hootenanny & *Grandpa Jones* Rollin Along. *In* SO! *2:8, 44:4 &* Reprints *#3,* Golden Ency of FS, Gr Legal FakeB, 1001 Jumbo S & S Am Sings. OY48

Sailing Down this Golden River

Sailing down this golden river, sun & water all my own
  Yet I was never alone
Sun & water old life givers, I'll have you where'ere I roam
  And I was not far from home

D Bm Em A / D EmA D - :II

Sunlight glancing on the water, life & death are all my own
  Yet I was never alone
Life to raise my sons & daughters, golden sparkles in the foam / **And I was not far from home**

Sailing down my winding highway, travelers from near & far
  Yet I was never alone
Exploring all the little byways, sighting all the distant stars / **And I was not far from home**

— Pete Seeger

 On his Rainbow Race & Circles & Seasons. *In his* WHATFG *& on* WHATFG & Seeds (S. of Pete Seeger v.3). OY49

Starlight on the Rails

I can hear the whistle blowing
High & lonesome as can be
Outside the rain is softly falling
Tonight it's falling just for me

C G / - C / F C / G C

Looking back along the road I've travelled
The miles can tell a million tales
Each year is like some rolling freight train
And cold as starlight on the rails

G C / / CF C / G C

I think about a wife & family
My home & all the things it means
The black smoke trailing out behind me
Is like a string of broken dreams

A man who lives out on the highway
Is like a clock that can't tell time
A man who spends his life just ramblin'
Is like a song without a rhyme

— Bruce ("Utah") Phillips

© Scruggs Music. Used by permission. — On his Good Though! *(Philo) & in* Starlight on the Rails. *On Rosalie Sorrels* If I Could Be the Rain. OY50

Thirsty Boots

You've long been on the open road, you've been sleepin' in the rain
From the dirt of words & mud of cell, your clothes are dark and stained
But the dirty words & muddy cells will soon be judged insane
So only stop & rest yourself til you'll be off again

C ↓ F G / C ↓ Dm G / 1st / C FC Dm G -

Then take off your thirsty boots & stay for awhile
Your feet are hot & weary from a dusty mile
And maybe I can make you laugh, maybe if I try
I'm just lookin' for the evenin' & the mornin' in your eyes

C F C F / C ↓ Dm G / 1st / C ↓ Dm G C -

But tell me of the ones you saw as far as you could see
Across the plain from field to town a-marchin' to be free
And of the rusted prison gates that tumbled by degree
Like laughin' children one by one who looked like you & me

I know you are no stranger down the crooked rainbow trails
From dancing cliff-edged shattered sills of slander shackled jails
But the voices drift up from below as the walls they're being scaled
All of this & more my friend, your song shall not be failed

— Eric Anderson

© 1965 United Artists Music Co., Inc. International copyright secured. Made in USA. All rights reserved. Used by permission of CPP Belwin Inc. — On his 'Bout Changes 'n Things Best S & Best of. *On John Denver* I Want to Live *& Judy Collins* 5th Alb *& in her* SB. *In* SO! *16:1 & Reprints #10.* OY51

Truck Drivin' Woman

You see me on the highway & you nearly shift your load
You take another look good buddy & you nearly leave the road
Ain't you never seen a truck drivin' woman
90 lbs. of fire in a 5 foot frame
And you better move on over
'Cause I'm right behind you in the left-hand lane

D - - -/- - - D7/G7 -/- - D -/A -/G - D - (A -)

You see me at the truck stop & my long hair hangs in curls
Don't you try to buy my coffee 'cause I ain't no good time girl
I'm a truck drivin' mama
Children waiting when I end my run
And I got to get moving
Got to be in Georgia with the rising sun

So when you see me on the highway & you hear my diesel moan
Don't you whistle at me buddy 'cause you know I'm not alone
I got my man *[a woman]* beside me
Working together, that's the way we feel
I'm a truck drivin' woman
Night haul from Pittsburgh with a load of steel

— Si Kahn

© Joe Hill Music (ASCAP). All rights reserved. Used by permission. — On his New Wood, *Judy Gorman-Jacobs* Right Behind You...Lane *(OneSky), Cathy Winter & Betsy Rose* As Strong As Anyone Can Be *(GW), Bobbie McGee* Bread & Raises *& Bright Morning Star* Arisin. *In* Here's to the Women. OY52

Wabash Cannonball

By the great Atlantic Ocean on the wide Pacific shore
Heard the Queen of flowing mountains to the South Belle by the shore
She's long, tall & handsome, she's loved by one & all
She's a modern combination called the Wabash Cannonball

E - - A / B7 - - E :||

Listen to the jingle, the rumble & the roar
Riding thru the woodlands, thru the hills & by the shore
Hear the mighty rush of engines, hear the lonesome hobo squall
Riding thru the jungles on the Wabash Cannonball

Now the eastern states are dandies so the western people say
From New York to St. Louis & Chicago by the way
Thru the hills of Minnesota where the rippling waters fall
No chances can be taken on the Wabash Cannonball

Here's to Daddy Claxton, may his name forever stand
And will he be remembered thru parts of all our land
When his earthly race is over & the curtain round him falls
We'll carry him on to victory on the Wabash Cannonball

— trad. (USA – hobo song)

In SO! *16:4 & Reprints #11, Phillips* Starlight on the Rains, S for Pickin & Singin, *A Lomax* FS of NAm, *BA Botkin* Lay My Burden Down, *V Randolph* Ozark FS & FSEncyV2. *On Pete Seeger (& in)* Am Fav Bals V1 *(FW2320) & his* Prec Friend *(w Arlo Guthrie). On Carter Fam* The Orig & Great & Clinch Mtn Bals *(Pine Mtn), Phillips* Good Though! *(Philo), Doc Watson* Memories & On Stage, *Jack Elliott* Country Style, *B Oswald & C Collins* That's Country, *Art Thieme* On the Wilderness Rd, *Jean Richie & Doc Watson* At Folk City. OY53

Wanderin'

My daddy is an engineer, my brother drives a hack
My sister takes in washin' & the baby balls the jack
And it looks like I'm never gonna cease my wanderin'

C - Em - / Am - F G // C - Em - F G C -

My daddy longs to see me home, my brother'd share his bed
My sister yearns for me to have a roof above my head

I've been wandering early & late
From Singapore to the Golden Gate

I've worked on freighters & I worked on a farm
And all I got to show for it is the muscles in my arm

There's snakes on the mountain & eels in the sea
I let a red headed woman make a fool out of me

— trad. (US) adap by Sammy Kaye

© 1950 by Republic Music Corp. Copyright renewed 1977 by World Music Inc. PO Box 1319, Fair Lawn NJ 07410. International copyright secured. All rights reserved. Used by permission. — "Balls the jack" = an early jazz step. This evolved out of a much older song "My Father's Lawyer". In Sandburg Am SBag 1927, *A Lomax* FS of NAm & FSEncyV2. *On Josh White* Live!, *Earl Robinson* Strange Unusual Eve *& Dave Van Ronk* Just Dave. OY54

Wild Rover

I've played the wild rover for many a year
I've spent all my money on whiskey & beer
Now I'll save up my wages, keep money in store
And I never will play the wild rover no more

D A D G / D A7 - D :||

And it's no, nay, never / No, nay never, no more
For I've played the wild rover / But I'll never, no more

A7 - - - / D - G - / /D A7 D -

I went to an alehouse where I used to frequent
I told the landlady my money was spent
I asked her to trust me, her answer was "Nay
Such a custom as yours we can get any day"

Then out of my pockets I took sovereigns bright
And the landlady's eyes opened wide with delight
She said "I have whiskeys & wines of the best
And the words that I said, sure were only in jest"

"You can keep all your whiskey & your beer likewise too
For not another penny am I spending with you
For the money I've got, I'm taking good care
And I never will play the wild rover no more"

Now if I had all the money that I left in your care
It would plough all my lands & my family rear
It would thatch all my houses, it would build me a barn
It would buy me a coat for to keep my back warm

I'll go home to my parents & I'll tell what I've done
And I'll ask them to pardon their prodigal son
And if they forgive me, as they've oft done before
O it's ne'er will I play the wild rover no more

— trad. (Australian / Irish)

The above verses fit several rather different versions of the melody. These chords & chorus are from the variant found in the Clancy Bros. Irish SB, *on their* In Ireland & Gr H *& on Burl Ives* Men. *Also in* SO! *10:1 (version fr the singing of A.L. Lloyd) &* Reprints #8, Wind That Shakes the Barley & Dubliners SB. *On Irish Tradition* The Times We've Had *(GreenLinnet), Judy Small* Reunion, *& John Faulkner* Kind Providence *(GreenLinnet).* OY55

Willin'

I been warped by the rain, drivin' by the snow
I'm drunk & dirty don't you know
That I'm still — willin'

I was out on the road late at night
I seen my pretty Alice in every headlight
Alice — Dallas Alice

G D / Em C / G C G (D) :||

I've been from Tucson to Tucumcari, Tehatchapi to Tonapah
Drivin' every kind of rig that's ever been made
Driven the back roads so I wouldn't get weighed
And if you give me weed, whites & wine, & show me a sign
I'll be willing to be moving

C D - G / - - C - / - - D -
C D G - D - / G C G (GD)

I've been kicked by the wind, robbed by the sleet
Had my head stoved in, but I'm still on my feet
And I'm still — willing

I smuggled some smokes & folks from Mexico
Baked by the sun every time that I go
To Mexico — and I'm still

— Lowell George

 — On Little Feat *& their* Dixie Chicken *&* Waiting for Columbus. *On Linda Ronstadt* Heart Like a Wheel *& Jim Ringer* Good to get Home *(Philo).* OY56

You Were on My Mind

Woke up this morning, you were on my mind
And you were on my mind
Got some aches & got some pains &
Got some wounds to bind

I: C FG CG G / F C G - / CF (2x) / CF C G -

Went to the corner, just to ease my pain
It was just to ease my pain
I got drunk & I got sick &
I came home again

I got a feelin' down in my shoes
It's a way down in my shoes
Got to move on, got to travel
Walk away my blues

II: C FG CG FG / F Em Dm G / C FG (2x) / C G -

— Sylvia Fricker

 — On Ian & Sylvia Northern Journey, Best of & You Were On My Mind. *In* Gr FSingers of the '60s. *Version II adapted by We Five.* OY57

There are a number of hobo & other travel songs in RICH & POOR. Other travel or transportation-related songs include: "America" [Simon] (AMER) "Come Take a Trip in My Airship" (DREAM) "Rivers of Babylon" (FREE) "Moon River," "My Rambling Boy" (FRIEND) "Traveling Man" (FUN) "It's a Long Long Way to Tipperary," "Keep the Home Fires Burning" (GOLD) "Rambling Rover" (GOOD) "Life is Like a Mtn RR" (GOSP) "House of the Rising Sun" (HARD) "Back Home Again" (HOME) "Spanish is the Loving Tongue" (LOVE) "Hobo's Lullaby" (LULL) "Jenny's Gone Away," "My Home's Across the Blue Ridge Mtns" (MTN) Happy Wanderer (OUT) "I've Been Workin' on the RR," "Ridin' in my Car" (PLAY) "Down at the Station," "To Stop the Train" (ROUND) "Babylon" (SACR) "Amelia Earhart" (WOMEN) & "Drill Ye Tarriers" (WORK).

Because All Men Are Brothers

Because all men are brothers, wherever men may be
And women all are sisters, forever proud & free
No tyrant shall defeat us, no nation strike us down
And all who toil shall greet us the whole wide world around

(TD ↑ 6) F Dm G C Am E Am / /
F G F C F Dm A - / G Am D G F G C -

My brothers & my sisters, forever hand in hand
Where chimes the bell of freedom, there is my native land
My brothers' fears are my fears, yellow, white or brown
My sisters' tears are my tears, the whole wide world around

Let every voice be thunder, let every heart be strong
Until all tyrants perish, our work will not be done
Let every pain be token, the lost years shall be found
Let slavery's chains be broken, the whole wide world around

— w: Tom Glazer — m: J.S. Bach ("Passion Chorale")

 — aka: "The Whole Wide World Around." Chorale is fr St Matthews Passion. These adapted lyrics are by the author. Tune can be found in hymnals as "O Sacred Head Now Wounded." On Peter Paul & Mary See What Tomorrow Brings. OU01

Christmas Morning

It's winter & light is alive on the Earth
Wake up! It's Christmas morning
Starlight & firelight & sunlight give birth
Wake up! The Christ child's a-borning

Dm A Dm A / Dm A Dm - :||

He's man & he's woman, he's old & he's young
He's Buddhist & Christian & Jew
She's wealthy, she's poor & she's black & she's white
And o yes, the Christ child is you

F - A - / Dm Gm Dm - / - A Dm A / Dm A Dm -

Sisters & brothers, whatever your sleep / **Wake up...**
Bring with you dreams for the daylight to keep / **Wake...**

Jesus was good & he lived long ago...
You are good too & are living now so...

— Carol Bemmels & Ross Flanagan

 — In S of the Spirit & S On Our Way Out. *On* Sounds Good *(tape).* OU02

The Color Song

Why do they call you yellow man? You're not yellow at all
Yellow is the color of the morning sun & dandelions & chicken soup & legal pads & fearful minds
Yes yellow is the color of all these things but people are not the same
You remind me of the Golden Rule **whenever I say your name-o**
Bum bumbum bum bum (4x)

C - FC G / FC C - - - - CG G
C - - G / C - F FG / CG (4x)

Why do they call you red man? You're not red at all
Red is the color of the climbing rose & traffic lights & tomatoes & chickenpox & bloody nose & angry words
Yes red **is the color of all these things but people...same**
I can see the rosy future **whenever I say your name-o...**

Why do they call you black man?...
Black is the color of light not there & Daddy's shoes & Mommy's hair & bowling balls & question marks & blind despair / **Yes black is the color...**
I have had the deepest thoughts **whenever...**

Why do they call you white man?...
White is the color of petticoats & Elmer's glue & billy goats & falling snow & burning shame / **Yes white is...**
I have seen the clearest light **whenever...**

So what do you call your fellow man if color doesn't matter at all?
Anything! so long as it's in the name of love & forgiveness & hopefulness & lasting peace & dignity & brotherhood
For many are the colors of all these things but people...
We're each others' brothers & sisters & we all have one...

— Patricia Shih

 On her 7x1 *(c/o author, 27 Oakland St, Huntington NY 11743), John Bell* Deep Blue Sea, *Gail Rundlett* Just in Time. *In* SO! *31:1* & Broadside *#158.* OU03

Common Thread

In a many colored garden we are growing side by side
We will rise all together, we will rise
With the sun & rain upon us, not a row will be denied
We will rise all together, we will rise
We will rise like the ocean, we will rise like the sun
We will rise all together... (repeat after each line)
In our many colored fabrics, made from strands of common thread / **We will...rise!**

D D7 G Bm / G D Asus A / 1st / G A D -
D - G D / " / D D7 G Bm / " /

We can feed our grain to cattle, & the rich man will be fed
We will rise...
Or we'll feed our grain to people so that millions will have bread / **We will rise...**
We will rise like the ocean, we will rise like the sun...
No more will there be hunger in these strands of common thread...

In the cold of fear and hatred clothed in dignity we stand
We have pieced this quilt together linking hearts with stitching hands
We will rise like the ocean...sun / We are spirits drawn together tightly by our common threads

From our children to our elders, from all nations, we will rise
May respect for all our differences enhance our common ties
We...ocean...sun / We will build a global family strengthened by our common threads

— Pat Humphries

 On her Same Rain *(Moving Forward Music) & in* SO! *33:1.* OU04

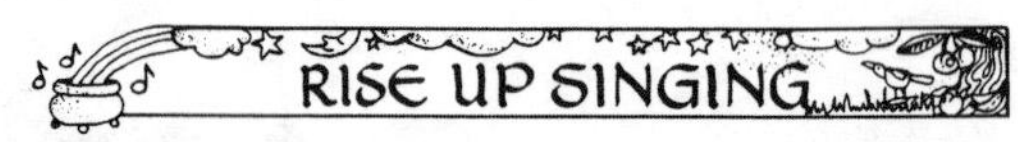

Everything Possible

We have cleared off the table, the leftovers saved
Washed the dishes & put them away
I have told you a story & tucked you in tight
At the end of a knockabout day
As the moon sets its sails to carry you to sleep
Over the midnight sea
I will sing you a song no one sang to me
May it keep you good company

(in D) A - G D / A G D - / A - Bm - / C - A -

D - G D / G Em A - / D G D G / D A G -

You can be anybody you want to be
You can love whomever you will
You can travel any country where your heart leads
And know I will love you still
You can live by yourself, you can gather friends around
You can choose one special one
And the only measure of your words & your deeds
Will be the love you leave behind when you're done

D A G A/G A D - :‖ - Bm Em A/G Em A -/ 1st 2

There are girls who grow up strong & bold
There are boys quiet & kind
Some race on ahead, some follow behind
Some go in their own way & time
Some women love women, some men love men
Some raise children, some never do
You can dream all the day never reaching the end
Of everything possible for you

(bridge) Don't be rattled by names, by taunts, by games
But seek out spirits true
If you give your friends the best part of yourself
They will give the same back to you

Bm - F♯ -/ G - D -/G - F♯m -/Em G Em A

— **Fred Small**

© 1983 Pine Barrens Music (BMI). All rights reserved. Used by permission. "A lesbian friend asked me to write a song she could sing to her 9-year old son. This is it." On his "No Limit" & in his Breaking fr the Line. *On Fink & Marxer* Nobody Else Like Me. *In* SO! *37:4.* OU05

Friends Forever

It's a jigsaw puzzle world with walls & borders
Broken lines on maps of men
But the world is just one place & all the strangers on its face
Belong to God – who calls us to be friends

G - C - / D C G - / - - C - / G CD G -

And we are friends forever, we are friends forever
And our work on Earth is just begun
Thru the pain & pleasure we will stand together
We are friends forever, we are one

C D Em C / Am D G - / C D Em G / C D G -

All the barbwire in the world cannot divide us
Only fear can build a fence
So a spirit that can reach across the fence around us each
Is sent from God, so we can live as friends

It's a simple faith that binds us all together
With a love that never ends
And together we will join our hands & reach around the world
We are the Lord's & we shall live as friends

— **John W. Carter**

© 1985 John W. Carter. Used by permission. — On his Rise Up. *On & in* Go Cheerfully *(cassette & SB pub by Friends United Press).* OU06

Gay Spirit

When we were born they tried to cover our eyes
Then they tried to tell us all what to see
We are discovering that did not work
For we were born to be free

(in C) G FC / G F :‖

There's a gay spirit singing in our hearts
Leading us thru these troubled times
There's a gay spirit moving 'round this land
Calling us to a time of open love

F Am / Dm G / F Am / Dm G F C

When we were born they tried to put us in a cage
And tell our bodies what to feel
But we have chosen to feel all the truth
That our bodies do reveal

You run & tell those old patriarchs
We're no longer blind to their ways
Run & tell them we've stolen the keys
To the prison they have made

Sometimes it gets too hard to feel the joy
In the face of all the pain we see
But there's a healing place within our hearts
It's coming alive in you & me

— **Charlie Murphy**

© 1981 Charlie Murphy (BMI) Used by permission. — On his Catch the Fire *& Bright Morning Star* Live in the US. OU07

I'm a Little Cookie

I'm a little cookie, **yes I am, I was made by the** cookie **man**
On my way from the cookie pan, a li'l piece broke offa me
A li'l piece broke offa me, **uh-huh (2x)**
But I can taste just as good, uh-huh, as a regular cookie **can**

A7 - D - / A7 - - D / 1st / GDdim DB7 EA D

I'm a little chocolate bar, **yes I am, I was made by the** chocolate **man**
On my way to the chocolate stand, I got a little bend in me
Got a li'l bend in me, **uh-huh (2x)**
But I can taste just as good, uh-huh, as a regular chocolate **can**

I'm a little Tootsie Roll, **yes...**Tootsie Roll **man**
On my way from Tootsie Roll Land, I got a little twist in me...

I'm a little gum drop, **yes...by the** gum drop **man**
On my way from the sugar can, I got a li'l dent in me...

I'm a little cookie... / ...pan, a li'l piece broke offa me
Now I'm not as round as I might be
but I taste good, just wait & see! and
I can love back just twice as hard as a regular cookie can

— **Larry Penn**

TRO © 1978 & 1984 Devon Music Inc., NY, NY. International copyright secured. Made in USA. All rights reserved incl. public performance for profit. Used by permission. — On his I'm a Little Cookie *(Collector1937),* Am Melody *(AM103) & in* SB Treasure & Blues. *On Peter Alsop* Take Me With You *(MooseSch) &* Take Me with You, *Claudia Schmidt* New Goodbyes & Old Helloes *(FF),* Ginni Clemens *(FF), Musical Friends* All Together *(GW), P Alsop* Take Me With You, *Cathy Finke* Granda's Patchwork Quilt & Swords Into Plowshares *(FTrad) & on John McCutcheon* Family Garden. *In* SO! Bulletin *Dec '82.* OU08

In Christ There Is No East Nor West

In Christ there is no East or West
In him no South or North
But one great fellowship of love
Thru out the whole wide earth

F - G C / Dm F G - / F G C Am / Dm G C -

In him shall true hearts ev'rywhere
Their high communion find
His service is the golden cord
Close binding all mankind *[our kind]*

Join hands then, brothers *[people]* of the faith
What e'er your race may be
Who serves my Father as a son *[Christ as a child of God]*
Is surely kin to me

In Christ now meet both East & West
In him meet South & North
All Christly souls are one in him
Thru out the whole wide earth

— w: John Oxenham, 1908 — m: Alexander R Reinagle, 1836
In hymnals. OU09

In the Very Middle

In the very middle you're a lot like me
A shining personality
The clothes & the skin are just a coverin'
In the very middle you're a lot like me

C GC :|| **(4x)**

God made souls * 1, 2, 3 * / Loved 'em all * equally *
Souls need homes * like bodies do * / One got me *
one got you * and: **(*=echo after each phrase in verses)**

C - Dm - / G - C - / 1st / G - - -

Some got castles, some got shacks
Some got dresses, some got slacks
Some got white, some got black
But the most important fact, is:

Royal blue, army green / Rhinestone cowboy, disco queen
Hula skirts, denim jeans / Not so different as it seems &

It helps me not to be afraid
Knowing we're so much the same
The road we take leads to the stars
We're just driving different cars, and

— Carol Johnson
 On her Isn't It Good To Know. OU10

Let's Get Together

Love is but a song we sing, fear's the way we die
You can make the mountains ring or make the angels cry
Tho' the bird is on the wing & you may not know why
C'mon people now, smile on your brother
Ev'rybody get together, try to love one another, right now!

D - - C / / // G A / D GA D -

Some will come & some will go, we shall surely pass
When the one that left us here, returns for us at last
We are but a moment's sunlight, fading in the grass

If you hear the song I sing, you will understand
You hold the key to love & fear in your trembling hand
Just one key unlocks them both, it's there at your command

— Chet Powers
 — Rec by the Youngbloods. On Indigo Girls Strange Fire. OU11

Little Bit of Light

I've got some of the light in me
You've got some of the light in you
And a little bit of light from everyone
Is enough to see us thru

(in C) C Dm / DmG C / F C / F G

Substitute: truth, love

(bridge) There is nobody with a handle on it all
No one place the answers can be found
But everybody has a gift & everyone can share
Put them all together, we can turn this world around

F G C Am / F G C - / 1st / Dm F Dm G

— Carol Johnson
 — aka: "I've Got Some Of The Light." On her Might As Well Make It Love. *In* Children's S for a Friendly Planet. OU12

Magic Penny

Love is something if you give it away
Give it away, give it away
Love is something if you give it away
You end up having more

D - / A D :||

It's just like a magic penny
Hold it tight & you won't have any
Lend it, spend it & you'll have so many
They'll roll all over the floor, for

G D / A D / G D / E A

Money's dandy & we like to use it
But love is better if you don't refuse it
It's a treasure & you'll never lose it
Unless you lock up your door, for

So let's go dancing til the break of day
And if there's a piper we can pay
For love is something if you give it away
You end up having more

(this v. only:) G D / A D :||

Food tastes better if you pass it around
Pass it around, pass it around
Food tastes...around / It always seems like more!

It's just like a loaf of rye bread
Hold it tight & it ends up dry bread
Pass it around & it ends up inside bread
Til everybody's full!

— Malvina Reynolds (new cho. & v. Wayne Lauser)
 — In her SB , Little Boxes *& on her* Held Over & Sings the Truth. *On Sally Rogers* Peace by Peace *(KidsRecs), Tickle Tune Typhoon "Circle Around", Fred Holstein "Holstein" & Bluestein Fam* Horse Named Bill *(Greenhays). In* SO! *5:4,* S of the Spirit, Quaker SB & A Time for Singing. OU13

The More We Get Together

The more we get together, together, together
The more we get together, the happier we'll be!
For your friends are my friends & my friends are your friends
The more we get together, the happier we'll be!

(in 3/4) D - A D / / A D A D / 1st /

— trad.
On Raffi Singable S for the V Young. OU14

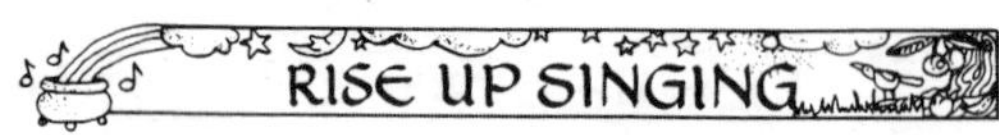

Old Devil Time

Old Devil Time I'm gonna fool you now
Old Devil Time you'd like to bring me down
When I'm feelin' low, **my lovers gather round**
And help me rise to fight you one more time!

C D G - / CD G D - / 1st / C D G (CD G -)
(in 6/8)

Old Devil Fear, you with your icy hands
Old Devil Fear, you'd like to freeze me cold
But when I'm afraid, **my lovers gather round...**

Old Devil Pain, you often pinned me down
You thought I'd cry & beg you for the end
But at that very time, **my lovers...**

Old Devil Hate, I knew you long ago
Then I found out the poison in your breath
Now when we hear your lies, **my lovers...**

No storm or fire can ever beat us down
No wind that blows but carries us further on
And you who fear, o lovers, gather round
And we can rise to sing it one more time!

— **Pete Seeger**

© 1969, 1970 Fall River Music, Inc. & Sigma Productions. All rights reserved. Used by permission. — Composed for the Otto Preminger movie Tell Me That You Love Me Junie Moon. *On his* Rainbow Race *& his* Sing Along Demonstration Conc *& Claudia Schmidt* New Goodbyes Old Hellos. *In his* Where Have All the Flowers Gone, SO! *19:5 &* Survival SB. *On Kim & Reggie Harris'* Guide My Feet *&* S of Pete Seeger V.2. *Pat Humphries rec on* S of Pete Seeger V.3. ©U15

One Man's Hands

Just my hands can't tear a prison down
Just your hands can't tear a prison down
But if two & two & fifty make a million
We'll see that day come round (2x)

C - G - / - - C - / F - C / G Am / F G C -

Just my voice can't shout to make them hear
Just your voice can't shout to make them hear...

(additional verses – for as many good causes as time permits!)
Just my strength can't ban the atom bomb...
Just my strength can't break the color bar...
Just my feet can't walk around this land...
Just my hands can't build a bridge of peace...
Just my heart can't turn this world to love...
Just my eyes can't see the way *[road]* ahead...

— **m: Pete Seeger orig. lyrics: Alex Comfort**
— **new lyrics adapted by Pete Seeger and Alice & Staughton Lynd**

© 1962 Fall River Music Inc. All rights reserved. Used by permission. — These lyrics have been adapted by Alice & Staughton Lynd and Pete Seeger and are included here in this version at Mr. Seeger's request. In SO! *12:2 &* Reprints #5, WHATFG, Bells of Rhymney, Sing for Freedom, How Can We Keep fr Singing, S of the Spirit, Children's S for a Friendly Planet *&* Quaker SB. ©U16

A Place in the Choir *(All God's Critters)*

All God's critters got a place in the choir
Some sing low, some sing higher
Some sing out loud on the telephone wire and
Some just clap their hands or paws or anything they got now

E - / B7 E / A AE / EB7 E - (verse is only: EB7 E)

Listen to the bass, it's the one on the bottom
Where the bullfrog groans & the hippopotamus
Moans & groans with a big to-do
The old cow just goes moo

The dogs & the cats they take up the middle
The hummingbird hums & the cricket fiddles
The donkey brays & the pony neighs
And the old coyote howls

Listen to the top where the little birds sing
On the melody with the high note ringing
The hoot owl hollers over everything
And the jay bird disagrees

Singing in the nighttime, singing in the day
The little duck quacks & is on his way
The possum ain't got much to say
And the porcupine talks to himself

It's a simple song, a living song everywhere
By the ox & the fox & the grizzly bear
The grumpy alligator & the hawk above
The sly raccoon & the turtle dove

— **Bill Staines**

© Mineral River Music (BMI). Used by permission. — On his Bridges, The Whistle of the Jay *& in his* If I Were A Word, *J McCutcheon* Howjadoo, *Bright Morning Star* Live in the US, *Susan Stark* Rainbow People. *Also on* Going to the Zoo, Peace Gathering S *(NSL) &* All Together *(GW). In* SO! *44:4,* Sing the Good Earth, V Fav of the V Young *&* Children's S for a Peaceful Planet. ©U17

Reach Out and Touch Somebody's Hand

Reach out & touch somebody's hand
Make this world a better place if you can (repeat)

(in 3/4) Am7 Dm7 G Cmaj7 / Am7 Dm7 G C / 1st / Am7 Dm7 G Em7 (last cho add: Am7 Dm7 - - Cmaj7)

(Just try) Take a little time out of your busy day
To give encouragement to someone who's lost the way
(Just try) Or would I be talking to a stone
If I asked you to share a problem that's not your own
(We can change things if we start giving, why don't you)

Em7 Am7 Cmaj7 F / Faug F6 Dm7 Em / " / Faug F6 Dm7 Gm7 A7 // C7 F Am Dm7 G

Just try) If you see an old friend on the street,
And he's down remember, his shoes could fit your feet
Just try a little kindness & you'll see
It's something that comes very naturally / **(We can...)**

— **Nickolas Ashford & Valerie Simpson**

© 1970 Jobete Music Co. Inc. 6255 Sunset Blvd., Hollywood CA 90028 International copyright secured. Made in USA. All rights reserved. Used by permission of CPP Belwin Inc. — On Diana Ross All the Gr H. ©U18

Same Boat Now

We may have come here on different ships
But we're in the same boat now (repeat)

Am G F E / D E Am - :||

Some of us came here for freedom from hunger & from hate
Some of us came here to make it rich & some of us came in chains
We gathered in the cities, claimed the new frontier
We pulled the cotton from the land we watered with our tears

Am G F E (2x) / Am G F E Dm - E -
Bm E AmD F G C - / Bm E Am F Dm Em F -

Some grew rich by toil & trade, some grew rich by vice
And some grew rich in power & all of us paid the price
And in the name of progress how we ground each other down
But no one is the winner when you're building on bloody ground

Women of all colors from every walk of life
We bore the hidden burden as workers, daughters & wives
Hired when we were needed, sent home when jobs ran down
They think we're waiting on the shore, but we're turning the boat around

We're a people born of many shores, our journeys so entwined
And we'll be on a sinking ship if we leave anybody behind
Don't want to be a melting pot, we're a rainbow family
And it's gonna take everything we've got to set each other free

— **Betsy Rose**

 OU19

Sing Along

I get butterflies in my stomach whenever I start to sing
And when I'm at a microphone I shake like anything
But if you'll sing along with me I'll holler right out loud
'Cause I'm awf'ly nervous lonesome, but I'm swell when I'm a crowd

C - F C / F C D G / C - F C / F C G C

Sing along, sing along
And just sing "la la la la la" if you don't know the song
You'll quickly learn the music, you'll find yourself a word
'Cause when we sing together we'll be heard

F - C - / - - - G / C - F C / - FG C -

O when I need a raise in pay & have to ask my boss
If I go see him by myself I'm just a total loss
But if we go together I'll do my part right pretty
'Cause I'm awf'ly nervous lonesome, but I make a fine committee

My congressman's important, he hobnobs with big biz
He soon forgets the guys & gals who put him where he is
I'll just write him a letter to tell him what I need
With a hundred thousand signatures, why even he can read

And when I say "together," I don't mean just we two
But Black, Brown, White, Red, Yellow, Christian, Muslim, Jew
The worker in the factory, the sailor on the sea
From mine & mill, both him & her, & you & you & me

O life is full of problems, the world's a funny place
I sometimes wonder why the hell I joined the human race
But when we work together, it all seems right & true
I'm an awful nothing by myself, but I'm OK with you

— **Malvina Reynolds**

 OU20

Somos El Barco

The stream sings it to the river, the river sings it to the sea
The sea sings it to the boat that carries you & me

Somos el barco, somos el mar
Yo navego en ti, tu navegas en mí
We are the boat, we are the sea
I sail in you, you sail in me

F G C - / // / / / /

Now the boat we are sailing in was built by many hands
And the sea we are sailing on, it touches many sands

O the voyage has been long & hard & yet we're sailing still
With a song to help us pull together, if we only will

So with our hopes we raise the sails to face the winds once more
And with our hearts we chart the waters never sailed before

El arroyo le canta al río, el río le canta al mar
Y el mar le canta al barco, que lejos nos va a llevar

— **Lorre Wyatt**

 OU21

Step By Step

Step by step, the longest march can be won, can be won
Many stones can form an arch, singly none, singly none
And in union what we will, can be accomplished still
Drops of water turn a mill, singly none, singly none

Dm - CDm AmDm / / Dm - DmGm GmA / 1st

— **Waldemar Hille & Pete Seeger**

 OU22

Turning of the World

1. **Let us sing this song for the turning of the world**
   That we may turn as one
   With every voice, with every song, we will move this world along
   And our lives will feel the echo of our turning
   With every voice, with every song, we will move this world along (2x)
   And our lives will feel the echo of our turning

(capo up) G D Em Bm / C G D - / 1st / C G D G

D - G - C G D - / G D Em Bm / C G D G

2. loving/love 3. healing/heal 4. dreaming/dream

For last v. go backwards repeating:
And our lives will feel the echo of our dreaming
And our...healing / ...loving / ...turning

— **Ruth Pelham**

 OU23

Under One Sky

We're all a family under one sky
We're a family under one sky **(repeat)**

A D / E A :||

1. **We're** people * **we're** animals *
   We're flowers * **and we're** birds in flight*
   Well **we're** people * **we're** animals *
   We're flowers * & birds in flight* (*=echo)

D - A - / E - AD A (AD A) / 1st / E - A -
= **echo**

2. plumbers / doctors / farmers / & we're teachers too
   And we're artists / electricians / waitresses / and we're astronauts
3. sisters / brothers / friends / & neighbors too
   grandmas / grandpas / grandchildren / & we're parents too
4. lions / puppies / kittycats / & we're horses too
   cows / sheep / snakes / & we are pigs **(make the sounds)**
5. happy / angry / frightened / & we're tender too
   sad / curious / embarrassed / & we're really excited!
   (pantomime these feelings)
6. Americans / Russians / Ethiopians / & Vietnamese
   Israelis / Palestinians / Nicaraguans / & we're Chinese

— **Ruth Pelham**

 OU24

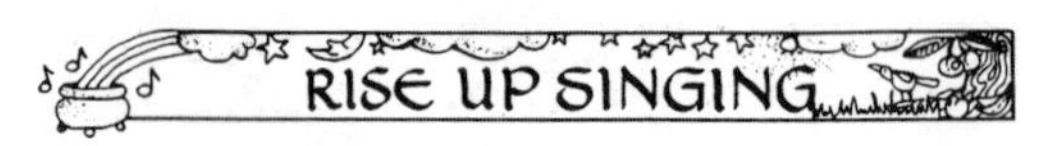

What You Do with What You've Got

You must know someone like him, he was tall & strong & lean
Body like a greyhound, mind so sharp & keen
But his heart just like a laurel, grew twisted on itself
Til almost everything he did brought pain to someone else

DG D DG D / / / /

It's not just what you're born with
It's what you choose to bear
It's not how large your share is
But how much you can share
It's not the fights you dream of
But those you really fought
It's not just what you're given
But what you do with what you've got

DG D / DG D / DG D / Em G :|| **(TD ↑ 9)**

For what's the use of two strong legs if you only run away
What good is the finest voice if you've nothing good to say
What good are strength & muscles if you only push & shove
What's the use of two good ears if you can't hear those you love

Between those who use their neighbors & those who use a cane
Between those in constant power & those in constant pain
Between those who run to evil & those who cannot run
Tell me which ones are the cripples & which ones touch the sun? **(last 2 lines tune=as chorus)**

— Si Kahn

© Joe Hill Music (ASCAP). All rights reserved. Used by permission. — Written espec. for SO! 29:1 (spec issue on FM & disabled people honoring the Internatl Yr of Disabled Persons). On his Unfinished Portraits, *Ginni Clemmens* Lopin' Along thru the Cosmos *& Bok, Muir & Trickett* Minneappolis Concert *(FSI 110). In* New Folk Favs. OU25

When All Thy Names Are One

I'll begin tomorrow, I'll be on my way
Thy light, Thy will be done
Bid farewell to sorrow, I will sing & pray
When all Thy names are one
When all Thy names are one, O Lord
All Thy names are one
Bid farewell to sorrow, I will sing & pray
(repeat 3rd line of each verse) / When...

C Am F C / - Am G - / 1st / CF CG C -
C F C Am / C Dm C G / C - F C / " /

For those who long for the days gone by / **Thy light...**
And for those who gaze at the starry skies / **When...**

O the whole world 'round they still praise Thy name...
In a thousand tongues still they sound the same...

We all live in one building tho' some preach of doom...
Why must all Thy children live in separate rooms...

We all drink water from the same old well...
How can one man's heaven be another one's hell?...

— w: Bob Zentz — m: trad (gospel)

© 1984 Bob Zentz. All rights reserved. Used by permission. — On his forthcoming album (tentatively titled It's Not Time*). On* Scott Alarik *(Swallowtail) & rec by Ed Trickett.* OU26

When I Needed a Neighbor

When I needed a neighbor were **you there, were you there?**
When I needed a neighbor **were you there?**
And the creed & the color & the name won't matter
Were you there?

(capo up or play in Em) Am F C E / Am FAm Dm G
C Am CF CE / Am - - -

I was hungry & thirsty were you there, **were you there?...**
I was cold, I was naked...
When I needed a shelter...
When I needed a healer...
Wherever you travel, I'll be there, I'll be there...

— Sydney Carter

© 1965 Stainer & Bell, Ltd. Used by permission of Galaxy Music Corp. NY, NY, sole U.S. agent. — Based on Matthew 25:31-46. In support of "Christian Aid". In his Green Print for Song. *Also in* S of the Spirit *&* Quaker SB. OU27

There are other songs on brother/sisterhood & community in FREEDOM, FRIENDSHIP, HOPE, MEN, PEACE, STRUGGLE, & WOMEN. See also: "I Live in a City" (CITY) "My Rainbow Race," "We Are All One Planet" (ECO) "If You Don't Love Your Neighbor," "Will the Circle Be Unbroken" (GOSPEL) "Building Bridges," "Circle Chant," "Shalom Chaverim" (SACR) "Wayfaring Stranger" (HARD) "River" (TIME) & "Bread Song" (WORK).

Amelia Earhart's Last Flight

Like a ship out o'er the ocean, like a speck against the sky
Amelia Earhart flying past that day
With her partner Capt. Noonan on the second of July
Her plane fell in the ocean far away

G C / D G :||

There's a beautiful, beautiful field
Far away in a land that is fair
Happy landings to you Amelia Earhart
Farewell, first lady of the air

C G / - D / G C / D G

Half an hour later, an S.O.S. was heard
Her signal weak, but still her voice was brave
In shark-infested waters her plane went down that night
In the blue Pacific to a watery grave

Now you have heard the story of that awful tragedy
We pray that she may fly home safe again
In days to come tho' others blaze a trail across the sea
We'll ne'er forget Amelia & her plane

— David McEnery

© 1939 Stasny Music. Copyright renewed. All rights administered by Bug Music Inc. Used by permission. — Earhart (1898-1937) was the first person to fly solo fr Hawaii to the mainland. She disappeared on a 1937 flight around the equator. In SO! 15-3 *&* Reprints #10, Liberated Woman's SB *&* Here's to the Women. *On* Greenbriar Boys *(Vang),* New Harmony Sisterhood Band *Ain't I A Woman?,* Faith Petric *As We Were &* Jim Kweskin *America.* OU28

Ballad of Erica Levine

When Erica Levine was seven & a half
Up to her door came Jason Metcalf
And he said "Will you marry me, Erica Levine?"
And Erica Levine said "What do you mean?"
"Well my father & mother say a fellow ought to marry
And my father said his brother, who is my Uncle Larry
Never married & he said Uncle Larry is a dope
So will you marry me?" Said Erica "Nope!
My piano teacher's smart & she never had to marry
And your father may be right about your Uncle Larry
But not being married isn't what made him a dope
Don't ask me again, 'cause my answer's 'Nope!'"

C F / C G / C F / C GC
||: FC GC / / " / " :||

When Erica Levine was 17
She went to the prom with Joel Bernstein
And they danced by the light of a sparkling bobby-sock
'Cause the theme of the prom was the history of rock
And after the prom Joel kissed her at the door
And he said "Do you know what that kiss was for?"
And she said "I don't know, but you kiss just fine"
And he said "What it means is that you are mine"
And she said "No I'm not!" & she rushed inside
And on the way home Joel Bernstein cried
And she cried too & wrote a letter to *Ms.*
Saying "This much I know: I am mine, not his"

When Erica Levine was 23
Her lover said "Erica, marry me
This relationship is answering a basic need
And I'd like to have it legally guaranteed
For without your precious love, I would truly die
So why can't we make it legal?" Erica said "Why?
Basic needs, at your age, should be met by you
I'm your lover, not your mother, let's be careful what we do
If I should ever marry, I will marry to grow
Not for tradition or possession or protection. No
I love you, but your needs are a very different issue"
Then he cried, & Erica handed him a tissue

When Erica was 30, she was talking with Lou
Discussing & deciding what they wanted to do
"When we marry, should we move into your place or mine?
Yours is rent-controlled, but mine is on the Green Line"
And they argued & they talked & they finally didn't care
And they bought a condominium near Harvard Square
[They joined a small cooperative near Central Square]
And their wedding was a simple one, they wanted it that way
And they thought alot about the things they would choose to say
"I will live with you & love you but I'll never call you mine"
Then the judge pronounced them married & everyone had wine
And a happy-ever-after life is not the kind they got
But they tended to be happy more often than not

— **Bob Blue**

© 7/27/1981 Bob Blue (copyright#Pau319-708) Used by permission. On his Erica Levine & Friends *(BlackSocks) &* Erica Levine *(priv issue), Kim Wallach* The Coldest Winter In Living Memory *(BlackSocks) &* Coldest Winter, *Frankie Armstrong* I Heard A Woman Singing *(FF) & Peter Alsop* Fan Club Favs *(FF). In* SO! *30:3.* OU29

Battle Hymn of Women

Mine eyes have seen the glory of the flame of women's rage
Kept smoldering for centuries, now burning in this age
We no longer will be prisoners in that same old gilded cage
That's why we're marching on
Move on over or we'll move on over you (3x)
For women's time has come!

G - / C G / - GEm / CD G :||

You have told us to speak softly, to be gentle & to smile
Expected us to change ourselves with every passing style
Said the only work for women was to clean & sweep & file...

It is we who've done your cooking, done your cleaning, kept your rules
We gave birth to all your children & we taught them in your schools
We've kept the system running but we're laying down our tools

You think that you can buy us off with crummy wedding rings
You never give us half the profit that our labor brings
Our anger eats into us, we no longer bow to kings...

We have broken thru our shackles, now we sing a battle song
We march for liberation & we're many thousand strong
We'll build a new society, we've waited much too long...

— **w: Meredith Tax** — **m: "Battle Hymn of the Republic"**

© Meredith Tax. Used by permission. For tune see "John Brown's Body" (FREE). OU30

Beware, Oh Take Care

They say young men are bold & free
Beware o take care
They'll tell you they're friends but they're liars you see
Beware o take care
Beware young ladies, they're foolin' you
Trust them not, they're foolin' you
Beware young ladies, they're foolin' you
Beware o take care

C - / G C :||: F C / G C :||

They smoke, they chew, they wear fine shoes / **Beware...**
And in their pocket is a bottle of booze / **Beware...**

Around their necks they wear a guard...
And in their pocket is a deck of cards...

They put their hands up to their hearts, they sigh o they sigh!...
They say they love no one but you, they lie o they lie...

— **authorship unknown**

First printed source is 1892. On Lavender Jane Loves Women, Blind Alfred Reed *(Rounder), New Lost City Ramblers* Old Timey S for Children *(FC7064) & their* SB *& Faith Petric* As We Were. *In Vince Randolph* FS of the Ozarks, All Our Lives, 1004 FS, FSEncyV1 *&* SO! *35:1.* OU31

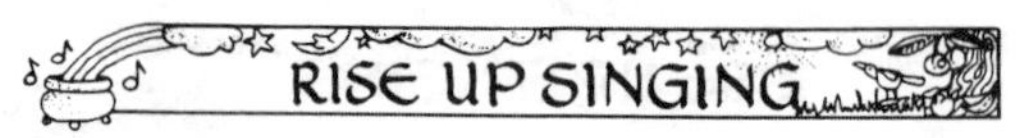

Bread and Roses

As we go marching marching in the beauty of the day
A million darkened kitchens, a thousand mill lots gray
Are touched with all the radiance that a sudden sun discloses
For the people hear us singing: bread & roses, bread & roses!

I: C G - C / - G FG C / Am G F C / F C G C

As we go marching marching, we battle too for men
For they are women's children & we mother them again
[For men can ne'er be free til our slavery's at an end]
Our lives shall not be sweated from birth until life closes
Hearts starve as well as bodies, give us bread but give us roses

As we go marching marching, unnumbered women dead
Go crying thru our singing their ancient call for bread
Small art & love & beauty their drudging spirits knew
Yes it is bread we fight for, but we fight for roses too

As we go marching, marching, we bring the greater days
The rising of the women means the rising of the race
No more the drudge & idler, ten that toil where one reposes
But a sharing of life's glories – bread & roses, bread & roses!

II: C - F G / C - D G / 1st / C Am F G C -
(v.3: C Am FG C -)

— w: James Oppenheim
— m: I: Caroline Kohsleet, II: Mimi Fariña

Inspired by a banner in the huge 1912 walkout of textile workers in Lawrence, Mass. In SO! *2:7 & 25:1,* S of Work & Protest, *(in & on)* Carry It On, Here's to the Women, Liberated Woman's SB, FSEncy V1 *&* All Our Lives. *On Judy Collins* Bread & Roses *(Mimi Fariña version),* First 15 Yrs, *Arlington St. Women's Caucus* Honor Thy Womanself, *Phillips* We Have Fed You All, Sings the S of the IWW, *Shays Rebellion* Daniel Shays Highway *(FF), Faith Petric* As We Were, *Bobbie McGee* Bread & Raises *& Bluestein Fam* Trav Blues. OU32

Custom Made Woman Blues

Well I tried to be the kind of woman / you wanted me to be
And it's not your fault that I tried to be
What I thought you wanted to see
Smilin' face & shinin' hair
Clothes that I thought you'd like me to wear
Made to please & not to tease:
It's the custom-made woman blues

D D7 / G D / D - / E A
/ " / " // G DB7 / EA D

Yes I tried to be the kind of woman / you wanted me to be
And I tried to see life your way
And say the things you'd like me to say
Lovin' thoughts, gentle hands
All guaranteed to keep a hold of your man / Made...

And now you say you're tired of me
And all those things I thought you wanted me to be
Is it true you want someone who
Knows how to think & do on her own?
Lord it's hard to realize
The lessons I learned so young were nothin' but lies...

— Alice Gerrard

 On her Hazel & Alice *(w/Hazel Dickens). In* SO! *21:6,* Here's to the Women & All Our Lives. OU33

Don't Shut My Sister Out

Don't shut my sister out! Trust her choices
Her women's wisdom & her will to grow
Don't shut my sister out! Trust her vision
Her intuition of her own way to go

Am EAm F Am / F GF Am E
Am EAm F C / F G E Am

Well a woman's rhythm is an ebb & a flow
It's a coming together & a letting go
Like the tides of the moon & the seasons of earth
We sing of our cycle of death & rebirth

Am - AmE Am / F G F Am
Am - AmF Am / D F E Am

Sometimes I find myself taking a stand
It's like finding rocks among the shifting sand
And sisters gather round holding hand in hand
Saying this is our story, this is our land

Sometimes I find I have to walk away
There are inner voices that I have to obey
And they lead me lonely & they lead me cold
And they lead me away from the sister fold

One thing I've learned is never to assume
That every woman I meet is gonna sing my tune
I want respect, I want to give you the same
This is a struggle for survival & not a party game

I see pointing fingers, I hear calling names
I see our strength being shattered by fear & pain
Can't you see the writing on the wall:
If we don't join together, well we're all gonna fall!

You are a special woman, shouldn't have to hide
I want to know you & grow with you right by my side
Won't you come as you are, won't you do what you must?
Won't you help build a sisterhood we all can trust!

— Betsy Rose

 On her Sweet Sorcery *(w/Cathy Winter), Meg Christian & Chris Williamson* At Carnegie Hall *(Olivia) & on* Judy Gorman-Jacobs. OU34

Fight Back

By day I lived in terror / By night I lived in fright
For as long as I can remember
A lady don't go out alone at night **(2x)**

A - / - EA / A - / Em A / /

And so we've got to fight back! in large numbers
Fight back! I can't make it alone
Fight back! in large numbers
Together we can make a safe home (2x)

F#m F#mE / / / DE A / /

Women all around the world / Every color, religion & age
One thing we've got in common
We can all be battered & raped **(2x)**

Some have an easy answer / Buy a lock & live in a cage
But my fear is turning to anger
And my anger is turning to rage
And I won't live my life in a cage – no!

— Holly Near

 On her Imagine My Surprise. *In* SO! *37:2.* OU35

Glad to Be a Woman

Fmaj7 Eaug

So many years I've been bitter
Wanting to be someone else
Nature had formed me & the world had conformed me
Into thinking I was less than the bravest & the best
Better find me a nest to take care of
And let somebody stronger take care of me, but now I'm:

Fmaj7 Eaug* Am C7 / / Fmaj7 Em Am C7 / 1st / / F Am D G

Glad to be a woman / Glad to be alive **(* or use E7)**
Glad for the children to take my place
Glad for the will to survive

C Em Fmaj7 G / / C E Am F / D G C -

Books that I read made me angry
And the life that I led made me blue
The face in the mirror looked hollow with fear
With the eyes painted blind, but a spirit behind
Saying let your light shine, let it shine
But I was still a young girl & it took some time to be:

(bridge) Well I never saw myself to be that strong
I was loving & tender 'cause that got me along
Until the storm swept around, Lord it shook my world down
And I stood in the ruins with no one to turn to
I turned to myself & that's when I found that I was:

C_{maj7} - F_{maj7} - / /D_m C D_m C/F_{maj7} D C E/A_m C F G

— Betsy Rose **(TD ↑ 11, in 3/4)**

© 1975 Betsy Rose. All rights reserved. Used by permission. On her & Cathy Winter Sweet Sorcery *(Ladyslipper), M Christian & C Williamson* At Carnegie Hall *(Olivia) & on* Judy Gorman-Jacobs. *In* SO! *28:4.* OU36

God's Gift to Woman

I don't want no handsome man, 'cause he won't treat me right
Always flirtin' & cheatin' & stayin' out half the night
Everybody wants him, but that don't mean it's good I'd
Rather have a plain lookin' man who loves me like he should

D - G D / - - E A / 1st / D B_m E_mA D

God's gift to woman, that's what they think they are
God's gift to woman, just like a movie star
Everybody wants him, but that don't mean it's good
I'd rather have a plain lookin' man who loves me like he should

A plain man likes his lovin', but a handsome man makes you beg
He wants to see you crawlin', kneelin' by his leg
He always keeps you waitin', 'cause he don't have much to give
He thinks you should be grateful for havin' him to dig

A plain man will be faithful, he's into bein' true
He don't need no fancy car, he just wants to make love to you
He won't win no beauty contest, but that's just not what counts
You need lots of tender lovin' by the pound & not the ounce

— Rory Block

© 1987 Happy Valley Music. Used by permission. On her Black Rhinestones & Steel Strings *(Rounder). In* SO! *31:2.* OU37

Good Old Dora

There's not a person who could hold me here
It's like trying to hold onto a river
Not a man nor a mountain could make me insecure
No way to separate *[sever]* us ever

Good Old Dora, she nurses me when I'm ill
Good Old Dora, she flatters me when I'm well
She brings the bucket & I bring the sponge
And together we're gonna clean up this old town!

A D E A/D E A -:|| G - D -/ /E - A -/D E A -

I watch the fish a-movin' like quick silver
They never take a wrong or awkward turn
They never ask what's received or who's the giver
They reveal there's so much more we could learn

Autumn is a fine time for long talks in the evening
And having all your friends & music handy
There's no use sighing about the summer's leaving
Because every season has her home & family

Looking down the lane & wondering how to go
I pause to check my sense of direction
One rugged mile, I'm gonna take it kinda slow
Next stop we make is at perfection

— Casse Culver

© 1974 Casse Culver. Published by Sweet Alliance Music. All rights reserved. So, how come the pictures of God in your Sunday School/Hebrew School books were always old men? Note what the initials of the title spell out. On her 3 Gypsies *& Ginni Clemmens* Long Time Friends. *In* SO! *25:6.* OU38

Housewife's Lament

One day I was walking, I heard a complaining
And saw an old woman, the picture of gloom
She gazed at the mud on her doorstep ('twas raining)
And this was her song as she wielded her broom

O life is a toil & love is a trouble
Beauty will fade & riches will flee
Pleasures they dwindle & prices they double
And nothing is as I would wish it to be **(in 3/4)**

G - C G/D - - G :|| G - B_7 -/E_m - D_7 -/1st 2

There's too much of worriment goes to a bonnet
There's too much of ironing goes to a shirt
There's nothing that pays for the time you waste on it
There's nothing that lasts us but trouble & dirt

In March it is mud, it is slush in December
The midsummer breezes are loaded with dust
In the fall the leaves litter, in muddy September
The wallpaper rots & the candlesticks rust

There are worms on the cherries & slugs on the roses
And ants in the sugar & mice in the pies
The rubbish of spiders no mortal supposes
And ravaging roaches & damaging flies

It's sweeping at 6 & it's dusting at 7
It's victuals at 8 & it's dishes at 9
It's potting & panning from 10 to 11
We scarce break our fast til we plan how to dine

With grease & with grime from corner to center
Forever at war & forever alert
No rest for a day lest the enemy enter
I spend my whole life in struggle with dirt

Last night in my dreams I was stationed forever
On a far little rock in the midst of the sea
My one chance of life was a ceaseless endeavor
To sweep off the waves as they swept over me

Alas! 'twas no dream, ahead I behold it
I see I am helpless my fate to avert
She lay down her broom, her apron she folded
She lay down & died & was buried in dirt

— w: adap fr Mrs Sara A Price m: anon. (mid 19th c.)

aka: "Life Is A Toil." This song is copied from the diary of Mrs Price, of Ottawa, Ill. She had 7 children & lost them all. Some of her sons were killed in the Civil War. On a rec by Walt Robertson (Folkways). Some of the words here are fr his version, rather than fr Mrs Price. In SO! *6:4 &* Reprints #1, Liberated Women's SB, Hootenanny SB, All Our Lives, Here's to the Women, *Lomax* FS of NA *&* FS EncyV2. *On Peggy Seeger* Penelope Isn't Waiting Anymore *(Rounder) &* Songs of the Working People *(FF483) as "Life Is A Toil."* OU39

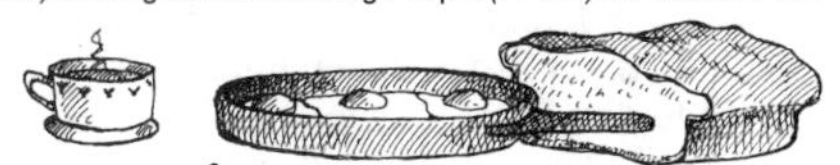

I Am a Woman

1. **I am a woman here on planet Earth**
   I have the breath of life in me, a gift given at birth
   No one, no body, no powers that be
   Can ever, ever, ever take this gift away from me

DA GD GA D / /A GD G A / 1st /

2. **I am a woman here on planet Earth**
   I have a song to sing in me, a song sung birth to birth
   No one...be / Can...take this song away from me
3. Flesh, bones & blood is me, before & after birth
4. I have the will to live in me, I learned that at my birth
5. I have the breath of life in me, a gift given at birth
   (repeat last 2 lines with: ...this life away from me)

— Ruth Pelham

© 1983 Silver Crane Music (ASCAP), PO Box 6024 Albany NY 12206. Used by permission. On her Look to the People *(FF399).* OU40

The I.P.D.

I'll sing you all a song about a wondrous new device
The nation's latest contraceptive plan
That funny little object they call the I.U.D.
Has recently been changed to fit a man

C G / FC G / C G / CG C

(It's) the I.P.D., the I.P.D.
It may not feel too good to you but it's not hurting me
So every time the pain begins to fill your eyes with tears
Remember I put up with it for years!

C F / C G / C F / G C

They tested it on whales & they tried it out on mice
They used it in the poorer parts of town
It's the cleverest invention since the automatic lift
Guaranteed to never let you down

It was proven to be safe for the average human male
Tho' testing showed some minor side effects
There were two died of infection & six were sterilized
But only ten percent were too depressed – from the...

But you know some people are never satisfied
So scientists are working once again
They've got something even better than the good old I.P.D.
It's called the morning after pill for men

(last cho) It's the pill, it's better than **the I.P.D.**
It may not be too safe but we'll just have to wait & see
So put away your worries & put away your fears
And **remember I put up with it for years!**

— w: Lian Tanner **— m: Sue Edmonds**

 In SO! *31:3 & on Judy Small* One Voice in the Crowd *(Redwood).* OU41

I'm Gonna Be an Engineer

When I was a little girl, I wished I was a boy
I tagged along behind the gang & wore me corduroys
Everybody said I only did it to annoy
But I was gonna be an engineer

G - / G GD (:‖ v. 2 only) G - / A_7 D_7

Mama told me "Can't you be a lady?
Your duty is to make me the mother of a pearl
Wait until you're older dear & maybe
You'll be glad that you're a girl"

G AB_7 / CG A_mD / G B_7C_7 / GD G

Dainty as a Dresden Statue
Gentle as a Jersey cow
Smooth as silk, gives creamy milk
Learn to coo, learn to moo
That's what you do to be a lady now _ **(*extra beat)**

E_mB_m E_m / E_m B_m / C_m G / C G / E_m* A_m D

When I went to school I learned to write & how to read
Some history, geography & home economy
And typing is a skill that every girl is sure to need
To while away the extra time until the time to breed
And then they had the nerve to say "What would you like to be?"
I says "I'm gonna be an engineer!"
No, you only need to learn to be a lady
The duty isn't yours for to try & run the world
An engineer could never have a baby!
Remember, dear, that you're a girl
She's smart! for a woman
I wonder how she got that way?
You get no choice, you get no voice
Just stay mum, pretend you're dumb
That's how you come to be a lady today!

So I become a typist & I study on the sly
Working out the day & night so I can qualify
And every time the boss come in he pinched me on the thigh
Say's "I've never had an engineer!"
You owe it to the job to be a lady
It's the duty of the staff to give the boss a whirl
The wages that you get are crummy maybe
But it's all you get 'cause you're a girl

Then Jimmy come along & we set up a conjugation
We were busy every night with loving recreation
I spent my day at work so HE could get his education
And now he's an engineer!
He says "I know you'll always be a lady
It's the duty of me darling to love me all her life
Could an engineer look after or obey me?
Remember, dear, that you're my wife"

Well as soon as Jimmy got a job, I began again
Then happy at me turret-lathe a year or so & then
The morning that the twins were born, Jimmy says to them
"Kids, your mother WAS an engineer"
You owe it to the kids to be a lady
Dainty as a dish-rag, faithful as a chow
Stay at home, you got to mind the baby
Remember you're a mother now

Well everytime I turn around it's something else to do
It's cook a meal or mend a sock or sweep a floor or two
I listen in to Jimmy Young, it makes me want to spew
I was gonna be an engineer!
I really wish that I could be a lady
I could do the lovely things that a lady's 'sposed to do
I wouldn't even mind if only they would pay me
And I could be a person too
What price – for a woman?
You can buy her for a ring of gold
To love & obey (without any pay)
You get a cook & a nurse (for better or worse)
You don't need a purse when a lady is sold

Ah but now that times are harder & me Jimmy's got the sack
I went down to Vicker's, they were glad to have me back
But I'm a third-class citizen, my wages tell me that
And I'm a first-class engineer
The boss he says "We pay you as a lady
You only got the job 'cause I can't afford a man
With you I keep the profits high as may be
You're just a cheaper pair of hands"
You got one fault: you're a woman
You're not worth the equal pay
A bitch or a tart, you're nothing but heart
Shallow & vain, you got no brain
You even go down the drain like a lady today

Well I listened to my mother & I joined a typing pool
I listened to my lover & I put him thru his school
But if I listen to the boss, I'm just a bloody fool
And an underpaid engineer!
I been a sucker ever since I was a baby
As a daughter, as a wife, as a mother & a "dear"
But I'll fight them as a woman, not a lady
I'll fight them as an engineer!

— Peggy Seeger

 Note: "Engineers" in the UK are "machinists" in the US. On her Different Therefore Equal, At the Pres Moment *(w/Ewan McColl), Pete Seeger* Circles & Seasons *& (on & in)* Carry It On, *Judy Gorman-Jacobs* Live at Folk City, *Bobbie McGee* Bread & Raises *& Bluestein Fam* Let the Dove Come In. *In* SO! *22:6,* All Our Lives, New S, New Time *&* Here's to the Women. OU42

I'm Gonna Wash That Man

I'm gonna wash that man right outa my hair (3x)
And send him on his way

D Em7 D GA / /D Em7 D G / D A D -

I'm gonna wave that man right outa my arms...

(bridge #1) Don't try to patch it up, tear it up, tear it up!
Wash him out, dry him out, push him out, fly him out
Cancel him / & let him go (yea sister!) / **I'm gonna wash...**

G - - - / / D - E7 - / A F E♭ A7

(verses are in 3/4 time)

1. If the man don't understand you
 If you fly on separate beams
 Waste not time! Make a change
 Ride that man right off your range
 Rub him outa roll call
 And drum him outa your dreams! Oh ho!

G - F D / G F G - / C - - - / G - C G //

2. If you laugh at diff'rent comics A - E♭ - / D - - -
 If you root for diff'rent teams
 Waste no time, weep no more
 Show him what the door is for! / **Rub him outa...**

(bridge #2) You can't light a fire when the wood's all wet!
You can't make a butterfly strong
You can't fix an egg when it ain't quite good
And you can't fix a man when he's wrong!
You can't put back a petal when it falls from a flower
Or sweeten up a feller when he starts turning sour!
(oh no! oh no!)

G - F D / G F GD G / G - F G
Dm7 - Fmaj7 - / Em7 - E♭ - / F♯ - D - / B♭ - - - A7 - - -

3. If his eyes get dull & fishy
 When you look for glints & gleams
 Waste no time, make a switch
 Drop him in the nearest ditch / **Rub him...** (oh ho! oh ho!)

I went an' **washed that man...**

She went an' **washed that man...**

— w: Oscar Hammerstein II — m: Richard Rodgers

 Fr their musical South Pacific. OU43

The Lucretia Mott Song

On the island of Nantucket she was born beside the sea
All her long life she fought bravely to make slaves & women free
And she told us that where God dwells there must be true liberty
And her light still shines for me

G - - - / C - G - / - - - Em / C D G -

Thank thee kindly, Friend Lucretia (3x)
For thy light still shines for me

In the town of Philadelphia she hid the fleeing slaves
For the freedom of her sisters she dared cross the ocean waves
And she asked Ulysses Grant to grant a pardon for the braves

"Let's bring an end to poverty" the gentle Quaker pled
"Let's give the workers all a chance to earn their daily bread
Let nations live in peace again just as our Lord has said"

Thru out the busy cities & across the countryside
She preached one simple message "O let truth be e'er thy guide
Mind the light within thee & let love with thee abide"

— w: Margaret Hope Bacon
— m: "Battle Hymn of the Republic"

© Margaret Hope Bacon. Used by permission. Ms. Bacon is author of Valiant Friend: The Life of Lucretia Mott, *NY: Walker, 1980.* In Here's to the Women. OU44

My Mom's a Feminist

I pulled into the loading zone feeling nervous, I was all alone
Unloading my equipment before the show
I started wheeling it down the hall
 til I turned hearing a young man call
"Can I help, that must be heavy, I know?
I've been looking forward to your show"

D - G Em / A EmA D - / 1st / A - - - / Em A D -

My mom's a feminist so I understand
That's why I'm here today I've come to lend a hand
I was raised on equal rights & furthermore
She helped me see that equality is a goal worth fighting for

D - Bm - / Em A D - / - - G - / EmA (3x) D -

She decided she could do some good
 ringing doorbells in the neighborhood
Not for the Girl Scouts but for the ERA
Sometimes she takes her friends along
 she's only ten, but she's already strong
She's a mover & a shaker well on her way
When they ask what she's doing, this is what she'll say:

Different questions in the classroom now
 young seekers asking how
Things came to be & how they can change
Becoming women & becoming men
 may not ever be the same again
But the new ways won't be quite so strange
When the people they trust help them get it arranged
(this cho) Because you're **feminists so** you **understand...**

It's worth all the time you take what a difference
 your time can make
For the new generation still coming along
If our movement is to last we must see that the torch is passed
And today's young people will grow up strong
And thousands more will sing this song
(last cho:) "**My** dad's **a feminist...**" or "**My** friend's..." **etc.**

— Kristin Lem

© 1981 Kleine Ding Music. Used by permission. On her We Will Never Give Up. *In* Here's to the Women. OU45

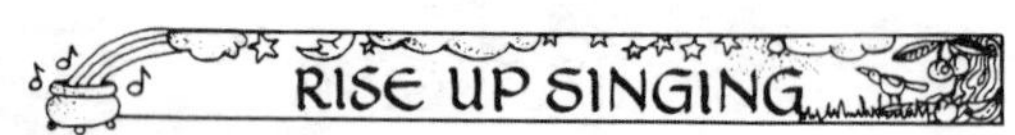

No Hole in My Head

Everybody thinks my head's full of nothin'
Wants to put his special stuff in
Fill the space with candy wrappers
Keep out sex & revolution, but **there's**
No hole in my head / Too bad

A - / /D7 - / A - // E7 - / A (E7)

Call me a dupe of this & the other
Call me a puppet on a string – They
They don't know my head's full of me and
That I have my own special thing **& there's...**

I have lived since early childhood
Figuring out what's going on – I
I know what hurts, I know what's easy
When to stand & when to run **& there's...**

So please stop shouting in my ear – There's
Something I want to listen to – There's
A kind of birdsong up somewhere – There's
Feet walking the way I mean to go **& there's...**

— Malvina Reynolds

The One About the Bird in the Cage

This bird is learning to fly
Soaring on the wings of her song
If sometimes she flies a bit too high
It's 'cause she was in a cage for so long

G - - C / - - - G :|| **(TD ↑ 1)**

And the man who kept her cage & fed her every day
Said "Little bird if you watch me, I'll show you the way
I'll teach you how to fly so free, I'll teach you how to sing
But if you want to be like me, I got to clip your wings"

C - G - / / / / **(this verse only)**

She said "I see you have the wisdom that must come with age
It must be 'cause you love me that you keep me in this cage"
Then one day the bird awoke to find her song was gone
And she said "What can it be? Did I do something wrong?"

G - C G / - - C D / C G C G / - D C G

And the man was very angry & he said "Bird hang your head
You're not singin' like you should, You cry all day instead
How can you behave so after all I've done for you?"
And the more she tried, the more she cried & wondered
what to do

But soon her tears of anguish turned to tears of rage
She said "How can I learn to fly if you keep me in this cage?
Now I know that if I stay, I'll never learn to sing
I am going far away, you can't teach me a thing

You know my freedom is not something you can give to me
I must take it for myself if I want to be free
I've got to trust my own wings if I want to learn to fly
In this cage I'll never sing, I've got to find the sky"

— Ruthy Taubb (formerly Ruthie Gorton)

Riverboat

I ain't gonna step down off of that riverboat (2x)
'Cause if I step down off of that riverboat
I don't think that I'm agonna float

D A D - / G - D A / D A Bm G / D A D -

'Cause there's mud just below that sparklin' water
Yes there's mud just below that sparklin' water
And it's soft, soft deep & warm
settled 'neath the river once in a storm
Mud just below that sparklin' water

Bm G D - / / D F# G E / D A D -

Once I had a daughter strong & fine
grew up & said she didn't want to be mine
I said I understood & I felt the same
Now she runs a school for girls
and each one tougher than a redwood burl
They're growin' up stronger than the world into which
they came / **So I ain't...**

D D7 G GD / D - A - / 1st / D A D -

When o when will I ever learn
it's not just fire that makes me burn?
It's not just ice that cools my flaming skin
But if I give up it'll cook me good
and that ain't the road to sisterhood
'Cause where I'm going ain't the same as where I've been

— Holly Near

The Road I Took to You

Bread & water, like some poor man's daughter
No never for me
Wine & money called me honey / Made me feel I was free
Like a glass raised too many times / I broke in two

C G Am C/F - C G / 1st / F - D G/F - G - / /

I was walking around in little pieces / and I never knew
That the way back home to me / was the road I took to you

C G F - / / C E Am F / - G C -

Winter saw me down & dragging my feet / thru the snow
Drinking, feeling like I was living on the street
With nowhere to go
And cracked in the coat I wore / I felt the cold come thru

And now somehow I've ended up with a cup / so full and
Overflowing all the time I know that is
Nothing I can hold in my hand
And it feels so good to me / just being true

— Barbara Keith

Sarah's Circle

1. We are weaving *[dancing]* Sarah's circle **(3x)**
   Sisters one & all *[Sisters, brothers all]*

C - - - / G - F C / - C7 F C / - G C -

2. We will all do our own naming **(3x) / Sisters...**
3. Every round a generation
4. Here we seek & find our history *[future]*
5. On & on the circle's moving
6. We are open, we are shining!

— w: Carol Etzler
— m: "Jacob's Ladder" (see SPIRS for sources)

Sister

Born of the earth, a child of God
Just one among the family
And you can count on me to share the load
  and I will always help you
Hold your burdens & I will be the one
  to help you ease your pain

C Dm B♭ F/Am B♭ C -/F G Em Am/Dm G F C

Lean on me, I am your sister
Believe in me, I am your friend **(repeat)**

Dm7 Em / Dm7 C :||

(bridge) I will fold you in my arms like a white wingèd dove
Shine in your soul, your spirit is crying

AmE Am7D / F Cmaj7

— **Cris Williamson**

© 1975 Bird Ankle Music. Used by permission. Orig written to be part of a musical about evangelist Aimee McPherson. On her Changer & the Changed *& in her* SB. OU51

Step it Out Nancy

Near Cheyenne in Wyoming there was a maiden fine & fair
Her eyes they shone like diamonds, she had long & golden hair
When the cattleman came riding, he came to her father's door
Mounted on a milk white pony, he came at the stroke of four
Step it out Nancy, pretty darlin', step it out, Nancy if you can
Step it out...darlin', show your legs to the wealthy man

Dm Am Dm F / Dm Am FAm Dm :|| 3x

I've come to court your daughter, Nancy of the golden hair
I have wealth & I have money, I have goods beyond compare
I will buy her silks & satins & a gold ring for her hand
I will build for her a mansion, she'll have servants to command

Can't you see I love a cowboy & I've promised him my hand?
I don't want your goods & money, I don't want your house
  & land
Nancy's father spoke up sharply, said you'll do as you are told
You'll be married on the Sunday, you will wear the ring of gold

The cattleman spoke with fury, said you will not have that man
And he rode for town in anger with his rifle in his hand
He came back from Colorado, on his pony was a sack
Deep red with the blood of the cowboy slung across the back

Pretty Nancy cried in anguish, she wept & tore her hair
She slipped into her father's room & found a pistol lying there
On the Sunday came the wedding, the townsfolk
  gathered at noon
They saw Nancy pull the pistol & shoot down that wealthy
  groom

Nancy said I am not sorry when the jury heard her tale
Tho' he rots beneath the ground & I shall rot in jail
There in the crowded courtroom, 12 good men took their stand
Said we will not hold you Nancy for killing that wealthy man

The moral of this story is not that murder pays
But that women must not be bought & sold, neither then
  nor nowadays
We will choose our lovers, we'll live out our own lives
We'll love whom we please with a passion & a sparkle in
  our eyes

— **Robin M. Williams & Jerome Clark (last v. Holly Near)**

© 1979 The New Music Times Inc. (BMI). Used by permission. Adap fr a trad ballad ("Step It Out Mary"). On Robin & Linda Williams Dixie Hwy Sign *(JuneAppal), Holly Near* Watch Out. *In SO! 27:5 & New Folk Favs.* OU52

Still Ain't Satisfied

Well they got women on TV, but I still ain't satisfied
'Cause co-optation's all I see, but I still ain't...
They call me "Ms.", they sell me blue jeans
They call it "Women's Lib", they make it sound obscene

Dm - G Dm / / A7 - Dm - / /

And I still ain't, whoa they lied (3x)
And I still ain't satisfied!

Dm DmG / / / DmG Dm

Well they got women prison guards, but...
With so many still behind bars &...
I don't plead guilt, I don't want no bum deal
I ain't askin' for crumbs, I want the whole meal

They liberalized abortion but...
'Cause it still costs a fortune &...
I'm singing about control of my own womb
And no reform is gonna change my tune

Abortion is still legal here but...
'Cause that might not be true next year &...
The right to life means no rights for us
If you agree, join in the chorus:

They give out pennies here & there but...
To set up centers for childcare &...
And while we work at slave wages
They brainwash our kids at tender ages

(as 2nd half of v.) I've got some pride & I won't be lied to
I did decide that half way won't do

— **Bonnie Lockhart**

© 1974 Paredon Records for Red Star Singers. Used by permission of author. On Red Star Singers Force of Life, *Robin Flower* More than Friends *(Spaniel) & on* Rosy's Bar & Grill *(BiscuitCity). In* SO! *28:3,* Out Loud, IWW S, New City Songster, Here's to the Women *&* All Our Lives. OU53

Testimony

There's godlike & warlike / And strong like only some show
And there's sadlike & madlike / And had like we know

Em Em (+D♯) / Em7 A / Cmaj7 Em / C D

But by my life be I spirit / And by my heart be I woman
And by my eyes be I open / And by my hands be I whole

Em D C CD / / / Em D C -

They say slowly brings the least shock
But no matter how slow I walk
There are traces, empty spaces / & doors & doors of locks

You young ones, you're the next ones
And I hope you choose it well
Tho' you try hard you may fall / Prey to the jaded jewel

Listen: there are waters hidden from us
In the maze we find them still
We'll take you to them, you take your young ones
May they take their own in turn

— **Ferron**

© 1980 Nemesis Publishing, Vancouver, Canada (PROCAN). Used by permission. Orig written for a friend's movie project, "This Film is about Rape". On her Testimony *(LucyRecs, distrib by Redwood), Ginni Clemmens* Lopin' Along *& Sweet Honey in the Rock* We All...Everyone. *In SO! 31:1.* OU54

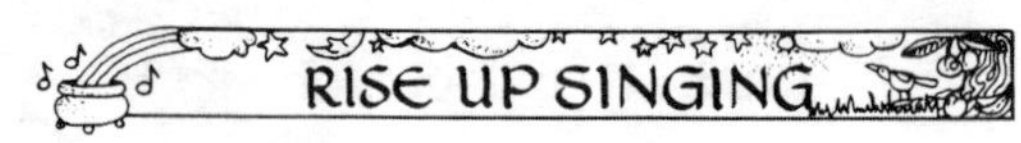

There Was a Young Woman

There was a young woman who swallowed <u>a lie</u>
We all know why she swallowed that lie
Perhaps she'll die

D - / Em A / AD D

There was a young woman who swallowed a rule
"Live to serve others" – she learned it in school
She swallowed the rule to hold up the lie / **& we all...**

D - / Em A ||: D - :|| * Em A / AD D

There was...swallowed some fluff* **as needed (later v.)**
Lipstick & candy & powder & puff
She swallowed the fluff to sweeten the rule **(go up verses)**

...a line / "I like 'em dumb baby, you suit me fine"
She swallowed the line to tie up the fluff...

...a pill / Her doctor said "I know that you will"
She swallowed the pill to go with the line...

...a ring / Looked like a princess & felt like a thing
She swallowed the ring to make up for the pill...

...some Spock / "Stay at home mother, take care of your flock"
She swallowed the Spock to go with the ring...

One day this young woman woke up & she said
"I've swallowed so much that I wish I were dead
I swallowed the Spock to go with the ring...
(go up list to:) I swallowed the rule to hold up the lie
Why in the world did I swallow that lie? / Perhaps I'll die"

She ran to her sisters, it wasn't too late
To be liberated, regurgitate!
She threw up the Spock & she threw up the ring
Looked like a princess & felt like a thing
She threw up the pill & she threw up the line
"I like 'em dumb baby, you suit me just fine"
She threw up the fluff & threw up the rule
"Live to serve others" (she learned it in school)
And last but not least, she threw up the lie
We all know why she threw up that lie / She will not die!

D - / Em A :|| 5x AD D

— w: Meredith Tax — m: Alan Mills (adap Peter Alsop)

 In SO! 20:3. On Alsop Asleep at the Helm *(under title "Young Woman Disco"). Also on* Virgo Rising: The Once & Future Woman *& rec by Seeger. For orig see "I Know an Old Lady" (PLAY).* OU55

They'll Be Comin' Round

Bumpy wagons moving thru the days & nights
They've been travelin' far in search of women's rights
Not much comfort or supporters but within this country's borders
They won't quit til they've won all of the fights

E - - - / - - B7 - / E E7 A - / B7 - E -

They'll be comin' round the mountain when they come
They'll be driving six white horses when they come
They'll be talkin' new solutions, women's suffrage, revolution
And we'll all go out to meet them when they come

In Colorado women sought a victory
Mrs. Stanton headed out with Susan B.
Organizing, speaking, writing, for us all they kept on fighting
Women won the vote out there in '93

Women rise & join your sisters on the line
It's been struggle after struggle all thru time
Keep your mind upon our heritage, your hearts upon the future
And we'll make it thru the tight spots every time!

— w: Eileen Abrams — m: trad. "She'll Be Comin'..."

 Original is in PLAY. OU56

We Don't Need the Men

(intro) It says in *Coronet Magazine*, June 1956, page 10
That married women are not as happy as women who have no men
Married women are cranky, frustrated & disgusted
While single women are bright & gay, creative & well-adjusted

G - Bm - / C - D G / - - Bm - / C G D G

We don't need the men, we don't need the men
We don't need to have them round, except for now & then
They can come to see us <u>when we need to move the piano</u>
Otherwise they can stay at home <u>& read about the White Sox</u>
We don't care about them, we can do without them
They'll look cute in a bathing suit on a billboard in Manhattan

G - Am - / D - - G :|| C G Am G / D - - G

We don't need the men, we don't need the men
We don't need to have them round, except for now & then
They can come to see us when they have tickets for the symphony
Otherwise they can stay at home & play a game of pinochle
We don't care about them, we can do without them
They'll look cute in a...on a billboard in Wisconsin

...see us when they're feeling pleasant & agreeable
Otherwise...& holler at the TV programs
We...them / They'll... Madagascar

...us when they're all dressed up with a suit on
Otherwise...& drop towels in their own bathroom
We... / They'll... Tierra del Fuego

— Malvina Reynolds

 On her Held Over (Cassandra), *in her* SB & Little Boxes. *Also in SO! 34:2,* All Our Lives & Here's to the Women. *On* Virgo Rising *(Thunderbird).* OU57

Witch Song

Who were the witches? Where did they come from?
Maybe your great, great, great grandmother was one
Witches were wise, wise women they say
And there's a little witch in ev'ry woman today

(in C) C Dm G C / / C Dm G Am / 1st

Witches knew all about flowers & weeds
How to use all their roots & their leaves & their seeds
When people grew weary from hardworkin' days
They made 'em feel better in so many ways

Am - G - / F - C - / Am - G - / F - Dm G

When women had babies the witches were there
To hold them & help them & give them sweet care
Witches knew stories of how life began
Don't you wish you could be one? Well maybe you can

Some people thought that the witches were bad
Some people were scared of the power they had
But power to help & to heal & to care
Isn't something to fear, it's a pleasure to share

— Bonnie Lockhart

 — aka: "Who Were the Witches?" On Kristin Lems We Will Never Give Up, *Nancy Schimmel* Plum Pudding *& Gary Lapow* Supermkt Shuffle. *In* Here's to the Women. OU58

The Woman in Your Life

The woman in your life will do what she must do
To comfort you & calm you down & let you rest now
The woman in your life, she can rest so easily
She knows everything you do
Because the woman in your life is you

C - F G / C - F G -

F G Am - Em - // Dm G / F G C -

The woman in your life knows simply what is true
She knows the simple way to touch to make you whole now
The woman in your life, she can touch so easily / **She...**

(bridge) And who knows more about your story
About your struggle in the world
And who cares more to bless your weary / shoulders than

F - C - / / Am Em Am - / Dm - G -

The woman in your life, she's trying to come thru
A woman's voice with messages, a woman's feelings
The woman in your life, she can feel so easily / **She...**

And who is sure to give you courage
And who will surely make you strong
And who will bear all the joy that's coming to you

If not the woman in your life, she's someone to pursue
She's patient & she's waiting & she'll take you home now
The woman in your life can wait so easily / **She...**

— **Alix Dobkin**

© 1973 Alix Dobkin. Used by permission. On Lavender Jane Loves Women, *her* Never Been Better *(both Women'sWaxWorks) & in her* Adventures in Women's Music *(TomatoPublics). Recs & SB avail fr: Ladyslipper Music, PO Box 3124, Durham NC 27705.* OU59

An excellent source of women's songs is Hilda Wenner & Elizabeth Freilicher Here's to the Women: 100 Songs for *& about* American Women, *Syracuse Univ Press, 1987. Two good but out-of-print sources are Joyce Cheyney, Marcia Deihl, & Deborah Silverstein,* All Our Lives *Diana Press, 1976, and Jerry Silverman,* The Liberated Woman's Songbook, *Macmillan, 1971.*

There are a number of songs about women's experience in WORK. See also: "Come All Ye Fair...Ladies," "Who's Gonna Shoe...Foot?" (BAL) "Farmer" (FARM) "Harriet Tubman" (FREE) "House of the Rising Sun" (HARD) "Can't Kill the Spirit" (HOPE) "Coal Mining Woman," "Mountain Song" (MTN) "Mothers Daughters Wives" (PEACE) "When I Was a Fair Maid" (SEA) "Woman at the Well" (SPIRS) "Eliz Gurley Flynn," "Hay Una Mujer" (STRUG) & "Truck Drivin' Woman" (TRAV).

All Used Up

I spent my whole life making somebody rich
I busted my ass for that son-of-a-bitch
And he left me to die like a dog in a ditch
And told me **I'm all used up**
He used up my labor, he used up my time
He plundered my body & squandered my mind
And gave me a pension of handouts & wine
And told me **I'm all used up** **(in 3/4)**

E - / A B7 / EB7 A / EB7 E // A E / 2nd → 4th

My kids are in hock to a God you call work
Slaving their lives out for some other jerk
My youngest in Frisco just made shipping clerk
And he don't know **I'm all used up**
Young people reaching for power & gold
Don't have respect for anything old
For pennies they're bought & for promises sold
Someday they'll all be **used up**

They use up the oil, they use up the trees
They use up the air & they use up the sea
Well, how about you, friend & how about me?
What's left when we're **all used up**?
I'll finish my life in this crummy hotel
It's lousy with bugs & my God, what a smell!
But my plumbing still works & I'm clear as a bell
Don't tell me **I'm all used up**

Outside my window the world passes by
It gives me a handout & spits in my eye
And no one can tell me, 'cause no one knows why
I'm livin', but **I'm all used up**
Sometimes in my dreams I sit by a tree
My life is a book of how things used to be
And kids gather 'round & they listen to me
And they don't think **I'm all used up**

And there's songs & there's laughter & things I can do
And all that I've learned I can give back to you
I'd give my last breath just to make it come true
No, I'm not **used up**
They use up the oil & they use up the trees
They use up the air & they use up the sea
Well, how about you, friend, & how about me?
What's left when we're **all used up**?

— **Bruce ("U. Utah") Phillips**

© 1981 by On Strike Music. All rights administered by Music Management, PO Box 174, Pleasantville NY 10570. Used by permission. — On his All Used Up *(Philo), Peter Alsop* Draw the Line. *In* Carry It On. OW02

Aragon Mill

At the east end of town, at the foot of the hill
Stands a chimney so tall, that says "Aragon Mill"
And the only tune I hear, is the sound of the wind
As it blows thru the town, weave & spin, weave & spin

C - Am - / G - F C :||

But there's no smoke at all, coming out of the stack
The mill has shut down & it ain't a-coming back

Well, I'm too old to work & I'm too young to die
Tell me, where shall we go, my old gal & I?

There's no children at all, in the narrow, empty street
The mill has closed down, it's so quiet I can't sleep

Yes, the mill has shut down, it's the only life I know
Tell me where will I go, tell me where will I go?

— **Si Kahn**

© Joe Hill Music (ASCAP). All rights reserved. Used by permission. — aka: "Weave & Spin." On his New Wood *(JuneAppal), Planxty* Words & Music *(Shanachie), Bok Muir & Trickett* Water Over Stone, *Peggy Seeger* Fr Where I Stand, *Hazel Dickens* Hard Hitting S for Hard Hit People, *Margaret Christi* Looking Towards Home, *Pete Seeger et al (on & in)* Carry It On, *Hans Theessink* Titanic, *Dry Branch Fire Squad* Fannin the Flames, *& Red Clay Ramblers* Chucking the Frizz. *In* SO! *28:4, 44:4 & in* New Folk Favs. OW03

Babies in the Mill

I used to work in factories, when things was movin' slow
When babies worked in cotton mills, each morning had to go
Ev'ry morning just at five, the whistle blew on time
To call those babies out of bed, at the age of 8 or 9
Get out of bed you sleepyheads, get you a bite to eat
The fact'ry whistle's calling you, there's no more time to sleep

(in 3/4) D - G D/- - E7 A ||: D - G D/- - A D :||

To their jobs those little ones was strictly forced to go
They had to be at work on time, thru rain & sleet & snow
Many times when things went wrong their bosses often frowned
Many times those little ones was kicked & shoved around

Our children they grew up unlearned, they never went to school
They never learned to read & write, they learned to spin and spool
Many times I close my eyes & see that picture still
When the textile work was carried out by babies in the mill

Old timer can't you see that scene, way back in years gone by
When babies had to go to work the same as you & I
Aren't you glad that things have changed & we have lots of fun
As we go in & do the jobs that babies used to run

— Dorsey Dixon

 On his Babies in the Mill *(Testament) & on Joe Glaser* Textile Voices *(Collector). In* SO! *29:3,* Carry It On *&* Here's to the Women. OW04

The Bread Song

Bread, where does it come from?
You find it on the shelf with a paper bag on
It comes from the ground & a factory too
Takes a whole lot of work just to get it to you
From the sun & the air & the water & the land
Lots of working people & lots of working hands (repeat)

D - A D :|| (4x) **cho:** ||: G - - - / D - A D :||

Lettuce, where does it come from?
You find it near the pickle in a hamburger bun
Someone picks it from the ground
That's a lot of hard work & a lot of bending down

Hamburger, where does it come from?
You eat it with mustard & ketchup on
A cow eats some grass & gets all fat
Takes a farmer & a butcher & a cook for that

Ice cream, where does it come from?
You eat it on a cone with sprinkles on
It used to be made from sugar & cream
Now they put in junk like gasoline

— Frente Music Collective

 — On Gary Lapow Supermarket Shuffle. *In* Friction in the System *&* SO! *28:3.* OW05

Casey Jones (Union Version)

The workers on the S.P. Line to strike sent out a call
But Casey Jones, the engineer, he wouldn't strike at all
His boiler it was leaking & its drivers on the bum
And his engine & its bearings they were all out of plumb

Casey Jones – kept his junkpile running
Casey Jones – was working double time
Casey Jones – got a wooden medal
For being good & faithful on the S.P. Line

A - / - B7E / A - / - EA :||

The workers said to Casey "Won't you help us with this strike?"
But Casey said "Let me alone, you'd better take a hike"
Then Casey's wheezy engine ran right off the wornout track
And Casey hit the river with an awful crack

Casey...hit the river bottom / ...broke his blooming spine
...became an angeleno
He took a trip to heaven on the S.P. Line

When Casey Jones got up to heaven to the Pearly Gate
He said "I'm Casey Jones, the guy that pulled the S.P. freight"
"You're just the man" said Peter "our musicians are on strike
You can get a job a-scabbing anytime you like"

...got a job in heaven / ...was doing mighty fine
...went scabbing on the angels
Just like he did to the workers on the S.P. Line

The angels got together & they said it wasn't fair
For Casey Jones to go around a-scabbing everywhere
The Angels Union No. 23, they sure were there
And they promptly fired Casey down the Golden Stair

...went to Hell a-flying / ...the Devil said "O fine
...get busy shoveling sulfur
That's what you get for scabbing on the S.P.Line"

— Joe Hill, 1911

For tune sources see under TRAV. OW06

The Chemical Worker Song

A process man am I & I'm telling you no lie
I work & breathe among the fumes that trail across the sky
There's thunder all around me & poison in the air
There's a lousy smell that smacks of Hell & dust all in me hair

Em - - - / - - - Bm / Em Am C Bm
EmBm EmAm EmBm Em

And it's go, boy, go, they'll time your every breath
And every day you're in this place you're two days nearer death / But yer go-o-o

EmBm Em **(2x)** / EmBm **(4x)** / Em -

I've worked among the spinners & I've breathed the oily smoke
I've shovelled up the gypsum & it nigh on makes you choke
I've stood knee deep in cyanide, gone sick with caustic burn
Been working rough & seen enough to make your stomach turn

There's overtime & bonus opportunities galore
The young lads like the money & they all come back for more
But soon you're knocking on & look older than you should
For every bob made on the job you pay with flesh & blood

— Ron Angel

 — On his alb (Tradition), Judy Gorman-Jacobs Right Behind You In The Left Hand Lane, *Magpie* Working My Life Away *& Lorre Wyatt* Roots & Branches. *In* SO! *29:3,* The Eng FSinger *(Collins) &* The Big Red SB. OW07

Coffee

When I wake up in the morning I will plug in the pot
If I choose to do it, drink my coffee hot
But I work in an office that is run by men
Who expect me to do it again & again

Coffee, the bane of my life
I am not paid to be an office wife
You've got hands & a modicum of sense & health
You can make your goddamn coffee for yourself

D - / A - / D - / A GD // D - / - A / **3rd & 4th** /

It's hard to be working in a paper life
To shuffle paper & to have to type
To file every morning & to balance the books
I'll be damned if I also have to cook

I receive all your visitors with charm & a smile
And I find important documents you lose in a file
Work overtime on call, draft reports you cannot do
And I make 10,000 less than you

If you're too important to make coffee or tea
Well that sure says what you must think of me
If the logic of this song doesn't filter thru
You drip, I still have grounds to sue!

— w: Cassandra Amesley — m: trad. "Simple Gifts"

 — On Solid Ground *(tape – Ladyslipper). Tune sources: see FAITH.* OW08

Cotton Mill Girls

I worked in the cotton mill all of my life
And I ain't got nothin' but a Barlow knife
It's a hard time cotton mill girls
It's a hard time everywhere
It's a hard time cotton mill girls (3x)
It's a hard time everywhere

D G / D A / D G / DA D :||

In 1916 you heard it said
Move to cotton country & get ahead / **& it's a hard time...**

Them country folk, they oughta be killed
For leavin' their farms & goin' to the mill...

They raised the wages up half a cent
And the poor old hands didn't know what it meant...

They raised the wages up half a cent more
But they went up a dime at the company store...

Us factory girls work ten hours a day
For 14 cenets of measly pay...

When I die, don't bury me at all
Just hang me up on the spinning room wall
Pickle my bones in alcohol
It's a hard time everywhere

— Hedy West

 — On her Hedy West *New Harmony Sisterhood Band* Ain't I a Woman? *& on* The Pennywhistlers. *In* SO! *12:2 & 27:7 &* Reprints #6, Liberated Women's SB, S that Changed the World, FS EncyV1 & Here's to the Women. OW09

Drill, Ye Tarriers, Drill

Ev'ry morning at 7 o'clock
There were twenty tarriers a-working at the rock
And the boss comes along & he says, "Keep still
And come down heavy on the cast iron drill!"

Am - / - E / Am - / AmEm CE

And drill ye tarriers, drill! / Drill ye tarriers drill!
O it's work all day for the sugar in your tay
Down behind the railway
And drill ye tarriers, drill! / And blast! & fire!

AmG Am - / / Am - / - E / AmG Am / - -

The boss was a fine man down to the ground
He married a lady six foot 'round
She baked good bread & she baked it well
But she baked it hard as the holes of hell!

Now the new foreman was Jim McGann
By God, he was a blamed mean man!
Last week a premature blast went off
And a mile in the air went big Jim Goff

The next time pay day came around
Jim Goff a dollar short was found
When he asked what for, came this reply
"You were docked for the time you were up in the sky"

— Thomas Casey & Connelly (vaudeville team, 1888)

In SO! *30:3,* Hootenanny SB, FS Abecedary, Golden Ency, S of Work & Protest, S for Pickin & Singin, S That Changed the World, Sing Along w World's Fav FS, FiresB of FS, *Lomax* FS of NAm, *JJ Geller* Farm S & Their Stories *(1931),* FiresB of Fun & Games *&* FS Ency V2. *On Weavers* On Tour & Traveling On, *Sam Hinton* The Real McCoy *(Decca) & Tim Rogers & Barry Luft* S of the Iron Trail. *Rec by Alan Lomax.* OW10

The Factory Girl

No more shall I work in the factory to greasy up my clothes
No more shall I work in the factory with splinters in my toes
It's pity me, my darling – pity me, I say
It's pity me, my darling & carry me away

D - - - / - - A D :||

No more shall I hear the bosses say "Boys you better daulf"
No more shall I hear...say "Spinners, you better clean off"

No more shall I wear that old black dress, greasy all around
No...wear the old black bonnet with holes all in the crown

No more shall I hear the whistle blow to call me up so soon
No...blow to call me from my home

No more shall I hear the drummer wheels a-rolling over my head
When factory girls are hard at work, I'll be in my bed

No more shall I see the super come all dressed up so fine
For I know I'll marry a country boy before the year is round

— coll, adap & arr by John A. Lomax & Alan Lomax

 — aka: "Pity Me My Darling." In Carry It On *& on Peggy Seeger* Penelope Isn't Waiting Anymore. OW11

Fifty-Nine Cents

High school daydreams come easy & free
When you're a working woman whatcha gonna be?
A senator, a surgeon, aim for the heights
But the guidance office says lower your sights to:

Am Am7 F E / / Am E G D / F - E -

59¢ for every man's dollar
59¢ it's a lowdown deal
59¢ makes a grown woman holler
They give you a <u>diploma</u>* it's your paycheck they steal
*** (2nd cho: degree 3rd: title)**

/ " / / Am Am7 D E / Am C E - → 1st

She's off to college, the elite kind
To polish her manners, sharpen her mind
Honors in English, letter in lacrosse
Teaches her to type for her favorite boss at:

Junior executive on her way up
Special assistant to the man at the top
She's one in a million & all she found
Was her own secretary now to order around at:

But the word is being processed in the typing pool
A working woman ain't nobody's fool
She's telling the boss on Secretary's Day
You can keep your flowers, buddy, give me a raise more than

(last cho) 59¢ for every man's dollar
59¢ – oh the deal has changed
59¢ makes a grown woman holler
You can keep your flowers, buddy, give us a raise!

— Fred Small

 On his Love's Gonna Carry Us *& in his* Breaking fr the Line. *Also on Bobbie McGee* Bread & Raises. *In* Carry It On. OW12

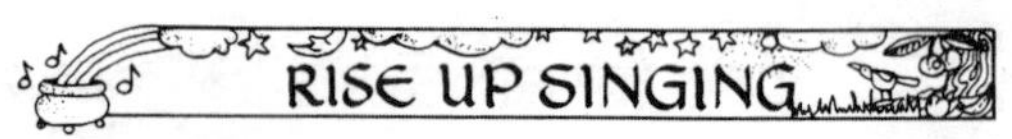

Forty Hour Week

There are people in this country who work hard every day
Not for fame or fortune do they strive
But the fruits of their labor are worth more than their pay
And it's time a few of them were recognized

C - G C / F C G - / 1st / F G C -

Hello Detroit auto workers, **let me thank you for your time**
You work a 40 hour week for a living, just to send it on down the line
Hello Pittsburgh steel mill workers, **let me thank...time**
You work a 40 hour week for a living, just to...line

FC C F C / F C - G C - :||

(1st bridge) This is for the one who swings the hammer driving home the nail
Or the one behind the counter, ringing up the sale
Or the one who fights the fires, the one who brings the mail
For everyone who works behind the scenes

G - F C / / Am - Em F / G - - -

You can see them every morning in the factories & the fields
In the city streets & the quiet country towns
Working together like spokes inside a wheel
They keep this country turning around

(2nd cho) Hello Kansas wheatfield farmer, **let me...**
You work... / Hello West Virginia coal miner... **/ You...**

(2nd bridge) This is for the one who drives the big rig up & down the road
Or the one out in the warehouse, bringing in the load
Or the waitress, the mechanic, the policeman on patrol
For everyone who works behind the scenes
With a spirit you can't replace with no machine

(last line add:) G - - -

(tag) Hello America – **let me thank you for your time!**

C - Dm G C -

— Dave Loggins, Don Schlitz & Lea Silver

 — aka: "For a Livin'." On Alabama 40 Hr. Wk & Gr H *(RCA).* OW13

Gallo Song

I was having dinner the other night
With the Bishop of Idaho
He served roast beef & mashed potatoes
And a bottle of Paisano

D - / - A7 / - - / - D

And I said "Paisano* **is a Gallo wine**
You got to take that bottle back
And you cannot drink it until Gallo signs
You got to take that bottle back" * (Thunderbird**, etc.)**

I was walking thru this alley the other night
And these were the words I heard
"Give me all your money 'cause I got to go
Buy a bottle of Thunderbird"

I was at a concert the other night
When I felt the tap on my arm
I took the joint, but I refused
The bottle of Boone's Farm

I was lying in bed the other night
Talking with my friend named Jane
I brought out the baby oil
And she brought out Andre Champagne

So when friends & family & relatives too
Take Gallo off the rack
Don't be afraid to step right up
And tell them to take it back
(last cho) Just say "Didn't you see that's a Gallo wine?"

— Steve & Peter Jones

 — On their Steve & Peter Jones *(CloudsRecs). Although a 3-year contract was signed between Gallo & the United Farmworkers in 2000, the union continues to battle the winery over health benefits & other issues.* OW14

Go to Work on Monday

I did my part in World War II, got wounded for the nation
Now my lungs are all shot down, there ain't no compensation

C - - F / /

I'm gonna go to work on Monday, one more time
I'm gonna go to work on Monday, one more time, one more time
I'm gonna go to work on Monday, one more time

C CF C - / C - F C / 1st /

The doctor says I smoke too much, he says that I'm not trying
He says he don't know what I've got, but we both know he's lying

The last time I went near my job, I thought my lungs were broken
Chest bound down like iron bands, I couldn't breathe for choking

The politicians in this state, they're nothing short of rotten
They buy us off with fancy words, & sell us out to cotton

The doctor says both lungs are gone, there ain't no way to shake it
But I can't live without a job, somehow I've got to take it

They tell me I can't work at all, there ain't no need of trying
But living like some used up thing, is just this short of dying

Sitting on my front porch swing, I'm like someone forgotten
Head all filled with angry thoughts & lungs filled up with cotton

— Si Kahn

 On his Doing My Job *(FF).* OW15

I am a Union Woman

I am a union woman, just as brave as I can be
I do not like the bosses & the bosses don't like me
Join the N.M.U. *[C.I.O.]*, **come join the N.M.U.** *[C.I.O.]***!**

Am - Em Am / Em Am E Am // - - E Am

I was raised in old Kentucky, in Kentucky born & bred
And when I joined the union they called me a Rooshian Red

This is the worst time on earth that I have ever saw
To get killed out by gun thugs & framed up by the law

The bosses ride big fine hosses while we walk in the mud
Their flag it is the dollar sign while ours is striped in blood

When my husband asked the boss for a job, this is the words he said
"Bill Jackson, I can't work you, sir, your wife's a Rooshian Red"

We are many thousand strong & I'm glad to say
We are getting stronger & stronger every day

— w: Aunt Molly Jackson — m: trad. ("Lay the Lily Low")

 — Same tune as "Which Side Are You On?" On S & Stories of Aunt Molly Jackson *(Folkways), Pete Seeger* Can't You See This System Isn't... *& (on & in)* Carry It On, *Bobbie McGee* Bread & Raises.. *In* SO! *10:4,* Liberated Women's SB, All Our Lives & Here's to the Women. OW16

Joe Hill

I dreamed I saw Joe Hill last night, alive as you & me
Says I "But Joe, you're 10 years dead"
"I never died" says he **(2x)**

A - D A / D EA / B7 E / - A

"In Salt Lake, Joe" says I to him, him standing by my bed
"They framed you on a murder charge"
Says Joe "But I ain't dead"...

"The Copper Bosses shot you Joe, they killed you Joe" says I
"Takes more than guns to kill a man" / Says Joe "I didn't die"

And standing there as big as life, & smiling with his eyes
Joe says "What they could never kill / went on to organize"

"Joe Hill ain't dead" he says to me "Joe Hill ain't never died
When workers strike & organize / Joe Hill is by their side"

From San Diego up to Maine, in every mine & mill
Where workers stand up for their rights
It's there you'll find Joe Hill

— w: Alfred Hayes m: Earl Robinson

 — On Earl's Strange Unusual Evening, Alive & Well *(Aspen) &* Walk In the Sun *(FW2324). On Joe Glazer* Sings Labor S & S of Joe Hill. *On Joan Baez* Fr Every Stage, Carry It On, One Day At A Time *& in her* SB. *On Pete Seeger* Can't You See This System... *& Utah Phillips* Sings the S of the IWW & We Have Fed You All *(Philo). In* Peoples SB, *(in & on)* Carry It On, S of Work & Protest, Treas of FS, & FiresB of FS. OW17

The Jute Mill Song

O dear me, the mill is running fast
And we poor shifters cannot get no rest
Shiftin' bobbins coarse & fine
They fairly make you work for your 10 & 9

D - - - / G - - A / D - - G / D - G A

O dear me, I wish the day were done
Running up & down the pass is no fun
Shiftin', piecin', spinnin', warp, weft & twine
To feed & clothe my babies off of 10 & 9

O dear me, the world is ill divided
Them that work the hardest are the least provided
But I must bide contented dark days or fine
There's no much pleasure livin' off of 10 & 9

— Mary Brookbank with new w & new m adap by Mike Jones, Cindy Kent, Mansel Davies & John Fyffe

 — aka:"Ten & Nine, O Dear Me The Mill." Brookbank wrote the original around 1920 abt her experiences of millwork during WWI. She worked for years in a Dundee (Scotland) jute mill. She died in 1978. "Ten & nine" is the scant daily wage of 10 shillings, 9 pence. In SO! 27:5. *On Magpie* Working My Life Away *(Collector), Shays Rebellion* Daniel Shay's Highway, *Liam Clancy* Ten & Nine *& Golden Ring* 5 Days Singing, V2 *(FolkLeg).* OW18

Mary Got a New Job

Mary got a new job, workin' on the line
Help to make the automobile
Wasn't very long til the job was going fine
And she liked the way it made her feel
It gave her independence to drive into the lot
And pull her heavy work clothes on
She liked the rush & clatter, she liked her new friends
And her fav'rite was a man named John

D - / - A / - - / - D
D - / D7 G / - D / A D **(last cho add:** A D **)**

John was like a brother, workin' at her side
And they both came on the job the same day
Learned the job together, how the ropes were tied
Went together down to draw their first pay
Opening up his packet, Johhny dropped his cash
Money was all over the floor
Mary saw the money, saw to her surprise
Johnny had a whole lot more, and she said:

"Who's been matching you sweat for sweat?
Who's been working on the line
Who's been earning what she ain't got yet?
All I want is what's mine
I've got hands & eyes & a back like you
And I use them hard the whole day
I stand here working just as hard as you do
And I want my equal pay"
(add after last cho: And I want my E.R.A.!"**)**

Johnny was a good man – Mary knew that
Taught to think of women as queens
Now here stood Mary in her yellow hard hat
And her broken down faded blue jeans
He liked her more than anybody he knew
He was close to understanding why
She didn't cuss or spit or even raise her voice
She just looked him straight in the eye & she said:

— Tom Paxton

 — On his Paxton Report. OW19

The Mill Was Made of Marble

I dreamed that I had died & gone to my reward
A job in heaven's textile plant on a golden boulevard
The mill was made of marble, the machines were made of gold
And nobody ever got tired & nobody ever grew old

(in 3/4) CG C F C / F CAm G C :||

This mill was built in a garden, no dust or lint could be found
The air was so fresh & so fragrant with flowers & trees all around

It was quiet & peaceful in heaven, there was no clatter or boom
You could hear the most beautiful music as you worked at the spindle & loom

There was no unemployment in heaven, we worked steady all thru the year
We always had food for our children, we never were haunted by fear

When I woke from this dream about heaven, I wondered if someday there'd be
A mill like that one down below here on earth for workers like you & me

— Joe Glazer

 — In (& on) Carry It On *& in* S of Work & Protest. OW20

WORK

Millworker

Now my grandfather was a sailor, he blew in off the water
My father was a farmer, & I his only daughter
Took up with a no good millworkin' man, from Massachusetts
Who dies from too much whiskey & leaves me these three faces to feed

Millwork ain't easy, millwork ain't hard
Millwork it ain't nothin' but an awful boring job
I'm waiting for a daydream to take me thru the morning
And put me in a coffee break where I can have a sandwich and remember

(open D tuning) D Dmaj7 G Dmaj7
D A(D) G A(D) / / D A(D) G A7 D -

Then it's me & my machine for the rest of the morning
For the rest of the afternoon, for the rest of my life

C - G Em / Gm - A - D -

Now my mind begins to wander to the days back on the farm
I can see my father smilin' at me swingin' on his arm
I can hear my grandad's stories of the storms out on Lake Erie
Where vessels & cargos & fortunes & sailor's lives were lost

Yes but it's my life has been wasted & I have been the fool
To let this manufacturer use my body for a tool
I can ride home in the evening, starin' at my hands
Swearin' by my sorrow that a young girl ought to stand a better chance

(bridge) O may I work the mills just as long as I am able
And never meet the man whose name is on the label

C - G Em / Gm - A -

— James Taylor

© 1979 Country Road Music, Inc (BMI) All rights reserved. Used by permission. — On his Flag *(CBS). Fr the musical* Working *(based on the powerful book by Studs Terkel consisting of in-depth interviews with a vast variety of US workingpeople on what their life on the job is actually like). Also on Frankie Armstrong* I Heard a Woman Singing *& Prisc Herdman* Forgotten Dreams. OW21

Nicolia

(intro) If Nicolia had a boat, if Nicolia made it her home
If Nicolia sang a song, she would sing "O – harbor me"

D - - A / D - F G D -

Nicolia girl worked inside a factory
She never saw the sun, never felt the summer sea
She dreamed someday she'd meet a prince
but she's been real disappointed since
Nicolia girl got a big idea somehow
And she's sailing, sailing now

D - A - / / G D G DA / D - A - / F G D -

Nicolia girl found a book called "Organize!"
And she understood every word to her surprise
So with an old sail & a novice crew, she's made a great big wave on the ocean blue / **Nicolia...**

Nicolia girl sings her favorite working song
To let the people know now's the time to move along
Small boats on a mighty sea, small girls in a factory
Nicolia girl... / And they're sailing, sailing now

(as intro) Now Nicolia has a boat, Nicolia's made it her home
Nicolia sings a song, & she sings "O – harbor me!"

(tag) O – won't you harbor me? Harbor me, harbor me!

𝄆 G F G F 𝄇

— w: Holly Near **— m: Jeff Langley**

© 1975 Hereford Music (ASCAP). Used by permission. On her You Can Know all I Am *& in her* Words & Music. OW22

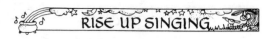

Old J.P. He Ain't What He Used to Be

1. Old J.P. he ain't what he used to be **(3x)**
 Old J.P. he ain't what he used to be, now we've organized
 Now we've organized, now we've organized
 Old J.P. he ain't what he used to be, now we've organized

E - B7 E / / E - A E / 1st

2. Roanoke Rapids ain't what it used to be...
3. Stevens profits ain't what they...
4. All of us just ain't what we...

— w: Stevens workers with James Orange & Si Kahn
— m: "The Old Grey Mare"

© Joe Hill Music (ASCAP). All rights reserved. Used by permission. In Stevensongs. *Substitute your own company name, hometown, etc.* OW23

Our Life Is More Than Our Work

Look all around you, say, look all around you
See all there is just to be alive about
Look all around you at the people around you
See all there is just to being alive

D - / G D / - - / G AD

O our life – is – more than our work
And our work – is – more than our jobs
You know that our life – is... work / And our work...jobs

D A G D / / / /

Time clocks & bosses, investments & losses
How can we measure our living in numerals?
Time...losses / How can we measure our life in this way

Think how our life could be, feel how our life could flow
If just for once we could get into letting go
Think...flow / If just for once we could let ourselves go

So let go what holds you back, close your eyes, take a dive
We got a universe we got to keep alive
Let go what holds you back, close your eyes, take a dive
We got a universe fighting to live

— Charlie King

© 1978 Charlie King/Pied Asp Music (BMI). Used by permission. — On his Somebody's Story *& his* Two Good Arms. *In* SO! *28:5.* OW24

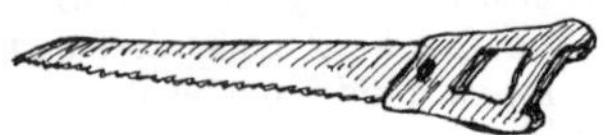

Please Tip Your Waitress

Sixteen tables, four chairs at each one
Two shows every night she's on the run
Three coffees here, five desserts there, let's go
And some jerk over there says she's too slow

C - G - / - - C - 𝄇

Please tip your waitress, she's workin' hard for you
She'll walk a few miles before she's thru
She's got bills to pay & food to buy like you
Please tip your waitress 'cause she's workin' hard for you

F - C - / G - C - 𝄇

It's "honey" this & "dear" that all the time
But that's not half as bad as all those lines
She's a strong woman & her temper's gonna perk
If one more guy asks when she gets off work

When she gets home from work she still can't rest
'Cause tomorrow at the college there's a test
She's up early in the morning as a rule
Making sure the kids get off to school

Her paycheck's low, she does the work of two
When something's wrong folks blame you know who
And then they say "Come on now, where's your smile?"
While the owner's gettin' richer all the while

— **Willie Sordill**

 On his Please Tip..., Walls to Roses *(Folkways alb of new men's music) & Bobbie McGee* Bread & Raises. *In* SO! *28:1 &* Here's to the Women. OW25

Rise Again

I can feel the spirit building
Soft as a whisper but loud as a roar
I can feel something a-stirring
Like I never have before
We've been quiet too long my friends
But the working folks of this country will rise again

D - - - / G - D - / 1st / E - A - / G - D - / DG DA D -

We've been quiet for thirty years now
You had the work & you gave us the pay
But with hard times round the corner
You think we've seen our better day
But we're not going back to where we began
And the working folk of this country will rise again

And now you say that you don't need me
You lay me off, no work you say
You expect to see my head a-hanging
As I pack & walk away
But with my brothers & sisters, so proudly we'll stand
As the working folks of this country rise again

And I've heard tell of Big Bill Haywood
And Elizabeth Gurley Flynn
They were old time union warriors
And gave no thought to giving in
We will rekindle that spirit again
And the working folks of this country will rise again!

— **Tom Juravich**

 — On his Rising Again *& on AFL-CIO* S for Labor. *In* Carry It On & Labor Heritage SB. *In* SO! *34:2.* OW26

Roll the Union On

We're gonna roll, we're gonna roll
We're gonna roll the union on! (repeat)

D - / - A7 / - - / - D

If the boss **is in the way we're gonna roll it* over him**
We're gonna roll it over him (2x)
If the boss **is in the way we're gonna roll it over him**
We're gonna roll the union on!

D - / A7 D :|| (* or "right")

If the scab **is in the way...**
If the sheriff's **in the way...**

Substitute others who are in the way ending with final verse:
Whoever's in the way, we're gonna roll right over him

— **John L. Handcox & Lee Hays**

 — SO! *31:3,* FS Ency V1, *(on & in)* Carry It On & S of Work & Protest. *On Almanac Singers* Talking Union. OW27

The Runaway Shop Song

I wish I was in the land of cotton
Wages there are on the bottom
Look away (3x) Dixie land
Down there where the air is sunny
You can make all kinds of money / **Look away...**

A - / D - / A - E A :||

I'll move my plant to Dixie, today, today
I'll lock the gates & close the doors – goodbye to union wages
Away, away, away we'll go to Dixie (2x)

A D B7 E / A D A E / A E A EA / /

Down among the alligators
Where there's friendly legislators / **Look away...**
Folks will smile & call you neighbor
You can't buy no cheaper labor / **Look...**

Union folks up North don't like me
All they want to do is strike me...
Now it's my turn to get even
Go down South like J.P.Stevens...

— **w: Si Kahn** — **m: trad ("Dixie")**

 — Thru out history whenever workers have battled successfully for union contracts, decent wages, work safety laws, etc., management has responded by moving to areas where workers are less organized and legislation more backward. This has happened from New England to the Southeastern US & later from there to Japan, to Taiwan, to Singapore, etc. Reinforces the idea none of us can be free til we are all *free "the whole wide world around!"* OW28

The Sick Note

Dear Sir, I write this note to you, to tell you of my plight
For, at the time of writing, I am not a pretty sight
My body is all black & blue, my face a deathly grey
And I write this note to say, why Paddy's not at work today

D - A D / G D E A / G D Em G / 1st /

Whilst working on the 14th floor, some bricks I had to clear
To throw them down from such a height, was not a good idea
The Foreman wasn't very pleased, the bloody awkward sod
And he said I'd have to cart them down the ladders in my hod

Now clearing all these bricks by hand, it was so very slow
So I hoisted up a barrel & secured the rope below
But in my haste to do the job, I was too blind to see
That a barrel full of building bricks was heavier than me

And so, when I untied the rope, the barrel fell like lead
And clinging tightly to the rope, I started up instead!
I shot up like a rocket til to my dismay I found
That halfway up I met the bloody barrel, coming down!

The barrel broke my shoulder, as toward the ground it sped
And when I reached the top I banged the pulley with my head
I hung on tightly, numb with shock from this almighty blow
And the barrel spilled out half the bricks, 14 floors below

Now when those bricks had fallen from the barrel to the floor
I then outweighed the barrel & so started down once more
Still clinging tightly to the rope, my body racked with pain
When, halfway down, I met the bloody barrel once again!

The force of this collision, halfway up the office block
Caused multiple abrasions & a nasty state of shock
Still clinging tightly to the rope, I fell towards the ground
And I landed on the broken bricks the barrel scattered round

I lay there, groaning on the ground, I thought I'd passed the worst
But the barrel hit the pulley-wheel & then the bottom burst
A shower of bricks rained down on me, I hadn't got a hope
As I lay there bleeding on the ground, I let go the bloody rope!

The barrel was free to fall & down it came once more
And landed right across me, as I lay upon the floor
It broke three ribs & my left arm & I can only say
That I hope you understand why Paddy's not at work today!

— **w: Pat Cooksey**

— **m: trad. ("In the Garden Where the Praties Grow")**

 — aka: "Paddy & the Barrel," "The Bricklayer Song," "Why Paddy's Not at Work Today." Before the New Deal in the US, however, companies routinely fired workers who were disabled on the job with no compensation or means of supporting their families whatsoever. In SO! *30:3,* The Furey's SB *& on a Furey Bros. album. Dubliners double 25th anniversary alb.* OW29

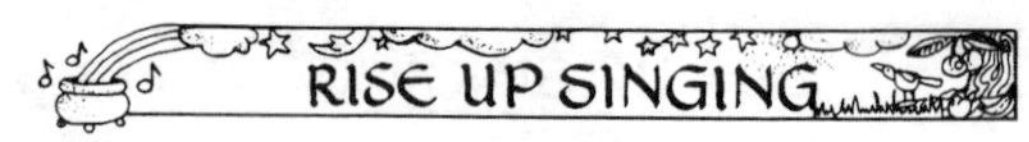

Stevens Don't Allow

Stevens* don't allow no organizing round here (2x)
We don't care what Stevens don't allow, gonna organize anyhow
Stevens don't allow no organizing round here

D A D - / - - A - / - D_7 G - / D A D -

Stevens don't allow no unions around here (2x)
We don't care what...gonna have our union **anyhow...**

Put in other things your company doesn't allow:
leaflets / pass out leaflets, blue cards / sign those blue cards, contracts / get a contract, dignity / live with dignity, sick pay / win our sick pay, **etc.**

— w: adapted by Si Kahn — m: trad ("Mama Don't Allow...")

** Fill in the name of your own favorite unionbusting company! Joe Hill Music (ASCAP). All rights reserved. Used by permission. For tune sources see CREAT.* OW30

Taft-Hartley

Part of me says we shouldn't be striking
But most of me says we should
'Cause when the owners get together with the U.S. Government
You know it ain't gonna do me no good
And if they keep on handing us a yellow-dog contract
We're gonna have to turn it down
Mr. Taft can dig it, Mr. Hartley can haul it
'Cause I'm gonna leave it in the ground

C - / F C / C↓ / D G / C - / F C // F C / G C

Mr. Taft can dig it, Mr. Hartley can haul it
Mr. Carter can supervise the crew
And if they find it too hard they got the National Guard
To fix their bayonets & shovel like fools
It's gonna take a lot longer than 80 short days
For this miner to cool on down / Mr. Taft can dig it...

/ " / " / G - / FG C / " / " / " / " /

The mine-owner don't worry 'bout safety regulations
He's walking in the sun all day
But when you're down in the mine the first thing you learn
You gotta stay alive if you want to spend that pay
So if we sign away our right to be wildcat strikin'
You know they're gonna push us around / **Mr. Taft...**

Well they took away our food-stamps, our medical plan
I got a mortgage I just can't pay
But the folks here in town are gonna give me credit
'Cause they know I'll be back on my feet some day
And if some gun-totin' thug takes to totin' for the owners
Better find himself another town / **Mr...**

Now my daddy's pensioned off at 80 bucks a week
It seems to get smaller every year
If every time the kids are sick I'm reachin' in my pocket
You know that pay raise is gonna disappear
No owner can outsmart me with his Taft & his Hartley
While the coal supply is running down
He may own the coal, but he don't own me
And I'm gonna leave it in the ground!

— Charlie King

© 1978 Charlie King/Pied Asp Music (BMI). Used by permission. — The Taft-Hartley Act of 1948 wiped out many of the progressive labor laws of the 1930s & largely stacked the cards in favor of management in its efforts to resist union organizing ever since. The law permits the govt to order an 80 day "cooling off" period in hopes of breaking a strike. This song was written during the 114 day miners' strike in 1977-78. On his Somebody Else's Story *& his* 2 Good Arms *& Peggy Seeger* Fr Where I Stand. OW31

Too Old to Work

You work in the factory all of your life
Try to provide for your kids & your wife
When you get too old to produce anymore
They hand you your hat & they show you the door

(in 3/4) C - F C/C A_m D G/C - F C/ - G - C

Too old to work, too old to work
When you're too old to work & you're too young to die
Who will take care of you, how'll you get by
When you're too old to work & you're too young to die?

C - F - / " / " / " /

You don't ask for favors when your life is thru
You've got a right to what's coming to you
Your boss gets a pension when he is too old
You helped him retire – you're out in the cold

They put horses to pasture, they feed them on hay
Even machines get retired some day
The bosses get pensions when their days are thru
Fat pensions for them, brother, nothing for you

There's no easy answer, there's no easy cure
Dreaming won't change it, that's one thing for sure
But fighting together we'll get there some day
And when we have won we will no longer say:

— Joe Glazer

© 1950 Joe Glazer. Used by permission. — On his 8 Songs for Labor *& Earl Robinson* Strange Unusual Eve. *In* SO! *6:4 &* Reprints *#2 &* S of Work & Protest. OW32

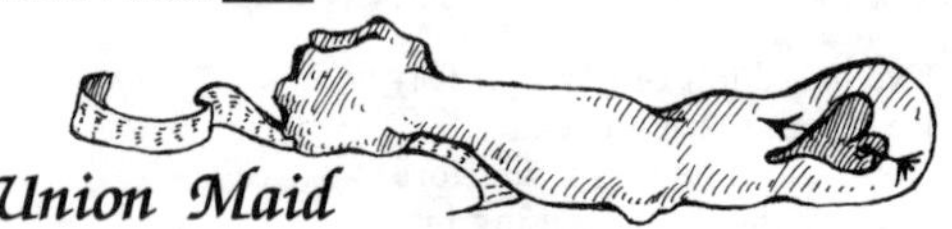

Union Maid

There once was a union maid who never was afraid
Of goons & ginks & company finks & the deputy sheriffs who made the raids
She went to the union hall when a meeting it was called
And when the company boys came 'round she always stood her ground

C - F C / G C D G / C - F C / G C G C

O you can't scare me, I'm sticking to the union
I'm sticking to the union, I'm sticking to the union
O you can't scare me, I'm sticking to the union
I'm sticking to the union til the day I die

F - C - / G - C - :||

This union maid was wise to the tricks of company spies
She never got fooled by a company stool, she'd always organize the guys
She always got her way, when she struck for higher pay
She'd show her card to the company guard & this is what she'd say:

You women who want to be free, take a little tip from me
Break outa that mold we've all been sold, you got a fighting his-to-ree
The fight for women's rights with workers must unite
Like Mother Jones, move those bones to the front of every fight!

— w: Woody Guthrie (new v. Cappie Israel)
— m: trad. ("Redwing")

TRO © 1961 & 1963 Ludlow Music, Inc, NY, NY. International copyright secured. Made in USA. All rights reserved incl. public performance for profit. Used by permission. — On his Hard Travelin, We Ain't Down Yet *& in his* SB, *New Harmony Sisterhood* Ain't I a Woman, *Seeger* Sings Woody Guthrie, *(on & in)* Carry It On, *Glazer* Sings Labor S, *Earl Robinson* Strange Unusual Eve, *Almanac Singers* Talkin Union, *Bobbie McGee* Bread & Raises *& on* Tribute to Woody Guthrie V2. *In* SO! *28:1,* Hootenanny SB, S of Work & Protest & Bells of Rhymney, Liberated Women's SB & Here's to the Women. OW33

We Are Building a Strong Union

We are building a strong union **(3x) / Workers in the mill!**

A - - - / E - D A / A A7 D A / - E A -

Every member makes us stronger **(3x) / Workers...**
We won't budge until we conquer...
We shall rise & gain our freedom...

— w: Marion (N.C.) textile workers — m: "Jacob's ladder"

Written by striking millworkers in a 1929 textile strike. Workers received $10 for a 72 hr. work week & revolted when the company tried to increase each shift fr 12 hrs to 12 hrs & 20 mins. The strike was smashed by state militia who shot & killed 6 workers & wounded 25 others. In S of Work & Protest. OW34

We Shall Not Be Moved

We shall not, we shall not be moved (2x)
Just like a tree that's planted by the water
We shall not be moved

D - A - / - - D D7 / G - D - / - A D -

1. For the union is behind us, **we shall not be moved (2x)**
   Just like a tree...
2. We're fighting for our freedom...
3. We're fighting for our children...
4. We'll build a mighty union...
5. ______ is our leader...
6. We are black & white together...
7. We are young & old together...

Fuertes, fuertes, fuertes somos ya (2x)
Como un arbol firma junto al rio / Fuertes somos ya

1. Luchamos por librarnos, **fuertes somos ya...**
2. Luchamos por los hijos...

(a 2nd Spanish version) No, no, no nos moverán (2x)
Como un arbol firme junto al rio / **no nos moverán**

1. Y el que no crea que haga la prueba, no nos mover n...
2. Unidos en la lucha...
3. Unidos en la huelga...
4. Unidos en sindicatos...
5. Construyendo el socialismo...
6. Y con un golpe de estado...

— w: textile workers

—m: Black Spiritual ("I Shall Not Be Moved")

1st Sp version is fr the United Farmworkers. 2nd is fr a Salvadoran union organizer who fled the death squads to take "Sanctuary" in the U.S. In Peoples SB, S of Work & Protest *&* Am Fav Bal, Children's S for a Friendly Planet, FS Ency V1 *&* S That Changed the World. *On Seeger* The Essential..., Talking Union *& (on & in)* Carry It On, *Joe Glazer* Sings Labor S, *Baez* Gracias A La Vida *(as No Nos Mover n), Carter Fam* Their Last Recording *(PineMtn) & Almanac Singers* Talking Union. OW35

Which Side Are You On?

Come all of you good workers, good news to you I'll tell
Of how the good old Union has come in here to dwell
Which side are you on? Which side are you on? (2x)

Am - E Am / Em A E Am // Am - E Am / /

My daddy was a miner, he's now in the air & sun
And I'll stick with the union til every battle's won

They say in Harlan County, there are no neutrals there
You're either with the union, or a thug for J.H. Blair

O workers can you stand it? O tell me how you can?
Will you be a crummy scab or lend us all a hand?

Don't scab for the bosses, don't listen to their lies
Us poor folks haven't got a chance, unless we organize

— w: Florence Reece — m: trad. ("Lay the Lily Low")

 — Reece, the wife of UMW organizer Sam Reece, wrote this song in the 1930s during the struggles of the UMW to organize Harlan Co mines. On P Seeger They'll Never Keep Us Down *(Rounder), Almanac Singers* Talking Union, Gr H *& (on & in)* Carry It On, *Seeger* Can't You See the System, *Carawan* S of Struggle & Celeb *(FF), Earl Robinson* Strange Unusual Eve *& McCutcheon* Barefoot Boy. *In* SO! *20:6,* Voices fr the Mtns, S That Changed the World, Peoples SB, S of Work & Protest, Here's to the Women, *&* Am Fav Bal. *Same tune as "I Am a Union Woman."* OW36

The White Collar Holler

Well I rise up every morning at a quarter to 8
Some woman who's my wife tells me not to be late
I kiss the kids good-bye I can't remember their names
And week after week it's always the same

E - - - / - - A B7 / E - - - / - - C B7

And it's ho boys, can't you code it & program it right
Nothing ever happens in this life of mine
I'm hauling up the data on the Xerox line

E - - - A B7 / E - - B7 / E - B7 E

Then it's code in the data, give the keyboard a punch
Then cross-correlate & a break for some lunch
Correlate, tabulate, process & screen
Program, printout, regress to the mean

Then it's home again, eat again, watch some TV
Make love to my woman at 10:53
I dream the same dream when I'm sleeping at night
I'm soaring over hills like an eagle in flight

Someday I'm gonna give up all the buttons & things
I'll punch that time clock til it can't ring
Burn up my necktie & set myself free
'Cause no-one's gonna fold, bend, or mutilate me

— Nigel Russell

 — Melody is a variant of "16 Tons". On Stan Rogers Betw the Breaks-Live! *& in his* S fr Fogarty's Cove. *On Reid Miller* Storytelling Minstrel. *In* SO! *36:2.* OW37

The Winnsboro Cotton Mill Blues

Old man Sargent, sitting at the desk
The damn' old fool won't give us a rest
He'd take the nickels off a dead man's eyes
To buy Coca Cola & Eskimo pies

D - / - EA / E - / ADm AdimA7

I got the blues (2x), I got the Winnsboro cotton mill blues
Lordy, Lordy, spoolin's hard
You know & I know, I don't have to tell
You work for Tom Watson, got to work like hell
I got the blues (2x), I got the Winnsboro Cotton Mill Blues

D - - D7 / G Gm / D - / BmE A
D - DA D

When I die, don't bury me at all
Just hang me up on the spool-room wall
Place a knotter in my hand
So I can spool in the Promised Land

When I die, don't bury me deep
Bury me down on 600 Street
Place a bobbin in each hand
So I can doff in the Promised Land

— w: anon. m: "Alcoholic Blues"

Written by an unknown millhand in Winnsboro, NC, during the 1920s. Rec by Bill Wolff in 1939 while he was teaching a summer course at the Southern Schl for Workers in NC. A woman in the gp sang him this song (new words to a popular blues song of the time). In SO! *10:4 &* Reprints #6, Hootenanny SB, FS Ency V2 *&* S of Work & Protest. *A parody is in* SO! *3:2. On Magpie* Working My Life Away *(Collector).* OW38

The Work of the Weavers

We're all met together here to sit & to crack
With our glasses in our hands & our wark upon our backs
There's nay a trade among them that can mend or can mak
If it wasna for the wark o' the weavers

G - C G / - - C D / G - C G / - - D G

If it wasna for the weavers what would ye do?
You wouldna hae a claith that was made o' woo'
You wouldna hae a coat o' the black or the blue
If it wasna for the wark o' the weavers

G D Em Bm / C G C D / " / " /

There's soldiers & there's sailors & glaziers & all
There's doctors & there's ministers & them that live by law
And our friends in South America tho' them we niver saw
But we ken they wear the wark o' the weavers

The weaving's a trade that niver can fail
As long as we need claithes for to keep another hale
So let us all be merry o'er a pitcher of good ale
And we'll drink to the health of the weavers!

— trad. (Scottish)

This is one of a whole genre of British folksongs in which different occupational groups express pride in their special contributions to society. In SO! *5:2 & Reprints #2,* FSEncyV2, 1004 FS, *Ewan McColl* The Shuttle & Cage. *In Clancy Bros* SB *& on their* with Tommy Makem *(Topic). On* Cilla Fisher & Artie Trezise *(Autogram).* ⊙W39

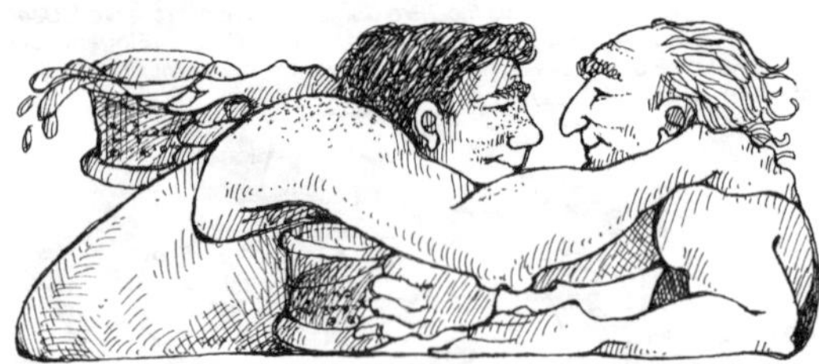

Working Girl Blues

I got the early Monday mornin' workin' blues
I put on my ragged, worn out workin' shoes
Well the weekend was too short, but I can't choose
When the Lord made the working girl, he made the blues

A - E - / - - A - :||

I'm tired of workin' my life away-ay-ay
Giving somebody else all of my pay, hey hey hey
While they get rich on the profits that I lose
Leavin' me here with the working girl blues
Ah-dee-yodel-ay-hee, workin' girl blues
And I can't even afford a new pair of shoes
While they can live in any old penthouse they choose
And all that I've got is the working girl blues

D - A - / E - A - / 1st / E - - A - :||

My boss says a raise is due most any day
But I wonder will my hair be all turned gray?
Before he turns that dollar loose & I get my dues
And lose a little bit of these working girl blues

Well my rent was raised again just the other day
Altho' my landlord's a millionaire they say
The poor get poorer & the rich get richer it's true
When the Lord made the working girl he made the blues

— Hazel Dickens

© 1986 Hazel Dickens / Happy Valley Music (BMI). Used by permission. — On her & Alice Gerrard, *Anne Romaine* Take a Stand *(FF 323), Magpie* Working My Life Away *(Collector) & on* Reel World String Band. *In* SO! *24:3,* Carry It On & New Folk Favs. ⊙W40

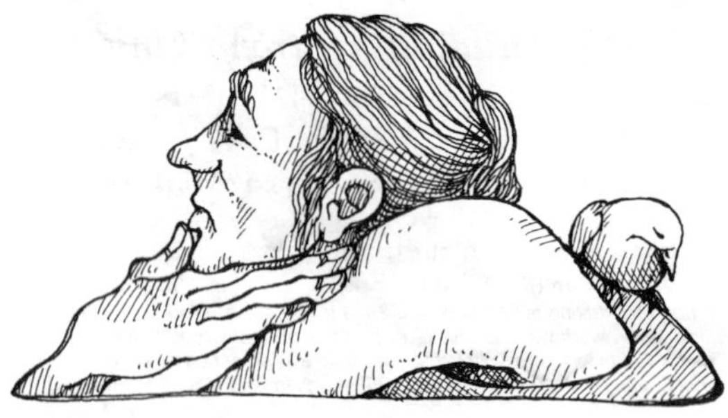

You Gotta Go Down

1. You gotta **go down and join the union**
   You gotta go join it by yourself
   Nobody here can join it for you
   You gotta go down & join the union by yourself

G - - - / D - G - / C - G - / G Em A D G -

2. Your brother's gotta **go down & join the union** / He's...
3. Your sister's gotta **go...**
4. I'm gonna **go down...**

5. And when the road gets rough & rocky
   And the hills get steep & high
   We can sing as we go marching
   And we'll win our big union by & by

— words & new music adap by Woody Guthrie

TRO © 1963 Ludlow Music, Inc, NY, NY. International copyright secured. Made in USA. All rights reserved incl. public performance for profit. Used by permission. — Adap fr "(Jesus Walked This) Lonesome Valley" (See FAITH for a more extended Guthrie version of this song.) In his SB, Peoples SB *&* S of Work & Protest. *On Pete Seeger* Talking Union *& Almanac Singers* Talking Union. ⊙W41

There are two excellent collections available of songs about working people and union struggles. The most recent gem is Pete Seeger & Bob Reiser Carry It On *("a history in song & picture of the working men & women of America"), Sing Out Publications, 1991, $14.95 – written to commemorate the centennial of the Haymarket Square Massacre, which took place in Chicago in May 1886. The older "classic" is Edith Fowke & Joe Glazer* Songs of Work & Protest *("100 fav songs of Am workers compete w/ music & historical notes"), Dover 1973 (orig pub by Labor Ed Div of Roosevelt U.) Some excellent recordings include Almanac Singers* Talking Union *(Folkways), John Greenway* Amer FS of Protest *(1953), Kornbluh* Rebel Voices *(1964), Joe Glazer's labor albums on Collector, "U.Utah" Phillips recordings of Wobbly (I.W.W.) songs & Tom Juravich's albums.*

There are lots of work songs in FARM & PRAIRIE (incl. songs on migrant work), MOUNTAIN VOICES (miners' experience & U.M.W.), and SEA. There are more union songs in RICH & POOR and in STRUGGLE. Other songs on this subject include: "My Hometown" (CITY) "Take This Hammer" (HARD) "Black Fly Song" (OUT) "Hard Travelin'" (TRAV) "Step by Step" (UNITY) "Bread & Roses," & "I'm Gonna Be an Engineer" (WOMEN).

ARTIST INDEX

We have included six different indices to make this book as easy to use as possible. We've included chapters (in caps following each song title) as well as page numbers after each song since (as you've probably already figured out) songs are in alphabetical order within each chapter. The chapters themselves are also in alphabetical order. The ARTIST INDEX will help you locate songs composed by a specific artist or group. The CULTURES INDEX lists songs from other countries, in different languages and even from a few special musical traditions. After the HOLIDAYS INDEX and MUSICAL INDEX is a SUBJECT INDEX which will help you better understand how the songs are grouped by chapters in the book. Finally, we have the TITLE INDEX which includes cross listings by first line and alternate titles, as well as the title you'll find the song under in this collection.

ARTIST INDEX

This index enables you to find all the songs in the book written by a given artist. If the composer(s) of a song are members of a group, you'll find the listing under the group name (eg. "Beatles") rather than the individual composers (eg. "Lennon" or "McCartney"). For reasons of space, we have limited this listing to only artists with more than one song in this book. A more detailed Artist and Composer Index is available from Sing Out! Please send a self-addressed stamped envelope. Adaptations of or new verses to traditional songs are indicated by the abbreviations "adap." or "new v." respectively.

RISE UP SINGING

ARTIST INDEX

CULTURE INDEX

These listings include songs in a specific foreign language, songs by artists from a given country or other grouping, songs about the given country or group listed, or songs from a specific musical, religious or cultural tradition where we felt this would be helpful. See also the SUBJECT INDEX and the notes at the end of each chapter.

CULTURE INDEX

CULTURE INDEX

HOLIDAY INDEX

For songs on birth, weddings, funerals and other life passages see the listings at the end of TIME & CHANGES.

MUSICALS INDEX

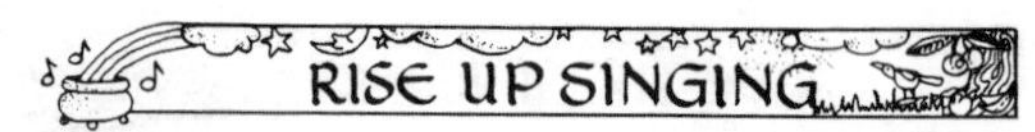

SUBJECT INDEX

As you get the feel for how the songs have been grouped in the book, you can turn directly to the chapter in which you feel the song is likely to be found (the chapters are arranged alphabetically), and then locate the song (the songs are also arranged alphabetically within each chapter). This index, along with the descriptive notes in the Table of Contents, can help you to better understand the chapter/subject system used in the book. (Please note that there are also cross-listing notes at the ends of many chapters.)

TITLE INDEX

also includes: First Lines and Alternate Titles

Titles as they appear in the book are given in bold; alternate titles are in regular type and first lines are italicized. We have used the first line of the chorus where we felt it would be easier to locate that way. Also please ignore initial articles (for example: "A" and "The") in both title and first lines.

A

TITLE INDEX

B

RISE UP SINGING

H

I

J

K

TITLE INDEX

L

M

N

O

Y

Z